HOUSE OF COMMONS
LIBRARY
DISPOSED OF
BY AUTHORITY

D0504327

GUIDE TO THE HOUSE OF COMMONS

MAY 2005

Editors

Tim Hames, Assistant Editor, The Times

Valerie Passmore, Editor, Dod's Parliamentary Companion

TIMES BOOKS

in association with

DOD'S PARLIAMENTARY COMMUNICATIONS

First published in 2005 by Times Books
HarperCollins*Publishers*
77–85 Fulham Palace Road, London W6 8JB

SPECIAL ACKNOWLEDGEMENTS AND THANKS TO
Tim Austin, Matthew Parris, Peter Riddell and Philip Webster

MP and constituency sketches
Daisy Ayliffe, Thom Cunningham-Burley, Paul Fuller, Caroline McGinn, David Roe, Maggie Sinclair, Mark Ward, Harry Watkinson, Louis Weinstock, Caroline Weston

MPs' photographs
Dod's Parliamentary Communications. Selected MP photos supplied by UPPA, copyright UPPA/Photoshot

Map
APC Design

Printed and bound in Great Britain by the Bath Press Ltd.

British Library Cataloguing in Publication Data.
A Catalogue record for this book is available from the British Library.

ISBN 0 00 721182 1

CONTENTS

ANALYSIS AND COMMENT

RESULTS BY CONSTITUENCY

STATISTICS

MANIFESTOS

GENERAL ELECTION 2005

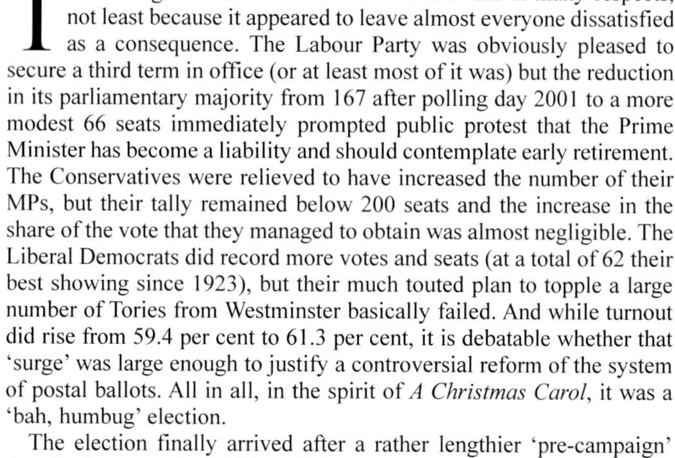

The 2005 general election was a curious event in many respects, not least because it appeared to leave almost everyone dissatisfied as a consequence. The Labour Party was obviously pleased to secure a third term in office (or at least most of it was) but the reduction in its parliamentary majority from 167 after polling day 2001 to a more modest 66 seats immediately prompted public protest that the Prime Minister has become a liability and should contemplate early retirement. The Conservatives were relieved to have increased the number of their MPs, but their tally remained below 200 seats and the increase in the share of the vote that they managed to obtain was almost negligible. The Liberal Democrats did record more votes and seats (at a total of 62 their best showing since 1923), but their much touted plan to topple a large number of Tories from Westminster basically failed. And while turnout did rise from 59.4 per cent to 61.3 per cent, it is debatable whether that 'surge' was large enough to justify a controversial reform of the system of postal ballots. All in all, in the spirit of *A Christmas Carol*, it was a 'bah, humbug' election.

The election finally arrived after a rather lengthier 'pre-campaign' than is the norm in British politics. Tony Blair and Michael Howard were engaged in explicit electioneering from the very beginning of 2005 and arguably from the party conference season three months previously. It can be asserted that this most prolonged warm-up actually served to make the final election proper a little flatter than it might have been. The first ten days of the formal campaign did not seem especially exciting, indeed the manifesto 'launches' did not really place any of those documents into political orbit. These initial skirmishes were followed by a week in which the war in Iraq, its legality, the motives behind it, the failure to find weapons of mass destruction and the messy aftermath of the conflict, became more prominent than had been anticipated, largely because of a series of media leaks plainly designed to embarrass the Prime Minister. Exactly who leaked what when and with what in mind remains one of the best mysteries of a contest which otherwise rather lacked for drama.

Exactly how large the Iraq factor was in voting is unclear. The broad thrust of the results were, however, defections from the Labour Party but mostly in the direction of the Liberal Democrats and a number of 'other', allegedly fringe, parties and not to the Conservatives. This movement was most pronounced in seats in university areas and in parts of the nation (notably London) where the middle-class intelligentsia was to be found in disproportionately sizeable numbers. The anti-Labour mood was not as potent in Scotland, Wales or the north of England. As a rule, working class voters seemed to be less aggrieved than their more affluent counterparts, but it was still a struggle to entice them to the polling stations at all.

The election outcome thus had a number of paradoxical dimensions to it. The Labour Party won what should be a solid majority but with less than 36 per cent of the ballots cast across the United Kingdom. This is an unprecedented development and one which may yet trigger fresh interest in proportional representation. The Conservatives failed for the third election in a row to seize more than one in three votes – an ignominy that again has never been experienced by the Tories before. The Liberal Democrats, who had failed to take any seats from Labour in

1997 and then a single one (Chesterfield) in 2001, snatched a dozen this time, but had a net loss of seats in their exchanges with the Tories. The established rules of British politics were bent if not entirely broken.

Part of that process involved the votes obtained by the minor parties. At more than one in ten, this was the best showing for the fringe in British political history. In numbers in the House of Commons, by contrast, the impact was much more muted. The SNP increased their representation but Plaid Cymru did not. Dr Richard Taylor, an independent, held the Wyre Forest seat that he had obtained in a staggering manner in 2001. He was joined by George Galloway, who triumphed for his Respect party after a bruising battle in Bethnal Green and Bow and by Peter Law, who was, in effect, independent Labour, who stood and was victorious in the previously ultra-safe Welsh Labour constituency of Blaenau Gwent. Mr Law objected to an all-women shortlist being imposed in the valleys. The voters agreed.

The electors with the most cause for discontent in this poll were a comparatively small group left out of the 5 May exercise. The sad death of the Liberal Democrat contender in Staffordshire South, which occurred after nominations had closed, meant that the general election had to be cancelled and a by-election held only after the new Parliament had assembled. That result is included in this volume as if it had taken place as originally proposed in May.

That new House of Commons will be a fascinating place over the next four to five years. The Labour Party has, since 1997, been accustomed to governing with massive and hence relatively pliant majorities on the green benches. It has had a much more difficult time with those sitting on the red benches in the House of Lords. The next House of Commons will not be as undisciplined as some of Mr Blair's internal opponents would like but it will certainly be less predictable than it has been. There is an 'awkward squad' in Westminster which could deprive the Cabinet of a majority of some issues. If the House of Commons indicates that it is prepared to be more independent in its behaviour, then that in turn is bound to embolden the House of Lords. It is tempting to conclude that the net effect of the 2005 general election will be a return to 'politics as normal'. In truth, though, the politics of the next few years could be most abnormal.

STATE OF THE PARTIES

Party	Election May 2005	Dissolution May 2005	Election May 2001
Labour	355*	410	412
Conservative	197	162	166
Liberal Democrat	62	54	52
Democratic Unionist Party	9	7	5
Scottish Nationalist Party	6	5	5
Sinn Féin	5	4	4
Social Democratic and Labour Party	3	3	3
Plaid Cymru	3	4	4
Independent	2	3	1
Ulster Unionist Party	1	5	6
Respect	1		
The Speaker	1	1	1
Total	645†	659	659

*Includes 29 Labour/Co-operative MPs, excludes Speaker
†By-election pending in South Staffordshire

Her Majesty's Government

THE CABINET

Prime Minister, First Lord of the Treasury and Minister for the Civil Service	Tony Blair
Deputy Prime Minister and First Secretary of State	John Prescott
Chancellor of the Exchequer	Gordon Brown
Secretary of State for Foreign and Commonwealth Affairs	Jack Straw
Secretary of State for Work and Pensions	David Blunkett
Secretary of State for Environment, Food and Rural Affairs	Margaret Beckett
Secretary of State for Transport and Secretary of State for Scotland	Alistair Darling
Secretary of State for Defence	Dr John Reid
Leader of the House of Commons, Lord Privy Seal	Geoffrey Hoon
Secretary of State for Health	Patricia Hewitt
Secretary of State for Culture, Media and Sport	Tessa Jowell
Chief Whip	Hilary Armstrong
Secretary of State for the Home Department	Charles Clarke
Secretary of State for Northern Ireland and for Wales	Peter Hain
Minister without Portfolio	Ian McCartney
Leader of the House of Lords and Lord President of the Council	Baroness Amos
Secretary of State for Constitutional Affairs and Lord Chancellor	Lord Falconer of Thoroton QC
Secretary of State for International Development	Hilary Benn
Secretary of State for Trade and Industry	Alan Johnson
Secretary of State for Education and Skills	Ruth Kelly
Chancellor of the Duchy of Lancaster	John Hutton
Chief Secretary to the Treasury	Des Browne
Minister of Communities and Local Government, Office of the Deputy Prime Minister	David Miliband
Also attending Cabinet	
Lords Chief Whip	Lord Grocott
Attorney General	Lord Goldsmith
Minister for Europe, Foreign and Commonwealth Office	Douglas Alexander

DEPARTMENTAL MINISTERS AND WHIPS

CABINET OFFICE
Chancellor of the Duchy of Lancaster
JOHN HUTTON
Parliamentary Secretary
JIM MURPHY

CONSTITUTIONAL AFFAIRS
Secretary of State and Lord Chancellor
LORD FALCONER OF THOROTON QC
Minister of State
HARRIET HARMAN
Parliamentary Under-Secretaries of State
BARONESS ASHTON OF UPHOLLAND, BRIDGET PRENTICE

CULTURE, MEDIA AND SPORT
Secretary of State
TESSA JOWELL
Minister of State
RICHARD CABORN
Parliamentary Under-Secretaries of State
DAVID LAMMY, JAMES PURNELL

DEFENCE
Secretary of State
DR JOHN REID
Minister of State
ADAM INGRAM
Parliamentary Under-Secretaries of State
DON TOUHIG, LORD DRAYSON

OFFICE OF THE DEPUTY PRIME MINISTER
Deputy Prime Minister and First Secretary of State
JOHN PRESCOTT
Ministers of State
DAVID MILIBAND, YVETTE COOPER, PHIL WOOLAS
Parliamentary Under-Secretaries of State
JIM FITZPATRICK, BARONESS ANDREWS

EDUCATION AND SKILLS
Secretary of State
Ruth Kelly
Ministers of State
JACQUI SMITH, BILL RAMMELL, BEVERLEY HUGHES
Parliamentary Under-Secretaries of State
PHIL HOPE, MARIA EAGLE, LORD ADONIS

ENVIRONMENT, FOOD AND RURAL AFFAIRS
Secretary of State
MARGARET BECKETT
Minister of State
ELLIOTT MORLEY
Parliamentary Under-Secretaries of State
BEN BRADSHAW, LORD BACH, JIM KNIGHT

FOREIGN AND COMMONWEALTH OFFICE
Secretary of State
JACK STRAW
Ministers of State
DOUGLAS ALEXANDER, KIM HOWELLS, IAN PEARSON (also DTI)
Parliamentary Under-Secretary of State
LORD TRIESMAN

HEALTH
Secretary of State
PATRICIA HEWITT
Ministers of State
ROSIE WINTERTON, JANE KENNEDY, LORD WARNER
Parliamentary Under-Secretaries of State
CAROLINE FLINT, LIAM BYRNE

HOME OFFICE
Secretary of State
CHARLES CLARKE
Ministers of State
HAZEL BLEARS, BARONESS SCOTLAND OF ASTHAL QC, TONY MCNULTY
Parliamentary Under-Secretaries of State
PAUL GOGGINS, FIONA MACTAGGART, ANDY BURNHAM

INTERNATIONAL DEVELOPMENT
Secretary of State
HILARY BENN
Parliamentary Under-Secretary of State
GARETH THOMAS

LAW OFFICERS' DEPARTMENT
Attorney General
LORD GOLDSMITH QC
Solicitor General
MIKE O'BRIEN
Advocate General for Scotland
LYNDA CLARK QC

LEADER OF THE HOUSE OF COMMONS
Leader of the House of Commons and Lord Privy Seal
GEOFF HOON
Deputy Leader of the House of Commons
NIGEL GRIFFITHS

LEADER OF THE HOUSE OF LORDS AND LORD PRESIDENT OF THE COUNCIL
BARONESS AMOS
Deputy Leader of the House of Lords
LORD ROOKER

MINISTER WITHOUT PORTFOLIO AND LABOUR PARTY CHAIR
IAN MCCARTNEY

NORTHERN IRELAND OFFICE
Secretary of State
PETER HAIN
Ministers of State
DAVID HANSON, LORD ROOKER
Parliamentary Under-Secretaries of State
ANGELA SMITH, SHAUN WOODWARD

PRIVY COUNCIL OFFICE
Lord President of the Council and Leader of the House of Lords
BARONESS AMOS

SCOTLAND OFFICE
Secretary of State
ALISTAIR DARLING
Parliamentary Under-Secretary of State
DAVID CAIRNS

TRADE AND INDUSTRY
Secretary of State
ALAN JOHNSON
Ministers of State
ALUN MICHAEL, MALCOLM WICKS, IAN PEARSON
Parliamentary Under-Secretaries of State
GERRY SUTCLIFFE, BARRY GARDINER, LORD SAINSBURY OF TURVILLE, MEG MUNN

TRANSPORT
Secretary of State
ALISTAIR DARLING
Minister of State
DR STEPHEN LADYMAN
Parliamentary Under-Secretaries of State
DEREK TWIGG, KAREN BUCK

TREASURY

Chancellor of the Exchequer
Gordon Brown
Chief Secretary to the Treasury
Des Browne
Paymaster General
Dawn Primarolo
Financial Secretary
John Healey
Economic Secretary
Ivan Lewis

WALES OFFICE

Secretary of State
Peter Hain
Parliamentary Under-Secretary of State
Nick Ainger

WORK AND PENSIONS

Secretary of State
David Blunkett
Ministers of State
Margaret Hodge, Stephen Timms
Parliamentary Under-Secretaries of State
Lord Hunt of Kings Heath, Anne McGuire, James Plaskitt

WHIPS

HOUSE OF COMMONS

Chief Whip *(Parliamentary Secretary to the Treasury)*
Hilary Armstrong
Deputy Chief Whip *(Treasurer of HM Household)*
Bob Ainsworth
Whips
Comptroller of HM Household
Thomas McAvoy
Vice-Chamberlain of HM Household
John Heppell
Lord Commissioners
Gillian Merron, Vernon Coaker, Tom Watson, Dave Watts, Joan Ryan
Assistant Whips
Frank Roy, Ian Cawsey, Alan Campbell, Claire Ward, Parmjit Dhanda, Tony Cunningham, Kevin Brennan

HOUSE OF LORDS

Lords Chief Whip *(Captain of the Honourable Corps of the Gentlemen-at-Arms)*
Lord Grocott
Deputy Chief Whip *(Captain of the Queen's Bodyguard of the Yeomen of the Guard)*
Lord Davies of Oldham
Whips
Lords in Waiting
Lord Bassam of Brighton, Lord Evans of Temple Guiting CBE, Lord McKenzie of Luton
Baronesses in Waiting
Baroness Farrington of Ribbleton, Baroness Crawley, Baroness Royall of Blaisdon

The House of Commons

The following were elected Members of the House of Commons in the 2005 general election and a June by-election

C – Conservative
DUP – Democratic Unionist Party
Ind – Independent
Ind KHHC – Independent Kidderminster Hospital and Health Concern
Lab – Labour
Lab/Co-op – Labour Co-operative
LD – Liberal Democrats
PlC – Plaid Cymru
Respect – Respect, Equality, Socialism Peace, Environment, Community, Trade Unionism
SDLP – Social Democratic and Labour
SF – Sinn Féin
SNP – Scottish National Party
UUP – Ulster Unionist Party

A

Abbott, Diane Hackney North and Stoke Newington Lab
Adams, Gerry Belfast West SF
Afriyie, Adam Windsor C
Ainger, Nick Carmarthen West and South Pembrokeshire Lab
Ainsworth, Bob Coventry North East Lab
Ainsworth, Peter East Surrey C
Alexander, Danny Inverness, Nairn, Badenoch and Strathspey LD
Alexander, Douglas Paisley and Renfrewshire South Lab
Allen, Graham Nottingham North Lab
Amess, David Southend West C
Ancram, Michael Devizes C
Anderson, David Blaydon Lab
Anderson, Janet Rossendale and Darwen Lab
Arbuthnot, James North East Hampshire C
Armstrong, Hilary North West Durham Lab
Atkins, Charlotte Staffordshire Moorlands Lab
Atkinson, Peter Hexham C
Austin, Ian Dudley North Lab
Austin, John Erith and Thamesmead Lab

B

Bacon, Richard South Norfolk C
Bailey, Adrian West Bromwich West Lab/Co-op
Baird, Vera Redcar Lab
Baker, Norman Lewes LD
Baldry, Tony Banbury C
Balls, Ed Normanton Lab/Co-op
Banks, Gordon Ochil and South Perthshire Lab
Barker, Gregory Bexhill and Battle C
Barlow, Celia Hove Lab
Baron, John Billericay C
Barrett, John Edinburgh West LD
Barron, Kevin Rother Valley Lab
Battle, John Leeds West Lab
Bayley, Hugh City of York Lab
Beckett, Margaret Derby South Lab
Begg, Anne Aberdeen South Lab
Beith, Alan Berwick-upon-Tweed LD
Bell, Stuart Middlesbrough Lab
Bellingham, Henry North West Norfolk C
Benn, Hilary Leeds Central Lab
Benton, Joe Bootle Lab
Benyon, Richard Newbury C
Bercow, John Buckingham C
Beresford, Paul Mole Valley C
Berry, Roger Kingswood Lab
Betts, Clive Sheffield Attercliffe Lab
Binley, Brian Northampton South C
Blackman, Liz Erewash Lab
Blackman-Woods, Roberta City of Durham Lab
Blair, Tony Sedgefield Lab
Blears, Hazel Salford Lab
Blizzard, Bob Waveney Lab
Blunkett, David Sheffield Brightside Lab
Blunt, Crispin Reigate C
Bone, Peter Wellingborough C
Borrow, David South Ribble Lab
Boswell, Timothy Daventry C
Bottomley, Peter Worthing West C
Bradshaw, Ben Exeter Lab
Brady, Graham Altrincham and Sale West C
Brake, Tom Carshalton and Wallington LD

Brazier, Julian Canterbury C
Breed, Colin South East Cornwall LD
Brennan, Kevin Cardiff West Lab
Brokenshire, James Hornchurch C
Brooke, Annette Mid Dorset and Poole North LD
Brown, Gordon Kirkcaldy and Cowdenbeath Lab
Brown, Lyn West Ham Lab
Brown, Nick Newcastle upon Tyne East and Wallsend Lab
Brown, Russell Dumfries and Galloway Lab
Browne, Des Kilmarnock and Loudoun Lab
Browne, Jeremy Taunton LD
Browning, Angela Tiverton and Honiton C
Bruce, Malcolm Gordon LD
Bryant, Chris Rhondda Lab
Buck, Karen Regent's Park and Kensington North Lab
Burden, Richard Birmingham Northfield Lab
Burgon, Colin Elmet Lab
Burnham, Andy Leigh Lab
Burns, Simon Chelmsford West C
Burrowes, David Enfield Southgate C
Burstow, Paul Sutton and Cheam LD
Burt, Alistair North East Bedfordshire C
Burt, Lorely Solihull LD
Butler, Dawn Brent South Lab
Butterfill, John Bournemouth West C
Byers, Stephen North Tyneside Lab
Byrne, Liam Birmingham Hodge Hill Lab

C

Cable, Vincent Twickenham LD
Caborn, Richard Sheffield Central Lab
Cairns, David Inverclyde Lab
Calton, Patsy Cheadle LD
Cameron, David Witney C
Campbell, Alan Tynemouth Lab
Campbell, Gregory East Londonderry DUP
Campbell, Menzies North East Fife LD
Campbell, Ronnie Blyth Valley Lab
Carmichael, Alistair Orkney and Shetland LD
Carswell, Douglas Harwich C
Cash, William Stone C
Caton, Martin Gower Lab
Cawsey, Ian Brigg and Goole Lab
Challen, Colin Morley and Rothwell Lab
Chapman, Ben Wirral South Lab
Chaytor, David Bury North Lab
Chope, Christopher Christchurch C
Clapham, Michael Barnsley West and Penistone Lab
Clappison, James Hertsmere C
Clark, Greg Tunbridge Wells C
Clark, Katy North Ayrshire and Arran Lab
Clark, Paul Gillingham Lab
Clarke, Charles Norwich South Lab
Clarke, Kenneth Rushcliffe C
Clarke, Tom Coatbridge, Chryston and Bellshill Lab
Clegg, Nick Sheffield Hallam LD
Clelland, David Tyne Bridge Lab
Clifton-Brown, Geoffrey Cotswold C
Clwyd, Ann Cynon Valley Lab
Coaker, Vernon Gedling Lab
Coffey, Ann Stockport Lab
Cohen, Harry Leyton and Wanstead Lab
Connarty, Michael Linlithgow and East Falkirk Lab
Conway, Derek Old Bexley and Sidcup C
Cook, Frank Stockton North Lab
Cook, Robin Livingston Lab
Cooper, Rosie West Lancashire Lab
Cooper, Yvette Pontefract and Castleford Lab
Corbyn, Jeremy Islington North Lab
Cormack, Patrick South Staffordshire C
Cousins, Jim Newcastle upon Tyne Central Lab
Cox, Geoffrey Torridge and West Devon C
Crabb, Stephen Preseli Pembrokeshire C
Crausby, David Bolton North East Lab
Creagh, Mary Wakefield Lab
Cruddas, Jon Dagenham Lab
Cryer, Ann Keighley Lab
Cummings, John Easington Lab
Cunningham, James Coventry South Lab
Cunningham, Tony Workington Lab
Curry, David Skipton and Ripon C
Curtis-Thomas, Claire Crosby Lab

D

Darling, Alistair Edinburgh South West Lab
Davey, Edward Kingston and Surbiton LD
David, Wayne Caerphilly Lab
Davidson, Ian Glasgow South West Lab/Co-op
Davies, David Monmouth C
Davies, Philip Shipley C
Davies, Quentin Grantham and Stamford C
Davis, David Haltemprice and Howden C
Dean, Janet Burton Lab
Denham, John Southampton Itchen Lab
Dhanda, Parmjit Gloucester Lab
Dismore, Andrew Hendon Lab
Djanogly, Jonathan Huntingdon C
Dobbin, Jim Heywood and Middleton Lab/Co-op
Dobson, Frank Holborn and St Pancras Lab
Dodds, Nigel Belfast North DUP

Doherty, Pat West Tyrone SF
Donaldson, Jeffrey Lagan Valley DUP
Donohoe, Brian Central Ayrshire Lab
Doran, Frank Aberdeen North Lab
Dorrell, Stephen Charnwood C
Dorries, Nadine Mid Bedfordshire C
Dowd, Jim Lewisham West Lab
Drew, David Stroud Lab/Co-op
Duddridge, James Rochford and Southend East C
Duncan, Alan Rutland and Melton C
Duncan Smith, Iain Chingford and Woodford Green C
Dunne, Philip Ludlow C
Dunwoody, Gwyneth Crewe and Nantwich Lab
Durkan, Mark Foyle SDLP

E

Eagle, Angela Wallasey Lab
Eagle, Maria Liverpool Garston Lab
Efford, Clive Eltham Lab
Ellman, Louise Liverpool Riverside Lab/Co-op
Ellwood, Tobias Bournemouth East C
Engel, Natascha North East Derbyshire Lab
Ennis, Jeffrey Barnsley East and Mexborough Lab
Etherington, Bill Sunderland North Lab
Evans, Nigel Ribble Valley C
Evennett, David Bexleyheath and Crayford C

F

Fabricant, Michael Lichfield C
Fallon, Michael Sevenoaks C
Farrelly, Paul Newcastle-under-Lyme Lab
Farron, Tim Westmorland and Lonsdale LD
Featherstone, Lynne Hornsey and Wood Green LD
Field, Frank Birkenhead Lab
Field, Mark Cities of London and Westminster C
Fisher, Mark Stoke-on-Trent Central Lab
Fitzpatrick, Jim Poplar and Canning Town Lab
Flello, Robert Stoke-on-Trent South Lab
Flint, Caroline Don Valley Lab
Flynn, Paul Newport West Lab
Follett, Barbara Stevenage Lab
Forth, Eric Bromley and Chislehurst C
Foster, Don Bath LD
Foster, Michael Jabez Hastings and Rye Lab
Foster, Michael John Worcester Lab
Fox, Liam Woodspring C
Francis, Hywel Aberavon Lab
Francois, Mark Rayleigh C
Fraser, Christopher South West Norfolk C

G

Gale, Roger North Thanet C
Galloway, George Bethnal Green and Bow Respect
Gapes, Mike Ilford South Lab/Co-op
Gardiner, Barry Brent North Lab
Garnier, Edward Harborough C
Gauke, David South West Hertfordshire C
George, Andrew St Ives LD
George, Bruce Walsall South Lab
Gerrard, Neil Walthamstow Lab
Gibb, Nick Bognor Regis and Littlehampton C
Gibson, Ian Norwich North Lab
Gidley, Sandra Romsey LD
Gildernew, Michelle Fermanagh and South Tyrone SF
Gillan, Cheryl Chesham and Amersham C
Gilroy, Linda Plymouth Sutton Lab/Co-op
Godsiff, Roger Birmingham Sparkbrook and Small Heath Lab
Goggins, Paul Wythenshawe and Sale East Lab
Goldsworthy, Julia Falmouth and Camborne LD
Goodman, Helen Bishop Auckland Lab
Goodman, Paul Wycombe C
Goodwill, Robert Scarborough and Whitby C
Gove, Michael Surrey Heath C
Gray, James North Wiltshire C
Grayling, Christopher Epsom and Ewell C
Green, Damian Ashford C
Greening, Justine Putney C
Greenway, John Ryedale C
Grieve, Dominic Beaconsfield C
Griffith, Nia Llanelli Lab
Griffiths, Nigel Edinburgh South Lab
Grogan, John Selby Lab
Gummer, John Suffolk Coastal C
Gwynne, Andrew Denton and Reddish Lab

H

Hague, William Richmond (Yorkshire) C
Hain, Peter Neath Lab
Hall, Mike Weaver Vale Lab
Hall, Patrick Bedford Lab
Hamilton, David Midlothian Lab
Hamilton, Fabian Leeds North East Lab
Hammond, Philip Runnymede and Weybridge C
Hammond, Stephen Wimbledon C
Hancock, Mike Portsmouth South LD
Hands, Greg Hammersmith and Fulham C
Hanson, David Delyn Lab
Harman, Harriet Camberwell and Peckham Lab

Harper, Mark Forest of Dean C
Harris, Evan Oxford West and Abingdon LD
Harris, Tom Glasgow South Lab
Harvey, Nick North Devon LD
Haselhurst, Alan Saffron Walden C
Havard, Dai Merthyr Tydfil and Rhymney Lab
Hayes, John South Holland and The Deepings C
Heal, Sylvia Halesowen and Rowley Regis Lab
Heald, Oliver North East Hertfordshire C
Healey, John Wentworth Lab
Heath, David Somerton and Frome LD
Heathcoat-Amory, David Wells C
Hemming, John Birmingham Yardley LD
Henderson, Doug Newcastle upon Tyne North Lab
Hendrick, Mark Preston Lab/Co-op
Hendry, Charles Wealden C
Hepburn, Stephen Jarrow Lab
Heppell, John Nottingham East Lab
Herbert, Nick Arundel and South Downs C
Hermon, Sylvia North Down UUP
Hesford, Stephen Wirral West Lab
Hewitt, Patricia Leicester West Lab
Heyes, David Ashton under Lyne Lab
Hill, Keith Streatham Lab
Hillier, Meg
Hackney South and Shoreditch Lab/Co-op
Hoban, Mark Fareham C
Hodge, Margaret Barking Lab
Hodgson, Sharon
Gateshead East and Washington West Lab
Hoey, Kate Vauxhall Lab
Hogg, Douglas Sleaford and North Hykeham C
Hollobone, Philip Kettering C
Holloway, Adam Gravesham C
Holmes, Paul Chesterfield LD
Hood, Jimmy Lanark and Hamilton East Lab
Hoon, Geoffrey Ashfield Lab
Hope, Phil Corby Lab/Co-op
Hopkins, Kelvin Luton North Lab
Horam, John Orpington C
Horwood, Martin Cheltenham LD
Hosie, Stewart Dundee East SNP
Howard, Michael Folkestone and Hythe C
Howarth, David Cambridge LD
Howarth, George
Knowsley North and Sefton East Lab
Howarth, Gerald Aldershot C
Howells, Kim Pontypridd Lab
Hoyle, Lindsay Chorley Lab
Hughes, Beverley Stretford and Urmston Lab
Hughes, Simon
North Southwark and Bermondsey LD
Huhne, Chris Eastleigh LD
Humble, Joan Blackpool North and Fleetwood Lab
Hunt, Jeremy South West Surrey C
Hurd, Nick Ruislip Northwood C
Hutton, John Barrow and Furness Lab

I

Iddon, Brian Bolton South East Lab
Illsley, Eric Barnsley Central Lab
Ingram, Adam
East Kilbride, Strathaven and Lesmahagow Lab
Irranca-Davies, Huw Ogmore Lab

J

Jack, Michael Fylde C
Jackson, Glenda Hampstead and Highgate Lab
Jackson, Stewart Peterborough C
James, Sian Swansea East Lab
Jenkin, Bernard North Essex C
Jenkins, Brian Tamworth Lab
Johnson, Alan Hull West and Hessle Lab
Johnson, Boris Henley C
Johnson, Diana Hull North Lab
Jones, David Clwyd West C
Jones, Helen Warrington North Lab
Jones, Kevan Durham North Lab
Jones, Lynne Birmingham Selly Oak Lab
Jones, Martyn Clwyd South Lab
Jowell, Tessa Dulwich and West Norwood Lab
Joyce, Eric Falkirk Lab

K

Kaufman, Gerald Manchester Gorton Lab
Kawczynski, Daniel Shrewsbury and Atcham C
Keeble, Sally Northampton North Lab
Keeley, Barbara Worsley Lab
Keen, Alan Feltham and Heston Lab/Co-op
Keen, Ann Brentford and Isleworth Lab
Keetch, Paul Hereford LD
Kelly, Ruth Bolton West Lab
Kemp, Fraser Houghton and Washington East Lab
Kennedy, Charles Ross, Skye and Lochaber LD
Kennedy, Jane Liverpool Wavertree Lab
Key, Robert Salisbury C
Khabra, Piara Ealing Southall Lab
Khan, Sadiq Tooting Lab
Kidney, David Stafford Lab
Kilfoyle, Peter Liverpool Walton Lab
Kirkbride, Julie Bromsgrove C

Knight, Greg Yorkshire East C
Knight, Jim South Dorset Lab
Kramer, Susan Richmond Park LD
Kumar, Ashok Middlesbrough South and East Cleveland Lab

L

Ladyman, Stephen South Thanet Lab
Laing, Eleanor Epping Forest C
Lait, Jacqui Beckenham C
Lamb, Norman North Norfolk LD
Lammy, David Tottenham Lab
Lancaster, Mark Milton Keynes North East C
Lansley, Andrew South Cambridgeshire C
Law, Peter Blaenau Gwent Ind
Laws, David Yeovil LD
Laxton, Bob Derby North Lab
Lazarowicz, Mark Edinburgh North and Leith Lab/Co-op
Leech, John Manchester Withington LD
Leigh, Edward Gainsborough C
Lepper, David Brighton Pavilion Lab/Co-op
Letwin, Oliver West Dorset C
Levitt, Tom High Peak Lab
Lewis, Ivan Bury South Lab
Lewis, Julian New Forest East C
Liddell-Grainger, Ian Bridgwater C
Lidington, David Aylesbury C
Lilley, Peter Hitchin and Harpenden C
Linton, Martin Battersea Lab
Lloyd, Tony Manchester Central Lab
Llwyd, Elfyn Meirionnydd Nant Conwy PlC
Lord, Michael Central Suffolk and North Ipswich C
Loughton, Tim East Worthing and Shoreham C
Love, Andrew Edmonton Lab/Co-op
Lucas, Ian Wrexham Lab
Luff, Peter Mid Worcestershire C

M

McAvoy, Thomas Rutherglen and Hamilton West Lab/Co-op
McCabe, Steve Birmingham Hall Green Lab
McCafferty, Christine Calder Valley Lab
McCarthy, Kerry Bristol East Lab
McCarthy-Fry, Sarah Portsmouth North Lab/Co-op
McCartney, Ian Makerfield Lab
McCrea, William South Antrim DUP
McDonagh, Siobhain Mitcham and Morden Lab
McDonnell, Alasdair Belfast South SDLP
McDonnell, John Hayes and Harlington Lab
MacDougall, John Glenrothes Lab
McFadden, Pat Wolverhampton South East Lab
McFall, John West Dunbartonshire Lab/Co-op
McGovern, Jim Dundee West Lab
McGrady, Eddie South Down SDLP
McGuinness, Martin Mid Ulster SF
McGuire, Anne Stirling Lab
McIntosh, Anne Vale of York C
McIsaac, Shona Cleethorpes Lab
Mackay, Andrew Bracknell C
McKechin, Ann Glasgow North Lab
McKenna, Rosemary Cumbernauld, Kilsyth and Kirkintilloch East Lab
Mackinlay, Andrew Thurrock Lab
Maclean, David Penrith and The Border C
McLoughlin, Patrick West Derbyshire C
MacNeil, Angus Na h-Eileanan An Iar SNP
McNulty, Tony Harrow East Lab
MacShane, Denis Rotherham Lab
Mactaggart, Fiona Slough Lab
Mahmood, Khalid Birmingham Perry Barr Lab
Main, Anne St Albans C
Malik, Shahid Dewsbury Lab
Malins, Humfrey Woking C
Mallaber, Judy Amber Valley Lab
Mann, John Bassetlaw Lab
Maples, John Stratford-on-Avon C
Marris, Rob Wolverhampton South West Lab
Marsden, Gordon Blackpool South Lab
Marshall, David Glasgow East Lab
Marshall-Andrews, Robert Medway Lab
Martin, Michael Glasgow North East Speaker
Martlew, Eric Carlisle Lab
Mates, Michael East Hampshire C
Maude, Francis Horsham C
May, Theresa Maidenhead C
Meacher, Michael Oldham West and Royton Lab
Meale, Alan Mansfield Lab
Mercer, Patrick Newark C
Merron, Gillian Lincoln Lab
Michael, Alun Cardiff South and Penarth Lab/Co-op
Milburn, Alan Darlington Lab
Miliband, David South Shields Lab
Miliband, Ed Doncaster North Lab
Miller, Andrew Ellesmere Port and Neston Lab
Miller, Maria Basingstoke C
Milton, Anne Guildford C
Mitchell, Andrew Sutton Coldfield C
Mitchell, Austin Great Grimsby Lab
Moffat, Anne (contested as Anne Picking) East Lothian Lab
Moffatt, Laura Crawley Lab

Mole, Chris Ipswich Lab
Moon, Madeleine Bridgend Lab
Moore, Michael
Berwickshire, Roxburgh and Selkirk LD
Moran, Margaret Luton South Lab
Morden, Jessica Newport East Lab
Morgan, Julie Cardiff North Lab
Morley, Elliot Scunthorpe Lab
Moss, Malcolm North East Cambridgeshire C
Mountford, Kali Colne Valley Lab
Mudie, George Leeds East Lab
Mulholland, Gregory Leeds North West LD
Mullin, Chris Sunderland South Lab
Mundell, David
Dumfriesshire, Clydesdale and Tweeddale C
Munn, Meg Sheffield Heeley Lab/Co-op
Murphy, Cor Newry and Armagh SF
Murphy, Denis Wansbeck Lab
Murphy, Jim East Renfrewshire Lab
Murphy, Paul Torfaen Lab
Murrison, Andrew Westbury C

N

Naysmith, Doug Bristol North West Lab/Co-op
Newmark, Brooks Braintree C
Norris, Dan Wansdyke Lab

O

Oaten, Mark Winchester LD
O'Brien, Mike North Warwickshire Lab
O'Brien, Stephen Eddisbury C
O'Hara, Edward Knowsley South Lab
Olner, Bill Nuneaton Lab
Öpik, Lembit Montgomeryshire LD
Osborne, George Tatton C
Osborne, Sandra Ayr, Carrick and Cumnock Lab
Ottaway, Richard Croydon South C
Owen, Albert Ynys Môn Lab

P

Paice, Jim South East Cambridgeshire C
Paisley, Ian North Antrim DUP
Palmer, Nick Broxtowe Lab
Paterson, Owen North Shropshire C
Pearson, Ian Dudley South Lab
Pelling, Andrew Croydon Central C
Penning, Mike Hemel Hempstead C
Penrose, John Weston-Super-Mare C
Picking, Anne (see Moffat, Anne)
Pickles, Eric Brentwood and Ongar C
Plaskitt, James Warwick and Leamington Lab
Pope, Greg Hyndburn Lab
Pound, Stephen Ealing North Lab
Prentice, Bridget Lewisham East Lab
Prentice, Gordon Pendle Lab
Prescott, John Hull East Lab
Price, Adam Carmarthen East and Dinefwr PlC
Primarolo, Dawn Bristol South Lab
Prisk, Mark Hertford and Stortford C
Pritchard, Mark The Wrekin C
Prosser, Gwyn Dover Lab
Pugh, John Southport LD
Purchase, Ken
Wolverhampton North East Lab/Co-op
Purnell, James Stalybridge and Hyde Lab

R

Rammell, Bill Harlow Lab
Randall, John Uxbridge C
Raynsford, Nick Greenwich and Woolwich Lab
Redwood, John Wokingham C
Reed, Andrew Loughborough Lab/Co-op
Reed, Jamie Copeland Lab
Reid, Alan Argyll and Bute LD
Reid, John Airdrie and Shotts Lab
Rifkind, Malcolm Kensington and Chelsea C
Riordan, Linda Halifax Lab/Co-op
Robathan, Andrew Blaby C
Robertson, Angus Moray SNP
Robertson, Hugh Faversham and Mid Kent C
Robertson, John Glasgow North West Lab
Robertson, Laurence Tewkesbury C
Robinson, Geoffrey Coventry North West Lab
Robinson, Iris Strangford DUP
Robinson, Peter Belfast East DUP
Rogerson, Dan North Cornwall LD
Rooney, Terry Bradford North Lab
Rosindell, Andrew Romford C
Rowen, Paul Rochdale LD
Roy, Frank Motherwell and Wishaw Lab
Ruane, Chris Vale of Clwyd Lab
Ruddock, Joan Lewisham Deptford Lab
Ruffley, David Bury St Edmunds C
Russell, Christine City of Chester Lab
Russell, Bob Colchester LD
Ryan, Joan Enfield North Lab

S

Salmond, Alex Banff and Buchan SNP
Salter, Martin Reading West Lab

Sanders, Adrian Torbay LD
Sarwar, Mohammed Glasgow Central Lab
Scott, Lee Ilford North C
Seabeck, Alison Plymouth Devonport Lab
Selous, Andrew South West Bedfordshire C
Shapps, Grant Welwyn Hatfield C
Shaw, Jonathan Chatham and Aylesford Lab
Sheerman, Barry Huddersfield Lab/Co-op
Shepherd, Richard Aldridge-Brownhills C
Sheridan, Jim Paisley and Renfrewshire North Lab
Short, Clare Birmingham Ladywood Lab
Simmonds, Mark Boston and Skegness C
Simon, Siôn Birmingham Erdington Lab
Simpson, Alan Nottingham South Lab
Simpson, David Upper Bann DUP
Simpson, Keith Mid Norfolk C
Singh, Marsha Bradford West Lab
Skinner, Dennis Bolsover Lab
Slaughter, Andy Ealing, Acton and Shepherd's Bush Lab
Smith, Andrew Oxford East Lab
Smith, Angela Sheffield Hillsborough Lab/Co-op
Smith, Angela Evans Basildon Lab
Smith, Geraldine Morecambe and Lunesdale Lab
Smith, Jacqui Redditch Lab
Smith, John Vale of Glamorgan Lab
Smith, Robert West Aberdeenshire and Kincardine LD
Snelgrove, Anne South Swindon Lab/Co-op
Soames, Nicholas Mid Sussex C
Soulsby, Peter Leicester South Lab
Southworth, Helen Warrington South Lab
Spellar, John Warley Lab
Spelman, Caroline Meriden C
Spicer, Michael West Worcestershire C
Spink, Bob Castle Point C
Spring, Richard West Suffolk C
Squire, Rachel Dunfermline and West Fife Lab
Stanley, John Tonbridge and Malling C
Starkey, Phyllis Milton Keynes South West Lab
Steen, Anthony Totnes C
Stewart, Ian Eccles Lab
Stoate, Howard Dartford Lab
Strang, Gavin Edinburgh East Lab
Straw, Jack Blackburn Lab
Streeter, Gary South West Devon C
Stringer, Graham Manchester Blackley Lab
Stuart, Gisela Birmingham Edgbaston Lab
Stuart, Graham Beverley and Holderness C
Stunell, Andrew Hazel Grove LD
Sutcliffe, Gerry Bradford South Lab
Swayne, Desmond New Forest West C
Swinson, Jo East Dunbartonshire LD
Swire, Hugo East Devon C
Syms, Robert Poole C

T

Tami, Mark Alyn and Deeside Lab
Tapsell, Peter Louth and Horncastle C
Taylor, Dari Stockton South Lab
Taylor, David North West Leicestershire Lab/Co-op
Taylor, Ian Esher and Walton C
Taylor, Matthew Truro and St Austell LD
Taylor, Richard Wyre Forest Ind KHHC
Teather, Sarah Brent East LD
Thomas, Gareth Harrow West Lab/Co-op
Thornberry, Emily Islington South and Finsbury Lab
Thurso, John Caithness, Sutherland and Easter Ross LD
Timms, Stephen East Ham Lab
Tipping, Paddy Sherwood Lab
Todd, Mark South Derbyshire Lab
Touhig, Don Islwyn Lab/Co-op
Tredinnick, David Bosworth C
Trickett, Jon Hemsworth Lab
Truswell, Paul Pudsey Lab
Turner, Andrew Isle of Wight C
Turner, Des Brighton Kemptown Lab
Turner, Neil Wigan Lab
Twigg, Derek Halton Lab
Tyrie, Andrew Chichester C

U

Ussher, Kitty Burnley Lab

V

Vaizey, Ed Wantage C
Vara, Shailesh North West Cambridgeshire C
Vaz, Keith Leicester East Lab
Viggers, Peter Gosport C
Villiers, Theresa Chipping Barnet C
Vis, Rudi Finchley and Golders Green Lab

W

Walker, Charles Broxbourne C
Wallace, Ben Lancaster and Wyre C
Walley, Joan Stoke-on-Trent North Lab
Walter, Robert North Dorset C

Waltho, Lynda Stourbridge Lab
Ward, Claire Watford Lab
Wareing, Robert Liverpool West Derby Lab
Waterson, Nigel Eastbourne C
Watkinson, Angela Upminster C
Watson, Tom West Bromwich East Lab
Watts, David St Helens North Lab
Webb, Steve Northavon LD
Weir, Mike Angus SNP
Whitehead, Alan Southampton Test Lab
Whittingdale, John Maldon and Chelmsford East C
Wicks, Malcolm Croydon North Lab
Widdecombe, Ann Maidstone and The Weald C
Wiggin, Bill Leominster C
Willetts, David Havant C
Williams, Alan Swansea West Lab
Williams, Betty Conwy Lab
Williams, Hywel Caernarfon PlC
Williams, Mark Ceredigion LD
Williams, Roger Brecon and Radnorshire LD
Williams, Stephen Bristol West LD
Willis, Phil Harrogate and Knaresborough LD
Willott, Jenny Cardiff Central LD
Wills, Michael North Swindon Lab
Wilshire, David Spelthorne C
Wilson, Robert Reading East C
Wilson, Sammy East Antrim DUP
Winnick, David Walsall North Lab
Winterton, Ann Congleton C
Winterton, Nicholas Macclesfield C
Winterton, Rosie Doncaster Central Lab
Wishart, Peter Perth and North Perthshire SNP
Wood, Mike Batley and Spen Lab
Woodward, Shaun St Helens South Lab
Woolas, Phil Oldham East and Saddleworth Lab
Wright, Anthony David Great Yarmouth Lab
Wright, David Telford Lab
Wright, Iain Hartlepool Lab
Wright, Jeremy Rugby and Kenilworth C
Wright, Tony Wayland Cannock Chase Lab
Wyatt, Derek Sittingbourne and Sheppey Lab

Y

Yeo, Tim South Suffolk C
Young, George North West Hampshire C
Younger-Ross, Richard Teignbridge LD

ANALYSIS AND COMMENT

A PARLIAMENT PACKED FULL OF EVENTS AND DEEP DIVISIONS

by **Rosemary Bennett**
Deputy Political Editor, The Times

When Tony Blair was returned to power in 2001 with another thumping Labour majority he had one thing on his mind – transforming Britain's public services. He was well aware that voters were disappointed the Government had not done more to improve schools, hospitals, transport and criminal justice, but had been prepared to give him another chance. He called their verdict 'an instruction to deliver'.

Cabinet ministers were ordered to get to work straight away on major structural reforms in health and education, and a succession of delivery units were set up across Whitehall to drive through change.

Mr Blair embarked on a succession of speeches about the virtues of the private sector, the contribution they could make to the public services and what the country could learn from the business world.

It was not immediately clear what he had in mind, but the direction of travel was obvious. And it was not long before he ran into trouble.

It is hard to believe that with a Commons majority of 167, Mr Blair's second term would be characterised by a succession of backbench rebellions that threatened the most significant pieces of Government legislation.

But MPs returning to Westminster in June 2001 were in defiant mood. Attempts by the whips to replace two long-serving select committee chairman, Donald Anderson and Gwyneth Dunwoody, resulted in the 'peasants' revolt' of 40 Labour MPs, which forced business managers to reinstate the unlikely heroes.

This early test of wills appeared to give back benchers an appetite for rebellion, and they were egged on by fresh tensions at the top of Government over the direction public service reform should take.

Within months of the election Gordon Brown charged former banker Derek Wanless with conducting a sweeping review of NHS spending, making clear that, as far as he was concerned, it would remain a fully tax-funded system. Meanwhile Alan Milburn, the Health Secretary, began drawing up his plans for a radical overhaul of health care provision. At the heart would be new 'foundation hospitals' with enormous freedom from Whitehall control, able to borrow on the financial markets, hire, fire and set their own pay rates.

The stage was set for an early showdown.

In his 2002 budget Mr Brown announced a one percentage point increase in national insurance contributions to pay for a major increase in health spending. He made clear that as far as he was concerned there were limits to the involvement of markets in the health service.

But Mr Milburn battled on. Egged on by Mr Blair and encouraged by heavy opposition from trade unions to his reforms, he drew up more detailed plans for his foundation hospitals despite the Chancellor's opposition.

The matter came to a head shortly after the 2002 Labour Party conference when Mr Blair was forced to broker a deal between Mr Brown and the Health Secretary where the Chancellor prevailed. The plans were hobbled and it was agreed foundation hospitals would not be able to borrow freely on financial markets after all.

Despite this major concession the arguments rumbled on with MPs eager for a showdown with Government. The bill suffered nine separate rebellions as Labour MPs sounded their fury at the direction public service reform was taking. In the final vote in November 2003 the Government's majority was cut to 17.

Mr Milburn resigned as Health Secretary before the parliamentary battle reached a climax, citing personal reasons, robbing Mr Blair of another key Cabinet ally.

Stephen Byers, another New Labour 'outrider' for reform, had already quit the year before after being embroiled for months in a row about Railtrack, which he took back into Government hands. Peter Mandelson had been forced to resign for a second time in the previous Parliament.

The Prime Minister used a series of major speeches to say he had learnt his lesson and never again would he serve up radical public service reforms on an unsuspecting party.

But within weeks he was embroiled in another full-scale row, this time over the introduction of top-up fees for university students. Spearheaded by the Downing Street education adviser Andrew, now Lord, Adonis, the plans were designed to inject fresh funds into university education, which would eventually lead to 50 per cent of all young people attending.

It was also designed to show New Labour's radical edge with the introduction of market forces into universities, which would be able to charge variable fees reflecting the popularity of their different courses.

But education is a highly symbolic issue for Labour back benchers. MPs had already shown their disdain at the direction education policy was taking. An education bill, allowing for more 'specialist schools', including faith schools, was opposed by 46 MPs early in 2002.

Plans for scores of new city academies to improve the quality of urban comprehensive schools were also viewed with suspicion by backbenchers.

Legislation allowing universities to charge top-up fees became the rallying point for all the backbench disaffection with education reform.

One Education Secretary, Estelle Morris, had resigned before the bill was even drawn up, following a series of clashes with Downing Street. Charles Clarke, her successor, now weighed into the debate insisting that he review all options.

Mr Brown took advantage of a further delay to make sure MPs knew he was far from happy with plans. His views on the elite admissions practice of top universities were well known. Variable tuition fees would only serve to deter more students from poorer backgrounds aiming for the top.

Lengthy wrangling between Cabinet ministers wore on, resulting in the creation of a new regulator which would only permit universities to charge the top level of fees if they could prove they were doing their utmost to recruit students from poorer backgrounds.

But despite this and numerous other concessions Labour back benchers reduced the Government's majority to five.

In an attempt to curry favour with his truculent back benchers Mr Blair dangled the carrot of a hunting ban before them for almost the entire Parliament without ever quite letting it get to a definitive vote.

In the end his promises caught up with him and MPs voted for an immediate ban, refusing to back a last-minute attempt by the Government to postpone its implementation by two years.

Like many of his predecessors, Mr Blair found foreign affairs increasingly dominated the domestic agenda. Within months of the election his plans to concentrate on public service delivery were blown off course. Events 3,500 miles away on America's east coast set Mr Blair on the path to a war which would shape the entire Parliament, fracturing his relationship with the party and destroying the trust of hundreds of thousands of voters.

The Prime Minister was swift to recognise the significance of the 9/11 attacks on the World Trade Centre and the Pentagon. Within minutes he announced he would stand 'shoulder to shoulder' with President Bush, underlining the special relationship between the two nations, and between the New Labour Government and the right-wing Republican administration.

British forces were soon playing a leading role in air strikes on Afghanistan, the first battle in the 'war on terror' in retaliation for the 9/11 attacks.

There were profound domestic implications of the 9/11 attacks too. David Blunkett, the Home Secretary, promptly announced plans for a anti-terrorism legislation which would give the authorities new powers to detain foreign terror suspects without trial.

That legislation would haunt the Government throughout the second term as civil liberty activists challenged the new laws, eventually winning out in the House of Lords which said the detention of suspects in Belmarsh prison was 'disproportionate and discriminatory'.

However, Mr Blair was about to become embroiled in a much bigger crisis. Throughout 2002 it was apparent President Bush was preparing for an invasion of Iraq. Faced with sceptical MPs at home and resistance from European allies, the Government set about building a case for war resulting in the now infamous September dossier, which warned of Iraqi weapons of mass destruction that could be deployed within 45 minutes.

Mr Blair persuaded President Bush to try and get the backing of the UN before invading, a move that ultimately ended in failure. With the armed forces massing on Iraq's borders, over one million people took to the streets to march against the war, unconvinced that Iraq posed Britain any threat.

Mr Blair had promised MPs the final say and, with the clock ticking down to war, one of the most dramatic debates in Parliament's modern history took place on 18 March 2003.

After impassioned speeches by Mr Blair, Jack Straw and a host of Tory and Labour back benchers, including Robin Cook who had resigned as the Leader of the House of Commons over the war, 139 Labour MPs voted against the Government, the biggest rebellion of the Parliament.

But support from the Conservatives meant the Government had enough support and air strikes started within 48 hours.

The war was swift, with US forces reaching Baghdad less than a month later. But the aftermath for Mr Blair was long and bloody.

A BBC report which accused Downing Street of 'sexing up' the September dossier sparked a huge row between the Government and the BBC, fuelled by Alastair Campbell, the director of communications.

As the weeks rolled by and no chemical and biological weapons were found in Iraq, the increasingly ferocious row with the BBC proved a useful distraction for the Government.

But events took a tragic turn. Dr David Kelly, the Ministry of Defence weapons expert, was uncovered as the source of the BBC story and shortly afterwards took his own life. A rattled Mr Blair immediately launched an inquiry into the affair led by Lord Hutton, a little known judge from Northern Ireland.

Throughout the summer of 2003 ministers including Mr Blair, Geoff Hoon, the Defence Secretary, and senior Government and intelligence officials were subjected to cross-examination in a poky corner of the Royal Courts of Justice.

A host of secret documents, e-mails and Cabinet papers were also released to the public. They lifted the lid on the casual way Mr Blair conducted business in Downing Street, showing how serious decisions of state were frequently taken in unminuted meetings in the Downing Street 'den', with officials with Mr Blair holding court on the sofa.

Mr Blair, the Government and senior intelligence officials were, to the astonishment of some, cleared of all charges, from embellishing the dossier to exposing Dr Kelly's identity to the press. The BBC was severely criticised, prompting the immediate resignation of Gavyn Davies, the chairman, and Greg Dyke, the director general.

However, the Government's triumphalist reaction, led by Mr Campbell, who had since resigned from Downing Street, made sure hostility towards Mr Blair and the Government lingered on right until polling day when the many thousands of opponents of the war finally got their chance to give the Prime Minister 'a bloody nose'.

The stresses and strains of the war and Hutton Inquiry clearly took their toll on Mr Blair. He was admitted to hospital in October 2003 suffering from an irregular heartbeat. His family had had a wretched time. His wife, Cherie, was forced to apologise and admit mistakes were made when she bought two flats in Bristol. The Blair children appeared increasingly to resent the exposure that came with their father's job.

As it became clear there would be no WMD found in Iraq, Mr Blair's integrity was damaged as never before. In the autumn of 2003 the Prime Minister told Mr Brown and John Prescott he was considering quitting. He spoke to them again the following spring, telling them he was thinking of announcing he would resign in the autumn at the party conference. Rearguard action from close Cabinet colleagues made him reconsider, and Mr Brown advised him it would be unwise to pre-announce that he was standing down. Better to just go in the autumn.

But over the summer Mr Blair's mood improved. Labour did better than expected in the June 2004 local elections, and Michael Howard, the Conservative leader who replaced the hapless Iain Duncan Smith, had failed to make much impact with voters. Mr Blair decided to stay on, infuriating Mr Brown who believe the Prime Minister had reneged on a deal.

The relationship was further damaged when Mr Blair unexpectedly announced he would serve a full third term but not fight a fourth general election, an attempt to end speculation about his future before he underwent further heart treatment and confirmed he had bought a house in Bayswater.

The final blow to Mr Brown was the triumphant return to the Cabinet of his nemesis Mr Milburn, who was invited to mastermind the general election campaign, a job the Chancellor had held in the previous two elections. Relations between Number 10 and 11 Downing Street hit an all-time low.

Mr Brown was still considered the only contender to succeed the Prime Minister, despite Mr Milburn's return to the front line.

Mr Blunkett, one of the few figures who could have mounted a challenge, was forced to quit in December 2004 when it emerged Home Office officials had helped 'fast track' a visa for the nanny of his lover, Kimberly Quinn. That left his successor Mr Clarke, another possible leadership contender, the task of cobbling together emergency legislation to replace the anti-terror laws overturned by the courts.

New measures allowing the authorities to place 'control orders' on terror suspects, including house arrest, scraped through Parliament after a series of concessions and a deal with the opposition parties as the clock ticked down to the general election. That left another rival to Mr Brown decidedly on the back foot.

Mr Brown had plenty to recommend him as a future Prime Minister. He had successfully steered the economy throughout the parliamentary term, avoiding the damaging slowdown experienced in much of Europe and the US. He presided over a massive injection of funds into key public services, paid for by taxes edging up at every budget. He had stamped Treasury ownership on the decision of whether or not to join the euro. In June 2003, after a mammoth analysis of the famous five economic tests, Mr Brown announced the conditions had not been met and Britain would not join the single currency for the time being.

It soon became clear to Labour's election strategists that Mr Brown was more popular with voters than Mr Blair. By the time the election campaign got under way a miraculous reconciliation between the Prime Minister and Chancellor had been achieved. Mr Brown was back at the helm of the election campaign and accompanying Mr Blair around the country on his leader's tour.

The strategy paid off, blunting the Tories' attack on the Prime Minister and helping to reduce the damage of Iraq on election day. But Labour could not work miracles. Voters returned Mr Blair to power with a greatly reduced majority, leaving him with a lot to do to secure his longed-for legacy.

A SECOND TERM THAT LABOUR DID NOT BARGAIN ON

by **Alice Miles**
Columnist, The Times

On 8 June 2001, having just secured another landslide mandate with a majority of 167 seats, Tony Blair stood in Downing Street and said his second term would be an opportunity to build on the economic foundations laid in the first. This term would see the Government 'relentlessly' focusing on its priorities. It would be about reform of the welfare and criminal justice systems; engagement with Europe; and, above all, the modernisation of Britain's public services.

It was not.

It was about 11 September 2001, the day that Islamic terrorists flew aeroplanes into the Pentagon and the World Trade Centre. From that moment on, a term which had been expected to be dominated by the fight to reform the public sector in the face of resistance from the Labour left, and to take the country into the euro in the face of resistance from the British public, became instead about the fight against international terror – in the face, often, of resistance from both the Labour left and much of the British public.

It was a fight that took Britain into Afghanistan, to defeat the Taliban, and into Iraq, to tackle Saddam Hussein. And it took Tony Blair into battle with his party, and nearly defeated him.

Mr Blair was at the annual conference of Britain's trade unions, nervously preparing for a rough ride over his plans for public sector reform, when the planes struck the World Trade Centre. He immediately cancelled the speech and returned to London, declaring that Britain would stand 'shoulder to shoulder' with the United States: 'This mass terrorism is the new evil in our world.'

His second term was barely under way – and a new Conservative party leader, Iain Duncan Smith, had just been elected by party members, and the result would be announced within days – but already it was utterly changed. Mr Blair had intended to use Labour's second term to drive through reform of Britain's public services, and in particular to involve the private sector more in their delivery. But a month after the attack on the World Trade Centre Britain and the US launched air strikes on Afghanistan in retaliation for 9/11. When the Taliban abandoned Kabul a month later it signalled the end of the beginning of Mr Blair's fight with Al Qaeda and international terror, not the beginning of the end. In January 2002 President Bush branded Iraq, Iran and North Korea as the 'axis of evil' – and the long march into Baghdad, and the events that nearly destroyed Mr Blair, began.

It was a slow build-up. By the summer of 2002 President Bush was telling US forces to be ready for pre-emptive action against Saddam Hussein; France and Germany were demanding a UN mandate for any attack; and Mr Blair promised that Parliament would be consulted before British forces were involved. Over the summer unrest grew among the British left at the prospect of an attack. Mr Blair recalled Parliament in September and published a 'dossier' of evidence which concluded that the Baghdad regime had weaponry, including weapons of mass destruction, some of which 'could be activated within 45 minutes'. Two months later the UN passed resolution 1441, giving Iraq a final opportunity to comply with earlier resolutions demanding disarmament. The US responded by formally requesting assistance from Britain in any conflict with Iraq. In January 2003 the US sent thousands of marines to the Gulf.

In an attempt to win support for any action in Iraq, in February the British government published a second dossier on the existence of Iraqi WMD. As a million people demonstrated in London, Russia, France and

Germany called for UN weapons inspectors to be given more time. In the continuing build-up to the invasion Mr Blair faced the most crucial vote of his Parliamentary career. On 18 March 2003 he asked for MPs' backing for a motion allowing 'all means necessary to ensure the disarmament of Iraq's weapons of mass destruction'. The motion was passed, with the support of the Conservatives, by 412 votes to 149, but 139 Labour MPs also backed a Liberal Democrat amendment saying that the case for war had not yet been made, especially in the absence of specific UN authorisation. Two days later Britain joined the US in the invasion of Iraq, without the authority of a second UN resolution. Baghdad fell within three weeks.

And the story had barely begun for Mr Blair. On 29 May 2003 the BBC journalist Andrew Gilligan reported on the channel's flagship *Today* programme that an official involved in the preparation of the September 2002 dossier on WMD had told him the government had 'sexed up' the threat posed by Iraq. In a subsequent newspaper article Mr Gilligan wrote that the Prime Minister's communications chief Alastair Campbell was responsible for this.

The scene was set, over a long, hot summer, for probably the most sustained, ferocious onslaught on a prime minister that has ever been seen in British public life. A House of Commons committee investigated the Gilligan claims and declared them false, while newspapers reported the BBC journalist's source to be government scientist Dr David Kelly. Dr Kelly himself was shortly called before the same committee of MPs; three days later he was found dead in a wood near his Oxfordshire home. 'Have you got blood on your hands, Prime Minister?' asked a reporter travelling to Japan with a shattered-looking Mr Blair. The Prime Minister immediately announced an inquiry into Dr Kelly's death, to be headed by Lord Hutton.

In the hearings by Lord Hutton that summer a British prime minister was called into a witness box in a judicial inquiry for the first time. By the moment that Lord Hutton cleared the government of any wrong doing five months later, causing the chairman and the director-general of the BBC to resign, Saddam Hussein had been captured but the failure to find any WMD in Iraq was a new threat to Mr Blair's position at home. The Prime Minister was forced to set up a second inquiry, headed by Lord Butler of Brockwell, into the use of intelligence in the run-up to the Iraq war. Lord Butler would criticise the Government in his report five months later for the way it used intelligence on WMD and removed any caveats about the quality of that intelligence, but he did not say that Mr Blair had lied. He also attacked the Prime Minister's informal 'sofa' style of government.

All the questions had been asked and answered many times, but the lack of trust in Mr Blair among the country and his own MPs remained. Britain, and Britons, were still under threat from international terrorism. The British consul was killed by suicide bombers in Istanbul in November 2003; a British Airways flight to Washington was repeatedly cancelled in January 2004; a train bombing in Madrid killed 200 in March 2004, leading the Metropolitan Police chief to say that an attack on Britain was inevitable; two Britons living in Iraq, Kenneth Bigley and Margaret Hassan, were kidnapped and later killed by Islamist groups; an Algerian living in Britain, Kamel Bourgass, was convicted of planning to poison Britons with ricin; and draconian new anti-terror laws scraped through Parliament just before the election, but only after Mr Blair was forced to make heavy concessions to MPs and the House of Lords. The Prime Minister was heavily punished by the electorate in the 2005 poll for the way he led the nation into war.

And terror was the issue that wasn't even meant to be. The battle on the euro, by contrast, was expected to dominate the second, and in the event it never even began. In a statement to Parliament on 9 June 2003 the Chancellor Gordon Brown declared four of the five economic tests which had to be passed before Britain joined the euro, failed. Mr Blair may have wanted to take Britain into the heart of Europe in his second term, but he ran out of the political capital necessary to make that a reality. Ten months after the Chancellor's statement Mr Blair gave another hostage to fortune when he announced that there would be a referendum in the next Parliament on whether Britain should sign up to the new EU Constitution.

If Europe was the dog that didn't bark, the Chancellor was the rottweiler who did. Mr Blair and Mr Brown entered their second term in uneasy alliance, having spent much of their first term rowing. As the Prime Minister was weakened, the Chancellor flexed his muscles, at first behind the scenes and then openly. At issue was, foremost, the leadership. An incendiary new book in January 2005, written with the co-operation of Mr Brown's closest allies, claimed that the Prime Minister had offered to the Chancellor to resign in November 2003, admitting that he had lost trust over the war in Iraq. The Conservative opposition had just elected a new leader, Michael Howard, and the Prime Minister was at a low ebb, having recently entered hospital for treatment to deal with an irregular heartbeat.

Over the next few months the two men repeatedly discussed the timing of the handover to Mr Brown, with Mr Blair even suggesting pre-announcing an autumn departure. In the midst of these negotiations, in January 2004, the Prime Minister narrowly avoided losing a Commons vote on his controversial proposal to introduce variable university tuition fees, a move unpopular with the Labour left. He only won the vote, his closest in office, by 316-311 after the apparent intervention of Mr Brown, who urged close allies to support the Government.

However, as Mr Blair's mood improved over subsequent months, partly due to the Hutton report which cleared him of any wrong doing, and partly due to loyal Cabinet ministers' pleading with him not to go, the Prime Minister changed his mind. Instead of leaving that autumn he organised a snap reshuffle, bringing Mr Brown's arch enemy Alan Milburn back into the Cabinet in charge of Labour's election campaign, a role filled by the Chancellor in the past. The openly provocative move brought relations between the two men to a new low, with Mr Brown refusing any co-operation with No 10 or the election campaign managers until the final weeks of the 2005 campaign when he and the Prime Minister reached a rapprochement in order to rescue Labour's faltering position in the polls.

Mr Blair ended the term with his main ambitions unfulfilled. Europe was as distant as ever. There were huge increases in investment in public services, partly helped by a penny increase in national insurance, which brought more teachers, more nurses, more doctors, new or refurbished buildings and falling hospital waiting lists but, particularly in education, the public sector did not see the radical reform that the Prime Minister had envisaged. Britain's transport system remained choked. The private sector was significantly more involved in providing NHS services in areas such as radiology, MRI scans and £1 billion of planned, minor operations – but a drive to free hospitals from Whitehall control by turning them into 'foundation hospital' became bogged down in a row between Mr Brown and the then Health Secretary Mr Milburn. The new type of hospital eventually got the go-ahead, despite a revolt by 65 Labour MPs, but with significantly reduced freedoms. It was a potent symbol of the second, unresolved and fundamental, dispute between Mr Brown and Mr Blair – over the limits of the market in public services.

Foxhunting was banned in November 2004 after years of prevarication by the Prime Minister and failure to find a compromise, and to shrieks of protest from countryside campaigners, some of whom invaded the House of Commons chamber during earlier debates.

Mr Blair failed to make as clear an impact as he would have liked on the constitution, with the House of Lords left half-reformed, and the messy abolition of the post of Lord Chancellor and over-hasty announcement of a new Supreme Court which immediately ran into problems. The Government did, however, make great strides with a 'family friendly' agenda, with fathers given the right to paid paternity leave for the first time, longer maternity leave, the right for parents of young children to request flexible working, very popular 'Sure Start' schemes for disadvantaged infants and nursery places for all three year olds. The minimum wage rose by 18 per cent over the term to £5.05 an hour.

Mr Blair lost a clutch of his closest allies in his second term (some said because he failed to give them the support they needed under pressure), with the resignations of Education Secretary Estelle Morris, Transport Secretary Stephen Byers, Health Secretary Alan Milburn, Home Secretary David Blunkett, communications director Alastair Campbell and the departure of the Prime Minister's longstanding adviser Peter Mandelson to Brussels as Britain's new EU commissioner. Even the Prime Minister's wife, Cherie, came under personal attack over her purchase of a couple of flats in Bristol. Mr Blair's health waned as his popularity faded. In October 2004 he went into hospital for a heart operation and announced that he would stand down after serving another full term – a statement taken as a further declaration of war by the Chancellor, who saw himself in No 10 long before then.

The second term ended as it had begun: with the Prime Minister saying that he now knew what needed to be done to transform Britain's public services, and believed that he had secured the personal and political wherewithal to do it. Cordial relations with the Chancellor, restored for the duration of the election campaign, were not expected to survive far into the third term. The cardinal question was: would Mr Blair?

THREE LEADERS AND FOUR YEARS OF TORY STRIFE

by **Tim Hames**
Assistant Editor, The Times

The Conservative Party began the Parliament of 2001-05 with a leadership election. It would end it with at least some senior figures (correctly as matters would transpire) privately preparing for another contest. In between these two events, there was also a leadership deselection swiftly followed by an election of sorts – unopposed and virtually by acclamation. These opening sentences alone convey a sense of crisis and factionalism. They do not capture the whole of that discord. For as well as three leaders, the Conservatives also witnessed a series of figures arrive and depart from the helm at Conservative Central Office and beneath them a set of supposed electoral gurus who also came and went at bewildering speed. In the end, it is remarkable that the Conservatives actually managed to gain seats and a somewhat more modest additional number of votes when the hustings finally arrived, as expected, on 5 May 2005.

William Hague resigned within 24 hours of polls closing in the 2001 campaign. Having secured only a single extra seat in the House of Commons (and barely a higher percentage of the national ballot), he had little realistic choice but to depart with all the dignity that he could muster. Michael Portillo appeared to be the strong favourite for the succession, but he was reluctant to press his challenge. He virtually disappeared to Morocco during the weekend after the Tory defeat but was persuaded by his supporters to make himself available to the party. At one stage it looked as if he might be swept to victory with the backing of 100 or more MPs.

This was not to be. Mr Portillo was reluctant to make the sort of compromises that would render his ultimate triumph more probable. He had strong backing in the Shadow Cabinet but was weaker in the parliamentary party as a whole. Others took the temperature and then decided that it was worth their while to pursue a claim. Mr Portillo was joined by Ken Clarke (ex Chancellor and Home Secretary) for the Tory left, Iain Duncan Smith (the Shadow Defence Secretary) on the right, Michael Ancram (Conservative Party Chairman) from the middle and David Davis (Chairman of the Public Accounts Committee 1997-2001), who defied easy categorisation. The race could not start until a new Chairman of the 1922 Committee had emerged. He was the figure whom the constitution made the returning officer for the leadership election. When Sir Michael Spicer obtained that position he decided on a more deliberate, less forceful, timetable for the election. That decision inevitably hurt the frontrunner.

To be fair to Sir Michael, that frontrunner appeared intent on damaging himself. The Portillo campaign became dogged by minor controversies as his rivals succeeded in painting the Shadow Chancellor as dangerously, even flakily, liberal. He led on the first ballot of MPs but with only 49 of the 166 votes cast. He was followed by Mr Clarke and Mr Duncan Smith. In a farcical twist, though, Mr Ancram and Mr Davis tied for the last place on the ballot. In the absence of clear rules about what to do in that eventuality, a further round of voting with all five names still in the ring was ordered. Mr Ancram duly did come bottom and, surprising many, endorsed Mr Duncan Smith and not Mr Clarke. Mr Davis also plumped for the Shadow Defence Secretary. The third and final round of the parliamentary stage was agonisingly close. Mr Clarke won 59 votes, Mr Duncan Smith 54 votes and Mr Portillo 53 votes (and was thus eliminated).

"I'D DEFECT FROM THE TORIES IF ONLY SOMEBODY ELSE WOULD HAVE ME"

The leadership contest then moved to the 300,000 members in the country. The campaign was dominated by Europe – or more precisely the acceptability or not of Mr Clarke's outlook on that subject – although the ex-Chancellor attempted to make his relative electability a more salient question in the eyes of Tory activists. That initiative failed. When the result was finally announced – having been delayed for a day after the terrorist atrocities of 11 September 2001 – Mr Duncan Smith had romped home by a 61-39 per cent margin. There was no doubt that his distaste for the euro was key.

It thus fell to Mr Duncan Smith to form a Shadow Cabinet. Michael Howard returned as the Shadow Chancellor, Oliver Letwin became Shadow Home Secretary, Mr Ancram took on the role of Shadow Foreign Secretary (and Deputy Leader), while Mr Davis was placed in charge at Conservative Central Officers. A number of 'modernisers', most notably Francis Maude, the departing Shadow Foreign Secretary, declined to serve but to balance this, others who had been at the heart of the Portillo election effort were headhunted by Mr Duncan Smith to take senior posts at Smith Square. The most notable of these was Mark MacGregor, a successful businessman, who became chief executive.

The whole period of Mr Duncan Smith's tenure was fraught with difficulties. His initial party conference was completely overshadowed by 11 September 2001, and the bombing campaign in Afghanistan obliged Parliament to be recalled on the opening day of it. Mr Duncan Smith made a low-key speech and signalled an interest in focusing on the public services and making a political bid for the support of the 'vulnerable'. This was an interesting tack as his reputation had been that of a right-winger.

The apparant modernisation of Mr Duncan Smith continued apace with the appointment of Dominic Cummings, a young radical who had made an enormous success of the anti-euro Business for Sterling campaign, as Director of Strategy at Central Office. During his brief period of serious influence, Mr Cummings persuaded his leader to deliver a speech to the party spring conference at Harrogate which was a model of moderate tone and outlook. It quickly became evident that this was not a complete change of heart and Mr Cummings, convinced he would not win the turf war which he could see coming, would leave Central Office in October 2002, a mere eight months from his arrival.

The Tories made a modest advance in the May 2002 local elections. They did not allay doubts which regularly surfaced about Mr Duncan Smith's qualifications as a prospective prime minister. Some did not care for the backing that he was offering to Tony Blair as it became apparent that a war in Iraq was a serious possibility. The Tory leader was persuaded that his party chairman was the source of his difficulties. Mr Davis was demoted to shadow John Prescott, the Deputy Prime Minister, while Theresa May was appointed to be his successor. It looked as if the modernisers might have captured the leader again after all. Aware of that possibility, Lord Tebbit, who had preceded Mr Duncan Smith as the MP for Chingford, publicly urged him to conduct a purge of top officials at Central Office with Mr MacGregor the principal target.

At the party conference in early October, Ms May made a sensational speech in which she reminded (informed?) delegates that, fairly or not, they had become known as 'the nasty party' and something had to be done about this. Although her address was hailed by the media, it was unpopular with the traditionalist wing of the party and Mr Duncan Smith himself appeared to be in two minds about it. His own speech to his conference audience included the assertion that his supporters should not 'underestimate the determination of a quiet man'.

Life became noisier for him almost immediately. An avoidable row about the party's stance on opposing the notion of gay and unmarried couples adopting children led John Bercow, an up-and-coming moderniser, to quit the Shadow Cabinet and prompted a huge internal revolt with 44 MPs either rejecting the official line or abstaining. This triggered a real crisis for Mr Duncan Smith which he did not help by delivering a strange address in which he somberly informed Tories that they must either 'unite or die'. Death looked like the most credible of those options.

It would not happen quickly or without more bloodshed in several quarters. In February 2003 Mr Duncan Smith did indeed purge the modernisers at Central Office, forcing Mr MacGregor out, disposing of another senior official, Rick Nye, as well and temporarily threatening Steven Gilbert, the widely liked and highly respected national agent, from his portfolio. Mr Duncan Smith had intended to impose a friend and former MP, Barry Legg, in the place of MacGregor. He had reckoned without the firm opposition of members of the National Board who eventually ensured that Mr Legg could not continue. The results of the local elections in May were good enough to keep the leader in his place, despite one of his frontbenchers, Crispin Blunt, resigning on the night of the poll and urging that Mr Duncan Smith be brought down.

The assassination had merely been delayed. The poor performance of the Tories at the Brent East by-election in September, accusations that Betsy Duncan Smith had been improperly compensated by the taxpayers for services which she had never performed, and a surreal display of rebellion at the Blackpool party conference plunged the leader into ever deeper trouble. The tone he took before delegates indicated a shift back to hard-right themes. Once MPs had come back to Westminster, an attempt was made to acquire the signatures required for a no-confidence ballot. Once they existed, the party moved straight to a vote and by a margin of 90 to 75 the coup was executed.

Mr Howard would be the beneficiary of it. On the night that Mr Duncan Smith fell, Mr Davis and Tim Yeo, a possible contender from the liberal spectrum, made it plain that they would not fight the Shadow Chancellor for the crown. On the next day Mr Ancram also declined to make a contest of it. Tory MPs congratulated themselves on the transition that they had rendered possible and expressed hope that with the arrival of an experienced 'adult' in the leadership, their fortunes could be revived.

Mr Howard started vigorously. His introductory speech at the Saatchi Gallery (apparently penned by Mr Maude) made many noises in the direction of modernisation. He decided to appoint a much smaller (12-strong) more business-like Shadow Cabinet. It included Mr Letwin as Shadow Chancellor, Mr Davis as Shadow Home Secretary, Mr Ancram as Shadow Foreign Secretary, Mr Yeo combining health and education and Liam Fox and Lord (Maurice) Saatchi as the co-Chairmen of the Conservative Party. Not all were convinced of the wisdom of these moves but slightly stronger opinion poll ratings made Mr Howard seem even more powerful. He entered 2004 in remarkably decent shape.

This was not to last. Mr Howard could not overturn the Labour lead in the polls. He was uncertain in his response to the Hutton Report and his opposition to university top-up fees struck many observers as too opportunistic. He abandoned the strategy set out at the Saatchi Gallery in favour of strident opposition to the Government. He was soon being accused of a retreat to the 'core vote' approach of Mr Hague.

Mr Howard enjoyed a respectable performance in the local council elections of June 2004 but the strong showing by UKIP upstaged him in the ballot for the European Parliament. He conducted an unexpected reshuffle. Mr Yeo was effectively demoted to Shadow Environment Minister, allowing Andrew Lansley and Tim Collins to enter the Shadow Cabinet covering health and education respectively. Ms May was consigned to cover 'the Family'. David Willetts lost the policy aspect of his brief to David Cameron. There was no sign of a party revival as a consequence. The Tories were a poor third in both the by-elections of July and Mr Howard invited a degree of ridicule by appearing to retrospectively retract his backing for the conflict in Iraq.

Matters would get worse before they became better. In another reshuffle in September John Redwood returned to the Shadow Cabinet in charge of Deregulation while Nicholas Soames and Mr Cameron were elevated to it while retaining their existing positions. A series of disagreements led to Damian Green, John Bercow and Julie Kirkbride leaving the front bench. On the Thursday before the party conference opened the Tories came fourth in the Hartlepool by-election. Despite this, Mr Howard's first conference did not pass off badly. His speech implied that he certainly had the stomach for the coming battle.

This final stage involved one more change of personnel. Boris Johnson, arts spokesman, editor of the *Spectator* and television personality, was sacked for allegedly being less than wholly truthful to his leader about a supposed love affair. In a totally separate development, Mr Howard decided to wager on the talents of Lynton Crosby, a legendary Australian political operator, to steer the election campaign. Although this brought a wave of reports of tension between Mr Crosby and either or both of Mr Fox and Lord Saatchi, by the beginning of 2005 a new professionalism was evident. Mr Howard had latched on to a collection of populist (or 'dog-whistle' issues) such as immigration and the behaviour of travellers on illegal camps and was attracting considerable publicity for them. They were the basis for a reasonably successful 'pre-campaign' before the contest proper finally opened.

This was preceded by one last internal feud in which Howard Flight was first sacked as Deputy Chairman and then deselected as an MP for making a speech (covertly recorded) which could be read as boasting that the Conservatives had a secret agenda for spending reductions beyond those which Mr Letwin and David James, the man who had been brought in by Mr Howard to identify 'waste' in Whitehall, had outlined to the electorate. After all the exceptional fratricide of the previous four years, it was perhaps appropriate for the Tories to end the Parliament on this divisive note.

KENNEDY OPTED FOR UNITY AND STEADY PROGRESS, NOT BIG RISKS

by **Greg Hurst**

Political Correspondent, The Times

Charles Kennedy's purpose in becoming leader of the Liberal Democrats was to refashion his party as a fully independent political force. Only after the 2001 general election, freed from the constraints of an approaching campaign and with a mandate of his own as he returned with 52 MPs, did he feel at liberty to do so. He shrugged off years of speculation about a realignment of progressive parties, talk of an eventual merger with Labour and an assumption that Liberal Democrats wielded influence only when paying court to Tony Blair and set off in a different direction.

More by luck than judgement, Mr Kennedy swiftly overcame the perennial danger facing the Liberal Democrats between elections. Historically they simply disappeared from public view as two-party politics resumed its rituals. Three things helped him. Oddly, all came to a head on the same day late that first summer.

11 September 2001 was the day he and Mr Blair had agreed they would announce the suspension of the Joint Cabinet Committee. This was the forum discussing a shared programme of constitutional reforms set up by the Prime Minister and Paddy Ashdown. Its future had been the subject of much consultation by Mr Kennedy since the election but for him the decision was straightforward. With ministers stalling on Lords reform, and refusing to countenance Liberal Democrat demands of devolution to England's regions or proportional representation for Westminster or town halls, there was nothing to be gained and much to lose from being seen to have a link to the Government.

Their suspension of co-operation was confirmed later, freeing Mr Kennedy to pursue his pledge to mount 'effective opposition' to Labour.

By a quirk of fate on that same September day the polls closed as the Conservative Party finalised the election of Iain Duncan Smith as leader. The rejection by Tory members of Kenneth Clarke, a pugnacious, pro-European centrist and formidable politician, presented a massive strategic opportunity to the Liberal Democrats. The announcement of the Conservatives' new leader was likewise delayed, but the die was cast.

For Mr Kennedy and his party the terrorism attacks of 9/11 presented a particular challenge to which they rose, surprisingly to some, as President Bush's war on terrorism led to the bombing of Afghanistan, two tranches of contentious anti-terrorism legislation and ultimately the invasion of Iraq.

Liberal Democrats was the first party to gather for the conference season barely a dozen days after 9/11. They had serious discussions about whether to go ahead at all. They did so, of course, and found themselves the first political movement in Britain to articulate and debate the terrorist attacks that shocked the world numb. Mr Kennedy, controversially at the time, talked of being a 'candid friend' to President Bush while his party urged caution as Ministers advocated identity cards and new counter-terrorism controls.

Liberal Democrats supported the bombing campaign to oust the Taleban regime from Afghanistan. Confusingly by the year's end they ended up with an additional MP as Mr Kennedy opened to his arms to a

Labour MP, Paul Marsden, who fell out with his own side after opposing the military action. This caused some unease among Liberal Democrats, which found an echo during the 2005 campaign when Mr Kennedy embraced Brian Sedgemore, a retiring MP from Labour's unreconstructed hard Left who had criticised the founders of the SDP.

Liberal Democrats worked closely with the Conservatives to temper the first raft of post-9/11 anti-terrorism laws. They defeated the proposed offence of incitement to religious hatred and added sunset clauses to unprecedented powers of detention without trial for foreign nationals wanted on terrorism charges abroad.

Alongside these pressing events, Mr Kennedy faced the familiar strategic question of whether he led a party of the left or the centre. A post-election review of policy on public services, chaired by the MEP Chris Huhne, turned into a tussle between champions of public sector providers and an emerging pro-markets wing eager to explore private sector solutions. Mr Kennedy, apparently more instinctively at ease with the former, flirted with trade union critics of Mr Blair's public sector reforms, reinforcing alarm among some Liberal Democrats at being cast as defenders of producer interests, not service users.

The Huhne review's most important conclusions were in committing the Liberal Democrats to local control of public services and community or mutual ownership of hospitals or schools. Paradoxically, the party later opposed Government plans for independently run foundation hospitals, illustrating an ambiguous attitude towards reforming public services. The review's proposals for a health tax, based on the national insurance system, and regional assemblies, were later dropped after Gordon Brown's huge increases in health spending and the decision by voters in the North East to say no to a directly elected regional assembly.

Mr Kennedy's own circumstances changed significantly as he married his long-term girlfriend, Sarah Gurling, in the Commons chapel (the service was delayed by the late arrival of Mr Blair, one of their guests). Many colleagues saw her as an important stabilising influence on him.

A small group of bullish young MPs, several with centre-right instincts that contrasted with the liberal-left statism of many party activists, began urging him be more ambitious. As the Conservatives foundered under Mr Duncan Smith, at one point dipping to 28 per cent in opinion ratings, some of Mr Kennedy's advisers fretted that an historic opportunity lay before him that he must seize with greater urgency.

Against this backdrop he made one of his most important leader's speeches, telling his annual conference in autumn 2002 that the Liberal Democrats need not forever remain Britain's third political party. He thus set his sights on overtaking the Conservatives.

Much of Mr Kennedy's time in the Parliament's first half became devoted to Iraq. Not naturally at ease dealing with foreign affairs, he formed a group of advisers that often met daily. He relied too on the counsel of Sir Menzies Campbell, his respected foreign affairs spokesman who was forced to remain in touch by telephone over the winter of 2002 as he underwent treatment for cancer. Sir Menzies was elected the party's deputy leader early the following year.

The Liberal Democrats' eventual opposition to the invasion of Iraq grew out of the questioning tone struck by the party in a series of tense parliamentary debates. It was thrown into sharp relief by the Conservative Party's hawkish endorsement of pre-emptive military action advocated by Mr Duncan Smith.

The case articulated by Mr Kennedy was not that war with Iraq would be wrong but military action had yet to be justified; United Nations weapons inspectors should be given full rein to hunt for Saddam Hussein's alleged weapons of mass destruction. He hardened his position by addressing an anti-war rally in London as conflict loomed. Despite caveats about his position as he addressed the rally, his presence as the most senior mainstream politician at a mass demonstration against the war was a powerful symbol.

The logic of his position was, in fact, that the Liberal Democrats would have supported the war had the UN Security Council passed a second resolution authorising military action against Saddam; such an outcome would have triggered a split in Mr Kennedy's party, with many grassroots members and some parliamentarians refusing to endorse such a war.

The international diplomatic impasse meant this never arose; all 53 Liberal Democrat MPs voted against the war in the deciding Commons division in March 2003. During the debate Conservative MPs barracked Mr Kennedy, calling him a coward, an experience he found personally traumatic. Several colleagues noted that he appeared to go 'into his shell' in the weeks after the war, after television pictures of jubilant Shia Iraqis beating Saddam's fallen statue appeared to vindicate Mr Blair's stance and American and British figures talked confidently of finding illegal weapons in liberated Iraq.

Only as a vicious counter-insurgency in Iraq began to take root, and the prospect of finding banned weapons programmes began to fade, did it appear that the Liberal Democrats' opposition to the war might reap electoral dividends.

There were some swings to the Liberal Democrats in urban, ethnic minority communities in that year's local elections. The first real test, however, was a parliamentary by-election in Brent East. This was an apparently safe Labour seat where Liberal Democrats lay in poor third place, with little representation on the council and a weak membership base.

Incredibly, the Liberal Democrats won the by-election after flooding the constituency with activists throughout the summer and distributing anti-war leaflets carrying grainy photographs of President Bush beside Mr Blair, the first evidence that the Prime Minister's electoral appeal was becoming double-edged.

It was a turning point for Mr Kennedy's party. Having spent two years planning a general election campaign predominantly targeting Conservative-held seats in the shires and suburbs, where many of the majorities were slimmer, he began a strategic turn-around and to focus on Labour bastions in urban areas, particularly in the industrial North of England.

An emboldened Mr Kennedy, by nature collegiate and conscious that a small party cannot afford too many embittered MPs nursing a grievance, proceeded within weeks with the most radical reshuffle of his leadership.

Vince Cable, formerly chief economist with Shell, was appointed Treasury spokesman to give the Liberal Democrats a more credible economic message, replacing Matthew Taylor. Mark Oaten, a right-of-centre (in party terms) former public relations executive, became home affairs spokesman and set about trying to neutralise years of knee-jerk liberal policy-making, most recently under Simon Hughes, that left the party vulnerable to the charge 'soft on crime'.

For the first time in a generation the party sought cuts in Whitehall budgets to fund their spending priorities rather than rises in general taxation. Mr Cable and his able deputy David Laws identified £5 billion worth of savings including the abolition of the Department of Trade and Industry.

A bolder leader might have made such changes a year earlier. Perhaps he assumed the Tories would allow their party steadily to crumble while their opponents incrementally inched to take advantage.

When Tory MPs acted with sudden ruthlessness, evicting their leader in a vote of no confidence and proclaiming in his place a much more experienced, combative politician in Michael Howard, Liberal Democrats immediately found themselves eclipsed. The Conservatives enjoyed an extended honeymoon as the media sensed the smack of firm leadership returning to the official Opposition and ignored the pretenders who had snapped at its heels.

Mr Kennedy finally elbowed his way back into the political mainstream due to the continuing controversy over Iraq: what else? As Mr Howard went for broke, he held back from demanding the Prime Minister's resignation as the Commons debated Lord Hutton's report into the death of David Kelly, the Government scientist linked to allegations that the case for war was exaggerated.

Most significantly Mr Kennedy then refused to endorse Lord Butler of Brockwell's inquiry into pre-war intelligence, saying this fell short of the full inquiry into the invasion he wanted. This was an important decision. Within days Mr Howard performed an about-turn as he, too, withdrew his support from the Butler inquiry.

For these reasons Mr Kennedy had the wind in his sails as he prepared for his party's 2004 spring conference in Southport. Bizarrely, he within days almost found himself ship-wrecked.

On Budget day he awoke feeling unwell. Instead of staying at home or summoning a doctor, he struggled into the Commons. Hours later he gave up and left, giving 15 minutes' notice for Menzies Campbell to take his place at Prime Minister's Questions and little more for Vince Cable to respond to the Budget statement.

Mr Kennedy was unwell for the duration of the spring conference and struggled through his closing speech, perspiring heavily. He looked no more than uncomfortable in the conference hall, but close up on television looked truly dreadful. A rash of harsh newspaper headlines that followed so shocked younger MPs that briefly they entertained notions of asking Mr Kennedy to stand down and his deputy to lead them into the general election.

The storm quickly blew over but a chastened Mr Kennedy vowed to improve his diet, sleep patterns and fitness by hill-walking in the Scottish Highlands. He threw himself into campaigning for the European elections, from which he emerged with 12 MEPs and rapidly redeemed himself with a succession of by-elections that followed. Liberal Democrats won the inner city constituency of Leicester

South, another campaign dominated by the war, taking their tally of MPs to 55. They came runners-up in Birmingham Hodge Hill and, later, Peter Mandelson's seat of Hartlepool with large swings from Labour in each.

The 2001-05 Parliament was an important period for the Liberal Democrats in which they found their voice as a small but growing independent opposition force, most notably as the only main political party to oppose the Iraq war.

Further, minor developments, illustrated this transition. In 2001 Mr Kennedy introduced to his front bench the post of Shadow Chief Secretary to the Treasury, held first by Edward Davey and later Mr Laws, indicating a more rigorous attitude to public spending. A row with the Scottish Nationalists over select committee places led to the Liberal Democrats giving up their traditional role as negotiators with Government and Opposition whips on behalf of the Westminster's minority parties, who decided to represent themselves.

But the wider question remains, thrown into still sharper relief by his mixed results in the 2005 general election: could Mr Kennedy have made still more of the opportunities presented to him during this unique period? Had he been bolder early on in promoting abler and more challenging front bench spokesmen and radical rather than consensual in crafting policy, he might have exploited better the vacuum created for two years by a dispirited and directionless Conservative Party. Mr Kennedy opted instead for internal unity. Rather than an invading armada, he preferred to lead a convoy progressing at the pace of his slowest ships.

A STRANGE CAMPAIGN WITH FEW REAL WINNERS

by **Philip Webster**
Political Editor, The Times

The general election of 5 May 2005 was, even more than the two that preceded it, all about Tony Blair. By winning his last election as Labour leader he wrote his name in the history books as the first Labour prime minister to win three successive electoral terms.

But a visitor from another planet would have thought he had arrived in a lunatic asylum had he descended on post-election Britain the weekend after Mr Blair went back into Downing Street with a 67-seat majority.

On Friday morning, after an exhausting campaign, Michael Howard followed the trend of his predecessors as Tory leaders at elections in 1997 and 2001 and threw in the towel. He had made modest gains for his party but they remained below the 200-seat threshold, and did not even reach the low-water mark of 209 seats achieved by the hapless Michael Foot for Labour in 1983.

Over at Liberal Democrat headquarters there was quiet satisfaction rather than euphoria as Charles Kennedy lifted his party's seats total up to 62, the highest for the liberal tradition for 80 years. It was an advance but, in truth, well below his party's expectations only months before. Facing two unpopular leaders the Liberals probably had the chance of a lifetime to make a breakthrough. But it did not happen.

Labour was back with a majority which, though vastly slashed, would have been grabbed with relish by any of the Labour leaders that came before Mr Blair. The party had 355 MPs, a massive number by the standards of the previous century.

So what did his MPs do? They called for him to go. Nothing better illustrated the craziness and cruelty of politics than what happened to Mr Blair that torrid weekend after the poll.

It was Mr Blair, helped by Gordon Brown, who gave Labour its position of dominance by reinventing the party in a form that made it appeal to Middle England. Many of the MPs who got into Parliament in 1997 and 2001 owed their places to Mr Blair and no one else.

But this time 47 of those elected in 2001 failed to get back. Many of them blamed Mr Blair for their failure to do so and many of those who returned claimed they did it despite Mr Blair. In most cases those assertions would probably turn out to spurious if there was a way of finding out what was truly in the voters' minds when they marked their ballot papers.

"THAT LAST BOY WAS A GENIUS – HE ALMOST UNDERSTOOD LABOUR'S SPENDING PLANS"

Even so Mr Blair and his character was the issue that dominated this election campaign. His prolonged honeymoon with the electorate had long gone when he was re-elected in 2001. By 2005 he had lost his sheen completely, to the point where his handlers feared he had become a serious negative factor.

Over the years familiarity had bred something approaching contempt in the eyes of many voters. Mr Blair's almost perpetual smile, an attractive feature way back when, was now almost universally seen as a smirk, to the extent that posters calling on the electorate to wipe the smile off his face were a part of the Tory campaign. Mr Blair appeared to acknowledge that he might be approaching his sell-by date when he announced in the autumn of 2004 that the next election would be his last.

But it was the fact that Mr Blair had taken Britain into an unpopular war with Iraq that changed everything in his relationship with his party and the British people. In March 2003, having secured a Commons vote in favour with the help of the Conservatives, Mr Blair sent British forces into action. Much of the country did not like the idea.

There was rejoicing when Saddam Hussein was toppled in April. But the weapons of mass destruction that were supposed to be in Iraq, and on which Mr Blair based much of his case for war, never turned up. He was blamed for exaggerating their threat in a dossier. The suicide of a weapons inspector David Kelly, who had been the source of reports suggesting the dossier was sexed up, led to the Hutton inquiry and the astonishing sight of the prime minister of the day being questioned in court. Later the Butler inquiry was critical of the way the war intelligence had been used. Mr Blair could never escape Iraq in the years running up to the election and it was again to haunt him only days before Britain voted, with a carefully orchestrated leak of the war advice he had received.

So it was against that backdrop, of a prime minsiter who had clearly lost the trust of voters, that the 2005 campaign was fought.

Labour knew it only too well. It is possible that a third Labour victory was won when Alastair Campbell, back working for Labour as election strategist, paid an Easter bank holiday visit to Gordon Brown at his Scottish home.

Mr Blair and Mr Brown had fallen out badly over the preceding Parliament. The Chancellor believed that he had – again – received an assurance from Mr Blair that he would step down, but again he was disappointed. The mood was so bad that Mr Brown appeared unlikely to play the dominant role he had in the two previous campaigns.

In early March Mr Campbell and Philip Gould, the chief pollster, realised that Mr Blair needed Mr Brown beside him both to counter the anti-Blair feeling around and to send out the message of a powerful double act. Mr Brown had wooed the voters in his Budget and was popular. They paid a number of visits to Mr Brown who wanted a campaign fought around the economy and the public services. Whatever was said at that meeting on Easter Monday Mr Brown was soon to be back. Mr Blair needed him; Mr Brown needed the biggest possible majority because it was certain that, barring accidents, he would be Labour leader at the next election in 2009 or 2010.

It worked. The Blair-Brown show was a major feature of the election. They did press conferences together, appeared smiling at each other in political broadcasts, joint interviews and campaigned as a duo all over the country. The electors might easily have concluded that everything they had read about the alleged mutual loathing of these two men had been made up. In his election interview with *The Times* Mr Blair went as far as he could, or dare, to anoint Mr Brown as his eventual successor.

The dual leadership approach is believed to have paid heavy dividends for Labour and the strategists believed that without it Labour's majority could have been cut much further or even whittled away. And it took the Conservatives by surprise. Earlier in the year some Tories had come up with the slogan 'Vote Blair, get Brown' as a way of showing the weakness of Mr Blair's position. They swiftly dropped it when it appeared that the voters quite liked the idea of Mr Blair being replaced by Mr Brown.

For their campaign the Conservatives had brought in the Australian election stategist Lynton Crosby, who had helped John Howard in his election campaigns and planned a similar no-nonsense core vote-plus strategy over here.

One of the aces in their pack was the pledge of a tax-cutting package of £4 billion which they planned to use prominently.

But the plan was sensationally derailed even before the campaign got under way when Howard Flight, a Conservative deputy chairman, was caught on tape suggesting that the scale of Conservative spending cuts was far deeper than had been revealed. Mr Howard sacked him swiftly to limit the damage, and then ruthlessly ended his careeer as an MP by withdrawing the whip from him. Mr Flight refused to go quietly at first and the turmoil as a new candidate was chosen in his Arundel and South Downs seat was a diversion the Conservatives could ill afford.

The Flight fiasco was just what Mr Brown needed as he piled into the campaign with tirade after tirade over what he said were Conservative plans to cut spending by £35 billion. Day after day, well into the second week of the campaign, the Chancellor and Mr Blair drummed home the message that the Tory plans did not add up, and could be even worse than expected.

Mr Blair had called the election on 5 April, a day later than expected because of the death of Pope John Paul II. Labour began comfortably ahead in the polls and maintained its lead during the tumultuous weeks that followed. The final share of the vote, with Labour on 36 per cent, Conservatives on 33 per cent and the Liberal Democrats on 22 per cent, was not a long way from the indications from the polls, although the majority in the end was lower than the final polls predicted because of differential swings in the marginal seats.

The Conservatives based their appeal around achieving cleaner hospitals, school discipline, controlled immigration, cutting taxation and providing more police. Apart from the occasional appearance by Oliver Letwin, the Shadow Chancellor, and a handful of other shadow ministers it was very much Mr Howard's campaign. Other shadow ministers privately accused him of running a one-man band, but Mr Howard knew that he had one shot at securing power for the Tories and he was going to take it.

But soon he was being accused of running an over-harsh, negative line of attack. He unapologetically focused hard on immigration, accusing Mr Blair of pussyfooting around on the issue. He undoubtedly made ground, as Labour's own polling showed, and after two weeks Mr Blair decided he had to fight back by going to Dover and making one of his own keynote speeches, over which he took more care than any other, on immigration. He accused Mr Howard of frightening voters but his purpose was to show that Labour, too, understood their worries. But it was the only issue on which the Conservatives consistently maintained their lead over Labour.

With the polls refusing to budge Mr Howard took to a more personalised attack on Mr Blair. In his interview for *The Times* Mr Howard said that he had lost respect for Mr Blair because of his repeated lying.

To call the prime minsiter of the day a liar in the middle of the election campaign was a calculated gamble for Mr Howard, who needed a boost. Posters suggesting that if Mr Blair was prepared to lie to go to war he would lie to win an election were swiftly produced. And when the Attorney General's advice on the war was leaked a week before polling, and Mr Blair gave a less than convincing performance under sustained pressure on *Question Time*, Labour briefly lost control of the campaign. Right up to the final weekend the war returned to haunt Mr Blair. There was no obvious evidence that the public was interested but the concentration of the media on the issue that had obsessed them for the previous two years meant that Labour was finding it hard to get back on message.

The episode did not appear to have changed much. The polls suggested the public were not too keen on the 'liar' charge from Mr Howard and most did not believe it anyway. But it did succeed in getting the country talking about Mr Blair and his character again and that was clearly in the Conservatives' interests at the time.

For Charles Kennedy there was personal joy just as the campaign started. Even before he had launched his manifesto Mr Kennedy became a father for the first time. But young Donald Kennedy was to have an early political impact when his father, blaming tiredness caused by the new arrival, stumbled badly over the details of his flagship local income tax policy at the manifesto launch. The public would have forgiven him for that.

But while the Liberal Democrats were to progress, there was a general feeling both during the campaign, and when the results came in, that they could have done better. As the only main party to have opposed the Iraq war they clearly benefited when the issue flared into life late on. They were to make gains mainly at Labour's expense and to take a few Tory seats. But some of their main hopes failed to make it and their so-called 'decapitation' strategy of trying to remove leading members of the Shadow Cabinet secured only one victim, Tim Collins, the Shadow Education Secretary.

Within days of the result Mr Kennedy had announced a root-and-branch review of the policies on which the election was fought. Everying, including the local income tax, was put up for grabs.

So a new Parliament began with Mr Blair still in charge and no one knowing quite how long he would last. His pledge to stay on for the full Parliament looked shaky on that first weekend after the polls. His majority was 100 lower than it had been when he asked for Parliament to be dissolved. Mr Blair and his Cabinet were having to come to terms with the idea that parliamentary defeats could become commonplace in the months and years ahead. A potentially perilous European referendum was waiting round the corner. Mr Howard, having announced his departure, was waiting to sail off into the sunset, but only after his party had been given a chance to change its leadership rules and to replace him. The only certainty was that neither would be leading their parties into the next election.

FIRST CRACKS APPEAR IN BLAIR'S ELECTORAL COALITION

by **Peter Riddell**
Chief Political Commentator, The Times

The first cracks appeared in Labour's dominant electoral position on 5 May. The party lost 47 seats, and, for the first time for 22 years the Conservatives made substantial gains, while the Liberal Democrats achieved their highest total of MPs since December 1923, on the eve of the formation of the first Labour Government.

Yet the contest was mainly an adjustment of the familiar electoral landscape. The coloured map of constituencies looks remarkably similar to 1997 and 2001: Labour dominance in the big cities and industrial Britain; with the Tories spreading from rural and shire England into the more prosperous London suburbs and parts of the Home Counties; and the Liberal Democrats advancing in university seats and in some big cities.

Overall just 62 seats changed hands, or fewer than one in ten of the smaller total of 646 in the House of Commons (a reduction of 13 from the last parliament because of boundary changes in Scotland following devolution). This is more than double the 27 which shifted in 2001. In mainland Britain 56 seats moved between parties, up from 21 four years ago. As in 2001, a third of the 18 Ulster seats changed hands.

As a result Labour's majority fell from 167 to 67 (before taking account of Staffordshire South where the death of the Liberal Democrat candidate during the campaign meant a special election). This majority is higher than in nine other post-war elections, but less than in the seven landslides (that is 100-plus majorities), in 1945, 1959, 1966, 1983, 1987, 1997 and 2001, two of which were won by Tony Blair himself. The current Labour majority is larger than those won by the Tories in 1955, 1970 and 1979, all of which were regarded as comfortable at the time.

However, the total Labour vote of 9.56 million was 1.17 million lower than in 2001, and nearly 4 million less than in 1997. This is the lowest total for any governing party since the 1920s when the electorate was much smaller. The 2001 election was the first since 1929 when one of the two main parties did not receive more than 10 million votes. The Labour vote share of 35.2 per cent in the UK is not only 5.5 points less than in 2001, but is four points less the previous low for a party with an overall Commons majority.

Turnout increased slightly from the low of 59.4 per cent in 2001 to 61.3 per cent, probably because of the increased number of postal votes. But this is still well below the levels of turnout for virtually all the post-war era. However, the fall in its share of the vote means that Labour won the support of just 21.6 per cent of the total electorate, down from 24.2 per cent at the 2001 general election.

The Tories gained 33 more MPs, up to a total of 197, on a 0.6 point rise in vote share to 32.3 per cent. This is their third lowest vote share, only just above 1997 and 2001, in the history of the mass franchise. It is lower than the main Opposition party has won in any earlier post-war election apart from 1983 and 1987. The total Conservative vote of 8.77 million compares with 8.36 million in 2001, but is, otherwise, by more than 850,000 the lowest vote for the party since 1929, when the electorate was far smaller.

Moreover, the Tories' total number of MPs is still 12 fewer than the 209 won by Michael Foot's Labour Party in 1983 at the low point in its fortunes. It is 127 fewer than needed for a bare overall majority in the Commons. Looked at another way, the Tories are still only 64 per cent of the way towards office.

"I HOPE THEY SEND PEOPLE OVER TO MONITOR THE ELECTION IN BRITAIN"

The Liberal Democrats gained 11 MPs, up to a total of 62, the highest for the third party since 1923. Nearly half its gains were in university seats where both its opposition to the Iraq war and tuition fees were big influences. The Lib Dems' total vote of 5.98 million was nearly 1.2 million higher than in 2001. The party's share of the vote rose by 3.7 points to 22 per cent. This is the highest since the party's creation in its current form in 1988, but less than the old SDP/Liberal Alliance won in either 1983 (25.4 per cent) or 1987 (22.6 per cent).

The 2001 election also saw a further marked decline in the dominance of the Labour and Conservative parties. Their combined share of the vote was just 67.5 per cent, or only just over two-thirds. This compares with a combined share of 95.8 per cent in 1951. The last general election when the Tories and Labour together won over 85 per cent of the vote was 1970. Since then the two-party share has declined, with fluctuations depending on the performance of the third and minor parties.

Similarly, the two-party share of seats in the Commons has declined. The Conservatives and Labour now have 553 MPs between them, or 85 per cent of the Commons. This compares with a peak share of 97 per cent in 1951, and a figure as high as 93 per cent as recently as 1992.

This national picture masks big regional variations. The Conservatives gained slightly more votes in England than Labour, 8.1 million to 8.04 million, but won 193 seats, compared with 286 for Labour. Labour remains dependent on Scotland and Wales, where, despite big losses, the party still has 70 MPs.

The English results reflect the way that the electoral system continues to favour Labour. It took just 26,800 votes to elect a Labour MP in Britain as a whole, but 44,500 to elect a Conservative member, and nearly 96,500 voters to elect a Liberal Democrat MP. These differences not only reflect the familiar 'winner's bonus' under the first-past-the-post system, but also Labour's ability to concentrate its votes to maximum effect. Labour-held seats are smaller than Conservative ones. That is in itself partly the result of the way that boundary changes every ten years or so lag well behind population shifts away from the mainly Labour-held inner cities to more Tory suburbs and rural areas.

The Tories' best performance was in London, where the party gained eight seats, largely because of a sharp fall in the Labour vote of 8.4 points down to 38.9 per cent. The Tories' own share rose by just 1.4 points to 31.9 per cent. The Tories gained three affluent London suburban seats near the Thames (Hammersmith and Fulham, Putney and Wimbledon) and five in outer London (Bexleyheath and Crayford, Croydon Central, Enfield Southgate, Hornchurch and Ilford North). Enfield Southgate was particularly sweet for the Tories since it produced Labour's most memorable win of 1997 when Stephen Twigg beat Michael Portillo. Both left the Commons at the 2005 general election: Mr Twigg involuntarily and Mr Portillo voluntarily after five years at Kensington and Chelsea. The other changes in London were the Lib Dems' holding on to its 2003 by-election victory in Brent East, and the capture of Hornsey and Wood Green from Labour. The other big change in London was George Galloway's victory for Respect at Bethnal Green and Bow over Labour incumbent Oona King.

The Tories also did well in the South East, where the party increased its share of the vote by 2.1 per cent and gained five seats, at the expense of both Labour (Gravesham, Milton Keynes North East, and Reading East) and the Liberal Democrats (Guildford and Newbury). The Eastern region, mainly East Anglia, was also good territory for the Tories, which gained a number of commuter seats near London (Braintree, Harwich, Hemel Hempstead, Peterborough, St Albans and Welwyn Hatfield). The Liberal Democrats gained Cambridge.

In the South West the main battle involved the Lib Dems, who gained three seats (Bristol West and Falmouth and Cambourne from Labour, and Taunton from the Conservatives), while losing two (Torridge and Devon West, and Weston-Super-Mare) to the Conservatives. The only direct Labour/Tory swap was the Forest of Dean

However, elsewhere in the country the Tories did less well, barely increasing their share of the vote at all outside London, the South East and East Anglia, and losing votes in the three northern regions of England, where the Lib Dems gained most of the votes lost by Labour. No seats changed hands at all in the North East, despite a 6.5 point drop in Labour's share of the vote in the region. In the North West Labour lost 5.7 points in vote share, and the Liberal Democrats were the main gainers, both in votes (up 4.6 points) and seats (two from Labour: Manchester Withington and Rochdale, and Westmorland and Lonsdale from the Conservatives). The Conservatives gained a single seat, Lancaster and Wyre, from Labour. In Yorkshire and Humberside Labour lost three seats (Scarborough and Whitby, and Shipley to the Conservatives, and Leeds North West to the Liberal Democrats).

In the West Midlands Labour did better than many expected in defending seats in and around Birmingham following the closure of the Longbridge plant. While Labour's share of the vote fell by 6.1 points, the Tories advanced by only 0.1 point, but won four seats (Rugby and Kenilworth, Shrewsbury and Atcham, and The Wrekin from Labour, and Ludlow from the Lib Dems), none in the industrial heartlands of the region. The Lib Dems gained two seats (Birmingham Yardley from the Lib Dems and Solihull from the Conservatives).

In the East Midlands Labour lost 6.5 in its vote share and three MPs (in Kettering, Northampton South and Wellingborough). All three were won by the Conservatives, despite losing 0.3 point of its vote share in the region.

The political scene changed considerably in Scotland, where the number of MPs had been reduced by 13 to 59 following devolution, to bring the average size of electorates more closely into line with the average for England. Labour lost an estimated ten MPs as a result and then lost a further five in the election, two to the Liberal Democrats, two to the Scottish Nationalists (now with six MPs) and one to the Conservatives. As a result of both changes Labour's MPs fell from 56 out of 72 to 41 out of 59. The Lib Dems established themselves as the second party north of the border, not only with 11 MPs but also, for the first time, in share of the vote, rising 6.3 points to 22.6 per cent and overtaking the SNP, on 17.7 per cent, down 2.4 points on 2001.

Labour also did badly in Wales, losing five seats, to a mixture of the Conservatives (who went from zero to three), the Liberal Democrats, and an Independent. Plaid Cymru lost one of its previous four MPs, and its share of the vote fell by 1.7 points to 12.6 per cent.

Northern Ireland politics remained a world of its own. The main outcome was the virtual extinction at a Westminster level of the Ulster Unionist party, which lost five of its six MPs, including the Nobel prize winning David Trimble, who then resigned as party leader. Ian Paisley's Democratic Unionists gained four seats, up to nine, while Sinn Féin moved up one to five, none of whom will take their Commons seats. The SDLP just about held on at three, having lost one and gained one.

One of the striking features of the election was the number of seats which have now been held by all three main parties in the past decade or so. The transition has been from Conservative to Labour, and then to Liberal Democrat. The list includes Bristol West, Cambridge, Cardiff Central, Falmouth and Cambourne, Hornsey and Wood Green, and Leeds North West.

In social terms, based on the exit and other polling figures prepared by MORI and NOP, the Liberal Democrats were the main winners among the middle classes, moving fractionally ahead of Labour among professionals and managers, on 29 to 28 per cent, behind the Tories on 37 per cent. The Tories appear to have made no headway among the middle classes, though, because of the Labour decline, they are now ahead among white-collar, lower middle-class voters, where the Lib Dems have done less well. The Tories seem to have taken just a under a third of the working-class voters lost by Labour, with the Lib Dems getting most of the rest.

Women provided the mainstay of Labour support, possibly reflecting the party's stress on issues like health and childcare. The party took 38 per cent of the votes of women, down from 42 per cent in 2001. However, the Tory share of women's votes slipped by one point to 32 per cent, with the Lib Dem share up four points to 23 per cent. A YouGov poll shows a slightly different balance with Labour taking 37 per cent of women's vote, against 33 per cent for the Tories and 23 per cent for the Lib Dems

Labour did badly among men, where its vote declined by eight points to 34 per cent, according to MORI. The Tories gained two points, up to 34 per cent, with the Lib Dems up four points at 22 per cent. But according to YouGov Labour was still slightly ahead among men, at 36 per cent, compared with 33 per cent for the Tories, and 23 per cent for the Lib Dems.

The Lib Dems have made strong gains among young people aged 18 to 24, where their opposition to the Iraq war and to tuition fees played well. The Tories' main strength remained among voters aged over 55, who, according to MORI, made up 42 per cent of those who turned out and voted. According to YouGov the Tories and the Lib Dems were level pegging among 18 to 34 year olds (at 28 to 27 per cent, behind Labour on 37 per cent); Labour was well ahead with 35 to 54 year olds (on 41 per cent, against 29 per cent for the Tories and 22 per cent for the Lib Dems); but the Tories were the winners among the over 55 aged group (on 41 per cent, against 32 per cent for Labour and 20 per cent for the Lib Dems).

The 2001 election looks a transitional contest: the end of Labour dominance, but only the start of a Conservative recovery, and a Liberal Democrat advance, but not yet a breakthrough.

A NEW STYLE OF CAMPAIGN WHICH LEFT TOO MANY VOTERS OUTSIDE

by **Tom Baldwin**
Assistant Editor, The Times

This election campaign was like an iceberg drifting with the prevailing political current to a destination which ultimately satisfied none of those who had hoped to navigate a more conclusive route.

What was visible above the waterline was cold, jagged and forbidding enough. But the bulk of this campaign, a vast dark mass of party political activity, was hidden from sight beneath the surface.

Both Labour and the Tories diverted most of their £15-20 million election budgets to a hi-tech operation designed to make direct contact with potential swing voters in marginal seats. As Alan Milburn, Labour's campaign co-ordinator, said: 'At the last election [in 2001], many people thought that direct contact with the public was confined to Sharon Storer's meeting with Tony Blair and John Prescott's encounter with an egg-thrower. This time we want direct communication every day.'

This battle, which could be detected only with sonar rather than the radar of the national media, was very different from previous general elections. For instance, the crack troops were not voluntary party activists, the numbers of which have been in steep decline in recent years, but the paid mercenaries of professional telephone canvassing.

Labour's call-centre in Gosforth, Newcastle upon Tyne, is thought to have made as many as three million telephone contacts with voters in the 12 months before polling day. In addition, the centre also sent out up to 10 million items of direct mail and hundreds of thousands of DVDs – adapted to the needs of individual MPs – and usually sent to those same target voters in the marginal seats.

The Conservatives' telephone canvassing was conducted mostly from a call-centre at Coleshill Manor, positioned among electricity pylons and motorways near Coventry. The beige, glass-fronted office was protected by tight security because the Tories were deeply sensitive about their operation and refused to disclose any statistics about its scale and effectiveness. The party also spent major sums on direct mail and recorded telephone messages from Michael Howard.

Another key difference was the precision of the bombardment. Mr Howard was fond of saying the 'people who matter' in this may number just 838,000 – less than 2 per cent of voters. If they could be persuaded to switch from Labour in the 165 marginals his party targeted, he argued, the Tories would win an overall majority. His decision to concentrate on a few thousand people in each target seat reflected the success of US Republicans in the 2004 presidential election in using similar software to win over key voters in swing states such as Florida and Ohio.

"IT'S EITHER A NEW POPE OR NEXT DOOR'S BURNING MORE ELECTION LEAFLETS"

Both Labour and the Conservatives used 'data capture' computer programs to identify voters by collating information ranging from their postcodes to reading habits or even their choice of garden furniture. The 'Voter Vault' system bought by the Tory party could predict an individual's propensity to vote, as well as which party they would support, with an accuracy of 70 per cent.

This was based on a commercial program called 'Mosaic', also bought by Labour, which divides every household into a kaleidoscope of 11 broad social groups and 61 categories. Some of these were, perhaps, a tad insulting. For instance, the elderly woman living in sheltered accommodation who received a call from a nice young man representing the Conservative Party might have been interested to know that she is described as part of the 'twilight subsistence group' characterised by the stereotypes Percy and Edna. Mosaic's brochure has this to say about them: 'These people have few, if any, savings and investments and are on very low incomes. Due to their low residual life expectancy, they are of little interest as a market to most financial services organisations.'

But the main parties were very interested in pensioners, not least because they are disproportionately likely to vote.

Inside the call-centres the prosperous contemporaries of Percy and Edna were being nicknamed Edgar and Constance, from the 'grey perspectives' group. The more frail among them will have 'retreated to the security of a seaside apartment'. A sub-category is described as 'sepia memories'. They have the radio on 'for companionship as much as anything' and are likely to enjoy watching *Songs of Praise*.

Ben and Chloe are liberal-minded, cosmopolitan people. They include students from the 'urban intelligence' group who were probably upset about the Iraq war. Joseph and Agnes are 'welfare borderline', possibly Bangladeshi or Caribbean in descent, whose 'immediate environment often gives an air of neglect and danger'. Wayne and Noreen are in 'municipal dependency' on provincial inner-city social housing estates where they are 'reliant on buses for mobility and television for entertainment. These people lead particularly passive lives.'

Rupert and Felicity represent the 'symbols of success' group. They live in economically successful regions where their 'houses are well-built and spacious with four or more bedrooms'. Darren and Joanne are in 'happy families' and live in towns such as Swindon and Milton Keynes, a key section of the electorate who backed Labour at the last election. When they received a telephone call from the party at this election, it was because Mosaic described them as 'placing a high value on material possessions, and tend to need credit'.

Geoffrey and Valerie are the caricatures for the 'suburban comfort' zone who believe 'an Englishman's home is his castle [but] seldom earn enough money to accumulate significant wealth'. Lee and Noreen represent the old Labour 'ties of community' category, incorporating sub-groups such as 'Coronation Street and settled minorities' in 'rather old-fashioned' former industrial towns. Dean and Mandy represent 'blue-collar enterprise' around the M25 and in the Midlands, where they may have bought their council house and developed a Tory-friendly 'white van culture'.

The old characterisations of middle-class and working-class voters are long gone and, on occasions, this identification of the key sections of the electorate appeared to distort policy. The Tories' assault on illegal gypsy and traveller camps was a case in point. Although such an issue affected only tiny numbers of people, the party believed their tough approach would appeal to 'Dean and Mandy', 'Geoffrey and Valerie' as well as 'Darren and Joanne' in target seats. Along with the robust stance taken by the Conservatives over immigration and asylum, this was one of the 'dog whistle' policies of the last election. Lynton Crosby, the Australian political strategist imported to run the Conservative campaign, hoped to round up target voters with a message pitched at a frequency which only they could hear.

The new campaign techniques also made increasing use of new technology. Mr Blair took detailed advice from Joe Trippi, the American political guru behind Howard Dean's 2004 campaign for the Democratic presidential nomination.

He had built an anti-war coalition through the internet which, for a while, propelled Mr Dean to front-runner status in the race for the nomination. The campaign's army of 600,000 supporters raised tens of millions of dollars, mostly through an internet-based community of voters previously unengaged in politics. Mr Trippi also demonstrated that the internet enables parties to speak directly to reach parts of the electorate and individuals in a way that television and newspapers cannot.

Labour experimented with regular e-mails to around 100,000 registered supporters and tried to build web-based communities through publishing campaign blogs, including one ostensibly written by Mr Blair's own hand. The party believes this personal approach chimed with policies for the reform of public services, which it promises to 'tailor' according to individual needs. The reinvention of relations between state, citizen and party is likely to be a recurring theme of Labour thinking in the course of this Parliament.

However, while Labour and the Conservatives were concentrating their resources on this hidden campaign of individual voter contact, the Liberal Democrats – who had pioneered the technique of pavement politics – went the other way. For the first time since their inception, the Lib Dems had some sizeable money to spend. The party used several millions of pounds to buy up advertising billboards proclaiming they were the 'real alternative', while their competitors' spending on such national campaigning fell sharply.

One reason for this was, perhaps, that the party's brand was less tainted than that of its rivals. Significantly, all their posters included large images of Charles Kennedy, the Liberal Democrat leader. In contrast, Labour was reluctant to use pictures of Mr Blair while Mr Howard's face did not appear in Tory advertisements. Both leaders were seen as negative factors by many voters, so much so that on the final day of campaigning Labour published an advertisement which included a picture of Mr Howard and the Conservatives produced a newspaper advert featuring an unflattering picture of the Prime Minister.

There is some evidence to suggest the Liberal Democrats missed a trick in this respect. While the party succeeded in attracting Labour voters disillusioned with the Government over the Iraq war, their approach was too crude. In a swathe of target seats held by the Tories, the Lib Dems challenge faded away. Whereas in previous elections they had delivered slightly different messages to separate groups of voters through pavement politics and their Focus newsletters, this time they promoted a consistent national brand which was to the left of Labour. Unsurprisingly, Conservative voters were reluctant to back a party which now included the likes of Brian Sedgemore, a former hard left Labour MP and was promoting policies for a local income tax.

In the meantime Labour and the Tories fought each other to a stalemate in the key marginals. The Conservatives made substantial gains in London and the South East. They also appear to have performed better in seats where the local party had received money from a special fighting fund set up by Lord Ashcroft, the former Tory treasurer. But Labour can point to the way it held seats such as South Dorset, Selby, South Thanet, Gillingham, Enfield North and Redditch – all of which should have fallen to the Tories on a uniform 3 per cent swing.

Andrew Cooper, the director of Populus polls used by *The Times*, said: 'Both Labour and the Tories were trying to do the same thing: identify the key voters in swing seats and then bombard them with phone calls and direct mail. I suspect a lot of them just tuned out. In some ways this targeting of voters saw both parties neutralise the other. Of course, if either of them had not done it, then the result could have been different.'

But he suggested that Labour's campaign in the marginals 'probably had the edge over the Conservatives' and that the Government would have ended up with a bigger majority if many voters had not stayed at home because they assumed Mr Blair was going to win again.

The after-effects of this new campaign could yet go much further. There is already concern from data protection watchdogs over the use of telephone canvassing and direct mail on voters who do not wish to be 'targeted' in such a way. Labour has made formal complaints to the Information Commissioner about the Tories' use of recorded messages, which it claims were illegal unless telephone subscribers had given their explicit permission.

More importantly, the focus on not only marginal seats, but also just a few thousand voters within them, left many people feeling disenfranchised. Those living in safe seats, or even those firmly committed to one party or another, were largely ignored in this election. Campaigns used to be marked by a colourful array of posters going up in front windows across the country. This time, it would have been possible to be unaware an election was taking place in many seats.

Nina Temple, the director of Make Votes Count, which campaigns for proportional representation, has cited opinion polls showing nearly half of the electorate (48 per cent) believed their ballot paper was of no consequence to the result.

She said: 'It is no wonder that so many people do not bother to vote, when they are fully aware that their vote will not make any difference. Voters are becoming more aware that elections are decided by the swing voters in marginal seats as the parties have concentrated so much of their resources in that direction during this campaign.

'Nearly half the electorate now think that it is time to reform the voting system so that every vote counts equally. The government has set up a private review to look into this, but this is too important an issue for that. After the election, it is essential that there is a public debate about how to have a more inclusive electoral process and a more representative parliament.'

Stephen Twigg, one of the Labour MPs who lost his seat to the Tories, also agrees that the voting system needs to be changed. He points out that there will be a 'lot of low-hanging fruit' for the Tories in the form of small Labour majorities at the next election. As a long-standing advocate of electoral reform Mr Twigg says: 'We could be reaching the point where principle and self-interest meet.'

The Government will be reluctant to heed such calls, not least because of Mr Blair's post-election antipathy towards the Liberal Democrats, who would still be the chief beneficiaries of voting reform. But many ministers remain worried about turnout after an election where once again almost 40 per cent of the electorate did not bother to vote. Some of them privately admit that the new-style techniques used in 2001 may have helped further corrode the electorate's faith in the system.

If this campaign was an iceberg, democracy could yet be the *Titanic*.

THE E-CAMPAIGN AND THE FIRST BLOGGERS GENERAL ELECTION

by **Gabriel Rozenberg**
Economics reporter, The Times

Tony Blair notched up another first during the election campaign of 2005: he became the first prime minister to blog. It was not difficult for Mr Blair to claim the prize – after all, back in 1997 there had been no such thing, and even in 2001 internet-savvy voters would have found it difficult to explain what a blog was. But in 2005 they were everywhere: these web logs, essentially nothing more than online diaries, could act like mini-newspapers about anyone who had the time to write them. There were now some 50 million blogs online, and Mr Blair's was one of them.

Sadly, he proved not to be a diarist in the mould of Gladstone. 'Another whirlwind day buzzing around our key seats with Gordon,' began one entry, posted on Labour's website. 'I reminded people that it's only with Labour we can have a strong and stable economy.' Another time, the Prime Minister wrote: 'I could tell the minute I arrived at our hotel in Birmingham yesterday that I was not exactly the star attraction. The autograph hunters were there for Kylie who is currently on tour in Britain.'

The net surfer who found Mr Blair's blog insipid could flick over to conservatives.com, the Tories' website, and read the 'campaign diary' of Sandra Howard, the wife of the leader of the Opposition, which had the bonus that she had actually written it herself. She softened her husband's image with postings scribbled while travelling on the campaign helicopter, which ranged from digs at Cherie Blair's hair to concern at feeling 'a bit knicker-twisted' when facing an awkward question on a chat show. Fans of the Liberal Democrat leader, meanwhile, had the option of reading about his every move on a blog called kennedycampaign.org, written by researchers travelling with him.

But that was just the tip of the blog iceberg. More than 50 candidates, including several MPs in the previous Parliament, kept online diaries, allowing voters to track the daily movement of their would-be MPs for the first time in a British election. From Anne Begg in Aberdeen South to Marcus Wood in Torbay, the minutiae of local campaigns were faithfully recorded. Both Boris Johnson in Henley and his father Stanley Johnson in Teignbridge wrote blogs charting their progress. In some constituencies blogs went head to head: Michael Gove for the Conservatives and Rosalyn Harper for the Lib Dems both kept blogs of their respective campaigns to take Surrey Heath. Even John Prescott, that pioneer of the English language, had one put together by his team aboard the Deputy Prime Minister's battlebus.

" SHE EXPRESSLY SAID SHE DIDN'T WANT TO BE WOKEN UNTIL AFTER MAY 5th "

Other sites were more outlandish. One journal, The Awful Life of an MP's Wife, penned as an anonymous cri de coeur, was revealed during the campaign as the work of Linda McDougall, the wife of Austin Mitchell, the veteran Labour MP for Great Grimsby. Another site which kept readers guessing was a blog ostensibly written by Alastair Campbell. The site turned out to have been written by Anna Corp, a 30-year-old marketer, who described impersonating the Labour campaign's top spin doctor as easy. 'Sometimes I wrote stuff that sounded a bit too me-ish, so I just stripped out the pronouns and stuck in some expletives,' she explained. Other 'proxy blogs' were written for candidates whether they liked it or not; some of these were straightforwardly hostile, venomously attacking would-be MPs day by day.

But not all readers were so partisan. One of the most popular blogs throughout the campaign was politicalbetting.com, a site which concentrated solely on discussing the bookies' odds and spread bets available for different election outcomes. And then there were commentators in the wider 'blogosphere', with never-ending chatter that ranged from far-left to far-right. Connected to this were online quizzes such as whoshouldyouvotefor.com, which more than half a million voters tried out in the run-up to polling day, and websites offering tactical voters the chance to work together. Finally *The Times* hosted its first election blog, as did the BBC and other mainstream media.

Did any of this help anyone get elected? One person who should know is Lynne Featherstone, the Lib Dem who won Hornsey and Wood Green on a 15 per cent swing. 'It was a way of communicating to residents, journalists and opponents,' she said. 'If I needed to put out my side of an argument I had somewhere I could put that.' Taking half an hour to write out her thoughts every night was 'therapeutic', she said, and because journalists read her blog and wrote about what she posted the site had a significant role in raising her profile. Another prolific blogger was Iain Dale, who unsuccessfully fought North Norfolk for the Conservatives. Mr Dale, who himself founded a political website company, said he had been surprised at how many people he met on the doorstep had read his blog or visited his website. But he said: 'Politicians have got to understand what the potential of online campaigning is, because there are limits. It's only ever going to be complementary to other campaigning.'

The Conservatives tried to use their main website, conservatives.com, as a way of directing readers to find out more about their local candidates. The site, edited by Sheridan Westlake, a long-standing Central Office researcher, benefited from a regularly updated stream of news articles. These were similar to the press releases sent out to journalists, but toned down to suit a wider audience by John Deans, the Tories' media manager and a former chief political correspondent for the *Daily Mail*. Thanks to an innovation called RSS (Really Simple Syndication), local Conservative association websites could then automatically display rolling headlines from party HQ. The main site also featured billboard posters and adverts, and a separate site – www.conservatives.tv – featured short propaganda films tailor-made for cyberspace.

The Labour website was more restrained, and a survey during the campaign suggested the it was much less widely viewed than the Tory website. It too featured films, in which the Prime Minister, out on the campaign trail in Weymouth, showed his technological prowess by taking photos of himself with a mobile phone. U2's 'Beautiful Day' played on the soundtrack. But the Liberal Democrats managed the most outlandish attempt of the campaign to prove they could handle the very latest fads in technology. Their blog promoted the party's first Podcast, this being a downloadable version of a speech by Charles Kennedy which devotees could transfer to their iPods. History will not record quite how many voters, faced with the choice between a 15-minute declamation on Iraq and the latest hit single, opted to plug in to the Lib Dem leader.

Another trick the parties experimented with was cybersquatting, where they bought up domain names which might have been associated with their rivals. Labour quietly registered www.michaelhowardmp.org, www.michaelhowardmp.net and www.michaelhowardmp.org.uk, and then got cold feet: perhaps scared of being accused of dirty tricks, the party left the sites blank throughout the campaign. The Tories, meanwhile, launched www.libdempolicy.com, an attack site designed to look like a Lib Dem webpage. Some of this activity was pretty pointless in trying to win votes. When Labour unveiled their new slogan, If You Value It, Vote For It, the Conservatives bought up ifyouvalueitvoteforit.com and used it to post a link to the Tory website.

More useful was technology's ability to link activists together. The Tories, for example, ran no fewer than three extranet sites, accessible with a password. One contained resources for campaigners, such as briefing notes and graphics to put on leaflets, while another was for journalists. A third, called Conservatives Direct, was more clever: modelled on a US Republican Party initiative called Team Leader, it provided a toolbox for activists to influence debate. People who signed up to it were sent regular e-mails encouraging them to write to their local paper or put themselves forward for radio programmes, posing as ordinary, Conservative-minded, members of the public.

Some of the simplest technology was the most effective. Mark Pack, who for a second general election campaign was the Lib Dems' internet campaign manager, said the most popular feature on the party's low-budget website was a humble screensaver. The programme, which popped up with a few basic pictures and the latest Lib Dem headlines, was downloaded by thousands. And the Tories took a step backward in one regard: they brought back their Campaign Guide, the blue bible which had been scrapped in favour of an online version in 2001. As Mr Westlake put it: 'You can't beat a good old-fashioned big book which you can throw in the back of a car whilst you're on the campaign trail.'

As in 2001, e-mail was a key tool for all the major parties. Labour ran a sophisticated e-mail campaign overseen by Zack Exley, an American veteran of online campaigning who worked on John Kerry's presidential bid in 2004. Mr Exley gained notoriety in the US when he registered the domain name gwbush.com and used it to run a spoof campaign site, with fake pictures showing George Bush snorting cocaine. But his work for Labour was more cautious. He advised Labour that their e-mails should not bother trying to win over recruits; instead they should aim to get the vote out. So people who filled in their e-mail addresses on the party website were sent regular cheery messages from Labour headquarters enthusing them. Some e-mails were written by the broadcaster John O'Farrell, urging supporters to volunteer or donate money.

The party courted controversy by mining e-mail addresses from previous Labour campaigns to add bulk to their mailing lists. It ended up sending messages to many more people than just Labour supporters, raising accusations of sending out spam adverts, which it denied. Labour's messages were sent out by a British company called Email Reaction, which also manages electronic marketing for Barclays Bank and Penguin.

All three main parties used tracking technology to keep tabs on which of their e-mails were being read, and by whom. The parties also kept records of who was clicking through links on their e-mails to look at web pages. But it was unclear what use, if any, was made of the data, as data protection laws limited the parties' freedom of manoeuvre. Labour also requested people's postcodes, so they could send e-mails telling people when Cabinet members were visiting.

All parties tried to use postcodes to tell voters what was happening in their area: for any given address the Labour website listed the number of new nurses, doctors, and police officers nearby since 1997. A gizmo on the Lib Dem website took localisation a step further, offering to calculate how much you would pay under that party's proposals for a local income tax. That may have been a mistake: those voters who were told that 'your tax bill would be higher than under council tax', and presented with the precise size of their predicted bill, were unlikely to be encouraged to vote Lib Dem.

A few trends are noticeable overall. The first is that the internet and e-mail are here to stay as essential parts of any serious campaign. Websites provide a unique opportunity for any party to promote itself without having to work through the prism of the media or pay heavily for advertising space.

Another trend is that the internet, despite being accessible world-wide, can paradoxically help make campaigning more local. The committed voter, keen to find out what his or her local candidates were like, would previously have had to attend a local public meeting at a fixed time. But in 2005 for the first time voters could expect to be able to read full biographies of their local candidates, a list of their policies and even what they were doing daily, all from the comfort of their home or office. Online diaries are an intimate medium, and they allow constituents to get to know the personalities of their would-be MPs as well as their policies.

Finally, although it is dangerous to predict anything in such a fast-changing area, it does seem likely that digital video will become more prominent in the years ahead. The technology is already there – one pioneer this year was Iain Dale, whose online films mixed clips from BBC interviews with shots of him delivering leaflets in Norfolk villages. In the years ahead an ever-growing number of voters will be able to download such films quickly and easily. Expect local candidates to be transmitting regular party election broadcasts, live from your high street, on their websites in 2009-10.

But for all that 2005 was not the breakthrough year for online campaigning. What was remarkable about the first blogged election was how little new technology was used to upset any party's plans, in sharp contrast to the US presidential election the year before. There the blogosphere was instrumental in alerting the mainstream media to gaps in its coverage, most notably when bloggers exposed flaws in a report about President Bush's National Guard record. But while UK bloggers were primed to make use of any scandalous information that could blow an MP out of the water, none came. And Britain's politicians themselves helped by running what were, taken altogether, a tightly managed set of campaigns. Blogs gave prospective MPs far more scope to go off-message than ever before, but it was notable how carefully the candidates stuck to their scripts. Despite the morass of websites, e-mails and online wizardry, the 2005 e-campaign remained the blog that didn't bark.

MUCH CHANGE IN THE BATTLE BEYOND ENGLAND

This was the second post-devolution general election. The first had been a dull affair in Scotland and Wales with few seats changing hands. In 2005, however, there was much more change in both Scotland and Wales and an enormous shift in Northern Ireland.

Angus Macleod
on the campaign in Scotland

This was always going to be a general election campaign like no other in modern times in Scotland. As a direct result of the setting-up of the devolved Scottish Parliament, the number of Scottish constituencies was cut by the Boundaries Commission, from 72 to 59, ensuring at a stroke that Labour's Scottish representation fell by ten MPs before a vote was even cast.

The new map also meant that only three Scottish constituencies remained unchanged – East Renfrewshire (formely called Eastwood), Na-h-Eileanan An Iar (Western Isles) and Orkney and Shetland, and the first two of these underwent a change of name.

The other fascinating effect of the new order was to present Scotland with around ten constituencies which could be classed as highly marginal, thus giving this election the feel less of a national poll than of a series of local contests.

The changes were introduced to bring the average number of voters in Scottish constituencies up to the same as the rest of the UK. It was also an attempt by the Government to answer charges that Scotland, post-devolution, was grossly over-represented at Westminster.

If the campaign in Scotland started with a new set of electoral circumstances, it can fairly be said that it ended with a subtle change in Scotland's political make-up. The clear trend when voters finally went to the polls on 5 May was that the former tribal loyalty to Labour in Scotland was showing signs of being eroded, perhaps not among the traditional working class electorate, but certainly among those more prosperous voters who had supported Tony Blair in 1997 and 2001 and who were now looking around for an alternative.

The Liberal Democrats were the main beneficiaries of that shift; the Scottish Nationalists had a highly ambiguous result and the Scottish Tories were confirmed once again as also-rans.

The campaign in Scotland also had an entirely different feel from that in England. It became clear at an early stage that any attempt by the parties, especially Labour, to fight it on matters reserved to Westminster, such as the economy, was doomed. The Holyrood factor, in the shape of policy areas devolved to the Scottish Parliament, soon asserted itself mainly because voters insisted on talking about health, education, transport and law and order whether the politicians did or not.

Scottish Labour fought an increasingly defensive campaign aimed, it appeared, at holding on to what was left after the Boundary Commission's surgery and hoping that the emotive issue of the Iraq war and the Labour-led Scottish Executive's failure on NHS waiting times and lists (compared with the Government's success in these areas in England) lay dormant.

That strategy was undone when a gaffe in the party's Scottish manifesto exposed the fact that the waiting time target for treatment in the NHS in Scotland was twice as long as in England, despite record investment. When Mr Blair himself appeared at a London press conference to portray Scotland as an example of the way not to reform the NHS, Labour in Scotland tried to hide its embarrassment. Visits from several high-profile Cabinet ministers did nothing to dispel the feeling that the party knew that in this election in Scotland, the only way was down.

The Scottish Liberal Democrats have become experts in fighting local guerilla-style campaigns which have paid them dividends in the past and this election was no different. In spite of being in partnership with Labour in the ruling Scottish Executive, they paid no price, as the campaign gathered pace, for the public service delivery failures of the Holyrood coalition. They successfully emphasised their consistent stance against the Iraq war and their devolution policy successes in the areas of student finance and care for the elderly.

For the Scottish National Party, Westminster elections are always difficult. They are wide open to the charge that they, of all the major parties in Scotland, cannot form a Government. Their response, with a limited campaign budget, was to focus relentlessly on seats, mainly in the north-east of Scotland, where they were credible contenders.

Under Alex Salmond, who returned to the leadership in 2004 after a four-year absence, they ran an energetic if gimmicky campaign based on the slogan 'Make Scotland Matter', concentrating on their campaign to save Scotland's historic infantry regiments, making Scotland nuclear-free and setting themselves a target of winning six seats.

Labour, especially, responded by studiously ignoring the Nationalists in the hope that voters would too.

The Conservatives attempted early on to turn the campaign in Scotland into a mid-term referendum on the performance of the Labour/Liberal Democrat Scottish Executive in the areas of health, council tax and education. However, they ran into difficulties early on when the Tories in England concentrated so much fire on immigration.

Scotland's population trend is downwards and the country desperately wants to attract more skilled migrant workers. Thus, the Michael Howard dog whistle found no response in Scotland. Like the Nationalists, the Tories in Scotland concentrated their resources on around four seats where they had a chance and, again like the SNP, made much of the alleged Labour attack on the Black Watch and other regiments.

In the event, the big winners on election night in Scotland were the Liberal Democrats who won two seats from Labour and whose share of the vote leapt by six points to 22 per cent, putting them ahead of both the SNP and the Tories. Much of their advance (they came a good second in many West and Central Scotland constituencies and won the East Dumbartonshire seat just outside Glasgow) came mainly at the expense of Labour and they consolidated their long-time grip of the Highlands, Argyll and the Borders. In Edinburgh they were only one point behind Labour in vote share.

Labour, while winning 40 seats, had a poor result in comparison with 1997 and 2001, losing five seats and seeing their vote share drop by five points. There can be little doubt that the major problem for the party was the decision of many Labour supporters to switch allegiance on this occasion to the Liberal Democrats because of Iraq and the related issue of trust in the Prime Minister.

While Labour's Scottish fortifications have by no means crumbled, this election confirmed that cracks in the walls are appearing. The questions of whether the transfer of loyalties holds for the Scottish Parliament elections in 2007 or proves temporary, is a fascinating one.

The Scottish National Party met its six-seat target, taking two from Labour for the first time in 31 years. However, for the fourth election in Scotland in succession its share of the vote dropped and 50,000 fewer Scots voted Nationalist this time than in 2001. Such is their concentration of support in one area of Scotland, that it would not be all that misplaced to rename themselves the Scottish North-east Party. This performance does not indicate a breakthrough at Holyrood in two years' time.

The Scottish Conservatives had a dispiriting night. They ended with one MP, the same as in 2001, and their share of the vote at 15.1 per cent also remained almost unchanged. They failed to make any impact in their old heartlands of Perthshire and Angus and lost the Dumfries and Galloway seat fought by Peter Duncan, the Shadow Scottish Secretary.

For the umpteenth time in recent elections, the Conservatives in Scotland have had to go back to the drawing board to seek a solution to the problem of voter antipathy.

Tim Hames
on the campaign in Wales

The first Labour term in office had witnessed traumatic events in Wales. The referendum to establish an Assembly had been won by an extremely narrow margin but was to be followed by Ron Davis's 'moment of madness' which triggered his resignation both as Secretary of State for Wales and as the Labour nominee to head the new Assembly. A piece of shameless politics inspired from Downing Street allowed Alun Michael to become the First Minister but it was not be long before he felt obliged to resign in favour of the man whom he had denied that position, Rhodri Morgan. Despite all that upheaval, however, the 2001 general election results produced little overall change.

The pattern would be precisely the opposite in the 2001-05 Parliament and at the subsequent hustings. On the whole, Mr Morgan's brand of 'old Labour', or 'classic Labour' as he prefers to put it, has been popular enough with the electorate in the principality. In the 2003 Assembly elections the governing party did well enough to dispose of the services of the Liberal Democrats who had been their coalition ally.

Labour did not, though, have matters all their own way in the run-up to the 2005 ballot. As is typical of what might be harshly described as a 'one-party state', internal feuding takes the place of external competition. Labour managed to fall out with itself spectacularly over the imposition of all-women shortlists, especially when the women concerned had comparatively few local connections.

This row accounted for one of the most astonishing results ever recorded at a British general election. Labour managed to be defeated in Blaenau Gwent, its safest seat in Wales and the fifth safest seat for any party in the UK. In this former constituency of Michael Foot, Peter Law, a long-standing local politician, challenged the woman who had been selected by the shortlist mechanism. A similar resentment helped a Conservative, Stephen Crabb, snatch the seat of Preseli Pembrokeshire from the new Labour candidate, Sue Hayman (although pro-hunting sentiment may have had an influence as well). This was one of three seats snatched by the Conservatives. The other two were more predictable: Monmouth and Clwyd West, which have long been the most plausible parliamentary targets for the party.

If Labour had a relatively poor election, then Plaid Cymru had a worse one and the Liberal Democrats a far better outing. The Lib Dems captured Cerdigion from Plaid and Cardiff Central (the university seat) from Labour. This was a devastating defeat for the Welsh Labour Party. The seat did, admittedly, start with quite a small majority of 659 votes, but it was overturned comprehensively to leave a Liberal Democrat margin of 5,593. The war in Iraq and top-up fees were obviously significant here. Plaid also failed to capture Ynys Môn (Anglesey) from Labour partly because of the intervention of Peter Rogers, a former Conservative member of the Assembly who stood as an independent and split the anti-Labour electorate. This was one of few bright spots for the Government in Wales. Labour is now partly relying on 'divide and rule' for power.

Tim Hames
on the campaign in Northern Ireland

The four years from the 2001 election have been full of profound frustration for Northern Ireland politics. A brief restoration of devolved administration ended in the autumn of 2002 and a tentative deal to bring the institutions to life once more fell apart 12 months later. In the fresh elections for an Assembly (and by implication an Executive) the Democratic Unionist Party edged out the Ulster Unionists to become the largest pro-Union force in the Province while on the other side of the divide, Sinn Fein overtook the moderate nationalist SDLP as well. This polarised outcome did not bode well for the peace process, yet despite this another attempt at securing a 'grand bargain' which both Ian Paisley and Gerry Adams could accept nearly succeeded but fell at the last hurdle in an argument about what sort of photographic evidence should be used to demonstrate that the IRA had really engaged in comprehensive disarmament.

Any hope that this settlement could be shortly revisited was dashed when it was revealed that the main branch office of the Northern Bank in Belfast had been raided over the Christmas period and £26 million stolen, using techniques which pointed the finger of suspicion firmly in the IRA's direction. It was obvious by 1 January 2005 that all the parties would approach the general election as a political trial of strength and would not be interested in the prospect of compromise until afterwards.

In the early part of 2005 the republican movement was nevertheless placed on the defensive. The savage murder of Robert McCartney, an ordinary Roman Catholic from a family which normally supported Sinn Féin, provoked outrage across the sectarian divide. His fiancee and his five sisters led a high-profile campaign to demand that those who were involved in his killing, many of whom were believed to be associated with either the IRA or Sinn Féin, be brought to (British) justice. Mr Adams, although perhaps slow to recognise the damage done initially, sought to soothe their grievances and called on republicans to bring information forward. This was not popular in his own ranks and the IRA committed an astonishing public relations blunder when it announced that it had met the family and offered to shoot those who had attacked Mr McCartney. In a belated effort to reassert his and their credibility, Mr Adams started his election campaign with a speech in which he asked the IRA to put itself out of business. The Army Council of that organisation replied that it would think about it. Many deemed this exchange a cynical political exercise.

This series of political failures understandably provided the context for the ballot. And it was a momentus occasion. It witnessed the total victory of Mr Paisley's allies over the ex-First Minister David Trimble and his few remaining supporters in the Ulster Unionist Party. The DUP took 33.7 per cent of the overall votes cast and nine of the 18 Westminster seats available. This constituted an advance of four seats and more than 11 per cent of the poll compared with 2001. The UUP lost five out of the six constituencies that it had obtained four years earlier and had to suffer a slump in its vote as well. This was reduced to an embarrassing 17.7 per cent. Lady Sylvia Hermon managed to cling on to her North Down berth but Mr Trimble was soundly beaten in Upper Bann. He resigned shortly afterwards. It was a sad end to a brave career.

The outcome was not as decisive in the nationalist camp, although the evidence implies that had it not been for the Northern Bank raid and the McCartney affair, then it might have been. Sinn Féin captured Newry and Armagh from the SDLP quite easily and ran that party close in South Down as well. In total Mr Adams and his supporters had almost a quarter of the ballot while their nationalist rivals could only muster 17.5 per cent. The SDLP did retain command of John Hume's old patch in Foyle (probably assisted by some tactical voting by unionists) and were able to exploit the divisions between the two unionist parties to win Belfast South almost by default as well.

The conclusion, nonetheless, has to be that Northern Ireland has already switched from a four-party system to a three-party formula and it might not be long before the SDLP is as marginalised as the UUP today clearly is. Whether the triumph of the apparent extremes might, counter-intutively, be the condition necessary for a new and lasting political understanding in Ulster is an issue for the parliament to come.

PLENTY OF ACTION ON THE FRINGE BUT NOT MANY SEATS

by **Helen Rumbelow**
Political Correspondent, The Times

Sir Alan Herbert, the great mid-20th century independent MP said, 'I'm sure the party system is right and necessary, there must be some scum.' If you believe that, then the tidemark of scum reached a new low in the House of Commons this time, as the number of independent MPs jumped to two, or, counting George Galloway's lone victory for his Respect party, three. This is especially remarkable considering that between the time Sir Alan departed in 1950, and the arrival of Martin Bell in 1997, there was not a single independent MP.

The story of this new surge of independents (what do you call a group of free agents?) provided some of election night's greatest dramas, but something more profound was also going on.

Although the numbers of independent MPs are tiny, they hide the sudden popularity of free-thinkers among the British public. In 2005 a record number of 160 independent candidates stood, and the votes cast for them reached 141,903, the most votes polled for independents since 1885, probably ever.

And even if the three well-established other parties, the United Kingdom Independence Party, the Greens, and the British National Party, all, as expected, failed to win a seat, they each congratulated themselves on making good gains on 2001.

Why are voters being drawn from the centre to the fringe? A fascinating study by the Independent Network reveals some clues. This body was set up in 2005, with the patronage of one of the most famous modern independent MPs, Martin Bell, to support the growing phenomenon. When they looked at the voting pattern for independents, they found it correlated to periods of economic instability or war. The peaks are in 1918, after the Great War; in 1929, at the time of the Wall Street crash; in post-war 1945; in 1983, when the country was in the midst of a recession; and have at this election reached the highest peak. At times of crisis it seems people do not seek the comfortable refuge of the familiar parties. Some look elsewhere, in frustration or anger.

Except 2005 does not quite fit. The Iraq war certainly played a part, as seen by Reg Keys, standing as an independent in Tony Blair's Sedgefield constituency, in protest at the death of his son Tom in Iraq, and Rose Gentle, who opposed the Armed Forces minister Adam Ingram in East Kilbride, Strathaven and Lesmahagow over her son's death in that conflict. After the results in Sedgefield were read out, the Prime Minister had to stand, eyes fixed just past Mr Keys's left ear, as the grieving father blamed him for his loss.

This, as Mr Blair was all too painfully aware, was compelling viewing. Prime Ministers are used to eccentrics fighting them on their home turf, keen on a bit of reflected limelight. However, Keys came a close fourth, winning more than 4,000 votes in this safest of safe seats.

Iraq too was a theme of Mr Galloway's victory in Bethnal Green and Bow. This was a spectacular upset of election night, when the maverick from Glasgow, parachuted into the east London constituency of Oona King, just managed to wipe out Labour's 10,000 majority.

'Mr Blair, this is for Iraq,' boomed the victorious Mr Galloway, after one of the election's nastiest fights. Mr Galloway had lost the party whip in 2003 for refusing to toe the line on the war, responding by setting up his own party, the Respect, The Unity Coalition. He picked on the unfortunate Ms King because of her strong backing for the invasion, and also because her constituency had 45,000 Muslims whom he hoped would be receptive to his message.

"OH GREAT! HERE COMES ANOTHER CANVASSER"

But the war was also a focus for a kind of grudge match between Mr Galloway and new Labour. The same attempt to 'stick it up' a long-standing Blair government produced a startling result in Blaenau Gwent, where the independent Peter Law not only overturned Labour's 19,000 majority, but managed to construct a 9,000 majority of his own.

Like Mr Galloway, Mr Law is a former old Labour man – he used to be a Labour Welsh Assembly member. He departed to protest against the all-women shortlists the party used to select their candidate in the Labour stronghold of the Welsh valleys.

Mr Law inflicted such a crushing defeat that the Labour candidate conceded before she even arrived at the count, the victim of a culture clash between old Labour and new. 'It became a crusade,' said Mr Law, who added of his new life facing his old party in Parliament, 'no-one's going to intimidate me.'

By comparison with these Celtic firebrands, the election of the independent Dr Richard Taylor was a mild-mannered affair, passing without much notice. He held on to his Wyre Forest seat, which he won in 2001 on the single-issue of saving his local hospital. Then, the doctor in his white coat became the natural, gentlemanly, successor to the man in the white suit – Mr Bell, Parliament's single independent MP of 1997.

Mr Bell won a clear victory against a disgraced Conservative MP, when his campaign caught the spirit of the nation – to get the Tories out. But all three current independents embody the unpredictability of the modern electorate, less tribal in their allegiances, more confident in negotiating their own contract with their MP. It means the independents were able to bring off big upsets against the government with – especially in the case of Mr Law – barely a media bandwagon in sight.

All this seems a little unfair when you consider how much money and manpower the UKIP put into their campaign, desperate for their first Commons seat. They fielded the fourth largest number of candidates, after the main parties, almost one in every constituency. This entitled them to a party political broadcast, and they did their best to make it eye-catching, featuring a giant blue octopus on the rampage in Britain as a parable of the effect of Brussels on our once-great nation.

However, the party lost deposits in 451 seats, costing about £225,000. In the post-mortem some blamed the in-fighting that led to the departure of Robert Kilroy-Silk, the former broadcaster who joined them just before their wildly successful European Parliament elections of 2004. The Kilroy effect certainly netted them more votes, but at a cost. His failed leadership bid and departure to form his own party, Veritas, may have lost the UKIP their most powerful backer in Yorkshire millionaire Paul Sykes (to the Tories). It also contributed to a damaging impression of in-fighting and lost direction in the latter part of 2004.

But although their campaign did not benefit from the funds and celebrity endorsements of 2004, the major obstacle was convincing the electorate that a vote for the UKIP mattered in a domestic election. Britain's first-past-the-post electoral system militates against all the specialist parties, but the UKIP could possibly have done well if Europe had become a running theme of the election. It did not – with Mr Blair neutralising the debate by committing to a referendum on the European Constitution.

Looking on the bright side, the UKIP's national share of the vote increased from 0.34 per cent in 1997 to 2.38 per cent in 2005, with deposits saved up from one to 45 in that time. The Euro-sceptic think tank the Bruges Group argued that their influence was in the seats they blocked rather than gained. While the UKIP may have not won a seat, they may have prevented the Conservatives winning up to 27 seats.

Their analysis was simply based on the constituencies where the UKIP's vote was greater than the Labour majority. However, it does not hold water, because, as the UKIP state, their support comes from all political affiliations. They probably do draw mainly from the Conservative vote in the South, but attract sizeable numbers of Liberal Democrats in the South West, and Labour voters in the North. Taking this into account, the UKIP may have been a significant factor in several seats, such as South Thanet, where the Labour majority was as low as 664 and the UKIP polled 2,079.

Likewise the BNP may have helped Labour by attracting votes that could have gone to the Conservatives. The BNP's share of the vote was about 0.7 per cent, up substantially on 2001: with 192,850 votes overall they quadrupled their result. Of the 119 seats they contested, they did best in Barking, where their candidate came a close third behind the Tories. However, in nearby Hornchurch, a swing to the BNP – which came fourth, beating the UKIP – may have cost the Labour incumbent his seat.

The Greens had hoped to make a breakthrough in Brighton Pavilion, and ended up coming third, ahead of the Liberal Democrats, with 22 per cent of the vote, up from fourth at 2001.

However, one of the most poignant results was in Erewash, Derbyshire. This is where Mr Kilroy-Silk stood for his months-old party, Veritas, and by most standards did extremely well to come fourth with nearly 3,000 votes. But most standards are not those of Mr Kilroy-Silk – he hoped to beat Liz Blackman, the Labour candidate with a majority of just under 7,000, and his stony face on hearing the result became one of the images of the night. Some consolation for him – at least he beat his erstwhile party, the UKIP. Sometimes it is not always winning that counts, just the taking part.

THE OPINION POLLS WERE RIGHT, THE SYSTEM WAS WRONG

by **Dr Michael Hart**
Fellow, Exeter College, Oxford

The opinion polls got it right. The electoral system got it wrong. Within hours of the announcement of the election on 5 April five polls were declared (from ICM, Mori, NOP, Populus and You Gov). They all suggested that Labour was between 1 and 5 per cent ahead of the Conservatives. Throughout the campaign the polls varied little. Only two national polls put Labour at 40 per cent or over, only one put the Conservatives at under 30 per cent. They were more coherent than in 1997 and 2001, but they were mildly frustrated by their inability to detect local trends – which ultimately played such an important part on election night.

As the campaign progressed, so too the emphasis of issues changed. At the outset the Conservatives had set the tone on asylum and immigration, law and order; and the polls reflected it. Later the Conservatives switched their emphasis and the pollsters duly reflected this. It was an unusual election in that it was the opposition parties which drove the polling questions rather than the governing party. Labour's capacity in economic governance was overwhelmingly greater than that of the Conservatives, but this only magnified disenchantment with perceived failure to deliver better public services. Sky Television, for example, was inundated with viewers wanting to know about delays in medical operations, children not being admitted to schools of first parental choice, and closure of local services.

Throughout the month of the campaign no national poll put the Conservatives ahead of Labour, although YouGov twice produced polls (published on 8 April and 11 April) suggesting the two parties at level pegging on 36 per cent. However, unlike the elections of 1997 and 2001, Labour did not enjoy clear leads in polls. Not until 17 April and 19 April was Labour put as high as 40 per cent for ICM (*Sunday Telegraph*), Communication Research (*Independent on Sunday*), and Populus (*The Times*). Nor was Labour put so high again in any subsequent poll.

Pollsters used different methods. Most operated by telephone, cold-calling. Populus for *The Times* used a tracking poll. Mori tried to differentiate (for the *Observer*, 1 May) among those who said they were certain to vote, as opposed to those who simply named a party of preference. Occasionally newspapers reporting polls which went against what they hoped for relegated the results: on 24 April the *Sunday Telegraph*, using ICM, showed Labour with a six-point lead (39 to 33 per cent), but only printed this on page six of the paper.

"I LIED TO A POLLSTER"

Nevertheless, the polls were relatively consistent. By the end of the second week Labour was in the lead, the Conservatives were stable, and the Liberal Democrats were enjoying a small though steady rise in support. From these findings commentators drew conclusions, some of which were plausible but difficult to verify. ICM for the *Guardian* claimed on 14 April that the Iraq war and European issues were each ranked as important by only 3 per cent of voters. By the end of the campaign Iraq was plainly more significant, as Labour candidates acknowledged.

Further claims were made about a 'student vote'. It was alleged that students were likely to turn against Labour because of university fees. This was problematic either to verify or confound because so few students possess land-lines and are therefore difficult to poll. Nonetheless they are less problematic than, say, pensioners because students are geographically concentrated; and on election night the pollsters appeared to be vindicated – but more by intuition than survey.

A further problem for all polling organisations was to conduct national polls in an election which was plainly not 'national'. It was clear that regional and even local movements in voter loyalty were taking place, but questions asked in polls rarely identified this. The movement from Labour to the Liberal Democrats was pronounced in some sub-regions; in other places it was insignificant. Similarly, all polls suggested that Scotland and Wales were likely to vote without reference to England. And so they did.

Polls can rarely identify support for third parties, but this time they were more successful. The Liberal Democrats began the campaign measured at 19-20 per cent, and ended at 22-23 per cent. Unlike in the two previous elections, their support did not rise dramatically during the campaign but equally they entered the contest with marginally higher ratings than their actual result in 2001. *The Scotsman* predicted correctly that the Liberal Democrats would come second in the vote in Scotland, ahead of the SNP whose fortunes were in decline – though, as they had targeted constituencies so clearly, their representation remained stable.

Outside the main parties support for others was severely regional so that, although polls correctly estimated it at 8 to 9 per cent, the local impact was impossible to discern. Moreover, it was only after nominations closed that voters in individual constituencies knew how many candidates (and from which parties) were on offer to them. Various newspapers tried to lead opinion rather than simply reflect it.

Questions became more frequent about the personality of the Prime Minister and that of the leader of the Opposition. So too did questions concerning education, the NHS, and the Iraq war. In spite of these difficulties Labour's lead was not affected in the polls. This was true both of national and local polls, but it was overwhelmingly true in so far as those asked were not willing to embrace the Conservatives. No issue emerged which suggested that the Conservative campaign was overtaking Labour's.

By polling day, the polls suggested that Labour would win convincingly – but without enthusiastic endorsement. They therefore suggested that the Conservatives would lose, but without such evident hostility towards them as in 1997 and 2001. In the *Daily Telegraph* on 5 May (giving Labour 37 per cent over the Conservatives' 32 per cent) it was also suggested that the Conservative advantage was down on every issue polled from the beginning of the campaign. On the night the BBC and ITN exit poll correctly suggested that Labour was in the lead by 3 to 4 per cent. Other difficulties emerged for pollsters during the election.

One was the attempt to estimate the size of the turnout, historically low in 2001 at only just over 59 per cent. On this occasion pollsters were careful to attempt a measurement of those certain to vote, in itself a difficult proposition as more than six million people were registered for a postal vote. Ultimately there was no evidence that the increase in postal voting significantly altered the outcome; however, it did mean that the result of the election was probably decided even before polling booths opened.

With a higher level of postal ballots, the numbers voting in person on the day in 2005 were possibly fewer than for 2001, even though the total turnout was 2 per cent higher. Another problem was that the electorates in constituencies which returned Conservative MPs were on average substantially larger than those returning Labour MPs. By the time of the next election in 2009-10 this will have been rectified because of boundary changes. But in this election it was a problem which pollsters could not disentangle.

The final polls were largely correct. Some papers such as the *Sunday Times* were able to boast that their new methods – online polling – produced more accurate results than using traditional methods. As in the 2001 election Peter Kellner produced the most accurate forecast (for the *Sunday Times*) predicting an overall majority of 74 for Labour. In fact, it was 66. At 10 pm on 5 May, as the polling booths shut, the majority of 66 was absolutely accurately predicted by the BBC and ITN.

What could not be predicted from exit polls was the extraordinary difference among constituencies in different parts of the country. It could be argued that pollsters bore no blame for the curious behaviour of electors up and down the country. Tactical voting, encouraged by the unpredictability of individual constituency voting, threw up more results than ever which could not have been anticipated – even by the most skilled of pollsters or commentators. Polling is an art and not a science, and the artists provided the pundits with an accurate picture.

THE FINAL VERDICT

	Labour	Conservative	Lib Dem	Others
MORI	38	33	23	6
YouGov	37	32	24	7
ICM	38	32	22	8
NOP	36	33	23	8
Populus	38	32	21	9
GB vote	36	33	23	8

THE PRESS MGHT HAVE MOANED BUT IT STILL BACKED BLAIR AGAIN

by **Brian MacArthur**
Associate Editor, The Times

Nine of the ten national daily newspapers and seven of the nine Sunday papers declared against William Hague's Conservative Party in 2001 when Tony Blair's New Labour was given the most overwhelming endorsement by newspapers in the party's history. In 2005 Mr Blair still had a newspaper 'majority' but editors were much less enthusiastic about his premiership and mostly much kinder to Mr Hague's successor Michael Howard. Iraq was the issue that made voters squeamish about voting Labour, said the *Guardian*, the broadsheet with the highest proportion of Labour voters; its columnist Polly Toynbee even offered Guardianistas nosepegs to use as they made their reluctant vote for Blair.

So in 2005 five of the ten national daily newspapers, with almost 16 million readers – the *Sun*, *Daily Mirror*, *The Times*, the *Guardian*, and *Financial Times* – supported Mr Blair's Labour Party against three: the *Daily Mail*, *Daily Express* and *Daily Telegraph*, with 10 millon readers, who backed Mr Howard's Conservatives. The main change from 2001 was that Richard Desmond's *Daily Express* reverted to its historic role as a supporter of the Conservatives and his *Daily Star* made no endorsement. The Sunday papers split evenly – the *News of the World*, *Sunday Mirror*, the *People* and the *Observer*, with 9.4 million readers – backed Labour, while the *Sunday Times* and *Sunday Express* returned to the Tories, joining the ever-loyal *Mail on Sunday* and *Sunday Telegraph*, the four Tory supporters delivering 7 million readers.

Several papers supported tactical voting. Even the *Daily Mail*, throughout the campaign the most relentless critic of the 'overweeningly arrogant' Mr Blair, urged its readers to vote tactically – so it was OK to vote for the Lib Dems – to get the Labour candidate out. *The Times*, which endorsed Labour for only the second time in its 220-year history, wanted a smaller but viable Labour majority and a larger and renewed Tory opposition. On the other side of the spectrum the *Guardian* opted for Labour but with an increased Liberal Democrat presence. Voters delivered to the satisfaction of both papers. The *Independent* argued for a strengthening of the forces of Liberalism by a significantly larger force of Liberal Democrat MPs and the replacement of Mr Blair by Gordon Brown sooner rather than later.

The voters delivered to the satisfaction of all three papers. According to research on newspaper readers' voting intentions by MORI, indeed, the coverage of the election of the two papers that were most anguished about Iraq persuaded many of their readers into a tactical vote for the Lib Dems: during the campaign there was a shift of five points away from Labour to the Lib Dems among *Guardian* readers and eight from *Independent* readers.

The MORI research shows that only two newspapers, *The Times* and *FT*, voted differently from their readers. The *Sun* voted with its readers, 45 per cent of whom voted Labour on election day. Yet as the table also demonstrates, the voting intentions of newspapers' readers hardly change from election to election: unsurprisingly the *Daily Mirror* still has the highest proportion of Labour readers and the *Daily Telegraph* the highest proportion of Conservatives. The percentage of Conservative voters reading the *Independent* and the *Guardian*, at 11 per cent and 7 per cent respectively, is, however, notable as is the 6 per cent vote among *Guardian* readers for the Greens. On this occasion it was the *Daily Mirror* rather than the *Sun* which was rewarded with a five-page handwritten letter to start the campaign but it was the *Sun* which got a joint interview with both Blair and Gordon Brown and which also had the tackiest election interview ever with the Prime Minister and his wife in which Cherie Blair said size did matter and Mr Blair said that he was a five-times-a-night man. Who says the British press isn't dumbing down?

The *Sun*, which midway through the campaign asked if this was the dullest election ever, thought up several stunts to capture its readers' attention. There was a bare-breasted Page 3 girl for each of the three main parties and enlisting pop stars to 'Rock the Vote'. After the election of a new Pope only weeks earlier, it also announced its endorsement of Mr Blair with a puff of red smoke from a chimney over its offices in London's Wapping. Yet with sales of the red-tops declining year-by-year many editors believe that a political front page is nigh on commercial suicide. That was the view of Tina Weaver, editor of the *Sunday Mirror*, who said that a new and juicy sex scandal would always beat a strong exclusive story from an interview with the prime minister.

And it explains why during April more than three-quarters of tabloid front pages featured stories other than the election, according to research at Loughborough University reported in the *Guardian*. The *Sun* and the *Daily Mirror* each devoted more than ten times as many column inches to the marriage of the footballer David Beckham and his wife (aka 'Posh Spice') than to the leaking of the Attorney General Lord Goldsmith's advice on the legality of the Iraq war.

But if the election was seen as dull the politicians were at least as guilty as over-timid editors. It has become an increasingly familiar complaint from newspaper journalists, but never before has an election been quite so ruthlessly stage-managed for television, with newspapers relegated into a secondary role. The Tories' lost leader Kenneth Clarke suggested that the campaign became a series of exchanges between the three party leaders and an exclusive club of celebrity broadcasters; and as the *FT*'s Philip Stephens observed, the election battlebuses of the past have now made way for helicopters, and the travelling circuses of politicians and reporters for staged encounters between the leaders and media stars. That was why one constant theme in the newspapers was about the obstacles placed in the path of reporters trying to follow the party leaders. After a brush with Labour's bouncers at the start of the campaign *The Times*' Ben Macintyre wrote that the election was set to become the most controlled, sanitised and paranoid ever, an election in which the parties appealed directly to the voters, leap-frogged over the press pack and avoided questioning. He was still complaining three weeks later.

This was the first election in which the newspapers' online editions played a significant role in election coverage and were used by considerable numbers of voters, particularly the young. Usage of the BBC's website, albeit a news medium rather than a newspaper, showed how important online coverage is becoming.The BBC website received 69.7 million page impressions – up from 21.4 million in 2001 – during the campaign and there were 4.9 million unique users of the site on the day after the election. Online newspapers reported similarly impressive figures: on 6 May the *Guardian* website registered more than 700,000 unique users delivering 6.1 million page impressions, a 75 per cent increase on the previous Friday. *The Times* offered minute-by-minute results throughout election night. Voters seeking the result of the vote in their own constituencies are served much faster online than in newspapers published only once every 24 hours.

Online editors also had some ingenious ideas to make their election sites entertaining. *The Times* had Mandela or Mussolini? in which users could plot whether they were Labour, Tory or Liberal, a similar idea to the *Sun* Online's Election Blind Date game which asked readers to choose the policies they would vote for and then revealed which party they had chosen. Three young candidates – 'the 3 Bloggers' – wrote a blog about life on the front line of the campaign. Peter Riddell of *The Times* did a twice-weekly audio report on the election. Online reporting by newspapers will be still more important at future elections when use of the internet will be almost universal.

FIRST QUARTER 2005 – VOTING INTENTIONS

	All	Daily Express	Daily Mail	The Mirror	Daily Telegraph	Financial Times	The Guardian	The Independent	Daily Star	The Sun	The Times	None
Sample size	11786	564	1640	1000	700	109	552	246	291	1716	549	4517
% absolutely certain to vote	53%	67%	64%	54%	73%	58%	66%	65%	38%	44%	68%	47%
Conservative	34%	44%	57%	13%	64%	36%	7%	11%	17%	35%	44%	28%
Labour	39%	29%	24%	66%	14%	34%	48%	38%	53%	44%	27%	41%
Liberal Democrats	20%	20%	14%	15%	18%	23%	34%	43%	13%	10%	24%	24%
Scottish/Welsh Nationalist	2%	2%	1%	1%		1%	1%		7%	5%		2%
Green Party	2%	2%	1%	2%	1%		7%	4%	3%	1%	2%	2%
UKIP	2%	2%	2%	1%	2%	1%		1%	3%	3%	2%	2%
Other	1%	2%	1%	1%	1%	5%	4%	3%	4%	2%		1%
Labour lead	**5%**	**–15%**	**-33%**	**53%**	**–50%**	**–2%**	**41%**	**27%**	**36%**	**9%**	**–17%**	**12%**

TELEVISION STRUGGLED TO KEEP THE VIEWERS AWAKE

by **Joe Joseph**
Television critic, The Times

Long before it became perhaps the most powerful tool of modern democracy, television was often hailed as the first truly democratic culture, in that it is governed by what the people want; which is what makes it all the more startling to see what the people do actually want.

To judge from the television coverage of the 2005 general election, what the people apparently wanted was a series of stage-managed, sleekly choreographed set pieces by political party leaders. They wanted to see Jeremy Paxman talking to Tony Blair, Michael Howard and Charles Kennedy the way you would talk to a tailor who has made your trousers too short. They ached to glimpse Andrew Neil introduce his successful BBC political discussion show dressed in a purple tuxedo, frilly yellow shirt and feather boa, while singing the number one chart song of the moment, Tony Christie's 'Is This The Way To Amarillo?' And they wanted to see party leaders making speeches only for the eyes of tv cameras; addressing halls filled only with party loyalists; speaking only if they were standing in front of a backdrop of telegenic faces comprising a hand-picked selection of the young, the attractive, and the culturally diverse.

The people evidently also craved to see the three main party leaders appear on a joint special edition of David Dimbleby's *Question Time* – but one after the other, never actually meeting on stage, like three men theoretically dining together at the same restaurant, but each seated at a quite separate table. The people itched to watch Peter Snow once again getting so excited about his computer-created wizardry during the BBC's election night coverage that they almost forgot to switch channels to catch ITV's election night party boat moored on the River Thames, where they could eavesdrop on Nicholas Parsons and Germaine Greer, and hear the former boxer Chris Eubank offering political insights even his own wife might not be interested in hearing.

The reason elections are so prized by democracies is that they are a powerful test of a modern, advanced nation's robustness; because a country has to be in very good shape to be able to withstand having that kind of nonsense and havoc thrown at it every four or five years. And television is the biggest window on that havoc. It's the messenger that has replaced open-to-all public meetings, and eclipsed the candidate blaring through a bullhorn on the high street.

So as soon as the election was called a wave of resignation ran through a nation still dazed by dawn-to-dusk TV coverage of the death of the Pope and the Prince of Wales' wedding. There was a feeling that beneath the superficial sea of apathy on Britain's sofas lurked an even deeper sea of apathy. It was if the country sensed, from the moment Mr Blair got the Queen's consent to dissolve parliament, that the most important thing about the 2005 election campaign was not which party would win, but that it would definitely all be over by 6 May.

Indeed, it was this sense of a third Labour victory foretold that goaded tv channels to seek novel ways of luring audiences away from potentially more exciting tv fare; such as, say, repeats of *House Doctor*. Where once the networks covered election campaigns as part of their commitment to Reithian values, in this age of fickle, remote-flipping viewers, broadcasters take on the air of fairground attendants trying to drum up custom on a wet Wednesday afternoon.

"IF YOU'D LIKE US TO HECKLE MICHAEL HOWARD EVEN MORE PLEASE PRESS YOUR RED BUTTON NOW...."

And with the two major parties confining themselves through much of the 2005 campaign to a couple of key themes apiece – while also choosing when and where they would unveil these themes to a select audience of TV camera crews – broadcasters often found themselves chewing at bones on which even powerful microscopes would struggle to reveal any remaining meat.

A party's message-of-the-day would be previewed on the breakfast news broadcasts; later the lunchtime bulletins would show footage of the party leaders delivering that previewed message; and the evening news programmes would then summarise the message the party leaders had delivered. The repetition left tv viewers feeling as if thy were watching a GCSE revision course.

But if new Labour irritated the media with its news management (Sky News' political editor, Adam Boulton, complained about 'the arrogance, the mendacity of Labour's handling of the press'), it also provided the media and TV audiences with one of the most memorable broadcasting moments of the campaign when it screened its debut party election broadcast. This short film showed Mr Blair and Gordon Brown chatting like bosom buddies, when it was an open secret that the two architects of new Labour now got on about as well as Monica Lewinsky and Hillary Clinton. Mr Blair and Mr Brown resembled a couple posing for a happy-family photo opportunity after one of the spouses has been caught canoodling with a hooker by a Sunday tabloid.

The film, directed by Anthony Minghella, was a clear signal that the phoney war was over, and that the phoney sincerity had begun. The Conservatives' response was an advert portraying Mr Blair as a smug, smirking, deceitful halfwit who bares enough teeth when he grins to scare Little Red Riding Hood. A second Labour election broadcast portrayed Mr Howard as someone behaving as if he had forgotten to take his medication. It presented the Conservative leader as a man who divided the nation: while some people would hate Mr Howard for all he had done since entering parliament, the film seemed to be saying, there would be others who would detest him.

Another reliable generator of headlines was Mr Paxman's trio of special *Newsnight* interviews with the main party leaders, during which he routinely flaunted his incredulity at their replies to his questions by wincing the way he might after having just eaten a bad oyster. Elections are the one certain chance that the grand inquisitors of tv current affairs, men like Mr Paxman, get to speak to Mr Blair who, for the rest of the four or five years between elections, avoids them the way Wynona Ryder used to avoid department store security guards.

Mr Paxman's opening bouncer to Mr Blair was, 'Is there anything you'd like to apologise for?' The Prime minister's reply in summary? 'Not much'. When it came to Mr Howard's turn, the Conservative leader faced Mr Paxman with the jauntiness of a party leader whose election campaign was gaining momentum – even if it was only the sort of momentum that develops naturally in any object heading downhill. Mr Paxman's broad mission, with his three prime-time interviews with party leaders, seemed to be to demonstrate that if it is, indeed, the case that voters get the politicians they deserve, then the people of Britain must have been behaving very badly indeed.

By the time election night came along, broadcasters were both relieved to see the finishing line finally come into view at last, but also determined to make one last push to seduce audiences into staying up until they could greet their milkman in person at dawn.

BBC One's election night coverage was anchored by Mr Dimbleby. The host on ITV1 was Jonathan Dimbleby, his younger brother. There being no emergency back-up Dimblebys to call on, Sky News chose Julie Etchingham and political editor Adam Boulton to front their broadcast. But the scale of the challenge facing all three presenting teams was underlined when, at 10 pm, an NOP/MORI exit poll predicted the outcome to within a whisker of the actual result. Whatever doubts and tension lingered as to the poll's outcome evaporated like water on a hot griddle.

In their eagerness to sustain audiences' interest regardless, presenters resorted to behaving like plate-spinners at a circus, busily pretending that a shock result was always still possible. Television studios jangled with virtual swingometers, dazzling graphics, giant screens, interactive services and election night parties brimming with celebrities.

In *Why Politicians Can't Tell the Truth*, one of many election-flavoured documentaries screened during the campaign, Peter Oborne, political editor of the *Spectator*, hissed that the difficulty journalists faced buttonholing party leaders – combined with the way politicans had all said the same banal things in a bid to woo the same electors in the same marginal seats – had resulted in the 2005 campaign being 'the first election of the post-democratic era'.

Journalists did break through the protective armour. For example, ITN's political editor, Nick Robinson, pounced on misleading claims in a Labour election poster to ask Mr Blair and Mr Brown, 'Can you only win this election by distorting your opponents' policies?'

But such breaches were rare. The 2005 election – geared to tv cameras, and with each party's strategy more carefully choreographed than a Miss World contest – was the climax of a trend which had begun when Tim, now Lord, Bell stepped in to revamp the brittle image of the Conservatives' then new leader, and would-be prime minister, Margaret Thatcher. Mr Bell restyled her hair; tweaked her voice; allowed tv cameras to film her doing the dishes and shopping for groceries, and sold the nation a political leader the same way he sold products in his day job at the advertising agency Saatchi & Saatchi, changing the ground rules of politics forever.

The Labour Party had taken a while to catch on, rejecting such modern marketing techniques. In another documentary screened during the 2005 campaign, *How To Win Power*, Lord Bell said this was because Labour 'thought it would contaminate their philosophy and their purity.'

Jim Callaghan had snorted at what the Tories were up to with Mrs Thatcher: 'I don't intend to end this campaign packaged like cornflakes.' Neil Kinnock glimpsed the light, but went and ruined it all by shrieking so scarily at that televised Sheffield rally that they had to send in marksmen with tranquilliser darts to bring him under control. Then came Mr Blair, ready to be packaged as whichever breakfast cereal his focus groups suggested, if that would put Labour into power.

With the political parties' slick marketing strategies, their glossily-staged media conferences, and their targeting of bulletin-watching television audiences to get their slogans across, British election campaigns are gaining some of the flavour of American presidential elections. Celebrities have become more prominent in British tv coverage: ITV1's election night boat party was full of chat-show-sofa faces. Broadcasters are straining to lend some glamour to politics. So far, though, no sign of any British network following the example set by Italian television, which injected some zip into the first European elections by reporting it entirely with naked women. A matter of time?

SOME LEFT QUITE WILLINGLY AND OTHERS DID NOT

by David Charter

Chief Political Correspondent, The Times

It is not every election that voters kick out a Nobel Peace Prize winner but that was the fate of David Trimble, the Ulster Unionist leader, who became the most high-profile MP dumped by the electorate on 5 May. Mr Trimble was the first sitting party leader rejected in a general election since 1931, leading an exodus of 62 defeated MPs and 82 pre-poll retirements.

Some of the Commons' most colourful and experienced characters bowed out voluntarily, including ten former Cabinet ministers and another former party leader and Nobel peace laureate, John Hume of the SDLP. Father of the House Tam Dalyell was the most prominent retiree after 47 years as a thorn in the side of successive prime ministers.

But the voters then inflicted more damage than many expected, jettisoning 47 Labour MPs, five Liberal Democrats, five Ulster Unionists, three Conservatives and one each from Plaid Cymru and the SDLP.

Labour's casualties included three young ministers just beginning to make their mark, including Stephen Twigg, the schools minister, talisman of the party's landslide of 1997 when he memorably ousted Michael Portillo in Enfield Southgate. Other ministerial losers were Chris Leslie, a parliamentary under-secretary at the Constitutional Affairs department, who had been the youngest MP of the 1997 intake at 24, and Melanie Johnson, the public health minister.

The polls also led to the demise of Peter Bradley, parliamentary private secretary to the Rural Affairs Minister, who was claimed as a scalp by the pro-hunting lobby incensed at the ban on fox hunting. Other PPS casualties included Geraint Davies, defeated by 75 votes in Croydon Central, Gareth Thomas who lost Clwyd West by 133, Lawrie Quinn (Scarborough and Whitby) and Roger Casale (Wimbledon).

Barbara Roche, a former immigration minister, lost to a massive Liberal Democrat swing in Hornsey and Wood Green while in Bethnal Green and Bow Oona King, one of the 'Blair babe' MPs who joined in 1997, fell victim to anti-war sentiment and the challenge of George Galloway, the founder of the Respect party who had been expelled from Labour two years earlier. Lorna Fitzsimons, another of Mr Blair's female contingent from 1997, was shown the door by her constituents in Rochdale. Other Blair babes departing the Commons before election day included Diana Organ (Forest of Dean), Julia Drown (South Swindon), Jackie Lawrence (Preseli Pembrokeshire), Lynda Clark (Edinburgh Pentlands) and Jane Griffiths, who was deselected from her seat in Reading East.

Several MPs who consistently voted against the Labour whip departed voluntarily, including Alice Mahon, the virulently anti-war MP for Halifax, Harry Barnes (North East Derbyshire), Hilton Dawson (Lancaster and Wyre), Harold Best (Leeds North West), Iain Coleman (Hammersmith and Fulham) and finally Brian Sedgemore (Hackney South and Shoreditch), who once caused uproar by describing some of his female colleagues as Stepford Wives with 'a chip inserted in their brains to keep them on message'. He promptly joined the Liberal Democrats.

The voters dispatched another 'awkward squad' MP in John Cryer (Hornchurch). Other voluntary departures from the Labour benches included Donald Anderson (Swansea East), the long-serving foreign affairs select committee chairman, Ivor Caplin (Hove), a junior defence minister, Jean Corston (Bristol East), Ross Cranston (Dudley North), Denzil Davies (Llanelli), Win Griffiths (Bridgend) George Foulkes (Carrick, Cumnock and Doon Valley), the former international development minister David Hinchliffe (Wakefield), the health select committee chairman Kevin McNamara (Hull North), Martin O'Neill (Ochil) and Clive Soley (Ealing, Acton and Shepherd's Bush).

Two Labour defectors from the Conservatives also bowed out: Alan Howarth (Newport East) and Robert Jackson (Wantage). Voters also saw off Tony McWalter (Hemel Hempsted) and Alan Hurst (Braintree).

In the run-up to the ballot Paul Boateng quit as Chief Secretary to the Treasury in Cabinet to become British high commissioner in South Africa. Helen Liddell, the former Scottish Secretary, had already announced that she was leaving to become British high commissioner in Australia.

Four other of Labour's ex-Cabinet ministers decided to call it a day: Jack Cunningham, who was Tony Blair's 'Cabinet enforcer' as Chancellor of the Duchy of Lancaster in 1998-99; Chris Smith, Britain's first openly gay Cabinet member who was Culture Secretary from 1997-2001; Estelle Morris who served as Education Secretary in 2001-02 and became pro-vice-chancellor at Sunderland University; and Ann Taylor, who was chief whip from 1998-2001.

The ages of those who quit ranged from 37 – Paul Marsden, the Lib Dem who defected from Labour in 2001 but returned just as Parliament was winding down – to 73, the Labour veteran Tom Cox who represented Tooting for 31 years. Chris Leslie at 32 was the youngest to be sent packing by the electorate.

At the polls the Tories lost one of their rising stars in Tim Collins, shadow education secretary, who was the only victim of a much-publicised Liberal Democrat 'decapitation' campaign aimed at senior Conservatives. The other two Conservative MPs who were dismissed, again by Lib Dems, were John Taylor after 22 years in Solihull and Adrian Flook in Taunton.

Michael Portillo was the most prominent of the Tories who retired. He had returned in 2001 as MP for Kensington and Chelsea after his 1997 defeat but decided to have nothing more to do with front-bench politics after being thwarted in his second attempt at the Tory leadership.

Three further Conservative ex-Cabinet members bade the Commons farewell and, unlike Mr Portillo, headed straight for the red benches of the Lords: Virginia Bottomley, who had been Health and then Heritage Secretary; Gillian Shephard, who held four Cabinet posts (employment, agriculture, education and the education and employment portfolio); and Sir Brian Mawhinney (transport, then party chairman) – once described as having a 'chillingly mirthless smile'.

Archie Norman, the former chief executive of Asda, once seen as the man to 're-invent' the Tories, quit after two Parliaments – a case of a businessman who could not adjust to political life. Sir Teddy Taylor, first elected in 1964 and once described as the elder statesman of Tory Eeuro-phobes, retired from his Rochford and Southend East seat.

Howard Flight (Arundel and South Downs), who suggested that there was a secret Tory agenda of public spending cuts in the run-up the the election, was sacked as a candidate by Michael Howard in an attempt to close down a campaigning gift for Labour.

Nick Hawkins had been deselected in Surrey Heath and Jonathan Sayeed stood down in Mid Bedfordshire citing health reasons after he was criticised by a parliamentary committee for misconduct. Andrew Hunter, who left the Conservatives for the Democratic Unionists in Basingstoke, also stood down.

The other Tory retirements were David Atkinson (Bournemouth East), Sir Sydney Chapman (Chipping Barnet), James Cran (Beverley and Holderness), Richard Page (SW Hertfordshire), Dame Marion Roe (Broxbourne), Michael Trend (Windsor) and John Wilkinson (Ruislip Northwood).

Also calling it a day was Paul Tyler, the former chief whip of the Liberal Democrats, who had one of the longest interruptions to a parliamentary career – a gap of more than 17 years between the end of his first spell for Bodmin between February and October 1974 and his election for North Cornwall in 1992.

Another former party chief whip who retired was the Lib Dems' Sir Archy Kirkwood in Roxburgh and Berwickshire. The Lib Dems also lost one of their most outspoken MPs in Jenny Tonge (Richmond Park), who told a pro-Palestinian lobby that she 'might just consider' becoming a suicide bomber if she had to live in their situation. The other retiring Liberal Democrats were Richard Allan (Sheffield Hallam), John Burnett (Torridge and West Devon), David Chidgey (Eastleigh) and Nigel Jones (Cheltenham), survivor of a sword attack in his constituency office in 2000 when his assistant Andrew Pennington was killed.

Northern Ireland witnessed the retirement of two other long-serving MPs besides John Hume in the shape of his SDLP deputy leader Séamus Mallon and former Ulster Unionist chief whip, the Rev Martin Smyth.

Perhaps the most bitter-sweet departure was that of Labour's Tony Banks, who retired as MP for West Ham after years of colourful comment-making which enlivened politics. He famously called William Hague, then Tory leader, a 'foetus'. On another occasion he described the portly Nicholas Soames as 'a one-man food mountain'. But on vacating his seat, he declared: 'I most certainly won't miss the constituency work. It was 22 years of the same cases, but just the faces and the people changing. It might sound a little disparaging to say this, but I got no satisfaction from this at all.'

Tam Dalyell was not quite so censorious about his constituents. He saved that for Tony Blair, whom he described as 'by far the worst' of the eight Prime Ministers he knew and tormented from the back-benches. The 72-year-old old Etonian concluded: 'Enoch Powell was right. All political careers end in failure. No-one can claim complete success or anything approaching it. There will always be much to be done.' Tam did more than most, asking more parliamentary questions than anyone before on subjects as varied as Iraq, devolution, Lockerbie, Bosnia, the *Belgrano*, nuclear power, the Westland affair, the Gibraltar IRA shootings and air traffic control.

But the Powellism he quoted will be ringing in the ears of Mr Trimble, who not only lost his own seat but along with it most of his party's representation at Westminster. The UUP were reduced from six seats to one, blaming the failure of the Government to force the disarmament issue during the implementation of the Good Friday Agreement. Mr Trimble mused: 'There is no security of tenure in politics. You are at the mercy of the electorate all the time and you are also at the mercy of events.'

It was a sage valediction from a man rejected by voters despite being decorated with one of the highest honours that humanity can bestow.

THE LORDS MAY NOT BE A'LEAPING BUT THEY ARE NOW MUCH MORE LIVELY

by **Greg Hurst**
Political Correspondent, The Times

If Tony Blair thought removing most hereditary peers would make it easier to get his legislation through the House of Lords, he miscalculated gravely. Stripped of all but 92 members whose presence was by accident of birth, the largely appointed chamber that remained responded as though the Prime Minister had conferred it with greater legitimacy. The Lords defeated the Government over details of its legislation in the 2001-05 Parliament with such frequency, especially on questions of individual liberty and constitutional powers, that Ministers resolved again to clip the wings of the unelected House.

In the first session there were 56 such defeats, rising to 88 in the second, with 64 in the third and 37 in the final truncated session before the general election. The Government resorted to appointing an extra whip in the Lords to marshal Labour's peers in the division lobbies. As this exceeded their quota, a complicated formula was introduced of paying the incumbent the salary of a junior Minister on the understanding that the premium over a whip's salary was repaid, to avoid new legislation to authorise such a post.

Yet again, however, the question of how to reform the Lords could not command agreement. Having previously tried and failed with a Royal Commission on Lords reform, Mr Blair produced a Government White Paper proposing that 20 per cent of its members be elected. Reformers blew a collective raspberry at this, thinking it too timid. The Prime Minister instead asked Parliament to find a solution.

A large joint committee of both Houses, chaired by Jack Cunningham, finally came up with five options: a wholly appointed house or elections for 20, 60, 80 or 100 per cent of its members. More were added later, muddying the waters further. On the eve of votes in both House in February 2003 Mr Blair intervened to make clear his support for an all-appointed chamber which reformers blamed for the disaster that followed.

Unsurprisingly, peers voted for the status quo. But MPs torpedoed the opportunity by failing to agree on one course, voting down each option. An 80 per cent elected House was rejected by a handful of votes.

The failure to find a formula steeled the will of the Lords, whose defiance of the Government became still more entrenched. One focus became the Constitutional Reform Bill, with which Mr Blair tried abruptly to scrap the historic post of Lord Chancellor, replace the Law Lords with a supreme court and establish a commission to appoint judges. Simultaneously he sacked Lord Irvine of Lairg, his former pupil master and mentor, and appointed in his place Lord Falconer of Thoroton, his one-time flatmate and ministerial trouble-shooter.

Confusion engendered by the uncertain manner in which the changes were announced turned to farce when Lord Falconer announced he would refuse to sit on the Woolsack to preside over Lord proceedings but concentrate on running his renamed department as Secretary of State for Constitutional Affairs. Within days he was perched on the Woolsack in borrowed wig and court dress. Tradition had out-foxed reform.

The Lords delayed the Bill with the unusual device of sending it to a special select committee, and secured numerous concessions before it finally became law. The question of who should preside over the Upper House remained unresolved after a recommendation by a cross-party committee for the election of a paid post of Lord Speaker was opposed by traditionalists and provoked fears across the Palace that it would rival the authority of the Commons Speaker.

After the customary debate on that year's Queen's Speech, Conservative peers introduced another rare move by tabling a successful amendment striking from the programme a Bill seeking to remove the remaining hereditary peers among their number. Ministers later gave up and withdrew the Bill.

Fox-hunting, inevitably, generated an additional point of conflict with the Commons as peers consistently blocked Government Bills to outlaw hunting with dogs. Pro-hunting peers were offered an olive branch when it appeared a compromise might be reached over a so-called middle way to allow hunting to continue in heavily regulated form. They rejected it. Ministers accordingly made good on repeated threats and resorted to the Parliament Act for the third time in Mr Blair's tenure to force the ban into law.

In this transitional period the issuing of writs of summons to new members of the Lords was the subject of mounting criticism and ridicule. Lists of working peers, invariably dominated by Labour appointees and in which Liberal Democrats were given parity with or even precedence over the Conservatives, were greeted with howls of hostility from parliamentary reformers.

Mr Blair's experimental system for appointing crossbenchers, via an independent commission, effectively fell into disuse after the public relations disaster that greeted its first list of members in spring 2001. With members of the public able for the first time to apply for membership or nominate friends, speculation gathered – unchecked – that 'people's peers' would comprise hairdressers and taxi drivers. There was a backlash when the inaugural list read like roll call from *Who's Who*.

After a hiatus of three years the House of Lords Appointments Commission issued a further list of seven crossbench peers in spring 2004 and appointed just two more members to the Lords a year later. Most mocked of all, however, was the system invoked on the death of a hereditary peer. Six by-elections were held between 2003-05 in which the candidates were drawn from the ousted hereditary peers of their party. These followed the deaths of the Viscount of Oxfuird, Lord Milner of Leeds, Lord Vivian, the Earl Russell, Lord Burnham and Lord Aberdare. In the case of the Labour and Liberal Democrat parties, this meant an electorate of four or five.

Over the Parliament the number of Tory peers fell, largely due to the greater average age, but those on the Labour's benches rose only marginally with the Liberal Democrat group slightly larger.

In July 2001 there were 223 Conservatives, 195 Labour peers, 61 Liberal Democrats, 173 crossbenchers, 26 bishops and 31 others. By April 2005, just before Parliament was dissolved, they stood at 205 Conservatives, 199 Labour peers, 69 Liberal Democrats, 181 crossbenchers, 25 bishops and 12 others. The ability of Tory and Liberal Democrat peers to combine forces and defeat Government business, and on other occasions alliances of Conservatives and crossbenchers, proved wearying for Labour members in the Lords.

At one of their weekly meetings during the penultimate session Labour peers decided to go ahead and draft reform proposals themselves, electing a working group under their chairmanship of Lord Hunt of King's Heath. Their report, which deliberately excluded the matter of the Lords' composition, suggested codifying the conventions to prevent their misuse and restricting further its delaying powers.

Although their proposals were taken up in Labour's manifesto, the act of unelected peers entering the debate on Lords reform was a symptom of their frustration with their leadership in the second chamber. For the first half of the Parliament the Leader of the Lords was Lord Williams of Mostyn, whose intellect and political skills were widely admired. His death from a heart attack in September 2003 ushered in a period of less assured leadership.

His replacement, Baroness Amos, was appointed after just a few months' experience in the Cabinet as International Development Secretary and did not command the same respect in the Lords. Similarly her Chief Whip, Lord Grocott, previously Mr Blair's parliamentary private secretary in the Commons, did not find it as easy to take the temperature of the House as had his predecessor Lord Carter, whom he replaced in 2002. The suspicion remained that real power in the Lords lay with Lord Falconer.

The pair also faced a canny opponent in Lord Strathclyde, leader of the Conservative peers, a shrewd parliamentarian and political strategist as befits a former Opposition Chief Whip. His large group of peers, whom William Hague had alienated by opposing the compromise to spare 92 hereditary peers in 1999 and remained sceptical of the Conservative policy endorsing a largely elected second chamber, became under his leadership a powerful brake on the Government's plans.

The Liberal Democrat peers, the smallest and probably most cohesive political group, were led by Baroness Williams of Crosby until 2004. The post, which is subject to election by Liberal Democrat peers, was taken by her deputy Lord McNally. Lord Wallace of Saltaire and Lord Dholakia tied in a dead head in an election for deputy leader, and so shared the role.

In February 2005, as most eyes turned to the prospect of a May election, it emerged that Lady Amos had been nominated by Mr Blair for the post of head of the United Nations Development Programme. Speculation thus turned to her likely successor, only to be confounded when the nomination was unsuccessful.

In Mr Blair's post-election Cabinet she remained as Leader of the Lords, a post she had been ready to leave. Lord Rooker, a Minister of State at the Northern Ireland Office, was promoted to become her deputy, replacing Baroness Symons of Vernham Dean who stood down at the election after being tipped to become leader herself.

The most controversial appointment was that of Andrew Adonis, the Prime Minister's senior adviser on education and public services and the architect of university top-up fees, who was made a junior education minister. He was raised to the peerage to make policy at the Dapertment for Education and Skills and defend it in the Lords, rather than operate behind the scenes in Downing Street.

Also appointed to Government for the first time was Lord Drayson, formerly chief executive of a pharmaceuticals company and donor of more than £1.1 million to the Labour Party, who was made Minister for Defence Procurement. These new members could look forward to being part of a House that has now come into its own.

A STRANGE ACT: CONFESSIONS OF A PARLIAMENTARY SKETCHWRITER

by **Ann Treneman**
Parliamentary Sketchwriter, The Times

There is a great deal of talk about how wonderful democracy is but, it must be said, that up close and personal it is a very strange beast indeed. Before I came to Westminster, democracy was something of an abstract, a noble concept that had spawned revolution and war and inspired some of the greatest writers and orators of all time. I arrived with what I now realise were much too inflated expectations. I wasn't planning on seeing Edmund Burke in the chamber, obviously, but I was anticipating informed debate with lashings of brilliance and wit.

This lead to terrible confusion during my initial weeks. My first day in the press gallery involved watching defence questions with Geoff Hoon. At the time Mr Hoon was in serious trouble over the Hutton Inquiry and the word 'embattled' was attached to him like a ball and chain. In the chamber that day he had cloaked himself in a dull arrogance that seemed most inappropriate. He stood at the despatch box, learning forward, his nose in the air like a pointer who has spotted a bird in the undergrowth. He was sorry for nothing, he was responsible for even less and yet, somehow, he was in charge. His manner was that of a dull functionary and his body language so constrained that I thought he was being held in with invisible wires.

What was going on? It wasn't supposed to be like this. At first I thought it was just me. I was going to the chamber at the wrong time. If only I could find the secret door, then all would become clear. And so I began to pop in to the chamber at random intervals: in mid-afternoon, in late afternoon, at tea time and, indeed, at closing time. I went to Commons committees and even standing committees, where people were getting into heated discussions about the wording of footnotes and kept using the word 'heretofor'. I tarried in Westminster Hall, the alternative chamber where chairs are placed in a horseshoe in an effort to create a non-confrontational atmosphere. I soon saw that non-confrontational just does not work in this country: no one goes to Westminster Hall unless they absolutely have to.

I am not sure how long it took me to realise that I was not the problem. It was Parliament. 'I am not sure that a dull man giving a dull speech to an almost empty chamber is any way to run a country,' I commented, rather pompously (it is catching), to a press gallery colleague after a particularly gruelling session. In response he gave me a strange look. 'That's what everyone says at first,' he said, with a shrug.

I soldiered on. I began to recognise the faces of the dull men and to realise that it had been ridiculously naïve to assume that the basic purpose of the departmental question times was to answer questions. The idea of the truth, as I had always regarded it at least, featured mainly as a plaything here, a mouse that is chased round the Chamber by politicians who believe that this is the great game that they were born to play.

It is only on very important occasions – such as the various debates on Iraq and the subsequent inquiries – that the idea of the truth becomes substantial and real. Most of the time it is hidden behind cloaking devices that would do Harry Potter proud. When asked about oranges Ministers talk about apples and, when pressed about apples, they talk about carrots. In fact, this is exactly how I came to discover that, for the purposes of the free fruit in schools policy, the government had reclassified carrots as a fruit. What a shock that was: politics may have to be the art of the practical but dishing out carrots to kids expecting lovely juicy apples is just plain sadistic.

I also began to realise that, in its dysfunctional way, Parliament does work. The subjects that matter to people (and not, on the whole, to the press) are raised with at times tedious regularity. Not a week, and during some stretches of the year not a day, went by without an MP sharing with us the story about some mad post office closure. If government had its way no one would ever talk about NHS dentistry again (in fact, talking can be difficult without teeth and so it might get its way eventually) and yet sometimes health questions seems to be dental questions. Public drunkenness is a perennial favourite. I laughed out loud the first time I heard there was an 'alcohol harm reduction strategy' but, after about the thousandth mention, I began to welcome it like an old friend. It's important to have a strategy when you don't have a clue what to do.

Sketchwriters, by our very job description, concentrate on performance. It is amazing how appalling some politicians are in the Chamber. They mumble, stumble, and bumble. Some Ministers read their speeches at dictaphone speed, never looking up. Others become mired in jargon. I can no longer hear the word 'stakeholder' without physically recoiling. My colleagues at *The Times* are always assuring me that this or that MP is, actually, an incredibly bright and affable fellow. Then they always add this phrase 'when you get to know him'. But for those of us who have to watch these people in what passes for action, that really does not seem relevant.

There is nothing inherently cruel about the Chamber but it is a kind of theatre and that means that good performers, such as William Hague or Robin Cook, are made all the larger for it. But woe betide the shy and the maladroit. Some of my most painful moments were spent watching Iain Duncan Smith at the despatch box. It was like observing a dyslexic child try to spell a word in front of an audience of bullies. I kept waiting for someone to rush in and say: 'Stop! Enough!' But no one does that in politics. They shoot horses, don't they, but in politics they wait for them to collapse on their own.

I had known that the Prime Minister had an appalling voting record but I had not realised how little he is in the chamber other than during PMQs. (That may change for the new Parliament as his interest may increase in proportion to his decreased majority.) Question time, so painful during the IDS reign, was a lot more fun with Michael Howard, though at times he and the Prime Minister were just two barristers fighting over the placement of a comma, which was a bit dull for the rest of us.

Everyone says that PMQs is the highlight of the parliamentary week (which is not a week at all but four days) but it took me a long time to get used to the tribal lunacy of this half hour. To observe it some weeks is to see grown men and women screeching like monkeys in the wild. Some of the sessions got very frantic. During David Blunkett's various troubles the Opposition leader brought in a biography in which Mr Blunkett had criticised his colleagues. After brandishing it at the Prime Minister, he left it on the despatch box. When the chaotic session ended Hilary Armstrong, the chief whip, whose jaw always seems to be jutting, reached over and threw the book at the Tory front bench. Perhaps it was unintentional, but it just missed the groin of dapper little Alan Duncan.

The Government had such a large majority that almost all the real opposition came from behind them. During the contentious debates, such as tuition fees or the terror legislation, Ministers resembled owls as they swivelled their heads round to face their rebellious backbenchers. Eventually the Speaker would warn: 'The secretary of state should address the whole house.' The secretary of state reluctantly would rotate his head back round but, gradually and at first imperceptibly, the head would turn back round a little and then a lot.

Gordon Brown has been a constantly moving weather pattern over the past few years, as he wrestled with the fact that he is not the prime minister. I think, actually, that he may have set the international record for sulking. But, no matter how large the black cloud is that travels with him, he always perked up for Treasury questions. MPs who believe that he is the true leader gather for this like some sort of prayer service. It must be said that, for drama, Mr Brown is quite good value. He scuttles in, carrying a haystack of papers. The pages try to escape from him and an alarmingly large number succeed. The front bench, after Treasury questions, is a mess.

The most dramatic debates of the Parliament were on the war and the various inquiries into aspects of it. The Commons is at its best when it is serious. On evening, after the death of several soldiers in Iraq, Ministers hastened to the Commons for a short statement. The gravity of the situation was etched on the proceedings. It was an occasion for humanity and sadness and, as I watched, I was struck by how rarely you see such scenes in the political world. There is something about the Commons at such times that is grand and intimate. Politics as usual had been abandoned, for a while.

The chamber has been infiltrated twice. The latter, by hunt protesters in September 2004, should have been frightening. But as men in penguin suits tackled the protesters it seemed more comic than anything else. The purple flour attack, though, was something else. For a few seconds at 12.18 pm on 19 May 2004, no one knew if what had just happened was dangerous or not.

The chamber was packed for PMQs. On that day I sketched that Mr Howard had been taunting Mr Blair, saying he had been 'stitched up like a kipper' by his own Cabinet. Mr Blair had teased back: 'It is interesting, isn't it, how we never wants to discuss the issues! And I wonder why! I wonder why!'

There were shouts from the gallery reserved for members of the House of Lords and guests. A man stood up and threw something. A stream of purple shot through the air, partially disintegrating. No one panicked. The Prime Minister barely afforded it a glance before readjusting his spectacles. Another burst of purple shot through the air. A lavender haze hung over the benches. We could all see that the purple powder had hit Mr Blair in the back. The Speaker suspended the House. Only four seconds – four very long seconds – had elapsed since Mr Blair's 'I wonder why' and the Speaker's shout. At the time I wrote: 'Much could have happened in those seconds. We had absolutely no idea if it had.' In retrospect, what happened was that the Commons was confronted by its own vulnerability.

The most chaotic debate was the two-day madness that engulfed the Prevention of Terrorism Bill. This was introduced on the hoof, with very little time for debate. Many Labour backbenchers were furious, as was the House of Lords. The Home Secretary often seemed to be making it up as he went along and the whips were in overdrive, reeling around the Chamber creating little eddies of plots everywhere they went.

The Government thought the Lords did not have the stamina to stay up all night. How wrong it was. I have never seen so many happy old people as on that morning after the all-night sitting. For they are all expert cat-nappers and looked far fresher than the MPs did. In Parliamentary terms, on that morning, it was still Thursday as Friday did not exist. This was ridiculous but within the Palace of Westminster no one seemed to think this all that strange. The fractious session until a compromise was finally reached very late in this, the longest day.

My favourite debate, though, was about lunch. It took place, fittingly, at lunchtime. The session was ostensibly about Commons hours (whether to revert to a 2.30 pm start time) but it became a breadsticks-at-dawn duel between those who lunched and those who didn't. 'When I got this job, I used to say that any MP who had time for lunch wasn't worth talking to,' cried Paul Tyler, the Liberal Democrat. A Tory MP kept trying to intervene and Mr Tyler sneered: 'All right, I will give way to the luncher.'

Mr Cook tried, as ever, to raise the tone. He noted that on the way to the Chamber MPs walked past the statues of great parliamentarians. 'They will have passed Fox and Burke and Pitt frozen for all time in attitudes of declamation against each other. Their great debates on human rights, the French Revolution, Britain's place in Europe, all took place in the morning and the afternoon. None of them complained that the scrutiny of these issues would be better at 10 pm,' cried Mr Cook, with what may have been despair. 'What we do is far more important than when we do it,' he said, eyebrows arched into chalet roof peaks. 'There is no law that says the quality of our speeches improves the later in the day we make them.'

Up in the press gallery, I found myself nodding vigorously in agreement.

TONY BLAIR, THE POLITICIAN. A VERY PERSONAL ASSESSMENT

by **Matthew Parris**
Columnist, The Times

The memorable victories can be the least interesting. They are often the victor's first. Who can forget Margaret Thatcher on the steps of Downing Street in May 1979, clutching her infernal Prayer of St Francis of Assisi? Who can forget that famous 'Blair Babes' picture – Tony Blair with his backdrop of smiling women – in May 1997?

Yet in the right circumstances winning once is not difficult. Anybody can sweep an unpopular government from office. Anybody could have beaten Labour in 1979: it didn't need to be Mrs Thatcher. Anybody could have beaten the Tories in 1997: it didn't need to be Mr Blair.

What confirmed Mrs Thatcher as the electoral colossus she became was two more victories, in 1983 and 1987, both with majorities of more than a hundred. Those campaigns are less remembered perhaps only because they confirmed what we already knew: that the Prime Minister was capable of getting and keeping a popular majority behind her leadership. And in just the same way, what has confirmed Mr Blair as a formidable vote-getting machine has been two unmemorable general elections: a powerful majority in 2001, and even this time in 2005, a substantial margin of victory.

There are those who say his latest victory was won despite and not because of him, and on the most obvious level this is true: by 2005 Mr Blair's name had ceased to be an asset on the doorsteps, and to many (including this writer) he himself had become as irritating as a bluebottle in the kitchen. Familiarity stales. But Mr Blair can claim credit for more than the now-tainted Blair brand itself: it is to him we owe the look, shape and feel of a whole style of government: 'third way' politics – folksy, populist, empathising, undemanding and ideologically light on its feet. That sort of politics and those sorts of politician were what won again on 5 May 2005, and Mr Blair made them: they have been created in his image.

Once tried and tested in office, a democratic leader's electoral appeal becomes a many-stranded rope. Personality is part of it, but without good judgement, personality alone will not carry you for long. You need to choose your ground and your direction in politics, and to choose right.

A third strand is skill: by which I mean a lower art than judgement, which is strategic, and something closer to cunning, which is tactical. This is the art of anticipating, alliance-building, dodging, blowing hot and cold.

Finally – and if your electoral appeal is to endure – you must get results. In the end there is no substitute for solid achievement, and this carried Mrs Thatcher onward when personal charm had failed, judgement had faltered and even her shrewd sense of tactics had gone awry. She just kept pointing to the record.

Let us start with personality: the most obvious strand and in Mr Blair's case all-important in the early stages. Voters' reaction to personality in politicians is a complicated response: charm is not the only weapon (Disraeli had it, Gladstone didn't; Attlee lacked it, Wilson had it, Mrs Thatcher lacked it) but it is a weapon Mr Blair has wielded with practised ease. Mostly he has been a canny judge of public mood, with a truly thespian knack of reading his audience right. As do many great actors (and confidence tricksters) Mr Blair has responded to his audiences' moods with his whole being, becoming the thing they want him to be, inhabiting roles rather than playing them.

"RELAX! WE'RE PLAYING LIB DEMS VERSUS LABOUR"

This is not tactics: it is his nature. The catch in the throat at Diana's funeral was genuine. The grim-faced warrior during the bombing of Kosovo was real. The playful humour and knowing wink which has greeted journalists at press conferences has not been feigned. Rich business people have come away from private meetings convinced he admired wealth-creation and did not begrudge money-makers wealth of their own. When he has moved among the poor or distressed they have sensed he feels their pain. The 'pretty straight kind of a guy' on John Humphrey's sofa, meant it.

On one level at least, nobody was fooling anybody. On another I might argue that Mr Blair has been fooling himself; but nobody can dispute the results: people – individually and en masse – have warmed to him. He caught a tide in our country's affairs and in its mood: an incoming tide of rising prosperity, rising security, a post-Thatcherite shudder at everything cold or brutal in politics, and an increasingly classless mass culture in which a comfortable people wanted to be amused, occasionally moved, and always entertained. He understood the role of celebrity in this, both becoming one, and associating himself with others: pop-stars, celebrity chefs, deceased royalty, Mr Blair has never been far from the spotlight and, like a modern Mahommed, when the spotlight refuses to come to Mr Blair, Mr Blair moves to the spotlight.

To the second strand in the electoral rope, judgement, Mr Blair can lay serious claim. His tactics (I shall suggest) have often been poor, but his strategy was, from the start, triumphantly right. He moved his party into the centre ground. He sensed Britain had edged rightwards during the Thatcher years and he shamelessly followed. I say 'shamelessly' because it was brazen but I do not believe it was unprincipled. Mr Blair's own true instincts were Christian-conservative, and he followed them, confident that the time was right politically. And it was.

How about skill? Sheer cunning can augment – even substitute for – charm. The skilful in democratic politics see trouble coming and know when to duck. Though the public have tended to see Mr Blair as a consummate ducker and weaver, a typical politician, the last word in guile, I question that. His approach has been short-termist, hand-to-mouth, sometimes self-defeatingly so. He relied (as he has from childhood) on charm to get him out of tricky situations.

Mr Blair's charm has exceeded his skill, rescuing him from blunders. The skilful underwrite their popularity by investing in tomorrow's votes; they see trouble coming and take a hit today in order to deflect a bigger hit tomorrow. They avoid hostages to fortune, resisting the temptation to make promises they are in no position to keep. They cultivate the friendship of potential troublemakers, and when awkward decisions are necessary they are careful to bind their enemies in.

But I believe history will judge Mr Blair a rather careless politician. He made enemies unnecessarily, lost friends he needed to keep, and showed an impatience (and, surprisingly, a candour) which did not serve him well. He had no time for alliances. He said of himself that 'I have no reverse gear' and it was true. He needed one.

Coalitions at home (or abroad) were not built for the work he needed to do on Lords reform, on reforming the delivery of public services, on student maintenance – and, critically, on Iraq.

Iraq was not an exercise of principle, it was a failure of tactical sense. Over-impressed by a new US president, the Prime Minister backed himself into a corner and gave undertakings for which there was no need. All else – the misleading, the over-egging, the wriggling, the vague sense of disgrace – followed. Even to those who supported Britain's involvement in the war I would argue that it was a bad mistake to allow the impression to arise that we had been dragooned. It suited both sides of this argument to assume that Britain faced a simple choice: back America or turn our back on her. In fact there was a wealth of available Foreign Office fudge between those alternatives, and Mr Blair missed it.

As I write this Mr Blair lurches on. A so-far strong economy and a sense that he has governed from the political centre, combined with a fading but still tangible public sentiment that, rascal or not, he's a moderate and he's a political winner, have lent him the momentum on which he now runs.

A huge song and dance has been made in recent years, triggered by the Iraq war and the issue of weapons of mass destruction, about the matter of trust. Undoubtedly Mr Blair has lost it, except in this one important regard: most people do trust him to do what he believes is in the nation's interests. I believe that is what saved him from a much worse result in 2005.

On the debit side there are as yet few obvious monuments to Blairism (beyond his transformation of his own party) on which he can rest his appeal to that most severe of electorates: the judgement of history. It is getting late for their construction.

But from the strands from which a politician's electoral appeal may be constructed, I missed one which was once important to Mr Blair. Luck.

It may be that historians will record that Mr Blair's luck – and with it his hopes of being remembered as more than just the best vote-gatherer in the story of the Labour Party – died on 18 July 2003 with Dr David Kelly in an Oxfordshire wood.

RESULTS BY CONSTITUENCY

HOUSE OF COMMONS, MAY 2005

The heart of The Times Guide to the House of Commons is the results of the 2005 general election. This section lists all of those which occurred on 5 May 2005 and the by-election in Staffordshire South which took place shortly afterwards. Each of the 646 constituencies is listed along with the relevant statistical data on voting figures, turnout and swings compared with the outcomes in June 2001. There is also a brief biographical summary for all Members of Parliament and a short demographic and geographical profile of each seat as well. The map which accompanies this book should help readers track down the constituencies which interest them.

Constituencies are listed in alphabetical order according to the significant element of their name: 'North', 'South', 'East' and 'West' and 'City of' at the beginning of a constituencies' names are disregarded and so West Suffolk appear under S and City of York under Y. 'St' is treated as 'Saint'.

In England and Wales (and Northern Ireland) there were no changes in constituency boundaries between 2001 and 2005 – there will be at the next election – which makes statistical comparisons straightfoward. The same is not true for the Scottish seats which were extensively redrawn. This means the actual outcome must be set against a notional calculation of what it is thought would have happened if these constituencies had been fought four years ago. This is an inevitably imperfect exercise.

In the biographical details, company directorships and similar postions are not generally listed if they are in the Register of Members Interests. That interesting document is available, along with a treasure trove of other information, on the parliamentary website (www.parliament.uk).

Tim Hames

PARTY ABBREVIATIONS

Parties with MPs: C Conservative; **DUP** Democratic Unionist Party; **Ind KHHC** Independent Kidderminster Hospital and Health Concern; **Lab** Labour; **Lab/C** Labour Co-operative; **LD** Liberal Democrat; **Pl C** Plaid Cymru; **Respect** Respect – The Unity Coalition; **SDLP** Social Democratic and Labour Party; **SF** Sinn Féin; **SNP** Scottish National Party; **UUP** Ulster Unionist Party

Minor parties: AFC Alliance for Change; **All** Alliance; **Anti-CF** Anti-Corruption Forum; **AP** Alternative Party; **Baths** Save the Bristol North Baths Party; **BMG** Blair Must Go Party; **BNP** British National Party; **BPP** British Public Party; **Bridges** Build Duddon and Morecambe Bridges; **Burnley** Burnley First Independent; **CAP** Community Action Party; **CD** Christian Democratic Party; **CG** Community Group; **CGB** Communist Party of Great Britain; **Clause 28** Clause 28 Children's Protection Christian Democrats; **CMEP** Church of the Militant Elvis Party; **Comm** Communist Party; **CP** Civilisation Party; **CPA** Christian People's Alliance; **CRD** Campaigning for Real Democracy; **Croydon** Croydon Pensions Alliance; **Currency** Virtue Currency Cognitive Appraisal Party; **DCSP** Direct Customer Service Party; **DDTP** Death, Dungeons and Taxes Party; **Dem Lab** Democratic Labour Party; **Dem Soc All** Democratic Socialist Alliance – People Before Profit; **DWSB** Defend the Welfare State against Blairism; **EC** Extinction Club; **EDP** English Democratic Party; **EEP** English Parliamentary Party; **Eng Dem** English Democrats Party; **England** English Democrats – Putting England First; **FDP** Fancy Dress Party; **FFUK** familiesfirst.uk.net; **Fit** Fit Party For Integrity And Trust; **Forum** Open Forum; **FP** Freedom Party; **Free** Free Party; **Free Scot** Free Scotland Party; **FW** Forward Wales Party; **GBB** Get Britain Back Party; **Green S** Alliance for Green Socialism; **Greens** Green Party; **Honesty** Demanding Honesty in Politics and Whitehall; **Ind** Independent; **IOW** Isle of Wight Party; **IP** Imperial Party; **Iraq** "Iraq War, Not In My Name"; **IWCA** Independent Working Class Association; **IZB** Islam Zinda Baad Platform; **Jam** Jam Wrestling Party; **JLDP** John Lillburne Democratic Party; **JP** Justice Party; **LCA** Legalise Cannabis Alliance; **LEDP** Lower Excise Duty Party; **LG** Life of Latgale; **Lib** Liberal; **LibP** Liberated Party; **Local** Local Community Party; **Loony** Official Monster Raving Loony Party; **Masts** Removal of Tetra masts in Cornwall; **MC** Millennium Council; **MebK** Mebyon Kernow (the party for Cornwall); **MNP** Motorcycle News Party; **Mus** Muslim Party; **NACVP** Newcastle Academy with Christian Values Party; **NBrit** New Britain Party; **NEP** New English Party; **NF** National Front; **NIUP** Northern Ireland Unionist Party; **NIWC** Northern Ireland Women's Coalition; **NMB** New Millennium Bean Party; **Northern** Northern Progress For You; **OCV** Operation Christian Vote; **Online** Seeks a Worldwide Online Participatory Directory; **Paisley** Pride in Paisley Party; **PCP** Pensioner Coalition Party; **PDP** Progressive Democratic Party; **PEurC** Pro Euro Conservative Party; **PHF** People of Horsham First; **PJP** People's Justice Party; **Power** Max Power Party; **PPS** Pensioners' Party Scotland; **Progress** Peace and Progress Party; **ProLife** Pro-Life Alliance; **Protest** Protest Vote Party; **PRTYP** Personality And Rational Thinking? Yes! Party; **Publican** Publican Party – Free to Smoke (Pubs); **PUP** Progressive Unionist Party; **RA** Residents Association; **R2000** Reform 2000; **RMGB** Residents and Motorists of Great Britain; **RNRL** Rock 'N' Roll Loony Party; **RP** Rate Payer; **SA** Socialist Alliance; **SAP** Socialist Alternative Party; **Scot Lab** Scottish Labour; **Scot Senior** Scottish Senior Citizens Party; **Senior** Senior Citizens Party; **SFRP** Scottish Freedom Referendum Party; **Silent** Silent Majority Party; **SLP** Socialist Labour Party; **SNH** Safeguard The National Health Service; **Soc EA** Socialist Environmental Alliance; **Soc Unity** Socialist Unity Network; **Socialist** Socialist; **SOS** SOS! Voters against Overdevelopment of Northampton; **SSCUP** Scottish Senior Citizens' Unity Party; **SSP** Scottish Socialist Party; **St Albans** St Albans Party; **Stuckist** Stuckist Party; **Sun Rad** Sunrise Radio; **SUP** Scottish Unionist Party; **TCP** CountrySide Party; **telepath** telepathicpartnership.com; **TEPK** Tigers Eye the Party for Kids; **TGP** Grey Party; **Third** Third Way; **TP** Their Party; **TPP** The Peace Party – non-violence, justice, environment; **Truth** Truth Party; **UKC** UK Community Issues Party; **UKIP** UK Independence Party; **UKP** United Kingdom Pathfinders; **UKPP** UK Pensioners Party; **UKUP** United Kingdom Unionist Party; **UPP** Unrepresented Peoples Party; **UTW** Ulster Third Way; **Veritas** Veritas; **Vote Dream** Vote for yourself rainbow dream ticket; **VYP** Vote for Yourself Party; **WesR** Wessex Regionalists; **Work** The People's Choice Making Politicians Work; **World Rev** World Revolutionary Party; **WP** Workers' Party; **WRP** Workers' Revolutionary Party; **XPP** Xtraordinary People Party; **YPB** Your Party (Banbury).

ABERAVON — Lab hold

		Electorate	Turnout	Change from	2001	Electorate	Turnout
		51,080	58.9%	2001		49,524	61%
Francis H	**Lab**	**18,077**	**60.1%**	**-3%**	**Lab**	**19,063**	**63.1%**
Waller C	LD	4,140	13.8%	4.1%	PIC	2,955	9.8%
Evans P	PIC	3,545	11.8%	2%	LD	2,933	9.7%
Rees-Mogg A	C	3,064	10.2%	2.6%	C	2,296	7.6%
Wright W	Veritas	768	2.6%		RP	1,960	6.5%
la Vey M	Greens	510	1.7%		NMB	727	2.4%
					SA	256	0.8%
Lab to LD swing	**3.6%**	**30,104**		**Lab maj 13,937**		**30,190**	**Lab maj 16,108**
				46.3%			53.4%

HYWEL FRANCIS b 6 June 1946. MP 2001-. Member Welsh Affairs select cttee 2001-. All-party groups: chair steel and cast-metal 2005-, vice-chair further and adult education, joint sec children in Wales 2001-, sec muscular dystrophy 2004. Member: Socialist Education Assocn 1999-, Co-operative Party 1999-. Vice-pres Friends of Cyprus. Member European standing cttee B 2003-. Dept/research asst. Adult education: tutor, lecturer, dir, professor. Sec of State Wales special adviser 1999-2000. Ed BA hist, PhD, Univ of Wales, Swansea.

Aberavon is dominated by Port Talbot, which is easily the main community in the constituency. The constituency is situated just to the east of Swansea Bay on the Bristol Channel. Since the decline of the mining industry, attempts have been made to revitalise the local economy with significant success, certainly in bringing down unemployment. Aberavon is clearly a Labour stronghold and seems set to remain so for the foreseeable future.

ABERDEEN NORTH — Lab hold

		Electorate	Turnout		2001
		65,714	55.8%		
Doran F	**Lab**	**15,557**	**42.5%**		No comparable results due to boundary changes
Delaney S	LD	8,762	23.9%		
Stewart K	SNP	8,168	22.3%		
Anderson D	C	3,456	9.4%		
Connon J	SSP	691	1.9%		
Lab to LD swing	**9.2%**	**36,634**		**Lab maj 6,795**	
(notional)				18.6%	

FRANK DORAN b 13 April 1949. MP for Aberdeen South 1987-92, for Aberdeen Central 1997-2005, for Aberdeen North 2005-. PPS to Ian McCartney 1997-99, 1999-2001. Opposition spokes energy 1988-92. Member Culture, Media and Sport select cttee 2001-. All-party groups: treasurer oil and gas industry 2002-, sec fisheries 2003-. Sec: GMB Westminster parly group, Lab MPs trade union group. Scottish Legal Action group 1974. Chair Dundee mental health assocn 1979-82. Solicitor 1977-88. Ed Leith Academy, LLB, Dundee Univ.

The new seat of Aberdeen North extends south from the river Don to the city centre and the harbour, incorporating the 11 most northerly wards of now defunct Aberdeen Central. In the large council estates of Mastrick, Hilton, Seaton and St Machar Labour is mainly challenged by the SNP. Midstocket is affluent and decidedly Tory, but it is outvoted by the working-class areas of north and central Aberdeen.

ABERDEEN SOUTH — Lab hold

		Electorate	Turnout		2001
		67,012	62.1%		
Begg A	**Lab**	**15,272**	**36.7%**		No comparable results due to boundary changes
Harris V	LD	13,924	33.4%		
Whyte S	C	7,134	17.1%		
Watt M	SNP	4,120	9.9%		
Reekie R	Greens	768	1.8%		
Munro D	SSP	403	1%		
Lab to LD swing	**3.1%**	**41,621**		**Lab maj 1,348**	
(notional)				3.2%	

ANNE BEGG b 6 Dec 1955. MP for Aberdeen South 1997-2005, for new Aberdeen South 2005-. Member select cttees: Scottish Affairs 1997-2001, Work and Pensions 2001-, Chairmen's Panel 2002-. Chair all-party endometriosis group 2002-. Member: Lab Party NEC 1998-99, PLP Lab Party policy forum, Educational Inst of Scotland 1978-, Gen Teaching Council for Scotland 1994-97. Disabled Scot of the Year 1988. Teacher. Ed MA hist/politics, Aberdeen Univ; secondary teaching cert, Aberdeen Coll of Ed.

Labour and the Liberal Democrats vie for control of Aberdeen South, which stretches from the south harbour and city centre, through well-heeled suburban Peterculter and Cults to westerly rural wards just north of the river Dee. It includes some of Aberdeen's richest residential areas, a peripheral town, Tory rural bastions, and a substantial group of Labour-voting city wards, though the Liberal Democrats have made the largest gains since 2001.

WEST ABERDEENSHIRE AND KINCARDINE — LD hold

		Electorate	Turnout		2001
		65,548	63.5%		
Smith R	**LD**	**19,285**	**46.3%**		No comparable results due to boundary changes
Johnstone A	C	11,814	28.4%		
Barrowman J	Lab	5,470	13.1%		
Little C	SNP	4,700	11.3%		
Grant L	SSP	379	0.9%		
C to LD swing (notional)	**2.2%**	**41,648**		**LD maj 7,471** 17.9%	

SIR ROBERT SMITH b 15 April 1958. MP for W Aberdeenshire and Kincardine 1997-2005, for new W Aberdeenshire and Kincardine 2005-. Lib Dem: dep chief whip 2001-, whip 1999-2001, spokes Scotland 1999-2001. Member select cttees: Scottish Affairs 1999-2001, Procedure 2001-, Trade/Industry 2001-, Unopposed Bills 2001-, Standing Orders 2001-, Accommodation and Works 2003-. Cllr Aberdeenshire Council 1995-97. JP 1997. Vice-convener Grampian Joint Police Board 1995-97. Member Electoral Reform Soc. Family estate manager. Ed BSc, Aberdeen Univ.

West Aberdeenshire and Kincardine is a mixture of commuter-belt and farmland situated to the south and west of oil-rich Aberdeen. The seat covers territory which had been thought of as very safe for the Conservatives, including Balmoral and a sprinkling of wealthy commuter towns. As well as Royal Deeside it includes Aboyne, Banchory, Braemar, Ballater and Portlethen. The Liberal Democrats obtain considerable support from the Mearns farming communities and coastal Stonehaven.

AIRDRIE AND SHOTTS — Lab hold

		Electorate	Turnout		2001
		61,955	53.5%		
Reid J	**Lab**	**19,568**	**59%**		No comparable results due to boundary changes
Balfour M	SNP	5,484	16.5%		
Watt H	LD	3,792	11.4%		
Cottis S	C	3,271	9.9%		
Coats F	SSP	706	2.1%		
Rowan J	Ind	337	1%		
SNP to Lab swing (notional)	**1.5%**	**33,158**		**Lab maj 14,084** 42.5%	

JOHN REID b 8 May 1947. MP for Motherwell North 1987-97, for Hamilton North and Bellshill 1997-2005, for Airdrie and Shotts 2005-. Sec of State: Defence 2005-, Health 2003-05; Leader of HoC 2003, Minister without Portfolio and Party Chair 2002-03. Sec of State: NI 2001-02, Scotland 1999-2001. Minister of State: DETR 1998-99, MoD 1997-98. Opposition: Dep Sec of State Defence 1995-97, spokes 1989-97. Chair select cttee. Lab Party: NEC, research, Neil Kinnock adviser, trade unionists for Lab. PC 1998. Ed MA hist, PhD econ hist, Stirling Univ.

John Smith's old seat of Airdrie and Shotts covers a large area south-east of Glasgow, in what was once Scotland's industrial heartland. On either side of the M8, Airdrie (in the north-west of the seat) and Shotts (in the south-west), are heavily working-class and have not yet recovered from the demise of heavy industry. Labour's dominance is newly supplemented by the addition of Holytown and Newarthill from North Lanarkshire.

ALDERSHOT — C hold

		Electorate	Turnout	Change from	2001	Electorate	Turnout
		78,553	61.3%	2001		78,255	57.9%
Howarth G	**C**	**20,572**	**42.7%**	**0.5%**	**C**	**19,106**	**42.2%**
Collett A	LD	15,238	31.6%	4%	LD	12,512	27.6%
Linsley H	Lab	9,895	20.6%	-4.6%	Lab	11,394	25.2%
Rumsey D	UKIP	1,182	2.5%	0.7%	UKIP	797	1.8%
Cowd G	Eng Dem	701	1.5%		Greens	630	1.4%
Hope H	Loony	553	1.2%	0.3%	Ind	459	1%
					Loony	390	0.9%
C to LD swing	**1.8%**	**48,141**		**C maj 5,334** 11.1%		**45,288**	**C maj 6,594** 14.6%

GERALD HOWARTH b 12 Sept 1947. MP for Cannock and Burntwood 1983-92, for Aldershot 1997-. Shadow Minister for International Affairs 2003-. PPS to: Margaret Thatcher 1991-92, Sir George Young 1990-91, Michael Spicer 1987-90. Opposition defence spokes 2002-. Member select cttees on: Home Affairs 1997-2001, Defence 2001-03. Banker and loan arranger 1971-83. Ed Bloxham Sch, Banbury; BA English, Southampton Univ.

Aldershot is Britain's best known army town, and home to one of the largest military training centres in the UK. Defence interests also feature at Farnborough, famous for its air show, and in numerous high-tech companies. The constituency is a base for its highly mobile population of London commuters. Throughout the last century, Aldershot returned Conservative MPs and, in recent times, the centre left vote has been split between Labour and the Liberal Democrats.

ALDRIDGE-BROWNHILLS C hold

		Electorate	Turnout	Change from	2001	Electorate	Turnout
		61,761	64%	2001		62,361	60.6%
Shepherd R	**C**	**18,744**	**47.4%**	**-2.8%**	**C**	**18,974**	**50.2%**
Phillips J	Lab	13,237	33.5%	-6.7%	Lab	15,206	40.2%
Sheward R	LD	4,862	12.3%	3.7%	LD	3,251	8.6%
Vaughan W	BNP	1,620	4.1%		SA	379	1%
Eardley G	UKIP	1,093	2.8%				
Lab to C swing	**2%**	**39,556**		**C maj 5,507**		**37,810**	**C maj 3,768**
				13.9%			10%

RICHARD SHEPHERD b 6 Dec 1942. MP 1979-. Member select cttees on: Treasury, Modernisation of House of Commons 1997-, Public Administration 1997-2000, Human Rights 2001-. Introduced 4 Private Member's Bills. Member South East Economic Planning Council 1970-74. Co-chair Campaign for Freedom of Information. Underwriter Lloyds 1974-94 and grocer. Ed London School of Economics; MSc Economics, John Hopkins School of Advanced International Studies.

A predominantly middle-class, residential seat in the northern West Midlands, Aldridge-Brownhills is a longstanding Conservative seat. Richard Shepherd has represented the constituency since 1979, when he took it from Labour, and his Euro-scepticism has earned him a strong personal vote. The demographic of the constituency is almost exclusively white, and there is a high level of home ownership. The constituency, despite a low majority, is probably safe for the Tories.

ALTRINCHAM AND SALE WEST C hold

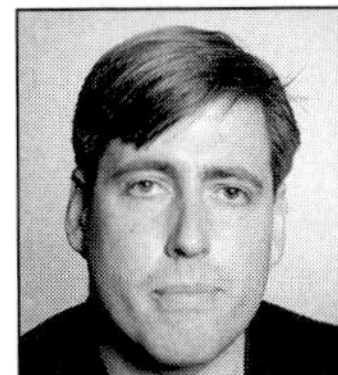

		Electorate	Turnout	Change from	2001	Electorate	Turnout
		67,247	65.9%	2001		71,861	60.6%
Brady G	**C**	**20,569**	**46.4%**	**0.2%**	**C**	**20,113**	**46.2%**
Stockton J	Lab	13,410	30.3%	-9.1%	Lab	17,172	39.4%
Chappell I	LD	9,595	21.6%	7.2%	LD	6,283	14.4%
Peart G	UKIP	736	1.7%				
Lab to C swing	**4.7%**	**44,310**		**C maj 7,159**		**43,568**	**C maj 2,941**
				16.2%			6.8%

GRAHAM BRADY b 20 May 1967. MP 1997-. Foreign Affairs Shadow Minister 2004-. PPS to: Michael Howard 2003-04, Michael Ancram 1999-2000. Opposition whip 2000. Opposition spokes on: employment 2000-01, schools 2001-03. Member select cttees on: Education and Employment 1997-2001, Office of Deputy Prime Minister 2004-. Career in PR and Centre for Policy Studies. Ed Altrincham Grammar Sch; BA law, Durham Univ.

Situated to the south of Manchester and to the north of Tatton, Altrincham and Sale West is, in the main, a residential constituency. Towns like Hale and Bowdon have retained their original character, proving to be attractive with commuters from the professional, managerial and technical sectors that form over half of the population. Formerly a regular five-figure majority seat for the Tories, this constituency will continue to return Conservative MPs, albeit with smaller margins.

ALYN AND DEESIDE Lab hold

		Electorate	Turnout	Change from	2001	Electorate	Turnout
		58,939	60.2%	2001		60,478	58.6%
Tami M	**Lab**	**17,331**	**48.8%**	**-3.5%**	**Lab**	**18,525**	**52.3%**
Hale L	C	8,953	25.2%	-1.1%	C	9,303	26.3%
Brighton P	LD	6,174	17.4%	4.5%	LD	4,585	12.9%
Coombs R	PlC	1,320	3.7%	0.4%	PlC	1,182	3.3%
Crawford W	UKIP	918	2.6%	1.2%	Greens	881	2.5%
Armstrong-Braun K	FW	378	1.1%		UKIP	481	1.4%
Kilshaw J	Ind	215	0.6%	-0.1%	Ind	253	0.7%
Davies G	Comm	207	0.6%		Comm	211	0.6%
Lab to C swing	**1.2%**	**35,496**		**Lab maj 8,378**		**35,421**	**Lab maj 9,222**
				23.6%			26%

MARK TAMI b 3 Oct 1962. MP 2001-. Member Northern Ireland Affairs select cttee 2001-. All-party groups: vice-chair manufacturing industry 2001-, sec aerospace 2001-. Treasurer Lab Friends of Australia. Member: European standing cttee B 2003-, TUC General Council 1999-2001. AEEU: research and communications head 1992-99, head of policy 1999-2001. Ed Enfield Grammar Sch; BA hist, Swansea Univ.

Alyn and Deeside is situated in north-east Wales, on the English border close to Chester. Despite being so close to England, it has a Welsh-speaking population of 14 per cent. It is part of a long chain of strongly-held Labour seats stretching across North Wales and Merseyside. This seat, having been a Labour seat since its inception, is unlikely to be gained by any other party in the foreseeable future.

AMBER VALLEY — Lab hold

		Electorate 75,376	Turnout 62.9%	Change from 2001	2001	Electorate 73,798	Turnout 60.3%
Mallaber J	**Lab**	**21,593**	**45.6%**	**-6.3%**	**Lab**	**23,101**	**51.9%**
Shaw G	C	16,318	34.4%	-1.3%	C	15,874	35.7%
Smith K	LD	6,225	13.1%	0.7%	LD	5,538	12.4%
Snell P	BNP	1,243	2.6%				
Stevenson A	Veritas	1,224	2.6%				
Price H	UKIP	788	1.7%				
Lab to C swing	**2.5%**	**47,391**		**Lab maj 5,275** 11.1%		**44,513**	**Lab maj 7,227** 16.2%

JUDY MALLABER b 10 July 1951. MP 1997-. Member select cttees on: Education and Employment 1997-2001, Treasury 2001, Trade and Industry 2003-. Chair all-party clothing and textiles group 1999-. Chair Labour Research Dept 1991-94. Vice-chair East Midlands Regional Group of Labour MPs 2002-. NUPE research officer 1975-85. Director local govt information unit 1987-95. Ed North London Collegiate Sch; BA, St Anne's Coll, Oxford.

The constituency embraces the three Derbyshire towns of Heanor, Alfreton and Ripley. The seat was a one-time industrial and mining area, but now has some light industry and serves as a commuting area for Derby and Nottingham. Amber Valley remains a predominantly working-class constituency, albeit one that has experienced rising affluence. It changed hands from Conservative to Labour in 1997 and has remained Labour ever since.

ANGUS — SNP hold

		Electorate 63,093	Turnout 60.5%		2001
Weir M	**SNP**	**12,840**	**33.6%**		No comparable results due to boundary changes
Bushby S	C	11,239	29.5%		
Bradley D	Lab	6,850	18%		
Rennie S	LD	6,660	17.4%		
Manley A	SSP	556	1.5%		
C to SNP swing (notional)	**1.3%**	**38,145**		**SNP maj 1,601** 4.2%	

MIKE WEIR b 24 March 1957. MP for Angus 2001-05, for new Angus 2005-. SNP spokes: trade and industry, health, environment, for work and pensions, energy and trade and industry 2005-. Member Scottish Affairs select cttee 2001-. Sec all-party Iraqi Kurdistan group 2002-. Cllr Angus DC 1984-88. Solicitor. Law Society of Scotland 1981. Ed Arbroath High Sch; LLB, Aberdeen Univ.

Angus occupies a sweep of eastern coastline from Montrose in the north down to Arbroath, but now stops short of Carnoustie, having lost SNP strongholds Monifieth and Carnoustie to Dundee. Reaching a good 50 kilometres inland, it includes thousands of hectares of Strathmore farmland, including Tory Brechin and Kirriemuir, and SNP-inclined Forfar. Those two parties are practically neck-and-neck in this extremely close marginal seat.

EAST ANTRIM — DUP gain

		Electorate 58,335	Turnout 54.5%	Change from 2001	2001	Electorate 60,897	Turnout 59.1%
Wilson S	**DUP**	**15,766**	**49.6%**	**13.6%**	**UUP**	**13,101**	**36.4%**
Beggs R	UUP	8,462	26.6%	-9.8%	DUP	12,973	36%
Neeson S	All	4,869	15.3%	2.8%	All	4,483	12.5%
O'Connor D	SDLP	1,695	5.3%	-2%	SDLP	2,641	7.3%
McKeown J	SF	828	2.6%	0.1%	Ind	1,092	3%
Kerr D	Vote Dream	147	0.5%		SF	903	2.5%
					C	807	2.2%
UUP to DUP swing	**11.7%**	**31,767**		**DUP maj 7,304** 23%		**36,000**	**UUP maj 128** 0.4%

SAMMY WILSON b 4 April 1953. MP 2005-. MLA for Belfast East 1998-2003, and for East Antrim 2003-. Member Northern Ireland Policing Board 2001-; Councillor East Belfast City Council 1981-: Lord Mayor 1986. Schoolteacher; head of economics at grammar school

This largely urban constituency nestles on the north-eastern coast of Ireland between the Antrim Hills and Belfast Lough. The seat is dominated by the large port town of Larne. The constituency is largely Protestant and unionist, with Catholics forming just over 13 per cent of the population. The spectacular re-alignment of Ulster politics was highlighted in East Antrim in the 2003 Assembly election with the DUP comfortably overtaking the Ulster Unionists.

NORTH ANTRIM — DUP hold

		Electorate	Turnout	Change from	2001	Electorate	Turnout
		74,450	61.7%	2001		74,451	66.1%
Paisley I	**DUP**	**25,156**	**54.8%**	**4.9%**	**DUP**	**24,539**	**49.9%**
McGuigan P	SF	7,191	15.7%	5.9%	UUP	10,315	21%
McCune R	UUP	6,637	14.4%	-6.6%	SDLP	8,283	16.8%
Farren S	SDLP	5,585	12.2%	-4.6%	SF	4,822	9.8%
Dunlop J	All	1,357	3%	0.4%	All	1,258	2.6%
DUP to SF swing	**0.5%**	**45,926**		**DUP maj 17,965**		**49,217**	**DUP maj 14,224**
				39.1%			28.9%

IAN PAISLEY b 6 April 1926. MP 1970-. DUP constitutional affairs spokes. Leader (co-founder) DUP 1971-. Member: Rex Cttee, European Parliament political cttee. NI Assembly 1973-74, 1982, 1998-. MP for Parl of NI (Stormont) 1970-72: opposition leader 1972. NI MEP 1979-2004. Ordained 1946. Moderator Free Presbyterian Church of Ulster 1951-. Founded Protestant Telegraph 1966. Constitutional Convention 1975-76. Co-chair World Congress of Fundamentalists 1978. Ed S Wales Bible Coll; Reformed Presbyterian Theological Coll, Belfast.

This mainly rural constituency is situated in the north-east of Northern Ireland. It is bounded to the north by the Antrim Coast and to the south by Lough Neagh. The seat is overwhelmingly Protestant and unionist. It is the parliamentary berth of the 'Big Man' in Northern Ireland politics, DUP leader Ian Paisley. The DUP hold on the seat seems unbreakable after the party took the top two positions in the 2003 Assembly elections.

SOUTH ANTRIM — DUP gain

		Electorate	Turnout	Change from	2001	Electorate	Turnout
		66,931	56.7%	2001		70,651	62.5%
McCrea W	**DUP**	**14,507**	**38.2%**	**3.4%**	**UUP**	**16,366**	**37.1%**
Burnside D	UUP	11,059	29.1%	-8%	DUP	15,355	34.8%
McClelland N	SDLP	4,706	12.4%	0.3%	SDLP	5,336	12.1%
Cushinan H	SF	4,407	11.6%	2.2%	SF	4,160	9.4%
Ford D	All	3,278	8.6%	4.1%	All	1,969	4.5%
					NIUP	972	2.2%
UUP to DUP swing	**5.7%**	**37,957**		**DUP maj 3,448**		**44,158**	**UUP maj 1,011**
				9.1%			2.3%

WILLIAM McCREA b 6 August 1948. MP 2005-. Civil servant Northern Ireland Department of Health and Social Services 1966-82; Member Northern Ireland Assembly 1982-86, MP for Mid Ulster 1983-87, for South Antrim 2000-01; MLA 1998-. Ed Cookstown Grammar School; Doctorate of divinity, Marietta Bible College, Ohio

This large rural seat lies at the heart of Ulster to the north of Belfast. It stretches from the river Bann and Lough Neagh in the west to the outskirts of Belfast. It includes Belfast international airport at Aldergrove. It was one of the seats lost by the UUP to the DUP in the 2005 general election that helped to confirm the DUP as the dominant force of unionist politics in Northern Ireland.

ARGYLL AND BUTE — LD hold

		Electorate	Turnout		2001
		67,325	64.2%		
Reid A	**LD**	**15,786**	**36.5%**		No comparable results due to boundary changes
McGrigor J	C	10,150	23.5%		
Manson C	Lab	9,696	22.4%		
Strong I	SNP	6,716	15.5%		
Henderson D	SSP	881	2%		
C to LD swing (notional)	**1.9%**	**43,229**		**LD maj 5,636** 13%	

ALAN REID b 7 Aug 1954. MP for Argyll and Bute 2001-05, for new Argyll and Bute 2005-. Lib Dem whip 2002-. Lib Dem Scotland spokes 2004-. Member Broadcasting select cttee 2001. Scottish Lib Dems 1981: vice-convener 1994-98, member exec cttee. Election agent George Lyon Scottish Parl election 1999. Cllr Renfrew DC 1988-96. Teacher 1976-77, computer programmer 1977-85, computer project programmer 1985-. Ed BSc maths, Strathclyde Univ; teacher training qualification, Jordanhill Coll; computer data processing, Bell Coll.

Argyll and Bute is vast, remote and beautiful. It comprises 26 inhabited islands off the west coast of Scotland, including Coll, Colonsay, Islay, Jura, Mull, Tiree and Bute, as well as a great swathe of the mainland reaching north from the Kintyre Peninsula to the moors of Argyll in the remote north. The Liberal Democrats have comfortably held off Labour and the Conservatives, though the addition of Helensburgh and Garelochead from Dumbarton could create a three-way marginal race.

ARUNDEL AND SOUTH DOWNS — C hold

		Electorate 72,535	Turnout 68.5%	Change from 2001	2001	Electorate 70,956	Turnout 64.7%
Herbert N	**C**	**24,752**	**49.8%**	**-2.4%**	**C**	**23,969**	**52.2%**
Deedman D	LD	13,443	27.1%	4.7%	LD	10,265	22.4%
Whitlam S	Lab	8,482	17.1%	-3.6%	Lab	9,488	20.7%
Moffat A	UKIP	2,700	5.4%	0.7%	UKIP	2,167	4.7%
Stack M	Protest	313	0.6%				
C to LD swing	**3.6%**	**49,690**		**C maj 11,309** 22.8%		**45,889**	**C maj 13,704** 29.9%

NICK HERBERT b 1963. MP 2005-. Contested Berwick-upon-Tweed 1997 general election. Political affairs British Field Sports Society 1990-96; Chief executive Business for Sterling 1998-2000; Director Reform 2002-05. Ed Haileybury; Law and land economy, Magdelene College, Cambridge

This is a quiet, predominantly rural constituency stretching across the north of the picturesque South Downs. Rolling agricultural land gives way to country towns and large villages. Arundel is the ancestral home of the Dukes of Norfolk and has a historic castle and Catholic cathedral. This prosperous corner of the traditional English countryside is natural territory for the Conservatives and is one of the safest Tory seats in the country, regardless of their choice of candidate.

ASHFIELD — Lab hold

		Electorate 73,403	Turnout 57.3%	Change from 2001	2001	Electorate 73,540	Turnout 53.5%
Hoon G	**Lab**	**20,433**	**48.6%**	**-9.5%**	**Lab**	**22,875**	**58.1%**
Inglis-Jones G	C	10,220	24.3%	-0.1%	C	9,607	24.4%
Johnson W	LD	5,829	13.9%	2.6%	LD	4,428	11.3%
Adkins R	Ind	2,292	5.4%		Ind	1,471	3.7%
Allsop K	Ind	1,900	4.5%	0.8%	SA	589	1.5%
Hemstock S	Veritas	1,108	2.6%		SLP	380	1%
Grenfell E	Ind	269	0.6%				
Lab to C swing	**4.7%**	**42,051**		**Lab maj 10,213** 24.3%		**39,350**	**Lab maj 13,268** 33.7%

GEOFFREY HOON b 6 Dec 1953. MP 1992-. Leader HoC and Lord Privy Seal 2005-, Defence Sec 1999-2005, Foreign and Commonwealth Office Min of State 1999, Lord Chancellor's Dept: Min of State 1998-99, Parliamentary Sec 1997-98. Opposition whip 1994-95. Opposition trade and industry spokes 1995-97. MEP Derbyshire 1984-94. Chair European Parliament Delegation for relations with China 1986-89, US 1989-83. Legal career 1976-84. PC 1999. Ed Nottingham High Sch; BA law 1976, MA, Jesus Coll, Cambridge.

The constituency lies to the north west of Nottingham, its main towns being Sutton-in-Ashfield, Kirby-in-Ashfield and Eastwood. It used to be a coalmining constituency. As a result of coal's decline the constituency's social character is changing. New private housing estates have been built and from these estates residents commute to work in Nottingham or Mansfield. This is a working class seat which has been Labour ever since its creation in 1955.

ASHFORD — C hold

		Electorate 79,493	Turnout 65%	Change from 2001	2001	Electorate 76,699	Turnout 62.5%
Green D	**C**	**26,651**	**51.6%**	**4.2%**	**C**	**22,739**	**47.4%**
Whitaker V	Lab	13,353	25.8%	-6.3%	Lab	15,380	32.1%
Took C	LD	8,308	16.1%	1%	LD	7,236	15.1%
Boden R	Greens	1,753	3.4%	0.6%	Greens	1,353	2.8%
Stroud B	UKIP	1,620	3.1%	0.5%	UKIP	1,229	2.6%
Lab to C swing	**5.3%**	**51,685**		**C maj 13,298** 25.7%		**47,937**	**C maj 7,359** 15.4%

DAMIAN GREEN b 17 Jan 1956. MP 1997-. Shadow Sec of State: Transport 2003-04, Education and Skills 2001-03. Opposition spokes: education and employment 1998-99, environment 1999-2001. Member select cttees on: Culture, Media and Sport 1997-98, Procedure 1997-98, Home Affairs 2004-. Member 1922 cttee exec 2004-. Chair Con parly mainstream group 2003-. Media career 1978-92. Special adviser PM's Policy Unit 1992-94. Ed Reading Sch; BA PPE, Oxford Univ.

The constituency includes some attractive countryside, set as it is between the North Downs, Romney Marsh in the East and the Weald of Kent in the south. But there are enormous pressures for development in this area as a result of the M20 and the high-speed rail link to the Channel Tunnel served by Ashford's international passenger terminal. The constituency has been a Conservative stronghold for as long as most can remember.

ASHTON UNDER LYNE — Lab hold

		Electorate 72,000	Turnout 51.3%	Change from 2001	2001	Electorate 72,820	Turnout 49.1%
Heyes D	**Lab**	**21,211**	**57.4%**	**-5.1%**	**Lab**	**22,340**	**62.5%**
Brown G	C	7,259	19.6%	0.5%	C	6,822	19.1%
Jones L	LD	5,108	13.8%	2%	LD	4,237	11.8%
Jones A	BNP	2,051	5.6%	1.1%	BNP	1,617	4.5%
Whittaker J	UKIP	768	2.1%		Greens	748	2.1%
Crossfield J	Local	570	1.5%				
Lab to C swing	**2.8%**	**36,967**		**Lab maj 13,952** 37.7%		**35,764**	**Lab maj 15,518** 43.4%

DAVID HEYES b 2 April 1946. MP 2001-. Member Public Administration select cttee 2001-. Cllr Oldham Metropolitan Borough Council 1992-: Labour Group sec 1993-2000, chair Personnel cttee 1994-2000, vice-chair Policy cttee 1999-2000. Local govt 1962-90, computer graphics 1990-95, development worker 1993-95, deputy district manager Manchester CAB 1995-2001. Ed Blackley Technical High Sch, Manchester; BA social sciences, Open Univ.

Situated to the east of Manchester Central and to the south of the two Oldham constituencies, Ashton under Lyne is a Labour stronghold, returning candidates for the entire period since the Second World War. A largely urban constituency, the textile and coal mining industries were the main employers, but with the decline in that field unemployment and other spectres of inner-city decay has arisen.

AYLESBURY — C hold

		Electorate 82,428	Turnout 62.4%	Change from 2001	2001	Electorate 80,002	Turnout 61.4%
Lidington D	**C**	**25,253**	**49.1%**	**1.8%**	**C**	**23,230**	**47.3%**
Jones P	LD	14,187	27.6%	0.7%	LD	13,221	26.9%
Khaliel M	Lab	9,540	18.5%	-4.7%	Lab	11,388	23.2%
Adams C	UKIP	2,479	4.8%	2.3%	UKIP	1,248	2.5%
LD to C swing	**0.6%**	**51,459**		**C maj 11,066** 21.5%		**49,087**	**C maj 10,009** 20.4%

DAVID LIDINGTON b 30 June 1956. MP 1992-. Shadow Sec of State: Northern Ireland 2003-, Environment, Food and Rural Affairs 2002-03. Agriculture and Fisheries Shadow Min 2002. PPS to: Michael Howard 1994-97, William Hague 1997-99. Member Education select cttee 1992-96. Special adviser to Douglas Hurd at Home Office 1987-89, at FCO 1989-90. Senior consultant at The Public Policy Unit 1991-92. Ed Haberdasher's Aske's Sch; MA hist PhD, Sidney Sussex Coll, Cambridge.

Aylesbury is prime commuter territory – attractive countryside within easy reach of London. But there is also substantial local employment in hi-tech industries. As well as the urban centre of Aylesbury the seat includes the Prime Minister's country residence at Chequers. This Buckinghamshire constituency is safe Conservative territory, with tactical voting from Labour supporters appearing to be the only way that serious inroads will be made into the Tory majority.

AYR, CARRICK AND CUMNOCK — Lab hold

		Electorate 73,448	Turnout 61.3%		2001
Osborne S	**Lab**	**20,433**	**45.4%**		No comparable results due to boundary changes
Jones M	C	10,436	23.2%		
Waugh C	LD	6,341	14.1%		
Brodie C	SNP	5,932	13.2%		
Sharp D	SSCUP	592	1.3%		
Steele M	SSP	554	1.2%		
McDaid J	Scot Lab	395	0.9%		
McCormack B	UKIP	365	0.8%		
Lab to C swing (notional)	**2.2%**	**45,048**		**Lab maj 9,997** 22.2%	

SANDRA OSBORNE b 23 Feb 1956. MP for Ayr 1997-2005, for Ayr, Carrick and Cumnock 2005-. PPS to: Helen Liddell 2002-03, George Foulkes 2001-02, Brian Wilson 1999-2001. Member select cttees: Information 1997-2000, Scottish Affairs 1998-99, European Scrutiny 2004-. Cllr: Kyle and Carrick DC 1990-95, South Ayrshire Council 1994-97. Chair Scottish regional group of Lab MPs 1999-. Community worker. Former TGWU branch sec. Ed Anniesland Coll; Jordanhill Coll; dip community ed, dip and MSc equality and discrimination, Strathclyde Univ.

Fanning south from its main town, Ayr, through 40 kilometres of coastline to the east, the Doon and Afton Valleys and rich Carrick farmland to the south, this seat combines picturesque seaside towns, prosperous farmland, and ex-mining towns. The less prosperous northern estates of Ayr, and the old industrial towns like Cumnock and Patna, have high unemployment and a large proportion of social housing. They outvote Conservative Carrick and the coast, providing Labour with an ample majority.

CENTRAL AYRSHIRE — Lab hold

		Electorate	Turnout	2001
		68,643	62.5%	
Donohoe B	**Lab**	**19,905**	**46.4%**	No comparable results due to boundary changes
Clark G	C	9,482	22.1%	
Kennedy I	LD	6,881	16.1%	
Hanif J	SNP	4,969	11.6%	
Morton D	SSP	820	1.9%	
Cochrane R	SLP	468	1.1%	
Groves J	UKIP	346	0.8%	
C to Lab swing (notional)	**0.7%**	**42,871**	**Lab maj 10,423** 24.3%	

BRIAN DONOHOE b 10 Sept 1948. MP for Cunninghame South 1992-2005, for Central Ayrshire 2005-. Member select cttees: Environment, Transport and Regional Affairs 1997-2001, Transport, Local Govt and Regions 2001-02, Transport 2002-. Chair Scottish Lab MPs group 1997-98. Apprentice engineer, Hunterston nuclear power station, ICI draughtsman. NALGO district officer 1981-92, chair TASS political/education cttee 1969-81, member TGWU parly campaigning group 1992-. Ed Irvine Royal Academy; nat cert engineering, Kilmarnock Tech Coll.

Spreading inland from the west coast to the edge of the Ayrshire coalfield, this seat has a smattering of prosperous rural towns, spectacular golf-courses and pretty seaside resorts – characteristic Conservative territory. A clutch of depressed ex-mining towns in the south-east and populous Irvine new town in the north have relatively high unemployment and tracts of social housing (especially in Irvine, designed to relieve housing pressure in nearby Glasgow. They provide Labour with a comfortable majority.

NORTH AYRSHIRE AND ARRAN — Lab hold

		Electorate	Turnout	2001
		73,737	60%	
Clark K	**Lab**	**19,417**	**43.9%**	No comparable results due to boundary changes
Connell S	C	8,121	18.4%	
Gurney T	SNP	7,938	18%	
White G	LD	7,264	16.4%	
Turbett C	SSP	780	1.8%	
Pursley J	UKIP	382	0.9%	
McDaid L	SLP	303	0.7%	
Lab to C swing (notional)	**2.7%**	**44,205**	**Lab maj 11,296** 25.6%	

KATY CLARK b 3 July 1967. MP 2005-. Contested Galloway and Upper Nithsdale 2001; Solicitor; Head of membership legal services, UNISON

This seat comprises the Isle of Arran, and the tranche of Ayrshire coastine which faces it across the Firth of Clyde. Agriculture, tourism and nuclear power are the main local industries now, although the villages of the Garnock valley were once dependent on mining and towns like Kilburnie and Dalry have suffered from the decline of the steel industry. Affluent Conservative commuting villages in the north of the seat are outvoted by the south which is firmly Labour.

BANBURY — C hold

		Electorate	Turnout	Change from	2001	Electorate	Turnout
		87,168	64.5%	2001		84,374	61.1%
Baldry T	**C**	**26,382**	**46.9%**	**1.7%**	**C**	**23,271**	**45.2%**
Sibley L	Lab	15,585	27.7%	-7.3%	Lab	18,052	35%
Patrick Z	LD	10,076	17.9%	2%	LD	8,216	15.9%
Duckmanton A	Greens	1,590	2.8%	0.3%	Greens	1,281	2.5%
Heimann D	UKIP	1,241	2.2%	0.9%	UKIP	695	1.3%
Starkey J	NF	918	1.6%				
Rowe C	YPB	417	0.7%				
Lab to C swing	**4.5%**	**56,209**		**C maj 10,797** 19.2%		**51,515**	**C maj 5,219** 10.1%

TONY BALDRY b 10 July 1950. MP 1983 -. MAFF Min of State 1995-97, Parly Under-Sec: FCO 1994-95, Dept of Environment 1990-94, Dept of Energy 1990. PPS to: Lynda Chalker 1985-87, John Wakeham 1987-90. Member select cttees on: Trade and Industry 1997-2001, Standards and Privileges 2001, Liaison 2001-, Chair Internat Devt 2001-. Exec member 1922 cttee 2001-02. Construction/legal career 1975-. Ed Leighton Park Sch, Reading; BA soc science, LLB, Sussex Univ; Lincoln's Inn.

Set in North Oxfordshire, this partly rural constituency has experienced significant urban growth in the expanding towns of Banbury and Bicester, where two-thirds of the electors now live. Nestling in the countryside lie a number of leafy and prosperous villages, popular with commuters who favour the area for its fast links to Birmingham, Oxford and London. This has long been a safe Conservative seat, and appears as if it will remain that way.

BANFF AND BUCHAN — SNP hold

		Electorate	Turnout	2001
		65,570	56.8%	
Salmond A	**SNP**	**19,044**	**51.2%**	No comparable results due to boundary changes
Wallace S	C	7,207	19.4%	
Anderson E	LD	4,952	13.3%	
Okasha R	Lab	4,476	12%	
Ross V	OCV	683	1.8%	
Kemp K	UKIP	442	1.2%	
Will S	SSP	412	1.1%	
C to SNP swing (notional)	**2.2%**	**37,216**	**SNP maj 11,837** 31.8%	

ALEX SALMOND b 31 Dec 1954. MP for Banff and Buchan 1987-2005, for new Banff and Buchan 2005-. MSP Banff and Buchan 1999-2001. SNP parly spokes: Constitution, economy, trade/industry, fishing 1992-97, constitution, fishing 1997-, Treasury 2001-. SNP Nat Exec 1981-: nat convener 1990-2000, 2004-. Leader Westminster parly group 2001-04. Vice-chair all-party fisheries group 2003-. Economist: Royal Bank of Scotland 1980-82, oil 1982-87. Hon vice-pres Scottish Centre for Economic and Social Research. Ed MA econ/hist, St Andrew's Univ.

Banff and Buchan is bounded by the north sea on two sides, from Cruden Bay via the major east coast ports of Peterhead and Fraserburgh, then turning through Rosehearty, Macduff and Portsoy in the north. Inland, the farming communities of New Pitsligo and Mintlaw are now joined by Turriff which shares their character and Tory inclinations, though Alex Salmond is very comfortably incumbent in what has become the safest SNP seat in Scotland.

BARKING — Lab hold

		Electorate	Turnout	Change from	2001	Electorate	Turnout
		57,658	50.1%	2001		55,229	45.5%
Hodge M	**Lab**	**13,826**	**47.8%**	**-13.1%**	**Lab**	**15,302**	**60.9%**
Prince K	C	4,943	17.1%	-5.9%	C	5,768	23%
Barnbrook R	BNP	4,916	17%	10.6%	LD	2,450	9.8%
Wickenden T	LD	3,211	11.1%	1.3%	BNP	1,606	6.4%
Jones T	UKIP	803	2.8%				
Cleeland L	Greens	618	2.1%				
Panton D	Ind	530	1.8%				
Saxby M	WRP	59	0.2%				
Lab to C swing	**3.6%**	**28,906**		**Lab maj 8,883** 30.7%		**25,126**	**Lab maj 9,534** 37.9%

MARGARET HODGE b 8 Sept 1944. MP by-election June 1994-. Minister of State: Dept for Work and Pensions 2005-, Dept for Education and Skills 2001-05. Parly Under-Sec Dept for Education and Employment 1998-2001. Member select cttees on: Education and Employment 1996-97 (chair 1997-98), Deregulation 1996-97, Liaison 1997-98. Cllr Islington 1973-94: leader 1982-92. Teaching/market research 1966-73, Price Waterhouse consultant 1992-94. MBE 1978, PC 2003. Ed Oxford High Sch; BSc economics LSE.

This seat in north-east London is both residential and industrial in character. The Dagenham Ford motor works are nearby, and many of Barking's voters are employed there. Social attitudes and political loyalties have changed radically. The 1980s witnessed Barking changing from Labour stronghold to Labour-Tory marginal. The vote is volatile with swings above the national average. It has reverted to being a safe Labour seat.

BARNSLEY CENTRAL — Lab hold

		Electorate	Turnout	Change from	2001	Electorate	Turnout
		60,592	47.2%	2001		60,086	45.8%
Illsley E	**Lab**	**17,478**	**61.1%**	**-8.5%**	**Lab**	**19,181**	**69.6%**
Crompton M	LD	4,746	16.6%	1.9%	LD	4,051	14.7%
Morel P	C	3,813	13.3%	0.2%	C	3,608	13.1%
Broadley G	BNP	1,403	4.9%		SA	703	2.6%
Wood D	Ind	1,175	4.1%				
Lab to LD swing	**5.2%**	**28,615**		**Lab maj 12,732** 44.5%		**27,543**	**Lab maj 15,130** 54.9%

ERIC ILLSLEY b 9 April 1955. MP 1987-. Opposition whip 1991-94. Opposition spokes: health 1994-95, local government 1995, Northern Ireland 1995-97. Member select cttees on: Procedure 1991-97, Foreign Affairs 1997-, Procedure 1997-, Chairman's Panel 2000-. Chair all-party caravanning group 2004-. Yorkshire area NUM official 1978-87. Ed Barnsley Holgate Grammar Sch; LLB, Leeds Univ.

The South Yorkshire constituency of Barnsley Central is comprised of the Town Centre, Monk Bretton, Cudworth, Ardsley, Lundwood, Kendray, Royston, Carlton, Smithies, New Lodge, Athersley, Wilthorpe and Pogmoor. The smallest of the three Barnsley constituencies, in both area and population, and with a smaller than average electorate, Barnsley Central is likely to remain a significant Labour stronghold in the future.

BARNSLEY EAST AND MEXBOROUGH — Lab hold

		Electorate	Turnout	Change from	2001	Electorate	Turnout
		66,941	49.3%	2001		65,655	49.5%
Ennis J	**Lab**	**20,779**	**62.9%**	**-4.6%**	**Lab**	**21,945**	**67.5%**
Brook S	LD	6,654	20.2%	4.3%	LD	5,156	15.9%
Abbott C	C	4,853	14.7%	2.3%	C	4,024	12.4%
Robinson T	SLP	740	2.2%		SLP	722	2.2%
					UKIP	662	2%
Lab to LD swing	**4.5%**	**33,026**		**Lab maj 14,125**		**32,509**	**Lab maj 16,789**
				42.8%			51.6%

JEFFREY ENNIS b 13 Nov 1952. MP for Barnsley East 1996-97, for Barnsley East and Mexborough 1997-. PPS to Tessa Jowell 1997-2001. Member Education and Skills select cttee 2001-. Chair all-party racing and bloodstock group 2001-. Cllr Barnsley Metropolitan Borough Council 1980-96: leader 1995-96. Chair South Yorkshire Fire and Civil Defence Authority 1995-96. Teacher 1976-96. Nat Assocn of Schoolmasters/Union of Women Teachers representative 1979-96. Ed Hemsworth Grammar Sch; CertEd, BEd, Redland Coll, Bristol.

The safe Labour seat covers a former mining area within South Yorkshire including the town of Grimethorpe. The mining towns and villages are now trying to survive without the mines which created them. Unemployment tends to hover well above the national average. Manual workers and their families form over 60 per cent of the population. Barnsley council is trying to attract new industry and they have undertaken a special reclamation and regeneration programme.

BARNSLEY WEST AND PENISTONE — Lab hold

		Electorate	Turnout	Change from	2001	Electorate	Turnout
		66,985	55%	2001		65,291	52.9%
Clapham M	**Lab**	**20,372**	**55.3%**	**-3.3%**	**Lab**	**20,244**	**58.6%**
Watkinson C	C	9,058	24.6%	1.8%	C	7,892	22.8%
Brelsford A	LD	7,422	20.1%	1.5%	LD	6,428	18.6%
Lab to C swing	**2.6%**	**36,852**		**Lab maj 11,314**		**34,564**	**Lab maj 12,352**
				30.7%			35.7%

MICHAEL CLAPHAM b 15 May 1943. MP 1992-. PPS to Alan Milburn 1997. Member Trade and Industry select cttee 1992-97, 2003-. Chair all-party groups: occupational safety and health 1995-, coalfield communities 1997-, fire safety 2001-. Chair Dodworth Lab Party branch 1984-86. Chair Barnsley Crime Prevention Partnership 1995-. Miner/lecturer. NUM member/official 1958-: head industrial relations 1983-92. Ed Darton Secondary Modern Sch; BSc sociology, Leeds Poly; PGCE, Leeds Univ; MPhil industrial relations, Bradford Univ.

The constituency stretches from the slopes of the Pennines eastwards down to the western outskirts of Barnsley. This is the most rural of the three Barnsley seats, with agriculture important in the uplands around Penistone and includes small towns on the outskirts of Barnsley. The constituency is well on its way to recovery from the loss of coalmining and heavy engineering. It will remain a Labour stronghold for the foreseeable future.

BARROW AND FURNESS — Lab hold

		Electorate	Turnout	Change from	2001	Electorate	Turnout
		61,883	59%	2001		64,746	60.3%
Hutton J	**Lab**	**17,360**	**47.6%**	**-8.1%**	**Lab**	**21,724**	**55.7%**
Dorman W	C	11,323	31%	0.7%	C	11,835	30.3%
Rabone B	LD	6,130	16.8%	4.6%	LD	4,750	12.2%
Beach A	UKIP	758	2.1%	0.3%	UKIP	711	1.8%
Bell T	Bridges	409	1.1%				
Greaves B	Veritas	306	0.8%				
Young H	Ind	207	0.6%				
Lab to C swing	**4.4%**	**36,493**		**Lab maj 6,037**		**39,020**	**Lab maj 9,889**
				16.5%			25.3%

JOHN HUTTON b 6 May 1955. MP 1992-. Chancellor Duchy of Lancaster 2005-. Dept of Health: Min of State 1999-2005, Parly Under-Sec 1998-99. PPS to Margaret Beckett 1997-98 as: President of Board of Trade and Trade and Industry Sec of State 1997-98, President of the Council and Leader of House of Commons 1998. Member Home Affairs select cttee 1994-97. Legal academic career 1980-92. PC 2001. Ed Westcliffe High Sch, Southend; BA law / BCL, Magdalen Coll, Oxford.

Barrow and Furness is situated in Cumbria, beyond the Lake District, across the bay from Morecambe. The seat takes in lush farmland and the small town of Ulverston as well as the port of Barrow itself. The town of Barrow is best known as a shipbuilding centre and was associated with Britain's nuclear submarine industry. It is a constituency that cuts across the political spectrum, though comfortably held by Labour at the moment.

BASILDON — Lab hold

		Electorate 73,912	Turnout 58.4%	Change from 2001	2001	Electorate 74,121	Turnout 55.1%
Smith A	**Lab/C**	**18,720**	**43.4%**	**-9.3%**	**Lab/C**	**21,551**	**52.7%**
Powell A	C	15,578	36.1%	2.3%	C	13,813	33.8%
Thompson M	LD	4,473	10.4%	1.4%	LD	3,691	9%
Colgate E	BNP	2,055	4.8%		UKIP	1,397	3.4%
Blythe A	UKIP	1,143	2.6%	-0.8%	SA	423	1%
Copping V	Greens	662	1.5%				
Gandy K	Eng Dem	510	1.2%				
Lab/C to C swing	**5.8%**	**43,141**		**Lab/C maj 3,142** 7.3%		**40,875**	**Lab/C maj 7,738** 18.9%

ANGELA SMITH b 7 Jan 1959. MP 1997-. Northern Ireland Office Parly Under-Sec 2002-. Joint PPS to Paul Boateng as Home Office Min of State 1999-2001. Asst govt whip 2001-02. Cllr Essex County Council 1989-97: chief whip 1993-96. Trainee accountant 1982-83, League Against Cruel Sports 1983-95, Alun Michael research asst 1995-97. Ed Chalvedon Comprehensive, Basildon; BA public administration, Leicester Poly.

Basildon New Town is at the heart of working-class Essex and all but the Pitsea neighbourhood is included within the constituency. A mixture of the industrial and the residential, the constituency also includes a large country park and sites of special scientific interest. Basildon is regarded as a seat in which voters choose carefully according to their perceived economic interests, and the constituency has never been a safe haven for any political party.

BASINGSTOKE — C hold

		Electorate 76,404	Turnout 63%	Change from 2001	2001	Electorate 75,300	Turnout 63.7%
Miller M	**C**	**19,955**	**41.5%**	**-1.2%**	**C**	**20,490**	**42.7%**
Harvey P	Lab	15,275	31.7%	-9.2%	Lab	19,610	40.9%
Smith J	LD	9,952	20.7%	6.8%	LD	6,693	13.9%
Effer P	UKIP	1,044	2.2%	-0.3%	UKIP	1,202	2.5%
Shirley D	Greens	928	1.9%				
Robertson R	BNP	821	1.7%				
Macnair R	MC	148	0.3%				
Lab to C swing	**4%**	**48,123**		**C maj 4,680** 9.7%		**47,995**	**C maj 880** 1.8%

MARIA MILLER b 26 March 1964. MP 2005-. Contested Wolverhampton NE 2001 general election. Advertising executive Grey Advertising Ltd 1985-90; Marketing manager Texaco 1990-94; Company director Grey Advertising Ltd 1994-99, The Rowland Company 1999-2003. Ed Brynteg Comprehensive, Bridgend; economics, London School of Economics

Situated in the M3 corridor in North Hampshire, Basingstoke has become an increasingly urban constituency as hi-tech industries, office developments, and London commuters have made it their home. The population has grown over fivefold since 1951 and the constituency boundary has contracted significantly in accordance. Despite these large changes in the size and composition of the seat, the Conservatives have been returned here without interruption for over 50 years.

BASSETLAW — Lab hold

		Electorate 69,389	Turnout 58.1%	Change from 2001	2001	Electorate 68,417	Turnout 56.8%
Mann J	**Lab**	**22,847**	**56.6%**	**1.3%**	**Lab**	**21,506**	**55.3%**
Sheppard J	C	12,010	29.8%	-0.4%	C	11,758	30.2%
Dobbie D	LD	5,485	13.6%	0.9%	LD	4,942	12.7%
					SLP	689	1.8%
C to Lab swing	**0.9%**	**40,342**		**Lab maj 10,837** 26.9%		**38,895**	**Lab maj 9,748** 25.1%

JOHN MANN b 10 Jan 1960. MP 2001-. Member select cttees on: Information 2001-, Treasury 2003-, Unopposed Bills (Panel) 2004-. Chair all-party groups: endangered species 2002, Kazakhstan 2003-. Cllr London Borough of Lambeth 1986-90. Head research and education AEEU 1988-90. National training officer TUC 1990-95. Liaison officer National Trade Union and Labour Party 1995-2000. Ed Bradford Grammar Sch; BA Econ, Manchester Univ.

Bassetlaw is the most northerly of Nottinghamshire's seats and historically a Labour stronghold. The seat covers a fairly large area, but it is the light industrial town of Worksop that dominates the economic landscape. That has not always been the case, since mining was important in many locations until the pit closures of the 1980s

BATH — LD hold

		Electorate	Turnout	Change from	2001	Electorate	Turnout
		66,824	68.6%	2001		71,371	64.9%
Foster D	**LD**	**20,101**	**43.8%**	**-6.7%**	**LD**	**23,372**	**50.5%**
Dawson S	C	15,463	33.7%	4.6%	C	13,478	29.1%
Ajderian H	Lab	6,773	14.8%	-0.9%	Lab	7,269	15.7%
Lucas E	Greens	2,494	5.4%	2.2%	Greens	1,469	3.2%
Crowder R	UKIP	770	1.7%	0.2%	UKIP	708	1.5%
Cobbe P	Ind	177	0.4%				
Walker G	Ind	58	0.1%				
LD to C swing	**5.7%**	**45,836**		**LD maj 4,638**		**46,296**	**LD maj 9,894**
				10.1%			21.4%

DON FOSTER b 31 March 1947. MP 1992-. Shadow Sec of State: Culture, Media and Sport 2003-, Transport 2002-03. Lib Dem spokes: education 1992-95, education and employment 1995-97; principal spokes: environment, transport, regions and social justice 1999-2001, transport, local govt and regions 2001-02. Member Education and Employment select cttee 1996-99. Academic/consultant. Ed Lancaster Royal Grammar Sch; BSc phys and psychology/CEd, Keele Univ; MEd, Bath Univ.

The picturesque and historic spa town of Bath commends itself as the archetype of a Conservative stronghold. However, this affluent constituency has not been held by the Tories since Chris Patten was ousted by the Liberal Democrats in 1992. Since then the Lib Dem hold on the seat has been strengthened, although they did have their majority halved in 2005.

BATLEY AND SPEN — Lab hold

		Electorate	Turnout	Change from	2001	Electorate	Turnout
		62,948	62.3%	2001		63,665	60.5%
Wood M	**Lab**	**17,974**	**45.8%**	**-4.1%**	**Lab**	**19,224**	**49.9%**
Light R	C	12,186	31.1%	-5.6%	C	14,160	36.7%
Bentley N	LD	5,731	14.6%	4.3%	LD	3,989	10.3%
Auty C	BNP	2,668	6.8%		Greens	595	1.5%
Lord C	Greens	649	1.7%	0.2%	UKIP	574	1.5%
C to Lab swing	**0.8%**	**39,208**		**Lab maj 5,788**		**38,542**	**Lab maj 5,064**
				14.8%			13.1%

MIKE WOOD b 3 March 1946. MP 1997-. Member Broadcasting select cttee 1997-98. Member Labour Party departmental cttees for: environment, transport and the regions 1997-2001, home affairs 1997-2001 and 2001-, international development 1997-2001. Probation officer, social/community worker 1965-97. Ed Nantwich and Acton Grammar Sch; Cert theol, Salisbury/Wells Theological Coll; CQSW, Leeds Univ; BA history and politics, Leeds Metropolitan Univ.

The constituency is an urban sprawl in between Huddersfield and Bradford. It has streets of traditional terraced housing and a still predominantly working class population. Manufacturing has declined, but is still well above the national average. Around 55 per cent of all households are headed by manual workers. The seat, currently in Labour's hands, has historically been and continues to be marginal.

BATTERSEA — Lab hold

		Electorate	Turnout	Change from	2001	Electorate	Turnout
		69,548	59%	2001		67,495	54.5%
Linton M	**Lab**	**16,569**	**40.4%**	**-9.9%**	**Lab**	**18,498**	**50.3%**
Schofield D	C	16,406	40%	3.5%	C	13,445	36.5%
Bhatti N	LD	6,006	14.6%	2.5%	LD	4,450	12.1%
Charlton H	Greens	1,735	4.2%		Ind	411	1.1%
Jones T	UKIP	333	0.8%				
Lab to C swing	**6.7%**	**41,049**		**Lab maj 163**		**36,804**	**Lab maj 5,053**
				0.4%			13.7%

MARTIN LINTON b 11 Aug 1944. MP 1997-. PPS to: Baroness Blackstone 2001-03, Peter Hain 2003-05, Dept Const Affairs team 2005-. Member select cttees on: Home Affairs 1997-2001, Administration 2001-, Modernisation of the House of Commons 2003-. Member Labour departmental cttees for: home affairs 1997-, parliamentary affairs 1997-. Chair Constituency Labour Party 1994-96. Cllr Wandsworth 1971-82. Journalist 1966-97. President Battersea Arts Centre. Ed Christ's Hospital, Sussex; MA PPE, Pembroke Coll, Oxford; Université de Lyon.

This inner-city seat used to be solidly working class, but has become increasingly gentrified: Clapham and Balham are very fashionable neighbourhoods. Despite this Labour won the seat back from the Tories with a massive 10.2 per cent swing in 1997. It demonstrated how Labour have managed to adapt the base of their support in inner London. But 2005 witnessed affluent professionals switching their ideological commitment, and in a nail biting finish, Labour held on to the seat with a wafer thin majority.

BEACONSFIELD

C hold

		Electorate 68,083	Turnout 63.9%	Change from 2001	2001	Electorate 68,894	Turnout 61%
Grieve D	**C**	**24,126**	**55.4%**	**2.6%**	**C**	**22,233**	**52.8%**
Chapman P	LD	8,873	20.4%	-1.2%	Lab	9,168	21.8%
Sobel A	Lab	8,422	19.4%	-2.4%	LD	9,117	21.6%
Fagan J	UKIP	2,102	4.8%	0.9%	UKIP	1,626	3.9%
LD to C swing	**1.9%**	**43,523**		**C maj 15,253** 35%		**42,144**	**C maj 13,065** 31.1%

DOMINIC GRIEVE b 24 May 1956. MP 1997-. Shadow Attorney General 2003-. Opposition spokes: constitutional affairs and Scotland 1999-2001, Home Office 2001-03. Member select cttees on: Joint Cttee on Statutory Instruments 1997-2001, Environmental Audit 1997-2001. Cllr London Borough of Hammersmith and Fulham 1982-86. Barrister. Vice-chair/director, Hammersmith and Fulham MIND. Ed BA modern history/MA, Magdalen Coll, Oxford; law diploma, Central London Poly.

Set in Buckinghamshire, Beaconsfield is one of the richest corners of the Home Counties. The constituency prospered in the 1980s, helped by its location in the M40 corridor with the M25 also passing through the constituency at its eastern end. An affluent middle-class seat and home to the aristocratic house of Cliveden and Pinewood Studios, Beaconsfield has been one of the safest Conservative constituencies since its creation in 1950.

BECKENHAM

C hold

		Electorate 74,738	Turnout 65.5%	Change from 2001	2001	Electorate 72,241	Turnout 63.1%
Lait J	**C**	**22,183**	**45.3%**		**C**	**20,618**	**45.3%**
Curran L	Lab	13,782	28.2%	-6.2%	Lab	15,659	34.4%
Foulger J	LD	10,862	22.2%	6.2%	LD	7,308	16%
Cartwright J	UKIP	1,301	2.7%	1%	Greens	961	2.1%
Reed R	Ind	836	1.7%		UKIP	782	1.7%
					Lib	234	0.5%
Lab to C swing	**3.1%**	**48,964**		**C maj 8,401** 17.2%		**45,562**	**C maj 4,959** 10.9%

JACQUI LAIT b 16 Dec 1947. MP for Hastings and Rye 1992-97, for Beckenham Nov 1997- (by-election). Shadow: Minister for London 2005-, Minister for Home Affairs 2004-05, Minister for Home, Constitutional and Legal Affairs 2003-04, Scotland Sec of State 2001-03. PPS to William Hague 1995-96. Asst govt whip 1996-97, opposition whip 1999-2000. Opposition pensions spokes 2000-01. Member select cttees 1992-2002. Member 1922 cttee 1998-99. PR / Govt Info Service / parly consultant and adviser. Ed Strathclyde Univ.

Beckenham is a residential seat, home to prosperous commuters of south-east London. The Crystal Palace and Penge and Cator wards have inner city characteristics, but further south the seat becomes thoroughly suburban. Swings to Labour in suburban London seemed to illustrate attitudinal changes among affluent voters, but in 2005 the result proved the Conservatives do not have anything to worry about in Beckenham. Boundary changes after the 2005 election also give them cause for comfort.

BEDFORD

Lab hold

		Electorate 70,629	Turnout 59.6%	Change from 2001	2001	Electorate 67,762	Turnout 59.9%
Hall P	**Lab**	**17,557**	**41.7%**	**-6.2%**	**Lab**	**19,454**	**47.9%**
Fuller R	C	14,174	33.7%	0.9%	C	13,297	32.8%
Headley M	LD	9,063	21.5%	5.7%	LD	6,425	15.8%
Conquest P	UKIP	995	2.4%	1.3%	Ind	973	2.4%
McCready J	Ind	283	0.7%	-1.7%	UKIP	430	1.1%
Lab to C swing	**3.6%**	**42,072**		**Lab maj 3,383** 8%		**40,579**	**Lab maj 6,157** 15.2%

PATRICK HALL b 20 Oct 1951. MP 1997-. Member select cttees on: Joint Cttee on Consolidation of Bills Etc 1997-2001, European Scrutiny 1999-2001, Environment, Food and Rural Affairs 2001- (Radioactive Waste Policy Sub-Cttee 2001-02). Chair all-party groups: patient and public involvement in health 1999-, town centre management 2004-. Cllr Beds County Council 1989-97. Local govt planning officer. Ed BA geog, Birmingham Univ; town planning post grad dip, Oxford Poly.

An industrialised market town that continues to grow, Bedford lies 50 miles north of London. Today the seat is in one of the most cosmopolitan areas outside the capital, with almost 50 separate ethnic groups represented in the borough that gives the seat its name. The seat has been Tory in the past and, with Labour's majority here now looking very fllmsy, the Conservatives will be working hard to make it so again.

MID BEDFORDSHIRE — C hold

		Electorate 73,768	Turnout 68.4%	Change from 2001	2001	Electorate 70,794	Turnout 65.9%
Dorries N	**C**	**23,345**	**46.3%**	**-1.1%**	**C**	**22,109**	**47.4%**
Chapman M	LD	11,990	23.8%	4.1%	Lab	14,043	30.1%
Lindsay M	Lab	11,351	22.5%	-7.6%	LD	9,205	19.7%
Joselyn R	UKIP	1,372	2.7%		UKIP	1,281	2.7%
Foley B	Greens	1,292	2.6%				
Martin H	Veritas	769	1.5%				
Ali S	Ind	301	0.6%				
C to LD swing	**2.6%**	**50,420**		**C maj 11,355** 22.5%		**46,638**	**C maj 8,066** 17.3%

NADINE DORRIES b 1958. MP 2005-. Contested Hazel Grove 2001 general election; Nurse; businesswoman; Adviser to Oliver Letwin MP

This safe Conservative constituency is predominantly rural. The population is largely reliant on shops and leisure facilities outside the constituency: in Bedford, north of the seat, Luton, to the south, Letchworth and Hitchin in the east, and in the west Milton Keynes. Within the constituency, jobs are provided in agriculture, education and tourism. Cranfield Institute of Technology and Silsoe College are situated in the constituency. Tourist attractions include Woburn Abbey and Safari Park.

NORTH EAST BEDFORDSHIRE — C hold

		Electorate 72,757	Turnout 68%	Change from 2001	2001	Electorate 69,877	Turnout 64.8%
Burt A	**C**	**24,725**	**49.9%**		**C**	**22,586**	**49.9%**
White K	Lab	12,474	25.2%	-5.8%	Lab	14,009	31%
Rutherford S	LD	10,320	20.8%	4.5%	LD	7,409	16.4%
May J	UKIP	1,986	4%	1.3%	UKIP	1,242	2.7%
Lab to C swing	**2.9%**	**49,505**		**C maj 12,251** 24.8%		**45,246**	**C maj 8,577** 19%

ALISTAIR BURT b 25 May 1955. MP for Bury North 1983-97, for North East Beds 2001-. Shadow Min for Local Govt and Communities 2005-; PPS: Michael Howard 2003-05, Iain Duncan Smith 2002-03; Minister of State DSS/Disabled People 1995-97; Parly Under-Sec DSS 1992-95; PPS to Kenneth Baker 1985-90. Opposition education/skills spokes 2001-02. Member select cttees: Internat Devt 2001, 2002-03, Procedure 2001-02, ODPM 2002. Cllr Haringey 1982-84. Chair: all-party Christian fellowship group 2003-. Solicitor/exec search consultant. Ed BA jurisprudence, St John's Coll, Oxford.

This solid Tory constituency is overwhelmingly rural. The historic towns of Biggleswade and Sandy are the largest centres of population. The accessible M1, A1, A6 and the train to King's Cross make this area a haven for wealthy commuters. The area has traditionally been a centre of brick-making and agriculture. These activities have more recently been supplemented by the development of industrial and technical parks.

SOUTH WEST BEDFORDSHIRE — C hold

		Electorate 74,096	Turnout 61.8%	Change from 2001	2001	Electorate 70,666	Turnout 62.1%
Selous A	**C**	**22,114**	**48.3%**	**6.2%**	**C**	**18,477**	**42.1%**
Still J	Lab	13,837	30.2%	-10.2%	Lab	17,701	40.4%
Strange A	LD	7,723	16.9%	2.1%	LD	6,473	14.8%
Wise T	UKIP	1,923	4.2%	1.5%	UKIP	1,203	2.7%
Francis K	Forum	217	0.5%				
Lab to C swing	**8.2%**	**45,814**		**C maj 8,277** 18.1%		**43,854**	**C maj 776** 1.8%

ANDREW SELOUS b 27 April 1962. MP 2001-. PPS to Michael Ancram 2004. Opposition whip 2004-. Member Work and Pensions select cttee 2001-. Vice-chair all-party poverty group 2001-. Bow Group 1982-. Chair Con Christian Fellowship 2001-. Director CNS Electronics Ltd 1988-94. Underwriter Great Lakes Re (UK) plc 1991-. TA officer Hon Artillery Company, Royal Regiment of Fusiliers 1981-94. Chartered insurer 1998. Ed BSc econ industry and trade, LSE.

This safe Conservative seat lies on the seat's eastern border with Luton. Dunstable is the constituency's largest town. Leighton Buzzard in the west of the seat is the only other main town. Dunstable's declining motor trade has created increasing reliance on tourism; Whipsnade Zoo, stately homes and the Chiltern Hills being the main attractions. In the rural areas employment can be found in a number of smaller manufacturing units as well as in agriculture.

BELFAST EAST — DUP hold

		Electorate 53,176	Turnout 58%	Change from 2001	2001	Electorate 58,455	Turnout 63%
Robinson P	**DUP**	**15,152**	**49.2%**	**6.7%**	**DUP**	**15,667**	**42.5%**
Empey R	UUP	9,275	30.1%	6.9%	UUP	8,550	23.2%
Long N	All	3,746	12.2%	-3.6%	All	5,832	15.8%
Devenny D	SF	1,029	3.3%	-0.1%	PUP	3,669	10%
Muldoon M	SDLP	844	2.7%	0.3%	SF	1,237	3.4%
Greer A	C	434	1.4%	-0.8%	SDLP	880	2.4%
Bell J	WP	179	0.6%	0.3%	C	800	2.2%
Gilby L	Vote Dream	172	0.6%		WRP	123	0.3%
					VYP	71	0.2%
DUP to UUP swing	**0.1%**	**30,831**		**DUP maj 5,877** 19.1%		**36,829**	**DUP maj 7,117** 19.3%

PETER ROBINSON b 29 Dec 1948. MP for Belfast East 1979- (resigned Dec 1985, re-elected Jan 1986 by-election). Minister for regional devt NI Assembly 1999-. Spokes constitutional affairs. Member NI Affairs select cttee 1994-97, 1997-2004. DUP: dep leader, foundation member, party exec member 1973-, sec central exec cttee 1974-79, gen sec 1975. Cllr Castlereagh BC 1977-: mayor 1986. Member: NI assembly 1982-86, new NI Assembly 1998-, NI Forum 1996-98, NI sports council. Estate agent. Ed Annadale Grammar Sch; Castlereagh Coll of Further Ed.

Belfast East has long symbolised the "Protestant ascendancy" in Northern Ireland. It contains Stormont, the seat of government and the devolved Assembly. The huge cranes, known locally as Samson and Goliath, of the Harland and Wolff shipyard have long dominated. The Titanic was built here. With the DUP in the ascendant as they are currently it seems highly unlikely to be won by another party in coming years.

BELFAST NORTH — DUP hold

		Electorate 52,853	Turnout 57.8%	Change from 2001	2001	Electorate 60,941	Turnout 67.2%
Dodds N	**DUP**	**13,935**	**45.6%**	**4.8%**	**DUP**	**16,718**	**40.8%**
Kelly G	SF	8,747	28.6%	3.4%	SF	10,331	25.2%
Maginness A	SDLP	4,950	16.2%	-4.8%	SDLP	8,592	21%
Cobain F	UUP	2,154	7.1%	-4.9%	UUP	4,904	12%
Hawkins M	All	438	1.4%		WP	253	0.6%
Delaney M	WP	165	0.5%	-0.1%	VYP	134	0.3%
Gilby L	Vote Dream	151	0.5%				
SF to DUP swing	**0.7%**	**30,540**		**DUP maj 5,188** 17%		**40,932**	**DUP maj 6,387** 15.6%

NIGEL DODDS b 20 Aug 1958. MP 2001-. Chief whip DUP HoC 2001-. Vice-chair all-party war graves and battlefield heritage group 2002-. Sec Ulster DUP. Cllr Belfast CC 1985-: Lord Mayor 1988-89, 1991-92. Member: NI Forum for political dialogue 1996-98, NI Assembly 1998-. Minister for Social Devt 1999-2000, 2001-02. Vice-pres Assocn of NI local authorities 1989-90. Barrister. European Parliament Secretariat 1984-96. OBE 1997. Ed BA law, St John's Coll, Cambridge; Cert PLS, Queens Univ, Belfast Inst of Professional Legal Studies.

The constituency is on the north shore of Belfast Lough and contains many infamous places associated with the Troubles. The seat, the most diverse of the four Belfast constituencies, is largely Protestant but has a substantial Catholic minority of 40 per cent. Just over one in 12 speaks Irish. A challenge to the DUP dominance of the seat could only come from a collapse in the SDLP vote in favour of Sinn Féin.

BELFAST SOUTH — SDLP gain

		Electorate 52,668	Turnout 60.8%	Change from 2001	2001	Electorate 59,436	Turnout 63.9%
McDonnell A	**SDLP**	**10,339**	**32.3%**	**1.7%**	**UUP**	**17,008**	**44.8%**
Spratt J	DUP	9,104	28.4%		SDLP	11,609	30.6%
McGimpsey M	UUP	7,263	22.7%	-22.1%	NIWC	2,968	7.8%
Maskey A	SF	2,882	9%	1.4%	SF	2,894	7.6%
Rice G	All	2,012	6.3%	0.9%	All	2,042	5.4%
Gilby L	Vote Dream	235	0.7%		PUP	1,112	2.9%
Lynn P	WP	193	0.6%	0.1%	WP	204	0.5%
					Vote Dream	115	0.3%
SDLP to DUP swing	**13.4%**	**32,028**		**SDLP maj 1,235** 3.9%		**37,952**	**UUP maj 5,399** 14.2%

ALASDAIR McDONNELL b 1 Sept 1949. MP 2005-. Contested six general elections and one by-election 1970-97; MLA for Belfast S 1998-. Deputy leader SDLP 2004-; Belfast City councillor 1985-. Hospital doctor, GP 1975-. Ed University College Dublin medical school.

This vibrant middle class constituency of Belfast South is seen as the least openly sectarian of the Belfast seats. It has a large student population based at Queen's University and contains many of the city's historic landmarks including City Hall, which is the base of Belfast City Council. Just over a third of the people are Catholics in a previously safe Unionist seat captured by the SDLP in 2005.

BELFAST WEST — SF hold

		Electorate	Turnout	Change from	2001	Electorate	Turnout
		53,831	64.2%	2001		59,617	68.7%
Adams G	**SF**	**24,348**	**70.5%**	**4.4%**	**SF**	**27,096**	**66.1%**
Attwood A	SDLP	5,033	14.6%	-4.3%	SDLP	7,754	18.9%
Dodds D	DUP	3,652	10.6%	4.2%	DUP	2,641	6.4%
McGimpsey C	UUP	779	2.3%	-3.9%	UUP	2,541	6.2%
Lowry J	WP	432	1.2%	-0.6%	WP	736	1.8%
Gilby L	Vote Dream	154	0.4%		UTW	116	0.3%
Kennedy L	Ind	147	0.4%		VYP	98	0.2%
SDLP to SF swing	**4.4%**	**34,545**		**SF maj 19,315**		**40,982**	**SF maj 19,342**
				55.9%			47.2%

GERRY ADAMS b 6 Oct 1948. MP for Belfast West 1983-92, 1997-. Member: New NI Assembly for Belfast West 1998-, NI Forum 1996, NI Assembly 1981. Sinn Fein: vice-pres 1978-83, pres 1983-. Member PEN. Politician, author, bartender. Founder member civil rights movement. West Belfast community festival, Feile an Phobail. Thorr peace prize 1996. Ed St Marys' Christian Brothers' Sch, Belfast.

The constituency of Belfast West is overwhelmingly Catholic and Nationalist with the highest proportion of Catholics in any Northern Ireland seat, at over 76 per cent. The seat is an icon of the Troubles, infamous for the very many murders that have blighted its streets over the last 30 years. It is one of the poorest seats in the province and has been described by a dissident republican as a one-party Sinn Féin state.

BERWICKSHIRE, ROXBURGH AND SELKIRK — LD hold

		Electorate	Turnout		2001
		71,702	63.3%		
Moore M	**LD**	**18,993**	**41.8%**		No comparable results due to boundary changes
Lamont J	C	13,092	28.8%		
Held S	Lab	7,206	15.9%		
Orr A	SNP	3,885	8.6%		
Hein J	Lib	916	2%		
McIver G	SSP	695	1.5%		
Neilson P	UKIP	601	1.3%		
LD to C swing	**5.9%**	**45,388**		**LD maj 5,901**	
(notional)				13%	

MICHAEL MOORE b 3 June 1965. MP for Tweeddale, Ettrick and Lauderdale 1997-2005, for Berwickshire, Roxburgh and Selkirk 2005-. Lib Dem Shadow: Sec of State Defence 2005-, Minister Foreign Affairs 2001-05. Lib Dem spokes 1997-2001. Member Scottish Affairs select cttee 1997-99. Dep leader Scottish Lib Dems 2003-. Parly Group Convener 2000-, Scottish Parliament elections campaign chair 1999/2003, Scottish MP representative Lib Dem policy cttee 2001-02. Accountant/MP research asst. Ed MA politics/mod hist, Edinburgh Univ.

This large rural seat is spread out along the English border, beginning 20 kilometres inland from Carlisle and extending along the Cheviot Hills to the fishing towns of the east coast. It is bounded in the north by the Lammermuir Hills and Dumfriesshire in the east. It includes all the major border towns: Hawick, Jedburgh, Kelso, Melrose, Galashiels and Selkirk, in an area famous for its rugby and its abbeys and now safe for the Liberal Democrats.

BERWICK-UPON-TWEED — LD hold

		Electorate	Turnout	Change from	2001	Electorate	Turnout
		56,944	63.4%	2001		56,918	63.8%
Beith A	**LD**	**19,052**	**52.8%**	**1.4%**	**LD**	**18,651**	**51.4%**
Elliott M	C	10,420	28.9%	0.8%	C	10,193	28.1%
Reynolds G	Lab	6,618	18.3%	0.6%	Lab	6,435	17.7%
					UKIP	1,029	2.8%
C to LD swing	**0.3%**	**36,090**		**LD maj 8,632**		**36,308**	**LD maj 8,458**
				23.9%			23.3%

ALAN BEITH b 20 April 1943. MP by-election Nov 1973-. Lib chief whip 1976-87. Lib/Alliance/SLD/Lib Dem spokes 1985-2002. Member select cttees on: Procedure 2000-01, (chair) Constitutional Affairs 2003-, Liaison 2003-. Chair all-party Sweden group 2001-. Deputy leader: Lib Party 1985-88, Lib Dem 1992-2003. Cllr: Hexham RDC 1969-74, Tynedale DC 1974-75. Lecturer. PC 1992. Ed King's Sch, Macclesfield; BA PPE, Nuffield Coll, Oxford; BLitt/MA, Balliol Coll, Oxford.

The constituency is on England's border with Scotland. Predominantly agricultural with fishing and tourist industries, the constituency stretches south of the border down the spectacular rugged Northumbrian coast and its hinterland, it encompasses the county town of Alnwick, as well as sea-ports, and former mining communities. Under Liberal Democrat control since 1973, the Conservatives pose no real threat here.

BETHNAL GREEN AND BOW — Respect gain

		Electorate	Turnout	Change from	2001	Electorate	Turnout
		85,950	51.2%	2001		77,478	49.6%
Galloway G	**Respect**	**15,801**	**35.9%**		**Lab**	**19,380**	**50.5%**
King O	Lab	14,978	34%	-16.5%	C	9,323	24.3%
Bakth S	C	6,244	14.2%	-10.1%	LD	5,946	15.5%
Dulu S	LD	4,928	11.2%	-4.3%	Greens	1,666	4.3%
Foster J	Greens	1,950	4.4%	0.1%	BNP	1,211	3.2%
Etefia E	AFC	68	0.2%		New Brit	888	2.3%
Pugh C	ND	38	0.1%				
Lab to Respect swing	**26.2%**	**44,007**		**Respect maj 823**		**38,414**	**Lab maj 10,057**
				1.9%			26.2%

GEORGE GALLOWAY b 16 August 1954. Member for Glasgow Hillhead 1987-97, for Glasgow Kelvin 1997-2005, for Bethnal Green and Bow 2005-. (Lab MP 1987-2003, Independent Lab 2003-04, Respect 2004-). General labourer Garden Works 1972; Production worker Michelin Tyres 1973; Labour organiser 1977-83; General secretary War on Want 1983-87. Chair Scottish Labour Party 1980-81. Ed Charleston Primary; Harris Academy

In the east End of London, much of this constituency is working class. It has one of the highest rates of council-rented accommodation, an ethnic minority population approaching 40 per cent and high levels of unemployment. The Iraq war proved to be the decisive single issue in the constituency in 2005, as the anti-war independent George Galloway dramatically unseated Labour's pro-war Oona King. The result illustrated the power of the Muslim vote in the constituency.

BEVERLEY AND HOLDERNESS — C hold

		Electorate	Turnout	Change from	2001	Electorate	Turnout
		77,460	64.8%	2001		74,741	62%
Stuart G	**C**	**20,434**	**40.7%**	**-0.6%**	**C**	**19,168**	**41.3%**
McManus G	Lab	17,854	35.6%	-4%	Lab	18,387	39.6%
Willie S	LD	9,578	19.1%	3.2%	LD	7,356	15.9%
Marriott O	UKIP	2,336	4.6%	1.5%	UKIP	1,464	3.2%
Lab to C swing	**1.7%**	**50,202**		**C maj 2,580**		**46,375**	**C maj 781**
				5.1%			1.7%

GRAHAM STUART b 12 March 1962. MP 2005-. Contested Cambridge 2001 general election. Councillor Cambridge City Council 1998-: Conservative group leader 2000. Sole proprietor Go Enterprises 1984; Managing director CSL Publishing Ltd 1987; Director Marine Publishing Co Ltd 1999. Ed Glenalmond College, Perthshire; BA law/philosophy, Selwyn College, Cambridge

This east Yorkshire seat takes in large stretches of country and coast on the Holderness peninsula, including the seaside towns of Hornsea and Withernsea. Farming is the major industry here. There is some industry based on industrial estates. Elsewhere there is a major BP chemical refinery and on the coast at Easington most of the country's natural gas is brought ashore. Tourism at the coastal resorts is important. It is a marginal Tory seat.

BEXHILL AND BATTLE — C hold

		Electorate	Turnout	Change from	2001	Electorate	Turnout
		69,676	67.2%	2001		69,010	64.9%
Barker G	**C**	**24,629**	**52.6%**	**4.5%**	**C**	**21,555**	**48.1%**
Varrall M	LD	11,180	23.9%	-0.8%	LD	11,052	24.7%
Jones M	Lab	8,457	18.1%	-1.3%	Lab	8,702	19.4%
Smith A	UKIP	2,568	5.5%	-2.3%	UKIP	3,474	7.8%
LD to C swing	**2.7%**	**46,834**		**C maj 13,449**		**44,783**	**C maj 10,503**
				28.7%			23.5%

GREGORY BARKER b 8 March 1966. MP 2001-. Opposition whip 2003-. Member select cttees on: Environmental Audit 2001-, Broadcasting 2003-. Vice-chair all-party Globe UK group 2002-. Member British-German Forum. Chair: Shoreham Young Conservatives 1982-83, Holloway Conservative Society 1986-87. Researcher/analyst/investor/company director/assoc partner 1987-2001. Ed BA modern history/economic history/politics, Royal Holloway Coll, London Univ.

The constituency sits on the East Sussex coast and countryside surrounding Hastings and Rye and includes numerous villages and hamlets, as well as the two towns after which it is named. The area contains part of the High Weald Area of Outstanding Natural Beauty, and many historical sites including several castles. With its elderly demographic profile economic regeneration is a growing issue but, politically, Bexhill and Battle remains a safe Conservative seat.

BEXLEYHEATH AND CRAYFORD — C gain

		Electorate	Turnout	Change from	2001	Electorate	Turnout
		65,025	65.5%	2001		63,580	63.5%
Evennett D	**C**	**19,722**	**46.3%**	**6.4%**	**Lab**	**17,593**	**43.6%**
Beard N	Lab	15,171	35.6%	-8%	C	16,121	39.9%
Raval D	LD	5,144	12.1%	1%	LD	4,476	11.1%
Dunford J	UKIP	1,302	3.1%	1.2%	BNP	1,408	3.5%
Lee J	BNP	1,241	2.9%	-0.6%	UKIP	780	1.9%
Lab to C swing	**7.2%**	**42,580**		**C maj 4,551**		**40,378**	**Lab maj 1,472**
				10.7%			3.6%

DAVID EVENNETT b 3 June 1949. MP for Erith and Crayford 1983-97, for Bexleyheath and Crayford 2005-; contested Hackney South and Shoreditch 1979, Bexleyheath and Crayford 1997 and 2001 general elections. PPS to educ sec 1996-97, to Home Office minister 1995-96, to Wales sec 1993-95, to educ minister 1992-93. Cllr London Borough of Redbridge 1974-78. Ed Buckhurst Hill County High School for Boys, Ilford; economics, politics, London School of Economics

The Bexleyheath part of this east London seat is typified by prosperous commuter suburbs, whereas Crayford has far more council housing and contains more industry, such as chemical works and factories. Commuters, and owner-occupiers, form the considerable majority of the electorate. Bexleyheath and Crayford has many of the characteristics of a safe Conservative seat of times gone by, but was held by Labour between 1997 and 2005.

BILLERICAY — C hold

		Electorate	Turnout	Change from	2001	Electorate	Turnout
		79,537	61.4%	2001		78,528	58.1%
Baron J	**C**	**25,487**	**52.2%**	**4.8%**	**C**	**21,608**	**47.4%**
Dodds A	Lab	14,281	29.2%	-7.2%	Lab	16,595	36.4%
Hibbs M	LD	6,471	13.2%	-0.7%	LD	6,323	13.9%
Robinson B	BNP	1,435	2.9%		UKIP	1,072	2.4%
Callaghan S	UKIP	1,184	2.4%				
Lab to C swing	**6%**	**48,858**		**C maj 11,206**		**45,598**	**C maj 5,013**
				22.9%			11%

JOHN BARON b 21 June 1959. MP 2001-. Shadow Min: Health 2004-, Public Services, Health and Education 2003-04, Health 2004. Opposition Health spokes 2002-03. Member Education and Skills select cttee 2001-02. Chair all-party free trade group 2003-. Captain Royal Regiment of Fusiliers 1984-87. Investment manager 1987-2001. Securities Institute member. Charity fundraiser. Ed BA history and economics Jesus Coll, Cambridge; Royal Military Coll, Sandhurst.

Billericay is situated just to the north of Basildon New Town in Essex and encompasses its Pitsea neighbourhood as well as the old town of Billericay itself. A relatively middle class and fairly affluent constituency with a high number of owner-occupiers, Billericay has many commuters who use the Liverpool Street to Southend Victoria line. This is Conservative territory and since its reconstitution in 1983 it has been represented solely by Tory MPs.

BIRKENHEAD — Lab hold

		Electorate	Turnout	Change from	2001	Electorate	Turnout
		57,097	48.7%	2001		60,026	48.3%
Field F	**Lab**	**18,059**	**65%**	**-5.5%**	**Lab**	**20,418**	**70.5%**
Kelly S	LD	5,125	18.4%	5.6%	C	4,827	16.7%
Morton H	C	4,602	16.6%	-0.1%	LD	3,722	12.8%
Lab to LD swing	**5.6%**	**27,786**		**Lab maj 12,934**		**28,967**	**Lab maj 15,591**
				46.6%			53.8%

FRANK FIELD b 16 July 1942. MP 1979-. Dept Soc Security (Welfare Reform) Min of State 1997-98. Opposition Education spokes 1980-81. Member select cttees on: Social Security (chair) 1990-97, Public Accounts 2002-. Chair all-party groups: new Europe 2001-, sub post offices 2002-; sec all-party historic churches group 2004-. Teacher 1964-69. Director: Child Poverty Action Group 1969-79, Low Pay Unit 1974-80. PC 1997. Ed BSc economics, Hull Univ.

The main town on the Wirral peninsula, Birkenhead is commonly known as the part of Liverpool situated south of the Mersey. Most of the docks have been redeveloped and the shipyard is now a major repairing facility. However, other traditional industries have declined and unemployment is high. One of Birkenhead's more distinctive features, albeit shared with most of Liverpool, is a truly unassailable Labour majority; the only contest worth watching here is for second place.

BIRMINGHAM EDGBASTON — Lab hold

		Electorate 64,893	Turnout 58%	Change from 2001	2001	Electorate 67,405	Turnout 56%
Stuart G	**Lab**	**16,465**	**43.8%**	**-5.3%**	**Lab**	**18,517**	**49.1%**
Alden D	C	14,116	37.5%	0.9%	C	13,819	36.6%
Dixon M	LD	5,185	13.8%	1.8%	LD	4,528	12%
Beck P	Greens	1,116	3%		Pro-Euro Con	454	1.2%
White S	UKIP	749	2%		SLP	431	1.1%
Lab to C swing	**3.1%**	**37,631**		**Lab maj 2,349** 6.2%		**37,749**	**Lab maj 4,698** 12.4%

GISELA STUART b 26 Nov 1955. MP 1997-. Health Parly Under-Sec 1999-2001. PPS to Paul Boateng 1998-99. Member select cttees on: Social Security 1997-98, Foreign Affairs 2001-. Parly rep Convention on Future of Europe 2002-05. Lab Party departmental cttees member: Soc Security 1997-2001, Treasury 1997-2001, Health 1999-2001. Deputy director London Book Fair 1983. Lawyer/lecturer Worcester Coll of Tech and Birmingaham Univ 1992-97. Ed Manchester Poly; London Univ (LLB).

Birmingham Edgbaston represented a landmark victory for Labour in 1997, with Gisela Stuart ending the longstanding Conservative control of the seat. Despite its affluent heritage social and economic contrasts have emerged, highlighting the constituency's diversity and importance for the parties nationally. Stuart has, for many years, been outspoken about the increasing drug problem the region faces. Birmingham Edgbaston looks set to remain both hotly and closely contested.

BIRMINGHAM ERDINGTON — Lab hold

		Electorate 64,951	Turnout 48.9%	Change from 2001	2001	Electorate 65,668	Turnout 46.6%
Simon S	**Lab**	**16,810**	**53%**	**-3.8%**	**Lab**	**17,375**	**56.8%**
Elvidge V	C	7,235	22.8%	-1.4%	C	7,413	24.2%
Evans J	LD	5,027	15.8%	4%	LD	3,602	11.8%
Ebanks S	BNP	1,512	4.8%		NF	681	2.2%
Hepburn R	UKIP	746	2.4%	0.7%	SA	669	2.2%
Williams T	NF	416	1.3%	-0.9%	UKIP	521	1.7%
					SLP	343	1.1%
Lab to C swing	**1.2%**	**31,746**		**Lab maj 9,575** 30.2%		**30,604**	**Lab maj 9,962** 32.6%

SIÔN SIMON b 23 Dec 1968. MP 2001-. Member Public Accounts select cttee 2003-. Chair all-party private equity and venture capital group 2004-. Trade union member: TGWU 1990-96, AEEU 1997-, NUJ 1997-. Research asst to George Robertson MP 1990-93. Senior manager Guinness PLC 1993-95. Freelance journalist 1995-97. Columnist/assoc editor The Daily Telegraph/Spectator 1997-2001. Founder board sec Choroideremia Research Foundation Inc 1999. Ed Handsworth Grammar Sch, Birmingham; BA PPE Magdalen Coll, Oxford.

A working-class constituency north east of Birmingham, Erdington has become a Labour safe seat, with Labour councillors representing all four wards. There are relatively high levels of unemployment, and an industrial base to the workforce. With council housing making up a sizeable proportion accommodation, regeneration is a key issue. Strong local election performances, and favourable voter demographics both point to Labour security.

BIRMINGHAM HALL GREEN — Lab hold

		Electorate 57,222	Turnout 60.4%	Change from 2001	2001	Electorate 57,563	Turnout 57.5%
McCabe S	**Lab**	**16,304**	**47.2%**	**-7.4%**	**Lab**	**18,049**	**54.6%**
Hughes E	C	10,590	30.7%	-3.8%	C	11,401	34.5%
Harmer R	LD	6,682	19.4%	10.6%	LD	2,926	8.8%
Melhuish D	UKIP	960	2.8%	0.7%	UKIP	708	2.1%
Lab to C swing	**1.8%**	**34,536**		**Lab maj 5,714** 16.6%		**33,084**	**Lab maj 6,648** 20.1%

STEVE MCCABE b 4 Aug 1955. MP 1997-. PPS to Charles Clarke 2003-05. Member select cttees on: Deregulation 1997-99, Northern Ireland Affairs 1998-2003, Joint Cttee on House of Lords Reform 2003-. Vice-chair all-party gun crime group 2003-. Cllr Birmingham City Council 1990-98. NALGO shop steward 1978-82. Social worker/lecturer/researcher 1977-97. Ed Certificate Qualification social work, Moray House Coll, Edinburgh; MA social work, Bradford Univ.

Another Labour win in 1997, Hall Green is an affluent suburban constituency on the south side of the city, with the smallest ethnic minority population in Birmingham. Falling national popularity for the Conservatives and waning voter turnout have combined to secure this seat for Labour. The recent closure of the Rover plant at Longbridge, and its impact on the relative prosperity of the constituents, will prove a defining issue in the coming few years.

BIRMINGHAM HODGE HILL

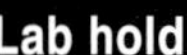

Lab hold

		Electorate	Turnout	Change from	2001	Electorate	Turnout
		53,903	52.7%	2001		55,254	47.9%
Byrne L	**Lab**	**13,822**	**48.6%**	**-15.3%**	**Lab**	**16,901**	**63.9%**
Davies N	LD	8,373	29.5%	21.4%	C	5,283	20%
Thomas D	C	3,768	13.3%	-6.7%	LD	2,147	8.1%
Adams D	BNP	1,445	5.1%	1.7%	BNP	889	3.4%
Duffen A	UKIP	680	2.4%	1.4%	PJP	561	2.1%
Begg A	Progress	329	1.2%		SA	284	1.1%
					UKIP	275	1%
					Mus	125	0.5%
Lab to LD swing	**18.4%**	**28,417**		**Lab maj 5,449**		**26,465**	**Lab maj 11,618**
				19.2%			43.9%

LIAM BYRNE b 2 Oct 1970. MP July 2004- by-election. Party Under-Sec Dept of Health 2005-. Member European Scrutiny select cttee 2005-. Adviser 1997 general election campaign. Sec all-party Kashmir group 2004-. Director Business Liaison, Office of Leader of Lab Party 1996-97. Member European Standing Cttee B 2005-. Leader Manchester Univ Students Union 1992-93. Andersen Consulting 1993, NM Rothschild 1997-99. Co-founder EGS Gp Ltd 2000-04. Member NVS national executive. Ed BA, Manchester Univ; MBA, Harvard Business Sch.

A predominantly working-class constituency, with a large Asian minority, Hodge Hill has remained a virtually unbroken Labour seat. In the 2004 by-election Labour's margin was heavily eroded, and activity from the People's Justice Party and British National Party make this an interesting constituency to watch. High levels of long-term unemployment, and the need for regeneration remain key political issues for voters.

BIRMINGHAM LADYWOOD

Lab hold

		Electorate	Turnout	Change from	2001	Electorate	Turnout
		70,977	46.8%	2001		71,113	44.3%
Short C	**Lab**	**17,262**	**51.9%**	**-17%**	**Lab**	**21,694**	**68.9%**
Khan A	LD	10,461	31.5%	23.3%	C	3,551	11.3%
Stroud P	C	3,515	10.6%	-0.7%	LD	2,586	8.2%
Nazemi A	UKIP	2,008	6%	5.1%	PJP	2,112	6.7%
					SLP	443	1.4%
					Mus	432	1.4%
					ProLife	392	1.2%
					UKIP	283	0.9%
Lab to LD swing	**20.2%**	**33,246**		**Lab maj 6,801**		**31,493**	**Lab maj 18,143**
				20.5%			57.6%

CLARE SHORT b 15 Feb 1946. MP 1983-. International Development Sec of State 1997-2003. Shadow Overseas Development Min 1996-97. Opposition spokes 1985-96. Lab Party NEC member 1988-98. Member Lab Party Departmental Cttee for Internat Devt 1997-2001. Chair human rights cttee of Socialist International 1996-98. Home Office civil servant 1970-75. Director: Youth Aid 1979-83, Unemployment Unit 1981-83. PC 1997. Ed Birmingham; Keele Univ; BA political science, Leeds Univ.

Ladywood is a large inner-city seat, complete with severe poverty and social deprivation, exceptionally high unemployment rates, and where ethnic minorities make up the majority of the population. Ladywood has become a Labour safe seat under Clare Short, and investment in the city centre has had a positive impact. The ward of Aston remains one of the most of deprived in the country.

BIRMINGHAM NORTHFIELD

Lab hold

		Electorate	Turnout	Change from	2001	Electorate	Turnout
		54,868	56.6%	2001		55,922	52.8%
Burden R	**Lab**	**15,419**	**49.6%**	**-6.4%**	**Lab**	**16,528**	**56%**
Ford V	C	8,965	28.9%	-0.7%	C	8,730	29.6%
Sword T	LD	4,171	13.4%	2.2%	LD	3,322	11.2%
Cattell M	BNP	1,278	4.1%		UKIP	550	1.9%
Chant G	UKIP	641	2.1%	0.2%	SA	193	0.7%
Rodgers R	Common Good	428	1.4%		SLP	151	0.5%
Houldey L	SAP	120	0.4%		CGB	60	0.2%
Sweeney F	WRP	34	0.1%				
Lab to C swing	**2.9%**	**31,056**		**Lab maj 6,454**		**29,534**	**Lab maj 7,798**
				20.8%			26.4%

RICHARD BURDEN b 1 Sep 1954. MP 1992-. PPS to Jeffrey Rooker 1997-2001. Motor Sports adviser to Richard Caborn 2002-. Member Trade and Industry select cttee 2001-. Chair all-party groups: electoral reform 1997-, motor group 1998-, Palestine 2002-. Chair Lab Campaign for electoral reform 1996-98. Founded Joint Action for Water Services 1985 to oppose water privatisation. NALGO 1979-1992: North Yorkshire branch organiser 1979-81, West Midlands district officer 1981-92. Ed BA politics, York Univ; MA industrial relations, Warwick Univ.

A predominantly working-class constituency in the south of the city, Northfield previously avoided a Labour backlash, enjoying comparatively high employment levels. Richard Burden's safety in his seat will undoubtedly be severely affected by the closure of the Longbridge Rover plant. Historically it is a seat prone to rapid change, with volatile employment issues playing a part in local and national elections over the past decade.

BIRMINGHAM PERRY BARR — Lab hold

		Electorate 70,126	Turnout 55.5%	Change from 2001	2001	Electorate 71,121	Turnout 52.6%
Mahmood K	**Lab**	**18,269**	**47%**	**0.5%**	**Lab**	**17,415**	**46.5%**
Hunt J	LD	10,321	26.5%	3.6%	C	8,662	23.1%
Khan N	C	6,513	16.7%	-6.4%	LD	8,566	22.9%
Naseem M	Respect	2,173	5.6%		SLP	1,544	4.1%
Claire R	SLP	890	2.3%	-1.8%	SA	465	1.2%
Balu B	UKIP	745	1.9%	1%	UKIP	352	0.9%
					Marxist	221	0.6%
					Mus	192	0.5%
Lab to LD swing	**1.6%**	**38,911**		**Lab maj 7,948** 20.4%		**37,417**	**Lab maj 8,753** 23.4%

KHALID MAHMOOD b 13 July 1961. MP 2001-. PPS to Tony McNulty 2004-. Member Broadcasting select cttee 2001-. Chair all-party Kuwait group 2004-. Vice-chair all-party Friends of Islam group 2003-. Vice-chair local constituency Lab Party. Cllr Birmingham City Council 1990-93 (chair: Race Relations). National member Lab Finance and Industry group. Adviser President of Olympic Council Asia. AEEU; former adviser Danish International Trade Union. Former engineer.

No longer a Labour safe seat, this constituency has seen an increase in competition from the Liberal Democrats. Perry Barr is home to Britain's second Muslim MP, Khalid Mahmood. A constituency of contrasts, the wards of Handsworth and Sandwell are typified by cultural diversity and economic deprivation, with Oscott and Perry Barr representing predominantly white, affluent populations.

BIRMINGHAM SELLY OAK — Lab hold

		Electorate 70,162	Turnout 59.5%	Change from 2001	2001	Electorate 71,237	Turnout 56.3%
Jones L	**Lab**	**19,226**	**46.1%**	**-6.3%**	**Lab**	**21,015**	**52.4%**
Tildesley J	C	10,375	24.9%	-1.7%	C	10,676	26.6%
Brighton R	LD	9,591	23%	6.7%	LD	6,532	16.3%
Smith B	Greens	1,581	3.8%	0.5%	Greens	1,309	3.3%
Burnett R	UKIP	967	2.3%	0.9%	UKIP	568	1.4%
Lab to C swing	**2.3%**	**41,740**		**Lab maj 8,851** 21.2%		**40,100**	**Lab maj 10,339** 25.8%

LYNNE JONES b 26 April 1951. MP 1992-. Member Science and Technology select cttee 1992-97 and 1997-2001. Chair all-party groups: mental health, pensioner incomes group 2004-. Member Lab Party Departmental Cttees: environment, transport and regions 1997-2001, trade and industry 1997-2001, Treasury 1997-, education and employment 1997-2001. Academic/housing/career. Ed BSc, PhD biochemistry, Birmingham Univ; post-grad housing studies dip, Birmingham Poly.

A suburban constituency under the leadership of Lynne Jones since 1992, Selly Oak is one of Labour's safer seats. The workforce has a largely commuter, professional base, with the Cadbury chocolate factory comprising an important economic ladmark. Low voter turnout has seen Labour's majority dwindle since 1997.

BIRMINGHAM SPARKBROOK AND SMALL HEATH — Lab hold

		Electorate 73,721	Turnout 51.8%	Change from 2001	2001	Electorate 74,358	Turnout 49.3%
Godsiff R	**Lab**	**13,787**	**36.1%**	**-21.4%**	**Lab**	**21,087**	**57.5%**
Yaqoob S	Respect	10,498	27.5%		LD	4,841	13.2%
Hussain T	LD	7,727	20.2%	7%	PJP	4,770	13%
Mirza S	C	3,480	9.1%	-1.7%	C	3,948	10.8%
Brookes J	UKIP	1,342	3.5%	1.8%	Ind	662	1.8%
Jamieson I	Greens	855	2.2%		UKIP	634	1.7%
Chaudhary A	Ind	503	1.3%	-0.5%	Mus	401	1.1%
					C	304	0.8%
Lab to Respect swing	**24.5%**	**38,192**		**Lab maj 3,289** 8.6%		**36,647**	**Lab maj 16,246** 44.3%

ROGER GODSIFF b 28 June 1946. MP for Birmingham Small Heath 1992-97, for Birmingham Sparkbrook and Small Heath 1997-. Cricket adviser to Richard Caborn 2002-. Chair all-party British-Japanese group 1999-. Co-operative Party member. IPU exec cttee member 1999. Cllr London Borough of Lewisham 1971-90: Lab chief whip 1974-77, mayor 1977. Chair Charlton Athletic Community Trust. Banking career 1965-70. Political officer APEX 1970-88. GMB senior research officer 1988-91. Ed Catford Comp Sch.

One of Labours safest seats, Sparkbrook and Small Heath is characterised by urban decay and a huge Asian population. There is little chance of Roger Godsiff losing out to another party, but calls from within the Labour ranks for a Muslim MP are growing stronger. This will remain a core seat to the Liberal Democrat campaign in the region, and a key source of support for the Justice Party.

BIRMINGHAM YARDLEY — LD gain

		Electorate	Turnout	Change from	2001	Electorate	Turnout
		50,975	57.7%	2001		52,444	57.2%
Hemming J	**LD**	**13,648**	**46.4%**	**8.1%**	**Lab**	**14,083**	**46.9%**
Innes J	Lab	10,976	37.3%	-9.6%	LD	11,507	38.3%
Uppal P	C	2,970	10.1%	-3%	C	3,941	13.1%
Purcell R	BNP	1,523	5.2%		UKIP	329	1.1%
Yaqub M	UKIP	314	1.1%		SLP	151	0.5%
Lab to LD swing	**8.9%**	**29,431**		**LD maj 2,672**		**30,011**	**Lab maj 2,576**
				9.1%			8.6%

JOHN HEMMING b 16 March 1960. MP 2005-. Contested Birmingham Hall Green 1983, Birmingham Small Heath 1987, Birmingham Yardley 1992, 1997, 2001 general elections. Birmingham City Council 1990-: Cllr 1990-, Group leader 1998-. Senior partner John Hemming and Company 1983. Ed King Edward's School, Birmingham; atomic, nuclear and theoretical physics, Oxford Univ

A suburban constituency typified by relatively low levels of unemployment and high levels of home ownership, Yardley stands in contrast to its neighbours. Labour looked far from comfortable here, with Estelle Morris standing down, and the contest for this seat between Labour and Liberal Democrats was tightly fought. John Hemming won this seat for his party at his fourth attempt.

BISHOP AUCKLAND — Lab hold

		Electorate	Turnout	Change from	2001	Electorate	Turnout
		67,534	56.5%	2001		67,368	57.2%
Goodman H	**Lab**	**19,065**	**50%**	**-8.8%**	**Lab**	**22,680**	**58.8%**
Foote Wood C	LD	9,018	23.6%	7.9%	C	8,754	22.7%
Bell R	C	8,736	22.9%	0.2%	LD	6,073	15.7%
Hopson M	UKIP	1,309	3.4%		Greens	1,052	2.7%
Lab to LD swing	**8.4%**	**38,128**		**Lab maj 10,047**		**38,559**	**Lab maj 13,926**
				26.4%			36.1%

HELEN GOODMAN b 2 January 1958. MP 2005-. Former head of strategy The Children's Society; Former civil servant HM Treasury; Chief executive Rail Safety and Standards Board. Ed Lady Manners School, Bakewell; Somerville College, Oxford

A diverse constituency stretching from former Durham coalfield towns westward to the wild and beautiful valleys of the Wear and Tees, it combines highly industrialised areas with historic towns and open countryside. The main industry in the rural areas is farming but with agriculture in decline many farms have diversified to take advantage of tourism but it's the mining interest that has ensured that Bishop Auckland has remained a safe Labour seat since 1935.

BLABY — C hold

		Electorate	Turnout	Change from	2001	Electorate	Turnout
		75,444	65.5%	2001		73,732	64.6%
Robathan A	**C**	**22,487**	**45.5%**	**-0.9%**	**C**	**22,104**	**46.4%**
Morgan D	Lab	14,614	29.6%	-3.8%	Lab	15,895	33.4%
Stephenson J	LD	9,382	19%	1.6%	LD	8,286	17.4%
Robinson M	BNP	1,704	3.4%	0.6%	BNP	1,357	2.8%
Young D	UKIP	1,201	2.4%				
Lab to C swing	**1.5%**	**49,388**		**C maj 7,873**		**47,642**	**C maj 6,209**
				15.9%			13%

ANDREW ROBATHAN b 17 July 1951. MP 1992-. Shadow Min: Defence 2004, International Development 2003, Trade and Industry 2002-03. PPS to Ian Sproat 1995-97. Member select cttees on: International Development 1997-2002, 2003-04. Member 1922 cttee executive 2001-02, 2003-04. Cllr London Borough of Hammersmith and Fulham 1990-92. City of London freeman. Coldstream Guards/SAS 1974-89, BP 1991-92. Ed Merchant Tylers' Sch, Northwood; BA modern history, Oriel Coll, Oxford; RMA, Sandhurst; Army Staff Coll.

This safe Conservative seat includes part of Leicester's suburbs, including the town of Blaby itself, Narborough, Enderby, Whetstone and Broughton Astley. Further south is a rural area and the small market town of Lutterworth. Agriculture is the traditional industry but declining and new industry is being attracted by the M1, M6 and A14 (M1/A1 link).

BLACKBURN — Lab hold

		Electorate 73,494	Turnout 56.9%	Change from 2001	2001	Electorate 72,611	Turnout 55.5%
Straw J	**Lab**	**17,562**	**42%**	**-12.1%**	**Lab**	**21,808**	**54.1%**
Ameen I	C	9,553	22.8%	-8.4%	C	12,559	31.2%
Melia A	LD	8,608	20.6%	12.5%	LD	3,264	8.1%
Holt N	BNP	2,263	5.4%		UKIP	1,185	2.9%
Murray C	Ind	2,082	5%	4.1%	SLP	559	1.4%
Baxter D	UKIP	954	2.3%	-0.6%	SA	532	1.3%
Carter G	Greens	783	1.9%		Ind	377	0.9%
Lab to C swing	**1.9%**	**41,805**		**Lab maj 8,009** 19.2%		**40,284**	**Lab maj 9,249** 23%

JACK STRAW b 3 Aug 1946. MP 1979-. Foreign Sec 2001, Home Sec 1997-2001. Shadow: Home Sec 1994-97, Environment Sec 1992-94, Education Sec 1987-92. Opposition spokes: Treasury and economic affairs 1980-83, environment 1983-87. 1999-. Lab Party NEC member 1994-95. Cllr Islington Borough Council 1971-78, Deputy leader Inner London Education Authority 1973. President NUS 1969-71. Barrister. PC 1997. Ed Brentwood Sch; LLB, Leeds Univ; Inns of Court Sch of Law.

An interesting former mill town in central Lancashire, Blackburn used to be the weaving centre of the world. Now the textile industry is much smaller, and a large engineering sector has developed. It has had the privilege of seeing both members who have represented the town since its creation in 1955 become significant figures in the Labour Party, and will undoubtedly keep returning Labour candidates for many years to come.

BLACKPOOL NORTH AND FLEETWOOD — Lab hold

		Electorate 74,975	Turnout 57.7%	Change from 2001	2001	Electorate 74,456	Turnout 57.2%
Humble J	**Lab**	**20,620**	**47.6%**	**-3.2%**	**Lab**	**21,610**	**50.8%**
Williamson G	C	15,558	35.9%	-1.4%	C	15,889	37.3%
Bate S	LD	5,533	12.8%	3.1%	LD	4,132	9.7%
Hopwood R	UKIP	1,579	3.6%	1.4%	UKIP	950	2.2%
Lab to C swing	**0.9%**	**43,290**		**Lab maj 5,062** 11.7%		**42,581**	**Lab maj 5,721** 13.4%

JOAN HUMBLE b 3 March 1951. MP 1997-. Member select cttees on: Social Security 1998-2001, Work and Pensions 2001. Chair all party-groups: personal social services 1999-, Myodil 2003-, university 2004-. Hon secretary: North West Lab MPs regional group 1999-, Lab Party departmental cttee for culture, media and sport 1997-. Cllr Lancs County Council 1985-87. JP, Preston Bench. Civil servant 1972-77. Ed Greenhead Grammar Sch, Keighley; BA history, Lancaster Univ.

Blackpool North now takes up very little of the seaside resort itself, although it is reliant on the tourism industry. Starting from the north of Blackpool's town centre, the seat goes on through Cleveleys to Fleetwood. This pleasant fishing port has been safe for Labour in recent years, but Blackpool North is one of the unusual instances of a relatively poor area being traditionally Conservative: the security of the seat is by no means certain.

BLACKPOOL SOUTH — Lab hold

		Electorate 73,529	Turnout 52.2%	Change from 2001	2001	Electorate 74,311	Turnout 52.2%
Marsden G	**Lab**	**19,375**	**50.5%**	**-3.8%**	**Lab**	**21,060**	**54.3%**
Winstanley M	C	11,453	29.9%	-3.1%	C	12,798	33%
Holt D	LD	5,552	14.5%	3.9%	LD	4,115	10.6%
Goodwin R	BNP	1,113	2.9%		UKIP	819	2.1%
Porter J	UKIP	849	2.2%	0.1%			
Lab to C swing	**0.4%**	**38,342**		**Lab maj 7,922** 20.7%		**38,792**	**Lab maj 8,262** 21.3%

GORDON MARSDEN b 28 Nov 1953. MP 1997-. PPS to: Tessa Jowell 2003-05, Lord Irvine of Lairg 2001-03. Member select cttees on: Deregulation 1997-99, Education and Employment 1998-2001 (Education sub-cttee 1998-2001). Chair all-party groups: future of Europe 1999-, Estonia 2002-. Pres British Resorts Assoc 1998-. Historian/lecturer. English Heritage public affairs adviser 1984-85. Ed MA history, New Coll, Oxford; combined historical studies, London Univ; Harvard Univ.

Blackpool is the quintessential resort for holidaymakers from Scotland and the north of England, and it is Blackpool South, rather than its northern neighbour constituency, which is home to the majority of the tourist areas. This seat would appear to have become fairly safe for Labour for the immediate future, with both the magnitude of the majority and the trends in local politics appearing more favourable than in the north division.

BLAENAU GWENT — Ind gain

		Electorate 53,301	Turnout 66.1%	Change from 2001	2001	Electorate 53,353	Turnout 59.5%
Law P	**Ind**	**20,505**	**58.2%**		**Lab**	**22,855**	**72%**
Jones M	Lab	11,384	32.3%	-39.7%	PIC	3,542	11.2%
Thomas B	LD	1,511	4.3%	-5%	LD	2,945	9.3%
Price J	PIC	843	2.4%	-8.8%	C	2,383	7.5%
Lee P	C	816	2.3%	-5.2%			
Osborne P	UKIP	192	0.5%				
Lab to Ind swing	**49%**	**35,251**		**Ind maj 9,121** 25.9%		**31,725**	**Lab maj 19,313** 60.9%

PETER LAW b 1 April 1948; MP 2005-; Member Nat Ass Wales for Blaenau Gwent 1999-: Sec for environment and local govt 1999-2000; Sec for local govt 2000; Cllr Nantyglo and Blaenau Urban DC 1970-74; Blaenau Gwent BC 1974-96, Mayor 1988-89, Blaenau Gwent County BC 1995-99; Justice of the Peace; Self-employed retail grocery 1964-87; Adviser in local govt and public authorities 1987-99; Ed Grofield Sec Modern School; King Henry School; Open Univ

This valleys constituency in south Wales, built on steel and coal, was previously represented by Old Labour icons Michael Foot and Nye Bevan. The seat includes the towns of Ebbw Vale and Tredegar. Before 2005 it was the safest Labour seat in Wales. It provided one of the most notable results of the election when the rebel local AM stood as an Independent and beat the official Labour candidate.

BLAYDON — Lab hold

		Electorate 62,413	Turnout 62.6%	Change from 2001	2001	Electorate 64,574	Turnout 57.4%
Anderson D	**Lab**	**20,120**	**51.5%**	**-3.3%**	**Lab**	**20,340**	**54.8%**
Maughan P	LD	14,785	37.9%	4.1%	LD	12,531	33.8%
Luckhurst D	C	3,129	8%	-3.4%	C	4,215	11.4%
Endacott N	UKIP	1,019	2.6%				
Lab to LD swing	**3.7%**	**39,053**		**Lab maj 5,335** 13.7%		**37,086**	**Lab maj 7,809** 21.1%

DAVID ANDERSON b 2 December 1953. MP 2005-. Engineer National Coal Board mines 1969-89; Elderly care worker Newcastle upon Tyne social services 1989-2004. Ed Maltby Grammar School; Mining and mechanical engineering, Durham Technical College; Doncaster Technical College; Durham University

The constituency of Blaydon is at the south-west edge of the Tyneside conurbation, and has been loyal to Labour since 1922, except for a brief interlude in 1931. Though technically included in the boroughs of Gateshead and Tyne and Wear, this seat fits the picture of a working-class corner of Durham steeped in Labour Party tradition and with a long history of Labour representation.

BLYTH VALLEY — Lab hold

		Electorate 63,640	Turnout 56.2%	Change from 2001	2001	Electorate 62,641	Turnout 55.2%
Campbell R	**Lab**	**19,659**	**55%**	**-4.7%**	**Lab**	**20,627**	**59.7%**
Reid J	LD	11,132	31.1%	6.7%	LD	8,439	24.4%
Windridge M	C	4,982	13.9%	-2%	C	5,484	15.9%
Lab to LD swing	**5.7%**	**35,773**		**Lab maj 8,527** 23.8%		**34,550**	**Lab maj 12,188** 35.3%

RONNIE CAMPBELL b 14 Aug 1943. MP 1987-. Member select cttees on: Public Administration 1997-2001, Catering 2001-. Secretary all-party boxing group 2002-. Member Lab Party departmental cttees on: health 1997-2001, Office of Public Service 1997-2001. Chair Lab MPs northern regional group 1999-. Cllr Blyth Borough Council 1969-74, Blyth Valley Council 1974-88. Miner 1958-86. NUM lodge sec 1982-86. Ed Ridley High Sch, Blyth.

Much of Northumberland is an area of outstanding natural beauty, with rugged moorlands, forested hillsides and examples of rare wildlife. Not so here. The landscape of power stations and disused collieries is less pleasing. However, offshore industries have been attracted to Blyth harbour, and the new town of Cramlington is symptomatic of growing economic activity in the area. Labour tends to do well in small seats, and this constituency is no exception.

BOGNOR REGIS AND LITTLEHAMPTON — C hold

		Electorate	Turnout	Change from	2001	Electorate	Turnout
		65,591	62.1%	2001		66,903	58.2%
Gibb N	**C**	**18,183**	**44.6%**	**-0.6%**	**C**	**17,602**	**45.2%**
O'Neill G	Lab	10,361	25.4%	-5.3%	Lab	11,959	30.7%
McDougall S	LD	8,927	21.9%	4.3%	LD	6,846	17.6%
Lithgow A	UKIP	3,276	8%	3.4%	UKIP	1,779	4.6%
					Greens	782	2%
Lab to C swing	**2.4%**	**40,747**		**C maj 7,822**		**38,968**	**C maj 5,643**
				19.2%			14.5%

NICK GIBB b 3 Sept 1960. MP 1997-. Shadow Min for Ed 2005-; Opposition spokes: Treasury 1998-99, trade and industry (energy, regulation, company law, competition) 1999-2001, transport, local govt and the regions 2001. Member select cttees on: Social Security 1997-98, Treasury 1998, public accounts 2001-03, education and skills 2003-. Vice-chair all-party groups: occupational pensions 1997-, energy studies 2001-, motor neurone disease 2002-, ageing and older people 2002-. Accountant 1984-97. Ed BA law, Durham Univ.

The seat covers a coastal strip of West Sussex where the South Downs fall away to the English Channel. The urban areas of Littlehampton and Bognor Regis are on either side of the river Arun. Stretching from the retirement and resort lands of Pagham Harbour and Aldwick, to the light industrial areas of Littlehampton, the constituency, with its significantly older than average population, is strong Conservative territory.

BOLSOVER — Lab hold

		Electorate	Turnout	Change from	2001	Electorate	Turnout
		67,568	57.3%	2001		67,237	56.9%
Skinner D	**Lab**	**25,217**	**65.2%**	**-3.4%**	**Lab**	**26,249**	**68.6%**
Hawksworth D	LD	6,780	17.5%	5.6%	C	7,472	19.5%
Imam H	C	6,702	17.3%	-2.2%	LD	4,550	11.9%
Lab to LD swing	**4.5%**	**38,699**		**Lab maj 18,437**		**38,271**	**Lab maj 18,777**
				47.6%			49.1%

DENNIS SKINNER b 11 Feb 1932. MP 1970-. Member Lab Party departmental cttees on: environment, transport and the regions 1997-2001, trade and industry 1997-2001, health. Chair Lab Party 1988-89 (vice-chair 1987-88). Lab Party NEC member 1978-92, 94-98, 1999-. President North East Derbyshire Constituency Lab Party 1968-71. Cllr Clay Cross UDC 1960-70; county cllr Derbyshire 1964-70. President Derbyshire Miners 1966-70. Miner 1949-70. Ed Tupton Hall Grammar Sch; Ruskin Coll, Oxford.

This Labour stronghold used to have more men employed in the mines than almost any other seat, but now there are no mines left. The number of households headed by manual workers is among the highest in the country, while the proportion headed by skilled non-manual workers is among the lowest. There are some agricultural areas in the constituency interspersed by small towns and villages which used to be supported by mines.

BOLTON NORTH EAST — Lab hold

		Electorate	Turnout	Change from	2001	Electorate	Turnout
		67,394	54.8%	2001		69,514	56%
Crausby D	**Lab**	**16,874**	**45.7%**	**-8.6%**	**Lab**	**21,166**	**54.3%**
Brierley P	C	12,771	34.6%	1.9%	C	12,744	32.7%
Killeya A	LD	6,044	16.4%	6.1%	LD	4,004	10.3%
Epsom K	UKIP	640	1.7%		Greens	629	1.6%
Ainscow A	Veritas	375	1%		SLP	407	1%
Lowe L	SLP	207	0.6%	-0.4%			
Lab to C swing	**5.3%**	**36,911**		**Lab maj 4,103**		**38,950**	**Lab maj 8,422**
				11.1%			21.6%

DAVID CRAUSBY b 17 June 1946. MP 1997-. Member select cttees on: Administration 1997-2001, Social Security 1999-2001, Defence 2001-. Member Lab Party departmental cttees on: foreign and commonwealth affairs 1997-2001, social security 1997-2001, trade and industry 1997-2001. Chair north west regional group PLP 2001-02. Cllr Bury Council 1979-92 (Housing chair 1985-92). Chair Amicus (AEEU) group. Shop steward/works convenor AEEU; full time works convenor 1978-97. Engineer. Ed Derby Grammar Sch, Bury; Bury Technical Coll.

Bolton North East was formerly a real knife-edge marginal, but was firmly pushed to the Labour Party by the boundary changes that occurred between the 1992 and 1997 general elections. The constituency comprises roughly half the town's urban area, with the northern and eastern extremes of the seat being more rural in character.

BOLTON SOUTH EAST — Lab hold

		Electorate 63,697	Turnout 50%	Change from 2001	2001	Electorate 68,140	Turnout 50.1%
Iddon B	**Lab**	**18,129**	**56.9%**	**-5%**	**Lab**	**21,129**	**61.9%**
Dunleavy D	C	6,491	20.4%	-3.8%	C	8,258	24.2%
Harasiwka F	LD	6,047	19%	7.5%	LD	3,941	11.5%
Bates F	UKIP	840	2.6%		SLP	826	2.4%
Jones D	Veritas	343	1.1%				
Lab to C swing	**0.6%**	**31,850**		**Lab maj 11,638** 36.5%		**34,154**	**Lab maj 12,871** 37.7%

BRIAN IDDON b 5 July 1940. MP 1997-. Member select cttees on: Environmental Audit 1997-2000, Science and Technology 2000-. Chair all-party groups: drugs misuse 1999-, chemical industry 2003-. Cllr Bolton Metropolitan District Council 1977-98 (chair housing cttee 1986-96). Member Inter-Parliamentary Union. Chemistry lecturer/demonstrator/reader 1964-97. Ed Southport Tech Coll; BSc chemistry, PhD organic chemistry, DSc, Hull Univ.

This seat is the most industrial of the three in Bolton, comprising mostly urban areas along with the town centre. Labour's safest Bolton seat looks set to stay that way for quite some time. Labour has held this seat, comfortably, since the Second World War and losing it is simply unthinkable.

BOLTON WEST — Lab hold

		Electorate 63,836	Turnout 63.5%	Change from 2001	2001	Electorate 66,033	Turnout 62.4%
Kelly R	**Lab**	**17,239**	**42.5%**	**-4.5%**	**Lab**	**19,381**	**47%**
Allott P	C	15,175	37.4%	3.8%	C	13,863	33.6%
Perkins T	LD	7,241	17.9%	-0.5%	LD	7,573	18.4%
Ford M	UKIP	524	1.3%		SA	397	1%
Ford M	Veritas	290	0.7%				
Griggs K	XPP	74	0.2%				
Lab to C swing	**4.2%**	**40,543**		**Lab maj 2,064** 5.1%		**41,214**	**Lab maj 5,518** 13.4%

RUTH KELLY b 9 May 1968. MP 1997-. Education and Skills Sec of State 2004-, Cabinet Office Min 2004. HM Treasury: Financial Sec 2002-04, Economic Sec 2001-02. PPS to Nick Brown 1998-2001. Member select cttees on: Treasury 1997-98 (Treasury Sub-Cttee 1998), Public Accounts 2002-04. The Guardian economics writer 1990-94, deputy head Inflation Report Division, Bank of England 1994-97. PC 2004. Ed Westminster Sch; BA PPE Queen's Coll, Oxford; MSc economics, LSE.

This seat includes little territory actually situated within the town of Bolton. Instead, its area covers the suburban and rural land between Bolton and Wigan, and is home to commuters and the majority of those in non-manual professions; hardly any of Bolton's industry is found in this seat. This is a true weather-vane seat; given the constituency's key demographic, it is likely that whichever party succeeds here will form the government.

BOOTLE — Lab hold

		Electorate 53,700	Turnout 47.7%	Change from 2001	2001	Electorate 55,910	Turnout 49.4%
Benton J	**Lab**	**19,345**	**75.5%**	**-2.1%**	**Lab**	**21,400**	**77.6%**
Newby C	LD	2,988	11.7%	3.2%	LD	2,357	8.5%
Moustafa W	C	1,580	6.2%	-1.8%	C	2,194	8%
Nuttall P	UKIP	1,054	4.1%		SLP	971	3.5%
Glover P	SAP	655	2.6%		SAP	672	2.4%
Lab to LD swing	**2.7%**	**25,622**		**Lab maj 16,357** 63.8%		**27,594**	**Lab maj 19,043** 69%

JOE BENTON b 28 Sept 1933. MP November 1990-. Opposition whip 1994-97. Member select cttees on: Education and Employment 1997-99 (Education and Employment Sub-Cttee 1997-99), Parliamentary Privilege (Joint Cttee) 1997-2000, Chairmen's Panel 1998-. Secretary all-party pro-life group 1997. Cllr Sefton Borough Council 1970-90: JP Bootle Bench 1969, education spokes 1977-86, leader Lab Group 1985-90. RAF national service 1955-57; Girobank 1982-90. Member RMT Parly Campaigning Group 2002-. Ed Bootle Technical Coll.

The safest seat in the country, Bootle is a Labour stronghold. It is situated on the mouth of the river Mersey, to the north of the Liverpool city seats. Home to disused docks and some of the most deprived housing in the UK, it also has very high unemployment, and a large proportion of those in employment are in unskilled labour jobs.

BOSTON AND SKEGNESS

C hold

		Electorate	Turnout	Change from	2001	Electorate	Turnout
		71,212	58.8%	2001		69,010	58.4%
Simmonds M	**C**	**19,329**	**46.2%**	**3.3%**	**C**	**17,298**	**42.9%**
Kenny P	Lab	13,422	32.1%	-9.5%	Lab	16,783	41.6%
Horsnell R	UKIP	4,024	9.6%	7.8%	LD	4,994	12.4%
Riley A	LD	3,649	8.7%	-3.7%	UKIP	717	1.8%
Russell W	BNP	1,025	2.4%		Greens	521	1.3%
Petz M	Greens	420	1%	-0.3%			
Lab to C swing	**6.4%**	**41,869**		**C maj 5,907**		**40,313**	**C maj 515**
				14.1%			1.3%

MARK SIMMONDS b 12 April 1964. MP 2001-. Shadow Minister: International Development 2005-, Foreign Affairs 2004-05, Education 2004, Public Services, Health and Education 2003-04. Member select cttees: Environmental Audit 2001-03, Education and Skills 2001-03. Secretary all-party Latin America group, treasurer all-party Venezuela group 2004-. Cllr London Borough of Wandsworth 1990-94 (chair: Property cttee 1991-92, Housing cttee 1992-94). Chartered surveyor. Ed BSc urban estate surveying, Trent Poly.

The market town of Boston is an important administrative and shopping centre for rural Lincolnshire. Its port is being developed as a gateway to the expanding East Midlands. Light industry and food processing are the major economic activities in the town and villages but elsewhere agriculture is dominant on some of the most fertile in the UK. An erstwhile Conservative stronghold, this seat now counts among their more vulnerable.

BOSWORTH

C hold

		Electorate	Turnout	Change from	2001	Electorate	Turnout
		71,596	66.3%	2001		69,992	64.4%
Tredinnick D	**C**	**20,212**	**42.6%**	**-1.8%**	**C**	**20,030**	**44.4%**
Herd R	Lab	14,893	31.4%	-8%	Lab	17,750	39.4%
Moore J	LD	10,528	22.2%	6%	LD	7,326	16.2%
Walker D	UKIP	1,866	3.9%				
Lab to C swing	**3.1%**	**47,499**		**C maj 5,319**		**45,106**	**C maj 2,280**
				11.2%			5.1%

DAVID TREDINNICK b 19 Jan 1950. MP 1987-. PPS to Sir Wyn Roberts 1991-94. Member select cttees on: Liaison 1997-, Joint Cttee on Statutory Instruments 1997-. Member Executive 1922 Cttee 2002-. Chair all-party integrated and complementary healthcare group 2002-. Chair British Atlantic group of young politicians, 1989-91. Army, account executive, consultant, manager 1968-87. Ed Graduate Sch of Business; MBA, Cape Town Univ; MLitt, St John's Coll, Oxford.

Bosworth, west of Leicester and east of Nuneaton, includes the ancient villages of Sheepy Parva and Fenny Drayton, while new housing in the Hinckley area has brought in more Conservative voters. The decline of coal in the region accounted for Labour's decline at the polls – they lost in 1970 and have not won since. Despite its suburban/rural nature, the seat is becoming increasingly unsafe for the Conservatives.

BOURNEMOUTH EAST

C hold

		Electorate	Turnout	Change from	2001	Electorate	Turnout
		63,426	59.3%	2001		60,454	59.2%
Ellwood T	**C**	**16,925**	**45%**	**1.7%**	**C**	**15,501**	**43.3%**
Garratt A	LD	11,681	31.1%	-2.6%	LD	12,067	33.7%
Stokes D	Lab	7,191	19.1%	-0.8%	Lab	7,107	19.9%
Collier T	UKIP	1,802	4.8%	1.7%	UKIP	1,124	3.1%
LD to C swing	**2.2%**	**37,599**		**C maj 5,244**		**35,799**	**C maj 3,434**
				14%			9.6%

TOBIAS ELLWOOD b 12 August 1966. MP 2005-. Contested Worsley 2001 general election. Cllr Dacorum Borough Council 1999; Chair Herts SW Con Assoc 1998. Army officer 1991-96; Researcher to Tom King MP 1996-97; Business manager London Stock Exchange 1999. Treasurer Bow Group 2000; Chair Con Insight 2000; CBI London Council 2000. Ed Vienna Int Sch; design and technology, Loughborough University of Technology; MBA City Univ

Bournemouth East is traversed by the river Stour which spills into Christchurch Bay on the constituency's boundary. This tourist hot spot has always been safe territory for the Conservatives and it would require tactical voting on a relatively large scale from Labour supporters to install the first Liberal Democrat MP in this south coast seat. The new Tory MP should have little to fear come the next election.

BOURNEMOUTH WEST — C hold

		Electorate 63,658	Turnout 53.3%	Change from 2001	2001	Electorate 62,038	Turnout 54.2%
Butterfill J	**C**	**14,057**	**41.4%**	**-1.4%**	**C**	**14,417**	**42.8%**
Renaut R	LD	10,026	29.6%	4.4%	Lab	9,699	28.8%
Williams D	Lab	7,824	23.1%	-5.7%	LD	8,468	25.2%
Maclaire-Hillier M	UKIP	2,017	6%	2.8%	UKIP	1,064	3.2%
C to LD swing	**2.9%**	**33,924**		**C maj 4,031** 11.9%		**33,648**	**C maj 4,718** 14%

SIR JOHN BUTTERFILL b 14 Feb 1941. MP 1983-. PPS to Dr Brian Mawhinney 1991-92, Cecil Parkinson 1988-90. Member select cttees: Trade and Industry 1992-2001, Chairmen's Panel 1997-, Court of Referees 1997-, Unopposed Bills (Panel) 1997. Chair all-party occupational pensions group 2001-. Chair: Conservative Group for Europe 1989-92, Conservative Party rules cttee 1997. Trustees Chairman, Parliamentary Members' Fund 1977-2002. Chartered surveyor. Kt 2004. Ed Caterham Sch; Coll of Estate Management, London.

Bournemouth West is home to much of town's tourist trade and receives a large amount of the estimated £250 million spent annually by visitors in Bournemouth. Like its twin seat to the East, Bournemouth West has always been safe Conservative territory. The real battle is between Labour and the Liberal Democrats, whose fight for second place is sufficiently close to ensure that neither can sustain a real challenge to the Tory MP.

BRACKNELL — C hold

		Electorate 80,657	Turnout 63.4%	Change from 2001	2001	Electorate 81,118	Turnout 60.7%
Mackay A	**C**	**25,412**	**49.7%**	**3.1%**	**C**	**22,962**	**46.6%**
Keene J	Lab	13,376	26.2%	-6.8%	Lab	16,249	33%
Glendon L	LD	10,128	19.8%	2.7%	LD	8,424	17.1%
Pearson V	UKIP	1,818	3.6%	1%	UKIP	1,266	2.6%
Roberts D	Ind	407	0.8%		ProLife	324	0.7%
Lab to C swing	**5%**	**51,141**		**C maj 12,036** 23.5%		**49,225**	**C maj 6,713** 13.6%

ANDREW MACKAY b 27 Aug 1949. MP for Birmingham Stechford 1977-79, for Berkshire East 1983-97, for Bracknell 1997-. Shadow Northern Ireland Sec of State 1997-2001, Shadow Cabinet member 1997-2001, PPS to Tom King 1986-1992. Member select cttees on: Procedure 1994-95, Selection 1994-97, Standards and Privileges 2002-, Foreign Affairs 2004. Deputy Chair (candidates) Con Party 2004-, Chair Northern Ireland Con Party Cttee 1997-. Public companies consultant. PC 1998. Ed Solihull Sch.

Bracknell is a former new town whose population expanded so rapidly that, just 40 years after its creation, it was designated a parliamentary constituency in its own right. Situated in the M4 corridor in the southern corner of Berkshire, the constituency is home to a number of affluent dormitory villages and the Royal Military Academy at Sandhurst. This safe Conservative seat is best known for the proliferation of hi-tech industries.

BRADFORD NORTH — Lab hold

		Electorate 64,515	Turnout 53.3%	Change from 2001	2001	Electorate 66,454	Turnout 52.7%
Rooney T	**Lab**	**14,622**	**42.5%**	**-7.2%**	**Lab**	**17,419**	**49.7%**
Ward D	LD	11,111	32.3%	12.5%	C	8,450	24.1%
Khong T	C	5,569	16.2%	-7.9%	LD	6,924	19.8%
Cromie L	BNP	2,061	6%	1.4%	BNP	1,613	4.6%
Schofield S	Greens	560	1.6%	-0.1%	Greens	611	1.7%
Yildiz U	Respect	474	1.4%				
Lab to LD swing	**9.9%**	**34,397**		**Lab maj 3,511** 10.2%		**35,017**	**Lab maj 8,969** 25.6%

TERRY ROONEY b 11 Nov 1950. MP Nov 1990-. PPS to: Michael Meacher 1997-2002, Keith Hill 2003-05. Member select cttees: Broadcasting 1991-97, House of Lords Reform Joint Cttee 2003-. Member Lab Party departmental cttees: education and employment 1997-2001, environment, transport and regions 1997-2001. Cllr Bradford City Council 1983-91: dep leader 1990-91. Commercial insurance broker/welfare rights worker. Ed Bradford Coll.

The seat, largely situated in the eastern part of the city, has a very substantial Asian population. There is high unemployment and much low quality housing and comparatively few voters fall into professional or managerial social strata. Labour holds the seat, but is increasingly threatened by the Liberal Democrats.

BRADFORD SOUTH — Lab hold

		Electorate	Turnout	Change from	2001	Electorate	Turnout
		67,576	54.2%	2001		68,449	51.3%
Sutcliffe G	**Lab**	**17,954**	**49.1%**	**-6.7%**	**Lab**	**19,603**	**55.8%**
Carter G	C	8,787	24%	-4.3%	C	9,941	28.3%
Doyle M	LD	5,334	14.6%	4%	LD	3,717	10.6%
Lewthwaite J	BNP	2,862	7.8%		UKIP	783	2.2%
Curtis D	Greens	695	1.9%		SLP	571	1.6%
Smith J	UKIP	552	1.5%	-0.7%	SA	302	0.9%
Muchewicz T	Veritas	421	1.2%		DWSB	220	0.6%
Lab to C swing	**1.2%**	**36,605**		**Lab maj 9,167**		**35,137**	**Lab maj 9,662**
				25%			27.5%

GERRY SUTCLIFFE b 13 May 1953. MP June 1994-. Trade and Industry Dept Parly Under-Sec of State 2003-. PPS to: Harriet Harman 1997-98, Stephen Byers 1998 / 1999. Asst govt whip 1999-2001, govt whip 200-03. Member select cttees: Public Accounts 1996-98, Unopposed Bills (Panel) 1997-99, Selection 2001-03. Member regional Lab Party executive. Cllr Bradford City Council 1982-94: leader 1992-94. Sales / advertising / printing career. SOGAT/GPMU deputy branch sec 1980-94. Ed Cardinal Hinsley Grammar Sch, Bradford.

Bradford South has been a Labour seat since 1945 but there have been some close contests, although not in recent years. This is a residential working class seat with above average numbers for all manual social groups. The seat has a sizeable Asian community, albeit smaller than the other Bradford constituencies.

BRADFORD WEST — Lab hold

		Electorate	Turnout	Change from	2001	Electorate	Turnout
		67,356	54%	2001		71,622	53.6%
Singh M	**Lab**	**14,570**	**40.1%**	**-7.9%**	**Lab**	**18,401**	**48%**
Rashid H	C	11,544	31.7%	-5.4%	C	14,236	37.1%
Ali M	LD	6,620	18.2%	11.8%	Greens	2,672	7%
Cromie P	BNP	2,525	6.9%		LD	2,437	6.4%
Darr P	Greens	1,110	3.1%	-3.9%	UKIP	427	1.1%
					All	197	0.5%
Lab to C swing	**1.3%**	**36,369**		**Lab maj 3,026**		**38,370**	**Lab maj 4,165**
				8.3%			10.9%

MARSHA SINGH b 11 Oct 1954. MP 1997-. Member Home Affairs select cttee 1997-. Hon secretary Lab Party departmental cttee for home affairs 1999-2001. Vice-chair all-party race and community group 2003-, treasurer all-party Kashmir group 1999-. Chair: Bradford West Lab Party 1986-91/1996-97, district Lab Party 1992. Bradford Community Heath senior development manager 1990-97. Ed Belle Vue Boys Upper Sch; BA languages, politics and economics of modern Europe, Loughborough Univ.

Most of Bradford's Asian community live here (31.9 per cent of this seat's population). The seat is one of great contrasts, stretching from the deprived inner city areas out to the more select and rural fringe of the city. Bradford found it difficult to recover from the decline in the textile trade and unemployment is still high. It is a far less safe Labour seat than previously.

BRAINTREE — C gain

		Electorate	Turnout	Change from	2001	Electorate	Turnout
		80,458	65.9%	2001		78,362	64.2%
Newmark B	**C**	**23,597**	**44.5%**	**3.2%**	**Lab**	**21,123**	**42%**
Hurst A	Lab	19,704	37.1%	-4.9%	C	20,765	41.3%
Turner P	LD	7,037	13.3%	2%	LD	5,664	11.3%
Abbott J	Greens	1,308	2.5%		Greens	1,241	2.5%
Lord R	UKIP	1,181	2.2%	0.7%	LCA	774	1.5%
Nolan B	Ind	228	0.4%		UKIP	748	1.5%
Lab to C swing	**4.1%**	**53,055**		**C maj 3,893**		**50,315**	**Lab maj 358**
				7.3%			0.7%

BROOKS NEWMARK b 8 May 1958. MP 2005-. Contested Newcastle upon Tyne Central 1997, Braintree 2001 general elections. Chair Southwark and Bermondsey Conservative Association 1990-93. Vice pres Lehman Brothers Inc 1984-87; Director Newmark Brothers Ltd 1988-93; Principal Stellican Ltd 1993-98; Partner Apollo Management LP 1998. Ed Bedford School; history, Harvard Univ; politics, Oxford Univ; finance, Harvard Business School

This had been considered a very safe Conservative constituency, keeping something of its rural flavour, unlike some of the Essex seats nearer London. The main towns, Braintree and Witham, retain traditional manufacturing industries, particularly engineering, but have also attracted new industries and office developments. Many residents are London commuters. A huge swing in 1997 gave the seat to Labour but the Tories reclaimed it in 2005.

BRECON AND RADNORSHIRE — LD hold

		Electorate 55,171	Turnout 69.5%	Change from 2001	2001	Electorate 53,247	Turnout 70.5%
Williams R	**LD**	**17,182**	**44.8%**	**8%**	**LD**	**13,824**	**36.8%**
Davies A	C	13,277	34.6%	-0.2%	C	13,073	34.8%
Veale L	Lab	5,755	15%	-6.4%	Lab	8,024	21.4%
Gwynfor M	PIC	1,404	3.7%	0.2%	PIC	1,301	3.5%
Phillips E	UKIP	723	1.9%	0.7%	Ind	762	2%
					UKIP	452	1.2%
					Ind	80	0.2%
C to LD swing	**4.1%**	**38,341**		**LD maj 3,905** 10.2%		**37,516**	**LD maj 751** 2%

ROGER WILLIAMS b 22 Jan 1948. MP 2001-. Lib Dem whip 2004-. Lib Dem rural affairs spokes 2002-. Member Welsh Affairs select cttee 2001-. All-party groups vice-chair: national parks 2001-, children in Wales 2001-, horse 2004-. Cllr: Powys CC 1981-2001, Brecon Beacons national park 1985- (chair 1991-95). Farmer. Former chair Brecon and Radnorshire NFU. Member Rural Wales devt board. Chair mid Wales agri-food partnership. Lay school inspector. Ed BA agriculture, Cambridge.

The largest seat in Wales geographically, making up the southern part of the large county of Powys, Brecon and Radnorshire is almost entirely rural and shares its eastern border with England. It is a very beautiful constituency, containing the Brecon Beacons National Park, the delightful market towns of Brecon, Builth Wells and Radnor as well as the spa town of Llandrindod Wells. It is gradually becoming a Lib Dem stronghold.

BRENT EAST — LD gain

		Electorate 56,227	Turnout 55.2%	Change from 2001	2001	Electorate 58,095	Turnout 49.9%
Teather S	**LD**	**14,764**	**47.5%**	**36.9%**	**Lab**	**18,325**	**63.2%**
Qureshi Y	Lab	12,052	38.8%	-24.4%	C	5,278	18.2%
Kwarteng K	C	3,193	10.3%	-7.9%	LD	3,065	10.6%
Ali S	Greens	905	2.9%	-1.8%	Greens	1,361	4.7%
Weininger M	Ind	115	0.4%		ProLife	392	1.4%
Weiss R	Vote Dream	39	0.1%		SLP	383	1.3%
					UKIP	188	0.6%
Lab to LD swing	**30.7%**	**31,068**		**LD maj 2,712** 8.7%		**28,992**	**Lab maj 13,047** 45%

SARAH TEATHER b 1 June 1974. MP September 2003-. Lib Dem Shadow Sec Communities and Local Govt 2005-. Lib Dem spokes: Health 2004, London 2004-. Chair Lib Dem health policy working group. Member Lib Dem national policy cttee. Cllr London Borough of Islington 2002-03. Macmillan Fund for Cancer Relief policy analyst to 2003. Ed Leicester Grammar Sch; BA pharmacology, St John's Coll, Cambridge.

Until September 2003 Brent East was best known as the London Mayor Ken Livingstone's former constituency. But this multi-ethnic area of North West London is now remembered for the sensational by-election in which the Liberal Democrats captured one of Labour's safest seats, ending New Labour's almost unbroken run of electoral success. No electoral future in Brent East is predictable as the Liberal Democrats gain momentum but take on a traditional Labour heartland.

BRENT NORTH — Lab hold

		Electorate 60,148	Turnout 59.3%	Change from 2001	2001	Electorate 58,789	Turnout 57.7%
Gardiner B	**Lab**	**17,420**	**48.8%**	**-10.6%**	**Lab**	**20,149**	**59.4%**
Blackman B	C	11,779	33%	3.7%	C	9,944	29.3%
Hughes H	LD	5,672	15.9%	4.6%	LD	3,846	11.3%
Ahmad B	Progress	685	1.9%				
Weiss R	Vote Dream	126	0.4%				
Lab to C swing	**7.2%**	**35,682**		**Lab maj 5,641** 15.8%		**33,939**	**Lab maj 10,205** 30.1%

BARRY GARDINER b 10 March 1957. MP 1997-. Parly Under-Sec Dept of Trade and Industry 2005-, Northern Ireland Office Parly Under-Sec of State 2004-05. PPS to Beverley Hughes 2002-04. Member select cttees on: Procedure 1997-2001, Broadcasting 1998-2001, Public Accounts 1999-2002, Consolidation of Bills etc Joint Cttee 2001-. Chair: Lab Friends of India 1999-2002, Lab Party departmental cttee for culture, media and sport 2002-04.Ed MA philosophy, St Andrews; Harvard Univ; research, Cambridge Univ.

The constituency covers an area north of the Wembley Stadium including suburbs such as Sudbury, North Wembley, and Queensbury (prosperous middle class residential areas). Labour-run Brent Council's 'loony left' reputation in the 1980s and early 1990s must have been anathema to Brent North's home-owning classes, and probably explains why this was a safe Conservative seat right up until 1997. Massive swings to Labour reflected the transformation of the party image locally as well as nationally, although their majority took a knock in 2005.

BRENT SOUTH — Lab hold

		Electorate 56,508	Turnout 52.7%	Change from 2001	2001	Electorate 55,891	Turnout 51.2%
Butler D	**Lab**	**17,501**	**58.8%**	**-14.5%**	**Lab**	**20,984**	**73.3%**
Allie J	LD	6,175	20.8%	10%	C	3,604	12.6%
Saha R	C	4,485	15.1%	2.5%	LD	3,098	10.8%
Langley R	Greens	957	3.2%		SA	491	1.7%
Wallace S	Ind	297	1%		RMGB	460	1.6%
Fernandez R	Ind	288	1%				
Weiss R	Vote Dream	61	0.2%				
Lab to LD swing	**12.3%**	**29,764**		**Lab maj 11,326** 38%		**28,637**	**Lab maj 17,380** 60.7%

DAWN BUTLER b 3 November 1969. Civil servant Job Centre 1993-96; recruitment officer and black women's officer Public and Commercial Services Union 1996-97; GMB: National officer, Regional equality officer, Regional race officer

A very safe Labour seat with one of the largest ethnic minority population of any seat in England and Wales. This North-west London seat is mainly residential but contains large trading estates and Wembley Stadium. The constituency is due to disappear and the majority of the seat is likely to be merged with parts of North Westminster. Despite low turnouts, the multi-cultural wards around Brent South will exert a strong pro-Labour force.

BRENTFORD AND ISLEWORTH — Lab hold

		Electorate 84,366	Turnout 54.5%	Change from 2001	2001	Electorate 84,049	Turnout 53%
Keen A	**Lab**	**18,329**	**39.8%**	**-12.5%**	**Lab**	**23,275**	**52.3%**
Northcote A	C	13,918	30.2%	1.1%	C	12,957	29.1%
Dakers A	LD	10,477	22.8%	9.3%	LD	5,994	13.5%
Hunt J	Greens	1,652	3.6%	0.6%	Greens	1,324	3%
Andrews P	Community	1,118	2.4%		UKIP	412	0.9%
Stoneman M	NF	523	1.1%		SA	408	0.9%
					Ind	144	0.3%
Lab to C swing	**6.8%**	**46,017**		**Lab maj 4,411** 9.6%		**44,514**	**Lab maj 10,318** 23.2%

ANN KEEN b 26 Nov 1948. MP 1997-. PPS to: Frank Dobson 1999-2001, Gordon Brown 2001-. Member Health select cttee 1997-99. Chair all-party theatre group 2002-, vice-chair all-party Singapore group 1998-. Member Lab Party departmental cttees for: health 1997-2001, home affairs 1997-2001, international development 1997-2001. Vice-chair Parly Lab Party trade union group. Community nursing sister. CancerBACUP Parly Figure of the Year. Ed PGCEA, Surrey Univ.

The constituency contains a diverse mix of communities. Unlike many seats in London, the area nearest to centre of the city, Chiswick, is the most attractive residential area, while the outer areas, such as Hounslow, have a more industrial 'inner city' character. Future Conservative victories seem unlikely in the medium term, because Labour has maintained its traditional support in working-class areas of Brentford, Hounslow and Gunnersbury. More middle-class areas are home to liberally-inclined urban professionals.

BRENTWOOD AND ONGAR — C hold

		Electorate 64,496	Turnout 68.4%	Change from 2001	2001	Electorate 64,693	Turnout 67.2%
Pickles E	**C**	**23,609**	**53.5%**	**15.5%**	**C**	**16,558**	**38%**
Stollar G	LD	11,997	27.2%	11.6%	Ind	13,737	31.5%
Adams J	Lab	6,579	14.9%	2.3%	LD	6,772	15.6%
Gulleford S	UKIP	1,805	4.1%	2.7%	Lab	5,505	12.6%
Appleton A	Ind	155	0.4%		UKIP	611	1.4%
					Ind	239	0.5%
					CMEP	68	0.2%
					Ind	52	0.1%
LD to C swing	**2%**	**44,145**		**C maj 11,612** 26.3%		**43,542**	**C maj 2,821** 6.5%

ERIC PICKLES b 20 April 1952. MP 1992-. Shadow: Local Govt Sec of State 2003-, Local Govt and the Regions Sec of State 2002-03, Transport Min 2001-02. Opposition spokes: Social Security 1998-2001. Member Environment, Transport and Regional Affairs select cttee 1997-98 (Transport Sub Cttee 1997-98). Vice-chair Con Party 1993-97. Cllr Bradford Metropolitan District Council 1979-91. Chair joint cttee against racism 1982-87. Industrial trainer. Ed Leeds Poly.

Just outside Greater London, in a relatively rural corner of Essex, the seat takes its name from Brentwood, the largest town in the area, and the small town of Chipping Ongar to the north of the constituency. Brentwood and Ongar has been a safe Conservative seat since its creation in 1974. The typical voter is middle-class and middle-aged with the majority of workers in managerial, technical and professional jobs.

BRIDGEND — Lab hold

		Electorate	Turnout	Change from	2001	Electorate	Turnout
		63,936	59.2%	2001		61,496	60.2%
Moon M	**Lab**	**16,410**	**43.4%**	**-9.1%**	**Lab**	**19,423**	**52.5%**
Baker H	C	9,887	26.1%	0.8%	C	9,377	25.3%
Warren P	LD	7,949	21%	6.6%	LD	5,330	14.4%
Clubb G	PIC	2,527	6.7%	-0.5%	PIC	2,653	7.2%
Spink J	Greens	595	1.6%		ProLife	223	0.6%
Rajan K	UKIP	491	1.3%				
Lab to C swing	**5%**	**37,859**		**Lab maj 6,523**		**37,006**	**Lab maj 10,046**
				17.2%			27.1%

MADELEINE MOON b 27 March 1950. MP 2005-. Bridgend borough councillor 1991-; Former mayor of Porthcawl; Residential care home inspector Care Standards Inspectorate. Member: Fabian Society, Amnesty International. Ed Whinney Hill School; Durham Girls School

The constituency is situated in South Wales, at the edge of the Vale of Glamorgan. It contains two major towns in Porthcawl and Bridgend itself. The latter is the more important of the two, providing the commercial, shopping and market centre of the area. It is now a safe Labour seat. It returned a Conservative MP in 1983 but in all but disastrous electoral circumstances for Labour they will continue to win here.

BRIDGWATER — C hold

		Electorate	Turnout	Change from	2001	Electorate	Turnout
		75,790	63.5%	2001		74,079	64.6%
Liddell-Grainger I	**C**	**21,240**	**44.2%**	**3.8%**	**C**	**19,354**	**40.4%**
Burchell M	Lab	12,771	26.6%	-0.2%	LD	14,367	30%
Main J	LD	10,940	22.7%	-7.3%	Lab	12,803	26.8%
Weinstein R	UKIP	1,767	3.7%	0.9%	UKIP	1,323	2.8%
Graham C	Greens	1,391	2.9%				
Lab to C swing	**2%**	**48,109**		**C maj 8,469**		**47,847**	**C maj 4,987**
				17.6%			10.4%

IAN LIDDELL-GRAINGER b 23 Feb 1959. MP 2001-. Member select cttees on: Public Administration 2001-, Scottish Affairs 2002-, Environment, Food and Rural Affairs 2003-. Vice-chair all-party groups: organophosphates 2001-, community media 2004-, horse 2004-. President Tyne Bridge Conservative Association 1993-96. Cllr Tynedale District Council 1989-95, Northern Area Council 1992-95. Company managing director. Ed South of Scotland Agricultural Coll, Edinburgh.

Taking its name from the small industrial town and port of Bridgwater, this seat stretches some 30 miles along north west Somerset to the Devon border, taking in part of Exmoor, the beautiful cliffs around Porlock and the resort town of Minehead. Despite boundary changes the Conservatives appear safe in this seat. Labour and the Liberal Democrats are close enough to each other to mean that tactical voting is unlikely to occur in the future.

BRIGG AND GOOLE — Lab hold

		Electorate	Turnout	Change from	2001	Electorate	Turnout
		67,364	63.2%	2001		64,647	63.5%
Cawsey I	**Lab**	**19,257**	**45.2%**	**-3.7%**	**Lab**	**20,066**	**48.9%**
Bean M	C	16,363	38.4%	-0.8%	C	16,105	39.2%
Johnson G	LD	5,690	13.4%	4.2%	LD	3,796	9.2%
Martin S	UKIP	1,268	3%	1.3%	UKIP	688	1.7%
					SLP	399	1%
Lab to C swing	**1.5%**	**42,578**		**Lab maj 2,894**		**41,054**	**Lab maj 3,961**
				6.8%			9.6%

IAN CAWSEY b 14 April 1960. MP 1997-. PPS to: Lord Williams of Mostyn 2001-02, David Miliband 2002-05. Asst govt whip 2005-. Member Home Affairs select cttee 1999-2001. Chair all-party animal welfare group 2001-, treasurer all-party steel group 2002-. Chair Lab Party home affairs departmental cttee 1997-2001. Elliot Morley MP asst 1987-97. Former IT consultant. Trustee Jerry Green Foundation 2004-. Vice-president Federation of Economic Development Authorities. Ed Wintringham Sch.

Brigg is a small market town on Lincolnshire's northernmost boundary. Goole in Yorkshire is far larger, the most inland port on the east coast. It is a highly industrialised town. Other industrial towns include Gunness and Flixborough, now home to large chemical works and burgeoning hi-tech industries. The rest of the seat is based on the rural Lincolnshire flatlands with isolated communities. The mixed nature of this Labour constituency ensures its marginality.

BRIGHTON KEMPTOWN — Lab hold

		Electorate 65,985	Turnout 60.2%	Change from 2001	2001	Electorate 67,621	Turnout 58%
Turner D	**Lab**	**15,858**	**39.9%**	**-7.9%**	**Lab**	**18,745**	**47.8%**
Symes J	C	13,121	33%	-2.3%	C	13,823	35.3%
Pepper M	LD	6,560	16.5%	6.1%	LD	4,064	10.4%
Williams S	Greens	2,800	7.1%	3.8%	Greens	1,290	3.3%
Chamberlain-Webber J	UKIP	758	1.9%	0.5%	UKIP	543	1.4%
O'Reilly C	TPP	172	0.4%		SLP	364	0.9%
McLeod J	SLP	163	0.4%	-0.5%	Free	227	0.6%
Cooke E	Ind	127	0.3%		ProLife	147	0.4%
Clarke P	SAP	113	0.3%				
Dobbs G	Ind	47	0.1%				
Lab to C swing	**2.8%**	**39,719**		**Lab maj 2,737** 6.9%		**39,203**	**Lab maj 4,922** 12.6%

DES TURNER b 17 July 1939. MP 1997-. Member Science and Technology select cttee 1997-. Chair all-party yacht club House of Commons group 2001-. Parly observer: Albanian elections 1997, Bosnian elections 1998. Cllr East Sussex County Council 1985-96, Brighton Borough Council 1994-96, Brighton and Hove Unitary Council 1996-99. Scientist. Ed BSc botany, MSc biochemistry, Imperial Coll, London; PhD biochemistry, Univ Coll, London; PGCE, Brighton Poly.

From the suburbia of Peacehaven and Saltdean to the heart of Brighton's vibrant gay community in Kemptown, from the expensive residential area of Rottingdean to the troubled council estates of Whitehawk and Moulsecoomb, this is a seat of dramatic contrasts. Traditionally a Conservative seat, (but the only Sussex seat ever to be won by Labour before 1997), Brighton Kemptown now appears to be undergoing a long-term shift towards Labour.

BRIGHTON PAVILION — Lab hold

		Electorate 68,087	Turnout 64%	Change from 2001	2001	Electorate 69,200	Turnout 58.8%
Lepper D	**Lab/C**	**15,427**	**35.5%**	**-13.2%**	**Lab/C**	**19,846**	**48.7%**
Weatherley M	C	10,397	23.9%	-1.2%	C	10,203	25.1%
Taylor K	Greens	9,530	21.9%	12.6%	LD	5,348	13.1%
Thorpe H	LD	7,171	16.5%	3.4%	Greens	3,806	9.3%
Crisp-Comotto K	UKIP	508	1.2%	0.3%	SLP	573	1.4%
Greenstein T	Green S	188	0.4%		Free	409	1%
Fyvie I	SLP	152	0.4%	-1%	UKIP	361	0.9%
Rooke C	Ind	122	0.3%		ProLife	177	0.4%
Jago K	Ind	44	0.1%				
Lab/C to C swing	**6%**	**43,539**		**Lab/C maj 5,030** 11.6%		**40,723**	**Lab/C maj 9,643** 23.7%

DAVID LEPPER b 15 Sept 1945. MP 1997-. Member select cttees on: Broadcasting 1997-2001 (chair 2001-), Public Administration 1999-2001, Environment, Food and Rural Affairs 2001- (Radioactive Waste Policy Sub-Cttee 2001-02), Liaison 2001-, Finance and Services 2001-. Chair all-party groups: English language teaching 2001-, Foyers 2004-. Cllr Brighton Council 1980-96: leader 1986-97, mayor 1993-94; Brighton and Hove Council 1996-97. Teacher 1969-96. Ed Kent Univ; Sussex Univ; Central London Poly.

Running westward from the Palace Pier and famous Pavilion towards Hove, and inland to the base of the South Downs at Patcham and Falmer, the constituency contains most of the town centre, the big hotels and the conference centre. Brighton is a tourist town with a developing business base and a large student population. Formerly safe Conservative territory, it has shifted towards Labour, for whom it may now be considered a safe seat.

BRISTOL EAST — Lab hold

		Electorate 68,096	Turnout 61.3%	Change from 2001	2001	Electorate 70,279	Turnout 57.4%
McCarthy K	**Lab**	**19,152**	**45.9%**	**-9.1%**	**Lab**	**22,180**	**55%**
James P	LD	10,531	25.2%	8.1%	C	8,788	21.8%
Manning J	C	8,787	21.1%	-0.7%	LD	6,915	17.1%
Krishna-Das A	Greens	1,586	3.8%	1%	Greens	1,110	2.8%
Smith J	UKIP	1,132	2.7%	1.3%	UKIP	572	1.4%
North P	Respect	532	1.3%		SLP	438	1.1%
					SA	331	0.8%
Lab to LD swing	**8.6%**	**41,720**		**Lab maj 8,621** 20.7%		**40,334**	**Lab maj 13,392** 33.2%

KERRY McCARTHY b 26 March 1965. MP 2005-. Councillor Luton Borough Council 1995-2003; Director London Luton Airport 1999-2003; member Labour National Policy Forum and Economic policy commission 1998-2005. Member The Law Society 1994-99; Head of public policy The Waterfront Partnership 2004-05 Ed. Russian, politics and linguistics, Liverpool Univ; CPE and final solicitors exams 1994

Along with Bristol South and Bristol West, Bristol East is one of the central constituencies that make up the Bristol conurbation. It is, however, neither as working-class as Bristol South, nor as affluent as Bristol West. These characteristics, combined with significant boundary changes in recent decades, explain the constituency's chequered political history. However, despite a big swing to the Liberal Democrats in 2005, Bristol East is still a safe Labour seat.

BRISTOL NORTH WEST — Lab hold

		Electorate	Turnout	Change from	2001	Electorate	Turnout
		77,703	61.1%	2001		76,903	60.4%
Naysmith D	**Lab/C**	**22,192**	**46.7%**	**-5.4%**	**Lab/C**	**24,236**	**52.1%**
Watson A	C	13,230	27.9%	-0.8%	C	13,349	28.7%
Hoyle B	LD	9,545	20.1%	4.2%	LD	7,387	15.9%
Lees C	UKIP	1,132	2.4%	-0.1%	UKIP	1,140	2.5%
Blundell M	EDP	828	1.7%		SLP	371	0.8%
Jones G	SAP	565	1.2%				
Lab/C to C swing	**2.3%**	**47,492**		**Lab/C maj 8,962**		**46,483**	**Lab/C maj 10,887**
				18.9%			23.4%

DOUG NAYSMITH b 1 April 1941. MP 1997-. Member select cttees: Regulatory Reform 1998-, Soc Security 1999-2001, Health 2001-. Vice-chair all-party groups: scientific 2002, stroke 2004-. Chair editorial cttee Science in Parliament 2000-, joint vice-chair Lab Party health and soc services departmental cttee 2000-. Chair Bristol District Lab Party 1991-97. Cllr Bristol City Council 1981-88. Past pres/sec Bristol AUT. Immunologist. Ed biology, Heriot-Watt Univ; BSc zoology, Edinburgh Univ.

Bristol North West is geographically the largest of the Bristol constituencies. Its diverse inhabitants can be described both as affluent and working class, a characteristic that has contributed to the constituency alternating between the Conservatives and Labour over the last 50 years. Given the electoral history of this weathervane constituency it is likely that it will remain in Labour hands until the party at large suffers a significant reversal in fortune.

BRISTOL SOUTH — Lab hold

		Electorate	Turnout	Change from	2001	Electorate	Turnout
		70,835	59.8%	2001		72,490	56.5%
Primarolo D	**Lab**	**20,778**	**49.1%**	**-7.8%**	**Lab**	**23,299**	**56.9%**
Barnard K	LD	9,636	22.8%	8%	C	9,118	22.3%
Hill G	C	8,466	20%	-2.3%	LD	6,078	14.8%
Bolton C	Greens	2,127	5%	2%	Greens	1,233	3%
Dent M	UKIP	1,321	3.1%	1.9%	SA	496	1.2%
					UKIP	496	1.2%
					SLP	250	0.6%
Lab to LD swing	**7.9%**	**42,328**		**Lab maj 11,142**		**40,970**	**Lab maj 14,181**
				26.3%			34.6%

DAWN PRIMAROLO b 2 May 1954. MP 1987-. HM Treasury Paymaster General 1999-, Financial Sec 1997-99. Opposition spokes: health 1992-94, Treasury and economic affairs 1994-97. Member Public Accounts select cttee 1997-98. Cllr Avon County Council 1985-87. Secretary/voluntary worker/student 1972-87. Patron: Terence Higgins Trust, Knowle West Against Drugs, Children's Hospice South West. PC 2002. Ed BA social science, Bristol Poly; Bristol Univ.

The most impoverished quarter of the city, Bristol South is solidly working-class and supportive of Labour. In fact, it is arguably their safest seat in the South West. Characterised by council estates, high crime and unemployment, the constituency encompasses more of the troubled urban areas of Bristol than its neighbours, Bristol West and Bristol East. The current MP should have no problem maintaining her parliamentary seat for as long as she wants.

BRISTOL WEST — LD gain

		Electorate	Turnout	Change from	2001	Electorate	Turnout
		81,382	70.5%	2001		84,821	65.6%
Williams S	**LD**	**21,987**	**38.3%**	**9.4%**	**Lab**	**20,505**	**36.8%**
Davey V	Lab	16,859	29.4%	-7.4%	LD	16,079	28.9%
Martin D	C	15,429	26.9%	-1.9%	C	16,040	28.8%
Quinnell J	Greens	2,163	3.8%	0.3%	Greens	1,961	3.5%
Muir S	UKIP	439	0.8%	-0.1%	SLP	590	1.1%
Kennedy B	SLP	329	0.6%	-0.5%	UKIP	490	0.9%
Reid D	Baths	190	0.3%				
Lab to LD swing	**8.4%**	**57,396**		**LD maj 5,128**		**55,665**	**Lab maj 4,426**
				8.9%			8%

STEPHEN WILLIAMS b 11 Oct 1966. MP 2005-. Contested Bristol South 1997, Bristol West 2001. Bristol City Council: Cllr 1995-99; Leader Liberal Democrat Group/Shadow Council Leader 1995-1997; Avon Council 1993-1996: Deputy Leader/Group Chair Liberal Democrat Group. Tax manager: Kraft Jacobs Suchard Ltd, Cheltenham Head Office 1995; Grant Thornton, Cheltenham Head Office 1996-1998; Grant Thornton, Bristol Office 1998-. Ed Mountain Ash Comprehensive School; BA history, Bristol University.

This is the most diverse of the city's constituencies, with its mixture of students, minorities, and wealthy professionals. Bristol West's varied character is reflected in its marginality and it was a genuine three-way fight in the election. The Liberal Democrat's opposition to tutition fees combined with the nationwide swing away from Labour was enough to give Bristol West its first Lib Dem MP since World War II.

BROMLEY AND CHISLEHURST — C hold

		Electorate	Turnout	Change from	2001	Electorate	Turnout
		71,173	64.8%	2001		68,763	62.9%
Forth E	**C**	**23,583**	**51.1%**	**1.6%**	**C**	**21,412**	**49.5%**
Reeves R	Lab	10,241	22.2%	-6.4%	Lab	12,375	28.6%
Brooks P	LD	9,368	20.3%	1.4%	LD	8,180	18.9%
Hooper D	UKIP	1,475	3.2%	0.3%	UKIP	1,264	2.9%
Garrett A	Greens	1,470	3.2%				
Lab to C swing	**4%**	**46,137**		**C maj 13,342**		**43,231**	**C maj 9,037**
				28.9%			20.9%

ERIC FORTH b 9 Sept 1944. MP for Mid Worcestershire 1983-97, for Bromley and Chislehurst 1997-. Shadow Leader of the House 2001-03; Education and Employment Dept Min of State 1995-97; Education Dept: Min of State 1994-95, Schools Parly Under-Sec of State 1992-94; Joint Parly Under-Sec: Employment Dept 1990-92, Trade and Industry Dept Industry and Consumer Affairs 1988-90. Member Chairmen's Panel 2003, joint Statutory Instruments select cttee 2003-. MEP Birmingham North 1979-84. Manager. PC 1997. Ed Glasgow Univ.

The area is dominated by commuters to London, while recent redevelopments have turned it into an attraction for shoppers. Containing the former Kent market town of Bromley and the wealthy residential area of Chislehurst, this is as close to a traditional suburb as can be found in London.

BROMSGROVE — C hold

		Electorate	Turnout	Change from	2001	Electorate	Turnout
		70,762	67.6%	2001		68,081	67.1%
Kirkbride J	**C**	**24,387**	**51%**	**-0.7%**	**C**	**23,640**	**51.7%**
Jones D	Lab	14,307	29.9%	-4%	Lab	15,502	33.9%
Haswell S	LD	7,197	15.1%	3.2%	LD	5,430	11.9%
Buckingham P	UKIP	1,919	4%	1.6%	UKIP	1,112	2.4%
Lab to C swing	**1.7%**	**47,810**		**C maj 10,080**		**45,684**	**C maj 8,138**
				21.1%			17.8%

JULIE KIRKBRIDE b 5 June 1960. Culture, Media and Sport Shadow Sec of State 2003-04. Member select cttees on: Catering 1998-, Trade and Industry 2004-. Vice-chair all-party childcare group 2002-. Member: Inter-Parliamentary Union executive cttee 2001-, Commonwealth Parliamentary Association UK branch 1999-. Journalist/researcher/producer 1983-97. Ed BA economics/history, MA, Girton Coll, Cambridge; Graduate Sch of Journalism, California Univ.

Typically a Conservative safe seat, Bromsgrove is a sleepy suburban constituency presided over by Julie Kirkbride. Housing development is a hotly debated issue for constituents, with many opposing plans to build on greenbelt areas. Stretching beyond suburbia, farming represents an important feature of the economy. The impact of Rover's disintegration on the managerial workforce of the constituency will be potentially damaging.

BROXBOURNE — C hold

		Electorate	Turnout	Change from	2001	Electorate	Turnout
		68,106	59.6%	2001		67,897	55.7%
Walker C	**C**	**21,878**	**53.8%**	**-0.3%**	**C**	**20,487**	**54.1%**
Bolden J	Lab	10,369	25.5%	-4.9%	Lab	11,494	30.4%
Porrer A	LD	4,973	12.2%	1.2%	LD	4,158	11%
Emerson A	BNP	1,929	4.8%	2.6%	UKIP	858	2.3%
Harvey M	UKIP	1,479	3.6%	1.3%	BNP	848	2.2%
Lab to C swing	**2.3%**	**40,628**		**C maj 11,509**		**37,845**	**C maj 8,993**
				28.3%			23.8%

CHARLES WALKER b 11 September 1967. MP 2005-. Contested Ealing North 2001 election. Communications director CSQ Plc 1997-2001; director Blue Arrow Ltd 1999-2001; director LSM Processing Ltd 2002-04; director Debitwise 2004-. Ed American School of London; politics and American history, Oregon University, USA.

Set in the heart of the Lea valley, the constituency of Broxbourne lies in a predominantly urban corner of south-east Hertfordshire. There has been some commercial development here but the constituency is mainly residential with most of its population based in a thin strip of commuter towns and villages running up the western side of the river Lea. Conservative since its creation, Broxbourne is firm ground for the Tories.

BROXTOWE — Lab hold

		Electorate 71,121	Turnout 68.6%	Change from 2001	2001	Electorate 73,665	Turnout 66.5%
Palmer N	**Lab**	**20,457**	**41.9%**	**-6.7%**	**Lab**	**23,836**	**48.6%**
Seely B	C	18,161	37.2%	0.5%	C	17,963	36.7%
Watts D	LD	7,837	16.1%	1.4%	LD	7,205	14.7%
Anderson P	Greens	896	1.8%				
Wolfe P	UKIP	695	1.4%				
Hockney D	Veritas	590	1.2%				
Gregory M	Ind	170	0.4%				
Lab to C swing	**3.6%**	**48,806**		**Lab maj 2,296** 4.7%		**49,004**	**Lab maj 5,873** 12%

NICK PALMER b 5 Feb 1950. MP 1997-. Dept for Environment, Food and Rural Affairs team PPS 2003-. Vice-chair all-party groups: animal welfare 2000-, world govt 2001-, fibromyalgia 2004-. Secretary all-party groups: Denmark 2001, internet 2001-, pluralism in education 2003-. National executive member Lab Animal Welfare Soc 1999-. Health and safety officer MSF Brighton 1975-76. Computing career. Ed maths / computing, Copenhagen Univ; maths PhD, Birkbeck Coll, London Univ.

This seat forms part of Nottingham's suburbs including the towns of Beeston and Stapleford. This is a relatively affluent area with high levels of owner occupation, a high percentage of full-time employees and low unemployment. Beeston is the main administrative centre with three main employers – Boots, GPT and Pafec. The seat was traditionally a Conservative stronghold, but has been in Labour hands since they took control in 1997.

BUCKINGHAM — C hold

		Electorate 70,265	Turnout 68.8%	Change from 2001	2001	Electorate 65,270	Turnout 69.4%
Bercow J	**C**	**27,748**	**57.4%**	**3.7%**	**C**	**24,296**	**53.7%**
Greene D	Lab	9,619	19.9%	-4.3%	Lab	10,971	24.2%
Croydon L	LD	9,508	19.7%	-0.3%	LD	9,037	20%
Williams D	UKIP	1,432	3%	0.9%	UKIP	968	2.1%
Lab to C swing	**4%**	**48,307**		**C maj 18,129** 37.5%		**45,272**	**C maj 13,325** 29.4%

JOHN BERCOW b 19 Jan 1963. MP 1997-. Shadow: Internat Devt Sec of State 2003-04, Treasury Chief Sec 2001-02. Opposition spokes: education and employment 1999-2000, home affairs 2000-01, work and pensions 2002. Member select cttees: Internat Devt 2004-, Procedure 2004-. Chair all-party Burma group 2004-. Exec 1922 cttee member 1998-99. Cllr Lambeth Borough Council 1986-90. Credit analyst/public affairs consultant/board director/adviser. Ed BA govt, Essex Univ.

This large and predominantly rural constituency is centred around the small market town of Buckingham, but most voters are scattered throughout many affluent villages. Although much of the constituency is rural, most of the residents commute to London or to nearby Milton Keynes. Industries include agriculture, car components and the service sector. Labour may have represented Buckingham in the past, but this is now one of the Conservatives' safest seats.

BURNLEY — Lab hold

		Electorate 65,869	Turnout 59.2%	Change from 2001	2001	Electorate 66,270	Turnout 55.7%
Ussher K	**Lab**	**14,999**	**38.5%**	**-10.8%**	**Lab**	**18,195**	**49.3%**
Birtwistle G	LD	9,221	23.6%	7.4%	C	7,697	20.9%
Brooks H	Ind	5,786	14.8%		LD	5,975	16.2%
Miah Y	C	4,206	10.8%	-10.1%	BNP	4,151	11.3%
Starr L	BNP	4,003	10.3%	-1%	UKIP	866	2.3%
Slater J	Ind	392	1%				
McDowell R	UKIP	376	1%	-1.3%			
Lab to LD swing	**9.1%**	**38,983**		**Lab maj 5,778** 14.8%		**36,884**	**Lab maj 10,498** 28.5%

KITTY USSHER b 18 March 1971. MP 2005-. Lambeth Council: Councillor 1998-2002; chair environment scrutiny committee 2000-01; chair finance scrutiny committee 2001-02. Parliamentary researcher 1993-97; Economist Intelligence Unit 1997-98; Centre for European Reform 1998-2000; chief economist Britain in Europe 2000-01; special adviser Patricia Hewitt/DTI 2001-04. Ed BA PPE, Balliol College Oxford; MSc economics, Birkbeck College London.

A safe Labour seat, Burnley is one of the East Lancashire towns linked by the M65 between Blackburn and Colne. The constituency includes some of the surrounding Pennine moors. Once a centre for textiles and mining that declined in the 1960s and 70s, the town's industries now include high technology, engineering and manufacturing in areas such as aerospace, plastics, electronics and car components.

BURTON — Lab hold

		Electorate	Turnout	Change from	2001	Electorate	Turnout
		78,556	61%	2001		75,194	61.8%
Dean J	**Lab**	**19,701**	**41.1%**	**-7.9%**	**Lab**	**22,783**	**49%**
Pepper A	C	18,280	38.2%	-0.4%	C	17,934	38.6%
Johnson S	LD	6,236	13%	3.4%	LD	4,468	9.6%
Russell J	BNP	1,840	3.8%		UKIP	984	2.1%
Lancaster P	UKIP	913	1.9%	-0.2%	ProLife	288	0.6%
Buxton B	Veritas	912	1.9%				
Lab to C swing	**3.8%**	**47,882**		**Lab maj 1,421**		**46,457**	**Lab maj 4,849**
				3%			10.4%

JANET DEAN b 28 Jan 1949. MP 1997-. Member select cttees: Home Affairs 1999-, Catering 1997-. Chair all-party lupus group 2000-; vice-chair all-party back care group 2002-. Vice-chair West Midlands regional Lab MPs group 2002-. Cllr: Staffordshire County Council 1981-97, East Staffordshire Borough Council 1991-97 (mayor 1996-97), Uttoxeter town council 1995-97. Member South-East Staffordshire health auth 1981-90. Clerk 1965-70. Ed Winsford Verdin Grammar Sch.

Following a Labour victory in 1997, Burton has become a key marginal, with strong Labour support in the urban centres of Burton upon Trent and Uttoxeter counterbalanced by Tory loyalty in the surrounding rural areas. Brewing forms the economic and cultural base of the constituency. Local elections have shown the Conservatives to be very competitive in this, and neighbouring constituencies.

BURY NORTH — Lab hold

		Electorate	Turnout	Change from	2001	Electorate	Turnout
		72,268	61.5%	2001		71,108	63%
Chaytor D	**Lab**	**19,130**	**43.1%**	**-8.1%**	**Lab**	**22,945**	**51.2%**
Nuttall D	C	16,204	36.5%	-0.1%	C	16,413	36.6%
Davison W	LD	6,514	14.7%	2.6%	LD	5,430	12.1%
Clough S	BNP	1,790	4%				
Silver P	UKIP	476	1.1%				
O'Neill R	SLP	172	0.4%				
Upton I	Veritas	153	0.3%				
Lab to C swing	**4%**	**44,439**		**Lab maj 2,926**		**44,788**	**Lab maj 6,532**
				6.6%			14.6%

DAVID CHAYTOR b 3 Aug 1949. MP 1997-. Member select cttees on: Education and Skills 2001-, Environmental Audit 2002-. Chair all-party groups: further education and lifelong learning 1999-, intelligent energy 2003-; sec all-party Globe UK group 2002-. Cllr Calderdale Council 1982-97 (chair: education/highways/economic development cttees). Academic career 1973-97. Ed Bury Grammar Sch; BA/MPhil, London Univ; PGCE, Leeds Univ.

Bury is one of the more relatively prosperous former textile towns in Lancashire, bolstered by alternative industries, and now part of the Manchester commuter belt. Although a relatively safe Labour seat, the Bury North division is the more marginal of the town's two seats, including as it does the small towns to the north of the town centre as well as Bury itself.

BURY SOUTH — Lab hold

		Electorate	Turnout	Change from	2001	Electorate	Turnout
		66,898	58.5%	2001		67,276	58.8%
Lewis I	**Lab**	**19,741**	**50.4%**	**-8.8%**	**Lab**	**23,406**	**59.2%**
Williams A	C	10,829	27.7%	0.8%	C	10,634	26.9%
D'Albert V	LD	6,968	17.8%	3.9%	LD	5,499	13.9%
Greenhalgh J	UKIP	1,059	2.7%				
Hossack Y	Ind	557	1.4%				
Lab to C swing	**4.8%**	**39,154**		**Lab maj 8,912**		**39,539**	**Lab maj 12,772**
				22.8%			32.3%

IVAN LEWIS b 4 March 1967. MP 1997-. Economic Sec HM Treasury 2005-. Education and Skills Dept Parly Under-Sec of State: Skills and Vocational Education 2003-05, Young People and Adult Skills 2002-03, Adult Learning and Skills 2002, Young People and Learning 2001-02; PPS to Stephen Byers 1999-2001. Chair Bury South Lab Party 1991-96. Cllr Bury Metropolitan Borough Council 1990-98. Charity exec. Chair Bury MENCAP 1989-92. Trustee Holocaust Educational Trust. Ed Stand Coll; Bury Further Education Coll.

Despite its name, Bury South does not have much to do with the town of Bury, but is instead centred on Radcliffe, a working-class town that is lumped in with its larger neighbour. It also includes Manchester's affluent northern suburbs, such as Prestwich. Although held by the Tories until the 1997 watershed, its massive and continuing swing to Labour means that it is now no longer the marginal seat that it once was.

BURY ST EDMUNDS — C hold

		Electorate	Turnout	Change from	2001	Electorate	Turnout
		79,658	66.1%	2001		76,146	66%
Ruffley D	**C**	**24,332**	**46.2%**	**2.7%**	**C**	**21,850**	**43.5%**
Monaghan D	Lab	14,402	27.4%	-11.1%	Lab	19,347	38.5%
Chappell D	LD	10,423	19.8%	5.9%	LD	6,998	13.9%
Howlett J	UKIP	1,859	3.5%	1.8%	UKIP	831	1.7%
Manning G	Greens	1,603	3.1%		Ind	651	1.3%
					SLP	580	1.2%
Lab to C swing	**6.9%**	**52,619**		**C maj 9,930**		**50,257**	**C maj 2,503**
				18.9%			5%

DAVID RUFFLEY b 18 April 1962. MP 1997-. Opposition whip 2004-. Special adviser to Ken Clarke MP as: Education and Science Sec of State 1991-92, Home Sec 1992-93, Chancellor of the Exchequer 1993-96. Vice-chair all-party groups: small business 2001-, BBC 2002-, Vietnam 2004-. Member 1922 Cttee Executive 2003-04. Conservative Party strategic economic consultant 1996-97. Solicitor. Ed Bolton Boys' Sch; BA law, Queen's Coll, Cambridge.

A fairly new constituency in everything but name, Bury St Edmunds encompasses a number of rural communities and market towns in northern Suffolk. The local economy largely revolves around the farming and refinement of agricultural produce and the town of Bury St Edmunds has the largest sugar beet factory in the country. Despite a near brush with Labour in 1997, the constituency has since reverted comfortably to Conservative representation.

CAERNARFON — PIC hold

		Electorate	Turnout	Change from	2001	Electorate	Turnout
		46,393	60.4%	2001		46,850	62%
Williams H	**PIC**	**12,747**	**45.5%**	**1.1%**	**PIC**	**12,894**	**44.4%**
Eaglestone M	Lab	7,538	26.9%	-5.4%	Lab	9,383	32.3%
ab Owain M	LD	3,508	12.5%	6.2%	C	4,403	15.2%
Opperman G	C	3,483	12.4%	-2.8%	LD	1,823	6.3%
Williams E	UKIP	723	2.6%	0.7%	UKIP	550	1.9%
Lab to PIC swing	**3.3%**	**27,999**		**PIC maj 5,209**		**29,053**	**PIC maj 3,511**
				18.6%			12.1%

HYWEL WILLIAMS b 14 May 1953. MP 2001-. Plaid Cymru spokes: work and pensions, social security, health, disability, 2001-, internat devt 2004-. Member Welsh Affairs select cttee 2004-. Plaid Cymru: policy cabinet 1999-, soc security and older people policy developer 1999-. Member: Welsh Cttee Central Council Education and Training in Soc Work, European standing cttee B 2002-04. Social worker, project worker, social work/policy lecturer, consultant, author. Ed Wales Univ: BSc psychology, Cardiff; CQSW social work, Bangor.

The constituency of Caernarfon covers a large rural area and has a long coastline, running from Caernarfon Bay to Cardigan Bay. It also includes the mountain of Snowdon and contains the impressive Caernarfon Castle. There are a very large number of Welsh speakers in the seat and there is a fierce sense of Welsh identity here which makes it a natural place to be a Plaid Cymru stronghold.

CAERPHILLY — Lab hold

		Electorate	Turnout	Change from	2001	Electorate	Turnout
		66,939	58.6%	2001		67,593	57.2%
David W	**Lab**	**22,190**	**56.6%**	**-1.6%**	**Lab**	**22,597**	**58.2%**
Whittle L	PIC	6,831	17.4%	-3.6%	PIC	8,172	21%
Watson S	C	5,711	14.6%	3.2%	C	4,413	11.4%
Ali A	LD	3,861	9.8%	0.4%	LD	3,649	9.4%
Beard G	FW	636	1.6%				
PIC to Lab swing	**1%**	**39,229**		**Lab maj 15,359**		**38,831**	**Lab maj 14,425**
				39.2%			37.3%

WAYNE DAVID b 1 July 1957. MP 2001-. PPS to Adam Ingram, MoD 2005-; Team PPS MoD 2005. Member select cttees: European Scrutiny 2001-, Standards and Privileges 2004. Chair all-party Poland group 2003-. 1994-98: leader European parly Lab Party, ex-officio Lab Party NEC member. Cllr Cefn Cribwr Community Council 1985-91: chair 1986-87. Vice-pres Cardiff UN assocn. MEP 1989-99. Pres Council for Wales of voluntary youth services. Teacher, tutor organiser, youth policy adviser. Ed Univ Coll, Cardiff: BA hist, Welsh hist, PGCE FE; econ hist research, Univ Coll, Swansea.

This constituency covers the lower half of the Rhymney Valley to the north of Cardiff. It includes areas of upland and rural countryside. Many of the towns and villages dotted along the valley owe their existence to the former mines and iron works. They include Bargoed, Ystrad Mynach, the town of Caerphilly itself, Bedwas, and Machen. This is a rock solid Labour seat and looks set to remain so.

CAITHNESS, SUTHERLAND AND EASTER ROSS — LD hold

		Electorate	Turnout		2001
		46,837	59.1%		
Thurso J	**LD**	**13,957**	**50.4%**		No comparable results due to boundary changes
Jamieson A	Lab	5,789	20.9%		
Shirron K	SNP	3,686	13.3%		
Ross A	C	2,835	10.2%		
Campbell G	Ind	848	3.1%		
Ivory L	SSP	548	2%		
Lab to LD swing (notional)	**7.6%**	**27,663**		**LD maj 8,168** 29.5%	

JOHN THURSO b 10 Sept 1953. MP for Caithness, Sutherland and Easter Ross 2001-05, for new Caithness, Sutherland and Easter Ross 2005-. Lib Dem Shadow Sec of State Transport and Scotland 2003-. Lib Dem whip 2001-02. Member House of Lords 1995-99. Lib Dem Lords spokes 1996-99, Scottish Lib Dem spokes 2001-. Lib Dem spokes 2001-03. Member Culture, Media and Sport select cttee 2001-. Member Lib Dem party federal policy cttee 1999-2001. Hotelier, chairman/dir. Pres/fellow Tourism Society 1999-. Ed HCIMA membership exam, Westminster Tech Coll.

Caithness, Sutherland and Easter Ross is the northernmost tip of the British mainland. Easter Ross (where the electorate is concentrated), depends on oil while Alness and Ardross bring a little light industry to the south of the seat. However, fishing and farming and tourism (especially at John O'Groats) mainly sustain these scattered northern communities. The extension of the southern boundary has increased Labour and SNP support, but the Liberal Democrats remain stronger than either challenger.

CALDER VALLEY — Lab hold

		Electorate	Turnout	Change from	2001	Electorate	Turnout
		71,325	67%	2001		69,870	67.9%
McCafferty C	**Lab**	**18,426**	**38.6%**	**-4.1%**	**Lab**	**20,244**	**42.7%**
Truss L	C	17,059	35.7%	-0.5%	C	17,150	36.2%
Ingleton L	LD	9,027	18.9%	2.9%	LD	7,596	16%
Gregory J	BNP	1,887	4%		Greens	1,034	2.2%
Palmer P	Greens	1,371	2.9%	0.7%	UKIP	729	1.5%
					LCA	672	1.4%
Lab to C swing	**1.8%**	**47,770**		**Lab maj 1,367** 2.9%		**47,425**	**Lab maj 3,094** 6.5%

CHRISTINE McCAFFERTY b 14 Oct 1945. MP 1997-. Member Internat Devt select cttee 2001-. Chair all-party groups: population, devt and reproductive health 1999-, girlguiding UK 2000-, Friends of Islam 2003-. Cllr Calderdale: MBC 1991-97, district council 1991-, Hebden Royd town council 1991-95. Panel member: Ind Education Appeals 1991-97, Ind Advisory 1991-97. Parly patron Women in Business Internat. Women's health counsellor. Ed Footscray High Sch, Melbourne, Australia.

This huge, sprawling constituency on the eastern side of the Pennines was won by Labour with an 11 per cent majority in 1997, and it remains a marginal seat. Nowadays textiles play little part in the economic well-being of Calder Valley, though agriculture survives in strength, as does engineering and furniture manufacture. Most of the seat's workers are employed in non-manual occupations, and there is low unemployment and a 75 per cent owner-occupancy rate.

CAMBERWELL AND PECKHAM — Lab hold

		Electorate	Turnout	Change from	2001	Electorate	Turnout
		55,739	52%	2001		53,687	46.8%
Harman H	**Lab**	**18,933**	**65.3%**	**-4.3%**	**Lab**	**17,473**	**69.6%**
Porter R	LD	5,450	18.8%	5.5%	LD	3,350	13.3%
Lee J	C	2,841	9.8%	-1.1%	C	2,740	10.9%
Ingram P	Greens	1,172	4%	0.8%	Greens	805	3.2%
Penhallow D	UKIP	350	1.2%		SA	478	1.9%
Sharkey M	SLP	132	0.5%	-0.2%	SLP	188	0.7%
Kulkarni S	WRP	113	0.4%	0.1%	WRP	70	0.3%
Lab to LD swing	**4.9%**	**28,991**		**Lab maj 13,483** 46.5%		**25,104**	**Lab maj 14,123** 56.3%

HARRIET HARMAN b 30 July 1950. MP for Peckham 1982-97, for Camberwell and Peckham 1997-. Minister of State Dept for Constitutional Affairs 2005-, Solicitor General 2001-05, Social Security Sec of State and Min for Women 1997-98. Shadow: Sec of State for Social Security 1996-97, Health 1995-96, Employment 1994-95; Chief Treasury Sec 1992-94; Social Services Min 1984 and 1985-87. Health spokes 1987-92. Lab Party NEC member 1993-98. QC 2001. PC 1997. Chair Childcare Commission 1999-. Legal officer 1978-82. Ed BA politics, York Univ.

In this inner city south London seat unemployment is high and manual and unskilled workers predominate. It has a reputation for deprivation and crime. However, it is a vibrant and diverse area, and there has been extensive regeneration of its worst areas in recent years. The Conservatives have failed to appeal to any major sectors of the community and Labour is still identified as the only party to represent its interests.

CAMBRIDGE — LD gain

		Electorate 70,154	Turnout 62.1%	Change from 2001	2001	Electorate 70,664	Turnout 60.6%
Howarth D	**LD**	**19,152**	**43.9%**	**18.8%**	**Lab**	**19,316**	**45.1%**
Campbell A	Lab	14,813	34%	-11.1%	LD	10,737	25.1%
Lyon I	C	7,193	16.5%	-6.4%	C	9,829	22.9%
Lucas-Smith M	Greens	1,245	2.9%	-0.4%	Greens	1,413	3.3%
Davies H	UKIP	569	1.3%	0.1%	SA	716	1.7%
Woodcock T	Respect	477	1.1%		UKIP	532	1.2%
Wilkinson G	Ind	60	0.1%				
Lab to LD swing	**15%**	**43,596**		**LD maj 4,339** 10%		**42,836**	**Lab maj 8,579** 20%

DAVID HOWARTH b 10 Nov 1958. MP 2005-. Cambridge City Council: Councillor 1987-2004, Leader Liberal Democrats 1990-2004, leader of opposition 1992-2000, leader 2000-04. Law lecturer, Cambridge University 1988-. Ed Queen Mary's Grammar School, Walsall; MPhil Cambridge University

Cambridge is world famous as being home to one of the two most prestigious universities in England. The university dominates the city in every way, although increasingly the high technology sector is also rising to prominence in the form of 'Silicon Fen'. Cambridge is a most unpredictable constituency and displays very few traits of loyalty to any one particular party. Its volatility served in favour of the Liberal Democrats in 2005

NORTH EAST CAMBRIDGESHIRE — C hold

		Electorate 85,079	Turnout 59.8%	Change from 2001	2001	Electorate 79,891	Turnout 60.1%
Moss M	**C**	**24,181**	**47.5%**	**-0.6%**	**C**	**23,132**	**48.1%**
Costain F	Lab	15,280	30%	-4.9%	Lab	16,759	34.9%
Dean A	LD	8,693	17.1%	3.1%	LD	6,733	14%
Baynes L	UKIP	2,723	5.4%	2.9%	UKIP	1,189	2.5%
					ProLife	238	0.5%
Lab to C swing	**2.2%**	**50,877**		**C maj 8,901** 17.5%		**48,051**	**C maj 6,373** 13.3%

MALCOLM MOSS b 6 March 1943. MP 1987-. Shadow Minister: the Family and Culture, Media and Sport 2005-, Home Affairs 2004-05, Home, Constitutional and Legal Affairs 2003-04, Culture, Media and Sport 2002-03, Transport 2002; Parly Under-Sec N Ireland Office 1994-97; PPS to: Sir Patrick Mayhew 1993-94, Tristan Garel-Jones 1991-93. Opposition whip 1997. Opposition spokes 1997-2002. Cllr: Wisbech Town 1979-87, Fenland DC 1983-87, Cambridgeshire CC 1985-87. Teacher/insurance consultant/MD. Ed BA geog, St John's Coll, Cambridge.

Agriculture, including horticulture and market gardening, is important, although a large proportion of the population is employed in food processing and other light industry. For a safe Tory seat the social mix is unusual: the percentage of white-collar employees is very low while 52.5 per cent of the population can be classified as skilled manual or partly skilled.

NORTH WEST CAMBRIDGESHIRE — C hold

		Electorate 79,694	Turnout 61.6%	Change from 2001	2001	Electorate 71,247	Turnout 61.7%
Vara S	**C**	**22,504**	**45.8%**	**-4%**	**C**	**21,895**	**49.8%**
Orhan A	Lab	12,671	25.8%	-5.6%	Lab	13,794	31.4%
Souter J	LD	11,232	22.9%	7.1%	LD	6,957	15.8%
Brown R	UKIP	2,685	5.5%	3.5%	UKIP	881	2%
					Ind	429	1%
Lab to C swing	**0.8%**	**49,092**		**C maj 9,833** 20%		**43,956**	**C maj 8,101** 18.4%

SHAILESH VARA b 4 Sept 1960. MP 2005-. Contested Birmingham Ladywood 1997, Northampton South 2001 general elections. Solicitor Richards Butler 1989-90; Senior legal adviser and business consultant London First 1998-99; Solicitor CMS Cameron McKenna; Vice-president Small Business Bureau. Ed Aylesbury Grammar School; law, Brunel University

The seat comprises half of Huntingdonshire District and the western region of Cambridgeshire. It extends to the western half of Peterborough. A prosperous region, with a fairly young population and much new, private housing, employment here is mostly in skilled and managerial positions. There are also large numbers of farmers working the richest crop-production soil in the country. Despite problems in Peterborough wards the Tories' grip on power here remains secure.

SOUTH CAMBRIDGESHIRE — C hold

		Electorate	Turnout	Change from	2001	Electorate	Turnout
		77,022	68.4%	2001		72,095	67.1%
Lansley A	**C**	**23,676**	**45%**	**0.8%**	**C**	**21,387**	**44.2%**
Dickson A	LD	15,675	29.8%	2.9%	LD	12,984	26.9%
Wilson S	Lab	10,189	19.4%	-4.9%	Lab	11,737	24.3%
Page R	UKIP	1,556	3%	1.2%	Greens	1,182	2.4%
Saggers S	Greens	1,552	3%	0.6%	UKIP	875	1.8%
					ProLife	176	0.4%
C to LD swing	**1.1%**	**52,648**		**C maj 8,001**		**48,341**	**C maj 8,403**
				15.2%			17.4%

ANDREW LANSLEY b 11 Dec 1956. MP 1997-. Shadow: Cabinet Member 2004-, Sec of State Health 2003-, Chancellor of Duchy of Lancaster 1999-2001, Min for Cabinet Office and Policy Renewal 1999-2001. Member select cttees: Health 1997-98, Trade and Industry 2001-04. Vice-chair Con Party 1998-99. DTI 1979-87: Sec of State DTI private sec 1984-85. Principal Private Sec to Norman Tebbit 1985-87. British Chambers of Commerce policy dir/dep dir-general. Dir: Con research dept, Public Policy Unit. CBE 1996. Ed BA politics, Exeter Univ.

The safe Tory constituency is largely based on the former South West Cambridgeshire seat held by the Conservatives since 1983. Strangely, given its rural nature, the seat includes the most middle-class Cambridge City wards – Trumpington and Queen Edith's. Moreover, only a fraction of those who live in this rural seat work on the land, largely due to the many commuter-dominated villages in the seat, such as Gamlingay, Melbourne, Sawston, Ickleton, Little Shelford and Grantchester.

SOUTH EAST CAMBRIDGESHIRE — C hold

		Electorate	Turnout	Change from	2001	Electorate	Turnout
		85,901	65.3%	2001		81,663	63.5%
Paice J	**C**	**26,374**	**47.1%**	**2.9%**	**C**	**22,927**	**44.2%**
Chatfield J	LD	17,750	31.7%	4.8%	LD	13,937	26.9%
Ross F	Lab	11,936	21.3%	-5.1%	Lab	13,714	26.4%
					UKIP	1,308	2.5%
C to LD swing	**1%**	**56,060**		**C maj 8,624**		**51,886**	**C maj 8,990**
				15.4%			17.3%

JIM PAICE b 24 April 1949. MP 1987-. Shadow: Minister for Agriculture 2005-, Sec of State for Agriculture, Fisheries and Food 2004-05. Shadow Minister: Home Affairs 2004, Home, Constitutional and Legal Affairs 2003-04. Parly Under-Sec: Dept for Education and Employment 1995-97, Dept of Employment 1994-95. PPS to: John Gummer 1990-94, Baroness Trumpington 1989-90. Chair all-party Singapore group 2000-. Farmer/farm manager and contractor. Training/gen manager. Ed Nat Agriculture Dip, Writtle Agricultural Coll.

This large, predominantly rural, staunchly Conservative constituency stretches from the Cambridge commuter-land villages of Histon, Milton and Fulbourn to Linton on the county's borders with Essex and the small cathedral city of Ely towards the Cambridgeshire-Suffolk border. Although the seat was only created in 1983, it roughly resembled the old Cambridgeshire seat which Francis Pym held from 1961. Many of the smaller towns in the West are populated by Cambridge commuters.

CANNOCK CHASE — Lab hold

		Electorate	Turnout	Change from	2001	Electorate	Turnout
		75,194	57.4%	2001		73,467	55.9%
Wright T	**Lab**	**22,139**	**51.3%**	**-4.8%**	**Lab**	**23,049**	**56.1%**
Collard I	C	12,912	29.9%	-0.2%	C	12,345	30.1%
Pinkett J	LD	5,934	13.8%		LD	5,670	13.8%
Jenkins R	UKIP	2,170	5%				
Lab to C swing	**2.3%**	**43,155**		**Lab maj 9,227**		**41,064**	**Lab maj 10,704**
				21.4%			26.1%

TONY WRIGHT b 11 March 1948. MP for Cannock and Burntwood 1992-97, for Cannock Chase 1997-. PPS to Lord Irvine 1997-98. Member select cttees: Liaison 1999- (Sub-cttee 2002-), Public Administration (chair) 2001-. Chair all-party constitution and citizen group 2002-. Vice-chair Lab Party Office of Public Service departmental cttee 1997-2000. Co-chair Campaign for Freedom of Info 1997-99. Lecturer. Ed BSc economics, LSE; Harvard Univ; Balliol Coll, Oxford.

Improving economic fortunes have secured this seat under Tony Wright. Predominantly working class, with a long manufacturing history, Cannock Chase is experiencing a growing commuter population, most probably owing to its outstanding natural beauty. Sustained investment in regeneration over recent years has lowered the unemployment rate, and bolstered the local economy.

CANTERBURY — C hold

		Electorate 72,046	Turnout 66%	Change from 2001	2001	Electorate 74,144	Turnout 60.9%
Brazier J	**C**	**21,113**	**44.4%**	**2.9%**	**C**	**18,711**	**41.5%**
Hilton A	Lab	13,642	28.7%	-8.2%	Lab	16,642	36.9%
Barnard-Langston J	LD	10,059	21.1%	3.3%	LD	8,056	17.8%
Meaden G	Greens	1,521	3.2%	1.2%	Greens	920	2%
Moore J	UKIP	926	2%	0.2%	UKIP	803	1.8%
van de Benderskum R	LCA	326	0.7%				
Lab to C swing	**5.6%**	**47,587**		**C maj 7,471** 15.7%		**45,132**	**C maj 2,069** 4.6%

JULIAN BRAZIER b 24 July 1953. MP 1987-. Shadow Min: Transport 2005-, International Affairs 2003-05, Home Affairs 2003, Work and Pensions 2002-03. PPS to Gillian Shephard 1990-1993. Opposition whip 2001-02. Chair all-party groups: adoption 2001-, adventure and recreation in society 2004-. President Con Family Campaign 1995-2001. TA 1972-82, 1989-92 (territorial decoration 1993). Charter Consolidated Ltd 1975-84, management consultant 1984-87. Ed BA maths/philosophy, Brasenose Coll, Oxford; London Business Sch.

The constituency of Canterbury is best known for the cathedral city from which it takes its name, but it also includes a number of surrounding villages, and the seaside town of Whitstable (famous for its oysters) on the North Kent coastline. Agriculture, tourism and light engineering are the major employers, along with a large education sector. Once rock solid Conservative territory, it is no longer the bastion of Tory support it was under its old boundaries.

CARDIFF CENTRAL — LD gain

		Electorate 61,001	Turnout 59.2%	Change from 2001	2001	Electorate 59,785	Turnout 58.3%
Willott J	**LD**	**17,991**	**49.8%**	**13.1%**	**Lab/C**	**13,451**	**38.6%**
Jones J	Lab/C	12,398	34.3%	-4.3%	LD	12,792	36.7%
Mohindra G	C	3,339	9.2%	-6.7%	C	5,537	15.9%
Grigg R	PIC	1,271	3.5%	-1.3%	PIC	1,680	4.8%
Hughes F	UKIP	386	1.1%		Greens	661	1.9%
Savoury A	Ind	168	0.5%		SA	283	0.8%
Beany C	NMB	159	0.4%		UKIP	221	0.6%
Taylor-Dawson C	Vote Dream	37	0.1%		ProLife	217	0.6%
Lab/C to LD swing	**8.7%**	**36,132**		**LD maj 5,593** 15.5%		**34,842**	**Lab/C maj 659** 1.9%

JENNY WILLOTT b 29 May 1974. MP 2005-. Contested Cardiff Central 2001 general election; councillor London Borough of Merton 1998-2000. Head of advocacy UNICEF UK 2001-03; Area manager Victim Support Wales 2003. Ed classics, St Mary's College, Durham; Development studies, London School of Economics

Cardiff Central comprises the city centre and includes the Castle, the University, the City Hall, the Law Courts, the National Museum, Cardiff Royal Infirmary and a large shopping area. The seat also includes the Millennium Stadium, the magnificent new home of Welsh rugby. The large student population is important here. In recent years the Lib Dems have made this their foothold in the Welsh capital.

CARDIFF NORTH — Lab hold

		Electorate 64,341	Turnout 70.5%	Change from 2001	2001	Electorate 62,634	Turnout 69%
Morgan J	**Lab**	**17,707**	**39%**	**-6.9%**	**Lab**	**19,845**	**45.9%**
Morgan J	C	16,561	36.5%	4.9%	C	13,680	31.6%
Dixon J	LD	8,483	18.7%	3.4%	LD	6,631	15.3%
Rowlands J	PIC	1,936	4.3%	-1.4%	PIC	2,471	5.7%
Hulston D	UKIP	534	1.2%	-0.2%	UKIP	613	1.4%
Hobbs A	FW	138	0.3%				
Taylor-Dawson C	Vote Dream	1					
Lab to C swing	**5.9%**	**45,360**		**Lab maj 1,146** 2.5%		**43,240**	**Lab maj 6,165** 14.3%

JULIE MORGAN b 2 Nov 1944. MP 1997-. Member select cttees: Welsh Affairs 1997-, Administration 2001, 2002-. Chair all-party groups: sex equality 2001-, children in Wales 2001-. Hon treasurer: Welsh regional group of Lab MPs 1999-, Parly Lab Party women's group. Cllr: South Glamorgan 1985-96, Cardiff 1996. Principal officer/devt officer W Glamorgan CC 1983-87, senior social worker 1985-87. Asst dir Child Care, Bernados 1987-. Ed BA Eng, King's Coll, London Univ; Manchester Univ; Postgrad Social Admin dip, CQSW, Cardiff Univ.

Cardiff North is commonly seen as the most middle-class of the four Cardiff seats. It contains the University Hospital of Wales and some of the most popular residential areas in the city. It has the highest rate of home-ownership in Wales at over 83% and the lowest unemployment rate in the principality. Historically a Labour/Conservative marginal seat it returned to that status at the 2005 general election.

CARDIFF SOUTH AND PENARTH — Lab hold

		Electorate 65,710	Turnout 56.2%	Change from 2001	2001	Electorate 62,627	Turnout 57.1%
Michael A	**Lab/C**	**17,447**	**47.3%**	**-8.9%**	**Lab/C**	**20,094**	**56.2%**
Green V	C	8,210	22.2%	0.4%	C	7,807	21.8%
Cox G	LD	7,529	20.3%	7.5%	LD	4,572	12.8%
Toby J	PIC	2,023	5.5%		PIC	1,983	5.5%
Matthews J	Greens	729	2%		UKIP	501	1.4%
Tuttle J	UKIP	522	1.4%		SAP	427	1.2%
Bartlett D	SAP	269	0.7%		ProLife	367	1%
Taylor A	Ind	104	0.3%				
Taylor-Dawson C	Vote Dream	79	0.2%				
Lab/C to C swing	**4.7%**	**36,912**		**Lab/C maj 9,237** 25%		**35,751**	**Lab/C maj 12,287** 34.4%

ALUN MICHAEL b 22 Aug 1943. MP 1987-. Min of State: Dept of Trade and Industry 2005-, Defra 2001-05. Sec of State Wales 1998-99. AM 1999-2000: First Secretary Wales 1999-2000. Minister of State Home Office 1997-98. Opposition: whip 1987-88, spokes: 1988-97. Member: Nat Exec, Co-operative Party, Commonwealth Parly Assocn. Cllr Cardiff CC 1973-89. JP Cardiff 1972-. Journalist, youth and community worker. NUJ branch sec 1967-70. PC 1998. Ed Colwyn Bar Grammar Sch; BA, Keele Univ.

The constituency of Cardiff South and Penarth includes four very distinct areas, in two local authorities. The wards in Cardiff include the old docklands, now reborn as the regenerated Cardiff Bay. These sections of the city are home to a multitude of ethnic groups. It also includes outer city suburbs such as Trowbridge and the pretty Victorian seaside resort of Penarth. The seat is a safe Labour constituency which has long been under the party's control.

CARDIFF WEST — Lab hold

		Electorate 59,847	Turnout 57.8%	Change from 2001	2001	Electorate 58,348	Turnout 58.4%
Brennan K	**Lab**	**15,729**	**45.5%**	**-9.1%**	**Lab**	**18,594**	**54.6%**
Baker S	C	7,562	21.9%	0.6%	C	7,273	21.3%
Goldsworthy A	LD	6,060	17.5%	4.4%	LD	4,458	13.1%
McEvoy N	PIC	4,316	12.5%	2.8%	PIC	3,296	9.7%
Callan J	UKIP	727	2.1%	0.7%	UKIP	462	1.4%
Taylor-Dawson C	Vote Dream	167	0.5%				
Lab to C swing	**4.9%**	**34,561**		**Lab maj 8,167** 23.6%		**34,083**	**Lab maj 11,321** 33.2%

KEVIN BRENNAN b 16 Oct 1959. MP 2001-. PPS to Alan Milburn 2004-05. Asst govt whip 2005-. Member Public Administration select cttee 2001-05. Chair all-party group 2003-. Member: Socialist Health Assocn, (exec) Lab campaign electoral reform. Chair Cardiff West constituency Lab Party 1998-2000. Cllr Cardiff CC. Editor/organiser Cwmbran Community Press 1982-84. Teacher, research officer/special adviser to Rhodri Morgan. Ed BA PPE, Pembroke Coll, Oxford; PGCE hist, Univ Coll of Wales, Cardiff; MSc education management, Glamorgan Univ.

Cardiff West is a residential constituency of mixed areas including the inner city wards of Riverside and Canton, the middle-class Radyr and St Fagans which, while socially middle class, politically at least, have tended to remain Labour, and the large council estates in Ely and Caerau on the city's south western edge. It is a safe Labour seat which would only be won by the Tories in landslide years such as 1983.

CARLISLE — Lab hold

		Electorate 59,508	Turnout 59.5%	Change from 2001	2001	Electorate 58,811	Turnout 59.4%
Martlew E	**Lab**	**17,019**	**48.1%**	**-3.1%**	**Lab**	**17,856**	**51.2%**
Mitchelson M	C	11,324	32%	-2.8%	C	12,154	34.8%
Tweedie S	LD	5,916	16.7%	5%	LD	4,076	11.7%
Cochrane S	UKIP	792	2.2%		LCA	554	1.6%
Gibson L	LCA	343	1%	-0.6%	SA	269	0.8%
Lab to C swing	**0.2%**	**35,394**		**Lab maj 5,695** 16.1%		**34,909**	**Lab maj 5,702** 16.3%

ERIC MARTLEW b 3 Jan 1949. MP 1987-. Shadow Defence Min 1992-97. PPS to: Dr David Clark 1997-98, Baroness Jay 1998-2001. Opposition whip 1996-97. Opposition spokes: defence, disarmament and arms control specially for RAF 1992-95. Chair all-party West Coast Main Line group 1998-. Cllr: Carlisle County Borough Council 1972-74, Cumbria County Council 1973-88 (chair 1983-85). Nestlé: laboratory technician/personnel manager 1966-87. Ed Carlisle Coll.

A comparatively safe Labour base, Carlisle is a predominantly urban constituency comprising the city itself, as well as outlying rural towns. Industry within the seat is predominantly focused on food manufacturing, with agriculture playing a role in the lives of many inhabitants. Tourism is also important with much historical interest attached to the city's Roman heritage, namely Hadrian's Wall (which bisects the city), and a castle where Mary, Queen of Scots was imprisoned.

CARMARTHEN EAST AND DINEFWR — PIC hold

		Electorate 53,484	Turnout 71.6%	Change from 2001	2001	Electorate 54,035	Turnout 70.4%
Price A	**PIC**	**17,561**	**45.9%**	**3.5%**	**PIC**	**16,130**	**42.4%**
Hendry R	Lab	10,843	28.3%	-7.3%	Lab	13,540	35.6%
Davies S	C	5,235	13.7%	0.8%	C	4,912	12.9%
Hughes J	LD	3,719	9.7%	2.3%	LD	2,815	7.4%
Squires M	UKIP	661	1.7%		UKIP	656	1.7%
Whitworth S	LCA	272	0.7%				
Lab to PIC swing	**5.4%**	**38,291**		**PIC maj 6,718** 17.5%		**38,053**	**PIC maj 2,590** 6.8%

ADAM PRICE b 23 Sept 1968. MP 2001-. Plaid Cymru spokes: economy and taxation, miners' compensation, regeneration, trade and industry, education and skills. Member Welsh affairs select cttee 2001-03. Research associate Univ of Wales Cardiff City and Regional Planning dept 1991-93. Exec dir: Menter an Busnes 1996-98, Newidiem economic devt consultancy 1998-. Spectator Inquisitor of the Year 2002. Ed Amman Valley Comp Sch; Saarland Univ; BA European community studies, Cardiff Univ.

This seat in south-west Wales is one of the few where most of the population are Welsh speakers. The eastern division of Carmarthen has a large rural population, but also includes part of the Amman Valley, the old anthracite coalfield. As is the case in most of the Wales seats, the contest here is between Plaid Cymru and Labour. Plaid Cymru won the seat in 2001 and increased their majority in 2005.

CARMARTHEN WEST AND SOUTH PEMBROKESHIRE — Lab hold

		Electorate 56,245	Turnout 67.3%	Change from 2001	2001	Electorate 56,518	Turnout 65.3%
Ainger N	**Lab**	**13,953**	**36.8%**	**-4.8%**	**Lab**	**15,349**	**41.6%**
Morris D	C	12,043	31.8%	2.5%	C	10,811	29.3%
Dixon J	PIC	5,582	14.7%	-4%	PIC	6,893	18.7%
Allen J	LD	5,399	14.3%	5.5%	LD	3,248	8.8%
MacDonald J	UKIP	545	1.4%	-0.1%	UKIP	537	1.5%
Daszak A	LCA	237	0.6%		DCSP	78	0.2%
Turner N	ND	104	0.3%				
Lab to C swing	**3.7%**	**37,863**		**Lab maj 1,910** 5%		**36,916**	**Lab maj 4,538** 12.3%

NICK AINGER b 24 Oct 1949. MP for Pembroke 1992-97, for Camarthen West and S Pembrokeshire 1997-. Parly Under-Sec Wales Office 2005-. PPS to: Paul Murphy 1999-2001, Alun Michael 1998-99, Ron Davies 1997-98. Govt whip 2001-05. Member select cttees: Broadcasting 1992-94, Welsh Affairs 1993-97, Administration 2001-. Cllr Dyfed CC 1981-93. British-Irish Interparly body 1993-2001. Branch sec TGWU. Marine and Port Services Ltd, Pembroke Dock 1977-92. Ed Netherthorpe Grammar Sch, Derbyshire.

The stunning coast and countryside constituency in south-west Wales includes the Pembrokeshire Coast National Park. The seat includes the resorts of Tenby, Saundersfoot, Oakwood and Folly Farm and the towns of Pembroke and Pembroke Dock. In its short life the constituency has been a Labour seat though the Conservatives Welsh recovery in 2005 has made the seat marginal and a big Tory target in future elections.

CARSHALTON AND WALLINGTON — LD hold

		Electorate 67,844	Turnout 63.5%	Change from 2001	2001	Electorate 67,339	Turnout 60.3%
Brake T	**LD**	**17,357**	**40.3%**	**-4.7%**	**LD**	**18,289**	**45%**
Andrew K	C	16,289	37.8%	4%	C	13,742	33.8%
Theobald A	Lab	7,396	17.2%	-1.2%	Lab	7,466	18.4%
Day F	UKIP	1,111	2.6%	1.4%	Greens	614	1.5%
Steel B	Greens	908	2.1%	0.6%	UKIP	501	1.2%
LD to C swing	**4.4%**	**43,061**		**LD maj 1,068** 2.5%		**40,612**	**LD maj 4,547** 11.2%

TOM BRAKE b 6 May 1962. MP 1997-. Lib Dem Shadow Sec of State: Transport 2005-, Internat Devt 2003-05. Lib Dem whip 2000-04. Lib Dem spokes: environment, transport in London and air transport 1997-99, environment, transport, the regions, social justice and London transport 1999-2001, transport, local govt and the regions 2001-02, transport 2002-03. Vice-chair all-party Globe UK group 2002-. Cllr London Boroughs of: Hackney 1988-90, Sutton 1994-98. IT manager. Ed BSc physics, Imperial Coll, London.

This a residential seat where office workers form a large part of the population. Carshalton Beeches in the south west is a comfortable neighbourhood, but there are poorer areas in Wrythe and Beddington. Most areas of this diverse constituency have in common a tendency to support the Liberal Democrats. The reult in 2005 confirms that Tom Brake seems to be conforming to a pattern of Liberal Democrat MPs who cultivate local support and hold on to unlikely gains.

CASTLE POINT — C hold

		Electorate 69,480	Turnout 65.9%	Change from 2001	2001	Electorate 68,108	Turnout 58.4%
Spink B	**C**	**22,118**	**48.3%**	**3.7%**	**C**	**17,738**	**44.6%**
Akehurst L	Lab	13,917	30.4%	-11.7%	Lab	16,753	42.1%
Sandbach J	LD	4,719	10.3%	2.5%	LD	3,116	7.8%
Hamper N	UKIP	3,431	7.5%	4.3%	UKIP	1,273	3.2%
Willis I	Greens	1,617	3.5%		Ind	663	1.7%
					Truth	223	0.6%
Lab to C swing	**7.7%**	**45,802**		**C maj 8,201** 17.9%		**39,766**	**C maj 985** 2.5%

BOB SPINK b 1 Aug 1948. MP 1992-97, 2001-. PPS to: Ann Widdecombe 1994-97, John Watts 1997. Member Science and technology select cttee 2001-. Chair all-party skills group 2005. Joint chair UNA UNESCO working cttee 1992-97. Director Parly Office of Science and Technology. RAF 1964-66. Engineer/company director 1966-. Ed Holycroft Sch, Keighley; PhD, CDipAF, BSc engineering, MSc industrial engineering, Manchester Univ/Cranfield Univ.

Situated on the Thames coastline of South East Essex, Castle Point is a largely residential constituency from which many commute to work in London. It has no large-scale industry or commerce, but there are a number of engineering and light industrial factories on industrial estates at Thundersley, Rayleigh Weir, Charfleet, and Leigh Beck. This was once safe Conservative territory, but came under Labour control in 1997, albeit temporarily. In 2001 it fell back into Tory hands and in 2005 the Conservative grip on power was galvanised once more, making the seat seem safe for the Torys again.

CEREDIGION — LD gain

		Electorate 53,493	Turnout 67.2%	Change from 2001	2001	Electorate 56,125	Turnout 61.7%
Williams M	**LD**	**13,130**	**36.5%**	**9.6%**	**PIC**	**13,241**	**38.3%**
Thomas S	PIC	12,911	35.9%	-2.4%	LD	9,297	26.9%
Harrison J	C	4,455	12.4%	-7%	C	6,730	19.4%
Davies A	Lab	4,337	12.1%	-3.3%	Lab	5,338	15.4%
Bradney D	Greens	846	2.4%				
Sheldon I	Veritas	268	0.8%				
PIC to LD swing	**6%**	**35,947**		**LD maj 219** 0.6%		**34,606**	**PIC maj 3,944** 11.4%

MARK WILLIAMS b 24 March 1966. MP 2005-. Contested Monmouth 1997 general election, Ceredigion 2000 by-election and 2001 general election. Member Welsh Lib Dem Executive 1991-92; Constituency assistant, Geraint Howells MP 1987-92; President, Ceredigion Lib Dems 1998-2000; Member, Welsh Lib Dems Campaign Cttee 2000. Teacher 1993-2000. Member NASUWT 1993-. Ed Richard Hale School, Hertford; University College of Wales, Aberystwyth (BSc politics and economics 1987); Plymouth University (PGCE primary education 1993)

This west Wales seat is predominantly rural in character. The county and constituency stretches from Eglwys-fach in the north to Cardigan town in the south. Its main towns are Abersystwyth, Aberaeron, Lampeter, Tregaron, Llandysul and Cardigan. Aberystwyth is the home of the National Library of Wales. The constituency has historically been held by the Liberals and they regained it from Plaid Cymru at the 2005 general election.

CHARNWOOD — C hold

		Electorate 76,274	Turnout 66.4%	Change from 2001	2001	Electorate 75,073	Turnout 64.3%
Dorrell S	**C**	**23,571**	**46.6%**	**-1.6%**	**C**	**23,283**	**48.2%**
Robinson R	Lab	14,762	29.2%	-3%	Lab	15,544	32.2%
King S	LD	9,057	17.9%	1.7%	LD	7,835	16.2%
Holders A	BNP	1,737	3.4%		UKIP	1,603	3.3%
Bye J	UKIP	1,489	2.9%	-0.4%			
Lab to C swing	**0.7%**	**50,616**		**C maj 8,809** 17.4%		**48,265**	**C maj 7,739** 16%

STEPHEN DORRELL b 25 March 1952. MP for Loughborough 1979-97, for Charnwood 1997-. Shadow Education and Employment Sec of State 1997-98; member Shadow Cabinet 1997-98. Sec of State: Health 1995-97, National Heritage 1994-95. Financial Sec 1992-94, Health Dept Parly Under-Sec of State 1990-92. PPS to Peter Walker 1983-87. Govt whip 1988-90, asst govt whip 1987-88. Millennium Commission chair 1994-95. Director family firm. PC 1994. BA law, Brasenose Coll, Oxford.

Created in 1995, Charnwood absorbed 15,000 electors from Blaby, Kirby and Leicester Forest East in the West, 14,000 electors from Bosworth, and others from suburbs of Leicester and the more rural Bradgate ward. Also part of the old Loughborough seat are the five wards of Birstall. The Charnwood electorate have twice chosen a Tory leader, and it seems support for the Conservatives here is stable.

CHATHAM AND AYLESFORD — Lab hold

		Electorate	Turnout	Change from	2001	Electorate	Turnout
		70,515	59.7%	2001		69,759	57%
Shaw J	**Lab**	**18,387**	**43.7%**	**-4.6%**	**Lab**	**19,180**	**48.3%**
Jobson A	C	16,055	38.2%	0.9%	C	14,840	37.3%
Enever D	LD	5,744	13.6%	1.8%	LD	4,705	11.8%
King J	UKIP	1,226	2.9%	0.4%	UKIP	1,010	2.5%
Russell M	England	668	1.6%				
Lab to C swing	**2.8%**	**42,080**		**Lab maj 2,332**		**39,735**	**Lab maj 4,340**
				5.5%			10.9%

JONATHAN SHAW 3 June 1966. MP 1997-. PPS to Ruth Kelly 2005-. Member Education and Skills select cttee 2001-. Chair all-party groups: paper industry 2000-, noise reduction 2004-, skills 2005-; vice-chair: children and young people in care and leaving care 2001-, eye health and visual impairment 2002-. Chair Lab Party departmental cttee for home affairs 2004-. Cllr Rochester 1993-98. Social worker. Ed Social Care Diploma, West Kent Coll of FE; Social Services Certificate, Bromley Coll.

The constituency comprises two contrasting areas. Chatham, a tough working-class town, rather in the shadow of neighbouring Rochester, has a long connection with the Royal Navy and strong Labour components. In complete contrast Aylesford, a fairly small town in the south of the constituency with its surrounding commuter villages and towns, is much more fertile Conservative territory. Since its conversion to Labour in 1997, this has become a marginal seat.

CHEADLE – BY ELECTION PENDING — LD hold

		Electorate	Turnout	Change from	2001	Electorate	Turnout
		68,123	69.6%	2001		69,001	63.2%
Calton P	**LD**	**23,189**	**48.9%**	**6.5%**	**LD**	**18,477**	**42.4%**
Day S	C	19,169	40.4%	-1.9%	C	18,444	42.3%
Miller M	Lab	4,169	8.8%	-5.2%	Lab	6,086	14%
Cavanagh V	UKIP	489	1%	-0.4%	UKIP	599	1.4%
Chadfield R	BNP	421	0.9%				
C to LD swing	**4.2%**	**47,437**		**LD maj 4,020**		**43,606**	**LD maj 33**
				8.5%			0.1%

PATSY CALTON 19 Sept 1948-29 May 2005. MP 2001-05. Lib Dem spokes: Northern Ireland 2001-02, Health 2002-05. Member House Administration select cttee 2001-05. Chair Stockport Metropolitan Lib Dems 1993-96, 1997-2000. Cllr Stockport Metropolitan Borough Council 1994-2002: deputy leader 1996-97, 1998-2001. Teacher. Ed BSc biochemistry, Manchester Univ Institute of Science and Technology; PGCE, Manchester Univ.

Cheadle is an attractive and affluent commuter area to the south of Stockport. The seat includes some of the wealthiest neighbourhoods in the country, such as Cheadle Hulme and Bramhall. A hotly contested seat between the Conservatives and the Liberal Democrats, it was the most marginal seat in the country before the 2005 general election. A considerable personal vote for the sitting MP gave the Lib Dems a useful majority, but her death soon after the election left it vulnerable in the subsequent by-election.

CHELMSFORD WEST — C hold

		Electorate	Turnout	Change from	2001	Electorate	Turnout
		82,489	61.9%	2001		78,073	61.7%
Burns S	**C**	**22,946**	**45%**	**2.5%**	**C**	**20,446**	**42.5%**
Robinson S	LD	13,326	26.1%	2.8%	Lab	14,185	29.5%
Kennedy R	Lab	13,236	25.9%	-3.6%	LD	11,197	23.3%
Wedon K	UKIP	1,544	3%	1.4%	Greens	837	1.7%
					UKIP	785	1.6%
					LCA	693	1.4%
C to LD swing	**0.2%**	**51,052**		**C maj 9,620**		**48,143**	**C maj 6,261**
				18.8%			13%

SIMON BURNS b 6 Sept 1952. MP for Chelmsford 1987-97, for Chelmsford West 1997-. Shadow Min: Health 2004-, Health and Education 2001-04. Health Dept Parly Under-Sec of State 1996-97. PPS to: Timothy Eggar 1989-1993, Gillian Shephard 1993-94. Govt whip 1995-96, asst govt whip 1994-95. Member Health select cttee 1999-. Exec member: 1922 cttee 1999, British American Parly group 2001-. MP asst 1975-81/company sec and director 1981-83/conference organiser 1983-87. Ed BA history, Worcester Coll, Oxford.

Chelmsford is a prosperous retail, administrative and manufacturing centre. It is the county town of Essex where the cricket team is based and both the district and county councils have their headquarters in the constituency. Many residents, who live in villages or attractive residential areas, commute to work in London using the A12 or trains into Liverpool Street Station. Chelmsford West has been and still is a safe Conservative seat.

CHELTENHAM — LD hold

		Electorate	Turnout	Change from	2001	Electorate	Turnout
		71,541	61%	2001		67,563	61.9%
Horwood M	**LD**	**18,122**	**41.5%**	**-6.2%**	**LD**	**19,970**	**47.7%**
Gearson V	C	15,819	36.3%	1.1%	C	14,715	35.2%
Evans C	Lab	4,988	11.4%	-0.6%	Lab	5,041	12%
Hodges R	Ind	2,651	6.1%	5.8%	Greens	735	1.8%
Bessant K	Greens	908	2.1%	0.3%	Loony	513	1.2%
Warry N	UKIP	608	1.4%	0.2%	UKIP	482	1.2%
Hanks D	Loony	525	1.2%		ProLife	272	0.7%
					Ind	107	0.3%
LD to C swing	**3.7%**	**43,621**		**LD maj 2,303**		**41,835**	**LD maj 5,255**
				5.3%			12.6%

MARTIN HORWOOD b 12 Oct 1962. MP 2005-. Contested Oxford East 1992 and Cities of London and Westminster 2001. Vale of White Horse district councillor 1991-95. Oxford Student Liberal Society: president 1983; Union of Liberal Students: Chair 1985-86. Marketing consultant. Member: Amnesty International, World Development Movement; Ashridge Management College Association. Ed Cheltenham College; Queen's College, Oxford.

This elegant and affluent spa town is situated on the edge of the Cotswold hills and is home to the Government Communications Headquarters (GCHQ), the town's largest employer. In 1992 Cheltenham relinquished its allegiance to the Conservatives when it flouted the national trend and elected a Liberal Democrat. Since then the Lib Dems have worked hard in the constituency to hold off the Conservative challenge and keep the seat.

CHESHAM AND AMERSHAM — C hold

		Electorate	Turnout	Change from	2001	Electorate	Turnout
		69,217	68%	2001		70,021	64.7%
Gillan C	**C**	**25,619**	**54.4%**	**3.9%**	**C**	**22,867**	**50.5%**
Ford J	LD	11,821	25.1%	0.8%	LD	10,985	24.3%
Huq R	Lab	6,610	14%	-4.8%	Lab	8,497	18.8%
Wilkins N	Greens	1,656	3.5%	1%	UKIP	1,367	3%
Samuel D	UKIP	1,391	3%		Greens	1,114	2.5%
					ProLife	453	1%
LD to C swing	**1.6%**	**47,097**		**C maj 13,798**		**45,283**	**C maj 11,882**
				29.3%			26.2%

CHERYL GILLAN b 21 April 1952. MP 1992-. Shadow Min: Home Affairs 2004-, Home, Constitutional and Legal Affairs 2003-04. Education and Employment Dept Parly Under-Sec of State 1995-97. PPS to Viscount Cranborne 1994-95. Opposition whip 2001-03. Opposition spokes: trade and industry 1997-98, foreign and Commonwealth affairs 1998-2001, internat devt 1998-. Chair Bow Group 1987-88. Marketing director/consultant. Ed Coll of Law; Chartered Institute of Marketing.

A land of comfortable towns and villages in the Chiltern hills, within commuting distance of London, Chesham and Amersham is the very model of a modern Conservative stronghold and one of their safest seats. It has been home to well-to-do London commuters since the Metropolitan Line was extended here in the 1920s. Chesham and Amersham is mainly residential but a number of national and international businesses also have their head offices in the constituency.

CITY OF CHESTER — Lab hold

		Electorate	Turnout	Change from	2001	Electorate	Turnout
		69,785	64.3%	2001		70,382	63.8%
Russell C	**Lab**	**17,458**	**38.9%**	**-9.6%**	**Lab**	**21,760**	**48.5%**
Offer P	C	16,543	36.8%	3.7%	C	14,866	33.1%
Jones M	LD	9,818	21.9%	7.2%	LD	6,589	14.7%
Weddell A	UKIP	776	1.7%	-0.3%	UKIP	899	2%
Abrams E	Eng Dem	308	0.7%		Ind	763	1.7%
Lab to C swing	**6.7%**	**44,903**		**Lab maj 915**		**44,877**	**Lab maj 6,894**
				2%			15.4%

CHRISTINE RUSSELL b 25 March 1945. MP 1997-. Member select cttees: Office of the Deputy Prime Min 2003-, Transport, Local Govt and Regions 2001-02, Environmental Audit 1999-2001. Vice-chair all-party groups: Theatre 2002-, Estonia 2002-, osteoporosis 2002-. Chair/President Chester Constituency Lab Party 1989-92. Cllr Chester City Council 1980-97. JP 1980. Member: CAB, Magistrate's Assoc. Librarian. Ed London Sch of Librarianship; North West London Poly.

Apart from the historic walled city, the City of Chester constituency includes smaller outlying areas such as Mollington, Saughall and Aldford. The urban population tend to be employed in the professional or managerial sectors but Chester's Roman heritage means that tourism is also a major industry here. Traditionally a Conservative stronghold, following the 1997 general election it has become a Labour seat.

CHESTERFIELD — LD hold

		Electorate	Turnout	Change from	2001	Electorate	Turnout
		74,007	59.6%	2001		73,252	60.7%
Holmes P	**LD**	**20,875**	**47.3%**	**-0.5%**	**LD**	**21,249**	**47.8%**
Rich S	Lab	17,830	40.4%	-1.6%	Lab	18,663	42%
Kreling M	C	3,605	8.2%	0.1%	C	3,613	8.1%
Brady C	UKIP	997	2.3%		SA	437	1%
Jerram I	Eng Dem	814	1.8%		SLP	295	0.7%
					Ind	184	0.4%
Lab to LD swing	**0.6%**	**44,121**		**LD maj 3,045**		**44,441**	**LD maj 2,586**
				6.9%			5.8%

PAUL HOLMES b 16 Jan 1957. MP 2001-. Lib Dem spokes: disability issues and work and pensions 2002-, disability issues 2001-02. Member Education and Skills select cttee 2001-. Treasurer all-party autism group 2004-. Euro election agent 1994. Cllr Chesterfield Borough Council 1987-95, 1999-2003. Vice-pres Local Govt Assocn 2001-. Chair Walton and West Community Forum, Chesterfield 2000-01. History teacher. Ed Firth Park Sch, Sheffield; BA hist, York Univ; PGCE, Sheffield Univ.

When Tony Benn stood down in 2001, the Liberal Democrats took the seat with a majority of 2,586 and retained it again in 2005. The constituency lies in North Derbyshire, south of Sheffield, and is largely urban and industrial in character. Chesterfield has a history of steel-, glass- and clay-making. The church of St Mary and All Saints is famous for its twisted steel spire, caused by the warping of the lead and wooden frame.

CHICHESTER — C hold

		Electorate	Turnout	Change from	2001	Electorate	Turnout
		78,645	66.6%	2001		77,703	63.8%
Tyrie A	**C**	**25,302**	**48.3%**	**1.3%**	**C**	**23,320**	**47%**
Hilliar A	LD	14,442	27.6%	3.5%	LD	11,965	24.1%
Austin J	Lab	9,632	18.4%	-3%	Lab	10,627	21.4%
Denny D	UKIP	3,025	5.8%	1%	UKIP	2,380	4.8%
					Greens	1,292	2.6%
C to LD swing	**1.1%**	**52,401**		**C maj 10,860**		**49,584**	**C maj 11,355**
				20.7%			22.9%

ANDREW TYRIE b 15 Jan 1957. MP 1997-. Shadow: Paymaster Gen 2004-05, Financial Sec 2003-04. Member select cttees: Joint Cttee on Consolidation of Bills Etc 1997-2001, Public Admin 1997-2001, Treasury 2001-03. Adviser to: Nigel Lawson 1986-89, John Major 1989-90. Senior economist European Bank for Reconstruction and Devt 1992-97. Member Public Accounts Commission 1997-. BP 1981-83, fellow Nuffield Coll, Oxford 1990-91. Ed BA PPE, Trinity Coll, Oxford; econ dip, Coll of Europe, Bruges; MPhil internat relations, Wolfson Coll, Cambridge.

The western-most constituency in West Sussex is largely rural, stretching north from the coast to the borders of Hampshire and Surrey. The cathedral city and county town of Chichester was the Roman Noviomagnus. This is a peaceful area of second homes, retirement homes and stately homes, including Cowdray Park, the international polo venue, and Goodwood with its beautiful racecourse. Unsurprisingly, it is a safe Conservative seat.

CHINGFORD AND WOODFORD GREEN — C hold

		Electorate	Turnout	Change from	2001	Electorate	Turnout
		61,386	63%	2001		63,252	58.5%
Duncan Smith I	**C**	**20,555**	**53.2%**	**5%**	**C**	**17,834**	**48.2%**
Wright S	Lab	9,914	25.6%	-7.8%	Lab	12,347	33.4%
Beanse J	LD	6,832	17.7%	2.2%	LD	5,739	15.5%
McGough M	UKIP	1,078	2.8%		BNP	1,062	2.9%
White B	Ind	269	0.7%				
Lab to C swing	**6.4%**	**38,648**		**C maj 10,641**		**36,982**	**C maj 5,487**
				27.5%			14.8%

IAIN DUNCAN SMITH b 9 April 1954. MP for Chingford 1992-97, for Chingford and Woodford Green 1997-. Leader: Con Party 2001-03, Opposition 2001-03. Shadow Sec of State: Defence 1999-2001, Soc Security 1997-99; Shadow Cabinet member 1997-2003. Vice-pres all-party British-American group 2002-. Chair Con Policy Board 2001-03. Chair Con Party social security cttee 1997-. Army 1975-81. Publishing director. PC 2001. Ed HMS Conway Cadet Sch; Universita per Stranieri, Perugia, Italy; RMA Sandhurst; Dunchurch Coll of Management.

This Greater London constituency is typical of suburbia. The residents are mainly white, and are well-off enough to be mainly owner-occupiers. There is plenty of green open space but the suburb is characterised more by its high streets and shopping arcades. Iain Duncan Smith's secure tenure indicates that the Thatcherism championed by Norman Tebbit remains popular with many voters, and it is unlikely this will change in a rather demographically static area.

CHIPPING BARNET — C hold

		Electorate	Turnout	Change from	2001	Electorate	Turnout
		66,143	64.1%	2001		70,217	60.5%
Villiers T	**C**	**19,744**	**46.6%**	**0.2%**	**C**	**19,702**	**46.4%**
Coakley-Webb P	Lab	13,784	32.5%	-7.5%	Lab	17,001	40%
Hooker S	LD	6,671	15.7%	2.1%	LD	5,753	13.6%
Poppy A	Greens	1,199	2.8%				
Kaye V	UKIP	924	2.2%				
Weiss R	Vote Dream	59	0.1%				
Lab to C swing	**3.9%**	**42,381**		**C maj 5,960**		**42,456**	**C maj 2,701**
				14.1%			6.4%

THERESA VILLIERS b 5 March 1968. MP 2005-. MEP for London 1999-2005: Legal Affairs Committee member 2004-05, Turkmenistan and Mongolia Delegation member 2004-05; Barrister Lincoln's Inn 1994-95. Ed Sarum Hall School, Francis Holland School, London; LLB Bristol University, BCL Jesus College, Oxford

This area of London is part of the stockbroker belt much sought after by successful City men seeking a near-rural retreat. The seat is largely residential and industry is limited almost entirely to retailing. It contains the old market town of Barnet in the north and the shopping area of North Finchley to the south. Having weathered the Labour storm in 1997 and retained their majority in 2005, this remains a reasonably safe bet for the Conservatives.

CHORLEY — Lab hold

		Electorate	Turnout	Change from	2001	Electorate	Turnout
		78,838	62.9%	2001		77,036	62.2%
Hoyle L	**Lab**	**25,131**	**50.7%**	**-1.6%**	**Lab**	**25,088**	**52.3%**
Mallett S	C	17,506	35.3%	0.6%	C	16,644	34.7%
Wilson-Fletcher A	LD	6,932	14%	2.8%	LD	5,372	11.2%
					UKIP	848	1.8%
Lab to C swing	**1.1%**	**49,569**		**Lab maj 7,625**		**47,952**	**Lab maj 8,444**
				15.4%			17.6%

LINDSAY HOYLE b 10 June 1957. MP 1997-. Member select cttees: Catering 1997-, Trade and Industry 1998-. Co-chair all-party fair and showgrounds group 2002-; vice-chair all-party Morocco group 2004-. Cllr: Adlington Town Council 1980-98; Chorley Borough Council 1980-98 (deputy leader 1994-97, Chorley Mayor 1997-98). Shop steward. Company director. Ed Horwich FE; Bolton TIC (City & Guilds Construction).

One of the real weathervane seats, Chorley has switched allegiance with the country as a whole since 1970. This seat in southern Lancashire incorporates the industrial town of Chorley and many small villages in the immediate vicinity. To the north it borders on the suburbs of Preston and Blackburn and to the south it is adjacent to the metropolitan towns of Greater Manchester, the closest being Wigan and Bolton.

CHRISTCHURCH — C hold

		Electorate	Turnout	Change from	2001	Electorate	Turnout
		74,109	69.6%	2001		73,447	67.5%
Chope C	**C**	**28,208**	**54.7%**	**-0.4%**	**C**	**27,306**	**55.1%**
Coman L	LD	12,649	24.5%	-3.3%	LD	13,762	27.8%
King J	Lab	8,051	15.6%	0.5%	Lab	7,506	15.1%
Hughes D	UKIP	2,657	5.2%	3.2%	UKIP	993	2%
LD to C swing	**1.5%**	**51,565**		**C maj 15,559**		**49,567**	**C maj 13,544**
				30.2%			27.3%

CHRISTOPHER CHOPE b 19 May 1947. MP for Southampton Itchen 1983-92, for Christchurch 1997-. Shadow Min: Environ and Transport 2003-05, for Transport 2002-03. Parly Under-Sec of State: Transport Dept (Roads and Traffic Min) 1990-92, Environ Dept 1986-90. PPS: Peter Brooke 1986. Opposition spokes 1997-2002. Member Trade and Industry select cttee 1999-2002, exec 1922 cttee 2001-05. Vice-chair Con Party 1997-98. Barrister/consultant. OBE 1982. Ed St Andrews Univ.

Situated to the east of Bournemouth on the Dorset coast, Christchurch is one of the archetypal Tory seats full of pensioners and owner-occupiers. It was also one of the signal sites of the Conservative collapse after the 1992 general election as the Liberal Democrats scored a sensational by-election victory. However, with Liberal Democrat support now on the wane it would be an even bigger shock for the Tories if they were to lose here again.

CITIES OF LONDON AND WESTMINSTER — C hold

		Electorate	Turnout	Change from	2001	Electorate	Turnout
		72,577	50.3%	2001		71,935	47.2%
Field M	**C**	**17,260**	**47.3%**	**1%**	**C**	**15,737**	**46.3%**
Lloyd H	Lab	9,165	25.1%	-8%	Lab	11,238	33.1%
Rossi M	LD	7,306	20%	4.6%	LD	5,218	15.4%
Smith T	Greens	1,544	4.2%	0.3%	Greens	1,318	3.9%
Merton C	UKIP	399	1.1%	-0.3%	UKIP	464	1.4%
Haw B	Ind	298	0.8%				
McLachlan J	CPA	246	0.7%				
Harris D	Veritas	218	0.6%				
Cass J	Ind	51	0.1%				
Lab to C swing	**4.5%**	**36,487**		**C maj 8,095**		**33,975**	**C maj 4,499**
				22.2%			13.2%

MARK FIELD b 6 Oct 1964. MP 2001-. Shadow Min: Treasury 2005-, London 2003-05. Opposition whip 2003-04. Member Constitutional Affairs select cttee 2003-04. Sec all-party groups: private equity and venture capital 2002-, German 2002-, Chinese in Britain 2003-. Member various standing cttees 2001-04. Association/ward officer Kensington/Chelsea/ Islington North Associations 1989-99. Former company director /solicitor. Ed Reading Sch; MA, St Edmund Hall, Oxford; Chester Coll of Law.

The seat is home to some of the world's most recognisable landmarks, including Buckingham Palace and St Paul's cathedral. The constituency straddles the boundary between Westminster and City of London councils. 1997 was probably the closest Labour will ever come to making a gain here. In 2005 the Conservatives strengthened their majority. The presence of many wealthy West End residents and a strong Tory supporting group should ensure Mark Field's future in Parliament for some time.

CLEETHORPES — Lab hold

		Electorate	Turnout	Change from	2001	Electorate	Turnout
		70,746	61.6%	2001		68,398	62%
McIsaac S	**Lab**	**18,889**	**43.3%**	**-6.3%**	**Lab**	**21,032**	**49.6%**
Vickers M	C	16,247	37.3%	1%	C	15,412	36.3%
Lowis G	LD	6,437	14.8%	2.8%	LD	5,080	12%
Hardie W	UKIP	2,016	4.6%	2.5%	UKIP	894	2.1%
Lab to C swing	**3.7%**	**43,589**		**Lab maj 2,642**		**42,418**	**Lab maj 5,620**
				6.1%			13.2%

SHONA McISAAC b 3 April 1960. MP 1997-. PPS to: Baroness Scotland of Asthal as Min of State, Home Office 2003, Northern Ireland Mins of State: Jane Kennedy 2001-03, Adam Ingram 2000-01. Member Standards and Privileges select cttee 1997-2001. Chair all-party fireworks group 2003-. Cllr London Borough of Wandsworth 1990-98. Sub-editor. Ed SHAPE Sch, Belgium; Barne Barton Sec Mod, Plymouth; Stoke Damerel High, Plymouth; BSc geography, Durham Univ.

Previously the fairly safe Conservative seat of Brigg and Cleethorpes, the loss of the former town to the new Brigg and Goole division transformed Cleethorpes into a marginal and Labour took the seat in 1997. This constituency comprises areas of heavy industry, particularly oil and gas on the Humber Estuary, a great deal of rural landscape, and some well-off commuter villages on the Lincolnshire Wolds. Cleethorpes itself is a seaside resort south of Grimsby.

CLWYD SOUTH — Lab hold

		Electorate	Turnout	Change from	2001	Electorate	Turnout
		52,353	62.9%	2001		53,680	62.4%
Jones M	**Lab**	**14,808**	**45%**	**-6.4%**	**Lab**	**17,217**	**51.4%**
Biggins T	C	8,460	25.7%	0.9%	C	8,319	24.8%
Burnham D	LD	5,105	15.5%	5.3%	PlC	3,982	11.9%
Strong M	PlC	3,111	9.4%	-2.5%	LD	3,426	10.2%
Humphreys A	FW	803	2.4%		UKIP	552	1.6%
Powell N	UKIP	644	2%	0.4%			
Lab to C swing	**3.7%**	**32,931**		**Lab maj 6,348**		**33,496**	**Lab maj 8,898**
				19.3%			26.6%

MARTYN JONES b 1 March 1947. MP for Clwyd SW 1987-97, for Clwyd South 1997-. Opposition whip 1988-92. Opposition spokes 1994-95. Member select cttees: Agriculture 1988-94, 1996-97, Liaison 1997- (chair) Welsh Affairs 1997-. Member: Christian Socialist Movt, Socialist environment and resources assocn, SERA. Cllr Clwyd CC 1981-89. Microbiologist. Chair TGWU parly group 2001-02. Vice-pres Federation of Economic Devt Authorities. Ed Liverpool Coll of Commerce; HND applied biology, Liverpool Poly; MIBiol, Trent Poly.

The constituency is in the north of Wales and incorporates the boundaries of three local authorities: Powys in the south of the region, Wrexham County to the east and Denbighshire to the north and west. It is largely rural in nature though there are old industrial pockets around Wrexham. Labour has a clear lead over the other political parties at local government level and they hold the parliamentary seat with a solid majority.

CLWYD WEST — C gain

		Electorate	Turnout	Change from	2001	Electorate	Turnout
		55,642	64%	2001		53,886	64.2%
Jones D	**C**	**12,909**	**36.2%**	**0.6%**	**Lab**	**13,426**	**38.8%**
Thomas G	Lab	12,776	35.9%	-2.9%	C	12,311	35.6%
Taylor F	LD	4,723	13.3%	1.9%	PIC	4,453	12.9%
Williams E	PIC	3,874	10.9%	-2%	LD	3,934	11.4%
Nicholson W	UKIP	512	1.4%		UKIP	476	1.4%
James J	Ind	507	1.4%				
Keenan P	SLP	313	0.9%				
Lab to C swing	**1.8%**	**35,614**		**C maj 133**		**34,600**	**Lab maj 1,115**
				0.4%			3.2%

DAVID JONES b 22 March 1952. MP 2005-. Contested Conwy 1997 general election, 1999 National Assembly for Wales election and City of Chester 2001 general election; AM for North Wales 2002-03. Senior partner David Jones & Company, Llandudno 1985-2005. Ed law, London University 1973

The constituency of Clywd West lies in the centre of North Wales. Its short coastline reaches from Colwyn Bay to Kinmel Bay and contains most of the voting population of the seat. The division stretches inland to take in the town of Ruthin and parts of rural Denbighshire and Conwy. Historically the seat was a Conservative stronghold. Its recapture from Labour in 2005 was a symbol of the Tory revival in Wales.

VALE OF CLWYD — Lab hold

		Electorate	Turnout	Change from	2001	Electorate	Turnout
		51,982	62.2%	2001		50,842	63.6%
Ruane C	**Lab**	**14,875**	**46%**	**-4%**	**Lab**	**16,179**	**50%**
Elphick F	C	10,206	31.6%	-0.6%	C	10,418	32.2%
Jewkes E	LD	3,820	11.8%	2.3%	LD	3,058	9.5%
Jones M	PIC	2,309	7.2%	0.1%	PIC	2,300	7.1%
Young M	Ind	442	1.4%		UKIP	391	1.2%
Khambatta E	UKIP	375	1.2%				
Ditchfield J	LCA	286	0.9%				
Lab to C swing	**1.7%**	**32,313**		**Lab maj 4,669**		**32,346**	**Lab maj 5,761**
				14.4%			17.8%

CHRIS RUANE b 18 July 1958. MP 1997-. PPS to Peter Hain 2002-. Member Welsh Affairs select cttee 1999-2002. Chair all-party heart disease group 2002-. Member Lab group of seaside MPs 1997-. Chair North Wales group of Lab MPs. Cllr Rhyl Town Council 1988-99. Founder member Rhyl: anti apartheid 1987, environmental assocn 1988, and district Amnesty Internat group 1989. Pres NUT: West Clwyd 1991, Vale of Clwyd 1997. Primary sch teacher 1982-97, dep head 1991-97. Ed BSc econ, hist, politics, Univ of Wales, Aberystwyth; PGCE, Liverpool Univ.

This north Wales constituency takes in the coastal resorts of Rhyl and Prestatyn as well as much of Denbighshire including the town of Denbigh itself. Historically a Conservative stronghold, the constituency has become a Labour seat since boundary changes were made before the 1997 general election. However, the collapse of the Conservative vote in Wales was a bigger reason than the boundary changes for the seat falling to New Labour.

COATBRIDGE, CHRYSTON AND BELLSHILL — Lab hold

		Electorate	Turnout		2001
		67,385	56.9%		
Clarke T	**Lab**	**24,725**	**64.5%**		No comparable results due to boundary changes
Ross D	SNP	5,206	13.6%		
Ackland R	LD	4,605	12%		
Paterson L	C	2,775	7.2%		
Kinloch J	SSP	1,033	2.7%		
Lab to SNP swing	**1.8%**	**38,344**		**Lab maj 19,519**	
(notional)				50.9%	

TOM CLARKE b 10 Jan 1941. MP for Coatbridge and Airdrie 1982-83, for Monklands West 1983-97, for Coatbridge and Chryston 1997-2005, for Coatbridge, Chryston and Bellshill 2005-. Minister of State Dept of Nat Heritage/for Culture, Media and Sport 1997-98. Shadow: Cabinet Minister 1995-97, Sec of State (two posts) 1992-94, Minister 1987-92. Opp Spokes 1993-94. Chair all-party groups. Cllr Coatbridge TC 1964-74, Monklands DC (provost) 1974-82. JP 1972. Scottish Film Council 1966-82. CBE 1980; PC 1997. Ed Scott Coll of Commerce.

This seat is essentially the old constituency of Coatbridge and Chryston combined with five wards centred on Bellshill. It curls around Glasgow's north-eastern and eastern periphery, now reaching south to include Old Monkhead, Viewpark and Bellshill. It is urban and suburban, and not particularly affluent. The only Conservative ward of the old seat has been moved across to East Dunbartonshire, and the five new wards are all solid Labour territory.

COLCHESTER

LD hold

		Electorate	Turnout	Change from	2001	Electorate	Turnout
		79,010	56.8%	2001		77,958	56.1%
Russell B	**LD**	**21,145**	**47.1%**	**4.5%**	**LD**	**18,627**	**42.6%**
Bentley K	C	14,868	33.1%	3.2%	C	13,074	29.9%
Bruni L	Lab	8,886	19.8%	-5.2%	Lab	10,925	25%
					UKIP	631	1.4%
					TGP	479	1.1%
C to LD swing	**0.7%**	**44,899**		**LD maj 6,277**		**43,736**	**LD maj 5,553**
				14%			12.7%

BOB RUSSELL b 31 March 1946. MP 1997-. Lib Dem whip 1999-2002, 2003-. Lib Dem spokes: home and legal affairs 1997-99, sport 1999-. Member select cttees: Home Affairs 1998-2001, Catering 2000-01, Home Affairs 2001-. Chair all-party groups: acquired brain injury 2002-, St Helena 2002-, road safety 2004-. Cllr Colchester Borough Council 1971-2002: mayor 1986-87, leader 1987-91. Journalist/publicity officer. Ed Proficiency Cert NCTJ, North-East Tech Coll.

Home to a university and an army garrison, Colchester is full of soldiers and students. Britain's earliest recorded town, the Roman Camulodunum, witnessed the submission of the British tribes to the Emperor Claudius in 43AD. Nearly two thousand years later it saw the submission of the Tory legions to an invading force of Liberal Democrats, in one of the most fascinating three-way fights of 1997. Labour has since faded but the Conservatives will challenge strongly.

COLNE VALLEY

Lab hold

		Electorate	Turnout	Change from	2001	Electorate	Turnout
		74,121	66%	2001		74,192	63.3%
Mountford K	**Lab**	**17,536**	**35.8%**	**-4.6%**	**Lab**	**18,967**	**40.4%**
Throup M	C	16,035	32.8%	2.3%	C	14,328	30.5%
Wilson E	LD	11,822	24.2%	-0.7%	LD	11,694	24.9%
Fowler B	BNP	1,430	2.9%		Greens	1,081	2.3%
Hedges L	Greens	1,295	2.6%	0.3%	UKIP	917	2%
Martinek H	Veritas	543	1.1%				
Mumford I	Loony	259	0.5%				
Lab to C swing	**3.5%**	**48,920**		**Lab maj 1,501**		**46,987**	**Lab maj 4,639**
				3.1%			9.9%

KALI MOUNTFORD b 12 Jan 1954. MP 1997-. PPS to Des Browne as Chief Sec to Treasury 2005-, Min of State: Home Office 2004-05, Work and Pensions Dept 2003-04. Member select cttees: Soc Security 1998-99, Treasury 2001-03, Administration 2005-. Vice-chair: CAB 1998-, Victim Support 1998-. CPSA: shop steward 1983-95, branch/regional sec 1985-92, Dept Employment Whitley Council Sec 1988-95, branch chair 1990-92, Trades Council Exec 1990-95. Pres Mehfal-E-Niswan 2000-. Ed Crewe Grammar Sch for Girls; DipHE, BA philosophy, psychology, sociology, Crewe and Alsager Coll.

The constituency includes Colne Valley and Holme Valley together with some areas of Huddersfield. Labour have controlled the seat since 1997, but political power in the Colne Valley has historically fluctuated between the three main parties and this see-sawing is reflected in the seat's marginality.

CONGLETON

C hold

		Electorate	Turnout	Change from	2001	Electorate	Turnout
		72,770	64.2%	2001		71,975	62.6%
Winterton A	**C**	**21,189**	**45.4%**	**-0.9%**	**C**	**20,872**	**46.3%**
Milton N	Lab	12,943	27.7%	-2.8%	Lab	13,738	30.5%
Key E	LD	12,550	26.9%	5.3%	LD	9,719	21.6%
					UKIP	754	1.7%
Lab to C swing	**1%**	**46,682**		**C maj 8,246**		**45,083**	**C maj 7,134**
				17.7%			15.8%

ANN WINTERTON b 6 March 1941. MP 1983-. Agriculture and Fisheries Shadow Min 2001-02. Opposition spokes: national drug strategy 1998-2001. Member select cttees on: Agriculture 1987-97, Chairmen's Panel 1992-98, Unopposed Bills (Panel) 1997-, Social Security 2000-01. Vice-chair all-party groups: Finland 2000-, Pro-Life 2002-. Representative, Organisation for Security and Co-operation in Europe. Patron East Cheshire NSPCC. Ed Erdington Grammar Sch for Girls.

Part of the genteel and wealthy county of Cheshire, Congleton is essentially an artist's impression of what a safe Conservative seat should look like. It is made up of a collection of small towns and villages and includes a number of affluent communities of which Congleton is the largest. Situated south of Tatton and north of Crewe it is very much part of the Cheshire commuter belt for the metropolitan areas to the north.

CONWY — Lab hold

		Electorate 53,987	Turnout 62.3%	Change from 2001	2001	Electorate 54,637	Turnout 62.9%
Williams B	**Lab**	**12,479**	**37.1%**	**-4.7%**	**Lab**	**14,366**	**41.8%**
Bebb G	C	9,398	27.9%	4.2%	C	8,147	23.7%
Roberts G	LD	6,723	20%	3.1%	LD	5,800	16.9%
Rowlinson P	PIC	3,730	11.1%	-5.4%	PIC	5,665	16.5%
Killock J	Greens	512	1.5%		UKIP	388	1.1%
Jones D	SLP	324	1%				
Khambatta K	UKIP	298	0.9%	-0.2%			
Evans T	LCA	193	0.6%				
Lab to C swing	**4.5%**	**33,657**		**Lab maj 3,081** 9.2%		**34,366**	**Lab maj 6,219** 18.1%

BETTY WILLIAMS b 31 July 1944. MP 1997-. Member Welsh Affairs select cttee 1997-. Commonwealth Parly Assocn, Inter-Parly Union. Chair Welsh regional group of Lab MPs 2003-. Cllr: Arfon BC 1970-91 (mayor 1990-91), Gwynedd County Council 1976-93. Freelance journalist/media researcher 1995-97. Vice-pres Univ of Wales, Bangor 2002-. Former member Snowdonia nat park cttee (northern). Y Cymro Prize 1994-95. Deacon Seion C Talysarn. Ed Ysgol Dyffryn Nantile, Penygroes; BA communications, Normal Coll, Bangor.

The constituency of Conwy extends along the North Wales coast from Penrhyn Bay in the east to beyond Bangor in the west. It has been represented at Westminster by a Conservative MP for most of the period since the Second World War but it was one of the many seats that fell to Labour in 1997. The ground gained by the Tories in 2005 means it looks back within their reach in the near future.

COPELAND — Lab hold

		Electorate 54,206	Turnout 62.3%	Change from 2001	2001	Electorate 53,526	Turnout 64.9%
Reed J	**Lab**	**17,033**	**50.5%**	**-1.3%**	**Lab**	**17,991**	**51.8%**
Whiteside C	C	10,713	31.7%	-5.8%	C	13,027	37.5%
Hollowell F	LD	3,880	11.5%	0.8%	LD	3,732	10.7%
Caley-Knowles E	UKIP	735	2.2%				
Earley B	Ind	734	2.2%				
Mossop A	Eng Dem	662	2%				
C to Lab swing	**2.3%**	**33,757**		**Lab maj 6,320** 18.7%		**34,750**	**Lab maj 4,964** 14.3%

JAMIE REED b 14 March 1973. MP 2005-. Media professional and anti-racism campaigner. Member GMB. Ed. Manchester and Leicester Universities

A coastal seat in western Cumbria, Copeland includes the southern tip of the Cumbrian Mountains and is mainly rural; there are urban areas on the coastline, such as the town of Whitehaven, which is a major fishing port. Copeland also includes some of the most spectacular Lake District scenery, England's deepest lake and tallest mountain, and controversially BNFL's plant at Sellafield.

CORBY — Lab hold

		Electorate 73,000	Turnout 66.5%	Change from 2001	2001	Electorate 72,594	Turnout 65%
Hope P	**Lab/C**	**20,913**	**43.1%**	**-6.2%**	**Lab/C**	**23,283**	**49.3%**
Griffith A	C	19,396	40%	2.8%	C	17,583	37.2%
Radcliffe D	LD	6,184	12.7%	2.6%	LD	4,751	10.1%
Gillman I	UKIP	1,278	2.6%	0.8%	UKIP	855	1.8%
Carey S	SLP	499	1%	-0.6%	SLP	750	1.6%
Morris J	Ind	257	0.5%				
Lab/C to C swing	**4.5%**	**48,527**		**Lab/C maj 1,517** 3.1%		**47,222**	**Lab/C maj 5,700** 12.1%

PHIL HOPE b 19 April 1955. MP 1997-. Parly Under-Sec: Dept of Education and Skills 2005-, Office of Deputy Prime Minister 2003-05. PPS to: Nick Raynsford 1999-2001, John Prescott 2001-03. Member select cttees: Public Accounts 1997-98, Selection 1999-2003. Lab party leadership campaign team member 1997-2001. Commonwealth Parly Assoc 1997-. Cllr: Kettering Borough Council 1983-87, Northants County Council 1993-97. Management and community work consultant. Ed BEd, St Luke's Coll, Exeter Univ.

The Northamptonshire town of Corby itself is industrial and votes Labour, but included in the constituency are 25,000 voters from the predominantly rural districts. Unemployment throughout the seat today stands at around 2.6 per cent, below the national average. The town was given Enterprise Zone and Assisted Area status and succeeded in establishing a diverse industrial and service economy involving over 600 companies.

NORTH CORNWALL — LD hold

		Electorate	Turnout	Change from	2001	Electorate	Turnout
		86,841	64.5%	2001		84,090	64.2%
Rogerson D	**LD**	**23,842**	**42.6%**	**-9.4%**	**LD**	**28,082**	**52%**
Formosa M	C	20,766	37.1%	3.3%	C	18,250	33.8%
Acton D	Lab	6,636	11.8%	2.1%	Lab	5,257	9.7%
Campbell Bannerman D	UKIP	3,063	5.5%	1.1%	UKIP	2,394	4.4%
Cole D	MebK	1,351	2.4%				
Eastwood A	Veritas	324	0.6%				
LD to C swing	**6.4%**	**55,982**		**LD maj 3,076**		**53,983**	**LD maj 9,832**
				5.5%			18.2%

DAN ROGERSON b 23 July 1975. MP 2005-. Contested Bedfordshire NE 2001 general election; Councillor Bedford Borough Council 1999-2002. Research assistant Bedford Borough Council 1996-98; administrative officer De Montfort University 1998-2002; campaigns officer Devon and Cornwall Liberal Democrats 2002-04. Ed BSc politics, University of Wales, Aberystwyth.

The constituency is large with a long coastline stretching from the holiday resort of Newquay, through Padstow, Wadebridge and Bude right up to the border with Devon. The main industries are agriculture and tourism and there is a heavy demographic bias to the over-65s. This was a Liberal Democrat stronghold but a Conservative revival in the election could give the Lib Dem MP future cause for concern.

SOUTH EAST CORNWALL — LD hold

		Electorate	Turnout	Change from	2001	Electorate	Turnout
		80,704	66.2%	2001		79,090	65.4%
Breed C	**LD**	**24,986**	**46.7%**	**0.8%**	**LD**	**23,756**	**45.9%**
Gray A	C	18,479	34.6%	-0.9%	C	18,381	35.5%
Binley C	Lab	6,069	11.4%	-1%	Lab	6,429	12.4%
Lucas D	UKIP	2,693	5%	1.2%	UKIP	1,978	3.8%
Sandercock G	MebK	769	1.4%	-0.9%	MebK	1,209	2.3%
Assheton-Salton A	Veritas	459	0.9%				
C to LD swing	**0.9%**	**53,455**		**LD maj 6,507**		**51,753**	**LD maj 5,375**
				12.2%			10.4%

COLIN BREED b 4 May 1947. MP 1997-. Lib Dem spokes 1997-. Member select cttees: European Scrutiny 1998-2004, Environment, Food and Rural Affairs 2001-. Vice-chair all-party groups: Methodist 2001-, Ethiopia 2001-, Jordan 2003-, leisure 2004-, beef and lamb 2004-. Exec cttee member Council for Advancement of Arab-British understanding. Cllr Caradon DC 1982-92; Saltash mayor 1989-90, 1995-96. Manager Midland Bank plc 1964-81. Managing dir/dir 1981-96. Member General Medical Council 1999-. Ed Torquay Boys Grammar Sch.

The attractive rural constituency of South East Cornwall has many small ports, and a thriving tourism industry. Like most south coast locations, it has a high proportion of retired people, and steadily rising housing costs. Despite all the efforts of the Conservatives this is a relatively safe Liberal Democrat seat. The MP has been able to act in concert with fellow Lib Dem MPs in the county on a range of key Cornish issues.

COTSWOLD — C hold

		Electorate	Turnout	Change from	2001	Electorate	Turnout
		71,039	66.6%	2001		68,140	67.5%
Clifton-Brown G	**C**	**23,326**	**49.3%**	**-1%**	**C**	**23,133**	**50.3%**
Beckerlegge P	LD	13,638	28.8%	4.6%	LD	11,150	24.2%
Dempsey M	Lab	8,457	17.9%	-4.7%	Lab	10,383	22.6%
Buckley R	UKIP	1,538	3.2%	0.3%	UKIP	1,315	2.9%
Derieg J	Ind	392	0.8%				
C to LD swing	**2.8%**	**47,351**		**C maj 9,688**		**45,981**	**C maj 11,983**
				20.5%			26.1%

GEOFFREY CLIFTON-BROWN b 23 March 1953. MP for Cirencester and Tewkesbury 1992-97, for Cotswold 1997-. Shadow Min: Local and Devolved Govt 2003-04, Local Govt 2002-03. PPS: Douglas Hogg 1995-97. Opposition whip 1999-2001, 2004-: Asst chief whip 2005-. Opposition spokes: environment, food and rural affairs 2001, transport, local govt and regions 2001-02, local govt, housing and planning 2002-03. Chair all-party wine and spirit group 2002-. Chartered surveyor. Ed Royal Agric Coll, Cirencester.

As the name implies, this constituency is nestled in the heart of the Cotswold hills. As a relatively affluent constituency populated mainly by country dwellers, it is little surprise that it is one of the Conservative's safest seats. Given the long and successful parliamentary careers of its two most recent former MPs, the current imcumbent should be representing the constituents here for quite some time to come.

COVENTRY NORTH EAST — Lab hold

		Electorate 70,225	Turnout 53%	Change from 2001	2001	Electorate 73,998	Turnout 50.4%
Ainsworth B	**Lab**	**21,178**	**56.9%**	**-4.1%**	**Lab**	**22,739**	**61%**
Birdi J	C	6,956	18.7%	-0.1%	C	6,988	18.8%
Field R	LD	6,123	16.5%	5.3%	LD	4,163	11.2%
Nellist D	SAP	1,874	5%		SAP	2,638	7.1%
Southeran P	UKIP	1,064	2.9%		BNP	737	2%
Lab to C swing	**2%**	**37,195**		**Lab maj 14,222** 38.2%		**37,265**	**Lab maj 15,751** 42.3%

BOB AINSWORTH b 19 June 1952. MP 1992-. Home Office Parly Under-Sec: Anti-Drugs Co-ordination and Organised Crime 2001-03, Dept of Environment, Transport and the Regions 2001. Whip: opposition 1995-97, govt 1997-: deputy chief 2003-. Member select cttees: Accommodation and Works 2003-, Selection 2003-, Finance and Services 2003-. Cllr Coventry City Council 1984-93: dep leader 1988-91. MSF: shop steward 1974, senior/joint shop stewards sec 1980-91, pres union branch 1983-87. Sheet metal worker. PC 2005. Ed Foxford Comp Sch, Coventry.

A secure Labour seat, Coventry North East is home to some of the region's worst economic deprivation. Although the safest of Labour's Coventry seats, declining turnout may prove to be a future thorn in Bob Ainsworth's side. Employment is focused on manufacturing, with Jaguar and Peugeot in neighbouring constituencies being key employers.

COVENTRY NORTH WEST — Lab hold

		Electorate 73,180	Turnout 59.4%	Change from 2001	2001	Electorate 76,652	Turnout 55.5%
Robinson G	**Lab**	**20,942**	**48.2%**	**-3.2%**	**Lab**	**21,892**	**51.4%**
Connell B	C	11,627	26.8%	0.9%	C	11,018	25.9%
Anderson I	LD	7,932	18.3%	4.6%	LD	5,832	13.7%
Clarke D	BNP	1,556	3.6%		Ind	3,159	7.4%
List S	UKIP	766	1.8%	0.3%	UKIP	650	1.5%
Downes N	SAP	615	1.4%				
Lab to C swing	**2.1%**	**43,438**		**Lab maj 9,315** 21.4%		**42,551**	**Lab maj 10,874** 25.6%

GEOFFREY ROBINSON b 25 May 1938. MP March 1976- by-election. Paymaster General HM Treasury 1997-98. Opposition spokes: science 1982-83, trade and industry and regional affairs 1983-87. Lab Party research asst 1965-68; MD Leyland Innocenti 1972-73; chief exec Jaguar Cars Coventry 1974-75, Triumph Motorcycles 1978-80; director West Midlands Enterprise Board 1982-85; chief exec TransTec plc 1986-97. Ed Emmanuel Sch, London; Clare Coll, Cambridge; Yale Univ, USA.

Historically the hub of the British automobile industry, Coventry North West is a relatively affluent constituency, with a high number of homeowners. Helped by high profile regeneration projects, including the building of a new home for Coventry City football club, Geoffrey Robinson is comfortable in this seat.

COVENTRY SOUTH — Lab hold

		Electorate 68,884	Turnout 59.1%	Change from 2001	2001	Electorate 72,527	Turnout 55.3%
Cunningham J	**Lab**	**18,649**	**45.8%**	**-4.4%**	**Lab**	**20,125**	**50.2%**
Wheeler H	C	12,394	30.5%	1%	C	11,846	29.5%
McKee V	LD	7,228	17.8%	3.7%	LD	5,672	14.1%
Windsor R	SAP	1,097	2.7%		SAP	1,475	3.7%
Brown W	UKIP	829	2%		Ind	564	1.4%
Rogers I	Ind	344	0.8%	-0.6%	SLP	414	1%
Rooney J	FFUK	144	0.4%				
Lab to C swing	**2.7%**	**40,685**		**Lab maj 6,255** 15.4%		**40,096**	**Lab maj 8,279** 20.6%

JAMES CUNNINGHAM b 4 Feb 1941. MP for Coventry South East 1992-97, for Coventry South 1997-. Member select cttees: Home Affairs 1993-97, Trade and Industry 1997-2001, Chairmen's Panel 1998-2001, Constitutional Affairs 2003-. Sec all-party funerals and bereavement group 2002-. Chair: Lab Party departmental cttee for Treasury 1999-; Coventry South East CLP 1977-79. Cllr Coventry City Council 1972-92: leader 1988-92. MSF shop steward 1968-88. Engineer. Ed Tillycoultry Coll, Ruskin Courses (Labour Movement, Industrial Law).

Coventry South is a highly diverse constituency, with extremely affluent suburban areas a stark contrast to the economically deprived inner city. The seat has been occupied by Jim Cunningham since its creation in 1997, when Labour Coventry South East was joined with Conservative South West. Local council swings make this seat far from safe, with a large student population being an obvious target for the Liberal Democrats.

CRAWLEY

Lab hold

		Electorate 71,911	Turnout 58.4%	Change from 2001	2001	Electorate 71,626	Turnout 55.2%
Moffatt L	**Lab**	**16,411**	**39.1%**	**-10.2%**	**Lab**	**19,488**	**49.3%**
Smith H	C	16,374	39%	6.8%	C	12,718	32.2%
Sheard R	LD	6,503	15.5%	2.8%	LD	5,009	12.7%
Trower R	BNP	1,277	3%		UKIP	1,137	2.9%
Walters R	UKIP	935	2.2%	-0.7%	Loony	383	1%
Burnham R	Dem Soc All	263	0.6%		JP	271	0.7%
Khan A	JP	210	0.5%	-0.2%	SLP	260	0.7%
					SA	251	0.6%
Lab to C swing	**8.5%**	**41,973**		**Lab maj 37** 0.1%		**39,517**	**Lab maj 6,770** 17.1%

LAURA MOFFATT b 9 April 1954. MP 1997-. PPS to: Lord Chancellors: Lord Irvine of Lairg 2001-03, Lord Falconer of Thoroton 2003-05, David Blunkett as SOS DWP 2005-. Member Defence select cttee 1997-2001. Chair all-party groups: depression 2004-, maternity 2004-; vice-chair all-party drugs misuse group 1999-. Cllr Crawley Borough Council 1984-96: mayor 1989-90. State registered nurse, Crawley Hospital 1975-97. President, Relate. Ed Hazelwick Sch, Crawley; Crawley Coll of Tech (pre nursing course).

Modern Crawley was designated a new town in 1946. The town is divided into a series of residential neighbourhoods around the town centre, each with its own schools, shops and community facilities. It grew rapidly during the 1960s and '70s in line with its major employer, Gatwick airport. Politically, a combination of boundary changes and national trends appeared to have made it reasonably safe for Labour, but the close 2005 result showed the electorate remains volatile.

CREWE AND NANTWICH

Lab hold

		Electorate 72,472	Turnout 60%	Change from 2001	2001	Electorate 69,040	Turnout 60.2%
Dunwoody G	**Lab**	**21,240**	**48.8%**	**-5.5%**	**Lab**	**22,556**	**54.3%**
Moore-Dutton E	C	14,162	32.6%	2.2%	C	12,650	30.4%
Roberts P	LD	8,083	18.6%	5.1%	LD	5,595	13.5%
					UKIP	746	1.8%
Lab to C swing	**3.9%**	**43,485**		**Lab maj 7,078** 16.3%		**41,547**	**Lab maj 9,906** 23.8%

GWYNETH DUNWOODY b 12 Dec 1930. MP for Exeter 1966-70, for Crewe 1974-83, for Crewe and Nantwich 1983-. Board of Trade Parly Sec 1967-70. Deputy Speaker Westminster Hall 1999-2000. Opposition spokes: foreign and Commonwealth affairs 1979-80, NHS 1980-83, parly campaigning and information 1983-84, transport 1984-85. Chair/member various select cttees 1997- incl chair Transport 2002-. MEP 1975-79: Vice-chair EP Social Affairs cttee Vice-pres Socialist Internat Women. Director Film Production Assoc of GB 1970-74. Ed Convent of Notre Dame.

This seat is very much an amalgamation of two separate entities. Crewe is the industrial centre for Cheshire, home to Rolls Royce and many industrial and business parks. Nantwich is a traditional market town, of great historic interest and beauty. It is famous for its many half-timbered Tudor buildings and 14th century parish church. The seat is currently a safe Labour seat, but the majority is not as rock-solid as it would seem.

CROSBY

Lab hold

		Electorate 54,255	Turnout 66.7%	Change from 2001	2001	Electorate 57,190	Turnout 64.5%
Curtis-Thomas C	**Lab**	**17,463**	**48.2%**	**-6.9%**	**Lab**	**20,327**	**55.1%**
Jones D	C	11,623	32.1%	-0.4%	C	11,974	32.5%
Murray J	LD	6,298	17.4%	6.3%	LD	4,084	11.1%
Whittaker J	UKIP	454	1.2%		SLP	481	1.3%
Bottoms G	Comm	199	0.6%				
Braid D	Clause 28	157	0.4%				
Lab to C swing	**3.3%**	**36,194**		**Lab maj 5,840** 16.1%		**36,866**	**Lab maj 8,353** 22.7%

CLAIRE CURTIS-THOMAS b 30 April 1958. MP 1997-. Member select cttees: Science and Technology 1997-2001, Regulatory Reform 2002-03, Home Affairs 2003-. Chair all-party abuse investigation group 2001-; vice-chair all-party groups: pro-life 2004-, rowing 2004-, army 2004-. Vice-chair North West regional group of Lab MPs. Cllr Crewe and Nantwich Borough Council 1995-97. Professional engineer. Shell Chemicals 1986-92. Ed BSc mechanical engineering, University Coll of Wales, Cardiff; MBA business administration, Aston Univ.

One of the more affluent Merseyside seats, the predominantly middle class constituency of Crosby was considered a safe Tory seat until 1997, and now looks set to join the long list of Merseyside's Labour strongholds. Embracing both Crosby and Formby, this seat lying to the north of Liverpool towards Southport is thoroughly suburban in nature with most residents commuting to Liverpool to work.

CROYDON CENTRAL — C gain

		Electorate 80,825	Turnout 60.6%	Change from 2001	2001	Electorate 77,568	Turnout 59.1%
Pelling A	**C**	**19,974**	**40.8%**	**2.3%**	**Lab**	**21,643**	**47.2%**
Davies G	Lab	19,899	40.6%	-6.6%	C	17,659	38.5%
Hargreaves J	LD	6,384	13%	1.8%	LD	5,156	11.2%
Edwards I	UKIP	1,066	2.2%	1%	UKIP	545	1.2%
Golberg B	Greens	1,036	2.1%		BNP	449	1%
Bowness M	Veritas	304	0.6%		Loony	408	0.9%
Cartwright J	Loony	193	0.4%	-0.5%			
Stears J	Work	101	0.2%				
Lab to C swing	**4.5%**	**48,957**		**C maj 75** 0.2%		**45,860**	**Lab maj 3,984** 8.7%

ANDREW PELLING b 20 Aug 1959. MP 2005-. Head of debt syndicate Nomura International Plc 1986-94; Member GLA 2000-; Head of syndicate Natwest Markets 1994-97; Head of origination UFJ International plc 1997-. Ed Trinity School, Croydon; PPE, New College, Oxford

Croydon is the most important site for shops and offices in the south of England outside central London. One of the outer London constituencies that changed to Labour in 1997 but was then won back by the Conservatives in 2005, it includes the expanding retail centre and sits as a key marginal between a safe Tory seat in Croydon South and Labour's healthy majority in Croydon North.

CROYDON NORTH — Lab hold

		Electorate 83,796	Turnout 52.3%	Change from 2001	2001	Electorate 76,575	Turnout 54.7%
Wicks M	**Lab**	**23,555**	**53.7%**	**-9.8%**	**Lab**	**26,610**	**63.5%**
Ahmad T	C	9,667	22.1%	-1.2%	C	9,752	23.3%
Gee-Turner A	LD	7,560	17.2%	6.8%	LD	4,375	10.4%
Khan S	Greens	1,248	2.8%		UKIP	606	1.4%
Pearce H	UKIP	770	1.8%	0.4%	SA	539	1.3%
Gibson P	Croydon	394	0.9%				
McKenzie W	Veritas	324	0.7%				
Rasheed F	Ind	197	0.4%				
Chambers M	Work	132	0.3%				
Lab to C swing	**4.3%**	**43,847**		**Lab maj 13,888** 31.7%		**41,882**	**Lab maj 16,858** 40.3%

MALCOLM WICKS b 1 July 1947. MP for Croydon North West 1992-97, for Croydon North 1997-. Minister of State Dept of Trade and Industry 2005-. Dept for Work and Pensions: Pensions Minister of State 2003-05, Parly Under-Sec 2001-03. Dept for Education and Employment Parly Under-Sec 1999-2001. Opposition spokes Social Security 1995-97. Member select cttees: Social Security 1994-96/97-98, Liaison 1998-99, Education and Employment (chair) 1998-99. Academic/research/analyst career. Ed BSc sociology, LSE.

Croydon North's extremely transitory population makes it electorally unpredictable. It is a template for Labour's success in the 1990s: building on a traditional support-base in poorer areas, aspirant voters and perceived strength on jobs and the economy has enabled the party to establish a large lead in the constituency. Malcolm Wicks looked safe in 2005, although with the Iraq factor it was also likely to swing a long way in a little time.

CROYDON SOUTH — C hold

		Electorate 76,872	Turnout 63.6%	Change from 2001	2001	Electorate 73,372	Turnout 61.4%
Ottaway R	**C**	**25,320**	**51.8%**	**2.6%**	**C**	**22,169**	**49.2%**
Smith P	Lab	11,792	24.1%	-5.8%	Lab	13,472	29.9%
Lawman S	LD	10,049	20.6%	2.3%	LD	8,226	18.3%
Feisenberger J	UKIP	1,054	2.2%		UKIP	998	2.2%
Dare G	Veritas	497	1%		Work	195	0.4%
Samuel M	Work	185	0.4%				
Lab to C swing	**4.2%**	**48,897**		**C maj 13,528** 27.7%		**45,060**	**C maj 8,697** 19.3%

RICHARD OTTAWAY b 24 May 1945. MP for Nottingham North 1983-87, for Croydon South 1992-. Shadow Environment Sec of State 2004. PPS to: Foreign and Commonwealth Office Mins of State 1985-87, Michael Heseltine 1992-95. Whip: govt 1995-97, opposition 1997. Opposition spokes: local govt and London 1997-99, defence 1999-2000, Treasury 2000-01. Member various select cttees 1996-. Vice chair all-party Olympics group 2003-. Vice-chair Con Party 1998-99. London mayoral nominee 2002. Solicitor. Royal Navy 1961-70. Ed LLB, Bristol Univ.

This part of the borough is known as 'commuterland'. The suburbs of Purley and Coulsdon are contained within its boundaries, and are typical of the comfortable middle-class residential nature of the seat as a whole. Croydon South is the most prosperous and least urban of the three Croydon seats. Retaining a healthy majority in the face of Labour's assault on outer London in 1997 shows how safe this seat is for the Conservatives.

CUMBERNAULD, KILSYTH AND KIRKINTILLOCH EAST — Lab hold

		Electorate	Turnout	2001
		64,748	60.4%	
McKenna R	**Lab**	**20,251**	**51.8%**	No comparable results due to boundary changes
Hepburn J	SNP	8,689	22.2%	
O'Donnell H	LD	5,817	14.9%	
Boswell J	C	2,718	7%	
O'Neill W	SSP	1,141	2.9%	
Elliott P	OCV	472	1.2%	
Lab to SNP swing (notional)	**1.1%**	**39,088**	**Lab maj 11,562** 29.6%	

ROSEMARY McKENNA b 8 May 1941. MP for Cumbernauld and Kilsyth 1997-2005, for Cumbernauld, Kilsyth and Kirkintilloch East 2005-. PPS: Brian Wilson 2001, (joint) Ministers of State 1999-2001. Member: select cttees, Scottish Exec and nat local govt cttee 1994-98. Cllr Cumbernauld and Kilsyth DC 1984-96: leader 1992-94. Member Scottish Enterprise 1993-97. Chair Scottish Libraries and Info Council 1998-2002. Pres Scottish Local Authorities Convention 1994-96. Teacher 1974-94. CBE. Ed dip primary education, Notre Dame Coll of Education.

The electorate of this largely working-class, heavily Labour-voting seat on the north-eastern margins of Glasgow is concentrated in Cumbernauld new town. Kirkintilloch is similarly typical of the Glasgow periphery, with a high concentration of social-housing for city overspill, while Kilsyth is an ex-mining town and retains some light industry. The seat now takes in some more rural areas, reaching the Campsie fells in the north-west. However, it remains largely urban, working-class and Labour voting.

CYNON VALLEY — Lab hold

		Electorate	Turnout	Change from 2001	2001	Electorate	Turnout
		45,369	58.7%			48,629	55.4%
Clwyd A	**Lab**	**17,074**	**64.1%**	**-1.5%**	**Lab**	**17,685**	**65.6%**
Benney G	PIC	3,815	14.3%	-3.1%	PIC	4,687	17.4%
Phelps M	LD	2,991	11.2%	1.8%	LD	2,541	9.4%
Dunn A	C	2,062	7.7%	0.1%	C	2,045	7.6%
Davies S	UKIP	705	2.6%				
PIC to Lab swing	**0.8%**	**26,647**		**Lab maj 13,259** 49.8%		**26,958**	**Lab maj 12,998** 48.2%

ANN CLWYD b 21 March 1937. MP May 1984- (by-election). Shadow Sec of State: Nat Heritage 1992-93, Wales 1992, Internat Devt 1989-92. Shadow Minister Education and Women's Rights 1987-88. Opposition spokes 1993-95. Asst to John Prescott 1994-95. Member Internat Devt select cttee 1997. Chair all-party groups. Member Lab Party NEC 1983-84. Chair PLP 2005-. Special envoy to PM on Iraq human rights 2003. Chair Tribune group 1986-87. Journalist, broadcaster, MEP 1979-84. PC 2004. Ed Univ Coll of Wales, Bangor.

This seat, previously known as Aberdare, and which encompasses the town of that name, is a former mining area and home to the last deep mine in Wales, the worker-owned Tower colliery. It is a poor and socially deprived area though investment is helping improve conditions. This is safe Labour territory: candidates of no other political persuasion have been elected here since 1922. This will not change in the near future.

DAGENHAM — Lab hold

		Electorate	Turnout	Change from 2001	2001	Electorate	Turnout
		60,141	51.3%			59,340	46.5%
Cruddas J	**Lab**	**15,446**	**50.1%**	**-7.1%**	**Lab**	**15,784**	**57.2%**
White M	C	7,841	25.4%	-0.3%	C	7,091	25.7%
Kempton J	LD	3,106	10.1%	-0.1%	LD	2,820	10.2%
Rustem L	BNP	2,870	9.3%	4.3%	BNP	1,378	5%
Batten G	UKIP	1,578	5.1%		SA	262	0.9%
					SLP	245	0.9%
Lab to C swing	**3.4%**	**30,841**		**Lab maj 7,605** 24.7%		**27,580**	**Lab maj 8,693** 31.5%

JON CRUDDAS b 7 April 1962. MP 2001-. Member Public Accounts select cttee 2003-. Sec all-party Olympics group 2003. Policy officer Lab Party Policy Directorate 1989-94; chief asst General Sec Lab Party 1994-97; deputy political sec PM's political office Downing St 1997-2001. TGWU 1989-2001: branch sec 1992-94. Ed Oaklands RC Comp, Portsmouth; BSc/MA/PhD Warwick Univ; USA visiting fellow, Wisconsin Univ, USA.

This east London seat is usually associated with the massive Ford motor works. There are, however, many more large companies based in the seat. This has led to the seat having a very large proportion of manual workers. However, the core demographic is changing in response to population increases and development, investment and regeneration in the Thames Gateway area. This is a safe Labour seat with strong local support.

DARLINGTON — Lab hold

		Electorate 65,281	Turnout 60.3%	Change from 2001	2001	Electorate 64,354	Turnout 62%
Milburn A	**Lab**	**20,643**	**52.4%**	**-3.9%**	**Lab**	**22,479**	**56.3%**
Frieze A	C	10,239	26%	-4.3%	C	12,095	30.3%
Adamson R	LD	7,269	18.4%	7.5%	LD	4,358	10.9%
Hoodless J	UKIP	730	1.8%		SA	469	1.2%
Davies D	Veritas	507	1.3%		Ind	269	0.7%
					SLP	229	0.6%
C to Lab swing	**0.2%**	**39,388**		**Lab maj 10,404** 26.4%		**39,899**	**Lab maj 10,384** 26%

ALAN MILBURN b 27 Jan 1958. MP 1992-. Chancellor Duchy of Lancaster 2004-05, Health Sec of State 1999-2003, Chief Sec Treasury 1998-99, Dept of Health Minister of State 1997-98. Opposition spokes: health 1995-96, Treasury/economic affairs (Shadow economic sec) 1996-97. Member Public Accounts select cttee 1994-95. Chair Newcastle Central Constituency Lab Party 1988-90. Pres MSF union NE region 1990-92. Senior business development officer N Tyneside Council 1990-92. PC 1998. Ed BA hist, Lancaster Univ; Newcastle Univ.

Darlington, an industrial and market town on Durham's southern border, is the largest town in County Durham. It was previously known as a railway town; the closure of the rail works in the mid-1960s was followed by a decline in other heavy industries; now business is focused on the technology and telecommunications industries. A constituency that has shown itself more than capable of switching political allegiance, it is, at the moment, a safe Labour seat.

DARTFORD — Lab hold

		Electorate 74,028	Turnout 63.2%	Change from 2001	2001	Electorate 71,758	Turnout 62.3%
Stoate H	**Lab**	**19,909**	**42.6%**	**-5.4%**	**Lab**	**21,466**	**48%**
Johnson G	C	19,203	41.1%	0.5%	C	18,160	40.6%
Bucklitsch P	LD	5,036	10.8%	2.3%	LD	3,781	8.5%
Croucher M	UKIP	1,407	3%	0.8%	UKIP	989	2.2%
Tibby M	NEP	1,224	2.6%		FDP	344	0.8%
Lab to C swing	**3%**	**46,779**		**Lab maj 706** 1.5%		**44,740**	**Lab maj 3,306** 7.4%

HOWARD STOATE b 14 April 1954. MP 1997-. PPS to: John Denham 2001-03, Estelle Morris 2003-05. Member Health select cttee 1997-2001. Chair all-party groups: men's health 2001-, pharmacy 2001-, primary care and public health 2001-, obesity (co-chair) 2002-, asthma 2004-. Vice-chair Dartford Fabian Soc. Cllr Dartford Borough Council 1990-99. General practitioner (GP Bexley Heath 1982-). Chair Bexley Ethics Research cttee 1995-97. Vice-chair Regional Graduate Education Board 1997-. Ed MBBS/MSc/DRCOG/FRCGP, King's Coll, London Univ.

Home to the extremely congested Dartford tunnels and bridge as well as the M25, and booming in jobs and population, Dartford is divided into parts which have a London type of social background, such as Dartford itself, and the more rural Kentish elements which are much more Conservative. This balance has made what was originally considered a fairly safe Labour seat much more unpredictable. It came very close to reverting to the Conservatives in 2005.

DAVENTRY — C hold

		Electorate 88,758	Turnout 68.1%	Change from 2001	2001	Electorate 86,510	Turnout 65.5%
Boswell T	**C**	**31,206**	**51.6%**	**2.4%**	**C**	**27,911**	**49.2%**
Hammond A	Lab	16,520	27.3%	-4.9%	Lab	18,262	32.2%
Saul H	LD	9,964	16.5%	0.4%	LD	9,130	16.1%
Mahoney B	UKIP	1,927	3.2%	0.8%	UKIP	1,381	2.4%
Wilkins B	Veritas	822	1.4%				
Lab to C swing	**3.7%**	**60,439**		**C maj 14,686** 24.3%		**56,684**	**C maj 9,649** 17%

TIMOTHY BOSWELL b 2 Dec 1942. MP 1987-. Shadow Min: Work and Pensions and Welfare Reform 2004-, Home Affairs 2004, Home, Consitutional and Legal Affairs 2003-04, Education and Skills (People with Disabilities). MAFF Parly Sec 1995-97, Education Dept Parly Under-Sec 1992-95. PPS to Peter Lilley 1989-90. Whip posts: asst govt 1990-92, govt 1992. Opposition spokes 1997-2001. Chair all-party progressive supranuclear palsy group 2004-. Farmer/economist. Ed MA classics/agricultural dip, New Coll, Oxford.

Daventry is an expanding town close to the M1, between Northampton and Rugby, and has grown up on the car industry. Most of the seat is rural, and the countryside harbours many prosperous small villages. Silverstone, home to the British Grand Prix, is in the region, as is Towcester, famous mainly for its racecourse. This seat has the lowest unemployment rate in the county and the highest proportions of professional and management/technical workers. It remains a Conservative stronghold.

DELYN — Lab hold

		Electorate 52,766	Turnout 64.4%	Change from 2001	2001	Electorate 54,732	Turnout 63.3%
Hanson D	**Lab**	**15,540**	**45.7%**	**-5.8%**	**Lab**	**17,825**	**51.5%**
Bell J	C	8,896	26.2%	-0.4%	C	9,220	26.6%
Jones T	LD	6,089	17.9%	2.5%	LD	5,329	15.4%
Thomas P	PlC	2,524	7.4%	0.9%	PlC	2,262	6.5%
Crawford M	UKIP	533	1.6%				
Williams N	Ind	422	1.2%				
Lab to C swing	**2.7%**	**34,004**		**Lab maj 6,644** 19.5%		**34,636**	**Lab maj 8,605** 24.8%

DAVID HANSON b 5 July 1957. MP 1992-. Minister of State NI Office 2005-. PPS to: Tony Blair as PM 2001-05. Parly Under-Sec Wales Office 1999-2001. PPS to Alastair Darling 1997-98. Asst govt whip 1998-99. Member Welsh Affairs select cttee 1992-95. Member leadership campaign team 1994-97. Cllr: Vale Royal BC 1983-91 (leader), Northwich Town Council 1987-91. Co-operative Union trainee 1980-81, manager Plymouth Co-operative 1981-82. Spastics Society 1982-89, dir Re-Solv 1989-92. Ed BA drama, Cert Ed, Hull Univ.

Close to the border in north-east Wales, this is linguistically one of the most anglicised parts of the principality. On a clear day England can be seen across the Dee Estuary which borders the constituency. There are several sizeable communities here: Holywell, Flint, and the market town Mold. There are a number of smaller villages in the Clwydian hills. A Tory seat until the 1992 general election, this is now a safe Labour seat.

DENTON AND REDDISH — Lab hold

		Electorate 68,267	Turnout 51.9%	Change from 2001	2001	Electorate 69,236	Turnout 48.5%
Gwynne A	**Lab**	**20,340**	**57.4%**	**-7.8%**	**Lab**	**21,913**	**65.2%**
Story A	C	6,842	19.3%	-0.3%	C	6,583	19.6%
Seabourne A	LD	5,814	16.4%	4%	LD	4,152	12.4%
Edgar J	BNP	1,326	3.7%		UKIP	945	2.8%
Price G	UKIP	1,120	3.2%	0.4%			
Lab to C swing	**3.8%**	**35,442**		**Lab maj 13,498** 38.1%		**33,593**	**Lab maj 15,330** 45.6%

ANDREW GWYNNE b 4 June 1974. MP 2005-. Councillor Tameside MBC 1996-. ICL 1990-92; National Computing Centre, Y2K team 1999-2000; researcher Andrew Bennett MP 2000-01; European co-ordinator Arlene McCarthy MEP 2000-01. Ed Egerton Park Community High School; politics and contemporary history, North East Wales Institute.

The little-known constituency of Denton and Reddish is situated on the immediate outskirts of Manchester, lending it proximity to the city's airport and industry on one side, and the moors on the other. The very high proportion of skilled manual workers residing within it probably helps the seat's Labour tendencies. By sequestering the core of Stockport's traditional support, the 1983 boundary review carved Labour an unmovable stronghold that is likely to continue in future elections.

DERBY NORTH — Lab hold

		Electorate 68,173	Turnout 64.3%	Change from 2001	2001	Electorate 75,926	Turnout 58%
Laxton B	**Lab**	**19,272**	**44%**	**-6.9%**	**Lab**	**22,415**	**50.9%**
Aitken Davies R	C	15,515	35.4%	0.4%	C	15,433	35%
Beckett J	LD	7,209	16.4%	2.3%	LD	6,206	14.1%
Bardoe M	Veritas	958	2.2%				
Medgyesy M	UKIP	864	2%				
Lab to C swing	**3.7%**	**43,818**		**Lab maj 3,757** 8.6%		**44,054**	**Lab maj 6,982** 15.8%

BOB LAXTON b 7 Sept 1944. MP 1997-. PPS to Alan Johnson 2001-. Member Trade and Industry select cttee 1997-2001. Treasurer all-party telecomms group 2004-. Member Lab Middle East Council. Lab Party Conference debate, local govt 1995. Cllr Derby City Council 1979-97: leader 1986-88/1994-97; chair East Midlands Local Govt Assocn to 1997. CWU member. Telecomms engineer (BT plc 1961-97). TU branch officer Communication Workers' union. Ed Woodlands Sec Sch; Derby Art and Technology Coll.

Derby North is more residential than its southern neighbour with some attractive middle class suburbs in Allestree and Darley while Mackworth contains large council estates and Breadsall both council estates and new private developments. Much of the census data for the constituency is near average although there are more professionals than in most constituencies. The seat has traditionally voted Labour, although history has proved that Derby North is by no means an impenetrable stronghold.

DERBY SOUTH — Lab hold

		Electorate	Turnout	Change from	2001	Electorate	Turnout
		70,397	61.6%	2001		76,708	56.2%
Beckett M	**Lab**	**19,683**	**45.4%**	**-11%**	**Lab**	**24,310**	**56.4%**
Care L	LD	14,026	32.3%	13%	C	10,455	24.3%
Brackenbury D	C	8,211	18.9%	-5.4%	LD	8,310	19.3%
Black D	UKIP	845	2%				
Leeming F	Veritas	608	1.4%				
Lab to LD swing	**12%**	**43,373**		**Lab maj 5,657**		**43,075**	**Lab maj 13,855**
				13%			32.2%

MARGARET BECKETT b 15 Jan 1943. MP for Lincoln 1974-79, for Derby South 1983-. Environment, Food and Rural Affairs Sec of State 2001-, Leader of House of Commons 1998-2001, Trade and Industry Sec of State 1997-98. Shadow: Board of Trade Pres 1995-97, Health Sec of State 1994-95. Opposition leader 1994, dep leader Lab Party and Opposition 1992-94. Shadow ministerial posts 1984-94. Parly Under-Sec of State Dept of Education and Science 1976-79. Chair HoC Modernisation 1998-2001. Metallurgist. PC 1993. Ed Manchester Science and Tech Coll; Poly.

The traditionally Labour constituency is home to Adtrans (the privatised British Rail Engineering Ltd), Rolls Royce Engines and Derby County FC's stadium. Derby South has a large non-white population constituting about one-fifth of its electorate. Margaret Beckett first won this seat in June 1983 having followed Walter Johnson who sat as Labour MP since 1970.

NORTH EAST DERBYSHIRE — Lab hold

		Electorate	Turnout	Change from	2001	Electorate	Turnout
		70,981	61.2%	2001		71,527	58.9%
Engel N	**Lab**	**21,416**	**49.3%**	**-6.3%**	**Lab**	**23,437**	**55.6%**
Johnson D	C	11,351	26.1%	-0.4%	C	11,179	26.5%
Snowdon T	LD	8,812	20.3%	2.5%	LD	7,508	17.8%
Perkins K	UKIP	1,855	4.3%				
Lab to C swing	**3%**	**43,434**		**Lab maj 10,065**		**42,124**	**Lab maj 12,258**
				23.2%			29.1%

NATASCHA ENGEL b 9 April 1967. MP 2005-. Trade union political fund ballot co-ordinator, Trade Union Co-ordinating Committee (TUCC). Newspaper journalist.

A mixed constituency, rural in the west and parts of the south and residential in areas that border the Peak District, nonetheless serves up a consistent Labour majority. Residential developments, combined with the disappearance of coal mining, continue to change the character of this constituency. In the north east are the fomer mining towns of Eckington and Killamarsh and in the south Clay Cross. Some engineering firms and other industries have survived.

SOUTH DERBYSHIRE — Lab hold

		Electorate	Turnout	Change from	2001	Electorate	Turnout
		85,049	65.6%	2001		81,217	64%
Todd M	**Lab**	**24,823**	**44.5%**	**-6.2%**	**Lab**	**26,338**	**50.7%**
Spencer S	C	20,328	36.4%	0.8%	C	18,487	35.6%
Newton-Cook D	LD	7,600	13.6%	3.5%	LD	5,233	10.1%
Joines D	BNP	1,797	3.2%		UKIP	1,074	2.1%
Spalton R	Veritas	1,272	2.3%		SLP	564	1.1%
					Ind	249	0.5%
Lab to C swing	**3.5%**	**55,820**		**Lab maj 4,495**		**51,945**	**Lab maj 7,851**
				8%			15.1%

MARK TODD b 29 Dec 1954. MP 1997-. PPS to Baroness Symons of Vernham Dean as Dep Leader House of Lords and Minister of State FCO and DTI 2002-05. Member select cttees: Agriculture 1997-2001, Environment, Food and Rural Affairs 2001-02. Chair all-party motor neurone disease group 2002-. Cllr Cambridge CC 1980-92: leader 1987-90. Dir Cambridge and District Co-operative Society 1986-89. Longman Group 1977-96. ASTMS (now AMICUS) union chairman at employers. Ed BA hist, Emmanuel Coll, Cambridge.

This Labour-Tory marginal seat is mainly agricultural with an industrial belt around Swadlincote, the largest town, historically based on coal and clay. Melbourne is at the centre of a fertile market gardening area. The coal mines have now closed, but new employment was created by the opening of a Toyota car assembly plant in 1992 at Burnaston close to Derby. About a third of households are headed by skilled manual workers.

WEST DERBYSHIRE

C hold

		Electorate 73,865	Turnout 69.2%	Change from 2001	2001	Electorate 74,651	Turnout 67.8%
McLoughlin P	**C**	**24,378**	**47.7%**	**-0.3%**	**C**	**24,280**	**48%**
Menon D	Lab	13,625	26.6%	-6.8%	Lab	16,910	33.4%
Dring R	LD	11,408	22.3%	6.6%	LD	7,922	15.7%
Cruddas M	UKIP	1,322	2.6%	1.3%	UKIP	672	1.3%
Delves N	Loony	405	0.8%	-0.1%	Loony	472	0.9%
Kyslun M	Ind	5	0%	-0.7%	Ind	333	0.7%
Lab to C swing	**3.3%**	**51,143**		**C maj 10,753** 21%		**50,589**	**C maj 7,370** 14.6%

PATRICK McLOUGHLIN b 30 Nov 1957. MP May 1986- (by-election). Parly Under-Sec: Dept of Trade and Industry 1993-94, (joint) Dept of Employment 1992-93, Dept of Transport 1989-92. PPS to: Lord Young of Graffham 1988-89, Angela Rumbold 1987-88. Whip: asst govt 1995-96, govt 1996-97, opposition pairing 1997-98, opposition dep chief 1998-. Member select cttees, incl Finance and Services 1998-. Young Cons nat vice-chair 1982-84. Cllr: Cannock Chase DC 1980-87, Staffs CC 1981-87. Agricultural worker 1974-79, NCB 1979-86. Ed Staffs Agriculture Coll.

The safe Tory seat of West Derbyshire covers a large part of the Peak District and includes the small towns of Belper, Matlock (spa town), and Wirksworth (quarrying). Chatsworth House is a leading tourist attraction in an area where tourism has become a major industry employing over 6,000 people and balancing out the decline in farming, textiles and quarrying industries. Unemployment levels consequently remain very low.

DEVIZES

C hold

		Electorate 86,168	Turnout 65.2%	Change from 2001	2001	Electorate 82,925	Turnout 64.2%
Ancram M	**C**	**27,253**	**48.5%**	**1.3%**	**C**	**25,159**	**47.2%**
Hornby F	LD	14,059	25%	2.9%	Lab	13,263	24.9%
Charity S	Lab	12,519	22.3%	-2.6%	LD	11,756	22.1%
Wood A	UKIP	2,315	4.1%	1.2%	UKIP	1,521	2.9%
					Ind	1,078	2%
					Loony	472	0.9%
C to LD swing	**0.8%**	**56,146**		**C maj 13,194** 23.5%		**53,249**	**C maj 11,896** 22.3%

MICHAEL ANCRAM b 7 July 1945. MP Berwickshire and E Lothian 1974, for Edinburgh S 1979-87, for Devizes 1992-. Shadow Sec of State: Defence 2005-, Internat Affairs 2003-05, Foreign and Commonwealth Affairs 2001-05. Dep Opposition leader 2001-. Northern Ireland/Scottish Office: ministerial posts 1983-97. Constitutional Affairs spokes 1997-98. Member Public Accounts select cttee 1992-93. Con Party: chair 1998-2001, dep chair 1998. Chair Con Party in Scotland 1980-83. QC. PC 1996. Ed BA hist, Christ Church, Oxford; LLB, Edinburgh Univ.

The epitome of rural charm, the Wiltshire constituency of Devizes is blessed with a multitude of prehistoric sites, barrows and white chalk horses. The Vale of Pewsey is perhaps the best example of the nature of the constituency and, along with the small market towns, is one of the major tourist attractions in the area. Despite the boundary changes at the 1997 general election, this remains the most solid of Conservative seats.

EAST DEVON

C hold

		Electorate 71,000	Turnout 69.4%	Change from 2001	2001	Electorate 69,542	Turnout 68.8%
Swire H	**C**	**23,075**	**46.9%**	**-0.5%**	**C**	**22,681**	**47.4%**
Dumper T	LD	15,139	30.7%	0.4%	LD	14,486	30.3%
Court J	Lab	7,598	15.4%	-1.3%	Lab	7,974	16.7%
McNamee C	UKIP	3,035	6.2%	0.6%	UKIP	2,696	5.6%
Way C	Ind	400	0.8%				
C to LD swing	**0.5%**	**49,247**		**C maj 7,936** 16.1%		**47,837**	**C maj 8,195** 17.1%

HUGO SWIRE b 30 Nov 1959. MP 2001-. Shadow Arts Min 2004-; PPS to Theresa May as Con Party chair 2003. Opposition whip 2003-04. Member Northern Ireland Affairs select cttee 2002-. All-party groups: chair political art 2002-, vice-chair: United Arab Emirates 2004-, world heritage sites 2004-, Lebanon (co-vice-chair) 2002-. Sec Con Middle East Council. Career: army 1979-83, MD 1983-85, financial consultant 1985-87, Nat Gallery head of development 1988-92, director Sotheby's 1997-2003. Ed Eton; St Andrew's Univ; RMA, Sandhurst.

The small strip of land on the coast east of Exeter makes up this affluent constituency of East Devon. This is retirement country, home to the third largest proportion of pensioners in England and Wales. They, like large numbers of older tourists, are attracted by the peace and quiet, warm climate and beautiful landscape. East Devon has always elected a Conservative MP and will, for the foreseeable future, continue to do so.

NORTH DEVON LD hold

		Electorate	Turnout	Change from	2001	Electorate	Turnout
		76,203	68.2%	2001		72,100	68.3%
Harvey N	**LD**	**23,840**	**45.9%**	**1.7%**	**LD**	**21,784**	**44.2%**
Fraser O	C	18,868	36.3%	-1.9%	C	18,800	38.2%
Cann M	Lab	4,656	9%	-1.1%	Lab	4,995	10.1%
Browne J	UKIP	2,740	5.3%	0.3%	UKIP	2,484	5%
Knight R	Greens	1,826	3.5%	1.1%	Greens	1,191	2.4%
C to LD swing	**1.8%**	**51,930**		**LD maj 4,972**		**49,254**	**LD maj 2,984**
				9.6%			6.1%

NICK HARVEY b 3 Aug 1961. MP 1992-. Lib Dem spokes: transport 1992-94, trade and industry 1994-97, constitution (English regions) 1997-99, health 1999-2001, culture, media and sport 2001-03. Member select cttees: Trade and Industry 1994-95, European Scrutiny 2004-. Chair: candidates cttee 1993-98, campaigns/communications 1994-99. Vice-pres Federation of Economic Devt Auths 2000-. Communications/marketing consultant/executive 1984-92. Ed Queen's Coll, Taunton; BA business studies, Middlesex Poly.

North Devon is the quintessential West Country constituency. It is a largely rural seat facing all the problems associated with living in such a remote place. Since the Second World War North Devon has been split fairly evenly between the Liberals and the Tories. The Lib Dems won it back in 1997 after 18 years of Conservatism and have since worked hard to hold onto the seat.

SOUTH WEST DEVON C hold

		Electorate	Turnout	Change from	2001	Electorate	Turnout
		71,307	68.6%	2001		70,922	66.1%
Streeter G	**C**	**21,906**	**44.8%**	**-2%**	**C**	**21,970**	**46.8%**
Evans J	LD	11,765	24.1%	5.7%	Lab	14,826	31.6%
Mavin C	Lab	11,545	23.6%	-8%	LD	8,616	18.4%
Williams H	UKIP	3,669	7.5%	4.3%	UKIP	1,492	3.2%
C to LD swing	**3.9%**	**48,885**		**C maj 10,141**		**46,904**	**C maj 7,144**
				20.7%			15.2%

GARY STREETER b 2 Oct 1955. MP for Plymouth Sutton 1992-97, for South West Devon 1997-. Shadow: Minister for Foreign Affairs 2003-05, Sec of State for Internat Devt 1998-2001. Parly Sec Lord Chancellor's Dept 1996-97. PPS to: Sir Nicholas Lyell 1994-95, Sir Derek Spencer 1993-95. Opposition spokes 1997-98. Asst govt whip 1995-96. Vice-chair all-party groups: Friends of Islam 2003-, North Korea 2004-. Vice-chair Con Party 2001-02. Cllr Plymouth CC 1986-92. Solicitor. Ed Tiverton Grammar Sch; LLB, King's Coll, London.

This is a varied constituency that incorporates part of the Devon city of Plymouth, part rural land and part coast. No matter what the Conservative Party do nationwide, there is little hope of Labour or the Liberal Democrats taking this seat soon. The issues that blight many rural constituencies are not so apparent here, because it is essentially a commuter constituency, totally unlike its truly rural neighbours.

TORRIDGE AND WEST DEVON C gain

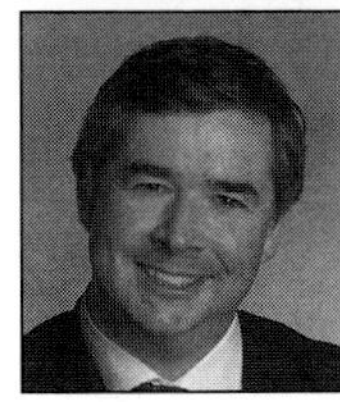

		Electorate	Turnout	Change from	2001	Electorate	Turnout
		83,489	70.2%	2001		78,976	70.5%
Cox G	**C**	**25,013**	**42.7%**	**2.7%**	**LD**	**23,474**	**42.2%**
Walter D	LD	21,777	37.2%	-5%	C	22,280	40%
Richards R	Lab	6,001	10.2%	-0.5%	Lab	5,959	10.7%
Jackson M	UKIP	3,790	6.5%	1.7%	UKIP	2,674	4.8%
Christie P	Greens	2,003	3.4%	1.1%	Greens	1,297	2.3%
LD to C swing	**3.9%**	**58,584**		**C maj 3,236**		**55,684**	**LD maj 1,194**
				5.5%			2.1%

GEOFFREY COX b 30 April 1960. MP 2005-. Contested Torridge and West Devon 2001 general election. Barrister, Thomas More Chambers 1982-2001; standing counsel of Mauritius 1996-2000. Ed Kings College, Taunton; English and law, Downing College, Cambridge.

There are very few places in the UK that are as rural as Torridge and Devon West and it has a strong agricultural industry. Based on the towns of Tavistock and Okehampton, and including large parts of Dartmoor National Park, this is currently the largest seat in the county. Previously strong Conservative territory, the Tories took this seat back in 2005 after eight years of Liberal Democrat control.

DEWSBURY — Lab hold

		Electorate	Turnout	Change from	2001	Electorate	Turnout
		62,243	62%	2001		62,345	58.8%
Malik S	**Lab**	**15,807**	**41%**	**-9.5%**	**Lab**	**18,524**	**50.5%**
Warsi S	C	11,192	29%	-1.2%	C	11,075	30.2%
Hill K	LD	5,624	14.6%	2.6%	LD	4,382	12%
Exley D	BNP	5,066	13.1%	8.6%	BNP	1,632	4.5%
Smithson B	Greens	593	1.5%		Greens	560	1.5%
Girvan A	Ind	313	0.8%		UKIP	478	1.3%
Lab to C swing	**4.2%**	**38,595**		**Lab maj 4,615**		**36,651**	**Lab maj 7,449**
				12%			20.3%

SHAHID MALIK b 24 November 1967. MP 2005-. Chair Urban Forum; Commissioner Commission for Racial Equality; Vice-chair UNESCO UK. Ed London Polytechnic; Durham Business School

The region was once almost solely reliant on the textile industry, but since its decline other industries, notably chemicals and engineering, have been established to maintain a firm economic base. A quarter of homes are rented from the council, and there is a significant Asian population (12.4 per cent), centred in Dewsbury itself. The seat has historically been marginal, and the drop in Labour support witnessed in 2005 ensured it will continue to be so.

DON VALLEY — Lab hold

		Electorate	Turnout	Change from	2001	Electorate	Turnout
		66,993	55%	2001		66,787	54.8%
Flint C	**Lab**	**19,418**	**52.7%**	**-1.9%**	**Lab**	**20,009**	**54.6%**
Duguid A	C	10,820	29.4%	0.8%	C	10,489	28.6%
Arnold S	LD	6,626	18%	6.8%	LD	4,089	11.2%
					Ind	800	2.2%
					UKIP	777	2.1%
					SLP	466	1.3%
Lab to C swing	**1.4%**	**36,864**		**Lab maj 8,598**		**36,630**	**Lab maj 9,520**
				23.3%			26%

CAROLINE FLINT b 20 Sept 1961. MP 1997-. Parly Under-Sec: Dept of Health 2005-. Home Office 2003-05. PPS to: John Reid 2002-03, Peter Hain 2001-02, joint PPS to Mins of State, FCO 1999-2001. Member select cttees: Education and Employment 1997-99, Admin 2001-05, Modernisation of HoC 2003. Chair Brentford/Isleworth Constituency Lab Party 1991-95. Council/Inner London Education Authority/trade union career. GMB senior researcher/political officer 1994-97. Ed BA American hist/lit and film studies, East Anglia Univ.

Although the coalmining industry is in sharp decline, such decline may serve only to strengthen the Labour vote. Other industries have been attracted to settle here in compensation for the loss of mining jobs, while engineering and agriculture were industries already established when coal was still king. Consequently, the majority of the workforce is involved in manual jobs, though not perhaps to the same extent as in the surrounding constituencies.

DONCASTER CENTRAL — Lab hold

		Electorate	Turnout	Change from	2001	Electorate	Turnout
		65,731	52.3%	2001		65,690	51.6%
Winterton R	**Lab**	**17,617**	**51.3%**	**-7.8%**	**Lab**	**20,034**	**59.1%**
Wilson P	LD	7,815	22.8%	9.9%	C	8,035	23.7%
Kerner S	C	6,489	18.9%	-4.8%	LD	4,390	12.9%
Wilkinson J	BNP	1,239	3.6%		UKIP	926	2.7%
Simmons A	UKIP	1,191	3.5%	0.8%	SA	517	1.5%
Lab to LD swing	**8.9%**	**34,351**		**Lab maj 9,802**		**33,902**	**Lab maj 11,999**
				28.5%			35.4%

ROSIE WINTERTON b 10 Aug 1958. MP 1997-. Dept of Health Min of State 2003-. Parly Sec Lord Chancellor's Dept 2001-03. Representative, PLP on Lab Party National Policy Forum. Member Lab Party Strategic Campaign cttee. Leader leadership campaign team 1998-99. Chair Transport and General Workers' parly group 1998-99. Parly officer 1986-90. Head of John Prescott private office as Lab Party dep leader 1994-97. MD Connect Public Affairs 1990-94. TGWU branch officer 1998-99. Ed Doncaster Grammar Sch; BA hist, Hull Univ.

Doncaster, like most of its neighbours a Labour stronghold, lies in the middle of one of the few worked coalfields left in the country, though mining in Doncaster has never amounted to much. Most industry is based on textiles and light engineering, but retail is also important as the town is a commercial centre for much of South Yorkshire as well as Nottinghamshire and Lincolnshire. The council-owned racecourse is also found in this seat.

DONCASTER NORTH — Lab hold

		Electorate 61,741	Turnout 51.2%	Change from 2001	2001	Electorate 62,124	Turnout 50.5%
Miliband E	**Lab**	**17,531**	**55.5%**	**-7.6%**	**Lab**	**19,788**	**63.1%**
Drake M	C	4,875	15.4%	0.7%	C	4,601	14.7%
Pickett D	LD	3,800	12%	1.4%	LD	3,323	10.6%
Williams M	CG	2,365	7.5%		Ind	2,926	9.3%
Haggan L	BNP	1,506	4.8%		UKIP	725	2.3%
Nixon R	UKIP	940	3%	0.7%			
Cassidy M	England	561	1.8%				
Lab to C swing	**4.2%**	**31,578**		**Lab maj 12,656** 40.1%		**31,363**	**Lab maj 15,187** 48.4%

ED MILIBAND b 24 December 1969. MP 2005-. Special adviser to Gordon Brown as Chancellor of the Exchequer 1997-2002; teacher of economics Harvard University 2002-04; chair Council of Economic Advisers 2004-05. Ed Oxford University; London School of Economics

This seat borders Lincolnshire, which explains the unchangingly level landscape stretching far into the distance. Towns and villages rarely impose themselves on this scene, communities there being based on farming or mining. This seat boasts one of the few remaining working pits in England, around Stainforth and Thorne, but the council is trying to attract new business to the area. Despite unemployment levels higher than the national average, Doncaster North remains a Labour stronghold.

MID DORSET AND POOLE NORTH — LD hold

		Electorate 65,924	Turnout 68.5%	Change from 2001	2001	Electorate 66,675	Turnout 65.6%
Brooke A	**LD**	**22,000**	**48.7%**	**6.7%**	**LD**	**18,358**	**42%**
Hayes S	C	16,518	36.6%	-4.5%	C	17,974	41.1%
Murray P	Lab	5,221	11.6%	-3.9%	Lab	6,765	15.5%
King A	UKIP	1,420	3.1%	1.7%	UKIP	621	1.4%
C to LD swing	**5.6%**	**45,159**		**LD maj 5,482** 12.1%		**43,718**	**LD maj 384** 0.9%

ANNETTE BROOKE b 7 June 1947. MP 2001-. Lib Dem whip 2001-03. Lib Dem spokes: home affairs 2001-04, children 2004-. Member Public Admin select cttee 2001-. Chair all-party microfinance/microedit group 2002-. Member European Standing Cttee B 2001-02. Cllr Poole BC 1986-2003: sheriff 1996-97, mayor 1997-98. Counsellor/tutor Open Univ 1971-91. Head of Economics Talbot Heath Sch Bournemouth 1984-94. Business partner/owner. Ed Romford Tech Coll; BSc econ, LSE; Cert Ed, Hughes Hall, Cambridge.

On the border between town and country, the constituency stretches from the suburban residential areas of Poole North to the smaller rural communities of Lytchett Matravers, Morden, and beyond to Bere Regis. A new creation for 1997, Mid Dorset and Poole North is predominantly a residential areas for commuters. It was narrowly held by the Conservatives in its inaugural year but has since fallen to the Liberal Democrats, who now appear relatively secure here.

NORTH DORSET — C hold

		Electorate 74,286	Turnout 71.1%	Change from 2001	2001	Electorate 71,412	Turnout 67%
Walter R	**C**	**23,714**	**44.9%**	**-1.8%**	**C**	**22,314**	**46.7%**
Gasson E	LD	21,470	40.6%	1.9%	LD	18,517	38.7%
Yarwood J	Lab	4,596	8.7%	-2.5%	Lab	5,334	11.2%
Frampton Hobbs R	UKIP	1,918	3.6%	1.5%	UKIP	1,019	2.1%
Arliss R	Greens	1,117	2.1%		LEDP	391	0.8%
					Ind	246	0.5%
C to LD swing	**1.9%**	**52,815**		**C maj 2,244** 4.2%		**47,821**	**C maj 3,797** 7.9%

ROBERT WALTER b 30 May 1948. MP 1997-. Opposition constitutional affairs (Wales) spokes 1999-2001. Member select cttees: Unopposed Bills (Panel) 1997-, Health 1997-99, European Scrutiny 1999, Internat Devt 2001-03, Treasury 2003-. Vice-chair various all-party groups. Member exec 1922 cttee 2002-. Vice-pres Con group for Europe 1997-2000. Member: Western European Union Assembly 2001-, Council of Europe Parly Assembly 2001-. Farmer/banker/East-West trade lecturer. City of London Freeman 1983. Ed BSc, Aston Univ, Birmingham.

Set in the splendour of the Dorset countryside to the north of Poole, the Dorset Downs and Cranbourne Chase have been designated areas of outstanding beauty. It is home to the small market towns of Wimborne Minster, Gillingham, Blandford Forum and Shaftesbury. North Dorset remains a Conservative seat, but another increase in Liberal Democrat support in the election has brought them within striking distance of the Tories.

SOUTH DORSET — Lab hold

		Electorate	Turnout	Change from	2001	Electorate	Turnout
		70,668	68.8%	2001		68,115	66.6%
Knight J	**Lab**	**20,231**	**41.6%**	**-0.4%**	**Lab**	**19,027**	**42%**
Matts E	C	18,419	37.9%	-3.7%	C	18,874	41.6%
Oakes G	LD	7,647	15.7%	1.3%	LD	6,531	14.4%
Chalker H	UKIP	1,571	3.2%	1.2%	UKIP	913	2%
Hamilton V	LCA	282	0.6%				
Parkes B	Respect	219	0.4%				
Kirkwood A	PRTYP	107	0.2%				
Bex C	Wes R	83	0.2%				
Marchesi D	SLP	25	0.1%				
C to Lab swing	**1.7%**	**48,584**		**Lab maj 1,812**		**45,345**	**Lab maj 153**
				3.7%			0.3%

JIM KNIGHT b 6 March 1965. MP 2001-. Parly Under-Sec Dept for Environment, Food and Rural Affairs 2005-. Dept of Health: team PPS 2004-05, PPS to Rosie Winterton 2003-04. Member Defence select cttee 2001-03. Chair all-party groups: minerals 2004-, leisure 2004-. Cllr: Frome Town Council 1993-2001 (mayor 1998-2001), Mendip DC 1997-2001 (dep leader 1999-2001). Dir: W Wiltshire Arts Centre Ltd 1990-91, Dentons Directories Ltd 1991-2001. Branch chair MSF 1997-2001. BA geog, social and political sciences, Fitzwilliam Coll, Cambridge.

South Dorset is centred primarily on the seaside resort of Weymouth, where tourism and defence are the biggest employers. The constituency is also home to some light industy, including the Wytch Farm offshore oilfield. South Dorset is something of an anomaly as the only seat held by Labour in the county. A very marginal constituency, the fight here between Labour and the Conservatives has been too close to call in recent elections.

WEST DORSET — C hold

		Electorate	Turnout	Change from	2001	Electorate	Turnout
		69,764	76.3%	2001		71,291	69.5%
Letwin O	**C**	**24,763**	**46.5%**	**1.9%**	**C**	**22,126**	**44.6%**
McGuinness J	LD	22,302	41.9%	0.1%	LD	20,712	41.8%
Roberts D	Lab	4,124	7.8%	-5.8%	Lab	6,733	13.6%
Guest L	UKIP	1,084	2%				
Greene S	Greens	952	1.8%				
LD to C swing	**0.9%**	**53,225**		**C maj 2,461**		**49,571**	**C maj 1,414**
				4.6%			2.9%

OLIVER LETWIN b 19 May 1956. MP 1997-. Shadow: Sec of State Environ, Food and Rural Affairs 2005-, Chancellor of Exchequer, Sec of State Economic Affairs 2003-05, Home Sec 2001-03, Chief Sec to Treasury 2000-01, Financial Sec 1999-2000. Opposition spokes: constitutional affairs, Scotland and Wales 1998-99, Treasury 1999-2000. Member Deregulation select cttee 1998-99. Special adviser to: Sir Keith Joseph, PM's Policy Unit. MD NM Rothschild & Son. PC 2002. Ed BA hist, MA, PhD philosophy, Trinity Coll, Cambridge; London Business Sch.

West Dorset is economically buoyant, with demand for land for industrial estates outstripping supply. The main town is Dorchester and the area as a whole has many attractions for tourists. Lyme Regis in particular is becoming an increasingly popular seaside resort. In what was once a bastion of Conservative support, the Liberal Democrats have closed the gap on the Tories significantly, but could not defeat Oliver Letwin in 2005.

DOVER — Lab hold

		Electorate	Turnout	Change from	2001	Electorate	Turnout
		70,884	67.6%	2001		68,994	65.2%
Prosser G	**Lab**	**21,680**	**45.3%**	**-3.5%**	**Lab**	**21,943**	**48.8%**
Watkins P	C	16,739	35%	-2.2%	C	16,744	37.2%
Hook A	LD	7,607	15.9%	4.5%	LD	5,131	11.4%
Wiltshire M	UKIP	1,252	2.6%	0.1%	UKIP	1,142	2.5%
Matcham V	Ind	606	1.3%				
Lab to C swing	**0.7%**	**47,884**		**Lab maj 4,941**		**44,960**	**Lab maj 5,199**
				10.3%			11.6%

GWYN PROSSER 27 April 1943. MP 1997-. Member select cttees: Information 2000-, Home Affairs 2001-. Chair all-party ports and Merchant Navy group 2002-. Member Parly Assembly of: Council of Europe 1997-2001, Western European Union 1997-2001. Cllr: Dover District Council 1987-97, Kent County Council 1989-97. Chartered marine engineer 1960-92. Civ servant 1993-96. Former member NUMAST NEC. MSF political officer. Ed Swansea Coll of Tech (Nat Dip, mech engineering, first class cert of competency, marine engineering).

Dover, a coastal strip rich in heritage and dominated by the famous white cliffs, is an extremely varied constituency both socially and economically. It includes the ferry port and old coalfield communities, as well as very attractive seaside spots and countryside, especially the North Downs with its Channel views. It has swapped between Labour and the Conservatives a number of times since the Second World War, but Labour seems to have consolidated since 1997.

NORTH DOWN — UUP hold

		Electorate 59,748	Turnout 54%	Change from 2001	2001	Electorate 63,212	Turnout 58.8%
Hermon S	**UUP**	**16,268**	**50.4%**	**-5.6%**	**UUP**	**20,833**	**56%**
Weir P	DUP	11,324	35.1%		UKUP	13,509	36.3%
Alderdice D	All	2,451	7.6%		SDLP	1,275	3.4%
Logan L	SDLP	1,009	3.1%	-0.3%	C	815	2.2%
Robertson J	C	822	2.6%	0.4%	Ind	444	1.2%
Carter C	Ind	211	0.6%	-0.6%	SF	313	0.8%
McCrory J	SF	205	0.6%	-0.2%			
UUP to DUP swing	**20.4%**	**32,290**		**UUP maj 4,944** 15.3%		**37,189**	**UUP maj 7,324** 19.7%

SYLVIA HERMON b 11 Aug 1955. MP 2001-. UUP spokes: home affairs 2001-, trade and industry 2001-02, youth and women's issues 2001-, culture, media and sport 2002-. Vice-chair all-party groups: police 2002-, dignity at work 2003-, pensioner incomes 2004-. Author/cttee member addressing Patten Report Criminal Justive Review 2000. Ulster Unionist Exec 1999. Constituency chair N Down Unionist Constituency Assocn 2001-03. Law lecturer 1978-88. Ed law, Aberystwyth Univ, Wales; Part II Solicitors' Qualifying Examinations.

This beautiful coastal constituency is on the Ards Peninsula bordering the southern shores of Belfast Lough, on the east of Northern Ireland. It is a predominantly Protestant, middle class and suburban dormitory area. It is most prosperous area of Northern Ireland with the UK's fourth largest yacht marina in its main town of Bangor, on the 'Gold Coast', but also contains pockets of deprivation. It is the once dominant UUP's last remaining seat.

SOUTH DOWN — SDLP hold

		Electorate 73,668	Turnout 65.4%	Change from 2001	2001	Electorate 73,519	Turnout 70.8%
McGrady E	**SDLP**	**21,557**	**44.8%**	**-1.5%**	**SDLP**	**24,136**	**46.3%**
Ruane C	SF	12,417	25.8%	6.1%	SF	10,278	19.7%
Wells J	DUP	8,815	18.3%	3.3%	UUP	9,173	17.6%
Nesbitt D	UUP	4,775	9.9%	-7.7%	DUP	7,802	15%
Crozier J	All	613	1.3%		All	685	1.3%
SDLP to SF swing	**3.8%**	**48,177**		**SDLP maj 9,140** 19%		**52,074**	**SDLP maj 13,858** 26.6%

EDDIE McGRADY b 3 June 1935. MP 1987-. NI Assembly Minister for Co-ordination 1974. Minister Chief whip SDLP 1979-. SDLP spokes: housing, local govt, environment. Member NI Affairs select cttee 1997-, NI Assembly 1973, 1982-86, 1998-2002, NI Forum 1996-98, NI Policing Board 2002-. SDLP founder member: first chair 1970-72. Cllr: Downpatrick Urban DC 1961-73 (chair 1964-73), Down DC 1973-89 (chair 1975). Chartered accountant. Ed St Patrick's High Sch, Downpatrick; Inst of Chartered Accountants.

This constituency is mainly Catholic, with Catholics accounting for nearly 62 per cent of the population. This sprawling rural and coastal constituency, wedged between the Irish Sea and the Republic of Ireland, has been a strong SDLP fiefdom for over a decade. While Sinn Fein continues to build up its vote in South Down it still seems to be some way off being able to overturn the SDLP majority.

DUDLEY NORTH — Lab hold

		Electorate 68,766	Turnout 60.2%	Change from 2001	2001	Electorate 68,964	Turnout 55.9%
Austin I	**Lab**	**18,306**	**44.2%**	**-7.9%**	**Lab**	**20,095**	**52.1%**
Hillas I	C	12,874	31.1%	-3.4%	C	13,295	34.5%
Lewis G	LD	4,257	10.3%	1.6%	LD	3,352	8.7%
Darby S	BNP	4,022	9.7%	5%	BNP	1,822	4.7%
Davis M	UKIP	1,949	4.7%				
Lab to C swing	**2.3%**	**41,408**		**Lab maj 5,432** 13.1%		**38,564**	**Lab maj 6,800** 17.6%

IAN AUSTIN b 6 March 1965. MP 2005-. Regional press officer West Midlands Labour Party 1995-98; Deputy director of communications Scottish Labour Party 1998-99; Special adviser to Gordon Brown as Chancellor of the Exchequer HM Treasury 1999-2005. Ed Dudley School

At the heart of the industrial Black Country, Dudley North is predominantly white, working class, and includes the poorest ward in Dudley. The seat is key in the Conservative bid for an overall majority in the House of Commons in 2009 or 2010.

DUDLEY SOUTH — Lab hold

		Electorate 65,228	Turnout 60.2%	Change from 2001	2001	Electorate 65,578	Turnout 55.4%
Pearson I	**Lab**	**17,800**	**45.3%**	**-4.5%**	**Lab**	**18,109**	**49.8%**
Longhi M	C	13,556	34.5%	3.4%	C	11,292	31.1%
Bramall J	LD	4,808	12.2%	-2.7%	LD	5,421	14.9%
Salvage J	BNP	1,841	4.7%		UKIP	859	2.4%
Benion A	UKIP	1,271	3.2%	0.8%	SA	663	1.8%
Lab to C swing	**4%**	**39,276**		**Lab maj 4,244** 10.8%		**36,344**	**Lab maj 6,817** 18.8%

IAN PEARSON b 5 April 1959. MP for Dudley West 1994-97, for Dudley South 1997-. Minister of State FCO and Dept of Trade and Industry 2005-. NI Parly Under-Sec 2002-05, PPS to Geoffrey Robinson 1997-98. Whip: asst govt 2001-02, govt 2002. Member select cttees: Treasury 1996-97, Deregulation 1996-97, Education and Employment 1999-2001. Cllr Dudley BC1984-87. Business and econ devt consultant. Ed BA PPE, Balliol Coll, Oxford; MA indust relats/PhD indust and business studies, Warwick Univ.

Another recent creation, Dudley South is a predominantly suburban seat occupied by Ian Pearson. The region has enjoyed huge investment in the recent past, with Merry Hill shopping centre and the Waterfront Complex representing massive regional employers, attracting further development. Although currently a comfortable Labour seat, local election results point to this being a constituency to watch.

DULWICH AND WEST NORWOOD — Lab hold

		Electorate 72,232	Turnout 58.1%	Change from 2001	2001	Electorate 71,621	Turnout 53.4%
Jowell T	**Lab**	**19,059**	**45.4%**	**-9.5%**	**Lab**	**20,999**	**54.9%**
Mitchell J	LD	10,252	24.4%	9.2%	C	8,689	22.7%
Humphreys K	C	9,200	21.9%	-0.8%	LD	5,805	15.2%
Jones J	Greens	2,741	6.5%	1.5%	Greens	1,914	5%
Atkinson R	UKIP	290	0.7%		SA	839	2.2%
Heather D	Veritas	241	0.6%				
Rose A	SLP	149	0.4%				
Weleminsky J	Fit	57	0.1%				
Lab to LD swing	**9.4%**	**41,989**		**Lab maj 8,807** 21%		**38,246**	**Lab maj 12,310** 32.2%

TESSA JOWELL b 17 Sept 1947. MP for Dulwich 1992-97, for Dulwich and West Norwood 1997-. Culture, Media and Sport Sec of State 2001-, Min for Women 1999-2001, Min of State: Education and Employment Dept 1999-2001, Health Dept 1997-99. Opposition whip 1994-95. Spokes: women 1995-96, health 1994-95/1996-97. Member select cttees: Social Security 1992, Health 1992-94. Cllr London Borough of Camden 1971-86. Chair Millennium Commission. Care/soc worker/charities/academic career. PC 1998. Ed Edinburgh Univ; Goldsmith's Coll, London Univ.

This is the residential part of Southwark and Lambeth, with industry concentrated further north near the Thames, but much of the housing is council-owned, and a good deal of it is in poor repair. Dulwich and West Norwood has alternated between the Conservatives and Labour since the 1945. However, the Secretary of State for Culture, Media and Sport Tessa Jowell has now turned it into a safe Labour seat with a large majority.

DUMFRIES AND GALLOWAY — Lab hold

		Electorate 74,273	Turnout 68.5%		2001
Brown R	**Lab**	**20,924**	**41.1%**		No comparable results due to boundary changes
Duncan P	C	18,002	35.4%		
Henderson D	SNP	6,182	12.2%		
Legg K	LD	4,259	8.4%		
Schofield J	Greens	745	1.5%		
Dennis J	SSP	497	1%		
Smith M	OCV	282	0.6%		
C to Lab swing (notional)	**2.7%**	**50,891**		**Lab maj 2,922** 5.7%	

RUSSELL BROWN b 17 Sept 1951. MP for Dumfries 1997-2005, for Dumfries and Galloway 2005-. PPS to: Alistair Darling 2005-, Leaders of Lords: Baroness Amos 2003-05, Lord Williams of Mostyn 2002-03. Member select cttees 1997-. Cllr: Dumfries and Galloway Regional Council 1986-96, Annandale and Eskdale DC 1988-96, Dumfries and Galloway Unitary Council 1995-97. ICI production supervisor 1974-97. Branch sec/branch chair TGWU 1979-85. Chair local community education project 1991-97. Ed Annan Academy.

In 2001 Galloway and Upper Nithsdale became the Tories' only Scottish seat when the party held off the SNP by just 74 votes. The addition of Dumfries, traditionally Labour-voting, transformed the political character of the seat and the tactical situation of its voters, 60 per cent of whom are scattered across the countryside in hamlets such as Stranraer, Newton Stuart, Kirkcudbright and Castle Douglas and 40 per cent of whom are in and around Dumfries.

DUMFRIESSHIRE, CLYDESDALE AND TWEEDDALE — C gain

		Electorate	Turnout		2001
		66,045	67.6%		
Mundell D	**C**	**16,141**	**36.2%**		No comparable results due to boundary changes
Marshall S	Lab	14,403	32.3%		
Kenton P	LD	9,046	20.3%		
Wood A	SNP	4,075	9.1%		
MacTavish S	SSP	521	1.2%		
Lee T	UKIP	430	1%		
Lab to C swing	**8%**	**44,616**		**C maj 1,738**	
(notional)				3.9%	

DAVID MUNDELL b 27 May 1962. MP 2005-. MSP for South of Scotland region since 6 May 1999. Scottish Conservative spokes for transport, telecommunications and IT 2002-; Member, Parly Cttee on Local Government and Transport 2003-. Corporate lawyer, Biggart Baillie & Gifford, Glasgow 1989-91; BT Scotland, Head of national affairs 1998-99. Ed law, Edinburgh University; MBA, Strathclyde University Business School

Dumfriesshire, Clydesdale and Tweeddale is the second-most rural seat in Scotland, stretching from the Solway coast and the English border in the south-west to the Edinburgh commuter zone in the north. Labour is strong in the east of the seat, especially in Kirkconnel, Douglas and Sanquhar, while the Liberal Democrats do well in Langholm and Peebles and the Conservatives in Lockerbie, Moffat and West Linton. In 2005 it became the Conservative's only Scottish seat.

EAST DUNBARTONSHIRE — LD gain

		Electorate	Turnout		2001
		64,763	72.2%		
Swinson J	**LD**	**19,533**	**41.8%**		No comparable results due to boundary changes
Lyons J	Lab	15,472	33.1%		
Jack D	C	7,708	16.5%		
Sagan C	SNP	2,716	5.8%		
Callison S	Greens	876	1.9%		
Page P	SSP	419	0.9%		
Lab to LD swing	**7.5%**	**46,724**		**LD maj 4,061**	
(notional)				8.7%	

JO SWINSON b 5 Feb 1980. MP 2005-. Contested Hull East 2001 general election, Strathkelvin and Bearsden 2003 Scottish Parliament election. Councillor Milngavie Community Council 2003-. Marketing executive Viking FM 2000-02; Marketing manager Spaceandpeople Ltd 2002-04; Development officer UK Public Health Association Scotland 2004-. Ed Douglas Academy, Glasgow; management, London School of Economics

Lying to the north of Glasgow and incorporating the most prosperous part of its commuter belt, East Dunbartonshire contains a larger proportion of homeowners than any other seat in Scotland. There are pockets of Labour voters in the less affluent east of the seat, but well-heeled suburbs like Bearsden and Milngavie predominate and this seat was a predictable gain from Labour for the Liberal Democrats in 2005.

WEST DUNBARTONSHIRE — Lab hold

		Electorate	Turnout		2001
		67,805	61.3%		
McFall J	**Lab/C**	**21,600**	**51.9%**		No comparable results due to boundary changes
Chalmers T	SNP	9,047	21.8%		
Walker N	LD	5,999	14.4%		
Murdoch C	C	2,679	6.4%		
Robertson L	SSP	1,708	4.1%		
Maher B	UKIP	354	0.8%		
Dawson M	OCV	202	0.5%		
SNP to Lab/C swing	**38%**	**41,589**		**Lab/C maj 12,553**	
(notional)				30.2%	

JOHN McFALL b 4 Oct 1944. MP for Dumbarton 1987-2005, for W Dunbartonshire 2005-. Parly Under-Sec NI Office 1998-99. Whip: opposition 1989-91, govt 1997-98. Opposition spokes Scottish affairs 1992-97. Select cttees member: Public Admin 2000-01, Treasury 2001- (chair 2001-), Liaison 2001-. Chair all-party Scotch whisky group 2003-. Member Co-op Party. Teacher: maths and chemistry, asst head –1987. PC 2004. Ed Paisley Coll of Tech; BSc chem, MBA, Strathclyde Univ; BA ed, Open Univ.

This seat combines the eastern portion of the old Dumbarton constituency, with the western portion of Clydebank and Milngavie. It reaches the bonnie banks of Loch Lomond in the north-west, though the population and the Labour vote are heavily concentrated in the south-east. Clydebank, containing half the constituency's electorate, was a shipbuilding town and industry remains integral though past its heyday. Dumbarton, the second-largest town, depends on whisky. Boundary changes will not noticeably dent the Labour majority.

DUNDEE EAST — SNP gain

		Electorate	Turnout		2001
		63,335	62.4%		
Hosie S	**SNP**	**14,708**	**37.2%**		No comparable results due to boundary changes
Luke I	Lab	14,325	36.2%		
Bustin C	C	5,061	12.8%		
Sneddon C	LD	4,498	11.4%		
Duke H	SSP	537	1.4%		
Low D	UKIP	292	0.7%		
Allison D	Ind	119	0.3%		
Lab to SNP swing	**1.1%**	**39,540**		**SNP maj 383**	
(notional)				1%	

STEWART HOSIE b 3 Jan 1963. MP 2005-. Contested Kirkcaldy 1992 and 1997 general elections, 1999 Scottish Parliament election; SNP spokes for Treasury, women and home affairs 2005-. SNP national secretary 1999-2003; organisation convener 2003-. IT career. Ed Carnoustie High School; HND computer studies, Bell Street Tech.

Dundee East is a largely urban and partly industrial port seat and a key battleground for Labour and the SNP. It is socially mixed, including tenement districts and large council estates along the Firth of Tay as well as middle-class pockets like Balgillo, Barnhill and Monifieth. In 2005 it lost four Labour-voting wards in the city centre and gained four SNP-voting wards on the north-east margins of the city and became one of the SNP's two gains from Labour.

DUNDEE WEST — Lab hold

		Electorate	Turnout		2001
		65,857	56.1%		
McGovern J	**Lab**	**16,468**	**44.6%**		No comparable results due to boundary changes
Fitzpatrick J	SNP	11,089	30%		
Garry N	LD	5,323	14.4%		
McKinlay C	C	3,062	8.3%		
McFarlane J	SSP	994	2.7%		
Lab to SNP swing	**4%**	**36,936**		**Lab maj 5,379**	
(notional)				14.6%	

JIM McGOVERN b 17 Nov 1956. MP 2005-; Elected representative Tayside Regional Council 1994-96; Glazier: Lynsey and Scott 1972-87, Dundee District Council 1987-97; GMB official 1997-; Ed Lawside Academy, Dundee

The addition of four staunch Labour wards in the city centre has bolstered Labour's natural support base in this interesting marginal, though a new rural ward in the north-west has also benefited the SNP. The Tayside west end is the only pocket of Conservative support and Dundee West is grittier than its eastern neighbour, being characterised by large enclaves of council housing from the older tenements of Lochee to housing in Mid Craigie and high rises in Ardler.

DUNFERMLINE AND WEST FIFE — Lab hold

		Electorate	Turnout		2001
		70,775	59.9%		
Squire R	**Lab**	**20,111**	**47.4%**		No comparable results due to boundary changes
Herbert D	LD	8,549	20.2%		
Chapman D	SNP	8,026	18.9%		
Smillie R	C	4,376	10.3%		
Archibald S	SSP	689	1.6%		
Borland I	UKIP	643	1.5%		
Lab to LD swing	**6.5%**	**42,394**		**Lab maj 11,562**	
(notional)				27.3%	

RACHEL SQUIRE b 13 July 1954. MP for Dunfermline West 1992-2005, for Dunfermline and West Fife 2005-. PPS to: Estelle Morris 1998-2001, Stephen Byers 1997-98. Member select cttees: Procedure 1992-97, Modernisation of HoC 1997-99, Defence 2001. Head Scottish Lab Party community care task force 1993-97. Chair Lab Party Scottish policy forum 1998-2002. Member Lab Movt in Europe. Soc worker Birmingham CC 1975-81. NUPE: area officer 1981-85, all of Scotland education officer 1985-92. Ed BA anthropology, Durham Univ, CQSW, Birmingham Univ.

Stretching about 10 miles inland, this constituency hugs the north bank of the Firth of Forth, from just before the Kincardine bridge to just beyond the Forth road bridge. It is centred on Dunfermline, once the Scottish capital, and the burial place of Robert the Bruce. The decline of the Rosyth dockyard and the closure of its naval base are symptomatic of the decline of the heavy industry so characteristic of this area, where Labour is dominant.

DURHAM NORTH — Lab hold

		Electorate	Turnout	Change from	2001	Electorate	Turnout
		67,506	55.3%	2001		67,755	56.9%
Jones K	**Lab**	**23,932**	**64.1%**	**-3.1%**	**Lab**	**25,920**	**67.2%**
Latham P	LD	7,151	19.2%	5.2%	C	7,237	18.8%
Watson M	C	6,258	16.8%	-2%	LD	5,411	14%
Lab to LD swing	**4.2%**	**37,341**		**Lab maj 16,781**		**38,568**	**Lab maj 18,683**
				44.9%			48.4%

KEVAN JONES b 25 April 1964. MP 2001-. Member Defence select cttee 2001-. Chair all-party groups: United Arab Emirates 2004-, cardiac risk in the young 2003-. Parly asst NH Brown MP 1985-89. Northern Region Lab Party chair 1998-2000, vice-chair 2000-. Member European Cities Environment cttee 1994-99. Cllr Newcastle City Council 1990-2001 (former dep leader). GMB: political officer 1989-2001, regional organiser 1992-99, senior organiser 1999-2001. Ed Portland Comp, Worksop; BA govt and public policy, Newcastle upon Tyne Poly.

A largely rural area, Durham North stretches from the village of Bournmoor, situated on the outskirts of the old market town of Chester-le-Street in the east, to a village called Tantobie, near the town of Stanley in the west. With a strong mining tradition, Durham North is a rock-solid Labour seat that has returned Labour MPs since 1945, and if lost, would indicate a major political upset.

CITY OF DURHAM — Lab hold

		Electorate	Turnout	Change from	2001	Electorate	Turnout
		71,441	62.1%	2001		69,610	59.6%
Blackman-Woods R	**Lab**	**20,928**	**47.2%**	**-8.9%**	**Lab**	**23,254**	**56.1%**
Woods C	LD	17,654	39.8%	16.1%	LD	9,813	23.7%
Rogers B	C	4,179	9.4%	-7.9%	C	7,167	17.3%
Martin A	Veritas	1,603	3.6%		UKIP	1,252	3%
Lab to LD swing	**12.5%**	**44,364**		**Lab maj 3,274**		**41,486**	**Lab maj 13,441**
				7.4%			32.4%

ROBERTA BLACKMAN-WOODS b 16 Aug 1957. MP 2005-. Former chair Newcastle East and Wallsend CLP; Chair City of Durham CLP. Professor of social policy and associate dean, Northumbria University. Ed BSc and PhD social science, Ulster University.

At the heart of this constituency is the attractive and ancient city of Durham, with its grand cathedral and esteemed university. However, the city, once home to one of the mightiest prelates in the land, contains only a minority of its electors. Designated a county constituency, the seat also includes the many ex-mining communities of Brandon and Byshottles, Coxhoe, and the Deerness Valley. This has become a major Lib Dem target seat

NORTH WEST DURHAM — Lab hold

		Electorate	Turnout	Change from	2001	Electorate	Turnout
		68,130	58%	2001		67,294	58.3%
Armstrong H	**Lab**	**21,312**	**53.9%**	**-8.6%**	**Lab**	**24,526**	**62.5%**
Ord A	LD	7,869	19.9%	5%	C	8,193	20.9%
Devlin J	C	6,463	16.4%	-4.5%	LD	5,846	14.9%
Stelling W	Ind	3,865	9.8%		SLP	661	1.7%
Lab to LD swing	**6.8%**	**39,509**		**Lab maj 13,443**		**39,226**	**Lab maj 16,333**
				34%			41.6%

HILARY ARMSTRONG b 30 Nov 1945. MP 1987-. Minister of State Dept of Environment, Transport and the Regions 1999-2001; PPS to John Smith 1992-94. Govt chief whip 2001-. Opposition spokes 1988-92, 1994-97. Member Education select cttee 1998. Member Lab Party NEC 1996-. Cllr Durham CC 1985-88. Chair ASTMS Northern Div Council 1981-88. Teacher/soc and community worker/lecturer/sec/researcher. UNICEF nat cttee member 1995-97. Vice-chair British Council 1994-97. PC 1999. Ed West Ham Coll of Tech; BSc sociology/soc work Dip, Birmingham Univ.

North West Durham is a large, sparsely populated Labour stronghold, combining small towns with beautiful natural areas. The landscape outside Consett has a stark beauty, and the Wear Valley and surrounding moors are increasingly attractive to tourists. The economy of this region was built solely on coal and steel but following its decline new industry, such as engineering, has developed.

EALING, ACTON AND SHEPHERD'S BUSH — Lab hold

		Electorate 70,454	Turnout 56.2%	Change from 2001	2001	Electorate 70,924	Turnout 52.5%
Slaughter A	**Lab**	**16,579**	**41.8%**	**-12.3%**	**Lab**	**20,144**	**54.1%**
Gough J	C	11,059	27.9%	2.8%	C	9,355	25.1%
Malcolm G	LD	9,986	25.2%	8.6%	LD	6,171	16.6%
Burgess G	Greens	1,999	5.1%		SA	529	1.4%
					UKIP	476	1.3%
					SLP	301	0.8%
					ProLife	225	0.6%
Lab to C swing	**7.6%**	**39,623**		**Lab maj 5,520** 13.9%		**37,201**	**Lab maj 10,789** 29%

ANDY SLAUGHTER b 29 Sept 1960. MP 2005-. Contested Uxbridge 1997 by-election. London Borough of Hammersmith and Fulham: Councillor 1986-, Deputy council leader 1991-96, Council leader 1996-. Barrister specialising in criminal, housing and personal injury law. Member: Co-operative Party; Amicus. Ed Exeter University

Ealing, Action and Shepherd's Bush is a real mixed bag of a seat, comprises Labour-leaning areas of a marginal Tory seat and parts of a safe Labour seat in West London. The seat witnessed a particularly sharp fall in the Labour vote in 2005.

EALING NORTH — Lab hold

		Electorate 78,298	Turnout 59.4%	Change from 2001	2001	Electorate 78,169	Turnout 57.5%
Pound S	**Lab**	**20,956**	**45.1%**	**-10.6%**	**Lab**	**25,022**	**55.7%**
Curtis R	C	13,897	29.9%	0.6%	C	13,185	29.3%
Fruzza F	LD	9,148	19.7%	8.5%	LD	5,043	11.2%
Outten A	Greens	1,319	2.8%	0.5%	Greens	1,039	2.3%
Lambert R	UKIP	692	1.5%		UKIP	668	1.5%
Malindine D	Veritas	495	1.1%				
Lab to C swing	**5.6%**	**46,507**		**Lab maj 7,059** 15.2%		**44,957**	**Lab maj 11,837** 26.3%

STEPHEN POUND b 3 July 1948. MP 1997-. Member select cttees: Broadcasting 1997-2001, Northern Ireland Affairs 1999-, Standards and Privileges 2003-. All-party groups: chair scout 1999-, vice-chair motorcycling 2001-. Cllr London Borough of Ealing 1982-98: mayor 1995-96. Seaman 1964-66, bus conductor 1966-68, hospital porter 1969-79, student 1979-84, housing officer 1984-97. COHSE branch sec 1975-79. T&GW (ACTS) branch officer 1990-96. Director Hanwell Community Centre. Ed Hertford Grammar Sch; BSc econ/indust relats dip, LSE.

Ealing North is a diverse constituency in west London, with one of the largest Polish populations as well as large Asian and Irish communities. Good communication links in the area have helped to replace manufacturing with warehousing and distribution as significant employers. It is considered a swing constituency, reflecting current national trends and is likely to remain a Labour seat as long as the party remains in power.

EALING SOUTHALL — Lab hold

		Electorate 83,738	Turnout 56.2%	Change from 2001	2001	Electorate 82,928	Turnout 56.5%
Khabra P	**Lab**	**22,937**	**48.8%**	**1.3%**	**Lab**	**22,239**	**47.5%**
Bakhai N	LD	11,497	24.4%	14.4%	C	8,556	18.3%
Nicholson M	C	10,147	21.6%	3.3%	SunR	5,764	12.3%
Edwards S	Greens	2,175	4.6%	0.1%	LD	4,680	10%
Bilku M	WRP	289	0.6%		Greens	2,119	4.5%
					Ind	1,214	2.6%
					Ind	1,166	2.5%
					SLP	921	2%
					Qari	169	0.4%
Lab to LD swing	**6.6%**	**47,045**		**Lab maj 11,440** 24.3%		**46,828**	**Lab maj 13,683** 29.2%

PIARA KHABRA b 20 Nov 1924. MP 1992-. Member International Development select cttee 1997-. Chair all-party India group 1997-. Member Lab Party departmental cttees: Foreign and Commonwealth Affairs 1997-2001, Home Affairs 1997-2001, International Development 1997-. Cllr London Borough of Ealing 1978-82. JP 1977-. Chair: Indian Workers' Assocn, Southall; Ealing law centre 1983-90. Cleric/teacher/ community worker 1964-91. Ed Khalsa High Sch, Punjab, India; BA soc sciences/BEd, Punjab Univ; teaching dip, Whitelands Coll, London.

Based in west London, Ealing Southall has the country's second largest Asian community. Its strategic location is convenient for both commuters and workers in outlying areas. The population is economically as well as ethnically diverse, with just under half the population working in professional, managerial or technical occupations.

EASINGTON — Lab hold

		Electorate	Turnout	Change from	2001	Electorate	Turnout
		61,084	52.2%	2001		61,532	53.6%
Cummings J	**Lab**	**22,733**	**71.4%**	**-5.4%**	**Lab**	**25,360**	**76.8%**
Ord C	LD	4,097	12.9%	2.6%	C	3,411	10.3%
Nicholson L	C	3,400	10.7%	0.4%	LD	3,408	10.3%
McDonald I	BNP	1,042	3.3%		SLP	831	2.5%
Robinson D	SLP	583	1.8%	-0.7%			
Lab to LD swing	**4%**	**31,855**		**Lab maj 18,636**		**33,010**	**Lab maj 21,949**
				58.5%			66.5%

JOHN CUMMINGS b 6 July 1943. MP 1987-. Opposition whip (Northern and Overseas Devt) 1994-97. Member select cttees: Environment, Transport and Regional Affairs 1997-2001, Chairmen's Panel 2000-, Transport, Local Govt and the Regions 2001-02, Office of the Deputy PM 2003-. Chair all-party groups: Czech Republic and Slovakia 2001-; local govt councillors 2001. Chair Northern Regional Lab MPs group 1999-. Cllr Easington District Council 1973-87: leader 1979-87. Murton Colliery 1958-87. Ed Easington and Durham Tech Colls 1958-62.

This coastal County Durham constituency includes Seaham Harbour, as well as large ex-coal mining villages such as Horden, Murton and Easington itself. The new town of Peterlee is also here. One of the safest seats in the country and a solid Labour stronghold, it is highly unlikely to be lost in the near future, especially as any credible opposition is lacking.

EAST HAM — Lab hold

		Electorate	Turnout	Change from	2001	Electorate	Turnout
		78,104	50.7%	2001		71,255	52.3%
Timms S	**Lab**	**21,326**	**53.9%**	**-19.2%**	**Lab**	**27,241**	**73.1%**
Mian A	Respect	8,171	20.6%		C	6,209	16.7%
Macken S	C	5,196	13.1%	-3.6%	LD	2,600	7%
Haigh A	LD	4,296	10.9%	3.9%	SLP	783	2.1%
Bamber D	CPA	580	1.5%		UKIP	444	1.2%
Lab to Respect	**19.9%**	**39,569**		**Lab maj 13,155**		**37,277**	**Lab maj 21,032**
				33.2%			56.4%

STEPHEN TIMMS b 29 July 1955. MP for Newham North East 1994-97, for East Ham 1997-. Minister of State Dept for Work and Pensions 2005-. Financial Sec HM Treasury 2004-05/1999-2001, Minister of State: DTI 2002-04, Education and Skills Dept 2001-02, Soc Security Dept 1999. Parly Under-Sec of State Dept of Soc Security 1998-99. PPS to: Marjorie Mowlam 1998, Andrew Smith 1997-98. Member select cttee. Cllr Newham 1984-97: leader 1990-94. Computer/telecomms career 1978-94. Ed MA maths, MPhil operational research, Emmanuel Coll, Cambridge.

A densely populated constituency in the East End of London, East Ham contains both high levels of diversity and unemployment. New developments, including London City Airport and the potential London bid for the 2012 Olympics, have changed the seat to some extent in an attempt to resolve some of the problems associated with inner-cities. As one of Labour's safer seats in recent elections, it is likely to remain secure.

EAST KILBRIDE, STRATHAVEN AND LESMAHAGOW — Lab hold

		Electorate	Turnout		2001
		75,132	63.5%		
Ingram A	**Lab**	**23,264**	**48.7%**		No comparable results due to boundary changes
Edwards D	SNP	8,541	17.9%		
Oswald J	LD	7,904	16.6%		
Lewis T	C	4,776	10%		
Robb K	Greens	1,575	3.3%		
Gentle R	Ind	1,513	3.2%		
Houston J	Ind	160	0.3%		
SNP to Lab swing	**0.8%**	**47,733**		**Lab maj 14,723**	
(notional)				30.8%	

ADAM INGRAM b 1 Feb 1947. MP for East Kilbride 1987-2005, for East Kilbride, Strathaven and Lesmahagow 2005-. Minister of State: MoD 2001-, NI Office 1997-2001. PPS to Neil Kinnock as Leader of Opposition 1988-92. Opposition whip 1988-89. Opposition spokes soc security, trade/industry 1993-97. Member Trade and Industry select cttee 1992-93. District cllr East Kilbride 1980-87: leader 1984-87. TGWU-supported MP 1987-. Full-time NALGO official 1977-87. Computer programmer/systems analyst 1967-77. PC 1999. Ed Cranhill Sec Sch.

East Kilbride, Scotland's first New Town, is the populous centre of the seat, which spreads southwards, mainly along the west side of the M74 as it heads south-west out of Glasgow. The more rural southern portion includes the villages of Chapelton and Glassford, the market town Strathaven, and villages Stonehouse and Blackwood. The SNP is the traditional challenger in this Labour-leaning seat on the Glasgow margins.

EASTBOURNE — C hold

		Electorate 74,628	Turnout 64.8%	Change from 2001	2001	Electorate 73,756	Turnout 60.7%
Waterson N	**C**	**21,033**	**43.5%**	**-0.6%**	**C**	**19,738**	**44.1%**
Lloyd S	LD	19,909	41.1%	1.8%	LD	17,584	39.3%
Jones A	Lab	5,268	10.9%	-2.4%	Lab	5,967	13.3%
Meggs A	UKIP	1,233	2.6%	0.6%	UKIP	907	2%
Gross C	Greens	949	2%		Lib	574	1.3%
C to LD swing	**1.2%**	**48,392**		**C maj 1,124** 2.3%		**44,770**	**C maj 2,154** 4.8%

NIGEL WATERSON b 12 Oct 1950. MP 1992-. Shadow Pensions Min 2003-. PPS to: Michael Heseltine 1996-97, Gerry Malone 1995-96. Opposition whip 1997-99. Opposition spokes: local govt and housing 1999-2001, trade and industry 2001-02. Member Work and Pensions select cttee 2003-. Chair all-party ageing and older people group 2002-. Chair: Bow Group 1986-87 (hon patron 1993-95), Hammersmith Con Assocn 1987-90. Cllr Hammersmith and Fulham 1974-78. Research asst to Sally Oppenheim MP 1972-73. Solicitor/barrister. Ed BA law, Queen's Coll, Oxford.

Eastbourne is an East Sussex seaside resort which prides itself on its quiet charm and elegance, home to a high proportion of senior citizens. Nevertheless, in the twenty-first century the town is growing faster than any in the region. The constituency also includes the dramatic headland of Beachy Head at the eastern end of the South Downs. Since 1990 the constituency has become a closely fought battleground between Conservatives and Liberal Democrats.

EASTLEIGH — LD hold

		Electorate 76,844	Turnout 64.8%	Change from 2001	2001	Electorate 74,603	Turnout 63.8%
Huhne C	**LD**	**19,216**	**38.6%**	**-2.1%**	**LD**	**19,360**	**40.7%**
Burns C	C	18,648	37.5%	3.2%	C	16,302	34.3%
Watt C	Lab	10,238	20.6%	-1.3%	Lab	10,426	21.9%
Murphy C	UKIP	1,669	3.4%	1.6%	UKIP	849	1.8%
					Greens	636	1.3%
LD to C swing	**2.7%**	**49,771**		**LD maj 568** 1.1%		**47,573**	**LD maj 3,058** 6.4%

CHRIS HUHNE b 2 July 1954. MP 2005-. Contested Reading E 1983, Oxford W and Abingdon 1987 general elections; MEP for SE 1999-2005: deputy leader Liberal Democrat Group, EP LD spokesman on economics 1999-2005. Trainee journalist 1975-77; journalist and editor 1977-94; managing director and founder Sovereign Risk Ratings IBCA Ltd 1994-. Ed Westminster School; PPE, Magdalen College, Oxford

Eastleigh is an old industrial Hampshire town. It has a working-class base and many of its residents commute into neighbouring Southampton. Historically it was home to a rail works and a Pirelli factory, but both these are in decline. The constituency is also home to numerous wealthy villages along the Solent and river Itchen. In 1997, the constituency became a three-way marginal, but now appears to have settled into a straight fight between Liberal Democrat and Conservative.

ECCLES — Lab hold

		Electorate 69,006	Turnout 50.2%	Change from 2001	2001	Electorate 68,764	Turnout 48.3%
Stewart I	**Lab**	**19,702**	**56.9%**	**-7.6%**	**Lab**	**21,395**	**64.5%**
Matuk T	C	6,816	19.7%	-1%	C	6,867	20.7%
Brophy J	LD	6,429	18.6%	3.8%	LD	4,920	14.8%
Reeve P	UKIP	1,685	4.9%				
Lab to C swing	**3.3%**	**34,632**		**Lab maj 12,886** 37.2%		**33,182**	**Lab maj 14,528** 43.8%

IAN STEWART b 28 Aug 1950. MP 1997-. PPS to: Stephen Timms 2003-, Brian Wilson 2001-03. Member select cttees: Information 1998-2001, Deregulation and Regulatory Reform 1997-2001. Chair all-party groups: community media 2004-, vaccine damaged children 2004-. Member: Soc of Internat Indust Relations, UK Soc of Industrial Tutors. Regional full-time officer TGWU. Ed Calder St Sec, Blantyre; Alfred Turner Sec, Irlam; Stretford Tech Coll; MPhil Management of change in progress, Manchester Metropolitan Univ.

To the south-west of Manchester, and in the middle of the three seats that make up the Borough of Salford, Eccles is a long way from the well-heeled constituencies that orbit the Manchester conurbation. The constituency is suburban and industrial, although following boundary changes the seat now incorporates some farmland either side of the M62. Its towns include Swinton, Irlam and Pendlebury, the home of artist L S Lowry. This is a firm Labour stronghold.

EDDISBURY — C hold

		Electorate	Turnout	Change from	2001	Electorate	Turnout
		72,249	63.2%	2001		69,181	64.2%
O'Brien S	**C**	**21,181**	**46.4%**	**0.1%**	**C**	**20,556**	**46.3%**
Green M	Lab	14,986	32.8%	-3.2%	Lab	15,988	36%
Crotty J	LD	8,182	17.9%	2.2%	LD	6,975	15.7%
Roxborough S	UKIP	1,325	2.9%	0.9%	UKIP	868	2%
Lab to C swing	**1.7%**	**45,674**		**C maj 6,195**		**44,387**	**C maj 4,568**
				13.6%			10.3%

STEPHEN O'BRIEN b 1 April 1957. MP July 1999- (by-election). Shadow: Minister for Skills 2005-, Sec of State for Industry 2003-05, Paymaster General 2002-03, Treasury Financial Sec 2002. PPS to: Iain Duncan Smith 2001, Michael Ancram 2000-01, Francis Maude 2000. Opposition whip 2001-02. Member Education and Employment select cttee 1999-2001. Chair all-party groups: minerals, Tanzania, headache disorders, malaria. Businessman/manufacturing industrialist/solicitor. Ed MA law, Emmanuel Coll, Cambridge; Coll of Law, Chester.

Winsford is the only large town in the seat, which is basically rural in character; commuters to Chester, Crewe and Wrexham find this an attractive area in which to settle. Eddisbury once thrived on salt-mining and sand quarrying, but is developing a service sector, and with picturesque landscapes, increasing numbers of tourists enjoy boating and canal holidays. Despite unfavourable boundary changes and the party's 1997 nadir, this has remained in Conservative hands.

EDINBURGH EAST — Lab hold

		Electorate	Turnout		2001
		64,826	61.2%		
Strang G	**Lab**	**15,899**	**40%**		No comparable results due to boundary changes
Mackenzie G	LD	9,697	24.4%		
Tymkewycz S	SNP	6,760	17%		
Brown M	C	4,093	10.3%		
Gillespie C	Greens	2,266	5.7%		
Grant C	SSP	868	2.2%		
Harris B	DDTP	89	0.2%		
Clifford P	ND	37	0.1%		
Lab to LD swing	**8.5%**	**39,709**		**Lab maj 6,202**	
(notional)				15.6%	

GAVIN STRANG b 10 July 1943. MP for Edinburgh East 1970-97, for Edinburgh East and Musselburgh 1997-2005, for Edinburgh East 2005-. Minister of State Dept of Environ, Transport and Regions 1997-98. Parly Sec Ministry of Agriculture 1974-79, Parly Under-Sec Energy 1974. Opposition spokes 1979-82, 1987-89, 1992-97. Chair all-party world govt group. Member Tayside econ planning consultative group 1966-68. Scientist Agricultural Research Council 1968-70. PC 1997. Ed BSc, PhD, Edinburgh Univ; DipAgfiSci, Churchill Coll, Cambridge.

This seat is another pie-slice of Edinburgh city council area. The thin end of the wedge includes some of Edinburgh's most noted tourist attractions – Arthur's Seat, St Giles' Castle and the Princes Street Garden. As the seat spreads outwards to the south and east it incorporates some rather less picturesque areas, such as the sprawling Craigmillar estate, heavily working-class and Labour-voting. It is socially mixed with pockets of deprivation and has traditionally been safe for Labour.

EDINBURGH NORTH AND LEITH — Lab hold

		Electorate	Turnout		2001
		68,038	62.7%		
Lazarowicz M	**Lab/C**	**14,597**	**34.2%**		No comparable results due to boundary changes
Crockart M	LD	12,444	29.2%		
Whyte I	C	7,969	18.7%		
Hutchison D	SNP	4,344	10.2%		
Sydenham M	Greens	2,482	5.8%		
Scott B	SSP	804	1.9%		
Lab/C to LD swing	**8.3%**	**42,640**		**Lab/C maj 2,153**	
(notional)				5%	

MARK LAZAROWICZ b 8 Aug 1953. MP for Edinburgh North and Leth 2001-05, for new Edinburgh North and Leith 2005. Member select cttees. Chair all-party debt/personal finance group. Cllr: Edinburgh DC 1980-96: leader 1986-93, City of Edinburgh council 1999-2001. Member: SERA, Co-op Party. Chair Scottish Lab Party 1989-90. Organiser Scottish Ed and Action for Devt 1978-80, 1982-86. Gen sec British Youth Council Scotland 1980-82. Advocate 1996-. Ed MA moral philosophy/medieval hist, St Andrews Univ; LLB, Edinburgh Univ; Dip Legal Practice.

Ranging from Princes Street to the elegant Georgian neo-classical streets of New Town to the historic port, Leith (once home to the heavy engineering industry) has had a yuppie makeover. Its new nickname, 'Leith-sur-mer' aptly suggests the vibrant bars and restaurants which now throng the waterfront. The Liberal Democrats do well here, but areas like Pilton are less vibrant and there Labour remains strong, although the addition of the Dean and Craigleith wards has diluted its support.

EDINBURGH SOUTH — Lab hold

		Electorate	Turnout	2001
		60,993	70%	
Griffiths N	**Lab**	**14,188**	**33.2%**	No comparable results due to boundary changes
MacLaren M	LD	13,783	32.3%	
Brown G	C	10,291	24.1%	
Sutherland G	SNP	2,635	6.2%	
Burgess S	Greens	1,387	3.2%	
Robertson M	SSP	414	1%	
Lab to LD swing (notional)	**6.5%**	**42,698**	**Lab maj 405** 1%	

NIGEL GRIFFITHS b 20 May 1955. MP for Edinburgh South 1987-2005, for new Edinburgh South 2005-. Dep Leader HoC 2005-. Parly Under-Sec Dept of Trade and Industry 1997-2005. Opposition: whip 1987-89, spokes 1989-97. Member select cttees 1999-2001. Member Lab Party nat policy forum 1999-. Pres EU Lab Club 1976-77. Cllr Edinburgh: DC 1980-97, Festival Council 1984-87, Health Council 1982-87. Rights adviser mental handicap pressure group 1979-87. Vice-pres Trading Standards Admin Inst 1994-. Ed MA, Edinburgh Univ; Moray House Coll of Education.

This affluent seat begins just south of the city centre in among the chic city apartments of Marchmont, Merchiston and Morningside. It stretches west to family-oriented Fairmilehead, on the outskirts of the city at the edge of the Braid hills. In the south it reaches the city by-pass and the peripheral council estates (and Labour strongholds) of Gilmerton, Kaimes and Moredun in the east. Boundary changes have added two south-eastern wards, strengthening the already considerable Liberal Democrat support base.

EDINBURGH SOUTH WEST — Lab hold

		Electorate	Turnout	2001
		67,135	65.4%	
Darling A	**Lab**	**17,476**	**39.8%**	No comparable results due to boundary changes
Buchan G	C	10,234	23.3%	
Clark S	LD	9,252	21.1%	
Elliot-Cannon N	SNP	4,654	10.6%	
Blair-Fish J	Greens	1,520	3.5%	
Smith P	SSP	585	1.3%	
Boys W	UKIP	205	0.5%	
Lab to C swing (notional)	**0.7%**	**43,926**	**Lab maj 7,242** 16.5%	

ALISTAIR DARLING b 28 Nov 1953. MP for Edinburgh Central 1987-2005, for Edinburgh South West 2005-. Sec of State: Scotland 2003-, Transport 2002-, Social Security/Work and Pensions 1998-2002. Chief Sec to Treasury 1997-98. Shadow Chief Sec to Treasury 1996-97. Opposition spokes: home affairs 1988-92, Treasury, economic affairs and City 1992-96. Member Lab Party economic commission 1994-97. Cllr Lothian Regional Council 1982-87. Solicitor 1978-82. Advocate 1984-. PC 1997. Ed Loretto Sch; LLB, Aberdeen Univ.

This new seat contains the south-western bulk of Edinburgh Pentlands but slices further into central Edinburgh than before, through the old tenement areas Dalry and Fountainbridge. It broadens out through council estates in Murray Burn, Sighthill and Firhill, to the suburbs of Colinton and Craiglockhart, crossing the by-pass to Tory village strongholds Balerno and Currie. Boundary changes have boosted the Labour core vote, with the Conservatives far from recovering what was once their safest seat in the Lothian region.

EDINBURGH WEST — LD hold

		Electorate	Turnout	2001
		65,741	68.8%	
Barrett J	**LD**	**22,417**	**49.5%**	No comparable results due to boundary changes
Brogan D	C	8,817	19.5%	
Ghaleigh N	Lab	8,433	18.6%	
Cleland S	SNP	4,124	9.1%	
Spindler A	Greens	964	2.1%	
Clark G	SSP	510	1.1%	
C to LD swing (notional)	**6.7%**	**45,265**	**LD maj 13,600** 30%	

JOHN BARRETT b 11 Feb 1954. MP for Edinburgh West 2001-05, for new Edinburgh West 2005-. Scottish Lib Dem spokes cross border transport 2001-, Lib Dem spokes internat devt 2002-. Sec all-party groups. Convener Lothian Region Lib Dems 1997-2000. Vice-pres Scottish Lib club 2000-. Member European standing cttee B 2003-. Cllr Edinburgh City Council 1995-2001. Director film-related organisations. Election agent Donald Gorrie MP 1997. Ed Forrester High Sch, Edinburgh; Telford Coll, Edinburgh; Napier Poly, Edinburgh.

This bulk of this prosperous seat is to the west and north-west of the city centre, though newly-accquired working-class Stenhouse and affluent Murrayfield jut into the city centre. The Liberal Democrats have eclipsed the Conservatives in this seat which broadens out through the leafy western suburbs of Costorphine, Gyle and Cramond. Reaching along the Firth of Forth to Queensferry, it also includes inland hamlets like Kirkliston and Ratho and Edinburgh airport.

EDMONTON — Lab hold

		Electorate 58,764	Turnout 59%	Change from 2001	2001	Electorate 61,788	Turnout 56.3%
Love A	**Lab/C**	**18,456**	**53.2%**	**-5.7%**	**Lab/C**	**20,481**	**58.9%**
Zetter L	C	10,381	29.9%	-0.9%	C	10,709	30.8%
Kilbane-Dawe I	LD	4,162	12%	5%	LD	2,438	7%
Armstrong N	Greens	889	2.6%		UKIP	406	1.2%
Rolph G	UKIP	815	2.4%	1.2%	R2000	344	1%
					SA	296	0.9%
					Ind	100	0.3%
Lab/C to C swing	**2.4%**	**34,703**		**Lab/C maj 8,075** 23.3%		**34,774**	**Lab/C maj 9,772** 28.1%

ANDREW LOVE b 21 March 1949. MP 1997-. PPS to: Jacqui Smith 2001-05. Member select cttees: Public Accounts 1997-2001, Regulatory Reform 1999-. Chair all-party groups: homelessness and housing need 1999-, Lebanon 2002-, Mexico 2004-, Sri Lanka 2004-. Chair Co-operative Parly Group 1999-2001. Cllr Haringey 1980-86. TGWU branch chair 1980-83. National Executive Member NACO 1989-92. Chartered sec. Co-operative Party parly officer. Ed Greenock High Sch; BSc physics, Strathclyde Univ; Assocn of Chartered Institute of Secretaries.

A typical outer London borough, Edmonton is a mixture of traditional working class areas and the more affluent suburbs, reflecting both its Hertfordshire and Tottenham borders. The constituency has considerable ethnic diversity, as well as containing a mixture of the residential and the industrial. The local support for Labour, combined with the relative deprivation of the area, suggests a continuing reign for the party is likely.

ELLESMERE PORT AND NESTON — Lab hold

		Electorate 68,249	Turnout 61.6%	Change from 2001	2001	Electorate 68,147	Turnout 60.9%
Miller A	**Lab**	**20,371**	**48.4%**	**-6.9%**	**Lab**	**22,964**	**55.3%**
Hogg M	C	13,885	33%	3.9%	C	12,103	29.1%
Cooke S	LD	6,607	15.7%	4.1%	LD	4,828	11.6%
Crocker H	UKIP	1,206	2.9%	0.9%	UKIP	824	2%
					Greens	809	1.9%
Lab to C swing	**5.4%**	**42,069**		**Lab maj 6,486** 15.4%		**41,528**	**Lab maj 10,861** 26.2%

ANDREW MILLER b 23 March 1949. MP 1992-. PPS to Dept of Trade and Industry Mins 2001-. Member select cttees: Science and Technology 1992-97, Information 1992-97/1997-2001, Joint Cttee on Human Rights 2001. Chair all-party justice for road traffic victims group 1999-. Pres Computing for Labour 1993-. Chair: Leadership Campaign Team 1997-98, North West Lab MPs group 1997-98. Member First Steps team. Technician/geology analyst. MSF regional official 1977-92. Ed Hayling Island Sec Sch; Highbury Tech Coll; industrial relations dip, LSE.

Administratively in Cheshire, this seat of Ellesmere Port and Neston is unequivocally within the social and economic orbits of the megolithic Merseyside to the north. It is squeezed between the marshy estuary of the Dee and Mersey. The seat is socially, but also physically, polarised – functional, industrial landscapes contrast with beautiful countryside and tourist spots. Like much of this area, the seat looks firmly to Labour for the near future.

ELMET — Lab hold

		Electorate 68,514	Turnout 68.8%	Change from 2001	2001	Electorate 70,121	Turnout 65.5%
Burgon C	**Lab**	**22,260**	**47.2%**	**-0.8%**	**Lab**	**22,038**	**48%**
Millard A	C	17,732	37.6%	-1.3%	C	17,867	38.9%
Kirk M	LD	5,923	12.6%	1.7%	LD	5,001	10.9%
Andrews T	BNP	1,231	2.6%		UKIP	1,031	2.2%
C to Lab swing	**0.3%**	**47,146**		**Lab maj 4,528** 9.6%		**45,937**	**Lab maj 4,171** 9.1%

COLIN BURGON b 22 April 1948. MP 1997-. Member select cttees: Joint Cttee on Statutory Instruments 1997-99, Accommodation and Works 1999-2000, Procedure 1999-2001, Northern Ireland Affairs 2000-01. Former chair Leeds Euro Constituency Lab Party. Teacher/local govt policy and research officer. Ed St Charles Sch, Leeds; St Michael's Coll, Leeds; City of Leeds and Carnegie Coll.

Elmet is situated on the eastern periphery of Leeds, and was created in 1983 mainly from the safer Conservative seat of Barkston Ash. It covers a large area comprising small towns and rural villages that hold a broad base of industries and a large commuter population. About 60 per cent of workers residing in the seat are non-manual, and 72 per cent of homes are owner-occupied. This west Yorkshire seat finally fell to Labour in 1997, but it remains marginal.

ELTHAM

Lab hold

		Electorate	Turnout	Change from	2001	Electorate	Turnout
		57,236	61.7%	2001		57,554	58.7%
Efford C	**Lab**	**15,381**	**43.6%**	**-9.2%**	**Lab**	**17,855**	**52.8%**
Drury S	C	12,105	34.3%	2.2%	C	10,859	32.1%
Gerrard I	LD	5,669	16.1%	3.9%	LD	4,121	12.2%
Elms J	UKIP	1,024	2.9%	0.8%	UKIP	706	2.1%
Roberts B	BNP	979	2.8%		Ind	251	0.7%
Graham A	Ind	147	0.4%	-0.3%			
Lab to C swing	**5.7%**	**35,305**		**Lab maj 3,276**		**33,792**	**Lab maj 6,996**
				9.3%			20.7%

CLIVE EFFORD b 10 July 1958. MP 1997-. Member select cttees: Procedure 1997-2001, Standing Orders 1999-2000, Transport 2002-. Vice-chair all-party groups: road passenger transport 2003-, transport forum 2004-. Vice-chair London Group of Lab MPs 2001-02. Member Lab Friends of India. Cllr London Borough of Greenwich 1986-98. Partner family-owned jewellery/watch repair business to 1987. London taxi driver 1987-97. Ed Walworth Comp Sch; Southwark Further Education Coll.

The south-east London constituency of Eltham in the south of Greenwich is a diverse mixture of working and lower middle class suburbia, containing some of the most as well as least deprived wards in England. While a swing to the Conservatives did occur in 2005, it was not of the scale seen elsewhere in the capital.

ENFIELD NORTH

Lab hold

		Electorate	Turnout	Change from	2001	Electorate	Turnout
		66,460	61.3%	2001		67,204	57%
Ryan J	**Lab**	**18,055**	**44.3%**	**-2.4%**	**Lab**	**17,888**	**46.7%**
de Bois N	C	16,135	39.6%	-1.1%	C	15,597	40.7%
Radford S	LD	4,642	11.4%	2.6%	LD	3,355	8.8%
Farr T	BNP	1,004	2.5%	0.9%	BNP	605	1.6%
Robbens G	UKIP	750	1.8%	0.7%	UKIP	427	1.1%
Burns P	Ind	163	0.4%	-0.7%	ProLife	241	0.6%
					None	210	0.5%
Lab to C swing	**0.7%**	**40,749**		**Lab maj 1,920**		**38,323**	**Lab maj 2,291**
				4.7%			6%

JOAN RYAN b 8 Sept 1955. MP 1997-. PPS to Andrew Smith 1998-2001. Whip: asst govt 2002-03, govt 2003-. Member Selection select cttee 2001-. Vice-chair all-party Namibia group 2004-. Chair London North European Constituency 1994-97. Cllr Barnet Council 1990-98: deputy leader 1994-98. Teacher. School governor. Ed St Joseph's Sec Sch; Notre Dame High Sch; BA history, sociology, City of Liverpool Coll; MSc sociology, Poly of South Bank, London.

The northernmost constituency in London, Enfield North is a diverse seat of lower middle class and aspiring working class constituents. The constituency is equally environmentally diverse, ranging from green belt and open countryside to a thriving industrial area. Owner-occupation is high, as is skilled non-manual and skilled manual social groups. Joan Ryan's narrow victory in the 2005 election means that Enfield North will remain a target for the Conservatives.

ENFIELD SOUTHGATE

C gain

		Electorate	Turnout	Change from	2001	Electorate	Turnout
		63,613	66.4%	2001		65,957	63.5%
Burrowes D	**C**	**18,830**	**44.6%**	**6%**	**Lab**	**21,727**	**51.8%**
Twigg S	Lab	17,083	40.5%	-11.3%	C	16,181	38.6%
Kakoulakis Z	LD	4,724	11.2%	4.2%	LD	2,935	7%
Doughty T	Greens	1,083	2.6%	1%	Greens	662	1.6%
Hall B	UKIP	490	1.2%	0.5%	UKIP	298	0.7%
					Ind	105	0.3%
Lab to C swing	**8.7%**	**42,210**		**C maj 1,747**		**41,908**	**Lab maj 5,546**
				4.1%			13.2%

DAVID BURROWES b 12 June 1969. MP 2005-. Councillor London Borough of Enfield 1994-2004: Shadow cabinet member 1999-2000, cabinet member 2002-04. Assistant solicitor, Shepherd Harris and Co, Enfield 1995-2001. Ed Highgate School, London; law, Exeter University

Epitomising Labour's sweeping 1997 victory with its shocking defeat of former Defence Secretary Michael Portillo, the north London seat of Enfield Southgate is relatively affluent, with mainly white, professional and home owning constituents, although there are significant Cypriot, Hindu and Jewish minorities. However, the constituency remains unpredictable, with Conservative David Burrowes' victory over Education Minister Stephen Twigg in 2005.

EPPING FOREST — C hold

		Electorate 72,776	Turnout 61.6%	Change from 2001	2001	Electorate 72,645	Turnout 58.4%
Laing E	**C**	**23,783**	**53%**	**3.9%**	**C**	**20,833**	**49.1%**
Charalambous B	Lab	9,425	21%	-8.3%	Lab	12,407	29.3%
Heavens M	LD	8,279	18.5%	-0.1%	LD	7,884	18.6%
Leppert J	BNP	1,728	3.8%		UKIP	1,290	3%
Smith A	UKIP	1,014	2.3%	-0.7%			
Tibrook R	Eng Dem	631	1.4%				
Lab to C swing	**6.1%**	**44,860**		**C maj 14,358** 32%		**42,414**	**C maj 8,426** 19.9%

ELEANOR LAING b 1 Feb 1958. MP 1997-. Shadow Sec of State for Scotland 2005-, Shadow Min: Women 2004-, Children 2003. Opposition whip 1999-2000. Opposition spokes: constitutional affairs and Scotland 2000-01, education and skills 2001-03. Member select cttees: Education and Employment 1997-98, Environment, Transport and Regional Affairs 1998-99, Office of Deputy Prime Minister 2004-05. Vice-chair all-party equalities group 2004. Special adviser to John MacGregor 1989-94. Solicitor. First woman pres Edinburgh Univ union. Ed BA/LLB, Edinburgh Univ.

Stretching from the edge of Greater London into the rural delights of Epping Forest, this constituency centres on commuter towns such as Loughton, Chigwell, and Waltham Abbey. This is classic commuter belt territory and has remained true to the Conservative Party over the years, electing such notable MPs as Winston Churchill. Though Labour made gains in 1997, Epping Forest remains a safe Tory seat.

EPSOM AND EWELL — C hold

		Electorate 75,515	Turnout 66%	Change from 2001	2001	Electorate 74,266	Turnout 62.8%
Grayling C	**C**	**27,146**	**54.4%**	**6.3%**	**C**	**22,430**	**48.1%**
Lees J	LD	10,699	21.4%	-0.7%	Lab	12,350	26.5%
Mansell C	Lab	10,265	20.6%	-5.9%	LD	10,316	22.1%
Kefford P	UKIP	1,769	3.6%	0.3%	UKIP	1,547	3.3%
LD to C swing	**3.5%**	**49,879**		**C maj 16,447** 33%		**46,643**	**C maj 10,080** 21.6%

CHRISTOPHER GRAYLING b 1 April 1962. MP 2001-. Shadow Leader HoC 2005-. Shadow Minister: Health 2005, Educ 2004-05, Public Services, Health and Education 2003-04. Opposition whip 2002. Shadow health spokes 2002-03. Member select cttees: Transport, Local Govt and the Regions 2001-02, Transport 2002. Vice-chair all-party rail group 2001-. Cllr Merton 1998-2002. Media career. Change consultant and European marketing director Burson Marsteller 1997-2001. Ed Royal Grammar Sch, High Wycombe; BA history, Sidney Sussex Coll, Cambridge.

A part of Surrey very much within the commuter belt, Epsom and Ewell is solidly middle-class and solidly Conservative. The constituency runs from Worcester Park in the north to Ashtead in the south. As with much of the area contained by the M25 there is little open countryside, as towns such as Epsom, Ewell, Ashtead and Stoneleigh merge into one another. The first does, however, possess a distinct identity originating in its famous wells and racecourse.

EREWASH — Lab hold

		Electorate 78,376	Turnout 64.5%	Change from 2001	2001	Electorate 78,484	Turnout 61.9%
Blackman L	**Lab**	**22,472**	**44.4%**	**-4.8%**	**Lab**	**23,915**	**49.2%**
Simmonds D	C	15,388	30.4%	-4.5%	C	16,983	34.9%
Garnett M	LD	7,073	14%	2.5%	LD	5,586	11.5%
Kilroy-Silk R	Veritas	2,957	5.8%		UKIP	692	1.4%
Graham S	BNP	1,319	2.6%	1.4%	BNP	591	1.2%
Kingscott G	UKIP	941	1.9%	0.5%	Loony	428	0.9%
Seerius R	Loony	287	0.6%	-0.3%	SLP	401	0.8%
Bishop D	CMEP	116	0.2%				
Lab to C swing	**0.2%**	**50,553**		**Lab maj 7,084** 14%		**48,596**	**Lab maj 6,932** 14.3%

LIZ BLACKMAN b 26 Sept 1949. MP 1997-. PPS to Geoff Hoon as Sec of State for Defence 2000-05. Member Treasury select cttee 1997-2001. Chair all-party autism group 2003-; vice-chair all-party markets industry group 2002-; treasurer all-party manufacturing industry group 1997-. Former deputy leader Broxtowe Borough Council. Teacher. Ed Carlisle County High Sch for Girls; Prince Henry's Grammar Sch, Otley; BEd, Clifton Coll, Nottingham.

The Erewash region is home to many East Midlands commuters, but also has a good deal of its own industry. Long Eaton is still a lace-making centre, and though coal-mining is no more, engineering, textile, and furniture-making industries remain. Most of the workforce are in manual trades, and Labour sit comfortably here, but a relatively low unemployment rate and a high level of owner-occupancy have previously given the Tories a solid support base.

ERITH AND THAMESMEAD — Lab hold

		Electorate 72,058	Turnout 52.2%	Change from 2001	2001	Electorate 66,371	Turnout 50.2%
Austin J	**Lab**	**20,483**	**54.4%**	**-4.9%**	**Lab**	**19,769**	**59.3%**
Bromby C	C	8,983	23.9%	-1.9%	C	8,602	25.8%
Toole S	LD	5,088	13.5%	2.1%	LD	3,800	11.4%
Ravenscroft B	BNP	1,620	4.3%		SLP	1,180	3.5%
Thomas B	UKIP	1,477	3.9%				
Lab to C swing	**1.5%**	**37,651**		**Lab maj 11,500** 30.5%		**33,351**	**Lab maj 11,167** 33.5%

JOHN AUSTIN b 21 Aug 1944. MP for Woolwich 1992-97, for Erith and Thamesmead 1997-. Member select cttees: Health 1994-97/1997-, Unopposed Bills (Panel) 1998-. Chair various all-party groups 2001. Co-chair Advancement of Arab-British Understanding council 1998-. Board member British Syria Soc. Cllr Greenwich 1970-94: leader 1982-87, mayor 1987-88/1988-89. Trustee various charities. Soc/community worker. Lab Party organiser/agent 1963-70. Ed Community and Youth Work Cert, Goldsmith's Coll, London; MSc policy studies, Bristol Univ.

A reasonably new seat in south east London, Erith and Thamesmead covers areas in Greenwich and Bexley and comprises council estates, industrial sites, Thames marshland, sewage works and a power station. A combination of poor communities, the area has high unemployment and low house ownership. The area has been marked for regeneration and development projects to ease the economic and social problems and Labour is likely to maintain its hold.

ESHER AND WALTON — C hold

		Electorate 76,926	Turnout 62.2%	Change from 2001	2001	Electorate 73,541	Turnout 61.9%
Taylor I	**C**	**21,882**	**45.7%**	**-3.3%**	**C**	**22,296**	**49%**
Marsh M	LD	14,155	29.6%	7.1%	Lab	10,758	23.6%
Taylor R	Lab	9,309	19.4%	-4.2%	LD	10,241	22.5%
Collignon B	UKIP	1,582	3.3%	-1.6%	UKIP	2,236	4.9%
Chinnery C	Loony	608	1.3%				
Cutler R	SLP	342	0.7%				
C to LD swing	**5.2%**	**47,878**		**C maj 7,727** 16.1%		**45,531**	**C maj 11,538** 25.3%

IAN TAYLOR b 18 April 1945. MP for Esher 1987-97, for Esher and Walton 1997-. Dept of Trade and Industry Parly Under-Sec of State 1994-97, PPS to William Waldegrave 1988-94. Opposition N Ireland spokes 1997. Member select cttees: Foreign Affairs 1987-89, Science and Technology 1998-2001. Chair: Tory Europe Network 2002-, European Movement 2001-. Governor British Assocn for Central and Eastern Europe 1997-2000. Company director/corporate finance consultant. MBE 1974. Ed BA econ, pol and mod hist, Keele Univ; research scholar, LSE.

Bordering Greater London, this Surrey constituency must be classed as one of the most exclusive of the stockbroker commuter belt. It is almost exclusively residential, and homes, particularly those overlooking the Thames, are very expensive. So it should come as no surprise that the seat has been and remains a Tory stronghold, even though the Liberal Democrats progressed significantly in the 2005 general election. The famous Hampton Court Palace sits just inside the constituency's northern boundary.

NORTH ESSEX — C hold

		Electorate 73,037	Turnout 65.7%	Change from 2001	2001	Electorate 71,605	Turnout 62.8%
Jenkin B	**C**	**22,811**	**47.6%**	**0.2%**	**C**	**21,325**	**47.4%**
Hughes E	Lab	11,908	24.8%	-6.7%	Lab	14,139	31.5%
Raven J	LD	9,831	20.5%	3%	LD	7,867	17.5%
Fox C	Greens	1,718	3.6%		UKIP	1,613	3.6%
Curtis G	UKIP	1,691	3.5%	-0.1%			
Lab to C swing	**3.5%**	**47,959**		**C maj 10,903** 22.7%		**44,944**	**C maj 7,186** 16%

BERNARD JENKIN b 9 April 1959. MP for N Colchester 1992-97, N Essex 1997-. Shadow Minister for Trade and Industry 2005-. Shadow Sec of State: The Regions 2003-05, Defence 2001-03; Shadow Minister for Transport 1998-2001. PPS to Michael Forsyth 1995-97. Opposition spokes: constitutional affairs, Scotland/Wales 1997-98, environment, transport and regions 1998. Member Soc Security select cttee 1993-97. Political adviser to Leon Brittan 1986-88. Venture capital manager. Ed BA Eng lit, Corpus Christi Coll, Cambridge.

The solid Conservative seat of North Essex forms a ring round the City of Colchester taking in Brightlingsea, the scene of protests over live animal exports, and Tiptree with its famous jam factory in the south-west corner. The northern perimeter of the seat forms the border with Suffolk and encompasses places, like Dedham Vale, made famous by Constable. The constituency is mainly affluent and rural.

EXETER — Lab hold

		Electorate 84,964	Turnout 64.8%	Change from 2001	2001	Electorate 81,946	Turnout 64.2%
Bradshaw B	**Lab**	**22,619**	**41.1%**	**-8.7%**	**Lab**	**26,194**	**49.8%**
Cox P	C	14,954	27.2%	-0.2%	C	14,435	27.4%
Underwood J	LD	11,340	20.6%	8.2%	LD	6,512	12.4%
Danks M	Lib	2,214	4%	-0.9%	Lib	2,596	4.9%
Brenan T	Greens	1,896	3.4%	1%	Greens	1,240	2.4%
Fitzgeorge-Parker M	UKIP	1,854	3.4%	1.3%	UKIP	1,109	2.1%
Stuart J	Ind	191	0.4%		SA	530	1%
Lab to C swing	**4.3%**	**55,068**		**Lab maj 7,665** 13.9%		**52,616**	**Lab maj 11,759** 22.3%

BEN BRADSHAW b 30 Aug 1960. MP 1997-. Dept for Environment, Food and Rural Affairs Parly Under-Sec of State 2003-, Parly Sec Privy Council Office 2002-03, Parly Under-Sec of State Foreign and Commonwealth Office 2001-02; PPS to John Denham 2000-01. Member European Scrutiny select cttee 1998-2001. Member: Lab Campaign for Electoral Reform, Lab Movement for Europe. Journalist (BBC correspondent during fall of Berlin Wall). BBC Radio 4 reporter 1991-97. Sony News Reporter Award 1993. Ed BA German, Sussex Univ; Freiburg Univ, Germany.

The constituency covers the whole of the city of Exeter and the university and represents a small island of New Labour urbanites surrounded by a sea of more rural Conservative and Liberal Democrat constituencies. Exeter is an expensive city for many low-income residents and there are many deep-seated employment and social issues to be tackled. Labour's future success in the seat depends on its long-term policies in these areas.

FALKIRK — Lab hold

		Electorate 76,784	Turnout 59.6%		2001
Joyce E	**Lab**	**23,264**	**50.8%**		No comparable results due to boundary changes
Love L	SNP	9,789	21.4%		
Chomczuk C	LD	7,321	16%		
Potts D	C	4,538	9.9%		
Quinlan D	SSP	838	1.8%		
Lab to SNP swing (notional)	**0.4%**	**45,750**		**Lab maj 13,475** 29.4%	

ERIC JOYCE b 13 Oct 1960. MP for Falkirk West Dec 2000 (by-election) -2005, for Falkirk 2005-. PPS to Margaret Hodge, DWP 2005-, Mike O'Brien, DTI 2003-05. Member select cttees: Scottish Affairs 2001-03, Procedure 2001-. Treasurer all-party Great Lakes region and genocide prevention group 2002-. Commission for racial equality 1999-2000. Former army Major. Private Black Watch regiment 1978-81. Ed Perth Academy; RMA, Sandhurst; BA religious studies, Stirling Univ; MA education, Bath Univ; MBA education, Keele Univ.

Set in Scotland's old industrial heartland, this seat combines populous Falkirk with several satellite towns and villages which are still partly characterised by manufacturing. Although it incorporates some more affluent rural wards in the south-east towards Edinburgh, the electorate is concentrated in Falkirk and its environs. Though tourism and investment, visibly symbolised by the remarkable Falkirk wheel, have helped revive the post-industrial economy, the seat remains poorer than average and overwhelmingly Labour in its political character.

FALMOUTH AND CAMBORNE — LD gain

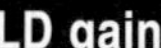

		Electorate 71,509	Turnout 67.2%	Change from 2001	2001	Electorate 72,833	Turnout 64.3%
Goldsworthy J	**LD**	**16,747**	**34.9%**	**10.4%**	**Lab**	**18,532**	**39.6%**
Atherton C	Lab	14,861	31%	-8.6%	C	14,005	29.9%
Crossley A	C	12,644	26.3%	-3.6%	LD	11,453	24.5%
Mahon M	UKIP	1,820	3.8%	1%	UKIP	1,328	2.8%
Mudd D	Ind	961	2%		MebK	853	1.8%
Holmes P	Lib	423	0.9%	-0.5%	Lib	649	1.4%
Wasley H	MebK	370	0.8%	-1%			
Gifford P	Veritas	128	0.3%				
Smith R	Masts	61	0.1%				
Lab to LD swing	**9.5%**	**48,015**		**LD maj 1,886** 3.9%		**46,820**	**Lab maj 4,527** 9.7%

JULIA GOLDSWORTHY b 10 Sept 1978. MP 2005-. Senior political adviser to Liberal Democrat Parliamentary Party (economy and education) 2003-04; Education researcher Truro College Business Centre 2004; Regeneration officer Carrick District Council 2004-. Ed Truro School, Cornwall; history, Fitzwilliam College, Cambridge; Japanese, Daiichi University of Economics; economics, Birkbeck College, London

The second most south-westerly constituency in England, Falmouth and Camborne extends from the north to the south coast of western Cornwall. Once the centre of the Cornish tin-mining industry, it is now best known for its busy port and booming tourism. A 9 per cent swing away from Labour in 2005 was enough to unseat their controversial MP and give the Liberal Democrats complete control of the Cornwall constituencies.

FAREHAM

C hold

		Electorate 72,599	Turnout 66.9%	Change from 2001	2001	Electorate 72,715	Turnout 62.5%
Hoban M	**C**	**24,151**	**49.7%**	**2.6%**	**C**	**21,389**	**47.1%**
Carr J	Lab	12,449	25.6%	-6%	Lab	14,380	31.6%
de Ste-Croix R	LD	10,551	21.7%	3%	LD	8,503	18.7%
Mason-Apps P	UKIP	1,425	2.9%	0.3%	UKIP	1,175	2.6%
Lab to C swing	**4.3%**	**48,576**		**C maj 11,702** 24.1%		**45,447**	**C maj 7,009** 15.4%

MARK HOBAN b 31 March 1964. MP 2001-. Shadow Min: Education 2004-, Public Services, Health and Education 2003-04. Opposition whip 2002-03. Member Science and Technology select cttee 2001-03. General election campaign manager 1987/1992. Member European Standing Cttee A 2001-. Hon vice-pres Soc of Maritime Industries. Chartered accountant (PricewaterhouseCoopers 1985-). Ed St Leonard's Comp Sch, Durham; BSc econ, LSE.

Situated between Southampton and Portsmouth, Fareham is predominantly suburban with areas such as Portchester, Warsash, and Titchfield each trying to retain their separate identity. With the Solent and river Hamble to the west, the constituency is home to some of the best British yachting. Portsmouth Harbour, typical of the shipbuilding and naval traditions of the area, marks the eastern edge of the constituency.

FAVERSHAM AND MID KENT

C hold

		Electorate 66,411	Turnout 65.7%	Change from 2001	2001	Electorate 67,995	Turnout 60.4%
Robertson H	**C**	**21,690**	**49.7%**	**4.1%**	**C**	**18,739**	**45.6%**
Bradstock A	Lab	12,970	29.7%	-5.8%	Lab	14,556	35.5%
Naghi D	LD	7,204	16.5%	3%	LD	5,529	13.5%
Thompson R	UKIP	1,152	2.6%	0.6%	UKIP	828	2%
Davidson N	Loony	610	1.4%		Greens	799	1.9%
					RNRL	600	1.5%
Lab to C swing	**5%**	**43,626**		**C maj 8,720** 20%		**41,051**	**C maj 4,183** 10.2%

HUGH ROBERTSON b 9 October 1962. MP 2001-. Shadow Sport Min 2005-. Special adviser security Shadow Northern Ireland Sec 1998-2001. Opposition whip 2002-04. Opposition sport spokes 2004-05. Vice-chair all-party South Caucasus group 2004-. Army officer (The Life Guards) 1985-95. Sultan of Brunei's Order of Merit 1992. Investment manager (asst director Schroder Investment Management 1995-2001). Ed BSc land management, Reading Univ; RMA Sandhurst.

Created in 1995, the constituency of Faversham and Mid Kent forms an uneasy coalition between the wedge of Labour wards from east Maidstone and the staunchly Tory Faversham, which abut a section of deeply Conservative countryside. With two motorways running through the seat, the M2 and M20, it is also ideally situated for commuters, but patrician Toryism has deep roots in this part of Kent and the seat appears reasonably safe for the Conservatives.

FELTHAM AND HESTON

Lab hold

		Electorate 75,391	Turnout 49.4%	Change from 2001	2001	Electorate 73,229	Turnout 49.4%
Keen A	**Lab/C**	**17,741**	**47.6%**	**-11.6%**	**Lab/C**	**21,406**	**59.2%**
Bowen M	C	10,921	29.3%	5.1%	C	8,749	24.2%
Khalsa S	LD	6,177	16.6%	2.8%	LD	4,998	13.8%
Kemp G	NF	975	2.6%		SLP	651	1.8%
Anstis E	Greens	815	2.2%		Ind	204	0.6%
Mullett L	UKIP	612	1.6%		Ind	169	0.5%
Prachar W	Ind	41	0.1%				
Lab/C to C swing	**8.4%**	**37,282**		**Lab/C maj 6,820** 18.3%		**36,177**	**Lab/C maj 12,657** 35%

ALAN KEEN b 25 Nov 1937. MP 1992-. Member select cttees: Education 1995-96, Deregulation 1995-96, Culture, Media and Sport 1997-. Chair all-party football group 2001-; vice-chair all-party groups: aviation 2001-, sport and leisure 2001-, sports 2002, football club 2003-, financial exploitation 2005-. Sec Lab First Past the Post group 1997-. Cllr London Borough of Hounslow 1986-90. Part-time tactical scout Middlesbrough FC 1967-85. Private industry and commerce (mainly fire protection industry) 1963-92. Ed St William Turner's Sch, Cleveland.

Close to Heathrow Airport, Feltham and Heston is characterised by light industry, large housing estates, and a 21 per cent Asian population. A largely middle class seat, the area has low unemployment and high house ownership. Recaptured by Labour in 1992 after a decade under the Conservatives, its Labour majority was on the increase, but the 2005 election suggests the seat may become vulnerable.

FERMANAGH AND SOUTH TYRONE — SF hold

		Electorate	Turnout	Change from	2001	Electorate	Turnout
		67,174	72.0%	2001		66,640	70%
Gildernew M	**SF**	**18,638**	**38.2%**	**4.1%**	**SF**	**17,739**	**34.1%**
Foster A	DUP	14,056	28.8%		UUP	17,686	34%
Elliott T	UUP	8,869	18.2%	-15.8%	SDLP	9,706	18.7%
Gallagher T	SDLP	7,230	14.8%	-3.9%	Ind	6,843	13.2%
SF to DUP swing	**12.4%**	**48,793**		**SF maj 4,582**		**51,974**	**SF maj 53**
				9.4%			0.1%

MICHELLE GILDERNEW b 28 March 1970. MP 2001-. Sinn Fein social devt spokes. New NI Assembly 1998-2002: Employment and Learning cttee, dep chair Social Devt cttee 1999-, Centre cttee 2000-. Sinn Fein: Internat Dept/Inter-Party talks team member, former women's issues spokes, press officer 1997, London office head 1997-98. Ed St Josephs PS, Caledon; St Catherine's Coll, Armagh; Ulster Univ, Coleraine.

This sprawling rural, border and somewhat peripheral seat of Fermanagh and South Tyrone is in the south west of the province. This was the seat that also provided the electoral victory of the IRA hunger striker Bobby Sands in 1981. Just over half the population is Catholic and Irish is spoken by nearly one in eight of the population. This has become a Sinn Fein held marginal after a long period of UUP dominance.

NORTH EAST FIFE — LD hold

		Electorate	Turnout		2001
		62,057	62.1%		
Campbell M	**LD**	**20,088**	**52.1%**		No comparable results due to boundary changes
Scott-Hayward M	C	7,517	19.5%		
King A	Lab	4,920	12.8%		
Campbell R	SNP	4,011	10.4%		
Park J	Greens	1,071	2.8%		
Pickard D	UKIP	533	1.4%		
Ferguson J	SSP	416	1.1%		
C to LD swing	**3.2%**	**38,556**		**LD maj 12,571**	
(notional)				32.6%	

MENZIES CAMPBELL b 22 May 1941. MP for North East Fife 1987-2005, for new NE Fife 2005-. Lib Dem Shadow Sec of State Foreign and Commonwealth Affairs 2001-. Lib/SLD/Lib Dem spokes 1987-2001. Member: select cttees 1990-99, Lib Dem Peel group 2001-. Dep leader Lib Dem Party 2003-. Chair Scottish Lib Party 1975-77. Advocate. Competed: 1964 Olympics, 1966 Commonwealth Games. UK athletics team capt. UK 100m record holder 1967-74. CBE 1987; PC 1999; Kt 2004. Ed MA arts, LLB law, Glasgow Univ; postgrad law studies, Stanford Univ, USA.

The sea bounds three sides of this seat, with coastline stretching from Leven in the Firth of Forth through Earlsferry, Elie, Pittenweem, Anstruther and St Andrews to the Firth of Tay. Inland, the East Neuk is studded with picturesque villages and spectacular golf courses. Like its famous university seat St Andrews, North East Fife is well-groomed and a little conservative, though it has been firmly in the hands of the Liberal Democrats since 1987.

FINCHLEY AND GOLDERS GREEN — Lab hold

		Electorate	Turnout	Change from	2001	Electorate	Turnout
		69,808	61.9%	2001		76,178	57.3%
Vis R	**Lab**	**17,487**	**40.5%**	**-5.8%**	**Lab**	**20,205**	**46.3%**
Mennear A	C	16,746	38.8%	1%	C	16,489	37.8%
Garden S	LD	7,282	16.8%	4.7%	LD	5,266	12.1%
Lynch N	Greens	1,136	2.6%	-0.6%	Greens	1,385	3.2%
Jacobs J	UKIP	453	1.1%	0.3%	UKIP	330	0.8%
Weiss R	Vote Dream	110	0.2%				
Lab to C swing	**3.4%**	**43,214**		**Lab maj 741**		**43,675**	**Lab maj 3,716**
				1.7%			8.5%

RUDI VIS b 4 April 1941. MP 1997-. Vice-chair all-party groups: Israel 1997-, war graves and battlefield heritage 2002-, Irish in Britain 2004-. Member: Lab Movement in Europe 1997-, European Movement 1999-. Member: Council of Europe, Western European Union, Council for advancement of Arab-British understanding 2000-. Cllr Barnet 1986-98. Dutch armed services/US Air Force 1960-66, academic career 1966-97. Member: CND/Friends of the Earth. Ed BSc econ, Univ of Maryland, USA; MSc econ, LSE; PhD econ, Brunel Univ, London.

A traditionally Tory seat in the affluent suburbs of North London, Finchley and Golders Green is well known for its large Jewish community and its famous former MP – Margaret Thatcher. It fell to Labour in 1997, but their hold was cut to under 1,000 in 2005. The residents experience low unemployment, well-paid jobs and high rates of home ownership.

FOLKESTONE AND HYTHE — C hold

		Electorate 70,914	Turnout 68.4%	Change from 2001	2001	Electorate 71,507	Turnout 64.1%
Howard M	**C**	**26,161**	**53.9%**	**8.9%**	**C**	**20,645**	**45%**
Carroll P	LD	14,481	29.9%	-2.2%	LD	14,738	32.1%
Tomison M	Lab	6,053	12.5%	-7.7%	Lab	9,260	20.2%
Dawe H	Greens	688	1.4%		UKIP	1,212	2.6%
Holdsworth P	UKIP	619	1.3%	-1.3%			
Jug T	Loony	175	0.4%				
Hylton-Potts R	GBB	153	0.3%				
Leon-Smith G	Senior	151	0.3%				
Dunn S	Progress	22	0.1%				
LD to C swing	**5.6%**	**48,503**		**C maj 11,680** 24.1%		**45,855**	**C maj 5,907** 12.9%

MICHAEL HOWARD b 7 July 1941. MP 1983-. Leader: Opposition 2003-, Con Party 2003-. Shadow: Chancellor of Exchequer 2001-03, Foreign and Commonwealth Affairs Sec of State 1997-99. Home Secretary 1993-97. Sec of State: Environment 1992-93, Employment 1990-92. Min of State: Housing and Planning 1989-90, Water and Planning 1988-89, Local Govt 1987-88. Parly Under-Sec Trade and Industry 1985-87. PPS to Sir Patrick Mayhew 1984-85. Contested Con Party leadership 1997. Member Con Policy Board 2001-. Barrister. PC 1990. Ed MA econ, Peterhouse, Cambridge.

This Kentish coastal constituency features the medieval 'Cinque' ports of Hythe and Romney, as well as the town of Folkestone, a scattering of pretty villages, and fertile areas such as Romney Marsh and the scenic Elham Valley further inland. A frontier mentality can be said to exist in a seat which effectively borders the rest of Europe. An ambitious Liberal Democrat target in 2005, Michael Howard comfortably saw off the challenge, doubling his majority in the process.

FOREST OF DEAN — C gain

		Electorate 67,225	Turnout 70.9%	Change from 2001	2001	Electorate 66,240	Turnout 67.3%
Harper M	**C**	**19,474**	**40.9%**	**2.1%**	**Lab**	**19,350**	**43.4%**
Owen I	Lab	17,425	36.6%	-6.8%	C	17,301	38.8%
Coleman C	LD	8,185	17.2%	4.3%	LD	5,762	12.9%
Hill P	UKIP	1,140	2.4%	0.9%	Greens	1,254	2.8%
Tweedie S	Greens	991	2.1%	-0.7%	UKIP	661	1.5%
Reeve A	Ind	300	0.6%		Ind	279	0.6%
Morgan G	EEP	125	0.3%				
Lab to C swing	**4.5%**	**47,640**		**C maj 2,049** 4.3%		**44,607**	**Lab maj 2,049** 4.6%

MARK HARPER b 26 June 1970. MP 2005-. Contested Forest of Dean 2001 general election. South Swindon Conservative Association: treasurer 1993-98; deputy chair 1998. Auditor KPMG 1991-95; Intel Corporation (UK) Ltd: senior finance analyst, 1995-97; finance manager 1997-2000, operations manager 2000-02; own accountancy practice 2002-. Ed Headlands School, Swindon; Swindon College; PPE, Brasenose College, Oxford.

This fascinating marginal in a tucked-away corner of England has a solid Labour past due to its history as a coal mining area, with villages clustered round its now defunct small pits. The seat was claimed by the Conservatives in 1979, who then held it until the Labour landslide of 1997. However, the Tories reclaimed the Forest of Dean in 2005 after a hard fought campaign.

FOYLE — SDLP hold

		Electorate 69,207	Turnout 65.9%	Change from 2001	2001	Electorate 70,943	Turnout 68.9%
Durkan M	**SDLP**	**21,119**	**46.3%**	**-3.9%**	**SDLP**	**24,538**	**50.2%**
McLaughlin M	SF	15,162	33.2%	6.6%	SF	12,988	26.6%
Hay W	DUP	6,557	14.4%	-0.8%	DUP	7,414	15.2%
McCann E	Soc EA	1,649	3.6%		UUP	3,360	6.9%
Storey E	UUP	1,091	2.4%	-4.5%	All	579	1.2%
Reel B	Vote Dream	31	0.1%				
SDLP to SF swing	**5.3%**	**45,609**		**SDLP maj 5,957** 13.1%		**48,879**	**SDLP maj 11,550** 23.6%

MARK DURKAN b 26 June 1960. MP 2005-. SDLP: Chair 1990-95, Leader 2001-; MLA for Foyle 1998-: Minister of Finance and Personnel 1999-2001; Deputy First Minister 2001-02; Councillor Derry City Council 1993-2000. Deputy President, Union of Students in Ireland 1982-84; assistant to John Hume MP 1984-98. Ed St Columb's College, Derry; Queen's University, Belfast

The constituency covers all the Derry district council area. Despite its name, after the local river, Foyle is really Derry, a much contested term between local Protestants and Catholics. The London prefix is seen as legitimising its plantation by Protestant settlers. It is the second city in Northern Ireland and the seat was held by SDLP stalwart John Hume for 22 years. The constituency has the second highest proportion of Catholics in Northern Ireland.

FYLDE — C hold

		Electorate 75,703	Turnout 60.1%	Change from 2001	2001	Electorate 73,460	Turnout 60.9%
Jack M	**C**	**24,287**	**53.4%**	**1.1%**	**C**	**23,383**	**52.3%**
Parbury W	Lab	11,828	26%	-4.8%	Lab	13,773	30.8%
Winlow B	LD	7,748	17%	2.2%	LD	6,599	14.8%
Akeroyd T	Lib	1,647	3.6%		UKIP	982	2.2%
Lab to C swing	**3%**	**45,510**		**C maj 12,459** 27.4%		**44,737**	**C maj 9,610** 21.5%

MICHAEL JACK b 17 Sept 1946. MP 1987-. Shadow Min Agric, Fisheries and Food 1997-98. Financial Sec Treasury 1995-97. Min of State: MAFF 1993-95, Home Office 1992-93. Soc Security Joint Parly Under-Sec 1990-92. PPS to John Gummer 1988-90. Opposition health spokes 1997. Member various select cttees; chair: Environment, Food and Rural Affairs 2003-, Information 2003. Member 1922 Cttee Exec 2000-03. Manager Proctor and Gamble, M&S 1975-80, Director LO Jeffs Ltd. PC 1997. Ed Bradford Tech Coll; BA econ/MPhil transport econ, Leicester Univ.

The Fylde constituency lies on the north bank of the river Ribble to the south and east of Blackpool. It is situated on and named after the Fylde peninsula, a low coastal plain 18 miles wide stretching between the Ribble and Morecambe Bay in the north. This mainly rural constituency is a popular retirement area, especially Lytham St Annes, and, unlike its robust neighbouring Blackpool constituencies, has remained faithfully Conservative.

GAINSBOROUGH — C hold

		Electorate 70,733	Turnout 64.6%	Change from 2001	2001	Electorate 65,870	Turnout 64.2%
Leigh E	**C**	**20,040**	**43.9%**	**-2.3%**	**C**	**19,555**	**46.2%**
Heath A	LD	12,037	26.4%	-0.3%	Lab	11,484	27.1%
Knight J	Lab	11,744	25.7%	-1.4%	LD	11,280	26.7%
Pearson S	UKIP	1,860	4.1%				
C to LD swing	**1%**	**45,681**		**C maj 8,003** 17.5%		**42,319**	**C maj 8,071** 19.1%

EDWARD LEIGH b 20 July 1950. Dept of Trade and Industry Parly Under-Sec 1990-93; PPS to John Patten 1990. Member select cttees: Soc Security 1995-97/1997-2000, Agriculture 1996-97, Deregulation 1997, Public Accounts 2000-01 (chair 2001-), Liaison 2001-. Chair all-party street children group 2001-. Cllr: Richmond BC 1974-78; GLC 1977-81. Barrister, arbitrator. Member: Con Research Dept 1973-75, Margaret Thatcher private office as Opposition Leader 1976-77. Ed Oratory Sch, Berks; French Lycee, London; BA hist, Durham Univ.

This safe Conservative seat, just north of Lincoln and bordered by the Trent to its West, includes some of the Lincolnshire Wolds and is typified by monotonously level agricultural land. Its main population centres are the ancient market towns of Gainsborough, Caistor and Market Rasen. Farming and associated trades are obviously the main industries, but the seat also holds many middle-class residents in angement/technical jobs.

GATESHEAD EAST AND WASHINGTON WEST — Lab hold

		Electorate 61,421	Turnout 56.4%	Change from 2001	2001	Electorate 64,041	Turnout 52.5%
Hodgson S	**Lab**	**20,997**	**60.6%**	**-7.5%**	**Lab**	**22,903**	**68.1%**
Hindle F	LD	7,590	21.9%	7%	LD	4,999	14.9%
Martin L	C	4,812	13.9%	-0.9%	C	4,970	14.8%
Batty J	UKIP	1,269	3.7%	1.5%	UKIP	743	2.2%
Lab to LD swing	**7.3%**	**34,668**		**Lab maj 13,407** 38.7%		**33,615**	**Lab maj 17,904** 53.3%

SHARON HODGSON b 1 April 1966. MP 2005-. Mitcham and Morden CLP 2000-05: constituency secretary 2002-05, organiser 2000-02; Labour North 1999-2000: regional organiser; Tyne Bridge CLP 1998-2000: women's officer. Payroll and accounting clerk 1982-99. Ed Heathfield Senior High School, Gateshead. HEFC English, Newcastle College; TUC diploma in Labour party organising, National Education Centre.

Greatly altered in 1995 to straddle the boroughs of Gateshead and Sunderland, this remains one of Labour's safest seats; a mixture of old and new working-class districts, this constituency consists of the eastern part of the post-industrial town of Gateshead and a very different set of neighbourhoods from the post-Second World War new town of Washington.

GEDLING — Lab hold

		Electorate 68,917	Turnout 64%	Change from 2001	2001	Electorate 68,519	Turnout 63.9%
Coaker V	**Lab**	**20,329**	**46.1%**	**-5%**	**Lab**	**22,383**	**51.1%**
Soubry A	C	16,518	37.5%	-0.8%	C	16,785	38.3%
Poynter R	LD	6,070	13.8%	3.2%	LD	4,648	10.6%
Margerison A	UKIP	741	1.7%				
Johnson D	Veritas	411	0.9%				
Lab to C swing	**2.1%**	**44,069**		**Lab maj 3,811** 8.6%		**43,816**	**Lab maj 5,598** 12.8%

VERNON COAKER b 17 June 1953. MP 1997-. PPS to: Tessa Jowell 2002-03, Estelle Morris 2002, Stephen Timms 1999-2002. Assistant govt whip 2003-. Member Social Security select cttee 1998-99. Co-chair all-party obesity group 2002-. Cllr Rushcliffe Borough Council 1983-97. Member: European Standing Cttee B 1998, Friends of the Earth, League Against Cruel Sports. Hon fellow UNICEF. Teacher 1976-97. Ed Drayton Manor Grammar Sch; BA politics, Warwick Univ; PGCE, Trent Poly.

The seat and borough take their name from the small town of Gedling in Nottinghamshire where the Domesday Book was compiled. The largest towns in the seat, Carlton and Arnold, offer comfortable suburban homes to some of the city's more prosperous commuters. Unemployment is below the national average and there are more non-manual workers than manual. Labour had consolidated here since winning the historically safe Conservative seat in 1997, but 2005 saw their wings clipped somewhat.

GILLINGHAM — Lab hold

		Electorate 72,223	Turnout 62.5%	Change from 2001	2001	Electorate 70,901	Turnout 59.5%
Clark P	**Lab**	**18,621**	**41.2%**	**-3.3%**	**Lab**	**18,782**	**44.5%**
Butcher T	C	18,367	40.7%	1.6%	C	16,510	39.1%
Stamp A	LD	6,734	14.9%	1.3%	LD	5,755	13.6%
Mackinley C	UKIP	1,191	2.6%	0.4%	UKIP	933	2.2%
Bryan G	Ind	254	0.6%		SA	232	0.5%
Lab to C swing	**2.5%**	**45,167**		**Lab maj 254** 0.6%		**42,212**	**Lab maj 2,272** 5.4%

PAUL CLARK b 29 April 1957. MP 1997-. PPS to: John Prescott as Deputy PM 2005-, Lord Falconer 2001-03. Joint PPS to Lord Irvine 1999-2001. Assistant govt whip 2003-05. Sec all-party Thames Gateway group 1997-. Member European Standing Cttees: A 1998, B 1998-2000. Cllr Gillingham Borough Council 1982-90. AAEU researcher to Pres and education officer 1980-86. Centre manager TUC, Nat Education Centre 1986-97. Ed Gillingham Grammar Sch; BA economics and politics, Keele Univ; DMS, Derby Univ.

Scrunched between the better known Medway Estuary towns of Rochester and Chatham, the urban constituency of Gillingham is densely populated and largely residential. Its estuary position attracted the Royal Naval Dockyard to the area in the seventeenth century, where it remained until its closure in 1984. The huge swing which allowed Labour to win the seat in 1997 was not entirely expected, and the seat has remained a Labour held marginal in subsequent elections.

VALE OF GLAMORGAN — Lab hold

		Electorate 68,657	Turnout 68.9%	Change from 2001	2001	Electorate 67,774	Turnout 66.7%
Smith J	**Lab**	**19,481**	**41.2%**	**-4.2%**	**Lab**	**20,524**	**45.4%**
Cairns A	C	17,673	37.3%	2.3%	C	15,824	35%
Hooper M	LD	6,140	13%	0.8%	LD	5,521	12.2%
Shaw B	PIC	2,423	5.1%	-1.2%	PIC	2,867	6.3%
Suchorzewski R	UKIP	840	1.8%	0.8%	UKIP	448	1%
Langford K	Lib	605	1.3%				
Mules P	SLP	162	0.3%				
Lab to C swing	**3.3%**	**47,324**		**Lab maj 1,808** 3.8%		**45,184**	**Lab maj 4,700** 10.4%

JOHN SMITH b 17 March 1951. MP for Vale of Glamorgan 1989-92, 1997-. PPS to: Dr John Reid 1997-99, Roy Hattersley as Lab Party dep leader 1989-92. Member Welsh Affairs select cttee 1990-92, 2000-01. Chair: all-party group 2002-, Wales Lab Party 1988-89. Member: Welsh Exec, Nat Policy Forum 1996. Former vice-chair Welsh parly Lab Party. Cllr Vale of Glamorgan BC 1979-91. Hon vice-pres rail users' federation. RAF 1967-71. Carpenter/joiner, tutor, lecturer, campaign manager. Ed Gwent Higher Ed Coll; BSc econ, Univ Coll of Wales, Cardiff.

This seat comprises a scenic area to the west of Cardiff in South Wales. Centred on the town of Barry, the seat has been won by the Conservatives in the past, but Labour currently hold the seat. The swing towards the Conservatives in the 2005 general election has re-established the division as a key marginal battleground for future electoral contests. If the Tory recovery continues it is seats like this that they will win.

GLASGOW CENTRAL — Lab hold

		Electorate	Turnout		2001
		64,053	43.8%		
Sarwar M	**Lab**	**13,518**	**48.2%**		No comparable results due to boundary changes
Nelson I	LD	4,987	17.8%		
Kidd B	SNP	4,148	14.8%		
Sullivan R	C	1,757	6.3%		
Masterton G	Greens	1,372	4.9%		
Gordon M	SSP	1,110	4%		
Hamilton W	BNP	671	2.4%		
Johnson I	SLP	255	0.9%		
Greig T	OCV	139	0.5%		
McKenzie E	CGB	80	0.3%		
Lab to LD swing (notional)	**7.4%**	**28,037**		**Lab maj 8,531** 30.4%	

MOHAMMED SARWAR b 18 Aug 1952. MP for Glasgow Govan 1997-2005, for Glasgow Central 2005-. Member Scottish Affairs select cttee 1999-. Chair all-party Kuwait group 2002-. Chair Scottish regional group of Lab MPs 2002-, member Scottish Lab Exec 1994-97. Constituency Lab Party: former branch chair, membership sec, trades union liaison officer. Cllr: Glasgow DC 1992-95, Glasgow City Council 1995-97. Retail shopkeeper 1976-83. Dir United Wholesale Ltd 1983-97. Ed BA political science, Faisalabad, Pakistan.

Glasgow Central is bounded by the M8 in the north and Rutherglen in the south, Bellahouston in the east and Dalmarnock in the west. Though it takes in the University of Strathclyde and its student village, Caledonian University and trendy Merchant City, it is largely poor, with easily the biggest ethnic minority of any Scottish seat. The Lib Dems are now Labour's nearest challenger but is no credible threat: Glasgow Central is safe for Labour.

GLASGOW EAST — Lab hold

		Electorate	Turnout		2001
		64,130	48.2%		
Marshall D	**Lab**	**18,775**	**60.7%**		No comparable results due to boundary changes
McNeill L	SNP	5,268	17%		
Jackson D	LD	3,665	11.8%		
Thomson C	C	2,135	6.9%		
Savage G	SSP	1,096	3.5%		
Lab to SNP swing (notional)	**1.5%**	**30,939**		**Lab maj 13,507** 43.7%	

DAVID MARSHALL b 7 May 1941. MP for Glasgow Shettleston 1979-2005, for Glasgow East 2005-. Member select cttees: Liaison 1987-92, 1997-2001, Scottish Affairs 1994-97 (chair 1997-2001), Unopposed Bills (Panel) 1997-2004. Chair all-party groups 2001-. Hon sec/treasurer Scottish Lab MPs group 1981-2001. Cllr: Glasgow Corp 1972-75, Strathclyde RC 1974-79. Chair Inter-Parly Union British group 1997-2000. Office worker, shepherd, tram/bus conductor. Chair TGWU 33 MPs group 1987-88. Ed Falkirk High Sch; Woodside Senior Sec Sch, Glasgow.

Glasgow East is the old Glasgow Baillieston plus four wards from Shettleston, one of which (Parkhead) contains Celtic Park, home of Celtic FC. It is bisected by the M8, which enters Glasgow from the East. It contains the vast and notorious Easterhouse council estate, which is solidly Labour-voting and extremely deprived. These are trends which characterise the whole of the constituency, whose sprawling concrete housing estates and dilapidated tower blocks are the outward show of serious poverty and depression.

GLASGOW NORTH — Lab hold

		Electorate	Turnout		2001
		55,419	50.4%		
McKechin A	**Lab**	**11,001**	**39.4%**		No comparable results due to boundary changes
Rodger A	LD	7,663	27.4%		
McLean K	SNP	3,614	12.9%		
Pope B	C	2,441	8.7%		
Bartos M	Greens	2,135	7.6%		
Tarlton N	SSP	1,067	3.8%		
Lab to LD swing (notional)	**8.7%**	**27,921**		**Lab maj 3,338** 12%	

ANN McKECHIN b 22 April 1961. MP for Glasgow Maryhill 2001-2005, for Glasgow North 2005-. PPS to Jacqui Smith 2005. Member select cttees: Scottish Affairs 2001-, Standing Orders 2001-, Information 2001-. Vice-chair heavily indebted poor countries group 2003-. Member WTO parly conference steering cttee, Co-operative Party. Glasgow Kelvin Lab Party women's officer 2000-01. Council member world development movement 1999-. Solicitor. Ed: Sacred Heart Sch, Paisley; Paisley Grammar Sch; LLB Scots law, Strathclyde Univ.

The new constituency takes in Charing Cross and Glasgow University then reaches west to Partick, through the chi-chi West End across the Great Western Road to posh Kelvindale and far-from-posh Maryhill and Ruchill, then to Summerston council estate on the edge of the city. It is contains more of a mixture of rich and poor than the other Glasgow seats, but the pockets of affluence are geographically and politically swamped by loyal Labour-voting working class areas and council estates.

GLASGOW NORTH EAST — Speaker hold

		Electorate	Turnout	2001
		62,042	45.8%	
Martin M	**Speaker**	**15,153**	**53.3%**	No comparable results due to boundary changes
McLaughlin J	SNP	5,019	17.7%	
Kelly D	SLP	4,036	14.2%	
Campbell G	SSP	1,402	4.9%	
Houston D	SUP	1,266	4.4%	
McLean S	BNP	920	3.2%	
Chambers J	Ind	622	2.2%	
Speaker to SNP swing (notional)	**6.6%**	**28,418**	**Speaker maj 10,134** 35.7%	

MICHAEL MARTIN b 3 July 1945. MP for Glasgow Springburn 1979-2005, for Glasgow North East 2005-. PPS to Denis Healey 1980-83. First Dep Chair Ways and Means (Dep Speaker) 1997-2000. Speaker 2000-. Member/chair select cttees 1987-2000. Joint pres: British American Parly group 2001-, Commonwealth Parly Assocn (UK) 2000-. Pres Hansard Soc for Parly govt 2000-. Chair HoC Commission 2000-. Cllr Glasgow: Corp 1973-74, DC 1974-79. AUEW shop steward, NUPE organiser, AEEU-sponsored MP. Metal worker. PC 2000. Ed St Patrick Boys Sch, Glasgow.

Glasgow North East begins immediately north of the city centre in Carntyne, Dennistounm Port Dundas and Sighthill. Further out are Riddie and Springburn and the Possil Park estate (one of Glasgow's most deprived), then on the very edge are the sizeable council estates of Barmulloch, Balomock, Milton and Robroyston. Labour has a large majority in every ward, though this will not contribute to a majority in the Commons as the seat is currently held by the Speaker.

GLASGOW NORTH WEST — Lab hold

		Electorate	Turnout	2001
		61,880	55%	
Robertson J	**Lab**	**16,748**	**49.2%**	No comparable results due to boundary changes
Graham P	LD	6,655	19.5%	
Hendry G	SNP	4,676	13.7%	
Roxburgh M	C	3,262	9.6%	
Wardrop M	Greens	1,333	3.9%	
Irwin A	SSP	1,108	3.2%	
Muir C	SLP	279	0.8%	
Lab to LD swing (notional)	**6.8%**	**34,061**	**Lab maj 10,093** 29.6%	

JOHN ROBERTSON b 17 April 1952. MP for Glasgow Anniesland Nov 2000 (by-election)-2005, for Glasgow North West 2005-. Member select cttees: Scottish Affairs 2001-, European Scrutiny 2003-. Chair all-party telecommunications group. Member: Commonwealth Interparly Assocn, Internat Parly Union. Chair Anniesland constituency Lab Party 1995-2000. CWU/NCU political/ed officer Glasgow branch. GPO/Post Office/BT. Election agent for Donald Dewar MP/MSP. Ed ONC electrical engineering, Langside Coll; HNC electrical engineering, Stow Coll.

Glasgow North West spreads along the north bank of the Clyde, from Partick to Whiteinch and Scotstoun, and inland to chic Jordanhill. Some older council estates like Knightswood and Yoker form the heart of the constituency, while newer ones such as the gargantuan Drumchapel estate litter the outskirts of the city.

GLASGOW SOUTH — Lab hold

		Electorate	Turnout	2001
		68,837	55.8%	
Harris T	**Lab**	**18,153**	**47.2%**	No comparable results due to boundary changes
Sanderson A	LD	7,321	19.1%	
MacLean F	SNP	4,860	12.6%	
McAlpine J	C	4,836	12.6%	
Allan K	Greens	1,692	4.4%	
Stevenson R	SSP	1,303	3.4%	
Entwistle D	SLP	266	0.7%	
Lab to LD swing (notional)	**4.9%**	**38,431**	**Lab maj 10,832** 28.2%	

TOM HARRIS b 20 Feb 1964. MP for Glasgow Cathcart 2001-05, for Glasgow South 2005-. PPS to: Patricia Hewitt 2005-, John Spellar 2003-05. Member Science and Technology select cttee 2001-04. Vice-chair all-party music group 2003-. Member Lab Friends of Israel. Press officer Scottish Lab Party 1990-92, Strathclyde RC 1993-96. Reporter. Senior media officer Glasgow CC 1996, PR manage E Ayrshire Council 1996-98. Chief PR/marketing officer Strathclyde Passenger Transport Exec 1998-2001. Ed HND journalism, Napier Coll, Edinburgh.

Glasgow South is more of a mixed bag than other Glaswegian seats, incorporating Maxwell Park, the only Conservative-voting ward in the city. Head south though, and the terrain becomes more typical, as the mixed residential neighbourhoods of Battlefield, Langside, Shawlands, Newlands and Cathcart give way to massive social housing projects such as Castlemilk and Carmunnock, at the edge of the city. Leafier areas like Carmunnock village are the exception, and Labour rules here despite low turnout.

GLASGOW SOUTH WEST

Lab hold

		Electorate	Turnout	2001
		62,005	50%	
Davidson I	**Lab/C**	**18,653**	**60.2%**	No comparable results due to boundary changes
Dornan J	SNP	4,757	15.4%	
Gordon K	LD	3,593	11.6%	
Brady S	C	1,786	5.8%	
Baldassara K	SSP	1,666	5.4%	
McConnachie A	Ind	379	1.2%	
Shaw V	SLP	143	0.5%	
SNP to Lab/C swing (notional)	**0.2%**	**30,977**	**Lab/C maj 13,896** 44.9%	

IAN DAVIDSON b 8 Sept 1950. MP for Glasgow Govan 1992-97, for Glasgow Pollok 1997-2005, for Glasgow South West 2005-. Member select cttees 1997-. Chair all-party groups. Member Co-operative Party. Chair: Co-operative Parly group 1998-99, Lab against the Euro 2002- (founder), Scottish regional group of Lab MPs 2003-04. Cllr Strathclyde RC 1978-92. Chair/pres student assocns, MEP researcher, project manager. Former chair MSF parly group. Sec Lab MPs trade union group 1998-2002. Member new Europe advisory council. Ed MA, Edinburgh Univ.

Glasgow Pollok is beefed up by three wards from Govan to form Glasgow South West which, like its predecessors, is Labour through and through. At its northern end is Govan, on the Clyde's south bank, and newly accquired Drumoyne and Ibrox, the latter home to Rangers FC. From the Clydeside ex-dockyards it stretches south through Cardonald, Crookston, and Penilee to the west of Pollok country park, then to Darnley and Nitshill at the city margins.

GLENROTHES

Lab hold

		Electorate	Turnout	2001
		66,563	56.1%	
MacDougall J	**Lab**	**19,395**	**51.9%**	No comparable results due to boundary changes
Beare J	SNP	8,731	23.4%	
Riches E	LD	4,728	12.6%	
Don B	C	2,651	7.1%	
Rodger G	PPS	716	1.9%	
Balfour M	SSP	705	1.9%	
Smith P	UKIP	440	1.2%	
Lab to SNP swing (notional)	**2.7%**	**37,366**	**Lab maj 10,664** 28.5%	

JOHN MacDOUGALL b 8 Dec 1947. MP for Central Fife 2001-05, for Glenrothes 2005-. Member select cttees: Consolidation of Bills Etc 2001-, Administration 2002-, Regulatory Reform 2003-, Scottish Affairs 2003-. Chair all-party group. Cllr Fife RC: leader of admin 1987-96, convener 1996-2001. JP. Member: Commonwealth parly assocn, Interparly Union, European network group COSLA, E of Scotland European Consortium (founder), Scottish OAPs Assocn, Fife economic forum. Boilermaker. Ed dip industrial management, Fife Coll.

This seat combines Glenrothes new town with a tranche of the Fife coal field to form a heavily Labour, predominantly working class constituency which stretches about 15 kilometres inland from the north coast of the Firth of Forth. After Glenrothes its main urban centres are the little coastal industrial towns of Buckhaven and Methil. Almost all of Fife Central (94 per cent) was combined with the eastern wards of Kircaldy and Dunfermline East to form the new constituency.

GLOUCESTER

Lab hold

		Electorate	Turnout	Change from	2001	Electorate	Turnout
		82,500	62.8%	2001		81,206	59.4%
Dhanda P	**Lab**	**23,138**	**44.7%**	**-1.1%**	**Lab**	**22,067**	**45.8%**
James P	C	18,867	36.4%	-1.3%	C	18,187	37.7%
Hilton J	LD	7,825	15.1%	0.8%	LD	6,875	14.3%
Phipps G	UKIP	1,116	2.2%	0.5%	UKIP	822	1.7%
Meloy B	Greens	857	1.6%		SA	272	0.6%
C to Lab swing	**0.1%**	**51,803**		**Lab maj 4,271** 8.2%		**48,223**	**Lab maj 3,880** 8%

PARMJIT DHANDA b 17 Sept 1971. MP 2001-. PPS to Stephen Twigg 2004-05. Asst govt whip 2005-. Member select cttees: Science and Technology 2001-03, Unopposed Bills (Panel) 2004-. Vice-chair all-party e-democracy group 2003-. Lab Party organiser West London, Hants and Wilts 1996-98. Member Lab Party NEC equal opps working group 1997-. Cllr Hillingdon 1998-2001. TUC trainer/officer. Asst national organiser Connect 1998-. Ed Mellow Lane Comp, Middlesex; BEng electronic engineering/MSc IT, Nottingham Univ.

The county seat of Gloucestershire is more diverse than Cheltenham, the county's other major town, both demographically and in its political history and complexion. This historic city is home to such landmarks as Gloucester Cathedral and Britain's most inland port. After almost three decades as a Conservative constituency Gloucester was taken by Labour in 1997.

GORDON — LD hold

		Electorate	Turnout		2001
		71,925	61.8%		
Bruce M	**LD**	**20,008**	**45%**		No comparable results due to boundary changes
Brotchie I	Lab	8,982	20.2%		
Atkinson P	C	7,842	17.6%		
Strathdee J	SNP	7,098	16%		
Paterson T	SSP	508	1.1%		
Lab to LD swing (notional)	**3.7%**	**44,438**		**LD maj 11,026** 24.8%	

MALCOLM BRUCE b 17 Nov 1944. MP for Gordon 1983-2005, for new Gordon 2005-. Lib Dem Shadow Sec of State: Environ, Food and Rural Affairs 2001-02, Trade and Industry 2003-05. Spokes 1985-99. Former member select cttees. Chair: all-party groups, Lib Dem Parly Party 1999-2001. Leader Scottish: Social and Lib Dems 1988-89 (pres 2000-), Lib Dems 1989-92. Barrister. Trainee journalist, buyer, research/info officer, dir, editor/publisher. Ed MA economics/political science, St Andrews Univ; MSc, Strathclyde Univ; CPE and Inns of Court Sch of Law.

Gordon spreads from the North Sea in the east through Oldmeldrum and Strathbogie to Huntly in the west. Forestry, agriculture and food processing including whisky distilleries are the most important industries. Beef production is important but was badly hit by the BSE crisis. Other industries include paper at Inverurie and engineering supplies for the oil and gas industries. Other towns include Huntly, Keith, Insch and Oldmeldrum and it now covers Aberdeen airport.

GOSPORT — C hold

		Electorate	Turnout	Change from	2001	Electorate	Turnout
		71,119	60.5%	2001		69,626	57.1%
Viggers P	**C**	**19,268**	**44.8%**	**1.2%**	**C**	**17,364**	**43.6%**
Williams R	Lab	13,538	31.5%	-5.6%	Lab	14,743	37.1%
Roberts R	LD	7,145	16.6%	1.5%	LD	6,011	15.1%
Bowles J	UKIP	1,825	4.2%	1.3%	UKIP	1,162	2.9%
Smith A	Greens	1,258	2.9%		SLP	509	1.3%
Lab to C swing	**3.4%**	**43,034**		**C maj 5,730** 13.3%		**39,789**	**C maj 2,621** 6.6%

PETER VIGGERS b 13 March 1938. MP 1974-. Northern Ireland Office Parly Under-Sec 1986-89. PPS to: Peter Rees 1983-85, Sir Ian Percival 1979-83. Member Defence select cttee 1992-97, 2000-01, 2003-. Chair all-party local hospitals group 2002-. Member exec 1922 cttee 1997-. UK delegate North Atlantic Assembly 1981-86, 2002-. Solicitor and company director/chair. RAF 1956-58, TA officer 1962-67. Chair Lloyd's pension fund 1996-. Vice-pres RNLI 1989-. Ed MA hist/law, Trinity Hall, Cambridge; Coll of Law, Guildford.

Gosport is a compact constituency on a peninsula formed by the western side of Portsmouth harbour and a coastline along the Solent facing the Isle of Wight. The Portsmouth Naval Base has employed Gosport's residents for hundreds of years, and strong psychological and economic ties to the armed services remain. Gosport is not demographically a natural Conservative stronghold and steady Labour progress had turned the seat into a marginal until they lost ground in 2005.

GOWER — Lab hold

		Electorate	Turnout	Change from	2001	Electorate	Turnout
		60,925	64.9%	2001		58,936	63.4%
Caton M	**Lab**	**16,786**	**42.4%**	**-4.9%**	**Lab**	**17,676**	**47.3%**
Murray M	C	10,083	25.5%	-2%	C	10,281	27.5%
Tregoning N	LD	7,291	18.4%	6.3%	LD	4,507	12.1%
Caiach S	PlC	3,089	7.8%	-2.5%	PlC	3,865	10.3%
Lewis R	UKIP	1,264	3.2%		Greens	607	1.6%
Griffiths R	Greens	1,029	2.6%	1%	SLP	417	1.1%
Lab to C swing	**1.5%**	**39,542**		**Lab maj 6,703** 17%		**37,353**	**Lab maj 7,395** 19.8%

MARTIN CATON b 15 June 1951. MP 1997-. Member select cttees: Welsh Affairs 1997-, Joint Cttee on Consolidation of Bills Etc 2001-, Chairmen's Panel 2003-. Chair all-party group. Member Socialist Health Assocn. Chair Welsh regional group of Lab MPs 2002-. Cllr: Mumbles Community Council 1986-90, Swansea CC 1988-95, Swansea City/County 1995-97. Agriculture/political (MEP) research. IPCS section treasurer/membership sec. Ed Norfolk Agriculture Sch; Nat Agriculture Cert, Higher Nat Cert applied biology, Aberystwyth Coll of Further Ed.

This seat includes not only the scenic holiday area of the Gower peninsula, with its attractive seaside villages and many sandy beaches, but also the inland industrial area of the Lliw valley, and the communities of Gorseinon, Pontarddulais, and Pontardawe therein. It is a safe Labour seat, thanks to the latter, while the former ensures that the Conservatives poll better here than in the majority of South Wales constituencies.

GRANTHAM AND STAMFORD — C hold

		Electorate 74,074	Turnout [illegible]	Change from 2001	2001	Electorate 75,500	Turnout 61.3%
Davies Q	**C**	**22,109**	**46.9%**	**0.8%**	**C**	**21,329**	**46.1%**
Selby I	Lab	14,664	31.1%	-5.2%	Lab	16,811	36.3%
O'Connor P	LD	7,838	16.6%	2.2%	LD	6,665	14.4%
Rising S	UKIP	1,498	3.2%		UKIP	1,484	3.2%
Brown B	Eng Dem	774	1.6%				
Andrews J	CRD	264	0.6%				
Lab to C swing	**3%**	**47,147**		**C maj 7,445** 15.8%		**46,289**	**C maj 4,518** 9.8%

QUENTIN DAVIES b 29 May 1944. MP for Stamford and Spalding 1987-97, for Grantham and Stamford 1997-. Shadow: N Ireland Sec of State 2001-03, Defence Min 2000-01, Paymaster General 1999-2000, Pensions Min 1998-99; PPS to Angela Rumbold 1988-91. Opposition spokes: soc security 1998-99, Treasury 1999-2000, defence 2000-01. Member various select cttees 1995-. Chair all-party German group 2001-. Diplomatic Service 1967-74. Manager/company director/consultant 1974-. Ed BA hist, Gonville and Caius Coll, Cambridge; Harvard Univ, USA.

Much of the constituency is rural, and even the largest and most Labour-oriented town, Grantham, has Tory credentials as the birthplace of Lady Thatcher. All three main towns (the others being Stamford and Bourne) have considerable historical associations and many protected buildings. Though employment is equally split between manual and non-manual occupations, and despite a good deal of industry in the division (from specialist tractor-making to shoes), most residents are comfortably-off.

GRAVESHAM — C gain

		Electorate 68,705	Turnout 65.8%	Change from 2001	2001	Electorate 69,588	Turnout 62.7%
Holloway A	**C**	**19,739**	**43.7%**	**4.9%**	**Lab**	**21,773**	**49.9%**
Pond C	Lab	19,085	42.2%	-7.7%	C	16,911	38.8%
Parmenter B	LD	4,851	10.7%	1.5%	LD	4,031	9.2%
Coates G	UKIP	850	1.9%	-0.2%	UKIP	924	2.1%
Nickerson C	Ind	654	1.4%				
Lab to C swing	**6.3%**	**45,179**		**C maj 654** 1.4%		**43,639**	**Lab maj 4,862** 11.1%

ADAM HOLLOWAY b 1965. MP 2005-. Commissioned Grenadier Guards 1987-92; presenter World in Action Granada TV 1992-93; reporter ITN 1993-97. Ed Cranleigh School, Surrey; Political science, Cambridge University; MBA, Imperial College, London

Centred on the north Kent towns of Gravesend and Northfleet, Gravesham's recent Labour majorities were supported by these Thameside strongholds especially North Gravesend, with its gritty urban wards. However, residents in the seat's picturesque hamlets always provided a sturdy counterweight to metropolitan control. Ethnically the most diverse in Kent, Gravesham is well-known as a bellwether seat but the 6.3 per cent swing here in 2005, resulting in a Conservative gain from Labour, exceeded the national trend this time.

GREAT GRIMSBY — Lab hold

		Electorate 63,711	Turnout 51.7%	Change from 2001	2001	Electorate 63,157	Turnout 52.3%
Mitchell A	**Lab**	**15,512**	**47.1%**	**-10.8%**	**Lab**	**19,118**	**57.9%**
Taylor G	C	7,858	23.8%	0.7%	C	7,634	23.1%
de Freitas A	LD	6,356	19.3%	0.3%	LD	6,265	19%
Fyfe S	BNP	1,338	4.1%				
Grant M	UKIP	1,239	3.8%				
Brookes D	Greens	661	2%				
Lab to C swing	**5.8%**	**32,964**		**Lab maj 7,654** 23.2%		**33,017**	**Lab maj 11,484** 34.8%

AUSTIN MITCHELL b 19 Sept 1934. MP for Grimsby 1977-83, for Great Grimsby 1983-. PPS to John Fraser 1977-79. Opposition: former whip, trade and industry spokes 1988-89. Member select cttees: Agriculture 1997-2001, Environment, Food and Rural Affairs 2001-. Chair/vice-chair various all-party groups 2001-. Chair Lab economic policy group. Vice-chair Hansard Soc. Member Public Accounts Commission 1997-. University lecturer/fellow. Journalist. Order of New Zealand 1991. Ed BA hist, Manchester Univ; MA/DPhil, Nuffield Coll, Oxford.

This long-term Labour seat is dominated by fishing, food and chemical industries. Grimsby is one of the largest container ports in the country, but is not dominated by its docks, however, and the town has its attractive areas with wide, tree-lined roads leading to the centre. The seat is home to the highest proportions of both part-time and partly-skilled workers in England and Wales, but unemployment is also high.

GREAT YARMOUTH — Lab hold

		Electorate	Turnout	Change from	2001	Electorate	Turnout
		68,887	60.1%	2001		69,131	58.4%
Wright A	**Lab**	**18,850**	**45.6%**	**-4.8%**	**Lab**	**20,344**	**50.4%**
Fox M	C	15,795	38.2%	-0.9%	C	15,780	39.1%
Newton S	LD	4,585	11.1%	2.7%	LD	3,392	8.4%
Poole B	UKIP	1,759	4.2%	2.1%	UKIP	850	2.1%
Skipper M	LCA	389	0.9%				
Lab to C swing	**2%**	**41,378**		**Lab maj 3,055**		**40,366**	**Lab maj 4,564**
				7.4%			11.3%

ANTHONY WRIGHT b 12 Aug 1954. MP 1997. PPS to Ruth Kelly as Financial Sec to Treasury 2002-03. Member Public Administration select cttee 2000-02. Chair all-party ME group 1999-. Lab Party organiser/agent 1983-97. Cllr Great Yarmouth Borough Council 1980-82, 1986-98: leader 1996-97. Member European Standing Cttee C 1999-. Engineer 1974-83. Director Seachange Trust 1995-. Ed Hospital Sec Sch, Great Yarmouth; City and Guilds mechanical engineer apprentice 1969-73.

Politically polarised between the declining seaside town of Great Yarmouth and the conservative villages of the constituency's rural hinterland, Great Yarmouth remains an important east coast port and a centre for the offshore and tourism industries. It was taken by Labour in 1997 after a huge swing, but persistent local issues, including crime and unemployment, have led the Conservatives to chip away at Labour's dominance in recent elections.

GREENWICH AND WOOLWICH — Lab hold

		Electorate	Turnout	Change from	2001	Electorate	Turnout
		64,033	55.6%	2001		62,565	52%
Raynsford N	**Lab**	**17,527**	**49.2%**	**-11.3%**	**Lab**	**19,691**	**60.5%**
Le Breton C	LD	7,381	20.7%	5.1%	C	6,258	19.2%
Craig A	C	7,142	20.1%	0.9%	LD	5,082	15.6%
Sharman D	Greens	1,579	4.4%		UKIP	672	2.1%
Bushell G	Eng Dem	1,216	3.4%		SA	481	1.5%
Gain S	UKIP	709	2%	-0.1%	SLP	352	1.1%
Nagalingam P	Ind	61	0.2%				
Lab to LD swing	**8.2%**	**35,615**		**Lab maj 10,146**		**32,536**	**Lab maj 13,433**
				28.5%			41.3%

NICK RAYNSFORD b 28 Jan 1945. MP for Fulham 1986-87, for Greenwich 1992-97, for Greenwich and Woolwich 1997-. ODPM: Min of State: Local and Regional Govt 2003-05, Local Govt and Regions 2002-03; Transport, Local Govt and Regions Dept Min of State 2001-02; Environ, Transport and Regions Dept: Min of State 1999-2001, Parly Under-Sec 1997-99. Former PPS to Roy Hattersley. Opposition spokes 1993-97. Cllr Hammersmith and Fulham 1971-75. Housing consultant. PC 2001. Ed BA hist, Sidney Sussex Coll, Cambridge; art and design dip, Chelsea Sch of Art.

A seat of economic contrasts, Greenwich and Woolwich is predominantly working class and a traditional Labour heartland. The famous local attractions present a deep contrast with the high levels of council housing, unemployment and significant ethnic minority population. A significant programme of investment in the area, combined with successful housing and regeneration projects, mean that the area is likely to remain loyal to Labour.

GUILDFORD — C gain

		Electorate	Turnout	Change from	2001	Electorate	Turnout
		75,566	68.3%	2001		76,296	62.7%
Milton A	**C**	**22,595**	**43.8%**	**2.4%**	**LD**	**20,358**	**42.6%**
Doughty S	LD	22,248	43.1%	0.5%	C	19,820	41.4%
Landles K	Lab	5,054	9.8%	-3.9%	Lab	6,558	13.7%
Pletts J	Greens	811	1.6%		UKIP	736	1.5%
Haslam M	UKIP	645	1.2%	-0.3%	TPP	370	0.8%
Morris J	TPP	166	0.3%				
Lavin V	Ind	112	0.2%				
LD to C swing	**1%**	**51,631**		**C maj 347**		**47,842**	**LD maj 538**
				0.7%			1.1%

ANNE MILTON b 1955. MP 2005-. Vice-chairman Conservative Medical Society. Councillor Reigate Borough 1999-2004. Nurse. Ed Haywards Heath Grammar School, West Sussex; St Bartholomew's Hospital, London.

Guildford's history goes back nearly 1,500 years. There is a medieval guildhall and, in contrast, a modern cathedral. The constituency contains some exceptionally beautiful countryside and the southernmost rural parts lie within the Surrey Hills, an area of outstanding natural beauty. London is only 30 miles to the north but Guildford has a thriving local economy. Once a safe Conservative seat, strong Tory traditions at grassroots are now counterbalanced by a significant Liberal Democrat presence.

HACKNEY NORTH AND STOKE NEWINGTON — Lab hold

		Electorate 59,200	Turnout 49.0%	Change from 2001	2001	Electorate 60,444	Turnout 47.8%
Abbott D	**Lab**	**14,268**	**48.6%**	**-12.4%**	**Lab**	**18,081**	**61%**
Blanchard J	LD	6,841	23.3%	9.2%	C	4,430	15%
Hurer E	C	4,218	14.4%	-0.6%	LD	4,170	14.1%
Borris M	Greens	2,907	9.9%	2.5%	Greens	2,184	7.4%
Vail D	Ind	602	2.1%		SLP	756	2.6%
Sen N	SLP	296	1%	-1.6%			
Barrow N	Loony	248	0.8%				
Lab to LD swing	**10.8%**	**29,380**		**Lab maj 7,427** 25.3%		**29,621**	**Lab maj 13,651** 46%

DIANE ABBOTT b 27 Sept 1953. MP 1987-. Member select cttees: Treasury and Civil Service 1989-97, Foreign Affairs 1997-2001. Chair all-party groups: Caribbean 2001-, race/community 2002-, gun crime 2003-. Member Lab Party NEC 1994-97. Cllr Westminster City 1982-86. Member: Greater London Assembly women and equality advisory cabinet 2000-, RMT parly campaigning group 2002-. Equality officer ACTT 1985-86. Admin trainee Home Office, race relats officer, journalist, press officer Lambeth Council. Ed BA hist, Newnham Coll, Cambridge.

One of the most deprived areas in London, Hackney North and Stoke Newington has a substantial proportion of ethnic minorities, lending the area a vibrant cultural and social mix. Although the area has high unemployment, those who are employed are predominantly skilled and partly skilled labourers. Labour continues to dominate the seat, with apparently little that other parties can do to shift its control.

HACKNEY SOUTH AND SHOREDITCH — Lab hold

		Electorate 64,818	Turnout 49.7%	Change from 2001	2001	Electorate 63,990	Turnout 47.4%
Hillier M	**Lab/C**	**17,048**	**52.9%**	**-11.3%**	**Lab**	**19,471**	**64.2%**
Baylis H	LD	6,844	21.2%	6.6%	LD	4,422	14.6%
Moss J	C	4,524	14%	0.2%	C	4,180	13.8%
Dan Iyan I	Greens	1,779	5.5%		SA	1,401	4.6%
Ryan D	Respect	1,437	4.5%		R2000	471	1.6%
Rae B	Lib	313	1%		CGB	259	0.9%
Goldman M	Comm	200	0.6%	-13.2%	WRP	143	0.5%
Leff J	WRP	92	0.3%	-0.2%			
Lab/C to LD swing	**9%**	**32,237**		**Lab/C maj 10,204** 31.6%		**30,347**	**Lab maj 15,049** 49.6%

MEG HILLIER b 14 February 1969. MP 2005-. Cllr London Borough of Islington, GLA member for North East London 2000-04. Journalist; merchant navy service; Freelance journalist 1998-2000. Ed PPE, Oxford; Journalism City University. Member TGWU, Fabian Society

Hackney South and Shoreditch is a safe inner-city Labour seat, adjoining the City of London. The constituency is young and multi-cultural, with the Shoreditch area becoming increasingly desirable, yet it is also one of the poorest seats in the country and receives high levels of government funding. It seems unlikely that Labour will relinquish its hold in the near future, even with a new MP for 2005.

HALESOWEN AND ROWLEY REGIS — Lab hold

		Electorate 65,748	Turnout 62.9%	Change from 2001	2001	Electorate 66,012	Turnout 59.5%
Heal S	**Lab**	**19,243**	**46.6%**	**-6.4%**	**Lab**	**20,804**	**53%**
Jones L	C	14,906	36.1%	1.9%	C	13,445	34.2%
Turner M	LD	5,204	12.6%	2.2%	LD	4,089	10.4%
Sinclaire N	UKIP	1,974	4.8%	2.4%	UKIP	936	2.4%
Lab to C swing	**4.2%**	**41,327**		**Lab maj 4,337** 10.5%		**39,274**	**Lab maj 7,359** 18.7%

SYLVIA HEAL b 20 July 1942. MP for Mid Staffs 1990-92, for Halesowen and Rowley Regis 1997-. PPS to: Geoffrey Hoon 1999-2000, Lord Robertson 1997-99. Deputy Shadow Min for Women 1991-92, Shadow Health Min 1991-92. First deputy chair Ways and Means and deputy speaker 2000-. NATO parly assembly 1997-2000. Social worker, national officer Carers National Association. JP. Member Action for South Africa. Ed Elfed Sec Modern Sch, North Wales; BSc econ, Univ Coll of Wales, Swansea.

Halesowen and Rowley Regis is a clearly divided constituency. It was a key seat in the Conservative failure to make a recovery in the Commons in 2001. This constituency represents an important hurdle for Tory recovery. The current bedrock of support for Sylvia Heal keeps Labour safer than appearances might suggest. As with many seats in the Midlands, the closure of the Rover manufacturing plant will see a significant rise in unemployment.

HALIFAX

Lab hold

		Electorate 64,861	Turnout 61.1%	Change from 2001	2001	Electorate 70,426	Turnout 57.4%
Riordan L	**Lab/C**	**16,579**	**41.8%**	**-7.2%**	**Lab**	**19,800**	**49%**
Hopkins K	C	13,162	33.2%	-0.6%	C	13,671	33.8%
Taylor M	LD	7,100	17.9%	3.3%	LD	5,878	14.6%
Wallace G	BNP	2,627	6.6%		UKIP	1,041	2.6%
Holmes T	NF	191	0.5%				
Lab/C to C swing	**3.3%**	**39,659**		**Lab/C maj 3,417** 8.6%		**40,390**	**Lab maj 6,129** 15.2%

LINDA RIORDAN b 31 May 1953. MP 2005-. Cllr Calderdale Metropolitan Borough Council; Chair Ovenden Initiative; Non-executive director Calderdale and Huddersfield NHS Trust; Board member Pennine Housing 2000; Private secretary to Alice Mahon MP. Ed Bradford University

Since wool, the textile up which Halifax grew up, has been in decline for some years now, food processing, machine-tool manufacture and engineering have become the key industries here. The seat was also home to the world's largest building society, before it became a bank. Although traditionally a Labour seat with a majority of blue collar workers and unemployment about the national average, Tory support here is bolstered by a 70 per cent owner-occupancy rate.

HALTEMPRICE AND HOWDEN

C hold

		Electorate 68,471	Turnout 70.2%	Change from 2001	2001	Electorate 66,733	Turnout 65.8%
Davis D	**C**	**22,792**	**47.4%**	**4.2%**	**C**	**18,994**	**43.2%**
Neal J	LD	17,676	36.8%	-2.1%	LD	17,091	38.9%
Hart E	Lab	6,104	12.7%	-3%	Lab	6,898	15.7%
Mainprize J	BNP	798	1.7%		UKIP	945	2.2%
Lane P	UKIP	659	1.4%	-0.8%			
LD to C swing	**3.2%**	**48,029**		**C maj 5,116** 10.6%		**43,928**	**C maj 1,903** 4.3%

DAVID DAVIS b 23 Dec 1948. MP for Boothferry 1987-97, for Haltemprice and Howden 1997-. Shadow: Home Sec 2003-, Home, Constitutional, Legal Affairs Sec of State 2003-04, Dep PM 2002-03. Minister of State FCO 1994-97, Parly Sec Office of Public Service/Science 1993-94, PPS to Francis Maude 1988-90. Asst govt whip 1990-93. Chair: Public Accounts select cttee 1997-2001, Con Party 2001-02. Tate & Lyle career. PC 1997. Ed BSc, Warwick Univ; MSc London Business Sch; AMP, Harvard Business Sch.

This marginal Tory seat is split between rural and residential elements. Howden is a small market town on agricultural land north of the Humber, whereas Haltemprice is one of Hull's more middle-class suburbs. Cottingham is another of Hull's cosier areas, and most of that city's more properous workers live in this seat – commuters are helped by the M62 which runs through it. Unemployment is low and 83 per cent of homes are owner-occupied.

HALTON

Lab hold

		Electorate 64,379	Turnout 53.1%	Change from 2001	2001	Electorate 63,742	Turnout 54.1%
Twigg D	**Lab**	**21,460**	**62.8%**	**-6.4%**	**Lab**	**23,841**	**69.2%**
Bloom C	C	6,854	20.1%	1.5%	C	6,413	18.6%
Barlow R	LD	5,869	17.2%	5%	LD	4,216	12.2%
Lab to C swing	**4%**	**34,183**		**Lab maj 14,606** 42.7%		**34,470**	**Lab maj 17,428** 50.6%

DEREK TWIGG b 9 July 1959. MP 1997-. Parly Under-Sec: Dept for Transport 2005-, Dept for Education and Skills 2004-05. PPS to: Stephen Byers 2001-02, Helen Liddell 1999-2001. Asst govt whip 2002-03, govt whip 2003-04. Member Public Accounts select cttee 1998-99. Chair NW regional group of Lab MPs 1999-2000. Cllr: Cheshire CC 1981-85, Halton BC 1983-97. Member European standing cttee B 1997-98. Civil servant Dept for Ed and Employment 1975-96, political consultant 1996. Branch sec/chair 1978-84. Ed Halton Coll of Further Education.

Very much a Merseyside seat, though part of Cheshire since the 1970s, Halton comprises the two towns of Widnes and Runcorn, both working-class in character and historically dominated by the chemical industry. Runcorn, originally developed as a canal port, is more modern than Widnes, and houses a large Liverpool overspill population. A strong Labour stronghold, this seat will return a candidate from no other party in the foreseeable future.

HAMMERSMITH AND FULHAM — C gain

		Electorate	Turnout	Change from	2001	Electorate	Turnout
		79,082	62.4%	2001		79,303	50.4%
Hands G	**C**	**22,407**	**45.4%**	**5.6%**	**Lab**	**19,801**	**44.3%**
Smallman M	Lab	17,378	35.2%	-9.1%	C	17,786	39.8%
Bullion A	LD	7,116	14.4%	2.6%	LD	5,294	11.8%
Harrold F	Greens	1,933	3.9%	0.7%	Greens	1,444	3.2%
Fisher G	UKIP	493	1%	0.2%	UKIP	375	0.8%
Lab to C swing	**7.4%**	**49,327**		**C maj 5,029**		**44,700**	**Lab maj 2,015**
				10.2%			4.5%

GREG HANDS b 1965. MP 2005-. Banker and local campaigner. Hammersmith and Fulham Borough Council, councillor 1998-, leader of the Conservative group 1999-. Ed Dr Challoner's Grammar School, Bucks; BA history, Cambridge University.

A mixed seat in south-west London, Hammersmith and Fulham contains both some of the poorest and most affluent areas in London. The seat is equally diverse ethnically, with around 20 per cent of the population identifying itself as an ethnic minority. The area has its economic and social problems, making it a prime (and successful) target for the Conservatives during the 2005 election campaign.

EAST HAMPSHIRE — C hold

		Electorate	Turnout	Change from	2001	Electorate	Turnout
		79,801	66.6%	2001		78,802	63.8%
Mates M	**C**	**24,273**	**45.7%**	**-1.9%**	**C**	**23,950**	**47.6%**
Bright R	LD	18,764	35.3%	5.4%	LD	15,060	29.9%
Broughton M	Lab	8,519	16%	-3.6%	Lab	9,866	19.6%
Samuel D	UKIP	1,583	3%	0.2%	UKIP	1,413	2.8%
C to LD swing	**3.7%**	**53,139**		**C maj 5,509**		**50,289**	**C maj 8,890**
				10.4%			17.7%

MICHAEL MATES b 9 June 1934. MP for Petersfield 1974-83, for East Hampshire 1983-. Min of State Northern Ireland Office 1992-93. Member select cttees: Defence (chair) 1987-92, Liaison 2001-, Northern Ireland Affairs (chair) 2001-. Member cttees: Intelligence and Security 1994-, Intelligence Review 2004. 1922 cttee: sec 1987-88, joint sec 1997-2001. Vice-chair all-party groups: Irish in Britain 2001-, theatre 2002-. UK delegate NATO Parly Assembly. Army 1954-74. PC 2004. Ed Blundell's Sch; King's Coll, Cambridge.

This is a mainly rural constituency. In the south the country town of Petersfield forms part of a richly farmed and deeply rural area of natural beauty. The region is home to rolling chalk downland and contrasting heavily wooded scarp slopes, which give way to the green and pleasant Meon and Rother Valleys. With a high employment rate, high home ownership, and general affluence, this is a classic Tory constituency, albeit with a growing Liberal Democrat vote.

NORTH EAST HAMPSHIRE — C hold

		Electorate	Turnout	Change from	2001	Electorate	Turnout
		72,939	64.8%	2001		71,304	61.6%
Arbuthnot J	**C**	**25,407**	**53.7%**	**0.5%**	**C**	**23,379**	**53.2%**
Carew A	LD	12,858	27.2%	4.2%	LD	10,122	23%
McGrath K	Lab	7,630	16.1%	-3.8%	Lab	8,744	19.9%
Birch P	UKIP	1,392	2.9%	-1%	UKIP	1,702	3.9%
C to LD swing	**1.9%**	**47,287**		**C maj 12,549**		**43,947**	**C maj 13,257**
				26.5%			30.2%

JAMES ARBUTHNOT b 4 Aug 1952. MP for Wanstead and Woodford 1987-97, for NE Hampshire 1997-. Shadow: Minister for Trade and Industry 2005-, Sec of State Trade 2003-05, Cabinet member 1997-2001; Minister of State Procurement, MoD 1995-97; Parly Under-Sec DSS 1994-95; PPS to: Peter Lilley 1990-92, Archie Hamilton 1988-90. Whip: asst govt 1992-94, opposition chief 197-2001. Member joint House of Lords Reform select cttee 2002-. Pres Cynon Valley Con Assocn 1983-92. Cllr Kensington and Chelsea 1978-87. Barrister. PC 1998. Ed Eton Coll; BA law, Trinity Coll, Cambridge.

Largely rural, North East Hampshire is a compact strip of land sandwiched between the constituencies of Aldershot to the east, and Basingstoke to the west. It stretches from Eversley on the Berkshire border through Fleet and Hook to Liphook, Selborne and Whitehill in the south, and is an area which is proud of its many military connections, including the Bordon Garrison and RAF Odiham. It has a consistent penchant for Conservative parliamentary representation.

NORTH WEST HAMPSHIRE — C hold

		Electorate	Turnout	Change from	2001	Electorate	Turnout
		79,763	64.3%	2001		78,793	61.7%
Young Sir George	**C**	**26,005**	**50.7%**	**0.6%**	**C**	**24,374**	**50.1%**
Tod M	LD	12,741	24.8%	3.6%	Lab	12,365	25.4%
Mumford M	Lab	10,594	20.7%	-4.7%	LD	10,329	21.2%
Sumner P	UKIP	1,925	3.8%	0.6%	UKIP	1,563	3.2%
C to LD swing	**1.5%**	**51,265**		**C maj 13,264**		**48,631**	**C maj 12,009**
				25.9%			24.7%

SIR GEORGE YOUNG b 16 July 1941. MP for Ealing Acton 1974-97, NW Hants 1997-. Shadow: HoC and Constitutional Affairs Leader 1999-2000, Chancellor of Duchy of Lancaster, HoC Leader 1998-99, Sec of State Defence 1997-98. Sec of State Transport 1995-97; Financial Sec Treasury 1994-95; Minister of State Dept of Environ 1990-94. Whip: opposition 1976-79, govt 1990. Parly Under-Sec 1979-86. Member select cttees (chair Standards and Privileges 2001-). Cllr 1968-73. Economist. PC 1993. Ed Eton; BA PPE, Christ Church, Oxford; MPhil econ, Surrey Univ.

North West Hampshire is deep in the county's Tory heartland, covering the northern part of the Test Valley, which includes scores of picturesque hamlets and a generous acreage of rolling Hampshire countryside. In the east the constituency now almost reaches Basingstoke. The town of Andover marks the centre of this constituency, and is the largest centre of population. The Conservative Party should be sitting comfortably here for many years to come.

HAMPSTEAD AND HIGHGATE — Lab hold

		Electorate	Turnout	Change from	2001	Electorate	Turnout
		68,737	55.5%	2001		71,084	49.8%
Jackson G	**Lab**	**14,615**	**38.3%**	**-8.6%**	**Lab**	**16,601**	**46.9%**
Wauchope P	C	10,886	28.5%	3.9%	C	8,725	24.6%
Fordham E	LD	10,293	27%	6.5%	LD	7,273	20.5%
Berry S	Greens	2,013	5.3%	0.6%	Greens	1,654	4.7%
Nielsen M	UKIP	275	0.7%	-0.2%	SA	559	1.6%
Weiss R	Vote Dream	91	0.2%		UKIP	316	0.9%
					None	144	0.4%
					ProLife	92	0.3%
					Ind	43	0.1%
Lab to C swing	**6.3%**	**38,173**		**Lab maj 3,729**		**35,407**	**Lab maj 7,876**
				9.8%			22.2%

GLENDA JACKSON b 9 May 1936. MP 1992-. Environment, Transport and the Regions Dept Parly Under-Sec of State 1997-99. Opposition transport spokes 1996-97. Member: Lab Party environment, transport and regions departmental cttee 1997-2001, Greater London Assembly advisory cabinet for homelessness 2000-. Actress (Oscars: 1971, 1974). Campaigner: Oxfam, Shelter, Friends of the Earth. Pres The National Toy Libraries Association. CBE 1978. Ed West Kirby County Grammar Sch for Girls; RADA.

Considered to contain some of the most fashionable postcodes in London, this seat in the north west of the capital also contains less affluent areas, as well as a sizeable ethnic minority population. Nevertheless, overall the population is wealthy and largely home owners. However, there is still support for Labour and for their Oscar-winning MP and the seat remains out of reach for the Conservatives.

HARBOROUGH — C hold

		Electorate	Turnout	Change from	2001	Electorate	Turnout
		74,583	64.2%	2001		73,300	63.3%
Garnier E	**C**	**20,536**	**42.8%**	**-1.9%**	**C**	**20,748**	**44.7%**
Hope J	LD	16,644	34.7%	1.3%	LD	15,496	33.4%
Evans P	Lab	9,222	19.2%	-0.8%	Lab	9,271	20%
King M	UKIP	1,520	3.2%	1.2%	UKIP	912	2%
C to LD swing	**1.6%**	**47,922**		**C maj 3,892**		**46,427**	**C maj 5,252**
				8.1%			11.3%

EDWARD GARNIER b 26 Oct 1952. MP 1992-. Shadow: Min for Home Affairs 2005-, Attorney General 1999-2001, Min Lord Chancellor's Dept 1997-99. PPS to: Roger Freeman 1996-97, Sir Nicholas Lyell/Sir Derek Spencer 1995-97, David Davis 1994-95, Alastair Goodlad 1994-95. Member Home Affairs select cttee 1992-95. Chair all-party groups: Italy 2004-, Liechtenstein 2004-. Member exec 1922 cttee 2002-. Vice-chair foreign affairs forum 1992-. Barrister. QC 1995. Ed Wellington Coll; BA mod hist/MA, Jesus Coll, Oxford; Coll of Law, London.

A largely rural seat with a sprinkling of market towns and villages, this Leicestershire consistency is now attracting London commuters taking advantage of the A6, which runs through the constituency. Concurrently its agricultural economy is in steep decline. The pleasant town of Market Harborough retains the air of a county farming centre, still boasting an ancient guildhall. Liberal Democrat support is increasing in this previously long-term Conservative stronghold.

HARLOW — Lab hold

		Electorate	Turnout	Change from	2001	Electorate	Turnout
		63,500	62.6%	2001		67,106	60.7%
Rammell B	**Lab**	**16,453**	**41.4%**	**-6.4%**	**Lab**	**19,169**	**47.8%**
Halfon R	C	16,356	41.2%	6.4%	C	13,941	34.8%
Spenceley L	LD	5,002	12.6%	-0.8%	LD	5,381	13.4%
Felgate J	UKIP	981	2.5%	-0.5%	UKIP	1,223	3%
Bennett A	Veritas	941	2.4%		SA	401	1%
Lab to C swing	**6.4%**	**39,733**		**Lab maj 97**		**40,115**	**Lab maj 5,228**
				0.2%			13%

BILL RAMMELL b 10 Oct 1959. MP 1997-. Minister of State Dept for Education and Skills 2005-, Parly Under-Sec FCO 2002-05, PPS to Tessa Jowell 2001-02. Asst govt whip 2002. Member select cttees: Education and Employment 1997-99, European Scrutiny 1998-2000/2000-01. Chair Lab Movement for Europe 1999-. Cllr Harlow Council 1985-97. Member European Standing Committee B 1998-. Vice-chair The European Movt 2001-. Academic/union/managerial career. Regional officer NUS 1984-87. Ed BA French and politics, Univ Coll of Wales, Cardiff.

Harlow is a west Essex constituency, with nearly 90 per cent of the constituency's voters living in the town of Harlow itself. Local employment is found mainly in retailing and distribution but with London's Liverpool Street station only 40 minutes away by train many workers commute to jobs in the City. The Tories lost Harlow to Labour in the landslide of 1997, who then managed to hang on in 2005 by the narrowest of margins.

HARROGATE AND KNARESBOROUGH — LD hold

		Electorate	Turnout	Change from	2001	Electorate	Turnout
		65,622	65.3%	2001		65,159	64.7%
Willis P	**LD**	**24,113**	**56.3%**	**0.7%**	**LD**	**23,445**	**55.6%**
Punyer M	C	13,684	31.9%	-2.7%	C	14,600	34.6%
Ferris L	Lab	3,627	8.5%	1.1%	Lab	3,101	7.4%
Royston C	UKIP	845	2%	0.2%	UKIP	761	1.8%
Banner C	BNP	466	1.1%		ProLife	272	0.6%
Allman J	AFC	123	0.3%				
C to LD swing	**1.7%**	**42,858**		**LD maj 10,429**		**42,179**	**LD maj 8,845**
				24.3%			21%

PHIL WILLIS b 30 Nov 1941. MP 1997-. Lib Dem Shadow Education and Skills Sec of State 2000-05. North, Midlands and Wales whip 1997-99. Lib Dem spokes: education and employment 1997-99, 1999-2000. Member Education and Employment select cttee 1999-2000. Chair all-party mobile comms group 2001-. Member Lib Dem Councillors Assocn. Cllr: Harrogate BC 1988-99 (leader 1990-97), North Yorkshire CC 1993-97 (dep group leader 1993-97). Ed Burnley Grammar Sch; Cert Ed, City of Leeds and Carnegie Coll; BPhil education, Birmingham Univ.

This Yorkshire constituency and its predecessor was represented by a Conservative from its creation after the war until 1997, when it became a Liberal Democrat gain. Harrogate's spa heritage, Victorian architecture and shopping attract tourists. It has also become a popular conferences and exhibitions venue following the extension of the Royal Hall in the 1980s. The typical voter here is middle class and middle aged or retired. The seat has a relatively high proportion of pensioners.

HARROW EAST — Lab hold

		Electorate	Turnout	Change from	2001	Electorate	Turnout
		84,033	60.5%	2001		81,575	58.9%
McNulty T	**Lab**	**23,445**	**46.1%**	**-9.2%**	**Lab**	**26,590**	**55.3%**
Ashton D	C	18,715	36.8%	4.6%	C	15,466	32.2%
Nandhra P	LD	7,747	15.2%	2.7%	LD	6,021	12.5%
Cronin P	UKIP	916	1.8%				
Lab to C swing	**6.9%**	**50,823**		**Lab maj 4,730**		**48,077**	**Lab maj 11,124**
				9.3%			23.1%

TONY McNULTY b 3 Nov 1958. Minister of State: Home Office 2005-, Transport Dept 2004-05; Parly Under-Sec: Transport Dept 2003-04, Housing, Planning and Regeneration, ODPM 2002-03; PPS to David Blunkett 1997-99. Whip: asst govt 1999-2001, govt 2001-02. Co-founder Lab Friends of India 1999-. Member Socialist Educational Assocn. Cllr Harrow 1986-97: leader 1995-97. Lecturer 1983-97. Ed Stanmore Sixth Form Coll; BA political theory and institutions, Liverpool Univ; MA political science, Virginia Poly Institute and State Univ, USA.

A mainly suburban and affluent seat in the north-west area of Greater London, Harrow East is mainly residential. Although a large ethnic minority lives in the area, the fact that it is mainly affluent, middle-class and Asian means that this is not a typical working class multi-cultural constituency. Labour's popularity was on the rise in recent years, but proposed boundary changes are more likely to affect the constituency's voting. The 2005 result is a warning.

HARROW WEST — Lab hold

		Electorate	Turnout	Change from	2001	Electorate	Turnout
		74,228	64.3%	2001		73,505	63.5%
Thomas G	**Lab/C**	**20,298**	**42.5%**	**-7.1%**	**Lab/C**	**23,142**	**49.6%**
Freer M	C	18,270	38.2%	1.8%	C	16,986	36.4%
Noyce C	LD	8,188	17.1%	4.2%	LD	5,995	12.9%
Cronin J	UKIP	576	1.2%	0.1%	UKIP	525	1.1%
Daver B	Ind	427	0.9%				
Lab/C to C swing	**4.5%**	**47,759**		**Lab/C maj 2,028**		**46,648**	**Lab/C maj 6,156**
				4.2%			13.2%

GARETH THOMAS 15 July 1967. MP 1997-. Dept for International Development Parly Under-Sec 2003-; PPS to Charles Clarke 1999-2003. Member Environmental Audit select cttee 1997-99. Chair Co-operative Party 2000-. Cllr Harrow 1990-97. Vice-chair Assocn of Local Govt Soc Services Cttee. Teacher. Ed Hatch End High Sch; Lowlands Coll; BSC econ/politics, Univ Coll of Wales, Aberystwyth; MA imperial and Commonwealth studies, King's Coll, London; PGCE, Greenwich Univ.

A largely residential corner at the north-west extreme of Greater London, Harrow West is relatively affluent, with many of its residents commuting to the city. The population is mainly professional or managerial, with an impressive reputation in education standards. Once a safe Conservative seat, it has been held by Labour since the 1997 landslide.

HARTLEPOOL — Lab hold

		Electorate	Turnout	Change from	2001	Electorate	Turnout
		68,776	51.5%	2001		67,654	56.2%
Wright I	**Lab**	**18,251**	**51.5%**	**-7.6%**	**Lab**	**22,506**	**59.1%**
Dunn J	LD	10,773	30.4%	15.4%	C	7,935	20.9%
Vigar A	C	4,058	11.4%	-9.5%	LD	5,717	15%
Ryder I	Greens	1,256	3.5%		SLP	912	2.4%
Harrison F	SLP	373	1.1%	-1.3%	Ind	557	1.5%
Hobbs J	Ind	288	0.8%		Ind	424	1.1%
Springer G	UKIP	275	0.8%				
Headbanger S	Loony	162	0.5%				
Lab to LD swing	**11.5%**	**35,436**		**Lab maj 7,478**		**38,051**	**Lab maj 14,571**
				21.1%			38.3%

IAIN WRIGHT MP Oct 2004- (by-election). Member Public Administration select cttee 2005-. Cllr Hartlepool Borough Council 2002-05: cabinet member for performance management. Member European Standing Cttee A 2005-. Chartered accountant. Ed Manor Comp Sch, Hartlepool.

The constituency includes the town and old port of Hartlepool itself plus the surrounding coastal area. Some of the coast is attractive, but most is dominated by the giant chemical factories that are part of the North-East industrial tradition. The area's heavy industries continue to decline, and unemployment remains high at around 10 per cent. Once a marginal seat, it is now in the Labour domain.

HARWICH — C gain

		Electorate	Turnout	Change from	2001	Electorate	Turnout
		80,474	62.6%	2001		77,590	62%
Carswell D	**C**	**21,235**	**42.1%**	**1.9%**	**Lab**	**21,951**	**45.6%**
Henderson I	Lab	20,315	40.3%	-5.3%	C	19,355	40.2%
Tully K	LD	5,913	11.7%	3.2%	LD	4,099	8.5%
Titford J	UKIP	2,314	4.6%	-0.5%	UKIP	2,463	5.1%
Tipple J	Respect	477	1%		Ind	247	0.5%
Humphrey C	ND	154	0.3%				
Lab to C swing	**3.6%**	**50,408**		**C maj 920**		**48,115**	**Lab maj 2,596**
				1.8%			5.4%

DOUGLAS CARSWELL b 3 April 1971. MP 2005-. Contested Sedgefield 2001 general election; Policy Unit Conservative Party 2004-. Chief project officer INVESCO Asset Management 1999-2003. Ed Charterhouse School, Surrey; BA history, University of East Anglia, MA King's College, London

As well as the port of Harwich this constituency includes the seaside resorts of Clacton, Frinton-on-Sea and Walton-on-the-Naze. Harwich is an important European ferry terminal but some of the dock work has gone and there are high unemployment levels. Labour ended more than 50 years of Conservative control in Harwich in 1997. However, a small swing to the Liberal Democrats in 2005 was enough to allow the Tories snatch this seat back.

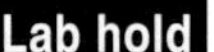

HASTINGS AND RYE — Lab hold

		Electorate	Turnout	Change from	2001	Electorate	Turnout
		63,437	67.8%	2001		70,734	58.3%
Foster M	**Lab**	**18,107**	**42.1%**	**-5%**	**Lab**	**19,402**	**47.1%**
Coote M	C	16,081	37.4%	0.8%	C	15,094	36.6%
Stevens R	LD	6,479	15.1%	4.8%	LD	4,266	10.3%
Grant T	UKIP	1,098	2.6%	0.4%	UKIP	911	2.2%
Phillips S	Greens	1,032	2.4%	0.7%	Greens	721	1.7%
Ord-Clarke J	Loony	207	0.5%		Ind	486	1.2%
					Loony	198	0.5%
					RNRL	140	0.3%
Lab to C swing	**2.9%**	**43,004**		**Lab maj 2,026**		**41,218**	**Lab maj 4,308**
				4.7%			10.5%

MICHAEL FOSTER b 26 Feb 1946. MP 1997-. PPS to: Harriet Harman 2001-03/2003-05, Lord Goldsmith 2001-03, 2003-, Ross Cranston 1999-2001, Lord Williams of Mostyn 1999-2001, John Morris 1999. Member select cttees: Standards and Privileges 1997-2004, Soc Security 1998-99. Member Soc of Lab Lawyers. Cllr: Hastings County BC 1971-74, Hastings BC 1973-79, 1983-87, East Sussex CC 1973-77/1981-97. Solicitor. GMB legal adviser. Member: Mensa, European Standing Cttee A 1998-. Ed Hastings Grammar Sch; LLM, Leicester Univ.

This pleasant seaside constituency in East Sussex consists of the three Cinque Ports of Hastings itself, Rye and Winchelsea. Not all coastline, the seat has a smattering of little towns and villages nestling in the rolling Sussex countryside between Ore and Winchelsea. The eastern boundary coincides with the Kent county boundary. Labour has reversed nearly a century of Tory incumbency, but the party political future of Hastings and Rye is by no means certain.

HAVANT — C hold

		Electorate	Turnout	Change from	2001	Electorate	Turnout
		68,545	60.3%	2001		70,246	57.6%
Willetts D	**C**	**18,370**	**44.4%**	**0.5%**	**C**	**17,769**	**43.9%**
Bogle S	Lab	11,862	28.7%	-4.8%	Lab	13,562	33.5%
Bentley A	LD	8,358	20.2%	1.6%	LD	7,508	18.6%
Dawes T	Greens	1,006	2.4%	0.4%	Greens	793	2%
Harris S	UKIP	998	2.4%	1%	UKIP	561	1.4%
Johnson I	BNP	562	1.4%		Ind	244	0.6%
Thomas R	Veritas	195	0.5%				
Lab to C swing	**2.7%**	**41,351**		**C maj 6,508**		**40,437**	**C maj 4,207**
				15.7%			10.4%

DAVID WILLETTS b 9 March 1956. MP 1992-. Shadow Sec of State: Trade and Industry 2005-, Welfare Reform 2004-05, Work and Pensions 2001-05, Soc Security 1999-2001, Education and Employment 1998-99. Office of Public Service: Paymaster Gen 1996, Parly Sec 1995-96. PPS to Sir Norman Fowler 1993-94. Whip: asst govt 1994-95, govt 1995. Opposition spokes 1997-98. Member Soc Security select cttee 1992-93. Head of Policy Co-ordination Con Party 2003-04. Political/policy/company director career. Ed BA PPE, Christ Church, Oxford.

Coastal Havant lies north east of Portsmouth North and Gosport, both of which fell to Labour in 1997. However, Labour wards are balanced here by private estates and a naturally Conservative grey population on Hayling Island. The densely populated constituency is centred on urban Havant. It clips a little of Waterlooville to the north east, and the western portion of Emsworth at its eastern boundary. Havant looks like a stalwart Tory seat for the foreseeable future.

HAYES AND HARLINGTON — Lab hold

		Electorate	Turnout	Change from	2001	Electorate	Turnout
		57,493	56.3%	2001		57,561	56.3%
McDonnell J	**Lab**	**19,009**	**58.7%**	**-7%**	**Lab**	**21,279**	**65.7%**
Worrall R	C	8,162	25.2%	1.1%	C	7,813	24.1%
Ball J	LD	3,174	9.8%	3.8%	LD	1,958	6%
Hazel T	BNP	830	2.6%	0.4%	BNP	705	2.2%
Haley M	UKIP	552	1.7%		SAP	648	2%
Outten B	Greens	442	1.4%				
Goddard P	Ind	220	0.7%				
Lab to C swing	**4.1%**	**32,389**		**Lab maj 10,847**		**32,403**	**Lab maj 13,466**
				33.5%			41.6%

JOHN McDONNELL b 8 Sept 1951. MP 1997-. Member select cttees: Deregulation and Regulatory Reform 1999-2002, Unopposed Bills (Panel) 1999-2004. Chair all-party Punjabi community in Britain group 1997-. Chair Lab Party Irish Soc. Cllr GLC 1981-86. Chair Britain and Ireland Human Rights Centre. NUM/TUC researcher/Camden council policy unit head. Chief exec: Assocn of London Authorities 1987-95, Assocn of London Govt 1995-97. Editor Labour Herald. Ed BSc govt/pol, Brunel Univ, London; MSc pol/sociology, Birkbeck Coll, London Univ.

In the western area of Greater London, Hayes and Harlington is relatively suburban and affluent. Although manufacturing has declined, its proximity to Heathrow Airport and several motorways mean it is well-connected and the airport also provides much of the employment. The furore over the airport's possible expansion and current MP John McDonnell's role in the campaign against it mean that the seat is likely to remain safe for Labour.

HAZEL GROVE — LD hold

		Electorate	Turnout	Change from	2001	Electorate	Turnout
		64,376	60.8%	2001		65,105	59.1%
Stunell A	**LD**	**19,355**	**49.5%**	**-2.5%**	**LD**	**20,020**	**52%**
White A	C	11,607	29.7%	-0.4%	C	11,585	30.1%
Graystone A	Lab	6,834	17.5%	1.3%	Lab	6,230	16.2%
Ryan K	UKIP	1,321	3.4%	1.7%	UKIP	643	1.7%
LD to C swing	**1.1%**	**39,117**		**LD maj 7,748**		**38,478**	**LD maj 8,435**
				19.8%			21.9%

ANDREW STUNELL b 24 Nov 1942. MP 1997-. Lib Dem whip: dep chief 1997-2001, chief 2001-. Lib Dem energy spokes 1997-. Member select cttees1997- incl Modernisation of HoC 1997-. Member Lib Dem federal/conference cttees 2001-. Cllr: Chester CC 1979-90, Cheshire CC 1981-91, Stockport MBC 1994-2002. Pres NW Constutional Convention 1999-. Vice-pres Local Govt Assocn 1997-. Vice-chair Assocn of County Councils 1985-90. Architectural asst/political sec. OBE 1995. Ed architecture RIBA pt. II exemption, Manchester Univ; Liverpool Poly.

This commuting dormitory to the south-east of Stockport and Manchester is mainly middle class and heavily residential. It contains a number of suburban communities including Bredbury, Romiley, and Marple beyond which moors and farms run into the Pennine foothills. The traditional cotton industry has been replaced with light industry and office-based employment. A strong history of Liberal sympathy suggests that only a substantial Tory revival could threaten a seat ranking one of the Liberal Democrats' safest.

HEMEL HEMPSTEAD — C gain

		Electorate	Turnout	Change from	2001	Electorate	Turnout
		73,095	64.4%	2001		72,743	63.1%
Penning M	**C**	**19,000**	**40.3%**	**1.8%**	**Lab/C**	**21,389**	**46.6%**
McWalter T	Lab/C	18,501	39.3%	-7.3%	C	17,647	38.5%
Grayson R	LD	8,089	17.2%	4.4%	LD	5,877	12.8%
Newton B	UKIP	1,518	3.2%	1.1%	UKIP	970	2.1%
Lab/C to C swing	**4.6%**	**47,108**		**C maj 499**		**45,883**	**Lab/C maj 3,742**
				1.1%			8.2%

MIKE PENNING b 28 Sept 1957. MP 2005-. Contested Thurrock 2001 general election. Former deputy chief press spokesperson Conservative Central Office. Fireman, journalist, lecturer. Ed Appleton School, Benfleet, Essex

In the heart of the Hertfordshire commuter belt, this new town of Hemel Hempstead is more than just a convenient dormitory for affluent city workers. The old town has been the scene for various period dramas, and it is one of the few places in England where you will see cows grazing a stone's throw from the town centre. Labour supporters switching to the Liberal Democrats allowed the Conservatives to take this seat back in 2005.

HEMSWORTH — Lab hold

		Electorate	Turnout	Change from	2001	Electorate	Turnout
		67,339	54.6%	2001		67,948	51.8%
Trickett J	**Lab**	**21,630**	**58.8%**	**-6.6%**	**Lab**	**23,036**	**65.4%**
Mortimer J	C	8,149	22.2%	1.2%	C	7,400	21%
Hall-Matthews D	LD	5,766	15.7%	4.4%	LD	3,990	11.3%
Burdon J	UKIP	1,247	3.4%		SLP	801	2.3%
Lab to C swing	**3.9%**	**36,792**		**Lab maj 13,481**		**35,227**	**Lab maj 15,636**
				36.6%			44.4%

JON TRICKETT b 2 July 1950. MP Feb 1996- by-election. PPS to Peter Mandelson 1997-98. Member select cttees: Unopposed Bills (Panel) 1997-, Education and Employment 2001, Public Accounts 2001-. All-party groups: chair gas safety 2001-, sec coalfield communities 2001-. Cllr Leeds City Council 1984-96: leader 1989-96. Member RMT Parly Campaigning Group 2002-. Plumber/builder 1974-86. Ed Roundhay Sch, Leeds; BA politics, Hull Univ; MA political sociology, Leeds Univ.

This safe Labour seat in Yorkshire was hit hard by pit closures. There is some farming, and the seat is also home to some of Wakefield's better-off commuters, but by far the greater proportion of the workforce are still skilled manuals. Since the decline of coal, service and distribution industries have developed, and some hi-tech companies have established themselves locally. Unemployment is therefore under control, and remains just above the national average.

HENDON — Lab hold

		Electorate	Turnout	Change from	2001	Electorate	Turnout
		71,764	58.3%	2001		70,212	52.2%
Dismore A	**Lab**	**18,596**	**44.4%**	**-8.1%**	**Lab**	**21,432**	**52.5%**
Evans R	C	15,897	38%	3.7%	C	14,015	34.3%
Boethe N	LD	5,831	13.9%	2.3%	LD	4,724	11.6%
Williams D	Greens	754	1.8%		UKIP	409	1%
Smallman M	UKIP	637	1.5%	0.5%	WRP	164	0.4%
Weiss R	Vote Dream	68	0.2%		PDP	107	0.3%
Stewart M	PDP	56	0.1%				
Lab to C swing	**5.9%**	**41,839**		**Lab maj 2,699**		**40,851**	**Lab maj 7,417**
				6.4%			18.2%

ANDREW DISMORE b 2 Sept 1954. MP 1997-. Member select cttees: Accommodation and Works 1997-99, Social Security 1998-2001, Standards and Privileges 2001-, Work and Pensions 2001-. Chair all-party groups: Far East prisoners of war and internees 2001-, Chinese in Britain 2003-, wine and spirit 2004-, British Virgin Islands 2005-. Vice-chair: Friends of Israel, Friends of India. Cllr Westminster City Council 1982-97. GMWU education dept 1976-78. Solicitor 1978-. Ed Bridlington Grammar Sch; LLB, Warwick Univ; LLM, LSE; Guildford Coll of Law.

Most famous for its police training college, the north-west London constituency of Hendon is a mixture of the affluent middle class and more working class council areas. There is similar environmental diversity, as green belt areas surround the edge of London. The area is also ethnically diverse with a large Jewish community.

HENLEY — C hold

		Electorate	Turnout	Change from	2001	Electorate	Turnout
		68,538	67.9%	2001		69,081	64.3%
Johnson B	**C**	**24,894**	**53.5%**	**7.4%**	**C**	**20,466**	**46.1%**
Turner D	LD	12,101	26%	-1%	LD	12,008	27%
Saeed K	Lab	6,862	14.8%	-6.3%	Lab	9,367	21.1%
Stevenson M	Greens	1,518	3.3%	0.7%	UKIP	1,413	3.2%
Gray-Fisk D	UKIP	1,162	2.5%	-0.7%	Greens	1,147	2.6%
LD to C swing	**4.2%**	**46,537**		**C maj 12,793**		**44,401**	**C maj 8,458**
				27.5%			19%

BORIS JOHNSON b 19 June 1964. MP 2001-. Shadow Min for the Arts 2004. Vice-chair all-party depression group 2004-. Vice-chair (campaigning), Con Party 2003-04. Member European Standing Cttee B 2003-. Journalist: Times, Wolverhamton Express, Star 1987-88, Daily Telegraph 1988-; editor Spectator 1999-. Editors' Editor of the Year 2003, British Press Awards Columnist of the Year 2004. Former Oxford Union president. Ed Eton Coll; classics/BA literae humaniores, Balliol Coll, Oxford.

Situated on the eastern fringes of Oxford and north east of Reading, Henley is a dormitory town on the Thames well served by motorways carrying commuters to both London and Reading. The constituency is probably most well-known for the famous Henley Regatta, an annual rowing and social event. The size of Conservative majorities had diminished markedly since the mid-1990s, as the Liberal Democrats consolidated and progressed, but 2005 saw a return to Conservative dominance.

HEREFORD — LD hold

		Electorate	Turnout	Change from	2001	Electorate	Turnout
		71,813	65.3%	2001		70,305	63.5%
Keetch P	**LD**	**20,285**	**43.3%**	**2.4%**	**LD**	**18,244**	**40.9%**
Taylor V	C	19,323	41.2%	2.5%	C	17,276	38.7%
Calver T	Lab	4,800	10.2%	-4.9%	Lab	6,739	15.1%
Lunt B	Greens	1,052	2.2%	-0.4%	UKIP	1,184	2.7%
Kingsley C	UKIP	1,030	2.2%	-0.5%	Greens	1,181	2.6%
Morton P	Ind	404	0.9%				
LD to C swing	**0.1%**	**46,894**		**LD maj 962**		**44,624**	**LD maj 968**
				2%			2.2%

PAUL KEETCH b 21 May 1961. MP 1997-. Lib Dem Defence Shadow Sec 1999-2005. Lib Dem spokes 1997-99. Member select cttees: Education and Employment 1997-99, Catering 1998-99, Environmental Audit 2000-01. Chair all-party groups: Lithuania 2001-, cider 2002-. Member Lib Dem federal exec cttee 2001-. OSCE observer Albanian elections 1996. Adviser Lithuanian local/nat elections 1995/96. Member Electoral Reform Society Council. Business consultant. Ed Hereford Sixth Form Coll.

Hereford is the administrative, commercial, cultural and retail centre for a large rural area. The cattle market is the second largest in the country and one of the biggest poultry processing units in Europe is also based here, as are cider-making and agricultural processing. Paul Keetch has held the seat for the Liberal Democrats since 1997 but it is very marginal and a Conservative revival would put him in serious jeopardy.

HERTFORD AND STORTFORD

C hold

		Electorate	Turnout	Change from	2001	Electorate	Turnout
		73,394	67.7%	2001		75,141	62.8%
Prisk M	**C**	**25,074**	**50.5%**	**5.8%**	**C**	**21,074**	**44.7%**
Henry R	Lab	11,977	24.1%	-8.7%	Lab	15,471	32.8%
Lucas J	LD	9,129	18.4%	-1.5%	LD	9,388	19.9%
Hart P	Greens	1,914	3.8%		UKIP	1,243	2.6%
Sodey D	UKIP	1,026	2.1%	-0.5%			
Lemay D	Veritas	572	1.2%				
Lab to C swing	**7.3%**	**49,692**		**C maj 13,097**		**47,176**	**C maj 5,603**
				26.4%			11.9%

MARK PRISK b 12 June 1962. MP 2001-. Shadow: Paymaster General 2003-04, Financial Sec 2002-03. Opposition whip 2004-. Member Welsh Affairs select cttee 2001-. Sec all-party airport for the South East group 2002-. Dep chair Con Party Hertfordshire area 1999-2000. Vice-pres First Defence 2004- (parly chair 2002-04). Chair Herts Countryside Partnership. Founder East Hertfordshire Business Forum. Member Prince's Trust. Founding chair Youth for Peace through NATO 1983-86. Chartered surveyor. Ed BSc land management, Reading Univ.

Picturesque villages and farmland separate the county town of Hertford and its neighbour Ware in the west from the market town of Bishop's Stortford in the north east of this semi-rural seat. Stansted Airport, just outside this affluent constituency, contributes to the constituency's economy and the pharmaceutical industry is also an important provider of jobs. Hertford and Stortford is one of the safest Conservative seats in the country.

NORTH EAST HERTFORDSHIRE

C hold

		Electorate	Turnout	Change from	2001	Electorate	Turnout
		72,190	65.6%	2001		68,718	65%
Heald O	**C**	**22,402**	**47.3%**	**3.2%**	**C**	**19,695**	**44.1%**
Harrop A	Lab	13,264	28%	-8.4%	Lab	16,251	36.4%
Coleman I	LD	10,147	21.4%	4.2%	LD	7,686	17.2%
Hitchman D	UKIP	1,561	3.3%	1%	UKIP	1,013	2.3%
Lab to C swing	**5.8%**	**47,374**		**C maj 9,138**		**44,645**	**C maj 3,444**
				19.3%			7.7%

OLIVER HEALD b 15 Dec 1954. MP for N Herts 1992-97, for NE Herts 1997-. Shadow: Sec of State Constitutional Affairs 2004-, Leader of the House 2003-, Min Work and Pensions 2002-03. Parly Under-Sec DSS 1995-97. PPS to: William Waldegrave 1994-95, Sir Peter Lloyd 1994. Opposition whip 1997-2000. Opposition spokes: home affairs 2000-01, health 2001-02. Member select cttees: Administration 1998-2000, HoC Modernisation 2003-. Member HoC Commission 2003-. Barrister. Ed Reading Sch; MA law, Pembroke Coll, Cambridge.

This safe Tory seat contains Letchworth, the first garden city, and now a growing residential, commercial and industrial town. Nearby Baldock is almost exclusively residential and contains many Georgian and older buildings. Royston, on the border with Cambridgeshire, is a traditional market town. An above average proportion of constituents in this seat live in council houses, concentrated mainly in Letchworth. There are also many commuters here, attracted by the good transport links to London.

SOUTH WEST HERTFORDSHIRE

C hold

		Electorate	Turnout	Change from	2001	Electorate	Turnout
		73,170	68.4%	2001		73,264	64.5%
Gauke D	**C**	**23,494**	**46.9%**	**2.6%**	**C**	**20,933**	**44.3%**
Featherstone E	LD	15,021	30%	3.7%	Lab	12,752	27%
Cross K	Lab	10,466	20.9%	-6.1%	LD	12,431	26.3%
Rodden C	UKIP	1,107	2.2%	0.4%	UKIP	847	1.8%
					ProLife	306	0.6%
C to LD swing	**0.6%**	**50,088**		**C maj 8,473**		**47,269**	**C maj 8,181**
				16.9%			17.3%

DAVID GAUKE b 8 October 1971. MP 2005-. Contested Brent East 2001 general election. Deputy chair, Brent East Conservative Association 1998-2000. Parliamentary research assistant to Barry Legg MP 1993-94; trainee solicitor and solicitor, Richards Butler 1995-99; solicitor, Macfarlanes 1999-. Ed Northgate High School, Ipswich, Law, Oxford Univ, Legal Practice course, College of Law, Chester.

The southern half of the seat, which comes within the Three Rivers District, contains the Metroland towns and villages of Rickmansworth, Chorleywood and Croxley Green which developed as commuter suburbs when London Underground's Metropolitan Line was built. In the north lies Berkhamsted, a largely residential town and Tring, an attractive market town. Local industries include milling and plastics. Despite its affluent, conservative character the seat has strong links with the radical 19th century Chartist movement.

HERTSMERE

C hold

		Electorate	Turnout	Change from	2001	Electorate	Turnout
		67,572	63%	2001		68,780	60.3%
Clappison J	**C**	**22,665**	**53.2%**	**5.4%**	**C**	**19,855**	**47.8%**
Tebb K	Lab	11,572	27.2%	-8.8%	Lab	14,953	36%
Davies J	LD	7,817	18.4%	3.2%	LD	6,300	15.2%
Dry J	SLP	518	1.2%	0.2%	SLP	397	1%
Lab to C swing	**7.1%**	**42,572**		**C maj 11,093** 26.1%		**41,505**	**C maj 4,902** 11.8%

JAMES CLAPPISON b 14 Sept 1956. MP 1992-. Shadow: Min for Treasury 2002, Min for Work 2001-02; Financial Sec 2000-01. Dept of Environment Parly Under-Sec 1995-97, PPS to Baroness Blatch 1992-95. Opposition spokes: home affairs 1997-99, education and employment 1999-2000, Treasury 2000-01. Member select cttees: Health 1992-94, Home Affairs 2002-, Constitutional Affairs 2003-. Barrister. Ed St Peter's Sch, York; BA PPE, The Queen's Coll, Oxford.

The south of this Conservative stronghold, which borders the London Boroughs of Barnet and Harrow, is urban in character. Outside the main towns attractive countryside and small rural communities can be found. Although industry and commerce have expanded here since the 1950s (many important companies, including O2, Pinnacle Insurance, Adecco Alfred Marks and Pizza Hut now have their head offices here) many constituents work in London.

HEXHAM

C hold

		Electorate	Turnout	Change from	2001	Electorate	Turnout
		60,374	68.8%	2001		59,807	70.9%
Atkinson P	**C**	**17,605**	**42.4%**	**-2.2%**	**C**	**18,917**	**44.6%**
Graham K	Lab	12,585	30.3%	-8.3%	Lab	16,388	38.6%
Duffield A	LD	10,673	25.7%	10.7%	LD	6,380	15%
Riddell I	Eng Dem	521	1.3%		UKIP	728	1.7%
Davison T	IP	129	0.3%				
Lab to C swing	**3.1%**	**41,513**		**C maj 5,020** 12.1%		**42,413**	**C maj 2,529** 6%

PETER ATKINSON b 19 Jan 1943. MP 1992-. PPS to: Lord Parkinson 1997-99, Jeremy Hanley 1994-96, Sir Nicholas Bonsor 1995-96. Opposition whip 1999-. Member select cttees: Scottish Affairs 1992-97/1997-2002, Deregulation 1995-97, Chairmen's Panel 1997-99/2002-04, Court of Referees 1997-, Procedure 2003-04, Catering 2002-. Cllr: Wandsworth 1978-82, Suffolk CC 1989-92. Member Wandsworth Health Auth 1982-89. Journalist. Public affairs director British Field Sports Society 1983-92. Ed Cheltenham Coll.

A safe seat, Hexham is the only remaining constituency in the North East to return Conservative candidates, and has been doing so for the past 80 years. England's second largest constituency geographically, Hexham stretches from the affluent commuter communities of Hexham and Ponteland outside Newcastle, across 1,100 square miles of sparsely populated countryside from Hadrian's Wall to the Durham, Cumbrian and Scottish borders.

HEYWOOD AND MIDDLETON

Lab hold

		Electorate	Turnout	Change from	2001	Electorate	Turnout
		71,510	54.6%	2001		73,005	53.1%
Dobbin J	**Lab/C**	**19,438**	**49.8%**	**-7.9%**	**Lab/C**	**22,377**	**57.7%**
Pathmarajah S	C	8,355	21.4%	-6.2%	C	10,707	27.6%
Lavin C	LD	7,261	18.6%	7.4%	LD	4,329	11.2%
Aronsson G	BNP	1,855	4.8%		Lib	1,021	2.6%
Burke P	Lib	1,377	3.5%	0.9%	CD	345	0.9%
Whittaker J	UKIP	767	2%				
Lab/C to C swing	**0.9%**	**39,053**		**Lab/C maj 11,083** 28.4%		**38,779**	**Lab/C maj 11,670** 30.1%

JIM DOBBIN b 26 May 1941. MP 1997-. Member select cttees: European Scrutiny 1998-, Joint Cttee on Consolidation of Bills Etc 2001-. Vice-chair all-party North Korea group 2004-. Hon treasurer North West regional group of lab MPs 1999-2004. Cllr Rochdale Metropolitan BC 1983-92, 1994-97: leader 1996-97. Member European Standing Cttee C 2002-. Microbiologist NHS 1966-94. Ed St Columba's High, Cowdenbeath; St Andrew's High, Kirkcaldy; BSc bacteriology/virology, Napier Coll, Edinburgh.

Situated between Manchester and Rochdale, this seat is effectively the second Rochdale seat, and a Labour stronghold. Once heavily reliant on textiles, the area has now undergone industrial diversification; engineering, plastics and chemicals are now important industries. Housing is varied, comprising the odd mansion in Norden, middle-class suburbs like Casleton, and council estates such as Langley in Middleton.

HIGH PEAK

Lab hold

		Electorate 75,275	Turnout 66.4%	Change from 2001	2001	Electorate 73,833	Turnout 65.2%
Levitt T	**Lab**	**19,809**	**39.6%**	**-7%**	**Lab**	**22,430**	**46.6%**
Bingham A	C	19,074	38.2%	0.9%	C	17,941	37.3%
Godwin M	LD	10,000	20%	3.9%	LD	7,743	16.1%
Schwartz M	UKIP	1,106	2.2%				
Lab to C swing	**4%**	**49,989**		**Lab maj 735** 1.5%		**48,114**	**Lab maj 4,489** 9.3%

TOM LEVITT b 10 April 1954. MP 1997-. PPS to: Hilary Benn 2003-, Baroness Amos 2003, Barbara Roche 1999-2003. Member Standards/Privileges select cttee 1997-2003. Chair all-party groups: charities/voluntary sector 2001-, Switzerland 2002-. Cllr: Cirencester town 1983-87, Stroud District 1990-92, Derbyshire County 1993-97. Teacher/research consultant. NUT school representative 1977-79, 1984-90, pres NUT local assocn 1985, pres NUT county div 1988. Ed BSc biological sciences, Lancaster Univ; PGCE, Oxford Univ.

High Peak is a sparsely populated, marginal Labour seat, covering much of the Peak District national park. Low unemployment is complemented by healthy proportions of professional and skilled non-manual workers. There is significant industry in Glossop and Buxton, and limestone quarrying elsewhere. The scenery and villages have attracted visitors for generations, and the seat also contains Derbyshire's premier tourist town, Buxton, whose spring waters are famous worldwide.

HITCHIN AND HARPENDEN

C hold

		Electorate 67,207	Turnout 70.5%	Change from 2001	2001	Electorate 67,196	Turnout 66.9%
Lilley P	**C**	**23,627**	**49.9%**	**2.6%**	**C**	**21,271**	**47.3%**
Hedges H	LD	12,234	25.8%	7.8%	Lab	14,608	32.5%
Orrett P	Lab	10,499	22.2%	-10.3%	LD	8,076	18%
Saunders J	UKIP	828	1.8%	0.5%	UKIP	606	1.3%
Rigby P	Ind	199	0.4%	-0.4%	Ind	363	0.8%
C to LD swing	**2.6%**	**47,387**		**C maj 11,393** 24%		**44,924**	**C maj 6,663** 14.8%

PETER LILLEY b 23 Aug 1943. MP for St Albans 1983-97, for Hitchin and Harpenden 1997-. Shadow Chancellor of Exchequer 1997-98. Sec of State: Soc Security 1992-97, Trade and Industry 1990-92. Treasury: Financial Sec 1989-90, Economic Sec 1987-89. PPS to: Nigel Lawson 1984-87, Lord Bellwin and William Waldegrave (joint) 1984. Dep Opposition leader 1998-99. Contested Con Party leadership 1997. Economic consultant/financial analyst. Chair Bow Group 1973-75. PC 1990. Ed Dulwich Coll; BA natural/economic sciences, Clare Coll, Cambridge.

This is affluent commuter belt and 'true blue' territory, with a high percentage of managers and professionals. Hitchin is described as one of the most visually satisfying towns in Hertfordshire. The town prospered largely through the wool trade and much of its medieval past has been preserved. Many workers commute to London. Employment can also be found in the adjoining towns of Stevenage and Letchworth and in nearby Luton.

HOLBORN AND ST PANCRAS

Lab hold

		Electorate 68,237	Turnout 50.4%	Change from 2001	2001	Electorate 68,205	Turnout 45.6%
Dobson F	**Lab**	**14,857**	**43.2%**	**-10.7%**	**Lab**	**16,770**	**53.9%**
Fraser J	LD	10,070	29.3%	11.3%	LD	5,595	18%
James M	C	6,482	18.9%	2%	C	5,258	16.9%
Oliver A	Greens	2,798	8.1%	2.1%	Greens	1,875	6%
Weiss R	Vote Dream	152	0.4%		SA	971	3.1%
					SLP	359	1.2%
					UKIP	301	1%
Lab to LD swing	**11%**	**34,359**		**Lab maj 4,787** 13.9%		**31,129**	**Lab maj 11,175** 35.9%

FRANK DOBSON b 15 March 1940. MP 1979-. Health Sec of State 1997-99. Shadow: Environment Sec 1994-97, Min for London 1993-97, Transport Sec 1993-94, Employment Sec 1992-93, Energy Sec 1989-92, HoC and Campaigns Co-ordinator 1987-89, Health Min 1983-87. Opposition spokes 1981-83, 1989-97. Chair all-party historic churches group 2004-. Cllr Camden BC: leader 1973-75. CEGB HQ 1962-70, Electricity Council 1970-75, Asst Sec Office of Local Ombudsman 1975-79. PC 1997. Ed Archbishop Holgate's Grammar Sch; BSc econ, LSE.

Holborn and St Pancras is an extremely diverse yet consistently Labour-supporting constituency with fashionable areas (Camden Town, Chalk Farm) populated by young professionals, wealthy neighbourhoods (Bloomsbury), and council estates (Kentish Town). Owner-occupation levels are low and other inner-city characteristics include a high number of single-parent families and large black, Asian and other non-white groups. The constituency is also home to four Hospital Trusts and has received nearly £1.5 million in Arts Council Lottery awards.

HORNCHURCH — C gain

		Electorate 59,773	Turnout 63.9%	Change from 2001	2001	Electorate 61,185	Turnout 58.3%
Brokenshire J	**C**	**16,355**	**42.8%**	**0.5%**	**Lab**	**16,514**	**46.4%**
Cryer J	Lab	15,875	41.6%	-4.8%	C	15,032	42.3%
Green N	LD	2,894	7.6%	-0.6%	LD	2,928	8.2%
Moore I	BNP	1,313	3.4%		UKIP	893	2.5%
Webb L	UKIP	1,033	2.7%	0.2%	Third	190	0.5%
Brown M	RA	395	1%				
Williamson G	Third	304	0.8%	0.3%			
Lab to C swing	**2.7%**	**38,169**		**C maj 480** 1.3%		**35,557**	**Lab maj 1,482** 4.2%

JAMES BROKENSHIRE b. 1968. MP 2005-. Solicitor. Ed Davenant Foundation Grammar School, Cambridge Centre for Sixth Form Studies; LLB law Exeter University.

Hornchurch residents seem especially loath to be classed as Londoners, despite their constituency's official position in the outer London borough of Havering and not in Essex. The marginal seat is largely residential in character with industry confined mainly to the Rainham district. The constituency is situated just to the east of Dagenham, and many workers at the Ford motor plant live here. 31 per cent of the economically active population are skilled manual workers.

HORNSEY AND WOOD GREEN — LD gain

		Electorate 76,621	Turnout 61.8%	Change from 2001	2001	Electorate 75,974	Turnout 58%
Featherstone L	**LD**	**20,512**	**43.3%**	**17.5%**	**Lab**	**21,967**	**49.9%**
Roche B	Lab	18,117	38.3%	-11.6%	LD	11,353	25.8%
Forrest P	C	6,014	12.7%	-3%	C	6,921	15.7%
Forbes J	Greens	2,377	5%	-0.1%	Greens	2,228	5.1%
Freshwater R	UKIP	310	0.6%		SA	1,106	2.5%
					SLP	294	0.7%
					R2000	194	0.4%
Lab to LD swing	**14.6%**	**47,330**		**LD maj 2,395** 5.1%		**44,063**	**Lab maj 10,614** 24.1%

LYNNE FEATHERSTONE b 20 Dec 1951. MP 2005-; Member GLA 2000-05: Chair, Assembly Committee on Transport 2003-05; Councillor, Haringey Council: Leader of the Opposition 1998-2003; Strategic design consultant 1987-97. Ed South Hampstead High School, London, Oxford Polytechnic 1974

Neighbouring plush Hampstead, this seat has its fair share of affluent middle-classes and very little native industry. But it does have large areas of council housing, high unemployment and a significant non-white population plus strong Jewish and Cypriot communities. Most of the seat is residential , although Wood Green, famous as being the original home of BBC television, is one of the capital's largest shopping and service centres. A previous Labour stronghold, it fell to the Lib Dems on a massive 14 per cent swing in 2005.

HORSHAM — C hold

		Electorate 80,974	Turnout 67.3%	Change from 2001	2001	Electorate 79,604	Turnout 63.8%
Maude F	**C**	**27,240**	**50%**	**-1.5%**	**C**	**26,134**	**51.5%**
Sharpley R	LD	14,613	26.8%	2.2%	LD	12,468	24.6%
Chishti R	Lab	9,320	17.1%	-3.1%	Lab	10,267	20.2%
Miller H	UKIP	2,552	4.7%	1.8%	UKIP	1,472	2.9%
Duggan J	PJP	416	0.8%		Ind	429	0.8%
Jeremiah M	PHF	354	0.6%				
C to LD swing	**1.9%**	**54,495**		**C maj 12,627** 23.2%		**50,770**	**C maj 13,666** 26.9%

FRANCIS MAUDE b 4 July 1953. MP for North Warwicks 1983-92, for Horsham 1997-. Shadow: Sec of State Foreign/Commonwealth Affairs 2000-01, Chancellor of Exchequer 1998-2000; Sec of State: Culture, Media, Sport 1997-98, Nat Heritage 1997. Financial Sec Treasury 1990-92. Min of State FCO 1989-90, Parly Under-Sec DTI 1987-89. PPS to Peter Morrison 1984. Govt whip 1985-87. Member Public Accounts select cttee 1990-92. Chair Con Party 2005-. Cllr Westminster 1978-84. Banker/barrister. PC 1992. Ed MA hist, Corpus Christi, Cambridge; Coll of Law.

Centred on the market town of Horsham, and well served by excellent communication links, the constituency also includes a number of charming small rustic villages. It is bordered in the north by Surrey, by the Downs along the southern border, by St Leonard's Forest and the High Weald to the east, and the Arun Valley in the west. The Conservatives maintain a position of considerable strength.

HOUGHTON AND WASHINGTON EAST — Lab hold

		Electorate 67,089	Turnout 51.7%	Change from 2001	2001	Electorate 67,946	Turnout 49.5%
Kemp F	**Lab**	**22,310**	**64.3%**	**-8.9%**	**Lab**	**24,628**	**73.2%**
Greenfield M	LD	6,245	18%	5.5%	C	4,810	14.3%
Devenish T	C	4,772	13.8%	-0.5%	LD	4,203	12.5%
Richardson J	BNP	1,367	3.9%				
Lab to LD swing	**7.2%**	**34,694**		**Lab maj 16,065** 46.3%		**33,641**	**Lab maj 19,818** 58.9%

FRASER KEMP b 1 Sept 1958. MP 1997-. Asst govt whip 2001-05. Member select cttees: Public Administration 1997-99, Selection 1997-99. Sec all-party space group 2000-. Lab Party: organiser Leicester 1981-86; asst regional organiser E Midlands; regional sec W Midlands 1986-94; nat general election co-ordinator 1994-96; sec Lab NEC campaigns and elections cttee 1995-96. Civil servant 1975-81. Full-time branch sec Civil and Public Services Assocn 1975-80. Pres Washington MIND. Ed Washington Comp.

South-west of Sunderland, the towns that comprise this seat are mostly ex-mining communities. Washington was designated a New Town in 1964 and is now famous for the Nissan car factory. Following the decline of the coal industry, light and service industries form the economic base of the seat, and companies such as Philips and Nike have set up in the area. Houghton and Washington East is one of Labour's top ten safest seats.

HOVE — Lab hold

		Electorate 69,939	Turnout 64%	Change from 2001	2001	Electorate 70,889	Turnout 59.2%
Barlow C	**Lab**	**16,786**	**37.5%**	**-8.4%**	**Lab**	**19,253**	**45.9%**
Boles N	C	16,366	36.5%	-1.8%	C	16,082	38.3%
Elgood P	LD	8,002	17.9%	8.8%	LD	3,823	9.1%
Ballam A	Greens	2,575	5.8%	2.5%	Greens	1,369	3.3%
Bower S	UKIP	575	1.3%	0.4%	SA	531	1.3%
O'Keefe P	Respect	268	0.6%		UKIP	358	0.9%
Dobbs B	Ind	95	0.2%	0.1%	Lib	316	0.8%
Franklin R	Silent	78	0.2%		Free	196	0.5%
Ralfe B	Ind	51	0.1%		Ind	60	0.1%
Lab to C swing	**3.3%**	**44,796**		**Lab maj 420** 0.9%		**41,988**	**Lab maj 3,171** 7.6%

CELIA BARLOW b 28 Sept 1955. MP 2005-. Contested Chichester 2001 general election; Constituency chair Chichester 1998. TV producer; Member NUJ 1977-. Ed MA archaeology and anthropology, Cambridge 1976; postgrad diploma journalism, University College, Cardiff 1978; postgrad diploma independent film and video, Central St Martins 1993

Hove is an almost entirely residential town on the East Sussex coast. It is quite stately, with Regency terraces, wide tree-lined avenues, bowling greens, and golf courses. The constituency contains the district of Portslade, the entrance to Shoreham Harbour and the southern-most reaches of the South Downs. Despite often being linked to its larger neighbour, Brighton, it possesses its own distinct character. A surprise Labour gain in 1997, the seat is now highly marginal.

HUDDERSFIELD — Lab hold

		Electorate 61,723	Turnout 56.6%	Change from 2001	2001	Electorate 64,350	Turnout 55%
Sheerman B	**Lab/C**	**16,341**	**46.8%**	**-6.4%**	**Lab/C**	**18,840**	**53.2%**
Bone E	LD	7,990	22.9%	7.9%	C	8,794	24.9%
Meacock D	C	7,597	21.7%	-3.2%	LD	5,300	15%
Stewart-Turner J	Greens	1,651	4.7%	1.2%	Greens	1,254	3.5%
Hanson K	BNP	1,036	3%		UKIP	613	1.7%
Quarmby T	Ind	325	0.9%		SA	374	1.1%
					SLP	208	0.6%
Lab/C to LD swing	**7.2%**	**34,940**		**Lab/C maj 8,351** 23.9%		**35,383**	**Lab/C maj 10,046** 28.4%

BARRY SHEERMAN b 17 August 1940. MP for Huddersfield East 1979-83, for Huddersfield 1983-. Shadow Min: Disability 1992-94, Home Affairs dep to Roy Hattersley 1987-92, Education and Employment 1983-87. Opposition spokes 1983-94. Select cttees: chair: Education and Employment 1999-2001, Education and Skills 2001-; member Liaison 1999-. Chair various all-party groups. Cllr Loughor and Lliw Valley Unitary DC 1972-79. Universtity lecturer 1966-79. Ed Hampton Grammar Sch; Kingston Tech Coll; BSc econ, LSE; London Univ.

Textiles, chemicals and engineering industries still survive in Huddersfield, but renovated buildings and a smoke-free zone encompassing the whole of Kirklees borough form part of a move to combat a stereotyped image of the industrial north. Moreover, a sizeable proportion of the workforce are non-manual. Labour's grip here is bolstered by a 17 per cent non-white population, 24 per cent council house occupancy and an unemployment rate that hovers around 10 per cent.

HULL EAST

Lab hold

		Electorate 65,407	Turnout 47.4%	Change from 2001	2001	Electorate 66,397	Turnout 46.5%
Prescott J	**Lab**	**17,609**	**56.8%**	**-7.8%**	**Lab**	**19,938**	**64.6%**
Sloan A	LD	5,862	18.9%	4%	LD	4,613	14.9%
Lindsay K	C	4,038	13%	-0.8%	C	4,276	13.8%
Siddle A	BNP	1,022	3.3%		UKIP	1,218	3.9%
Toker J	Lib	1,018	3.3%		SLP	830	2.7%
Morris G	Veritas	750	2.4%				
Noon R	Ind	334	1.1%				
Muir L	SLP	207	0.7%	-2%			
Wagner C	LCA	182	0.6%				
Lab to LD swing	**5.9%**	**31,022**		**Lab maj 11,747** 37.9%		**30,875**	**Lab maj 15,325** 49.6%

JOHN PRESCOTT b 31 May 1938. MP for Kingston-upon-Hull East 1970-83, for Hull East 1983-. First Sec of State 2001-, Sec of State for Environment, Transport and the Regions 1997-2001, Dep PM 1997-. Shadow Sec of State: Employment 1993-94, Transport 1988-93, Energy 1987-89, Employment 1984-87. PPS to Peter Shore 1974-76. Opposition spokes 1979-94. Dep leader: Lab Party 1994-, Lab Party NEC 1997-. Nat Union of Seamen/RMT union official to 2002. Merchant navy steward 1955-63. PC 1994. Ed DipEcon/Pol, Ruskin Coll, Oxford; BSc econ, Hull Univ.

John Prescott's constituency remains the safest of Labour's three Hull seats. Hull East is the most industrialised of the Hull constituencies, containing many of the old dockland areas. The area has benefited from Urban Development Grant Support, transforming old dockland warehouses into offices, retail arcades, light industrial units and housing. Unemployment is high, as is both the proportion of unskilled manual workers and of voters living in council houses.

HULL NORTH

Lab hold

		Electorate 62,590	Turnout 47.3%	Change from 2001	2001	Electorate 62,938	Turnout 45.5%
Johnson D	**Lab**	**15,364**	**51.9%**	**-5.3%**	**Lab**	**16,364**	**57.2%**
Healy D	LD	8,013	27.1%	7.4%	LD	5,643	19.7%
Rivlin L	C	3,822	12.9%	-4.2%	C	4,902	17.1%
Deane M	Greens	858	2.9%		UKIP	655	2.3%
Wainwright B	BNP	766	2.6%		SA	490	1.7%
Robinson T	Veritas	389	1.3%		LCA	478	1.7%
Veasey C	Northern	193	0.6%		Ind	101	0.4%
Wagner C	LCA	179	0.6%	-1.1%			
Lab to LD swing	**6.4%**	**29,584**		**Lab maj 7,351** 24.8%		**28,633**	**Lab maj 10,721** 37.4%

DIANA JOHNSON b 25 July 1966. MP 2005-. Cllr Tower Hamlets 1994-2002. Law clerk, Philadelphia, USA 1989; Paralegal Herbert Smith Solicitors 1990; Law clerk, Hamilton, Ontario, Canada 1991; Volunteer/locum lawyer Tower Hamlets Law Centre 1993-95; Family lawyer McCormacks 1994-95; Legal member Mental Health Act Commission 1995-98; Employment, immigration and education lawyer N Lewisham 1995-99; Employment lawyer Paddington LC 1999-. Ed Sir John Deans Sixth Form Coll, Cheshire; Modern hist, Brunel Univ; Law, Queen Mary College, London

Labour's grip on this essentially working-class seat is reinforced by the fact that many Conservative voters born in and around the town, or who work there now, live in pleasant suburbs outside the city boundaries. The university is the focus of the town. Unemployment in this seat is higher than in the rest of the city, and factories mingle with terraces and council estates in a mostly urban sprawl.

HULL WEST AND HESSLE

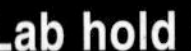

Lab hold

		Electorate 61,494	Turnout 45.2%	Change from 2001	2001	Electorate 63,077	Turnout 45.8%
Johnson A	**Lab**	**15,305**	**55%**	**-3.4%**	**Lab**	**16,880**	**58.4%**
Nolan D	LD	5,855	21.1%	6%	C	5,929	20.5%
Woods K	C	5,769	20.7%	0.2%	LD	4,364	15.1%
Wallis S	Veritas	889	3.2%		UKIP	878	3%
					Ind	512	1.8%
					SLP	353	1.2%
Lab to LD swing	**4.7%**	**27,818**		**Lab maj 9,450** 34%		**28,916**	**Lab maj 10,951** 37.9%

ALAN JOHNSON b 17 May 1950. MP 1997-. Sec of State: Trade and Industry 2005-, Work and Pensions 2004-05. Min of State Dept of Education and Skills 2003-04. Dept of Trade and Industry: Min of State 2001-03, Parly Under-Sec 1999-2001. PPS to Dawn Primarolo 1997-99. Member Trade and Industry select cttee 1997-98. Member Lab Party NEC 1995-97. Postman. TUC General Council member 1993-95. General sec: Union of Communication Workers 1993-95, (joint) Communication Workers Union 1995-97. PC 2003. Ed Sloane Grammar Sch, Chelsea.

Despite its title this safe Labour seat contains most of Hull's inner-city – a depressed area that is currently undergoing renovation. The area still has some way to go before it is fully restored to healthy economic life, and unemployment remains high – not helped by the declining fishing industry. Hessle is a quiet suburb to the west, conservative by nature, having little in common with its larger neighbour apart from working-class roots.

HUNTINGDON

C hold

		Electorate 83,843	Turnout 62.5%	Change from 2001	2001	Electorate 80,335	Turnout 61.1%
Djanogly J	**C**	**26,646**	**50.8%**	**0.9%**	**C**	**24,507**	**49.9%**
Huppert J	LD	13,799	26.3%	2.4%	LD	11,715	23.9%
Sartain S	Lab	9,821	18.7%	-4.1%	Lab	11,211	22.8%
Norman D	UKIP	2,152	4.1%	0.7%	UKIP	1,656	3.4%
C to LD swing	**0.8%**	**52,418**		**C maj 12,847** 24.5%		**49,089**	**C maj 12,792** 26.1%

JONATHAN DJANOGLY b 3 June 1965. MP 2001-. Shadow Solicitor General 2005-; Shadow Min: Home Affairs 2004-05, Home, Constitutional and Legal Affairs 2004. Member select cttees: Trade and Industry 2001-, Joint Cttee on Statutory Instruments 2001-02. Vice-chair/sec all-party thalidomide group 2003-. Vice-chair Westminster North Con Assocn 1993-94. Cllr Westminster City Council 1994-2001. Solicitor 1988-. Mail order retail business 1994-2002. Ed Univ Coll Sch; BA law and politics, Oxford Poly; Guildford Coll of Law.

Huntingdon, home to the notorious Huntingdon Life Sciences, was the seat of former Prime Minister John Major from 1979. His replacement held the seat comfortably in both the 2001 and 2005 election. The economy is still expanding, benefiting from the upgrading of the A1(M) as well as the knock on effect of the M11 link from London to Cambridge. Unemployment remains consistently low at 1.4 per cent

HYNDBURN

Lab hold

		Electorate 67,086	Turnout 58.8%	Change from 2001	2001	Electorate 66,533	Turnout 57.5%
Pope G	**Lab**	**18,136**	**46%**	**-8.7%**	**Lab**	**20,900**	**54.7%**
Mawdsley J	C	12,549	31.8%	-1.4%	C	12,681	33.2%
Greene B	LD	5,577	14.1%	4.5%	LD	3,680	9.6%
Jackson C	BNP	2,444	6.2%		UKIP	982	2.6%
Whittaker J	UKIP	743	1.9%	-0.7%			
Lab to C swing	**3.7%**	**39,449**		**Lab maj 5,587** 14.2%		**38,243**	**Lab maj 8,219** 21.5%

GREG POPE b 29 Aug 1960. MP 1992-. Whip: opposition 1995-97, asst govt 1997-99, govt 1999-2001. Member select cttees: Education 1994-95, Foreign Affairs 2001-. Cllr: Hyndburn BC 1984-88, Blackburn BC 1989-91. Co-ordinator Blackburn trade union unemployed centre 1983-85. Lancashire CC local govt officer 1987-92. Ed St Mary's Coll RC Grammar Sch, Blackburn; BA politics, Hull Univ.

Hyndburn encompasses the small Lancashire towns between Burnley and Blackburn, including Accrington, Oswaldtwistle and Great Harwood. The seat stretches down into Rossendale in the south, with attractive moorland around Haslingden. Engineering and cotton weaving were once major industries, but the area has diversified and tourism has become important as the area capitalises on its mill heritage and popularity with hill walkers. A largely working-class seat, it has traditionally voted Labour, but not overwhelmingly.

ILFORD NORTH

C gain

		Electorate 70,718	Turnout 60.8%	Change from 2001	2001	Electorate 68,893	Turnout 58.4%
Scott L	**C**	**18,781**	**43.7%**	**3.2%**	**Lab**	**18,428**	**45.8%**
Perham L	Lab	17,128	39.8%	-6%	C	16,313	40.5%
Gayler M	LD	5,896	13.7%	2%	LD	4,717	11.7%
Cross A	UKIP	902	2.1%	-9.6%	Ind	776	1.9%
Levin M	Ind	293	0.7%				
Lab to C swing	**4.6%**	**43,000**		**C maj 1,653** 3.8%		**40,234**	**Lab maj 2,115** 5.3%

LEE SCOTT b 6 April 1956. MP 2005-. Councillor London Borough of Redbridge, 1998-: cabinet member for regeneration and the community 2002; Director, Scott Associates 1998-; Campaign director/provincial director United Jewish Israel Appeal 1988-98. Ed Clarkes College, Ilford, Essex

Despite being by far the more affluent and more Conservative half of Ilford, Ilford North has since 1997 been a Tory/Labour marginal. The seat contains more open green space than urban area, and being on the London/Essex border attracts a good number of commuters. The houses tend to be owner-occupied, and inhabited by lower middle-class skilled non-manual workers. Unemployment is below the national average.

ILFORD SOUTH — Lab hold

		Electorate	Turnout	Change from	2001	Electorate	Turnout
		79,639	53.6%	2001		76,025	54.3%
Gapes M	**Lab/C**	**20,856**	**48.8%**	**-10.8%**	**Lab/C**	**24,619**	**59.6%**
Metcalfe S	C	11,628	27.2%	1.5%	C	10,622	25.7%
Lake M	LD	8,761	20.5%	9.2%	LD	4,647	11.3%
Rana K	BPP	763	1.8%		UKIP	1,407	3.4%
Taylor C	UKIP	685	1.6%	-1.8%			
Lab/C to C swing	**6.2%**	**42,693**		**Lab/C maj 9,228**		**41,295**	**Lab/C maj 13,997**
				21.6%			33.9%

MIKE GAPES b 4 Sept 1952. MP 1992-. PPS to: Lord Rooker 2001-02, Paul Murphy 1997-99. Member select cttees: Foreign Affairs 1992-97, Defence 1999-2001, Defence 2003-. Vice-chair United Nations group 2001-. Member Lab Party: nat policy forum 1996-, joint policy cttee 1999-. Chair Co-op Party parly group 2000-01. Member NATO parly assembly 2002-. Teacher/union official 1971-74. Lab students official/organiser 1975-80. Lab Party officer 1980-92. Ed MA econ, Fitzwilliam Coll, Cambridge; indust relats dip, Middlesex Poly, Enfield.

The town of Ilford is split into two constituencies. The southern half contains all of the town centre, and despite marginally more owner-occupiers the standard of housing here is poorer. Service and light industries are commonly found in the seat, which has more manual workers than North, as well as higher unemployment and a much higher ethnic minority population. Ilford South looks like a safe seat for Labour.

INVERCLYDE — Lab hold

		Electorate	Turnout		2001
		59,291	60.9%		
Cairns D	**Lab**	**18,318**	**50.8%**		No comparable results due to boundary changes
McMillan S	SNP	7,059	19.6%		
Herbison D	LD	6,123	17%		
Fraser G	C	3,692	10.2%		
Landels D	SSP	906	2.5%		
Lab to SNP swing	**2.5%**	**36,098**		**Lab maj 11,259**	
(notional)				31.2%	

DAVID CAIRNS b 7 Aug 1966. MP for Greenock and Inverclyde 2001-05, for Inverclyde 2005-. Parly Under-Sec Scotland Office 2005-. PPS to Malcolm Wicks 2003-05. Member Joint Cttee on Consolidation of Bills Etc 2001-. All-party groups: vice-chair brain injury 2002-, vice-pres Israel 2005-. Member Christian Socialist Movement (dir 1994-97). Cllr Merton 1998-2002. Member European standing cttee B 2003-. Priest 1991-94. Research asst to Siobhan McDonagh MP 1997-2001. Ed Gregorian Univ, Rome; Franciscan Study Centre, Canterbury.

Hugging the Clyde, this seat spreads inland from the once thriving docklands of Greenock and Port Glasgow to leafy Kilmacolm in the east. Harbourside developments have largely replaced heavy industry, and employment has shifted towards electronics and the service sector. This is a mixed seat, with pockets of poverty and prosperity.

INVERNESS, NAIRN, BADENOCH AND STRATHSPEY — LD gain

		Electorate	Turnout		2001
		69,636	63.6%		
Alexander D	**LD**	**17,830**	**40.3%**		No comparable results due to boundary changes
Stewart D	Lab	13,682	30.9%		
Thompson D	SNP	5,992	13.5%		
Rowantree R	C	4,579	10.4%		
MacLeod D	Greens	1,065	2.4%		
Lawson D	Publican	678	1.5%		
Macdonald G	SSP	429	1%		
Lab to LD swing	**6%**	**44,255**		**LD maj 4,148**	
(notional)				9.4%	

DANNY ALEXANDER b 15 May 1972. MP 2005-. Head of communications Cairngorms National Park 2004-; Head of communications Britain in Europe campaign 1999-2003; deputy director and head of communications, European Movement 1997-99; election aide to Jim Wallace MP 1997; press officer, European Movement 1996-97; press officer, Scottish Liberal Democrats 1993-95; researcher, Campaign for Freedom of Information 1991. Ed Lochaber High School, Fort William; PPE, Oxford.

Spreading inland from the Moray Firth, this is the southernmost of the three vast and remote Highland seats. Eastward along the coast is the pleasant seaside and golfing town of Nairn. Inland is Speyside and Grantown-on-Spey. However, the electorate is concentrated in Inverness (now united in a single constituency for the first time in two decades) where Liberal Democrats outnumbered Labour voters for the first time in 2005.

IPSWICH — Lab hold

		Electorate 68,825	Turnout 60.8%	Change from 2001	2001	Electorate 68,198	Turnout 57%
Mole C	**Lab**	**18,336**	**43.8%**	**-7.5%**	**Lab**	**19,952**	**51.3%**
West P	C	13,004	31.1%	0.6%	C	11,871	30.5%
Atkins R	LD	8,464	20.2%	5%	LD	5,904	15.2%
West A	UKIP	1,134	2.7%	1.1%	UKIP	624	1.6%
Kay J	Eng Dem	641	1.5%		SA	305	0.8%
Wainman S	Ind	299	0.7%		SLP	217	0.6%
Lab to C swing	**4.1%**	**41,878**		**Lab maj 5,332** 12.7%		**38,873**	**Lab maj 8,081** 20.8%

CHRIS MOLE b 16 March 1958. MP 2001-. Member select cttees: Regulatory Reform 2002-, Joint Cttee on Statutory Instruments 2002-, Office of the Deputy Prime Minister 2002-, Office of the Deputy Prime Minister (Urban Affairs Sub-Cttee) 2003-, Information 2004-. Vice-chair all-party telecommunications group 2004-. Leader Suffolk County Council 1993-2001. Telecoms research manager. Technologist Plessey Research 1979-81, research manager BT Labs 1981-88. Ed Dulwich Coll; BSc electronics, Kent Univ, Canterbury.

Previously marginal, and occasionally Conservative, this is an important and prosperous regional centre in Suffolk with a growing hi-tech sector. It has been safe for Labour since 1997, despite their majority falling in the by-election of November 2001, after the death of the popular Jamie Cann. The seat has one of the largest ethnic minority populations in East Anglia, at just under 10 per cent of the population.

ISLE OF WIGHT — C hold

		Electorate 109,046	Turnout 61.3%	Change from 2001	2001	Electorate 103,654	Turnout 61.2%
Turner A	**C**	**32,717**	**49%**	**9.3%**	**C**	**25,223**	**39.7%**
Rowlands A	LD	19,739	29.5%	-5.8%	LD	22,397	35.3%
Chiverton M	Lab	11,484	17.2%	2%	Lab	9,676	15.2%
Tarrant M	UKIP	2,352	3.5%	0.2%	UKIP	2,106	3.3%
Corby E	Ind	551	0.8%	-1.4%	Ind	1,423	2.2%
					Greens	1,279	2%
					IOW	1,164	1.8%
					SLP	214	0.3%
LD to C swing	**7.6%**	**66,843**		**C maj 12,978** 19.4%		**63,482**	**C maj 2,826** 4.5%

ANDREW TURNER b 24 Oct 1953. MP 2001-. Member Education and Skills select cttee 2001-. Member 1922 Cttee Exec 2001-03. Vice-pres Assocn of Con Clubs 2002-. Vice-chair (campaigning) Con Party 2003-. Cllr Oxford CC 1979-96. Sheriff of Oxford 1994-95. Teacher 1977-84, Con research specialist 1984-86, special adviser Soc Services Sec of State 1986-88. Director Grant-Maintained Schools Foundation 1988-97. Education consultant 1997-2001. Ed Rugby Sch; BA geog/MA, Keble Coll, Oxford; PGCE, Birmingham Univ; Henley Management Coll.

At over 100,000 the Island has the largest electorate of any constituency in the country. Inland it is rural with one large town – Newport. Most people live in the coastal resorts which include Ryde, Sandown and Shanklin. There is a large elderly population. The island is also well known for its three prisons, and the Cowes week regatta. Since the 1970s the seat has been traded between the Liberals/Liberal Democrats and the Conservatives.

ISLINGTON NORTH — Lab hold

		Electorate 58,427	Turnout 53.9%	Change from 2001	2001	Electorate 61,970	Turnout 48.8%
Corbyn J	**Lab**	**16,118**	**51.2%**	**-10.7%**	**Lab**	**18,699**	**61.9%**
Willoughby L	LD	9,402	29.8%	10.8%	LD	5,741	19%
Talbot N	C	3,740	11.9%	1.1%	C	3,249	10.8%
Nott J	Greens	2,234	7.1%	0.9%	Greens	1,876	6.2%
					SLP	512	1.7%
					R2000	139	0.5%
Lab to LD swing	**10.8%**	**31,494**		**Lab maj 6,716** 21.3%		**30,216**	**Lab maj 12,958** 42.9%

JEREMY CORBYN b 26 May 1949. MP 1983-. Member Social Security select cttee 1991-97. Vice-chair all-party groups: human rights 1997-, Iraqi Kurdistan 2002-, Latin America 2004. Cllr Haringey BC 1974-84. Former NUPE full-time organiser. Worked for Tailor and Garment workers and AUEW. Member RMT parly campaigning group 2002-. Ed Adams Grammar Sch, Newport, Shropshire.

Where once the London Borough of Islington had three seats, it now has two. With a 22 per cent non-white population this is a cosmopolitan inner-city seat, and not one of the more affluent at that. Accommodation is mainly found in rented or council houses, 41 per cent of homes are council-rented, and unemployment runs at 14.1 per cent. Holloway prison is also in this seat. Levels of deprivation continue to fortify Labour's grip here.

ISLINGTON SOUTH AND FINSBURY — Lab hold

		Electorate	Turnout	Change from	2001	Electorate	Turnout
		57,748	53.6%	2001		59,516	47.4%
Thornberry E	**Lab**	**12,345**	**39.9%**	**-14%**	**Lab**	**15,217**	**53.9%**
Fox B	LD	11,861	38.3%	10.2%	LD	7,937	28.1%
McLean M	C	4,594	14.8%	1.1%	C	3,860	13.7%
Humphreys J	Greens	1,471	4.8%		SA	817	2.9%
Theophanides P	UKIP	470	1.5%		Ind	276	1%
Gardner A	Loony	189	0.6%		Stuckist	108	0.4%
Gidden C	Ind	31	0.1%	-0.9%			
Lab to LD swing	**12.1%**	**30,961**		**Lab maj 484**		**28,215**	**Lab maj 7,280**
				1.6%			25.8%

EMILY THORNBERRY b 27 July 1960. MP 2005-. Member Mike Mansfield's Chambers: Tooks Court 1985-. Ed Law, Kent University

Home to the Blair family before they moved into Downing Street, this long-term Labour seat includes extreme contrasts of wealth and social status, with City high-fliers populating the plush Georgian squares, and interspersed among them low-paid public sector manual workers, large numbers of long-term welfare dependants, and a large poor non-white population. A massive 55 per cent of voters here are council tenants. Only 22 per cent of homes are owner occupied.

ISLWYN — Lab hold

		Electorate	Turnout	Change from	2001	Electorate	Turnout
		50,595	61%	2001		51,230	61.9%
Touhig D	**Lab/C**	**19,687**	**63.8%**	**2.3%**	**Lab/C**	**19,505**	**61.5%**
Criddle J	PlC	3,947	12.8%	0.9%	LD	4,196	13.2%
Dillon L	LD	3,873	12.6%	-0.6%	PlC	3,767	11.9%
Howells P	C	3,358	10.9%	2.9%	C	2,543	8%
					None	1,263	4%
					SLP	417	1.3%
PlC to Lab/C swing	**0.7%**	**30,865**		**Lab/C maj 15,740**		**31,691**	**Lab/C maj 15,309**
				51%			48.3%

DON TOUHIG b 5 Dec 1947. MP Feb 1995- (by-election). Parly Under-Sec: MoD 2005-, Wales Office 2001-05. Asst govt whip 1999-2001. Member Welsh Affairs select cttee 1996-97. Chair Co-operative parly group 1999. Member: Lab leadership campaign team 1996-97, Co-operative Party, European standing cttee B 1995-96. Hon sec Welsh regional group of Lab MPs 1995-99. Cllr Gwent CC 1973-95. Journalist, editor. Gen manager/editor in chief 1988-95. Pres nat old age pensioners Wales assocn. Papal Knight of the Order of St Sylvester. Ed Mid Gwent Coll.

Set in the Western valley of Gwent and part of Caerphilly, Islwyn, which is named after a Welsh language poet of the 19th century, includes the communities of Blackwood, Newbridge and Risca. Neil Kinnock's former seat, this is usually safe Labour territory, though Plaid Cymru sprang a major surprise in the National Assembly for Wales elections in 1999. It does seem to have been re-established as safe for Labour since 2003.

JARROW — Lab hold

		Electorate	Turnout	Change from	2001	Electorate	Turnout
		61,814	55%	2001		62,467	55.2%
Hepburn S	**Lab**	**20,554**	**60.5%**	**-5.6%**	**Lab**	**22,777**	**66.1%**
Schardt B	LD	6,650	19.6%	4.6%	LD	5,182	15%
Jack L	C	4,807	14.2%	-0.5%	C	5,056	14.7%
Badger A	UKIP	1,567	4.6%	2.5%	UKIP	716	2.1%
Nettleship R	SNH	400	1.2%		Ind	391	1.1%
					None	357	1%
Lab to LD swing	**5.1%**	**33,978**		**Lab maj 13,904**		**34,479**	**Lab maj 17,595**
				40.9%			51%

STEPHEN HEPBURN b 6 Dec 1959. MP 1997-. Member select cttees: Administration 1997-2001, Defence 1999-2001, Accommodation and Works 2003-, Northern Ireland Affairs 2004-. Chair all-party shipbuilding and ship repair group 2001-. Cllr South Tyneside 1985-: dep leader 1990-97. Labourer South Tyneside MBC. Research asst to Don Dixon MP. Ed Springfield Comp, Jarrow; BA, Newcastle Univ.

The south Tyneside constituency of Jarrow will forever be linked with the hunger marches of the 1930s. Traditional industries such as coal mining and shipbuilding have almost vanished and new light industry has been encouraged. By calling the area 'Catherine Cookson country', tourism is being promoted; the Venerable Bede lived and wrote in Jarrow town. In an area of staunch Labour support, a win for any other party would be a major event.

KEIGHLEY Lab hold

		Electorate	Turnout	Change from	2001	Electorate	Turnout
		68,229	67.9%	2001		68,331	63.4%
Cryer A	**Lab**	**20,720**	**44.7%**	**-3.5%**	**Lab**	**20,888**	**48.2%**
Poulsen K	C	15,868	34.3%	-4.7%	C	16,883	39%
Fekri N	LD	5,484	11.8%	0.9%	LD	4,722	10.9%
Griffin N	BNP	4,240	9.2%		UKIP	840	1.9%
C to Lab swing	**0.6%**	**46,312**		**Lab maj 4,852**		**43,333**	**Lab maj 4,005**
				10.5%			9.2%

ANN CRYER b 14 Dec 1939. MP 1997-. Member Constitutional Affairs select cttee 2003-. Chair all-party breast cancer group 2003-. Council of Europe Parly Assembly delegate 1997-2003. Member: Commonwealth Parly Assocn 1997-, Co-operative Party 1965-. Cllr Darwen Borough Council 1962-65. JP, Bradford bench (appointed 1996). Clerk 1955-64. PA to Bob Cryer MP/MEP 1974-94. Member: Soc Security Appeal Tribunal 1987-96; parly groups: ASLEF 2000-, RMT 2002-. Ed Spring Bank Sec, Darwin; Bolton Tech Coll; Keighley Tech Coll.

This Pennine seat encompasses the former textile town of Keighley, with a sizeable Asian minority, the contrasting spa and tourist resort of Ilkley, and a large rural area. It was traditionally a crucial marginal, changing hands several times, falling convincingly to Bob Cryer's widow Ann in 1997 (after Bob had held it for seven years) but swinging slightly back to the Tories in 2001. Despite a small swing in Labour's favour in 2005, the seat can just about be considered marginal again.

KENSINGTON AND CHELSEA C hold

		Electorate	Turnout	Change from	2001	Electorate	Turnout
		62,662	50%	2001		64,893	43.2%
Rifkind Sir Malcolm	**C**	**18,144**	**57.9%**	**3.5%**	**C**	**15,270**	**54.4%**
Kingsley J	LD	5,726	18.3%	2.6%	Lab	6,499	23.2%
Atkinson C	Lab	5,521	17.6%	-5.6%	LD	4,416	15.7%
Stephenson J	Greens	1,342	4.3%	0.1%	Greens	1,168	4.2%
Eilorat M	UKIP	395	1.3%	-0.2%	UKIP	416	1.5%
Bovill A	Ind	107	0.3%		ProLife	179	0.6%
Adams E	Green S	101	0.3%		Jam	100	0.4%
LD to C swing	**0.5%**	**31,336**		**C maj 12,418**		**28,048**	**C maj 8,771**
				39.6%			31.3%

SIR MALCOLM RIFKIND b 21 June 1946. MP for Edinburgh Pentlands 1974-97, Contested same 2001 general election. MP for Kensington and Chelsea 2005-. Shadow Sec of State Work and Pensions 2005-. Foreign Sec 1995-97; Defence Sec 1992-95; Transport Sec 1990-92; Scotland Sec 1986-90; PC 1986; Foreign Min 1983-86; Foreign Parly Under-Sec 1982-83; Scotland Min 1979-82. Lecturer University College of Rhodesia 1967-68; Barrister Scottish Bar 1970-; QC (Scotland) 1985. Ed George Watson's College, Edinburgh; LLB MSc law, Edinburgh Univ

Kensington and Chelsea is one of the most select, desirable and luxurious residential areas of London, even Europe. It has the highest proportion of privately-rented housing in the country, and is home to over 70 embassies. There is a retail side to the seat as well, with Chelsea once the haunt of the most dedicated followers of fashionable shops, centring on the Kings Road. The seat has been a Conservative stronghold for many years.

KETTERING C gain

		Electorate	Turnout	Change from	2001	Electorate	Turnout
		81,887	68%	2001		78,946	68.1%
Hollobone P	**C**	**25,401**	**45.6%**	**2.1%**	**Lab**	**24,034**	**44.7%**
Sawford P	Lab	22,100	39.7%	-5%	C	23,369	43.5%
Aron R	LD	6,882	12.4%	2.2%	LD	5,469	10.2%
Clark R	UKIP	1,263	2.3%	0.7%	UKIP	880	1.6%
Lab to C swing	**3.6%**	**55,646**		**C maj 3,301**		**53,752**	**Lab maj 665**
				5.9%			1.2%

PHILIP HOLLOBONE b 7 Nov 1964. MP 2005-. Contested Lewisham East 1997, Kettering 2001 general elections. Councillor London Borough of Bromley 1990-94, Kettering District Council 2003-. Investment bank analyst (various) 1987-2000. Ed Dulwich College, London; BA modern history and economics, Lady Margaret Hall, Oxford

A mixture of semi-industrial towns, small villages and countryside in Northamptonshire, it was won by Labour in 1997 with a big swing and a tiny majority. In 2001 this was technically Labour's most vulnerable seat, but the Tories failed to regain it, and Phil Sawford's majority actually increased. The Tories didn't make the same mistake twice though, re-taking the seat in 2005 with a slender majority.

KILMARNOCK AND LOUDOUN — Lab hold

		Electorate	Turnout	2001
		72,851	60.9%	
Browne D	**Lab**	**20,976**	**47.3%**	No comparable results due to boundary changes
Coffey D	SNP	12,273	27.6%	
Smith G	C	5,026	11.3%	
Lang K	LD	4,945	11.1%	
Kerr H	SSP	833	1.9%	
Robertson R	UKIP	330	0.7%	
Lab to SNP swing (notional)	**5.4%**	**44,383**	**Lab maj 8,703** 19.6%	

DES BROWNE b 22 March 1952. MP for Kilmarnock and Loudoun 1997-2005, for new Kilmarnock and Loudoun 2005-. Chief Sec to Treasury 2005-. Minister of State: Home Office 2004-, Dept for Work and Pensions 2003-04. Parly Under-Sec NI Office 2001-03. PPS to: Adam Ingram 2000, Donald Dewar 1998-99. Member select cttees 1997-2001. Solicitor, advocate (called to Scottish Bar 1993). Council member Scotland Law Soc 1988-92. Member Scottish Civil Liberties Council 1976-. Chair Scottish Child Law Centre 1988-92. Ed LLB, Glasgow Univ.

Kilmarnock and Loudoun is enlarged by four rural wards east of the A713 and to the south of Kilmarnock, the largest town. Kilmarnock and the smaller Hurlford are industrial and largely vote Labour, while the towns of Darvel, Newmilns and Galston – nestled in the Irvine Valley which runs east-west across the middle of the seat – favour the SNP. The addition of Mauchline, Auchinleck, Catrine and Muirkirk in the south has increased Labour's traditional support base.

KINGSTON AND SURBITON — LD hold

		Electorate	Turnout	Change from	2001	Electorate	Turnout
		72,671	68.5%	2001		72,683	67.5%
Davey E	**LD**	**25,397**	**51.1%**	**-9.1%**	**LD**	**29,542**	**60.2%**
Davis K	C	16,431	33%	4.8%	C	13,866	28.2%
Parrott N	Lab	6,553	13.2%	4.4%	Lab	4,302	8.8%
Thornton B	UKIP	657	1.3%	0.4%	Greens	572	1.2%
Hayball J	SLP	366	0.7%	0.1%	UKIP	438	0.9%
Henson D	Veritas	200	0.4%		SLP	319	0.6%
Weiss R	Vote Dream	146	0.3%		UPP	54	0.1%
LD to C swing	**7%**	**49,750**		**LD maj 8,966** 18%		**49,093**	**LD maj 15,676** 31.9%

EDWARD DAVEY b 25 Dec 1965. MP 1997-. Lib Dem Shadow: Sec of State Education and Skills 2005-, Chief Sec Treasury 2001-02. Whip 1997-2000. Lib Dem spokes: Treasury (public spending and taxation) 1997-99, economy 1999-2001, London 2000-03, ODPM 2002-. Member select cttees: Procedure 1997-2000, Treasury 1999-2001. Member: Federal Policy cttee 1994-95, Lib Dem Cllrs Assocn. Senior Lib Dem MPs economics adviser. Management consultant. Royal Humane Soc hon testimonial. Ed BA PPE, Jesus Coll, Oxford; MSc econ, Birkbeck Coll, London.

Kingston had elected a Conservative in every election since 1918 and similarly Surbiton since its creation in 1955. However, in 1997 the Liberal Democrats managed to overturn this long tradition with a majority of just 56 votes. They increased this hugely in 2001 and fell back to a still substantial majority in 2005. The seat is prosperous and mainly residential but the shopping facilities in Kingston's town centre attract people from a wider area. The major local employers are the Borough Council and Kingston University.

KINGSWOOD — Lab hold

		Electorate	Turnout	Change from	2001	Electorate	Turnout
		84,400	66.7%	2001		80,532	65.4%
Berry R	**Lab**	**26,491**	**47%**	**-7.9%**	**Lab**	**28,903**	**54.9%**
Inksip O	C	18,618	33.1%	4.7%	C	14,941	28.4%
Brewer G	LD	9,089	16.1%	1.4%	LD	7,747	14.7%
Knight J	UKIP	1,444	2.6%	0.5%	UKIP	1,085	2.1%
Burnside D	Ind	669	1.2%				
Lab to C swing	**6.3%**	**56,311**		**Lab maj 7,873** 14%		**52,676**	**Lab maj 13,962** 26.5%

ROGER BERRY b 4 July 1948. MP 1992-. Member select cttees: Deregulation 1994-95, Trade and Industry 1995-97, 1997-. Chair all-party Lithuania group 2001-. Chair south and west group of Lab MPs 1997-. Cllr Avon County Council: dep leader 1985-86. Chair AMICUS parly group 1997-98. Economics lecturer. Highland Park/Spectator backbencher of the year 1994. Ed Dalton County Junior Sch; Huddersfield New Coll; BSc econ, Bristol Univ; DPhil econ, Sussex Univ.

This constituency was created from parts of the Wansdyke and Bristol constituencies. Kingswood is split between urban and rural areas and profits directly from its proximity to Bristol. Though it was initially a very marginal seat, Labour's grip on Kingswood since 1992 has become increasingly secure. A return to marginality is not impossible, but a very strong Conservative revival would be necessary to cause the Labour MP any real concern.

KIRKCALDY AND COWDENBEATH

		Electorate	Turnout		2001
		71,606	58.4%		
Brown G	**Lab**	**24,278**	**58.1%**		No comparable results due to boundary changes
Bath A	SNP	6,062	14.5%		
Cole-Hamilton A	LD	5,450	13%		
Randall S	C	4,308	10.3%		
West S	SSP	666	1.6%		
Adams P	UKIP	516	1.2%		
Parker J	Scot Senior	425	1%		
Kwantes E	Ind	47	0.1%		
Sargent P	Ind	44	0.1%		
SNP to Lab swing	**1.8%**	**41,796**		**Lab maj 18,216**	
(notional)				43.6%	

GORDON BROWN b 20 Feb 1951. MP for Dunfermline East 1983-2005, for Kirkcaldy and Cowdenbeath 2005-. Chancellor of Exchequer 1997-. Shadow: Chancellor of Exchequer 1992-97, Chief Sec to Treasury 1987-89. Opposition spokes trade and industry 1985-87, 1989-92. Head gen election campaign (strategy) 1999-2001. Former member Lab Party NEC. Chair Scotland Lab Party 1983-84. Joint hon sec Commonwealth parly assocn (UK branch) 1999-. Rector, lecturer, journalist, editor. PC 1996. Ed Kirkcaldy High Sch; MA, PhD, Edinburgh Univ.

Kirkaldy and Cowdenbeath sweeps up along the Firth of Forth from Kirkaldy through Burntisland to Dalgety Bay near the Forth road bridge, where it tapers inland, occupying a narrow strip of ex-mining country which includes the 'little Moscows' of Cowdenbeath and Lochgelly, part of the heart of the Fife coalfield. This was the home of heavy industry and, in its Fife heartland, Labour's domination here comes as no surprise.

KNOWSLEY NORTH AND SEFTON EAST

Lab hold

		Electorate	Turnout	Change from	2001	Electorate	Turnout
		70,403	52.6%	2001		70,781	53%
Howarth G	**Lab**	**23,461**	**63.3%**	**-3.4%**	**Lab**	**25,035**	**66.7%**
Clucas F	LD	7,192	19.4%	5.6%	C	6,108	16.3%
Purewal N	C	5,064	13.7%	-2.6%	LD	5,173	13.8%
McDermott M	BNP	872	2.4%		SLP	574	1.5%
Whatham S	SLP	464	1.2%	-0.3%	Ind	356	0.9%
					Ind	271	0.7%
Lab to LD swing	**4.5%**	**37,053**		**Lab maj 16,269**		**37,517**	**Lab maj 18,927**
				43.9%			50.4%

GEORGE HOWARTH b 29 June 1949. MP for Knowsley North 1986-97, for Knowsley North and Sefton East 1997-. Parly Under-Sec: N Ireland Office 1999-2001, Home Office 1997-99. Opposition spokes: environment/environmental protection 1989-94, home affairs 1994-97. Member Public Accounts select cttee 2002-03. Chair all-party betting/gaming group 2002-. Cllr: Huyton Urban DC 1971-75; Knowsley BC 1975-86: dep leader 1982-83. Teacher/engineer. Chief exec Wales TUC sponsored co op centre, Cardiff 1984-86. Ed BA soc sciences, Liverpool Poly.

Despite the introduction of middle-class areas like Maghull and Aintree, the Merseyside constituency of Knowsley North and Sefton East remains staunchly Labour. Following slum clearances, families were relocated to the new council estates of Kirkby, including the infamous Cantril Farm (renamed Stockbridge Village in the early 1980s) and Tower Hill, merely transposing the problems of the inner-city to these out-of-town sites.

KNOWSLEY SOUTH

Lab hold

		Electorate	Turnout	Change from	2001	Electorate	Turnout
		70,726	51.5%	2001		70,681	51.8%
O'Hara E	**Lab**	**24,820**	**68.1%**	**-3.2%**	**Lab**	**26,071**	**71.3%**
Smithson D	LD	7,132	19.6%	6.6%	LD	4,755	13%
Leadsom A	C	4,492	12.3%	0.7%	C	4,250	11.6%
					SLP	1,068	2.9%
					Ind	446	1.2%
Lab to LD swing	**4.9%**	**36,444**		**Lab maj 17,688**		**36,590**	**Lab maj 21,316**
				48.5%			58.3%

EDWARD O'HARA b 1 Oct 1937. MP Sept 1990- (by-election). Dep Speaker Westminster Hall 2001-. Member select cttees: Education 1992-96, Education and Employment 1996-97, Chairmen's Panel 1997-. Chair all-party groups: Greece 1997-, ageing and older people 1999-. Member: Socialist Ed Assocn, Co-op Party, Lab Movt in Europe, Council of Europe. Cllr Knowsley BC 1975-91. Patron Knowsley Arts Trust 1999-. Higher ed lecturer 1970-90. Ed Liverpool Collegiate Sch; MA literae humaniores, Magdalen Coll, Oxford.

This Merseyside division, made up of small residential communities and large Liverpool overspill estates, is now best known for containing Ford's Jaguar factory in Halewood. The seat derives its name from Knowsley Park (in neighbouring Knowsley North), the ancestral seat of local aristocrats the Stanleys (the Earls of Derby). Strongly Labour, Knowsley South was, in its previous Huyton incarnation, the seat of Harold Wilson for almost 40 years.

LAGAN VALLEY — DUP gain

		Electorate	Turnout	Change from	2001	Electorate	Turnout
		70,742	60.2%	2001		72,671	63.2%
Donaldson J	**DUP**	**23,289**	**54.7%**	**41.3%**	**UUP**	**25,966**	**56.5%**
McCrea B	UUP	9,172	21.5%	-35%	All	7,624	16.6%
Close S	All	4,316	10.1%	-6.5%	DUP	6,164	13.4%
Butler P	SF	3,197	7.5%	1.6%	SDLP	3,462	7.5%
Lewsley P	SDLP	2,598	6.1%	-1.4%	SF	2,725	5.9%
UUP to DUP swing	**38.2%**	**42,572**		**DUP maj 14,117**		**45,941**	**UUP maj 18,342**
				33.2%			39.9%

JEFFREY DONALDSON b 7 Dec 1962. MP 1997- (for DUP Jan 2004-). Ulster Unionist spokes 1997-2003. Democratic Unionist spokes 2004-. NI Assembly 1985-86, 2003-. Member select cttees: NI Affairs 1997-2000, Environ, Transport, Regional Affairs 2000-01, Regulatory Reform 2001-, Statutory Instruments 2001-, Transport 2004-. Vice-pres Ulster Unionist Council 2000-03. NI Forum 1996-98. Partner financial services/estate agency business 1986-. MPs agent/personal asst 1983-85. Ulster Defence Regiment 1980-85. Ed Castlereagh Coll.

This prosperous Northern Ireland constituency lies to the south-west of Belfast and contains most of Lisburn and a small part of Banbridge district councils. Only one in seven of the population is Catholic. It was one of the safest seats in the UK for the UUP but the defection of the MP Jeffrey Donaldson to the DUP was a body blow to the UUP and presaged a major re-alignment of unionist politics.

LANARK AND HAMILTON EAST — Lab hold

		Electorate	Turnout	2001
		73,736	59.1%	
Hood J	**Lab**	**20,072**	**46.1%**	No comparable results due to boundary changes
Grieve F	LD	8,125	18.6%	
Wilson J	SNP	7,746	17.8%	
Pettigrew R	C	5,576	12.8%	
Reilly D	SSP	802	1.8%	
Mackay D	UKIP	437	1%	
McFarlane D	Ind	416	1%	
Mawhinney R	OCV	415	1%	
Lab to LD swing	**5.9%**	**43,589**	**Lab maj 11,947**	
(notional)			27.4%	

JIMMY HOOD b 16 May 1948. MP for Clydesdale 1987-2005, for Lanark and Hamilton East 2005-. Member select cttees: Liaison 1992-97, 1997-, Defence 1997-2001, Chairmen's Panel 1997-, (chair) European Scrutiny 1998-. Member: Scottish parly group Lab MPs, Co-operative Party. Cllr Newark and Sherwood DC 1979-87. NUM official 1973-87, leader Notts striking miners 1984-85 nat miners' strike. Mining engineer 1964-87. Ed Lesmahagow Higher Grade Sch; Coatbridge Coll; Nottingham Univ.

This seat begins south-east of the Glasgow periphery, widening into the tranquil Clyde Valley. The eastern half of Hamilton, Uddingston and Bothwell are the main towns of the urban strip, while the rural portion includes Carluke, Lanark and surrounding farms and villages. Though white-collar companies have replaced Clydeside heavy industry in this area, Labour and the SNP are the only parties with a significant support base, with Labour in ample majority.

WEST LANCASHIRE — Lab hold

		Electorate	Turnout	Change from	2001	Electorate	Turnout
		74,777	57.7%	2001		73,046	58.8%
Cooper R	**Lab**	**20,746**	**48.1%**	**-6.4%**	**Lab**	**23,404**	**54.5%**
Doran A	C	14,662	34%	2%	C	13,761	32%
Kemp R	LD	6,059	14%	2.4%	LD	4,966	11.6%
Freeman A	UKIP	871	2%		Ind	523	1.2%
Garrett S	Eng Dem	525	1.2%		Ind	317	0.7%
Braid D	Clause 28	292	0.7%				
Lab to C swing	**4.2%**	**43,155**		**Lab maj 6,084**		**42,971**	**Lab maj 9,643**
				14.1%			22.4%

ROSIE COOPER b 5 September 1950. MP 2005-. Contested Liverpool Broadgreen 1992 general election, NW region 2004 European Parliament election. PR and communications professional; Director Merseyside Centre for Deaf People. Liverpool City councillor 1973-2000. Lord Mayor of Liverpool 1992-93.

The constituency of West Lancashire lies to the north of the Merseyside conurbation. Largely rural, it includes the new town of Skelmersdale and the old town of Ormskirk. Like most of the seats in the locality, it is now in the large group of fairly safe Labour seats, although not as rock solid as the Merseyside divisions.

LANCASTER AND WYRE — C gain

		Electorate 80,739	Turnout 64.5%	Change from 2001	2001	Electorate 78,964	Turnout 66.3%
Wallace B	**C**	**22,266**	**42.8%**	**0.6%**	**Lab**	**22,556**	**43.1%**
Sacks A	Lab	18,095	34.8%	-8.3%	C	22,075	42.2%
Langhorn S	LD	8,453	16.2%	5.9%	LD	5,383	10.3%
Barry J	Greens	2,278	4.4%	1.4%	Greens	1,595	3%
Mander J	UKIP	969	1.9%	0.5%	UKIP	741	1.4%
Lab to C swing	**4.5%**	**52,061**		**C maj 4,171** 8%		**52,350**	**Lab maj 481** 0.9%

BEN WALLACE b 15 May 1970. MP 2005-. Ski instructor Austrian National Ski School 1988-89; Army officer Scots Guard 1990-98; EU and overseas director Qinetiq 2003-. Ed Millfield School, Somerset; Royal Military Academy, Sandhurst 1989

Created in 1995, this mainly rural and residential Lancashire seat is flanked on three sides by the staunch Tory strongholds of Fylde, Morecambe and Ribble Valley, and the Labour held Blackpool South on the other. The City of Lancaster is the largest urban area in the constituency and its University is one of the main employers. A marginal seat since its conception, it became a relatively solid Conservative seat following the 2005 general election.

LEEDS CENTRAL — Lab hold

		Electorate 62,939	Turnout 46.4%	Change from 2001	2001	Electorate 65,653	Turnout 41.6%
Benn H	**Lab**	**17,526**	**60.1%**	**-6.8%**	**Lab**	**18,277**	**66.9%**
Coleman R	LD	5,660	19.4%	6.2%	C	3,896	14.3%
Cattell B	C	3,865	13.2%	-1.1%	LD	3,607	13.2%
Collett M	BNP	1,201	4.1%		UKIP	775	2.8%
Sewards P	UKIP	494	1.7%	-1.1%	SA	751	2.8%
Dear M	Ind	189	0.6%				
Taiwo O	Ind	126	0.4%				
Fitzgerald J	AFC	125	0.4%				
Lab to LD swing	**6.5%**	**29,186**		**Lab maj 11,866** 40.7%		**27,306**	**Lab maj 14,381** 52.7%

HILARY BENN b 26 Nov 1953. MP June 1999- (by-election). Sec of State International Devt 2003-; Min of State Dept for Internat Devt 2003; PPS: Home Office 2002-03, Dept for Internat Devt 2001-02. Member Environment, Transport and Regional Affairs 1999-2001. Cllr London Borough of Ealing: dep leader 1986-90. Chair London Authorities Education Cttee Assocn 1989-90. MSF research officer/head of policy/comms 1975-97, David Blunkett special adviser 1997-99. PC 2003. Ed Holland Park Comp Sch; BA Russian/East European studies, Sussex Univ.

Surrounding the smart shopping areas and booming business quarter of Leeds city centre, this is nevertheless the city's most deprived constituency, and solidly Labour. Hilary Benn, Blairite son of Tony, won it in a by-election in 1999 after the premature death of Derek Fatchett, with the lowest peacetime turnout in history, less than 20 per cent. Even in 2005 the turnout was the tenth lowest in the country.

LEEDS EAST — Lab hold

		Electorate 54,691	Turnout 55%	Change from 2001	2001	Electorate 56,552	Turnout 51.4%
Mudie G	**Lab**	**17,799**	**59.2%**	**-3.7%**	**Lab**	**18,290**	**62.9%**
Tear A	LD	6,221	20.7%	7.2%	C	5,647	19.4%
Ponniah D	C	5,557	18.5%	-0.9%	LD	3,923	13.5%
Socrates P	Ind	500	1.7%	1.2%	UKIP	634	2.2%
					SLP	419	1.4%
					Ind	142	0.5%
Lab to LD swing	**5.5%**	**30,077**		**Lab maj 11,578** 38.5%		**29,055**	**Lab maj 12,643** 43.5%

GEORGE MUDIE b 6 Feb 1945. MP 1992-. Parly Under-Sec Dept for Education and Employment 1998-99. Whip: Opposition 1994-97, 1997-98. Member select cttees: Accommodation and Works 1992-98; Public Accounts 1994-95; Selection 1995-99, Finance and Services 1997-99, Treasury 2001-. Former leader Leeds City Council. NUPE engineer/union official. Ed local state schools.

George Mudie succeeded Denis Healey, erstwhile Chancellor and Deputy Leader of the Labour Party, in 1992 and has steadily increased his majority here. 38 per cent of housing is council property, the greatest proportion being in the Seacroft area. Harehills houses a large Asian community, whereas Halton contains almost solely white residents. Unemployment is above the national average, and those that do work are likely to do so in skilled manual trades.

LEEDS NORTH EAST — Lab hold

		Electorate	Turnout	Change from	2001	Electorate	Turnout
		63,304	65.5%	2001		64,263	61.9%
Hamilton F	**Lab**	**18,632**	**44.9%**	**-4.2%**	**Lab**	**19,540**	**49.1%**
Lobley M	C	13,370	32.2%	0.9%	C	12,451	31.3%
Brown J	LD	8,427	20.3%	4.4%	LD	6,325	15.9%
Foote C	Green S	1,038	2.5%		GreenS	770	1.9%
					UKIP	382	1%
					SLP	173	0.4%
					Ind	132	0.3%
Lab to C swing	**2.6%**	**41,467**		**Lab maj 5,262**		**39,773**	**Lab maj 7,089**
				12.7%			17.8%

FABIAN HAMILTON b 12 April 1955. MP 1997-. Member select cttees: Administration 1997-2001, Foreign Affairs 2001-. Chair all-party business services group 2001-. Vice-chair Lab Friends of Israel. Member Co-operative Party. Cllr Leeds City Council 1987-98. Taxi driver 1978-79, graphic designer 1979-94, Apple Mac consultant/dealer 1994-97. Ed Brentwood Sch; BA soc sciences, York Univ.

This seat represented the winning post for Labour in 1997. Half prosperous suburbs, half under-populated agricultural land, Leeds North East has gradually been prised from the Conservative grasp, eventually giving Labour a majority of just under 7,000 in 1997. This shift was helped by a growth in student and minority populations.

LEEDS NORTH WEST — LD gain

		Electorate	Turnout	Change from	2001	Electorate	Turnout
		71,644	62.4%	2001		72,941	58.2%
Mulholland G	**LD**	**16,612**	**37.2%**	**10.3%**	**Lab**	**17,794**	**41.9%**
Blake J	Lab	14,735	33%	-8.9%	C	12,558	29.6%
Lee G	C	11,510	25.7%	-3.9%	LD	11,431	26.9%
Hemingway M	Greens	1,128	2.5%		UKIP	668	1.6%
Knowles A	England	545	1.2%				
Sutton J	Green S	181	0.4%				
Lab to LD swing	**9.6%**	**44,711**		**LD maj 1,877**		**42,451**	**Lab maj 5,236**
				4.2%			12.3%

GREGORY MULHOLLAND b 31 August 1970. MP 2005. Leeds City Council: Councillor 2003-, Lead member, corporate services 2004-. Account director, several leading agencies 1997-2002. Member Institute of Sales Promotion 1999; Member CAMRA (Campaign for Real Ale); Co-founder CENA (Campaign for an English National Anthem); Campaigner CAFOD

In 1997 Labour snatched this middle-class, residential constituency from its long-standing Conservative representation with a comfortable majority of just under 4,000. They lost it in 2005 to the Lib Dems. The seat radiates out from Headingly in inner city Leeds, through the suburbs of Weetwood and Cookridge to the rural areas of Bramhope and Otley. Headingly, once a staunchly Conservative up-market part of the city, is now a combination of run down inner-city and student bedsitter-land. Leeds-Bradford Airport is situated here.

LEEDS WEST — Lab hold

		Electorate	Turnout	Change from	2001	Electorate	Turnout
		62,882	53.6%	2001		64,342	49.9%
Battle J	**Lab**	**18,704**	**55.5%**	**-6.6%**	**Lab**	**19,943**	**62.1%**
Finlay D	LD	5,894	17.5%	7.1%	C	5,008	15.6%
Metcalfe T	C	4,807	14.3%	-1.3%	LD	3,350	10.4%
Blackburn D	Greens	2,519	7.5%	-0.5%	Greens	2,573	8%
Day J	BNP	1,166	3.5%		UKIP	758	2.4%
Sewards D	UKIP	628	1.9%	-0.5%	Lib	462	1.4%
Lab to LD swing	**6.9%**	**33,718**		**Lab maj 12,810**		**32,094**	**Lab maj 14,935**
				38%			46.5%

JOHN BATTLE b 26 April 1951. MP 1987-. Minister of State: FCO 1999-2001, DTI 1997-99. Shadow Minister: Energy 1995-87, Science and Technology 1994-95, Housing 1993-94. Opposition whip 1990. Opposition environment spokes 1992-94. Member Internat Devt select cttee 2001-. Chair all-party groups: CAFOD 2001-, cast metal 2003-. Cllr Leeds CC 1980-87. Joint chair British Trade Internat Board 1999-2001. Research asst 1979-83. Church Action on Poverty nat co-ordinator 1983-87. PC 2002. Ed BA English, Leeds Univ.

This constituency, on the River Aire and Leeds to Liverpool canal, consists of mixed council and owner occupied housing stretching from the inner city out towards the edge of Leeds. There is light engineering and service industries in the constituency, although most workers travel into the city centre. Armley and Bramley have their own distinctive town centres.

LEICESTER EAST — Lab hold

		Electorate 66,383	Turnout 62.2%	Change from 2001	2001	Electorate 65,526	Turnout 62.1%
Vaz K	**Lab**	**24,015**	**58.1%**	**0.5%**	**Lab**	**23,402**	**57.6%**
Fernandes S	C	8,139	19.7%	-4.8%	C	9,960	24.5%
Cooper S	LD	7,052	17.1%	4.8%	LD	4,989	12.3%
Brown C	Veritas	1,666	4%		SLP	837	2.1%
Smalley V	SLP	434	1.1%	-1%	BNP	772	1.9%
					Ind	701	1.7%
C to Lab swing	**2.7%**	**41,306**		**Lab maj 15,876** 38.4%		**40,661**	**Lab maj 13,442** 33.1%

KEITH VAZ b 26 Nov 1956. MP 1987-. Min of State FCO 1999-2001; Parly Sec Lord Chancellor's Dept 1999; PPS to: Solicitors General Lord Falconer of Thoroton 1997-98, Ross Cranston 1998-99; John Morris as Attorney General 1997-99. Opposition environment spokes 1992-97. Chair: all-party Yemen group 2003-, Lab Party race action group 1983-. Lab Party regional exec 1994-96. British Council board member 1999-. Barrister. Ed Latymer Upper Sch, Hammersmith; BA law/MA/MCFI, Gonville and Caius Coll, Cambridge; London Coll of Law.

Of the three Leicester seats, East is safest for Labour. It has been called the 'city of a thousand trades'. Although the most famous of these trades – shoemaking – is now in decline, hosiery, knitwear and engineering continue to flourish. 56 per cent of the workforce are skilled or partly-skilled manual workers. Aside from industry, a residential element is matched by the third largest Asian population in the land.

LEICESTER SOUTH — Lab hold

		Electorate 72,310	Turnout 58.6%	Change from 2001	2001	Electorate 72,674	Turnout 58%
Soulsby P	**Lab**	**16,688**	**39.4%**	**-15.1%**	**Lab**	**22,958**	**54.5%**
Gill P	LD	12,971	30.6%	13.4%	C	9,715	23.1%
McElwee M	C	7,549	17.8%	-5.3%	LD	7,243	17.2%
Ridley Y	Respect	2,720	6.4%		Greens	1,217	2.9%
Follett M	Greens	1,379	3.2%	0.3%	SLP	676	1.6%
Roseblade K	Veritas	573	1.4%		UKIP	333	0.8%
Roberts D	SLP	315	0.7%	-0.9%			
Lord P	Ind	216	0.5%				
Lab to LD swing	**14.3%**	**42,411**		**Lab maj 3,717** 8.8%		**42,142**	**Lab maj 13,243** 31.4%

PETER SOULSBY b 27 Dec 1948. MP 2005-. Contested Leicester South 2004 by-election. Leicester City Council: Councillor 1973-2003, Council leader 1981-94, 1995-99. Special educational needs teacher 1973-90. Ed City of Leicester College; Leicester University

Once the most marginal seat in the country, Leicester South looked safe for Labour until a by-election in 2004 put the seat in Liberal Democrat hands. Labour won it back in the general election of 2005, but the seat is now firmly marginal. Its 26 per cent Asian population is smaller than in Leciester East, but is nonetheless massive. The seat is not affluent – more than half the working population are employed in manual occupations, levels of home ownership and car ownership are among the lowest in England and Wales and unemployment is above the national average.

LEICESTER WEST — Lab hold

		Electorate 62,389	Turnout 53.2%	Change from 2001	2001	Electorate 65,267	Turnout 50.9%
Hewitt P	**Lab**	**17,184**	**51.7%**	**-2.5%**	**Lab**	**18,014**	**54.2%**
Richardson S	C	8,114	24.4%	-0.8%	C	8,375	25.2%
Haq Z	LD	5,803	17.5%	2.2%	LD	5,085	15.3%
Forse G	Greens	1,571	4.7%	1.5%	Greens	1,074	3.2%
Score S	SAP	552	1.7%		SLP	350	1.1%
					SAP	321	1%
Lab to C swing	**0.9%**	**33,224**		**Lab maj 9,070** 27.3%		**33,219**	**Lab maj 9,639** 29%

PATRICIA HEWITT b 2 Dec 1948. MP 1997-. Sec of State: Health 2005-, Trade and Industry/Minister Women and Equality, 2001-05; Minister of State Dept of Trade and Industry 1999-2001, Econ Sec Treasury 1998-99. Member Soc Security select cttee 1997-98. Member Lab social justice campaign. Chair Science/Technology Council. Age Concern PR officer 1971-73. Gen sec Nat Civil Liberties Council 1974-83. Gen sec to Neil Kinnock 1983-89: press sec, policy co-ordinator; dep dir Public Policy Research Inst. PC 2001. Ed BA Eng lit, Newnham Coll, Cambridge.

Leicester West now has the second highest majority for Labour of all the city's three seats, following the decimation of the Labour vote in Leicester South. It was represented for many years by Greville Janner, who retired in 1997 and was succeeded by Patricia Hewitt (one-time adviser to Neil Kinnock). Unemployment is relatively high as half the workforce are in skilled or partly skilled employment. The ethnic population is smaller than in the neighbouring seats.

NORTH WEST LEICESTERSHIRE — Lab hold

		Electorate	Turnout	Change from	2001	Electorate	Turnout
		70,519	66.8%	2001		68,414	65.8%
Taylor D	**Lab/C**	**21,449**	**45.5%**	**-6.6%**	**Lab/C**	**23,431**	**52.1%**
Le Page N	C	16,972	36%	2.1%	C	15,274	33.9%
Keyes R	LD	5,682	12.1%	1.8%	LD	4,651	10.3%
Blunt J	UKIP	1,563	3.3%	1%	UKIP	1,021	2.3%
Potter C	BNP	1,474	3.1%		Ind	632	1.4%
Lab/C to C swing	**4.4%**	**47,140**		**Lab/C maj 4,477**		**45,009**	**Lab/C maj 8,157**
				9.5%			18.1%

DAVID TAYLOR b 22 Aug 1946. MP 1997-. Member select cttees: Modernisation of HoC 1999-2001, Environment, Food and Rural Affairs 2001-, Chairmen's Panel 2002-. Chair all-party smoking and health group 2003-. Member Lab electoral reform campaign. Cllr: NW Leics DC 1981-87, 1992-95. JP 1985-. NALGO dept steward/auditor 1985-97. Computer manager/accountant/lecturer. Ed Chartered Public Finance Accountant, Leicester Poly/Lanchester Poly; BA maths/computing, Open Univ.

North West Leicestershire covers much of the county's old coalfields. The largest town is Coalville and the traditional Conservative areas include the historic small town of Ashby de la Zouch and the area around Castle Donnington. A third of households are headed by skilled manual workers. The seat was Tory from 1983 to 1997, when Labour took it with a huge swing. Following a swing away from labour in 2005, the seat has reverted to its marginal status.

LEIGH — Lab hold

		Electorate	Turnout	Change from	2001	Electorate	Turnout
		72,473	50.4%	2001		71,054	49.7%
Burnham A	**Lab**	**23,097**	**63.3%**	**-1.2%**	**Lab**	**22,783**	**64.5%**
Wedderburn L	C	5,825	16%	-2.2%	C	6,421	18.2%
Crowther D	LD	4,962	13.6%	0.8%	LD	4,524	12.8%
Franzen I	CAP	2,189	6%		SLP	820	2.3%
Hampson T	LCA	415	1.1%		UKIP	750	2.1%
C to Lab swing	**0.5%**	**36,488**		**Lab maj 17,272**		**35,298**	**Lab maj 16,362**
				47.3%			46.4%

ANDY BURNHAM b 7 Jan 1970. MP 2001-. Parly Under-Sec Home Office 2005-, PPS to: Ruth Kelly 2004-05, David Blunkett 2003-04. Member Health select cttee 2001-03. Treasurer all-party rugby league group 2002-. Member Co-operative Party. Researcher to Tessa Jowell MP 1994-97. Parly officer NHS Confederation 1997. Football Task Force admininstrator 1997-98. Special adviser to Chris Smith 1998-2001. Chair Supporters Direct 2002-. Ed St Aelred's RC High Sch, Merseyside; BA English, Fitzwilliam Coll, Cambridge.

Leigh is on the old Lancashire coalfield, part of a series of such seats that have returned Labour MPs since the early twentieth century. The seat is to the south-west of Bolton and Wigan, nestled between Manchester and Liverpool and is made up of the eponymous town and several smaller working-class communities such as Atherton and Hindley. Light industry, in the form of printing and electronics, has replaced the declining mining and textile industries.

LEOMINSTER — C hold

		Electorate	Turnout	Change from	2001	Electorate	Turnout
		63,121	77.3%	2001		68,695	68%
Wiggin B	**C**	**25,407**	**52.1%**	**3.1%**	**C**	**22,879**	**49%**
Williams C	LD	12,220	25%	-1.8%	LD	12,512	26.8%
Bell P	Lab	7,424	15.2%	-1.6%	Lab	7,872	16.8%
Norman F	Greens	2,191	4.5%	0.9%	Greens	1,690	3.6%
Venables P	UKIP	1,551	3.2%	-0.2%	UKIP	1,590	3.4%
					Ind	186	0.4%
LD to C swing	**2.5%**	**48,793**		**C maj 13,187**		**46,729**	**C maj 10,367**
				27%			22.2%

BILL WIGGIN 4 June 1966. MP 2001-. Shadow: Sec of State Wales 2003-, Minister Environment, Food and Rural Affairs 2005, 2003. Member select cttees: Welsh Affairs 2001-03, Transport, Local Govt and Regions 2001-02, Environment, Food and Rural Affairs 2002-. Vice-chair all-party chocolate and confectionery industry group 2002-. Member 1922 cttee exec 2002-03. Governor Hammersmith and West London Coll 1995-98. Banker. Manager structured products Commerzbank 1998-. City of London Freeman. Ed Eton Coll; BA econ Univ Coll of North Wales.

Leominster is a safe Tory rural retreat, its landscape almost entirely agricultural, and farming providing the livelihood for a large proportion of the population. The few market towns are pretty, quaint affairs, Tenbury renowned for its half timbered architecture, while the only industry is found in Leominster. The scenery is often exquisite, with the Malvern Hills to the south and east, and the Welsh mountains visible to the west.

LEWES

LD hold

		Electorate 67,073	Turnout 69.4%	Change from 2001	2001	Electorate 66,332	Turnout 68.5%
Baker N	**LD**	**24,376**	**52.4%**	**-3.9%**	**LD**	**25,588**	**56.3%**
Love R	C	15,902	34.2%	-0.7%	C	15,878	34.9%
Black R	Lab	4,169	9%	1.7%	Lab	3,317	7.3%
Murray S	Greens	1,071	2.3%		UKIP	650	1.4%
Petley J	UKIP	1,034	2.2%	0.8%			
LD to C swing	**1.6%**	**46,552**		**LD maj 8,474** 18.2%		**45,433**	**LD maj 9,710** 21.4%

NORMAN BAKER b 26 July 1957. MP 1997-. Lib Dem Shadow Sec of State Environment 2002-. Environment and transport spokes 1997-. Member select cttees: Environmental Audit 1997-2000, Broadcasting 2000-01, Joint Cttee on Human Rights 2001-03. Chair: all-party environment group 2003-. Lib Dem HoC environment campaigner 1989-90. Cllr: Lewes DC 1987-99 (leader 1991-97), East Sussex County Council 1989-97. Teacher/lecturer/company dir 1978-83, 1985-97. Ed Royal Liberty Sch, Gidea Park; BA German, Royal Holloway Coll, London Univ.

This East Sussex constituency extends from Ditchling village on the western to Polegate on the eastern border. It stretches from rural Newick in the north to the port of Newhaven on the south coast. The picturesque town of Lewes is small but politically important. Many commute into Lewes but also to jobs in London or Brighton. The Liberal Democrats' progress has been remarkable here, overturning more than a century of Conservative tenure.

LEWISHAM DEPTFORD

Lab hold

		Electorate 59,018	Turnout 51.5%	Change from 2001	2001	Electorate 60,275	Turnout 48.3%
Ruddock J	**Lab**	**16,902**	**55.6%**	**-9.4%**	**Lab**	**18,915**	**65%**
Blango C	LD	5,091	16.8%	5.1%	C	3,622	12.4%
Cartlidge J	C	3,773	12.4%		LD	3,409	11.7%
Johnson D	Greens	3,367	11.1%	4.6%	Greens	1,901	6.5%
Page I	SAP	742	2.4%		SAP	1,260	4.3%
Holland D	UKIP	518	1.7%				
Lab to LD swing	**7.3%**	**30,393**		**Lab maj 11,811** 38.9%		**29,107**	**Lab maj 15,293** 52.5%

JOAN RUDDOCK b 28 Dec 1943. MP 1987-. Parly Under-Sec Women 1997-98. Opposition spokes: transport 1989-92, home affairs 1992-94, environmental protection 1994-97. Member select cttees: Modernisation of HoC 2001-, Environment, Food and Rural Affairs 2003-. Promoted various Bills 1999-2003. Vice-chair various all-party groups 2002-. Member IPU 2001-. Chair CND 1981-85. Dir: research/publications Shelter, Nat Homeless Campaign; Oxford Housing Aid Centre. Council officer/CAB manager. Ed BSc botany, Imperial Coll, London Univ.

This is a south London inner-city Labour stronghold with a 32 per cent non-white population, the vast majority of whom are black. Only 38 per cent of homes are owner-occupied. Unemployment runs at about twice the national average. The seat stretches from the Thames and Deptford in the north through New Cross and Brockley, Honor Oak Park and Ladywell in the south. Goldsmiths' College, part of the University of London, is situated in this seat.

LEWISHAM EAST

Lab hold

		Electorate 59,135	Turnout 52.6%	Change from 2001	2001	Electorate 56,657	Turnout 53%
Prentice B	**Lab**	**14,263**	**45.8%**	**-7.8%**	**Lab**	**16,116**	**53.6%**
Cleverly J	C	7,512	24.1%	0.3%	C	7,157	23.8%
Thomas R	LD	6,787	21.8%	5.4%	LD	4,937	16.4%
Baker A	Greens	1,243	4%		BNP	1,005	3.3%
Tarling A	UKIP	697	2.2%	1%	SA	464	1.5%
Franklin B	NF	625	2%		UKIP	361	1.2%
Lab to C swing	**4.1%**	**31,127**		**Lab maj 6,751** 21.7%		**30,040**	**Lab maj 8,959** 29.8%

BRIDGET PRENTICE b 28 Dec 1952. MP 1992-. Parly Under-Sec Dept for Constitutional Affairs 2005-. PPS to: Lord Irvine of Lairg 1999-2001, Brian Wilson 1998-99. Whip: opposition 1995-97, asst govt 1997-98, 2003-05. Member select cttees: Home Affairs 2001-03, Court of Referees 2002-. Leadership Campaign Team Co-ordinator 1995-96. Cllr Hammersmith and Fulham 1986-92. JP 1985-. Teacher 1974-86, careers head 1984-88. Ed MA Eng lit/mod hist Glasgow Univ; PGCE, London Univ; LLB, South Bank Univ, London.

Labour MP Bridget Prentice won Lewisham East in 1992 from former Sports Minister and Olympic rower, Colin Moynihan, with a majority of 1,095. In 1997 she dramatically increased it to 12,127. This is a socially mixed seat with affluent Blackheath in the north giving way to Grove Park and Downham in the south. About half the homes in the seat are owner-occupied, though a third are council-rented.

LEWISHAM WEST — Lab hold

		Electorate	Turnout	Change from	2001	Electorate	Turnout
		58,349	54.7%	2001		59,176	52.1%
Dowd J	**Lab**	**16,611**	**52%**	**-9.1%**	**Lab**	**18,816**	**61.1%**
Feakes A	LD	6,679	20.9%	7.4%	C	6,896	22.4%
McAnuff E	C	6,396	20%	-2.4%	LD	4,146	13.5%
Long N	Greens	1,464	4.6%		UKIP	485	1.6%
Winton J	UKIP	773	2.4%	0.8%	Ind	472	1.5%
Lab to LD swing	**8.3%**	**31,923**		**Lab maj 9,932**		**30,815**	**Lab maj 11,920**
				31.1%			38.7%

JIM DOWD b 5 March 1951. MP 1992-. Whip: opposition 1993-95, govt 1997-2001. Opposition spokes Northern Ireland 1995-97. Member Health select cttee 2001-. Chair all-party small shops group 2003-. Member Co-operative Party. Cllr London Borough of Lewisham 1974-94: mayor 1992. Member Lewisham and North Southwark District Health Authority. Member various charities. Electronics engineer (telecomms engineer Plessey Company 1973-92). Ed Sedgehill Comp Sch, London; London Nautical Sch.

This politically swinging part of Lewisham has some light industrial sites, but it is typified by having the better residential areas. Just over half the homes are owner-occupied, with council housing at 27 per cent being the lowest proportion in the borough. The black population, though nowhere near as large as that in Deptford, is significant at 14 per cent, and unemployment is high.

LEYTON AND WANSTEAD — Lab hold

		Electorate	Turnout	Change from	2001	Electorate	Turnout
		60,444	55%	2001		61,818	54.5%
Cohen H	**Lab**	**15,234**	**45.8%**	**-12.2%**	**Lab**	**19,558**	**58%**
Khan M	LD	8,377	25.2%	9.2%	C	6,654	19.7%
Foster J	C	7,393	22.2%	2.5%	LD	5,389	16%
Gunstock A	Greens	1,523	4.6%	1.5%	Greens	1,030	3.1%
Jones N	UKIP	591	1.8%	0.7%	SA	709	2.1%
Robertson M	Ind	155	0.5%		UKIP	378	1.1%
Lab to LD swing	**10.7%**	**33,273**		**Lab maj 6,857**		**33,718**	**Lab maj 12,904**
				20.6%			38.3%

HARRY COHEN b 10 Dec 1949. MP for Leyton 1983-97, for Wanstead 1997-. Member Defence select cttee 1997-2001. All-party groups: sec race and community 2002-, treasurer Tibet 2003-. Member UK delegation to North Atlantic Assembly 1992-. Cllr Waltham Forest BC 1972-83. Member Waltham Forest Health Authority 1972-83. Accountant/auditor (incl auditor NALGO). Ed George Gascoigne Sec Mod; East Ham Tech Coll Chartered Inst of Public Finance and Accountancy; MSc pol/admin, Birkbeck Coll, London Univ.

Leyton has a feel of the inner-city in an outer London borough, with a high ethnic minority population and overcrowded accommodation, much of it council-rented. Wanstead, however, is far more suburban and owner-occupied. The majority of the workforce is non-manual but of these, the number of professionals is only around the national average.

LICHFIELD — C hold

		Electorate	Turnout	Change from	2001	Electorate	Turnout
		65,565	66.7%	2001		63,794	65.3%
Fabricant M	**C**	**21,274**	**48.6%**	**-0.5%**	**C**	**20,480**	**49.1%**
Gardner N	Lab	14,194	32.4%	-6.1%	Lab	16,054	38.5%
Jackson I	LD	6,804	15.6%	4.9%	LD	4,462	10.7%
McKenzie M	UKIP	1,472	3.4%	1.8%	UKIP	684	1.6%
Lab to C swing	**2.8%**	**43,744**		**C maj 7,080**		**41,680**	**C maj 4,426**
				16.2%			10.6%

MICHAEL FABRICANT b 12 June 1950. MP for Mid-Staffs 1992-97, for Lichfield 1997-. Shadow Minister: Economic Affairs 2003-05, Trade and Industry 2003. Opposition whip 2005-. PPS to Michael Jack 1996-97. Member select cttees incl chair Information 2001-03. Chair all-party Royal Marines group 1999-. Member: 1922 cttee exec 2001-03, Con Way Forward, Inter-Parly Union. Lawyer/chartered electronics engineer. Ed BSc econ/law, Loughborough Univ; MSc systems/econometrics, Sussex Univ; PhD econometrics/forecasting, Oxford Univ/ London Univ/S California Univ, USA.

The cathedral city of Lichfield is in itself fairly conservative. The seat has a a majority of better-off non-manual workers. Council housing amounts to only about 15 per cent of the total, and unemployment is low. There is a little agricultural land, but the landscape outside Lichfield is typically made up of small towns – Burntwood is one of the largest urbanised parishes in the country.

LINCOLN

Lab hold

		Electorate	Turnout	Change from	2001	Electorate	Turnout
		65,203	56.5%	2001		66,299	56%
Merron G	**Lab**	**16,724**	**45.4%**	**-8.5%**	**Lab**	**20,003**	**53.9%**
McCartney K	C	12,110	32.9%	1.7%	C	11,583	31.2%
Gabriel L	LD	6,715	18.2%	5.5%	LD	4,703	12.7%
Smith N	UKIP	1,308	3.6%	1.3%	UKIP	836	2.3%
Lab to C swing	**5.1%**	**36,857**		**Lab maj 4,614**		**37,125**	**Lab maj 8,420**
				12.5%			22.7%

GILLIAN MERRON b 12 April 1959. MP 1997-. PPS to: Dr John Reid 2001-02, Ministers of State Ministry of Defence: Baroness Symons of Vernham Dean 1999-2001, Doug Henderson 1998-99. Whip: asst govt 2002-04, govt 2004-. Member Trade and Industry select cttee 1997-98. Member Co-operative Party. Chair E Mids regional Lab MPs group 1999-2002. Business devt adviser/local govt officer 1982-87. NUPE (now UNISON) official 1987-95; UNISON senior regional Lincolnshire officer 1995-97. Ed Wanstead High Sch; BSc management sciences, Lancaster Univ.

Lincoln is an ancient town, parts of it still surviving from Roman times, and with a magnificent cathedral that dates back to 1070. The Lincoln campus of the new University of Humberside opened here in 1996. More than a quarter of homes are council-rented, and manual workers make up the majority of the economically active population. Lincoln is looking a decreasingly safe Labour seat, with support for the Conservatives, the Liberal Democrats and UKIP creeping up.

LINLITHGOW AND EAST FALKIRK

Lab hold

		Electorate	Turnout		2001
		76,739	60.4%		
Connarty M	**Lab**	**22,121**	**47.7%**		No comparable results due to boundary changes
Guthrie G	SNP	10,919	23.5%		
Glenn S	LD	7,100	15.3%		
Veitch M	C	5,486	11.8%		
Hendry A	SSP	763	1.6%		
Lab to SNP swing	**1.2%**	**46,389**		**Lab maj 11,202**	
(notional)				24.2%	

MICHAEL CONNARTY b 3 Sept 1947. MP for Falkirk East 1992-2005, for Linlithgow and East Falkirk 2005-. PPS to Tom Clarke 1997-98. Member select cttees: Information 1997-2001, European Scrutiny 1998-. Chair: all-party groups, Stirlingshire Co-op Party 1990-92, Scottish Lab MPs group 1998-99. Internat Parly Union, Commonwealth Parly Assocn. Cllr Stirling DC: leader 1980-90. JP 1977-90. Pres student assocn, chair Stirling Economic Devt Co, teacher. Member Socialist ed assocn. Ed BA econ, Stirling Univ; Glasgow Univ; DCE, Jordanhill Coll of Ed.

The southern and Forthside parts of Falkirk East are combined with all but the south-eastern tip of Linlithgow to form this new seat in Scotland's central industrial belt. Labour comfortably outstripped the SNP in the old Linlithgow seat. However, the SNP does rather well in Grangemouth and Bo'ness. Bathgate and Armadale also favour the SNP in local elections, tightening the gap between the parties.

LIVERPOOL GARSTON

Lab hold

		Electorate	Turnout	Change from	2001	Electorate	Turnout
		63,669	54.9%	2001		65,094	50.2%
Eagle M	**Lab**	**18,900**	**54%**	**-7.4%**	**Lab**	**20,043**	**61.4%**
Keaveney P	LD	11,707	33.5%	10.4%	LD	7,549	23.1%
Rudd A	C	3,424	9.8%	-5.7%	C	5,059	15.5%
Kearney K	UKIP	780	2.2%				
Oatley D	WRP	163	0.5%				
Lab to LD swing	**8.9%**	**34,974**		**Lab maj 7,193**		**32,651**	**Lab maj 12,494**
				20.6%			38.3%

MARIA EAGLE b 17 Feb 1961. MP 1997-. Parly Under-Sec: Dept for Education and Skills 2005-, Dept for Work and Pensions (Minister for Disabled People) 2001-05; PPS to John Hutton 1999-2001. Member Public Accounts select cttee 1997-99. Constituency Lab party: Merseyside W Euro (incl press officer role) 1983-84; sec/press officer/political education officer 1983-85. Campaigns organiser Crosby 1993-96. Solicitor. Voluntary sector 1983-90. Ed BA PPE, Pembroke Coll, Oxford; Common Professional Exam, Law Soc Finals, London Coll of Law.

This southern Liverpool seat combines some of the most well-heeled residential areas in the city including Allerton and Woolton, as well as massive council estates such as Speke. Liverpool Garston is also the home to John Lennon airport and the Dockland area of Garston, the major employers in the area. Formerly a true Labour/Conservative marginal with a number of volatile swings, it is now firmly entrenched in the long list of safe Labour seats.

LIVERPOOL RIVERSIDE — Lab hold

		Electorate	Turnout	Change from	2001	Electorate	Turnout
		75,171	41.5%	2001		74,827	34.1%
Ellman L	**Lab/C**	**17,951**	**57.6%**	**-13.8%**	**Lab/C**	**18,201**	**71.4%**
Marbrow R	LD	7,737	24.8%	8.1%	LD	4,251	16.7%
Howatson G	C	2,843	9.1%	0.7%	C	2,142	8.4%
Cranie P	Greens	1,707	5.5%		SA	909	3.6%
Marshall B	SLP	498	1.6%				
Irving A	UKIP	455	1.5%				
Lab/C to LD swing	**11%**	**31,191**		**Lab/C maj 10,214**		**25,503**	**Lab/C maj 13,950**
				32.8%			54.7%

LOUISE ELLMAN b 14 Nov 1945. MP 1997-. Member select cttees: Environment, Transport and Regional Affairs 1997-2001, Transport, Local Govt and the Regions 2001-02, Transport 2002-. Vice-chair all-party groups: Israel 2002-, council against anti-semitism 2003-. Vice-chair Lab Friends of Israel. Cllr: Lancs CC 1970-97 (leader 1981-97), W Lancs DC 1974-87. Founder chair NW Regional Assocn 1991-92. Open Univ tutor/further education lecturer. Ed Manchester High Sch for Girls; BA sociology, Hull Univ; MPhil soc admin, York Univ.

This inner-city Liverpool constituency is one of the poorest and most deprived areas in the country. The seat includes the city centre with its cathedrals and universities, and, as its name suggests, the waterfront stretching from the working port to the north through the decayed old Dockland and to the more pleasant redeveloped Albert Dock and Festival Gardens. Despite being a safe Labour seat, the extremely low turnout here indicates a very disaffected electorate.

LIVERPOOL WALTON — Lab hold

		Electorate	Turnout	Change from	2001	Electorate	Turnout
		62,044	45%	2001		66,237	43%
Kilfoyle P	**Lab**	**20,322**	**72.8%**	**-5%**	**Lab**	**22,143**	**77.8%**
Reid K	LD	4,365	15.6%	1%	LD	4,147	14.6%
Buckle S	C	1,655	5.9%	-0.2%	C	1,726	6.1%
Moran J	UKIP	1,108	4%	2.4%	UKIP	442	1.6%
Wood D	Lib	480	1.7%				
Lab to LD swing	**3%**	**27,930**		**Lab maj 15,957**		**28,458**	**Lab maj 17,996**
				57.1%			63.2%

PETER KILFOYLE b 9 June 1946. MP July 1991- (by-election). Parly Under-Sec Ministry of Defence 1999-2000; Parly Sec: Cabinet Office 1998-99, Office of Public Service 1997-98. Opposition whip 1992-94. Opposition spokes: education 1994-96, education and employment 1996-97. Vice-chair all-party Vietnam group 2003-. Lab Party organiser 1986-91. Labourer 1965-70, 1973-75. Teacher 1975-85. Ed St Edward's Coll, Liverpool; Durham Univ; Christ's Coll, Liverpool.

This is the northernmost seat in Liverpool and is home to the football grounds of Liverpool (Anfield) and Everton (Goodison Park). An inner-city, largely residential seat with many of its wards high on the deprivation indices, Liverpool Walton has high levels of unemployment and a large proportion of unskilled workers. Unsurprisingly for Liverpool, it is one of the safest Labour seats in the country.

LIVERPOOL WAVERTREE — Lab hold

		Electorate	Turnout	Change from	2001	Electorate	Turnout
		69,189	50.8%	2001		72,555	44.3%
Kennedy J	**Lab**	**18,441**	**52.4%**	**-10.3%**	**Lab**	**20,155**	**62.7%**
Eldridge C	LD	13,268	37.7%	13.3%	LD	7,836	24.4%
Steen J	C	2,331	6.6%	-3%	C	3,091	9.6%
Bill M	UKIP	660	1.9%	0.8%	SLP	359	1.1%
Theys G	SLP	244	0.7%	-0.4%	SA	349	1.1%
Filby P	Dem Soc All	227	0.6%		UKIP	348	1.1%
Lab to LD swing	**11.8%**	**35,171**		**Lab maj 5,173**		**32,138**	**Lab maj 12,319**
				14.7%			38.3%

JANE KENNEDY b 4 May 1958. MP for Liverpool Broadgreen 1992-97, for Liverpool Wavertree 1997-. Minister of State: Dept of Health 2005-, Dept for Work and Pensions 2004-05, N Ireland Office 2001-04; Parly Sec Lord Chancellor's Dept 1999-2001. Whip: opposition 1995-97, asst govt 1997-98, govt 1998-99. Member select cttees: Soc Security 1992-94, Admin 1997-99. Chair Lab Friends of Israel 1997-98. NUPE: branch sec 1983-88, area organiser 1988-92. Child care officer/care asst. PC 2003. Ed Queen Elizabeth sixth form coll; Liverpool Univ.

Situated to the east of central Liverpool, the constituency of Wavertree is predominantly residential, with a large technology park at its centre. This is a relatively middle-class area, but has pockets with unemployment levels much higher than the national average. Liverpool Wavertree provides the Liberal Democrats with their best chance to break the stranglehold enjoyed by Labour in all the Liverpool seats, although it is highly unlikely to happen any time soon.

LIVERPOOL WEST DERBY — Lab hold

		Electorate	Turnout	Change from	2001	Electorate	Turnout
		64,591	47.2%	2001		67,921	45.5%
Wareing R	**Lab**	**19,140**	**62.8%**	**-3.4%**	**Lab**	**20,454**	**66.2%**
Maloney P	LD	3,915	12.8%	1.9%	Lib	4,601	14.9%
Radford S	Lib	3,606	11.8%	-3.1%	LD	3,366	10.9%
Garrett P	C	2,567	8.4%	0.4%	C	2,486	8%
Andersen K	SLP	698	2.3%				
Baden P	UKIP	538	1.8%				
Lab to LD swing	**2.7%**	**30,464**		**Lab maj 15,225**		**30,907**	**Lab maj 15,853**
				50%			51.3%

ROBERT WAREING b 20 Aug 1930. MP 1983-. Asst opposition whip 1987-92. Member Foreign Affairs select cttee 1992-97. Vice-chair all-party groups: Macedonia 2001-, Yugoslavia/ Serbia and Montenegro 2002-, diabetes 2002-. Pres Liverpool District Lab Party 1972-73, 1974-81. Cllr Merseyside CC 1981-86. Member: RMT parly campaigning group 2002-, Hansard Society. RAF 1948-50. Loc govt officer. Further education economics, politics and history lecturer. Ed Teacher's Cert, Bolton Coll of Education; BSc econ, London Univ (external).

This emphatically residential seat to the north-east of Liverpool is made up of both inner-city and suburban areas. The vast council estates of Norris Green and Dovecot are partly the result of inner-city slum clearance, whereas some quarters of Croxteth could be a model of suburban owner-occupation. This is a long-term Labour seat, where the Liberal Democrat Party comes a distant second.

LIVINGSTON — Lab hold

		Electorate	Turnout		2001
		76,353	58.1%		
Cook R	**Lab**	**22,657**	**51.1%**		No comparable results due to boundary changes
Constance A	SNP	9,560	21.6%		
Dundas C	LD	6,832	15.4%		
Ross A	C	4,499	10.2%		
Nimmo S	SSP	789	1.8%		
Lab to SNP swing	**1.2%**	**44,337**		**Lab maj 13,097**	
(notional)				29.5%	

ROBIN COOK b 28 Feb 1946. MP for Edinburgh Central 1974-83, for Livingston 1983-2005, for new Livingston 2005-. Leader HoC 2001-03, Sec of State Foreign and Commonwealth Affairs 1997-2001. Shadow Sec of State: Foreign and Commonwealth Affairs 1994-97, Trade/Industry 1992-94, Health, Soc Security 1987-92. Opposition spokes. Chair: select cttee. Lab Party: campaign co-ordinator 1984-86, NEC 1997. Member HoC Commission 2001-03. Cllr Edinburgh TC 1971-74. Tutor/organiser. PC 1996. Ed MA Eng lit, Edinburgh Univ.

Livingston, the only new town in Lothian, is at the heart of what was once a thriving mining industry. Nicknamed 'silicon glen', it depends on the electronics industry, with the highest proportion of Japanese companies of any British seat. Despite growth it suffers from unemployment, poor housing and a lack of services. Ex-mining towns such as Broxburn and Uphall vote Labour though the SNP has done well in New Town.

LLANELLI — Lab hold

		Electorate	Turnout	Change from	2001	Electorate	Turnout
		55,678	63.5%	2001		58,148	62.3%
Griffith N	**Lab**	**16,592**	**46.9%**	**-1.7%**	**Lab**	**17,586**	**48.6%**
Baker N	PlC	9,358	26.5%	-4.4%	PlC	11,183	30.9%
Phillips A	C	4,844	13.7%	4.2%	C	3,442	9.5%
Rees K	LD	4,550	12.9%	4.4%	LD	3,065	8.5%
					Greens	515	1.4%
					SLP	407	1.1%
PlC to Lab swing	**1.4%**	**35,344**		**Lab maj 7,234**		**36,198**	**Lab maj 6,403**
				20.5%			17.7%

NIA GRIFFITH b 4 December 1956. MP 2005-. Language teacher; Schools inspector. Ed Oxford University; University College of North Wales, Bangor

Llanelli is the largest town in Carmarthenshire, situated in the industrial south-east of the county; the constituency also includes the towns of Burry Port and Kidwelly. Traditionally Llanelli's main industries were steel and tinplate, giving it the nickname 'Tresosban' (saucepan town) and the rugby anthem 'sosban fach'. Historically a safe Labour constituency.

EAST LONDONDERRY — DUP hold

		Electorate 58,861	Turnout 60.3%	Change from 2001	2001	Electorate 60,215	Turnout 66.2%
Campbell G	**DUP**	**15,225**	**42.9%**	**10.8%**	**DUP**	**12,813**	**32.1%**
McClarty D	UUP	7,498	21.1%	-6.3%	UUP	10,912	27.4%
Dallat J	SDLP	6,077	17.1%	-3.7%	SDLP	8,298	20.8%
Leonard B	SF	5,709	16.1%	0.5%	SF	6,221	15.6%
Boyle Y	All	924	2.6%	-1.5%	All	1,625	4.1%
Samuel M	Ind	71	0.2%				
UUP to DUP swing	**8.6%**	**35,504**		**DUP maj 7,727** 21.8%		**39,869**	**DUP maj 1,901** 4.8%

GREGORY CAMPBELL b 15 Feb 1953. MP 2001-. New NI Assembly Minister for Regional Devt 2000-03. Whip 1998. Security spokes 1994. Member select cttees: Transport, Local Govt and Regions 2001-02, Transport 2002-04, NI Affairs 2004-. Cllr Londonderry City Council 1981-. Member: NI Assembly 1982-86, NI political dialogue forum 1996-98. New NI Assembly: 1998-, Enterprise, Trade and Investment cttee 1999-. Civil servant. Self-employed businessman 1994-. Ed Londonderry Tech Coll; extra-mural political studies cert, Magee Coll.

Despite its name, the constituency includes no part of the city of Londonderry, but is named after the county of the same name. This mainly rural and Protestant constituency lies to the east of Londonderry in the north-western part of the province. The main town is Coleraine, where the main campus of the University of Ulster is based. The seat has become a safe DUP division.

EAST LOTHIAN — Lab hold

		Electorate 70,989	Turnout 64.5%		2001
Moffat A	**Lab**	**18,983**	**41.5%**		No comparable results due to boundary changes
Butler C	LD	11,363	24.8%		
Stevenson B	C	7,315	16%		
McLennan P	SNP	5,995	13.1%		
Collie M	Greens	1,132	2.5%		
Galbraith G	SSP	504	1.1%		
Robb E	UKIP	306	0.7%		
Thompson W	OCV	178	0.4%		
Lab to LD swing (notional)	**7.5%**	**45,776**		**Lab maj 7,620** 16.6%	

ANNE MOFFAT (contested election as Anne Picking) b 30 March 1958. MP for East Lothian 2001-05, for new East Lothian 2005-. Member select cttees: Modernisation of HoC 2001-, Accommodation and Works 2001-, European Scrutiny 2004-. Vice-chair all-party Scottish football group 2003-. Member Lab Party NEC. Cllr Ashford BC 1994-98: group chair. Member: European standing cttee B 2003-, European scrutiny cttee. COHSE 1975-: member NEC 1990-. UNISON 1975-: member NEC 1999-2000, nat pres 1999-2000. Nurse. Ed Woodmill High Comp Sch.

Mussleburgh, newly accquired from Edinburgh East, has bolstered Labour support in this already safe seat, which now stretches from the outskirts of Edinburgh to the Lammermuir hills. The ex-mining communities of Prestonpans and Ormiston, and populous Musselburgh and Port Seton in the west contain more than half of the population. They outweigh the more prosperous east, characterised by tracts of farmland and the picturesque north eastern coast around Dunbar which includes Muirfield, home of the Scottish Open.

LOUGHBOROUGH — Lab hold

		Electorate 72,351	Turnout 63.8%	Change from 2001	2001	Electorate 70,078	Turnout 63.1%
Reed A	**Lab/C**	**19,098**	**41.4%**	**-8.3%**	**Lab/C**	**22,016**	**49.7%**
Morgan N	C	17,102	37.1%	1.8%	C	15,638	35.3%
Smith G	LD	8,258	17.9%	5.1%	LD	5,667	12.8%
Sherratt B	UKIP	1,094	2.4%	0.3%	UKIP	933	2.1%
McVay J	Veritas	588	1.3%				
Lab/C to C swing	**5.1%**	**46,140**		**Lab/C maj 1,996** 4.3%		**44,254**	**Lab/C maj 6,378** 14.4%

ANDREW REED b 17 Sept 1964. MP 1997-. PPS: to Margaret Beckett 2001-03 at Dept for Culture, Media and Sport 2000-01. Vice-chair various all-party groups 2000-. Chair E Mids Lab MPs regional group 2002-. Cllr Charnwood BC 1995-97. Vice-chair Loughborough Town Partnership 1995-97. Various posts NALGO 1988-/UNISON 1990-. Keith Vaz MP parly asst 1987-88. Leicester CC/Leicestershire CC 1988-97. Ed Longslade Community Coll, Leicestershire; BA public administration, Leicester Poly.

Loughborough is an industrial, university town between Leicester and Nottingham, with an economy based on the unusual combination of electrical engineering, chemicals, hi-tech research and development and bell-founding. The Wolds villages in the constituency are home to affluent middle-classes. 74 per cent of homes are owner-occupied, there is only 16 per cent council housing and unemployment is under 4 per cent. The seat is now a Labour-Tory marginal.

LOUTH AND HORNCASTLE — C hold

		Electorate	Turnout	Change from	2001	Electorate	Turnout
		75,313	62%	2001		71,556	62.1%
Tapsell P	**C**	**21,744**	**46.6%**	**-1.9%**	**C**	**21,543**	**48.5%**
Hodgkiss F	Lab	11,848	25.4%	-6.1%	Lab	13,989	31.5%
Martin F	LD	9,480	20.3%	0.2%	LD	8,928	20.1%
Pain C	UKIP	3,611	7.7%				
Lab to C swing	**2.1%**	**46,683**		**C maj 9,896**		**44,460**	**C maj 7,554**
				21.2%			17%

PETER TAPSELL b 1 Feb 1930. MP for Nottingham West 1959-64, for Horncastle 1966-83, for Lindsay East 1983-97, for Louth and Horncastle 1997-. Opposition spokes: foreign and Commonwealth affairs 1976-77, Treasury and economic affairs 1977-78. Member Unopposed Bills (Panel) select cttee 2004-. Member UN Business Advisory Council. PA to Anthony Eden (as PM) 1955. Adviser to central banks/internat companies 1960-. Fiscal Studies Inst council member. Stockbroker. Kt 1985. Ed Tonbridge Sch; BA mod hist/MA, Merton Coll, Oxford; Econ Dip.

The safe Tory seat in north-east Lincolnshire comprises agricultural villages, coastal resorts and some attractive and well-preserved market towns. There has been some small-scale industrial development in, but agriculture and tourism form the mainstay of the local economy. Tourists are attracted to the resort of Mablethorpe, The Wolds, and places of historical interest like the remains of Bolingbroke Castle, St James's Church, Louth and Somersby, the birthplace of Alfred, Lord Tennyson.

LUDLOW — C gain

		Electorate	Turnout	Change from	2001	Electorate	Turnout
		64,572	72.1%	2001		63,514	67.9%
Dunne P	**C**	**20,979**	**45.1%**	**5.7%**	**LD**	**18,620**	**43.2%**
Green M	LD	18,952	40.7%	-2.5%	C	16,990	39.4%
Knowles N	Lab	4,974	10.7%	-2.7%	Lab	5,785	13.4%
Gaffney J	Greens	852	1.8%	-0.2%	Greens	871	2%
Zuckerman M	UKIP	783	1.7%	-0.3%	UKIP	858	2%
LD to C swing	**4.1%**	**46,540**		**C maj 2,027**		**43,124**	**LD maj 1,630**
				4.4%			3.8%

PHILIP DUNNE b 14 August 1958. MP 2005-. Councillor South Shropshire District Council 2001-: member standards committee. Director: Juvenile Diabetes Research Foundation. Chair Ottaker's PLC. Ed PPE, Oxford University.

This marginal seat is a large constituency with few towns and a relatively small electorate. Although a majority of voters are middle class, a large proportion are employed in manual and unskilled jobs – presumably because of the dominance of agriculture. Ludlow and Bridgnorth are the constituency's only towns. Ludlow, with its castle, parish church, black and white buildings and Georgian streets has been described as the most beautiful and distinguished country town in England.

LUTON NORTH — Lab hold

		Electorate	Turnout	Change from	2001	Electorate	Turnout
		68,175	57.4%	2001		65,998	59.3%
Hopkins K	**Lab**	**19,062**	**48.7%**	**-8%**	**Lab**	**22,187**	**56.7%**
Hall H	C	12,575	32.1%	0.9%	C	12,210	31.2%
Jack L	LD	6,081	15.5%	5.8%	LD	3,795	9.7%
Brown C	UKIP	1,255	3.2%	0.8%	UKIP	934	2.4%
Gurney K	Forum	149	0.4%				
Lab to C swing	**4.5%**	**39,122**		**Lab maj 6,487**		**39,126**	**Lab maj 9,977**
				16.6%			25.5%

KELVIN HOPKINS b 22 Aug 1941. MP 1997-. Member select cttees: Broadcasting 1999-2001, Public Administration 2002-. Vice-chair all-party groups: opera 2001-, building societies and financial mutuals 2001-, humanist 2001-, jazz appreciation 2003-. Vice-chair central region Lab Party 1995-96. Adviser on yachting to Richard Caborn 2002-. Cllr Luton Borough 1972-76. Delegate Luton Trades Union Council. TUC Econ Dept 1969-70, 1973-77; NALGO/UNISON policy/research officer 1977-94. Ed BA pol/econ maths with stats, Nottingham Univ.

Luton North is an exclusively urban, residential and quasi-safe Labour constituency. Communications are good, with the M1 running across the west of the constituency and the Thameslink rail service to London. The population is relatively young, being the home of the highest percentage of school-age children in the county and a small proportion of pensioners. The seat has a significant ethnic minority population: 10 per cent are Asian, 5 per cent are black.

LUTON SOUTH — Lab hold

		Electorate	Turnout	Change from	2001	Electorate	Turnout
		71,949	54.1%	2001		70,349	55.9%
Moran M	**Lab**	**16,610**	**42.7%**	**-12.5%**	**Lab**	**21,719**	**55.2%**
Stay R	C	10,960	28.2%	-1.2%	C	11,586	29.4%
Hussain Q	LD	8,778	22.6%	11.7%	LD	4,292	10.9%
Lawman C	UKIP	957	2.5%	1%	Greens	798	2%
Scheimann M	Greens	790	2%		UKIP	578	1.5%
Ilyas M	Respect	725	1.9%		SA	271	0.7%
Lynn A	WRP	98	0.2%	-0.1%	WRP	107	0.3%
Lab to C swing	**5.7%**	**38,918**		**Lab maj 5,650**		**39,351**	**Lab maj 10,133**
				14.5%			25.8%

MARGARET MORAN b 24 April 1955. MP 1997-. PPS to: Andrew Smith 2002-03, Barbara Roche 2001-02, Baroness Morgan of Huyton 2001, Dr Mo Mowlam 1999-2001, Gavin Strang 1997-98. Asst govt whip 2003-05. Member select cttees: N Ireland Affairs 1998, Public Admin 1999-2000, Information 2001-. Member Lab: nat policy forum, women's network, housing group. Cllr Lewisham 1984-97: leader 1993-95. Housing/ local govt/soc services/education career. Former nat pres NALGO housing assocn. Ed BSocSc, Birmingham Univ.

This mainly urban seat was once known as a centre for hat-making but the constituency is now dominated by Luton airport and the university. Good communication links include rail services into London and proximity to the M25 and the M1 and companies such as Whitbread and Scholl Footwear have located head offices here. Despite a big swing to the Liberal Democrats in 2005 this is still a safe Labour seat.

MACCLESFIELD — C hold

		Electorate	Turnout	Change from	2001	Electorate	Turnout
		72,267	63.1%	2001		73,123	62.3%
Winterton N	**C**	**22,628**	**49.6%**	**0.7%**	**C**	**22,284**	**48.9%**
Carter S	Lab	13,227	29%	-4.1%	Lab	15,084	33.1%
O'Brien C	LD	8,918	19.6%	1.6%	LD	8,217	18%
Scott J	Veritas	848	1.9%				
Lab to C swing	**2.4%**	**45,621**		**C maj 9,401**		**45,585**	**C maj 7,200**
				20.6%			15.8%

NICHOLAS WINTERTON b 31 March 1938. MP Sept 1971- (by-election). Dep speaker Westminster Hall 1999-2001, 2002-. Member select cttees: Health (chair) 1991-92, Liaison 1997-, Procedure (chair) 1997-, HoC Modernisation 1997-, Chairmen's Panel 1997-. Joint chair/chair various all-party groups. 1922 cttee: exec member 1997-2001, joint vice-chair 2001-. Member exec cttee: Commonwealth parly assocn UK branch 1997-, inter-parly union UK branch 1997-. Cllr Warwicks CC 1967-72. Sales/general manager 1960-71. Kt 2002. Ed Rugby Sch.

With Manchester close to the north, and the seat being set in some delightful countryside, it can easily be seen why the area is so attractive to wealthy commuters. There is a little industry in Macclesfield, which is centred on textiles and pharmaceuticals, and the majority are either in professional or managerial roles. A Conservative seat since the 1918 general election, it is highly unlikely to change hands.

MAIDENHEAD — C hold

		Electorate	Turnout	Change from	2001	Electorate	Turnout
		63,978	71.7%	2001		69,837	62%
May T	**C**	**23,312**	**50.8%**	**5.8%**	**C**	**19,506**	**45%**
Newbound K	LD	17,081	37.2%	-0.2%	LD	16,222	37.4%
Pritchard J	Lab	4,144	9%	-6.2%	Lab	6,577	15.2%
Rait T	BNP	704	1.5%		UKIP	741	1.7%
Lewis D	UKIP	609	1.3%	-0.4%	Loony	272	0.6%
LD to C swing	**3%**	**45,850**		**C maj 6,231**		**43,318**	**C maj 3,284**
				13.6%			7.6%

THERESA MAY b 1 Oct 1956. MP 1997-. Shadow Sec of State: Culture, Media and Sport 2005-, the Family 2004-, Environment and Transport 2003-04, Transport 2002, Transport, Local Govt and the Regions 2001-02, Education and Employment 1999-2001; Shadow Schools Minister 1998-99. Opposition spokes 1998-2001. Member Education and Employment select cttee 1997-98. Chair Con Party 2002-03. Cllr Merton 1986-94. Payment clearing services career. Senior internat affairs adviser. PC 2003. Ed BA geog, St Hugh's Coll, Oxford.

Much of this seat's boundary is formed by the Thames and the attractive villages of Cookham, Hurley, Remenham, Wargrave and Sonning. This is a prosperous constituency – professional, managerial and technical social groups form almost 60 per cent of the total. The town of Maidenhead is an important shopping centre and in recent times has attracted many hi-tech and pharmaceutical companies.

MAIDSTONE AND THE WEALD — C hold

		Electorate	Turnout	Change from	2001	Electorate	Turnout
		74,054	65.8%	2001		74,002	61.6%
Widdecombe A	**C**	**25,670**	**52.6%**	**3%**	**C**	**22,621**	**49.6%**
Breeze B	Lab	10,814	22.2%	-4.8%	Lab	12,303	27%
Corney M	LD	10,808	22.2%	2.3%	LD	9,064	19.9%
Robertson A	UKIP	1,463	3%	0.9%	UKIP	978	2.1%
					Ind	611	1.3%
Lab to C swing	**3.9%**	**48,755**		**C maj 14,856**		**45,577**	**C maj 10,318**
				30.5%			22.6%

ANN WIDDECOMBE b 4 Oct 1947. MP for Maidstone 1987-97, for Maidstone and The Weald 1997-. Shadow: Home Sec 1999-2001, Health Sec of State 1998-99. Minister of State Home Office 1995-97. Dept of Employment: Minister of State 1994-95, Joint Parly Under-Sec 1993-94. Joint Parly Under-Sec DSS 1990-93. PPS to Tristan Garel-Jones 1990. Member select cttees 1997- incl Chairman's Panel 1998, 2001-. Cllr Runnymede DC 1976-78. Unilever 1973-75, administrator London Univ 1975-87. PC 1997. Ed BA Latin, Birmingham Univ; BA PPE, Lady Margaret Hall, Oxford.

This seat is home to commuters and light industry in Maidstone, and more agricultural pursuits on the Weald centred on small towns such as Cranbrook and Hawkhurst. The exclusive girls' school of Benenden is to be found here, as is Sissinghurst Castle. A much-changing constituency, it contains only part of Maidstone and part of the Weald, but is unchanging in one respect. It consistently elects Conservative MPs in general, and Ann Widdecombe in particular.

MAKERFIELD — Lab hold

		Electorate	Turnout	Change from	2001	Electorate	Turnout
		69,039	51.5%	2001		68,457	50.9%
McCartney I	**Lab**	**22,494**	**63.2%**	**-5.3%**	**Lab**	**23,879**	**68.5%**
Ranger K	C	4,345	12.2%	-5.4%	C	6,129	17.6%
Beswick T	LD	3,789	10.6%	-0.8%	LD	3,990	11.4%
Franzen P	CAP	2,769	7.8%		SA	858	2.5%
Shambley D	BNP	1,221	3.4%				
Atherton G	UKIP	962	2.7%				
C to Lab swing	**0.1%**	**35,580**		**Lab maj 18,149**		**34,856**	**Lab maj 17,750**
				51%			50.9%

IAN McCARTNEY b 25 April 1951. MP 1987-. Minister without Portfolio and Party Chair 2003-. Min of State: Pensions, Dept for Work/Pensions 2001-03, Cabinet Office 1999-2001, DTI 1997-99. Opposition spokes: NHS 1992-94, employment 1994-96, education and employment 1996-97. Member Soc Security select cttee 1991-92. Member Lab Party: NEC 1996-, joint policy commission. Chair Lab Party nat policy forum 2002-. Cllr Wigan 1982-87. TGWU: branch sec/shop steward/chair parly group. Sec to Roger Stott MP 1979-87. PC 1999. Ed state schools.

The Makerfield constituency comprises the town of Ashton-in-Makerfield plus a number of disparate, small, traditional, working-class communities on the old Lancashire coalfield. With the decline of coalmining, new industries such as engineering have developed here. A traditional white working-class constituency, this seat has a long historic link to the Labour Party.

MALDON AND CHELMSFORD EAST — C hold

		Electorate	Turnout	Change from	2001	Electorate	Turnout
		69,502	66.3%	2001		69,201	63.7%
Whittingdale J	**C**	**23,732**	**51.5%**	**2.3%**	**C**	**21,719**	**49.2%**
Tibballs S	Lab	11,159	24.2%	-5.9%	Lab	13,257	30.1%
Lambert M	LD	9,270	20.1%	4.2%	LD	7,002	15.9%
Pryke J	UKIP	1,930	4.2%	1.6%	UKIP	1,135	2.6%
					Greens	987	2.2%
Lab to C swing	**4.1%**	**46,091**		**C maj 12,573**		**44,100**	**C maj 8,462**
				27.3%			19.2%

JOHN WHITTINGDALE b 16 Oct 1959. MP for South Colchester and Maldon 1992-97, for Maldon and Chelmsford East 1997-. Shadow Sec of State: Culture, Media and Sport 2004-05, 2002-03, Agricult, Fisheries and Food 2003-04, Trade and Industry 2001-02. PPS to: William Hague 1999-2001, Eric Forth 1994-96. Opposition: whip 1997-98, Treasury spokes 1998-99. Member select cttees 1993-98, 2001. Margaret Thatcher political/private sec 1988-92. Political adviser/ researcher. Manager NM Rothschild & Sons. OBE 1990. Ed BSc econ, Univ Coll, London.

Maldon and Chelmsford East is composed of mainly flat countryside, bordered by a stretch of North Sea coastline to the east, and includes only two towns of any size – Maldon and Burnham-on-Crouch. The greater proportion of the seat's workforce belong to the well-paid middle-class management/technical social group and 78 per cent of homes are owner-occupied. Not surprisingly this is a safe Conservative constituency.

MANCHESTER BLACKLEY — Lab hold

		Electorate 60,229	Turnout 45.8%	Change from 2001	2001	Electorate 59,111	Turnout 44.9%
Stringer G	**Lab**	**17,187**	**62.3%**	**-6.6%**	**Lab**	**18,285**	**68.9%**
Donaldson I	LD	5,160	18.7%	7.3%	C	3,821	14.4%
Ahmed A	C	3,690	13.4%	-1%	LD	3,015	11.4%
Bullock R	UKIP	1,554	5.6%		SLP	485	1.8%
					SA	461	1.7%
					Anti-CF	456	1.7%
Lab to LD swing	**7%**	**27,591**		**Lab maj 12,027** 43.6%		**26,523**	**Lab maj 14,464** 54.5%

GRAHAM STRINGER b 17 Feb 1950. MP 1997-. Parly Sec Cabinet Office 199-2001. Govt whip 2001-02. Member select cttees: Environment, Transport and Regional Affairs 1997-99, Transport 2002-. Cllr Manchester CC 1979-98: leader 1984-96. Chair of Board Manchester Airport plc 1996-97. Analytical chemist. Branch officer/shop steward Union of Manufacturing, Science, Finance. Ed Moston Brook High Sch; BSc chemistry, Sheffield Univ.

Blackley covers the northern wards of Manchester, and borders Salford in the west and Rochdale and Oldham in the east. It extends from the open spaces of Heaton Park to central, urban wards like Cheetham, stretching into the city centre almost as far as Strangeways Prison. It is a residential centre of declining Manchester suburbs. One of Labour's safest seats.

MANCHESTER CENTRAL — Lab hold

		Electorate 69,656	Turnout 42%	Change from 2001	2001	Electorate 66,268	Turnout 39.1%
Lloyd T	**Lab**	**16,993**	**58.1%**	**-10.6%**	**Lab**	**17,812**	**68.7%**
Ramsbottom M	LD	7,217	24.7%	9%	LD	4,070	15.7%
Jackson T	C	2,504	8.6%	-0.4%	C	2,328	9%
Durrant S	Greens	1,292	4.4%	0.5%	Greens	1,018	3.9%
Kemp R	NF	421	1.4%		SLP	484	1.9%
O'Connor D	Ind	382	1.3%		ProLife	216	0.8%
Whittaker J	UKIP	272	0.9%				
Sinclair R	SLP	183	0.6%	-1.3%			
Lab to LD swing	**9.8%**	**29,264**		**Lab maj 9,776** 33.4%		**25,928**	**Lab maj 13,742** 53%

TONY LLOYD b 25 Feb 1950. MP for Stretford 1983-97, for Manchester Central 1997-. Opposition spokes: transport 1988-89, employment 1988-92, 1993-94, education 1992-94, environment and London 1994-95, foreign and Commonwealth affairs 1995-97. Chair all-party Russia group 2001-. Member parly Lab Party parly cttee 2001-. Leader UK delegation Council of Europe/W European Union parly assembly 2000-. Cllr Trafford District Council 1979-84. University lecturer. Ed Nottingham Univ (maths); Manchester Business Sch (business admin).

The safe Labour seat of Manchester Central includes the commercial, retail and business core of the city. Companies in the area include heavy engineering, wholesale clothing and toy firms. The seat also includes Strangeways Prison, Manchester University, Boddington's brewery, and Granada Studios (which houses Coronation Street and a replica House of Commons chamber).

MANCHESTER GORTON — Lab hold

		Electorate 64,696	Turnout 45%	Change from 2001	2001	Electorate 63,834	Turnout 42.7%
Kaufman G	**Lab**	**15,480**	**53.2%**	**-9.6%**	**Lab**	**17,099**	**62.8%**
Afzal Q	LD	9,672	33.2%	11.9%	LD	5,795	21.3%
Byrne A	C	2,848	9.8%	-0.1%	C	2,705	9.9%
Beaman G	UKIP	783	2.7%	1%	Greens	835	3.1%
Waller D	WRP	181	0.6%		UKIP	462	1.7%
Key M	RP	159	0.6%		SLP	333	1.2%
Lab to LD swing	**10.8%**	**29,123**		**Lab maj 5,808** 19.9%		**27,229**	**Lab maj 11,304** 41.5%

GERALD KAUFMAN b 21 June 1930. MP for Ardwick 1970-83, for Manchester Gorton 1983-. Shadow: Foreign Sec 1987-92, Home Sec 1983-87, Environment Sec 1980-83. Min of State Dept of Industry 1975. Parly Under-Sec: Dept of Industry 1975, Environment 1974-75. Opposition environment spokes 1979-80. Member select cttees: Liaison 1992-97, 1997-, (chair) Culture, Media and Sport 1997-. Member: Lab Party NEC 1991-92. Lab Party parly press liaison officer 1965-70. Journalist 1955-65. PC 1978, Kt 2004. Ed MA PPE, The Queen's Coll, Oxford.

Situated to the south and east of the city centre, Manchester Gorton takes in Fallowfield and Rusholme in the west (close to Manchester City's former Maine Road football ground), and Levenshulme in the east. Mainly residential in character, there is a minor light engineering industry in this solid Labour seat.

MANCHESTER WITHINGTON — LD gain

		Electorate	Turnout	Change from	2001	Electorate	Turnout
		67,781	55.3%	2001		67,480	51.9%
Leech J	**LD**	**15,872**	**42.4%**	**20.4%**	**Lab**	**19,239**	**54.9%**
Bradley K	Lab	15,205	40.6%	-14.3%	LD	7,715	22%
Bradley K	C	3,919	10.5%	-4.8%	C	5,349	15.3%
Candeland B	Greens	1,595	4.3%	-0.1%	Greens	1,539	4.4%
Gutfreund-Walmsley R	UKIP	424	1.1%		SA	1,208	3.4%
Benett I	Ind	243	0.6%				
Zalzala Y	Ind	153	0.4%				
Reed R	TP	47	0.1%				
Lab to LD swing	**17.4%**	**37,458**		**LD maj 667**		**35,050**	**Lab maj 11,524**
				1.8%			32.9%

JOHN LEECH b 11 April 1971; MP 2005-; Deputy leader of the opposition, Manchester City Council 1998-; Deputy leader, Manchester Lib Dems Group 2003-; Assistant restaurant manager McDonalds Restaurant Ltd 1995-97; Customer relations, RAC Ltd 1998-; Ed Manchester Grammar School; history and politics, Brunel University

This mainly residential seat to the south of Manchester city centre includes the areas of Didsbury, Withington and Chorlton. Once very desirable for Manchester's middle-aged middle classes many have now moved away and their old homes have been turned into flats for students and young professionals. After first deserting the Tories during the Thatcher years, a shock win for the Liberal Democrats has turned this once very safe Labour seat into a marginal.

MANSFIELD — Lab hold

		Electorate	Turnout	Change from	2001	Electorate	Turnout
		69,131	55.4%	2001		66,733	55.2%
Meale A	**Lab**	**18,400**	**48.1%**	**-9%**	**Lab**	**21,050**	**57.1%**
Wright A	C	7,035	18.4%	-8.8%	C	10,012	27.2%
Rickersey S	Ind	6,491	17%		LD	5,790	15.7%
Shelley R	LD	5,316	13.9%	-1.8%			
Harvey M	Veritas	1,034	2.7%				
Lab to C swing	**0.1%**	**38,276**		**Lab maj 11,365**		**36,852**	**Lab maj 11,038**
				29.7%			30%

ALAN MEALE b 31 July 1949. MP 1987-. Parly Under-Sec Dept of Environment, Transport and Regions 1998-99. PPS to John Prescott 1994-98. Opposition whip 1992-94. Member select cttees: Home Affairs 1990-92, Court of Referees 1999-2001. Chair PLP E Mids/central groups 1988-95. Member Co-op Party. Commonwealth War Groups commissioner 2003-. Author/editor/MP researcher. Michael Meacher parly/political adviser 1984-87. NACRO officer 1977-80, ASLEF gen sec asst 1979-84. Ed Durham Univ; Ruskin Coll, Oxford; Sheffield Hallam Univ.

Mansfield's history has been largely tied to its position on the north Nottinghamshire coalfield, first bringing economic well-being then political strife as many of the miners ignored Arthur Scargill's strike call in 1984. Many of those working miners found themselves jobless not ten years later, and it is other industries that the town must now rely upon. Unemployment is about average.

MEDWAY — Lab hold

		Electorate	Turnout	Change from	2001	Electorate	Turnout
		67,251	61.1%	2001		64,934	59.5%
Marshall-Andrews R	**Lab**	**17,333**	**42.2%**	**-6.8%**	**Lab**	**18,914**	**49%**
Reckless M	C	17,120	41.7%	2.5%	C	15,134	39.2%
Juby G	LD	5,152	12.5%	3.2%	LD	3,604	9.3%
Oakley B	UKIP	1,488	3.6%	1.1%	UKIP	958	2.5%
Lab to C swing	**4.7%**	**41,093**		**Lab maj 213**		**38,610**	**Lab maj 3,780**
				0.5%			9.8%

ROBERT MARSHALL-ANDREWS b 10 April 1944. MP 1997-. Member Joint Cttee on Consolidation of Bills Etc 1997-2001. Member Society of Labour Lawyers. Barrister. QC 1987, Bencher 1996. Crown Court Recorder 1982. Novelist. Spectator parly award 1997. Ed Mill Hill Sch; LLB, Bristol Univ.

A largely industrial and classic marginal seat made up of the historic town of Rochester and its surrounding towns and villages as well as the industrial Isle of Grain to the north east, Medway has swung backwards and forwards on the political tide for half a century, almost always following the national trend. Known internationally for its Dickensian connections, Rochester forms a significant contiguous urban area with neighbouring Chatham and Gillingham.

MERIONNYDD NANT CONWY — PlC hold

		Electorate	Turnout	Change from	2001	Electorate	Turnout
		33,443	61.7%	2001		32,969	63.9%
Llwyd E	**PlC**	**10,597**	**51.3%**	**1.7%**	**PlC**	**10,459**	**49.6%**
Jones R	Lab	3,983	19.3%	-3.4%	Lab	4,775	22.7%
Munford D	C	3,402	16.5%	-2.3%	C	3,962	18.8%
Fawcett A	LD	2,192	10.6%	1.7%	LD	1,872	8.9%
Wykes F	UKIP	466	2.3%				
Lab to PlC swing	**2.6%**	**20,640**		**PlC maj 6,614**		**21,068**	**PlC maj 5,684**
				32%			27%

ELFYN LLWYD b 26 Sept 1951. MP 1992-. Plaid Cymru spokes 1992-94, 1997-. Plaid Cymru parly whip 1995-2001. Member Welsh Affairs select cttees 1992-97, 1998-2001. Vice-chair all-party organophosphate group 2000-. Leader Plaid Cymru parly party 1997-. Member Plaid Cymru policy cabinet 1994-, British-Irish parly body, UNICEF parly panel, European standing cttee B 2004-05. Barrister. Ed LLB law, Univ Coll of Wales, Aberystwyth; Coll of Law, Chester.

A Plaid Cymru seat since 1974, the constituency covers a large rural area including much of the Snowdonia National Park in the north-west of Wales. Its main town is Blaenau Ffestiniog. Tourism and hill farming are the main activities. It has the smallest number of constituents of any seat in England and Wales, at 33,000.

MERIDEN — C hold

		Electorate	Turnout	Change from	2001	Electorate	Turnout
		77,342	60.1%	2001		73,787	60.4%
Spelman C	**C**	**22,416**	**48.2%**	**0.5%**	**C**	**21,246**	**47.7%**
Brown J	Lab	15,407	33.1%	-6.1%	Lab	17,462	39.2%
Laitinen W	LD	7,113	15.3%	4.2%	LD	4,941	11.1%
Brookes D	UKIP	1,567	3.4%	1.4%	UKIP	910	2%
Lab to C swing	**3.3%**	**46,503**		**C maj 7,009**		**44,559**	**C maj 3,784**
				15.1%			8.5%

CAROLINE SPELMAN b 4 May 1958. MP 1997-. Sec of State: Local and Devolved Govt Affairs 2004-, Environment 2003-04. Shadow: Min for Women 2001-04, Sec of State Internat Devt 2001-03. Opposition whip 1998-99. Opposition spokes: health 1999-2001, women's issues 1999. Member Science and Technology select cttee 1997-98. Vice-chair all-party Switzerland group 2002-. Board member Parly Office of Science and Technology 1997-2001. Sec/research fellow/business consultant. Ed BA European studies, Queen Mary Coll, London Univ.

This rural buffer between Coventry and Birmingham is a Tory seat, and despite the stark socio-economic contrasts between the outer Chelmsley City housing estate of Chelmsley Wood and the more affluent villages of South Solihull, sought after by the wealthier commuter. The M6 and M42 motorways cross here, there is Birmingham International rail station, and an airport that serves all major European and some American cities.

MERTHYR TYDFIL AND RHYMNEY — Lab hold

		Electorate	Turnout	Change from	2001	Electorate	Turnout
		54,579	54.9%	2001		54,919	57.7%
Havard D	**Lab**	**18,129**	**60.5%**	**-1.3%**	**Lab**	**19,574**	**61.8%**
Rees C	LD	4,195	14%	6.5%	PlC	4,651	14.7%
Turner N	PlC	2,972	9.9%	-4.8%	LD	2,385	7.5%
Berry R	C	2,680	8.9%	1.7%	C	2,272	7.2%
Greer N	Forward Wales	1,030	3.4%		Ind	1,936	6.1%
Parry G	UKIP	699	2.3%		SLP	692	2.2%
Marsden I	SLP	271	0.9%	-1.3%	ProLife	174	0.5%
Lab to LD swing	**3.9%**	**29,976**		**Lab maj 13,934**		**31,684**	**Lab maj 14,923**
				46.5%			47.1%

DAI HAVARD b 7 Feb 1950. MP 2001-. Member select cttees: Regulatory Reform 2001-, Defence 2003-. Sec all-party mountain rescue and search teams group 2004-. Welsh Lab Party joint policy cttee. Delegation leader, Wales Lab Party, Conferences. Member European standing cttee C. MSF union full time officer 1971-: studies tutor, researcher, education, official. Ed Cert Ed, St Peter's Coll, Birmingham; MA industrial relations, Warwick Univ.

This constituency runs from the Brecon Beacons national park through the Taff valley in South Wales. Most of the seat is contained in the area of Merthyr Tydfil County Borough Council with its remaining electors coming from the upper Rhymney valley area. There has been limited success in replacing mining and heavy industry with other activity and unemployment is high. This is a solid Labour constituency.

MIDDLESBROUGH — Lab hold

		Electorate	Turnout	Change from	2001	Electorate	Turnout
		65,924	48.8%	2001		67,662	49.8%
Bell S	**Lab**	**18,562**	**57.8%**	**-9.8%**	**Lab**	**22,783**	**67.6%**
Michna J	LD	5,995	18.6%	8.2%	C	6,453	19.1%
Flynn-Macleod C	C	5,263	16.4%	-2.7%	LD	3,512	10.4%
Armes R	BNP	819	2.6%		SA	577	1.7%
Landers M	UKIP	768	2.4%		SLP	392	1.2%
Elder J	Ind	503	1.6%				
Arnott D	Ind	230	0.7%				
Lab to LD swing	**9%**	**32,140**		**Lab maj 12,567**		**33,717**	**Lab maj 16,330**
				39.1%			48.4%

SIR STUART BELL b 16 May 1938. MP 1983-. PPs to Roy Hattersley 1983-84. Opposition spokes: N Ireland 1984-87, Trade and Industry 1992-97. Member select cttees: Liaison 2000-01, 2002-, Finance and Services (chair) 2000-. Second Church Estates commissioner 1997-. Member Lab Lawyers Soc. Founder member British Irish Inter-Parly body 1990. Vice-chair Interparly Union. HoC commission member 2000-. Cllr Newcastle CC 1980-83. Barrister/clerk/reporter/novelist. Kt 2004. Ed Hookergate Grammar Sch; Gray's Inn Legal Education Council.

The seat contains all but the southern part of this deprived Teesside town, centre of the late but unlamented County of Cleveland. Most of the industries it built its economic base on, such as steel and chemicals, are now in decline and the service sector is the main employer. Labour have been as unmovable from here as the famous Transporter Bridge, returning candidates since 1935.

MIDDLESBROUGH SOUTH AND EAST CLEVELAND — Lab hold

		Electorate	Turnout	Change from	2001	Electorate	Turnout
		71,883	60.8%	2001		71,542	61.5%
Kumar A	**Lab**	**21,945**	**50.2%**	**-5.1%**	**Lab**	**24,321**	**55.3%**
Brooks M	C	13,945	31.9%	-2.1%	C	14,970	34%
Minns C	LD	6,049	13.8%	3.1%	LD	4,700	10.7%
Groves G	BNP	1,099	2.5%				
Bull C	UKIP	658	1.5%				
Lab to C swing	**1.5%**	**43,696**		**Lab maj 8,000**		**43,991**	**Lab maj 9,351**
				18.3%			21.3%

ASHOK KUMAR b 28 May 1956. MP for Langbaurgh 1991-92, for Middlesbrough South and East Cleveland 1997-. PPS to Hilary Benn 2003-. Member select cttees incl Chairmen's Panel 2000-01. Dep chair all-party energy studies group 2002-. Chair Northern regional Lab MPs group 2004-. Board member Parly Office of Science/Technology 1997-. Cllr Middlesbrough BC 1987-97. Research fellow/scientist. Ed Rykenld Sch for Boys; Derby and District Art/Tech Coll; BSc chemical engineering/MSc process analysis/devt, PhD fluid mechanics, Aston Univ.

Middlesbrough South and East Cleveland is a mix of coastal, rural and suburban areas with an economy mainly reliant upon the farming and chemical industries. Population centres are found in the ancient market town of Guisborough and coastal resort of Saltburn, however, most residents are clustered around the south Middlesbrough suburbs. Although Labour has a healthy majority, there is enough Tory support to suggest that things may change if the Government has a downturn in fortunes.

MIDLOTHIAN — Lab hold

		Electorate	Turnout		2001
		60,644	62.2%		
Hamilton D	**Lab**	**17,153**	**45.5%**		No comparable results due to boundary changes
Mackintosh F	LD	9,888	26.2%		
Beattie C	SNP	6,400	17%		
McGill I	C	3,537	9.4%		
Gilfillan N	SSP	726	1.9%		
Lab to LD swing	**7%**	**37,704**		**Lab maj 7,265**	
(notional)				19.3%	

DAVID HAMILTON b 24 Oct 1950. MP for Midlothian 2001-05, for new Midlothian 2005-. Member select cttees: Broadcasting 2001-, Procedure 2001-, Scottish Affairs 2003-, Work and Pensions 2003-. Vice-chair all-party occupational safety and health group 2004-. Cllr Midlothian Council. Joint NUM chair 1981-87. Member: European standing cttee A 2003, RMT parly campaigning group 2002-. Miner, employment training scheme supervisor, placement/training officer, chief exec Craigmillar Opportunities Trust. Ed Dalkeith High Sch.

Spreading out southwards from the Edinburgh commuter belt, this ex-mining county is traditional Labour heartland. This is the old Midlothian seat, amplified by four south-westerly wards in Penicuik to form a rough diamond, now coextensive with the council area. In addition to Penicuik it contain the county town Dalkeith, and Bonnyrigg, Gorebridge and Loanhead. Labour dominates Midlothian in local and national elections.

MILTON KEYNES NORTH EAST — C gain

		Electorate	Turnout	Change from	2001	Electorate	Turnout
		78,758	63.6%	2001		72,909	64.6%
Lancaster M	**C**	**19,674**	**39.3%**	**1.2%**	**Lab**	**19,761**	**42%**
White B	Lab	18,009	35.9%	-6.1%	C	17,932	38.1%
Carr J	LD	9,789	19.5%	1.7%	LD	8,375	17.8%
Phillips M	UKIP	1,400	2.8%	0.6%	UKIP	1,026	2.2%
Richardson G	Greens	1,090	2.2%				
Vyas A	Ind	142	0.3%				
Lab to C swing	**3.7%**	**50,104**		**C maj 1,665**		**47,094**	**Lab maj 1,829**
				3.3%			3.9%

MARK LANCASTER b 12 May 1970. MP 2005-. Contested Nuneaton 2001 general election. Cllr Huntingdon District Council 1990-99. Army officer Royal Engineers 1988-90; Director Kimbolton Fireworks Ltd 1990-; Major Royal Engineers (TA) 1990-. Ed Kimbolton School, Huntingdon; Royal Military Academy, Sandhurst; BSc business studies, Buckingham University 1991; MBA Exeter University 1994

This marginal seat is more rural and affluent than its south-western neighbour. It has a much higher proportion of managers and professionals and a high rate of home ownership. As well as parts of the town of Milton Keynes the constituency covers Newport Pagnell, villages on Buckinghamshire's border with Northamptonshire and Bedfordshire, and Milton Keynes, the village after which the new town is named. The Open University has its headquarters at Walton Hall.

MILTON KEYNES SOUTH WEST — Lab hold

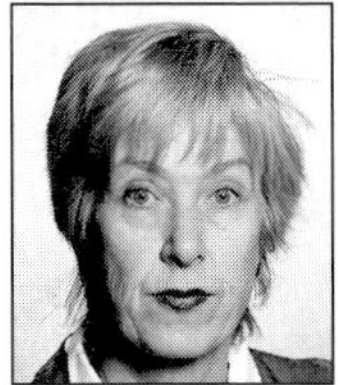

		Electorate	Turnout	Change from	2001	Electorate	Turnout
		82,228	59.2%	2001		72,823	62.3%
Starkey P	**Lab**	**20,862**	**42.8%**	**-6.7%**	**Lab**	**22,484**	**49.5%**
Stewart I	C	16,852	34.6%	0.4%	C	15,506	34.2%
Stuart N	LD	7,909	16.2%	5.6%	LD	4,828	10.6%
Harlock G	UKIP	1,750	3.6%	1.7%	Greens	957	2.1%
Francis A	Greens	1,336	2.7%	0.6%	UKIP	848	1.9%
					LCA	500	1.1%
					SA	261	0.6%
Lab to C swing	**3.6%**	**48,709**		**Lab maj 4,010**		**45,384**	**Lab maj 6,978**
				8.2%			15.4%

PHYLLIS STARKEY b 4 Jan 1947. MP 1997-. PPS: to Denis MacShane 2002-05, (team) FCO 2001-02. Member select cttees: Modernisation of HoC 1997-99, Foreign Affairs 1999-2001. Vice-chair all-party Iran group 2004-. Chair SE Lab MPs regional group 1998-. Lab cllrs nat policy representative 1995-97. Chair: Parly Office of Science and Tech 2002-. Cllr Oxford CC 1983-97: leader 1990-93. Research scientist/univ lecturer/science policy administrator/parly fellow 1974-98. Ed BA biochemistry, Lady Margaret Hall, Oxford; PhD, Clare Hall, Cambridge.

Milton Keynes, commissioned as a new town in 1967, was built around the existing towns of Stony Stratford, Wolverton and Bletchley, all of which fall within this constituency. The marginal seat has a relatively high proportion of local authority housing, but it also has a higher rate of owner occupation than some of the older new towns like Harlow and Stevenage. Smaller businesses and the service sector dominate the local economy.

MITCHAM AND MORDEN — Lab hold

		Electorate	Turnout	Change from	2001	Electorate	Turnout
		65,172	61.2%	2001		65,671	57.8%
McDonagh S	**Lab**	**22,489**	**56.4%**	**-4%**	**Lab**	**22,936**	**60.4%**
Shellhorn A	C	9,929	24.9%	0.8%	C	9,151	24.1%
Christie-Smith J	LD	5,583	14%	3.9%	LD	3,820	10.1%
Walsh T	Greens	1,395	3.5%	1.1%	Greens	926	2.4%
Roberts A	Veritas	286	0.7%		BNP	642	1.7%
Alagaratnam R	ND	186	0.5%		UKIP	486	1.3%
Lab to C swing	**2.4%**	**39,868**		**Lab maj 12,560**		**37,961**	**Lab maj 13,785**
				31.5%			36.3%

SIOBHAIN McDONAGH b 20 Feb 1960. MP 1997-. PPS to John Reid 2005-. Member select cttees: Social Security 1997-98, Health 2000-, Unopposed Bills Panel 2004-. Cllr London Borough of Merton 1982-97. Member Merton MIND. Vice-pres QUIT (smoking cessation charity). Clerical officer DHSS 1981-83, housing benefits asst 1983-84, Wandsworth homeless persons unit 1984-86, housing adviser 1986-88, Battersea church housing trust devt co-ordinator 1988-97. Ed Holy Cross Convent, New Malden; BA govt, Essex Univ.

This South London sprawl combines the borough of Merton with more up-market Wimbledon. Exemplary of the Labour project, the seat has since 1997 been solid red territory. The percentage of professional and managerial/technical voters is slightly below the national average, and manual workers constitute about half the electorate. The non-white population is around 20 per cent.

MOLE VALLEY — C hold

		Electorate	Turnout	Change from	2001	Electorate	Turnout
		68,181	72.5%	2001		68,316	68.9%
Beresford P	**C**	**27,060**	**54.8%**	**4.3%**	**C**	**23,790**	**50.5%**
Butt N	LD	15,063	30.5%	1.5%	LD	13,637	29%
Bi F	Lab	5,310	10.8%	-5.8%	Lab	7,837	16.6%
Payne D	UKIP	1,475	3%	0.2%	UKIP	1,333	2.8%
Meekins R	Veritas	507	1%		ProLife	475	1%
LD to C swing	**1.4%**	**49,415**		**C maj 11,997**		**47,072**	**C maj 10,153**
				24.3%			21.6%

SIR PAUL BERESFORD b 6 April 1946. MP for Croydon Central 1992-97, for Mole Valley 1997-. Parly Under-Sec Dept of Environment 1994-97. Member select cttees: Education 1992-94, Procedure 1997-2001, Environ, Transport and Regional Affairs 2000-01, Transport, Local Govt and Regions 2001-02, ODPM 2002-. All-party groups: (chair) transport integration 2004-, (vice-chair) South Pacific 2001-. Joint sec 1922 cttee 2002-. Cllr Wandsworth BC 1978-94: leader 1983-92. Dental surgeon. Kt 1990. Ed Waimea Coll, New Zealand; Otago Univ, New Zealand.

A highly prosperous, very middle-class corner of the home counties, incorporating the market town of Dorking and the surrounding Surrey Hills area of outstanding natural beauty, Leatherhead and a number of wealthy commuter villages, such as Brockham, Mole Valley is not quite as massively Conservative as it used to be. It is still Conservative enough, however, not to have shown any signs of the remarkable Liberal Democrat advance seen in next-door Guildford.

MONMOUTH — C gain

		Electorate	Turnout	Change from	2001	Electorate	Turnout
		63,093	72.4%	2001		62,280	71.4%
Davies D	**C**	**21,396**	**46.9%**	**5%**	**Lab**	**19,021**	**42.8%**
Edwards H	Lab	16,869	37%	-5.8%	C	18,637	41.9%
Hobson P	LD	5,852	12.8%	1.4%	LD	5,080	11.4%
Clark J	PIC	993	2.2%	-0.2%	PIC	1,068	2.4%
Bufton J	UKIP	543	1.2%	-0.3%	UKIP	656	1.5%
Lab to C swing	**5.4%**	**45,653**		**C maj 4,527**		**44,462**	**Lab maj 384**
				9.9%			0.9%

DAVID DAVIES b 27 July 1970. MP 2005-. Contested Brigend 1997 general election; Member Nat Ass for Wales for Monmouth 1999-. Deputy leader/ business secretary Welsh Conservative Party 1999-; Opposition spokes 1999-, for Education and Lifelong Learning 2003-; Opposition chief whip 1999-2001. Manager Burrow Heath Ltd (forwarded and tea importer) 1991-99. Ed Bassaleg Comprehensive, Newport

This is a largely rural constituency in east Wales bordering England, its main population centre is the town of Monmouth itself on the River Wye. The other main towns are Abergavenny, close to the Black Mountains, and Usk. This is a Conservative/Labour marginal seat which the Tories will hope to return to its former heartland status, having regained it in 2005.

MONTGOMERYSHIRE — LD hold

		Electorate	Turnout	Change from	2001	Electorate	Turnout
		46,766	64.4%	2001		44,243	65.5%
Öpik L	**LD**	**15,419**	**51.2%**	**1.8%**	**LD**	**14,319**	**49.4%**
Baynes S	C	8,246	27.4%	-0.5%	C	8,085	27.9%
Tinline D	Lab	3,454	11.5%	-0.4%	Lab	3,443	11.9%
ap Gwynn E	PIC	2,078	6.9%	0.1%	PIC	1,969	6.8%
Easton C	UKIP	900	3%	0.3%	UKIP	786	2.7%
					ProLife	210	0.7%
					Ind	171	0.6%
C to LD swing	**1.2%**	**30,097**		**LD maj 7,173**		**28,983**	**LD maj 6,234**
				23.8%			21.5%

LEMBIT ÖPIK b 2 March 1965. MP 1997-. Lib Dem Shadow Sec of State: Wales 2001-, Northern Ireland 1999-. Lib Dem spokes: Welsh affairs 1997-, young people 1997-2002, Northern Ireland 2001-. Member Agriculture select cttee 1999-2001. Chair all-party groups. Leader: Welsh Lib Dem parly party, Welsh Lib Dems. Member: federal exec cttee, federal finance admin cttee, Welsh Grand Cttee. Welsh vice-pres Lib Dem federal party 1999. Cllr Newcastle upon Tyne CC 1992. NUS exec 1987-88. Proctor and Gamble 1988-97. Ed BA philosophy, Bristol Univ.

Montgomeryshire is a rural constituency situated in the mid-Wales countryside. The seat has an elderly population centred on Newtown. The only other sizeable town is Welshpool. There are a large number of people involved in agriculture. This seat has a long Liberal history, only switching to the Tories for the 1979 parliament, and there is little reason to think that it will not stay true to that Liberal tradition.

MORAY — SNP hold

		Electorate	Turnout		2001
		66,463	58.4%		
Robertson A	**SNP**	**14,196**	**36.6%**		No comparable results due to boundary changes
Halcro-Johnston J	C	8,520	22%		
Hutchens K	Lab	7,919	20.4%		
Gorn L	LD	7,460	19.2%		
Anderson N	SSP	698	1.8%		
C to SNP swing (notional)	**4.1%**	**38,793**		**SNP maj 5,676** 14.6%	

ANGUS ROBERTSON b 28 Sept 1969. MP for Moray 2001-05, for new Moray 2005-. SNP spokes foreign affairs/ defence; for Europe and for ODPM 2005-. Member European Scrutiny select cttee 2001-. Vice-chair all-party groups. Nat organiser Student Nationalists Federation 1988. Member: nat exec young Scottish nationalists 1986, SNP internat bureau. SNP dep spokes constitutional/ external affairs 1998-99. European policy adviser SNP group Scottish Parl. Communication consultant, journalist. Ed Broughton High Sch, Edinburgh; MA politics/internat relations, Aberdeen Univ.

Moray's electorate is mainly found in the small towns and fishing villages which sprinkle its rural acres which spread from the Cairngorm Mountains up to the Moray Firth. It is also sprinkled with whisky distilleries, producing celebrated Speyside malts. For the last 30 years the Conservatives and the SNP have vied for control, though more recently Labour's support has increased, especially in Elgin.

MORECAMBE AND LUNESDALE — Lab hold

		Electorate	Turnout	Change from 2001	2001	Electorate	Turnout
		67,775	61.4%			68,159	61.1%
Smith G	**Lab**	**20,331**	**48.8%**	**-0.8%**	**Lab**	**20,646**	**49.6%**
Airey J	C	15,563	37.4%	0.1%	C	15,554	37.3%
Stone A	LD	5,741	13.8%	4.6%	LD	3,817	9.2%
					UKIP	935	2.2%
					Greens	703	1.7%
Lab to C swing	**0.5%**	**41,635**		**Lab maj 4,768** 11.4%		**41,655**	**Lab maj 5,092** 12.2%

GERALDINE SMITH b 29 Aug 1961. MP 1997-. Member select cttees: Deregulation 1997-99, Science and Technology 2001-. Chair North West regional Lab MPs group 2002-. Cllr Lancaster CC 1991-97. UK substitute delegate Council of Europe 1999-. Member European Standing Cttee C 1999-2002. Communication Workers Union NW area admin representative 1994-97. Postal officer 1980-97. Ed Morecambe High Sch; Dip business studies, Lancaster and Morecambe Coll.

Situated on the north west coast, Morecambe and Lonsdale had traditionally been a Conservative stronghold; in fact to suggest that this constituency would return a Labour MP would have been laughable before 1997. However, for the moment, it is a reasonably safe Labour seat. A seaside resort, its primary industry is tourism, although it has declined in recent years. The Heysham power station is also a major employer, as is the off-shore industries.

MORLEY AND ROTHWELL — Lab hold

		Electorate	Turnout	Change from 2001	2001	Electorate	Turnout
		72,248	58.8%			71,880	53.5%
Challen C	**Lab**	**20,570**	**48.4%**	**-8.6%**	**Lab**	**21,919**	**57%**
Vineall N	C	8,227	19.4%	-6.2%	C	9,829	25.6%
Golton S	LD	6,819	16.1%	1.9%	LD	5,446	14.2%
Finnigan R	Ind	4,608	10.8%		UKIP	1,248	3.2%
Beverley C	BNP	2,271	5.3%				
Lab to C swing	**1.2%**	**42,495**		**Lab maj 12,343** 29%		**38,442**	**Lab maj 12,090** 31.4%

COLIN CHALLEN b 12 June 1953. MP 2001-. Member select cttees: Environmental Audit 2001-, Joint Cttee on Consolidation of Bills Etc 2001-, Unopposed Bills (Panel) 2004-. Vice-chair all-party weight watchers group 2004-. Member Co-operative Party 1994-. Lab Party organiser 1994-2000. Member Socialist Environment Resources Assocn 1995-. Cllr Hull 1986-94. Supplier accountant RAF 1971-74. Postman/printer/publisher. Marketing devt worker Humberside Co-operative devt agency 1991-93. Ed Malton Grammar Sch; BA philosophy, Hull Univ.

Morley and Rothwell, largely the old Leeds South, is the latest incarnation of a seat with notable credentials: former MPs include Merlyn Rees, former Home Secretary, and Labour leader Hugh Gaitskell. It covers working-class, industrial terrain, and over a quarter of homes are council-rented. Here, 35 per cent of the economically active population are skilled manual workers, traditional Labour supporters, and this is generally reflected at the polls. Unemployment is below average.

MOTHERWELL AND WISHAW — Lab hold

		Electorate 66,987	Turnout 55.4%	2001
Roy F	**Lab**	**21,327**	**57.5%**	No comparable results due to boundary changes
MacQuarrie I	SNP	6,105	16.4%	
Snowden C	LD	4,464	12%	
Finnie P	C	3,440	9.3%	
MacEwan G	SSP	1,019	2.8%	
Carter D	Free	384	1%	
Thompson C	OCV	370	1%	
SNP to Lab swing (notional)	**2.4%**	**37,109**	**Lab maj 15,222** 41%	

FRANK ROY b 29 Aug 1958. MP for Motherwell and Wishaw 1997-2005, for new Motherwell and Wishaw 2005-. PPS to: Helen Liddell 2001, 1998-99, Dr John Reid 1999-2001. Asst govt whip 2005-. Member select cttees: Social Security 1997-98, Defence 2001-. Parly election agent to Dr Jeremy Bray 1987-92, PA to Helen Liddell MP 1994-97. Vice-pres federation of economic devt authorities. Steelworker 1977-91. Shop steward ISTC 1983-90. Ed HNC marketing, Motherwell Coll; BA consumer and management studies, Glasgow Caledonian Univ.

Motherwell in the Clyde valley, to the south-east of Glasgow, is solid Labour territory. Centred on Motherwell and Wishaw, its gloomy post-industrial character is leavened a little by Strathclyde county park, but this is an area which still suffers a great deal from the demise of heavy industry, particularly the closure in 1992 of the steel works at Ravenscraig which the constituency depended on for jobs, directly and in related industries.

NA H-EILEANAN AN IAR — SNP gain

		Electorate 21,576	Turnout 64.1%	Change from 2001	2001 (as Western Isles)		Turnout 60.1%
MacNeil A	**SNP**	**6,213**	**44.9%**	**8%**	**Lab**	**5,924**	**45%**
Macdonald C	Lab	4,772	34.5%	-10.5%	SNP	4,850	36.9%
Davis J	LD	1,096	7.9%	1.4%	C	1,250	9.5%
Hargreaves J	OCV	1,048	7.6%	7.6%	LD	849	6.5%
Maciver A	C	610	4.4%	-5.1%	SSP	286	2.2%
Telfer J	SSP	97	0.7%	-1.5%			
Lab to SNP swing	**9.3%**	**13,836**		**SNP maj 1,441** 10.4%		**13,159**	**Lab maj 1,074** 8.2%

ANGUS MacNEIL b 21 July 1970. MP 2005-. Contested Inverness East, Nairn and Lochaber 2001 general election. SNP spokes for transport, environment, food and rural affairs, fishing and toursim 2005-. Convener Lochaber branch SNP 1999. Education lecturer part-time Inverness College 1999-. Ed Strathclyde University (BEng civil engineering 1992); Jordanhill College (PGCE primary teaching and bilingualism 1996)

Stretching 130 spectacular miles from the Butt of Lewis in the north to Barra Head in the south, two thirds of the population of the Western Isles speaks Gaelic and many northern communities are devoutly Presbyterian. Crofting, fishing, whisky distilling, limited tourism and cottage industries are the basis of the local economy, along with Harris tweed. The SNP finally overturned two decades of Labour incumbency in 2005.

NEATH — Lab hold

		Electorate 57,607	Turnout 62.2%	Change from 2001	2001	Electorate 56,001	Turnout 62.5%
Hain P	**Lab**	**18,835**	**52.6%**	**-8.1%**	**Lab**	**21,253**	**60.7%**
Owen G	PIC	6,125	17.1%	-1.3%	PIC	6,437	18.4%
Waye S	LD	5,112	14.3%	4.8%	LD	3,335	9.5%
Davies H	C	4,136	11.6%	2.1%	C	3,310	9.5%
Jay S	Greens	658	1.8%		SA	483	1.4%
Brienza G	Ind	360	1%		ProLife	202	0.6%
Tabram P	LCA	334	0.9%				
Falconer H	Respect	257	0.7%				
Lab to PIC swing	**3.4%**	**35,817**		**Lab maj 12,710** 35.5%		**35,020**	**Lab maj 14,816** 42.3%

PETER HAIN b 16 Feb 1950. MP April 1991- (by-election). Sec of State Ireland 2005-. Leader of HoC/Lord Privy Seal 2003-05. Sec of State Wales 2002-. Minister: for Europe, FCO 2001-02, of State Dept of Trade and Industry 2001, FCO 1999-2001. Parly Under-Sec Welsh Office 1997-99. Opposition: whip 1995-96, spokes 1996-97. Chair Modernisation of HoC select cttee 2003-. Member Co-op. Leader Young Libs. Union of Communication Workers head of research. PC 2001. Ed BSc, political science, Queen Mary Coll, London Univ; MPhil, Sussex Univ.

The constituency is centred on the town of Neath, although there is a significant population in Dulais and in the Upper Swansea and Neath valleys. A safe Labour seat with a strong Labour history, this South Wales constituency has had to engage in major economic adjustment with some success.

NEW FOREST EAST — C hold

		Electorate 68,633	Turnout 65.9%	Change from 2001	2001	Electorate 66,723	Turnout 63.2%
Lewis J	**C**	**21,975**	**48.6%**	**6.2%**	**C**	**17,902**	**42.4%**
Dash B	LD	15,424	34.1%	0.7%	LD	14,073	33.4%
Roberts S	Lab	5,492	12.1%	-9.6%	Lab	9,141	21.7%
Davies K	UKIP	2,344	5.2%	2.7%	UKIP	1,062	2.5%
LD to C swing	**2.8%**	**45,235**		**C maj 6,551** 14.5%		**42,178**	**C maj 3,829** 9.1%

JULIAN LEWIS b 26 Sept 1951. MP 1997-. Shadow Minister: Defence 2005-, Cabinet Office 2004-05, Internat Affairs 2003-04. Opposition whip 2001-02. Shadow defence spokes 2002-03. Member select cttees: Welsh Affairs 1998-2001, Defence 2000-01. Exec member 1922 cttee 2001. Joint organiser of campaign against Lab Party militant infiltration. Royal Naval Reserve. Defence consultant/political researcher (dep dir Con research dept). Ed MA philosophy/politics, Balliol Coll, Oxford; DPhil strategic studies, St Anthony's Coll, Oxford.

This is a constituency of two halves, encompassing a broad swathe of the famous woodland and the tourist centres therein of Lyndhurst and Brockenhurst, and significant shipping and petrochemical industries and accompanying centres of population alongside Southampton Water. New Forest East has historically been a safe Conservative seat, but falling Conservative support coupled with a rock steady Liberal Democrat vote over a sustained period had turned this into a virtual marginal before the 2005 Conservative revival.

NEW FOREST WEST — C hold

		Electorate 69,232	Turnout 66.5%	Change from 2001	2001	Electorate 67,725	Turnout 65.1%
Swayne D	**C**	**26,004**	**56.4%**	**0.7%**	**C**	**24,575**	**55.7%**
Kaushik M	LD	8,719	18.9%	-6.9%	LD	11,384	25.8%
Hurne J	Lab	7,590	16.5%	1.8%	Lab	6,481	14.7%
Lawrence B	UKIP	1,917	4.2%	0.5%	UKIP	1,647	3.7%
Richards J	Greens	1,837	4%				
LD to C swing	**3.8%**	**46,067**		**C maj 17,285** 37.5%		**44,087**	**C maj 13,191** 29.9%

DESMOND SWAYNE b 20 Aug 1956. PPS to Michael Howard as Leader of Opposition 2004-. Shadow Minister: Northern Ireland 2004, International Affairs 2003-04. Opposition whip 2002-03. Opposition spokes: health 2001, defence 2001-02. Member select cttees: Scottish Affairs 1997-2001, Social Security 1999-2001, Procedure 2002-. System analyst/teacher. Manager Risk Management Systems Royal Bank of Scotland 1988-96. Major, TA. TD. Ed Bedford Sch; MA theology, St Mary's Coll, St Andrews Univ.

This seat contains the more populous areas of the Forest, in the towns of Lymington, Ringwood and New Milton. Forestry, farming and market gardening are prominent in much of the seat. Lymington serves as a ferry port for Yarmouth on the Isle of Wight, and also as a centre for those touring the forest. The constituency seems insulated against broader political trends and invariably votes overwhelmingly Conservative.

NEWARK — C hold

		Electorate 72,249	Turnout 63.2%	Change from 2001	2001	Electorate 71,061	Turnout 63.5%
Mercer P	**C**	**21,946**	**48%**	**1.5%**	**C**	**20,983**	**46.5%**
Reece J	Lab	15,482	33.9%	-3.6%	Lab	16,910	37.5%
Thompstone S	LD	7,276	15.9%	2.7%	LD	5,970	13.2%
Creasy C	UKIP	992	2.2%		Ind	822	1.8%
					SA	462	1%
Lab to C swing	**2.6%**	**45,696**		**C maj 6,464** 14.2%		**45,147**	**C maj 4,073** 9%

PATRICK MERCER b 26 June 1956. MP 2001-. Shadow Min Homeland Security 2003-. Member Defence select cttee 2001-03. Army career/journalist: Second Lieutenant to Colonel (mentioned in Despatches 1982), gallantry commendation 1991. Reporter BBC Radio 4 Today programme 1999. Member King's Coll London East Timor mission 2000. MBE 1993; OBE 1997. Ed King's Sch, Chester; MA mod hist, Exeter Coll, Oxford; RMA Sandhurst.

Newark-on-Trent is an old market town 20 miles north east of Nottingham. The main industries in this moderately safe Tory seat are engineering and food processing, while other main economic activities are agriculture based on the large rural area stretching from Newark and Southwell up to the small market town of East Retford in the north. There are some old mining villages in the north and newer residential developments in other villages such as Collingham and Winthorpe.

NEWBURY — C gain

		Electorate 75,903	Turnout 72%	Change from 2001	2001	Electorate 75,490	Turnout 67.3%
Benyon R	**C**	**26,771**	**49%**	**5.5%**	**LD**	**24,507**	**48.2%**
Rendel D	LD	23,311	42.6%	-5.6%	C	22,092	43.5%
Van Nooijen O	Lab	3,239	5.9%	-1%	Lab	3,523	6.9%
McMahon D	UKIP	857	1.6%	0.3%	UKIP	685	1.3%
Cornish N	Ind	409	0.8%				
Singleton B	Ind	86	0.2%				
LD to C swing	**5.6%**	**54,673**		**C maj 3,460** 6.3%		**50,807**	**LD maj 2,415** 4.8%

RICHARD BENYON b 4 Sept 1960. MP 2005-. Contested Newbury 1997 and 2001 general elections. Cllr Newbury District Council 1991-95: Leader Con Group 1994-95. Army 1980-85; land agent chartered surveyor1987-; Farmer 1990-. Ed Bradfield College, Reading; diploma, real estate management land economy, Royal Agricultural College

Newbury, a Tory – Lib-Dem marginal seat, has experienced acrimonious and well-publicised road protests. The constituency is largely rural. Newbury, the only sizeable town, is a market-town famous for its horse racing associations. Unemployment is low, and the constituency's social composition is quite heavily weighted towards professional and managerial and technical classes. Greenham Common, one-time UK base for Cruise missiles has now closed, but defence-related services continue to play an important part in the local economy.

NEWCASTLE-UNDER-LYME — Lab hold

		Electorate 68,414	Turnout 58.2%	Change from 2001	2001	Electorate 65,739	Turnout 58.8%
Farrelly P	**Lab**	**18,053**	**45.4%**	**-8%**	**Lab**	**20,650**	**53.4%**
Lefroy J	C	9,945	25%	-2.6%	C	10,664	27.6%
Johnson T	LD	7,528	18.9%	3.4%	LD	5,993	15.5%
Nixon D	UKIP	1,436	3.6%	2.1%	Ind	773	2%
Dawson J	BNP	1,390	3.5%		UKIP	594	1.5%
Dobson A	Greens	918	2.3%				
Harvey-Lover M	Veritas	518	1.3%				
Lab to C swing	**2.7%**	**39,788**		**Lab maj 8,108** 20.4%		**38,674**	**Lab maj 9,986** 25.8%

PAUL FARRELLY b 2 March 1962. MP 2001-. Member select cttees: Joint Cttee on Consolidation of Bills Etc 2001-, Science and Technology 2003-, Unopposed Bills (Panel) 2004-. Hornsey and Wood Green CLP: Sec 1992-94, vice-chair 1994-95. Newcastle-under-Lyme CLP 1998-: campaign co-ordinator and organiser, political ed officer. Member Socialist Ed Assocn. Manager corporate finance div Barclays De Zoete Wedd Ltd 1984-90. Reuters 1990-95, Independent on Sunday 1995-97, The Observer 1997-2001. Ed BA PPE, St Edmund Hall, Oxford.

Labour has held Newcastle-under-Lyme for over 70 years, although their grip has loosened recently. This diverse seat covers the Pennine foothills to the north, scenic Shropshire to the west and the Potteries conurbation to the east. Other industries range from electronics to textiles to bakeries. Some of its territory covers ex-mining areas like Silverdale. Skilled manual workers make up by far the greatest percentage of the workforce, and unemployment has dropped dramatically in recent years to 2 per cent.

NEWCASTLE UPON TYNE CENTRAL — Lab hold

		Electorate 62,734	Turnout 57.3%	Change from 2001	2001	Electorate 67,970	Turnout 51.3%
Cousins J	**Lab**	**16,211**	**45.1%**	**-9.9%**	**Lab**	**19,169**	**55%**
Stone G	LD	12,229	34.1%	12.4%	LD	7,564	21.7%
Morton W	C	5,749	16%	-5.3%	C	7,414	21.3%
Hulm J	Greens	1,254	3.5%		SLP	723	2.1%
Harding C	NACVP	477	1.3%				
Lab to LD swing	**11.2%**	**35,920**		**Lab maj 3,982** 11.1%		**34,870**	**Lab maj 11,605** 33.3%

JIM COUSINS b 23 Feb 1944. MP 1987-. Opposition spokes: trade and industry 1992-94, foreign and Commonwealth affairs 1994-95. Member select cttees: Trade and Industry 1989-92, Treasury 1997-. Chair all-party groups: Egypt 1998-, central Asia 1999-. Chair Northern Lab MPs group 1997-. Cllr: Wallsend BC 1969-73; Tyne and Wear CC: dep leader 1981-86. Industrial relations/research worker 1967-82. Lecturer Sunderland Poly 1982-87. Ed New Coll, Oxford; LSE.

Contrary to what the name suggests, Newcastle upon Tyne Central does not in fact encompass the true city centre, for although it includes Newcastle's lively East Quayside area, the majority of the constituency covers the land surrounding the large open space of Town Moor to the north. Newcastle Central may have once returned a Tory MP, but it became a safe Labour seat, though the Lib Dems reduced their majority by two-thirds in 2005.

NEWCASTLE UPON TYNE EAST AND WALLSEND — Lab hold

		Electorate 56,900	Turnout 55.7%	Change from 2001	2001	Electorate 61,494	Turnout 53.2%
Brown N	**Lab**	**17,462**	**55.1%**	**-8%**	**Lab**	**20,642**	**63.1%**
Ord D	LD	9,897	31.2%	11.6%	LD	6,419	19.6%
Dias N	C	3,532	11.2%	-0.6%	C	3,873	11.8%
Hopwood W	SAP	582	1.8%		Greens	651	2%
Levy M	CGB	205	0.6%		Ind	563	1.7%
					SLP	420	1.3%
					CGB	126	0.4%
Lab to LD swing	**9.8%**	**31,678**		**Lab maj 7,565** 23.9%		**32,694**	**Lab maj 14,223** 43.5%

NICK BROWN b 13 June 1950. MP for Newcastle upon Tyne East 1983-97, for Newcastle upon Tyne East and Wallsend 1997-. Minister of State for Work, Dept of Work and Pensions 2001-03, Minister of Agriculture, Fisheries and Food 1998-2001. Dep to Margaret Beckett 1992-94. Whip: opposition dep chief 1995-97, govt chief 1997-98. Opposition spokes 1985-95. Member select cttees: Broadcasting 1994-95, Selection 1996-97. Cllr Newcastle upon Tyne CC 1980-83. Legal adviser GMBATU. Proctor and Gamble advertising dept. PC 1997. Ed BA, Manchester Univ.

Of the four seats contained within the city boundaries, Newcastle upon Tyne East and Wallsend has suffered the most problems. The heavy industries, most notably shipbuilding, once the lifeblood of the local economy, are in steep decline and most new developments are situated elsewhere in the city. The Liberal Democrats have done well here in recent elections to take second place, but pose no threat to Labour dominance in Newcastle.

NEWCASTLE UPON TYNE NORTH — Lab hold

		Electorate 64,599	Turnout 59.5%	Change from 2001	2001	Electorate 63,208	Turnout 57.5%
Henderson D	**Lab**	**19,224**	**50%**	**-10.1%**	**Lab**	**21,874**	**60.1%**
Beadle R	LD	12,201	31.7%	12.3%	C	7,424	20.4%
Hudson N	C	6,022	15.7%	-4.7%	LD	7,070	19.4%
Wood R	NF	997	2.6%				
Lab to LD swing	**11.2%**	**38,444**		**Lab maj 7,023** 18.3%		**36,368**	**Lab maj 14,450** 39.7%

DOUG HENDERSON b 9 June 1949. MP 1987-. Minister of State: Armed Forces, Ministry of Defence 1998-99, FCO (Europe) 1997-98. Opposition spokes: trade and industry 1988-92, environment (local govt) 1992-94, Citizen's Charter 1994-95, home affairs 1995-97. Vice-chair all-party groups: Philippines 2003-, Malaysia 2004-. Chair northern regional Lab MPs group 2000-01. GMWU research officer 1973; GMB organiser 1975-87. Rolls Royce apprentice/British Rail clerk. Ed econ, Central Coll, Glasgow; econ, Strathclyde Univ.

As the name suggests, Newcastle upon Tyne North contains the northernmost parts of the city. Very little of the seat is composed of built-up districts, instead open countryside, villages and small towns north of the actual city cover most of the area, encompassing rural, industrial and residential areas. The seat is also home to both Newcastle airport and racecourse. Unsurprisingly, it is an area of strong Labour support.

NEWPORT EAST — Lab hold

		Electorate 54,956	Turnout 57.9%	Change from 2001	2001	Electorate 56,456	Turnout 55.4%
Morden J	**Lab**	**14,389**	**45.2%**	**-9.5%**	**Lab**	**17,120**	**54.7%**
Townsend E	LD	7,551	23.7%	9.7%	C	7,246	23.2%
Collings M	C	7,459	23.4%	0.2%	LD	4,394	14%
Asghar M	PIC	1,221	3.8%	-1.1%	PIC	1,519	4.9%
Thomas R	UKIP	945	3%	1.7%	SLP	420	1.3%
Screen L	SLP	260	0.8%	-0.5%	UKIP	410	1.3%
					CGB	173	0.6%
Lab to LD swing	**9.6%**	**31,825**		**Lab maj 6,838** 21.5%		**31,282**	**Lab maj 9,874** 31.6%

JESSICA MORDEN b 29 May 1968. MP 2005-. General secretary Welsh Labour Party. Member GMB. Ed Croefyceiliog Comprehensive School; Birmingham University.

The eastern division of the newest city in Wales is less prosperous that the west. There is still a problem with deprivation and poverty here, though ambitious regeneration plans are helping bring growth to the region and the city itself. Newport has achieved substantial improvement in recent years in both the local infrastructure and the prospects for its residents. The steel centre remains a safe Labour seat.

NEWPORT WEST

Lab hold

		Electorate 60,287	Turnout 59.3%	Change from 2001	2001	Electorate 59,742	Turnout 58.7%
Flynn P	**Lab**	**16,021**	**44.8%**	**-7.9%**	**Lab**	**18,489**	**52.7%**
Morgan W	C	10,563	29.6%	3.4%	C	9,185	26.2%
Flanagan N	LD	6,398	17.9%	6.2%	LD	4,095	11.7%
Salkeld T	PlC	1,278	3.6%	-3.6%	PlC	2,510	7.2%
Moelwyn Hughes H	UKIP	848	2.4%	1%	UKIP	506	1.4%
Varley P	Greens	540	1.5%		BNP	278	0.8%
Arjomand S	Ind	84	0.2%				
Lab to C swing	**5.7%**	**35,732**		**Lab maj 5,458** 15.3%		**35,063**	**Lab maj 9,304** 26.5%

PAUL FLYNN b 9 Feb 1935. MP 1987-. Opposition spokes: health and social security 1988-89, social security 1989-90. Member select cttees: Welsh Affairs 1997-98, Environmental Audit 2003-. Vice-chair all-party groups: drugs misuse, rheumatoid arthritis 2002-. Sec Welsh group of Lab MPs 1997-. Cllr: Newport Council 1972-81, Gwent CC 1974-83. Member UK delegation to Council of Europe and Western European Union 1997-. POST board member. Chemist, radio broadcaster, Labour MEP research officer. Ed Univ Coll of Wales, Cardiff.

Newport is Wales' newest city. This western division is a safe Labour seat in an area which has reinvented itself economically. The seat was created in 1983 when Newport was split into the current east and west divisions. This constituency includes the docks area which is undergoing major regeneration. Politically it seems that this seat will return a Labour MP for the foreseeable future despite being held by the Tories in the 1983 parliament.

NEWRY AND ARMAGH

SF gain

		Electorate 72,448	Turnout 70%	Change from 2001	2001	Electorate 72,466	Turnout 76.8%
Murphy C	**SF**	**20,965**	**41.4%**	**10.5%**	**SDLP**	**20,784**	**37.4%**
Bradley D	SDLP	12,770	25.2%	-12.2%	SF	17,209	30.9%
Berry P	DUP	9,311	18.4%	-1%	DUP	10,795	19.4%
Kennedy D	UUP	7,025	13.9%	1.6%	UUP	6,833	12.3%
Markey G	Ind	625	1.2%				
SDLP to SF swing	**11.4%**	**50,696**		**SF maj 8,195** 16.2%		**55,621**	**SDLP maj 3,575** 6.4%

CONOR MURPHY b 1963. MP 2005-. MLA for Newry and Armagh 1998-; Sinn Féin group leader, Northern Ireland Assembly. Contested Newry and Armagh 2001 general election. Councillor, Newry and Mourne District Council 1989-97. Ed St Colman's College, Newry; Queen's University, Belfast

Newry and Armagh is a large constituency between Belfast and the border of the Republic. It covers the whole of Armagh and most of Newry and Mourne district councils. In 2005 Sinn Fein gained the seat with a solid majority. The general trend in nationalist politics towards Sinn Fein will put the seat in the more hard-line nationalist camp for some time to come. The 2003 Assembly elections presaged this.

MID NORFOLK

C hold

		Electorate 81,738	Turnout 67%	Change from 2001	2001	Electorate 79,046	Turnout 66.5%
Simpson K	**C**	**23,564**	**43.1%**	**-1.7%**	**C**	**23,519**	**44.8%**
Zeichner D	Lab	16,004	29.2%	-6.9%	Lab	18,957	36.1%
Clifford-Jackson V	LD	12,988	23.7%	9.2%	LD	7,621	14.5%
Fletcher S	UKIP	2,178	4%	1.5%	UKIP	1,333	2.5%
					Greens	1,118	2.1%
Lab to C swing	**2.6%**	**54,734**		**C maj 7,560** 13.8%		**52,548**	**C maj 4,562** 8.7%

KEITH SIMPSON b 29 March 1949. MP 1997-. Shadow Minister: Foreign Affairs 2005-, Defence 2002-05. Opposition whip 1999-2001. Opposition spokes: defence 1998-99, environment, food and rural affairs 2001-02. Member select cttees: Catering 1998, Environment, Food and Rural Affairs 2001-02. Chair Con hist group 2003-. Member Strategic Studies Internat Inst. Spec adviser to Defence Secs of State 1988-90. Military historian/defence consultant. Sandhurst lecturer. Con research dept. Ed BA hist, Hull Univ; PGCE, King's Coll, London Univ.

Mid Norfolk takes in a large rural area north of Norwich and contains several prosperous suburbs. The seat arches across the heart of the county between West Lexham in the west and Acle and the Halvergate Marshes in the east. Industrial development has been planned, particularly around Dereham, but there remain more non-manual workers than manual. After running the Conservatives close in 1997 it now appears that Labour's chance here has passed.

NORTH NORFOLK — LD hold

		Electorate 80,784	Turnout 73%	Change from 2001	2001	Electorate 80,061	Turnout 70.2%
Lamb N	**LD**	**31,515**	**53.4%**	**10.8%**	**LD**	**23,978**	**42.7%**
Dale I	C	20,909	35.5%	-6.3%	C	23,495	41.8%
Harris P	Lab	5,447	9.2%	-4.1%	Lab	7,490	13.3%
Agnew S	UKIP	978	1.7%	0.6%	Greens	649	1.2%
Appleyard J	Ind	116	0.2%		UKIP	608	1.1%
C to LD swing	**8.6%**	**58,965**		**LD maj 10,606** 18%		**56,220**	**LD maj 483** 0.9%

NORMAN LAMB b 16 Sept 1957. MP 2001-. Lib Dem Shadow Sec of State Trade and Industry 2005-. Lib Dem spokes: Internat Devt 2001-02, Treasury 2002-. Member Treasury select cttee 2003-. All-party groups: chair state boarding schools 2002; vice-chair: epilepsy 2001-, Saudi Arabia 2002-. Cllr Norwich CC 1987-91. Member European Standing Cttee A. Solicitor/consultant 1982-. Ed Wymondham Coll, Norfolk; LLB, Leicester Univ.

North Norfolk covers a large area curling around the top of East Anglia and includes seaside tourist resorts, agricultural inland communities, a near-unspoilt coastline and the Norfolk Broads. The seat has the fourth highest number of second homes in England and Wales – testament to the attraction the area has with visitors. This once was a marginal seat but the Liberal Democrats have now secured themselves a sizeable majority in North Norfolk.

NORTH WEST NORFOLK — C hold

		Electorate 82,171	Turnout 61.6%	Change from 2001	2001	Electorate 77,387	Turnout 66.2%
Bellingham H	**C**	**25,471**	**50.3%**	**1.8%**	**C**	**24,846**	**48.5%**
Welfare D	Lab	16,291	32.2%	-9.5%	Lab	21,361	41.7%
Higginson S	LD	7,026	13.9%	5.5%	LD	4,292	8.4%
Stone M	UKIP	1,861	3.7%	2.3%	UKIP	704	1.4%
Lab to C swing	**5.7%**	**50,649**		**C maj 9,180** 18.1%		**51,203**	**C maj 3,485** 6.8%

HENRY BELLINGHAM b 29 March 1955. MP for Norfolk NW 1983-97, for NW Norfolk 2001-. Shadow Min: Economic Affairs 2003-05, Trade and Industry 2002-03. Opposition whip 2005-. PPS to Malcolm Rifkind 1991-97. Member select cttees: Northern Ireland Affairs 2001-02, Trade and Industry 2002-03. Chair Con Council on Eastern Europe 1989-93. Barrister. Pres British Resorts Assocn 1993-97. Company director/business consultant 1997-2001. Ed Eton Coll; BA, Magdalen Coll, Cambridge.

This mixed constituency contains the port of King's Lynn, many small farming communities, a sizeable amount of light industry, and the Sandringham Estate. Despite the royal connection, the Labour party was successful here in 1997. That result, however, now appears an aberration with the Conservatives once again sitting on a sizeable majority. Unemployment is high, and there is also more council housing than in the surrounding areas.

SOUTH NORFOLK — C hold

		Electorate 85,896	Turnout 68.7%	Change from 2001	2001	Electorate 82,710	Turnout 67.6%
Bacon R	**C**	**26,399**	**44.8%**	**2.6%**	**C**	**23,589**	**42.2%**
Mack I	LD	17,617	29.9%		LD	16,696	29.9%
Morgan J	Lab	13,262	22.5%	-2%	Lab	13,719	24.5%
Tye P	UKIP	1,696	2.9%	1.4%	Greens	1,069	1.9%
					UKIP	856	1.5%
LD to C swing	**1.3%**	**58,974**		**C maj 8,782** 14.9%		**55,929**	**C maj 6,893** 12.3%

RICHARD BACON b 3 Dec 1962. MP 2001-. Member select cttees: Public Accounts 2001-, European Scrutiny 2003-. Vice-chair all-party road traffic victims group 2004-. Co-founder Geneva Con gen election voluntary agency. Journalist and communications adviser. Barclays investment banker 1986-89. Founder English Word Factory 1999-. Ed BSc (Econ) politics and economics, LSE.

This large, safe Tory constituency consists of small towns and villages including Wymondham, Diss, Harleston and Loddon, providing attractive residential accommodation for Norwich commuters. It is more middle aged and more middle class than the average seat – 50 per cent are 40 or over and more than the national average can be categorised as professional, managerial or technical. Agriculture is of declining importance but still a mainstay of the local economy.

SOUTH WEST NORFOLK — C hold

		Electorate	Turnout	Change from	2001	Electorate	Turnout
		88,260	62.5%	2001		83,903	63.1%
Fraser C	**C**	**25,881**	**47%**	**-5.2%**	**C**	**27,633**	**52.2%**
Morgan C	Lab	15,795	28.6%	-5.9%	Lab	18,267	34.5%
Pond A	LD	10,207	18.5%	7.8%	LD	5,681	10.7%
Hall D	UKIP	2,738	5%	2.4%	UKIP	1,368	2.6%
Hayes K	Ind	506	0.9%				
Lab to C swing	**0.4%**	**55,127**		**C maj 10,086**		**52,949**	**C maj 9,366**
				18.3%			17.7%

CHRISTOPHER FRASER b 25 Oct 1962. MP for Mid Dorset and Poole North 1997-2001, for SW Norfolk 2005-. PPS to Lord Strathclyde as Shadow Leader of the House of Lords 1999-2001; Secretary Conservative Party committee for culture, media and sport 1997-2001. Chair International Communications group of companies. Ed Harrow College, Westminster University

Predominantly rural, the area includes a small part of the fens. Defence cuts have hit the area with the closure of air bases although the Ministry of Defence still owns a large tract of land still used as a Battle Training Area. The lack of large towns in the area explains the low numbers from office-based occupational groups such as the professions and skilled non-manuals.

NORMANTON — Lab hold

		Electorate	Turnout	Change from	2001	Electorate	Turnout
		65,129	57.5%	2001		65,392	52.2%
Balls E	**Lab/C**	**19,161**	**51.2%**	**-4.9%**	**Lab**	**19,152**	**56.1%**
Percy A	C	9,159	24.5%	-2.5%	C	9,215	27%
Butterworth S	LD	6,357	17%	2.4%	LD	4,990	14.6%
Aveyard J	BNP	1,967	5.3%		SLP	798	2.3%
Harrop M	Ind	780	2.1%				
Lab/C to C swing	**1.2%**	**37,424**		**Lab/C maj 10,002**		**34,155**	**Lab maj 9,937**
				26.7%			29.1%

ED BALLS b 25 February 1967. MP 2005-. Teaching fellow Department of Economics Harvard 1989-90; Economics leader writer and columnist Financial Times 1990-94; Economics adviser to Shadow Chancellor of Exchequer 1994-97; Secretary Labour Party Economic Policy Commission 1994-97; Economic adviser to Chancellor of Exchequer 1997-99; Chief economic adviser HM Treasury 1999-2004. Ed Nottingham High School; BA PPE, Keble College Oxford; MPA JFK School of Government, Harvard

Normanton is a safe West Yorkshire Labour seat north of Wakefield. The main industry was coalmining, but since the nationwide pit closure plan, there has been diversification, mostly into light industries. 35 per cent of the workforce are skilled manual, which with the history of coal is enough to give Labour all the support it needs. The almost entirely white population live mainly (70 per cent) in private homes.

NORTHAMPTON NORTH — Lab hold

		Electorate	Turnout	Change from	2001	Electorate	Turnout
		73,926	56.9%	2001		73,836	56.2%
Keeble S	**Lab**	**16,905**	**40.2%**	**-9.2%**	**Lab**	**20,507**	**49.4%**
Collins D	C	12,945	30.8%	0.4%	C	12,614	30.4%
Simpson A	LD	10,317	24.5%	6.8%	LD	7,363	17.7%
Howsam J	UKIP	1,050	2.5%	1.1%	UKIP	596	1.4%
Withrington P	SOS	495	1.2%		SA	414	1%
Otchie A	CPA	336	0.8%				
Lab to C swing	**4.8%**	**42,048**		**Lab maj 3,960**		**41,494**	**Lab maj 7,893**
				9.4%			19%

SALLY KEEBLE b 13 Oct 1951. MP 1997-. Parly Under-Sec: Dept for Internat Devt 002-03, Dept for Transport, Local Govt and Regions 2001-02. PPS to Hilary Armstrong 1999-2001. Member Agriculture select cttee 1997-99. Vice-chair all-party domestic violence group 2004-. Lab HQ press officer 1983-84. Cllr Southwark 1986-94: leader 1990-93. Asst dir ILEA external relations 1984-86. Head of communications GMB 1986-90. Public affairs consultant 1995-97. Journalist 1973-83. Ed BA theology, St Hugh's Coll, Oxford; BA sociology, Univ of S Africa.

The latter day Northampton North is socially mixed and entirely urban. A quarter of the voters are council house tenants, 5 per cent above the English and Welsh average. About 30 per cent are either professional or managerial/technical, down 8 per cent on the average. 53 per cent are manual workers, 5 per cent more than the average. Labour had enjoyed a healthy majority here since 1997, but this was halved in 2005.

NORTHAMPTON SOUTH — C gain

		Electorate 89,722	Turnout 60.7%	Change from 2001	2001	Electorate 83,848	Turnout 60.9%
Binley B	**C**	**23,818**	**43.7%**	**2.6%**	**Lab**	**21,882**	**42.9%**
Clarke T	Lab	19,399	35.6%	-7.3%	C	20,997	41.1%
Barron K	LD	8,327	15.3%	2.8%	LD	6,355	12.5%
Clark D	UKIP	1,032	1.9%	-0.5%	UKIP	1,237	2.4%
Green A	Veritas	508	0.9%		LibP	362	0.7%
Harrisson J	SOS	437	0.8%		ProLife	196	0.4%
Percival J	Loony	354	0.6%				
Fitzpatrick F	Ind	346	0.6%				
Webb T	CPA	260	0.5%				
Lab to C swing	**5%**	**54,481**		**C maj 4,419** 8.1%		**51,029**	**Lab maj 885** 1.7%

BRIAN BINLEY b 1 May 1942. MP 2005-. Northamptonshire CC: Shadow ed vice-chair 1997-98; Finance portfolio holder and member of shadow cabinet 1998-; Chair finance and resources scrutiny cttee 2001-. National sales manager Phonotas Services Ltd 1980-87; Managing director, founder BCC Marketing Services Ltd 1989-2001; Chair, founder Beechwood House Publishing Ltd 1993-2000; Chair BCC Marketing Services Ltd 2002-. Ed Finedon Mulso C of E Sec Modern

Northampton is a manufacturing town close to the M1. A rural and commuter hinterland remains to the south, with small villages offering very pleasant residences to the more affluent workers in Northampton and Milton Keynes. 72 per cent of homes are owner-occupied, and unemployment is relatively low. 1997 was the first time this seat had ever returned a Labour MP and their lack of historical depth proved fatal in 2005 when the Conservatives took the seat back again.

NORTHAVON — LD hold

		Electorate 81,800	Turnout 72.2%	Change from 2001	2001	Electorate 78,840	Turnout 70.7%
Webb S	**LD**	**30,872**	**52.3%**	**-0.1%**	**LD**	**29,217**	**52.4%**
Butt C	C	19,839	33.6%	-1.1%	C	19,340	34.7%
Gardener P	Lab	6,277	10.6%	-1%	Lab	6,450	11.6%
Blake A	UKIP	1,032	1.8%	0.5%	UKIP	751	1.3%
Pinder A	Greens	922	1.6%				
Beacham T	Ind	114	0.2%				
C to LD swing	**0.5%**	**59,056**		**LD maj 11,033** 18.7%		**55,758**	**LD maj 9,877** 17.7%

STEVE WEBB b 18 July 1965. MP 1997-. Lib Dem Shadow Sec of State: Health 2005-, Work and Pensions 2001-05. Lib Dem spokes: soc security and welfare (pensions) 1997-99, soc security 1999-2001. Member Lib Dem: tax and benefits working group, costings group, policy cttee. Member Commission on Social Justice. Specialist Soc Security select cttee adviser. Inst of Fiscal Studies researcher/programme dir 1986-95. Social policy prof, Bath Univ 1995-. Ed Dartmouth High Sch, Birmingham; BA PPE, Hertford Coll, Oxford.

Northavon is a mixture of suburbs and small towns, and covers a large area to the north of Bristol. Its position at a key point in Britain's motorway network with direct links to London, the West Midlands, South Wales, and the West Country has brought extensive residential and commercial development. Although the seat has been represented by all three major parties in recent times, it is now securely Liberal Democrat.

NORWICH NORTH — Lab hold

		Electorate 76,992	Turnout 61.1%	Change from 2001	2001	Electorate 77,158	Turnout 59.1%
Gibson I	**Lab**	**21,097**	**44.9%**	**-2.5%**	**Lab**	**21,624**	**47.4%**
Tumbridge J	C	15,638	33.2%	-1.4%	C	15,761	34.6%
Whitmore R	LD	7,616	16.2%	1.4%	LD	6,750	14.8%
Holmes A	Greens	1,252	2.7%	1%	Greens	797	1.7%
Youles J	UKIP	1,122	2.4%	1.4%	UKIP	471	1%
Holden B	Ind	308	0.6%	0.1%	Ind	211	0.5%
Lab to C swing	**0.6%**	**47,033**		**Lab maj 5,459** 11.6%		**45,614**	**Lab maj 5,863** 12.9%

IAN GIBSON b 26 Sept 1938. MP 1997-. Member select cttees: Science and Technology 1997-2001 (chair 2001-), Liaison 2002-. Chair all-party groups: cancer 2001-, Cuba 2003-. Chair: Parly Office of Science and Technology 1998-2001, MSF parly group 1998-2000. House magazine Backbencher of the Year 2004. Engineering Council Professors award 2004. ASTMS/MSF NEC 1972-96. Lecturer 1965-97. Biology dean 1991-97. Ed Dumfries Academy; BSc genetics/PhD, Edinburgh Univ.

Norwich North has less of an urban focus than the seat covering the southern half of the city. As well as containing a considerable amount of council housing in the Mousehold area of Norwich, the constituency takes in the suburbs of Sprowston and the rural area to the north surrounding Norwich airport.

NORWICH SOUTH — Lab hold

		Electorate	Turnout	Change from	2001	Electorate	Turnout
		70,409	59.9%	2001		65,792	64.7%
Clarke C	**Lab**	**15,904**	**37.7%**	**-7.8%**	**Lab**	**19,367**	**45.5%**
Aalders-Dunthorne A	LD	12,251	29%	6.4%	C	10,551	24.8%
Little A	C	9,567	22.7%	-2.1%	LD	9,640	22.6%
Ramsay A	Greens	3,101	7.4%	4%	Greens	1,434	3.4%
Ahlstrom V	UKIP	597	1.4%	0.3%	LCA	620	1.5%
Constable C	Eng Dem	466	1.1%		SA	507	1.2%
Barnard D	LCA	219	0.5%	-1%	UKIP	473	1.1%
Blackwell R	WRP	85	0.2%				
Lab to LD swing	**7.1%**	**42,190**		**Lab maj 3,653**		**42,592**	**Lab maj 8,816**
				8.7%			20.7%

CHARLES CLARKE b 21 Sept 1950. MP 1997-. Home Sec 2004-, Sec of State Education and Skills 2002-04, Lab Party Chair and Minister without Portfolio 2001-02. Minister of State Home Office 1999-2001, Parly Under-Sec Dept for Education and Employment 1998-99. Member Treasury select cttee 1997-98. Member: Lab Party nat policy forum 2001-, Joint Cttee on House of Lords Reform 2002-. Cllr Hackney 1980-86. Member NUS exec, pres 1975-77. Lecturer, researcher/chief of staff to Neil Kinnock 1981-92. PC 2001. Ed BA maths/econ, King's Coll, Cambridge.

The less secure of Norwich's two Labour seats, Norwich South takes in the majority of the city's historical features including its Norman castle and impressive cathedral. Inner city repopulation appears to be favouring the Conservatives in this seat. But the phenomenon has hardly troubled Charles Clarke, who remains relatively secure in Norwich South, despite a sizeable swing to the Liberal Democrats in 2005.

NOTTINGHAM EAST — Lab hold

		Electorate	Turnout	Change from	2001	Electorate	Turnout
		60,634	49.6%	2001		65,339	45.5%
Heppell J	**Lab**	**13,787**	**45.8%**	**-13.2%**	**Lab**	**17,530**	**59%**
Ghazni I	LD	6,848	22.8%	9.8%	C	7,210	24.3%
Thornton J	C	6,826	22.7%	-1.6%	LD	3,874	13%
Baxter A	Greens	1,517	5%		SA	1,117	3.8%
Ellwood A	UKIP	740	2.5%				
Radcliff P	Soc Unity	373	1.2%				
Lab to LD swing	**11.5%**	**30,091**		**Lab maj 6,939**		**29,731**	**Lab maj 10,320**
				23.1%			34.7%

JOHN HEPPELL b 3 Nov 1948. MP 1992-. PPS to: John Prescott 1998-2001, Lord Richard 1997-98. Govt whip 2001-. Member Selection select cttee 2001-. Cllr Notts CC 1981-93: dep leader 1989-92. Fitter: National Coal Board 1964-70, various firms 1970-75. British Rail diesel fitter 1975-78, workshop supervisor 1978-79. Ed Rutherford Grammar Sch; South East Northumberland Tech Coll; Ashington Tech Coll.

This safe Labour constituency is mostly an inner-city area with a young population. Only 50 per cent of the dwellings are owner-occupied, unemployment levels are amongst the highest in the country, as is the non-white population. Most of the workforce are either skilled or partly skilled manual employees. Two notable features within the constituency are the prison at Sherwood and the racecourse near the River Trent on the southern border.

NOTTINGHAM NORTH — Lab hold

		Electorate	Turnout	Change from	2001	Electorate	Turnout
		61,894	49.1%	2001		64,281	46.7%
Allen G	**Lab**	**17,842**	**58.7%**	**-5.8%**	**Lab**	**19,392**	**64.5%**
Patel P	C	5,671	18.7%	-5.1%	C	7,152	23.8%
Ball T	LD	5,190	17.1%	6.5%	LD	3,177	10.6%
Marriott I	UKIP	1,680	5.5%		SLP	321	1.1%
Lab to C swing	**0.4%**	**30,383**		**Lab maj 12,171**		**30,042**	**Lab maj 12,240**
				40.1%			40.7%

GRAHAM ALLEN b 11 Jan 1953. MP 1987-. Shadow Min: Environ 1996-97, Transport 1995-96, Media/Broadcasting 1994-95, Constitutional Affairs 1992-94, Soc Security 1991-92. Govt whip 1997-2001. Member select cttees: Public Accounts 1988-91, Selection 2000-01. Chair all-party camping/traveller management group 2004-. Officer: Lab Party research, local govt 1979-84. Political Fund ballots nat co-ordinator 1984-86. GMBATU research/education officer 1986-87. Ed BA pol/econ, City of London Poly; MA political sociology, Leeds Univ.

As the most working class of the three Nottingham constituencies, it is also unsurprisingly the safest for Labour. It is the only city constituency to contain a coalmine, albeit now disused. Two-thirds of the workforce are still employed in either skilled or unskilled manual trades. The amount of accommodation rented from the council, 43 per cent, is again the highest in Nottingham, and is mainly in Bilborough, Aspley and Strelley.

NOTTINGHAM SOUTH — Lab hold

		Electorate	Turnout	Change from	2001	Electorate	Turnout
		68,921	50.6%	2001		72,274	50.6%
Simpson A	**Lab**	**16,506**	**47.4%**	**-7.1%**	**Lab**	**19,949**	**54.5%**
Mattu S	C	9,020	25.9%	-1.3%	C	9,960	27.2%
Sutton T	LD	7,961	22.8%	6.2%	LD	6,064	16.6%
Browne K	UKIP	1,353	3.9%	2.2%	UKIP	632	1.7%
Lab to C swing	**2.9%**	**34,840**		**Lab maj 7,486**		**36,605**	**Lab maj 9,989**
				21.5%			27.3%

ALAN SIMPSON b 20 Sept 1948. MP 1992-. Member Environment, Food, Rural Affairs select cttee 2003-. Chair all-party groups: warm homes 2001-, soc science and policy 2002-. Board member Tribune newspaper 1996-. Vice-chair Socialist Lab MPs campaign. Chair Lab against the war 2001-. CND member. Tennis adviser to Richard Caborn 2002-. Asst gen sec Nottingham council of voluntary service 1970-74. Community worker 1974-78. Nottingham racial equality council research officer 1979-92. Ed BSc econ, Nottingham Trent Poly.

This safe Labour seat is a strange mix of estate-filled areas like Clifton and the inner-city Meadows area, and the more affluent, almost suburban districts around Wollaton and the university. Most of the city's golf courses and a deer park are here, yet the seat includes the central shopping area. It includes by far the largest proportion of the city's professional workers, but only 55 per cent of the housing is owner-occupied.

NUNEATON — Lab hold

		Electorate	Turnout	Change from	2001	Electorate	Turnout
		73,440	61.7%	2001		72,101	60.1%
Olner B	**Lab**	**19,945**	**44.1%**	**-8%**	**Lab**	**22,577**	**52.1%**
Pawsey M	C	17,665	39%	4.3%	C	15,042	34.7%
Asghar A	LD	5,884	13%	1.9%	LD	4,820	11.1%
Tyson K	UKIP	1,786	3.9%	1.9%	UKIP	873	2%
Lab to C swing	**6.2%**	**45,280**		**Lab maj 2,280**		**43,312**	**Lab maj 7,535**
				5%			17.4%

BILL OLNER b 9 May 1942. MP 1992-. Member select cttees: Environment, Transport and Regional Affairs 1997-2001, Chairmen's Panel 1998-, Standing Orders 1998-99, 2000-01, Foreign Affairs 2001-. Chair various all-party groups incl: cable/satellite 1997-, child abduction 2001-, engineering 2001-. Joint vice-chair exec cttee UK branch Commonwealth Parly Assocn 1995-99. Cllr Nuneaton BC 1971-92: leader 1982-87, mayor 1987-88. AEU/AMICUS branch sec 1972-92. Engineer. Ed City and Guilds mech engineering, N Warwicks Tech Coll.

This constituency has some very picturesque parts, popular local attractions such as Coombe Abbey and Country Park, and many much-frequented country-house-style hotels. Communication links are excellent, with ancient routes such as the Fosse Way and Watling Street along with the M6 passing through. Good links have enabled the towns of Nuneaton and Bedworth to expand both housing and business occupation. Traditionally Labour-voting, the seat is now a Labour–Tory marginal.

OCHIL AND SOUTH PERTHSHIRE — Lab hold

		Electorate	Turnout		2001
		70,731	66%		
Banks G	**Lab**	**14,645**	**31.4%**		No comparable results due to boundary changes
Ewing A	SNP	13,957	29.9%		
Smith E	C	10,021	21.5%		
Whittingham C	LD	6,218	13.3%		
Baxter G	Greens	978	2.1%		
Campbell I	SSP	420	0.9%		
Bushby D	UKIP	275	0.6%		
Kelly M	Free Scot	183	0.4%		
Lab to SNP swing	**0.2%**	**46,697**		**Lab maj 688**	
(notional)				1.5%	

GORDON BANKS b 14 June 1955. MP 2005-. contested Mid Scotland and Fife regional list 2003 Scottish Parliament election. Director Cartmore Building Supply Co Ltd 1986-; chief buyer Barratt Developments 1976-86. Ed Lornshill Academy, Alloa; City and Guilds construction technology and concrete practice, Glasgow College of Building; BA history and politics, Stirling University

This rural seat combines the Clackmannashire and Kinross area of the old Ochil seat with the rural parts of the old Perth seat. skirting Perth in the east and Stirling in the west. Auchterader (in the middle of the seat) and Crieff (in the north) are bastions of Conservative support, but the real contest here is between Labour and the SNP who vie for support in the Clackmannashire centes of Alloa and Alva, to the south-west of the constituency.

OGMORE — Lab hold

		Electorate	Turnout	Change from	2001	Electorate	Turnout
		52,349	57.8%	2001		52,185	58.2%
Irranca-Davies H	**Lab**	**18,295**	**60.4%**	**-1.6%**	**Lab**	**18,833**	**62%**
Radford J	LD	4,592	15.2%	2.4%	PIC	4,259	14%
Lloyd-Nesling N	C	4,243	14%	2.9%	LD	3,878	12.8%
Williams J	PIC	3,148	10.4%	-3.6%	C	3,383	11.1%
Lab to LD swing	**2%**	**30,278**		**Lab maj 13,703**		**30,353**	**Lab maj 14,574**
				45.3%			48%

HUW IRRANCA-DAVIES b 22 Jan 1963. MP Feb 2002-(by-election). PPS to Jane Kennedy 2003-. Member select cttees: Joint Cttee on Statutory Instruments 2002-04, Procedure 2002-. Treasurer all-party Iraq group 2003-. Vice-pres Neath constituency Lab Party to 2002. Leisure facility management. Swansea Institute of Higher Education senior lecturer and course director 1996-2002. Ed Gowerton Comp Sch; MSc European leisure resort management, Swansea Institute of Higher Education.

This is a typical former mining valley seat, named after Ogmore Vale and Ogmore Forest and embracing two valleys between Maesteg and Pontypridd. The largest town is Maesteg. Other communities include Pontycymer, Price Town, Gilfach Goch, Pencoed and Llanharan. No party other than Labour has a chance here and it has been solid socialist territory for decades. The other parties merely have close battles for a distant second place.

OLD BEXLEY AND SIDCUP — C hold

		Electorate	Turnout	Change from	2001	Electorate	Turnout
		68,227	65.3%	2001		67,841	62.1%
Conway D	**C**	**22,191**	**49.8%**	**4.4%**	**C**	**19,130**	**45.4%**
Moore G	Lab	12,271	27.5%	-10%	Lab	15,785	37.5%
O'Hare N	LD	6,564	14.7%	1%	LD	5,792	13.7%
Barnbrook M	UKIP	2,015	4.5%	1.1%	UKIP	1,426	3.4%
Sayers C	BNP	1,227	2.8%				
Peters G	Ind	304	0.7%				
Lab to C swing	**7.2%**	**44,572**		**C maj 9,920**		**42,133**	**C maj 3,345**
				22.3%			7.9%

DEREK CONWAY b 15 Feb 1953. MP for Shrewsbury and Atcham 1983-97, for Old Bexley and Sidcup 2001-. PPS to Ministers of State for: Employment 1992-93, Wales 1988-91. Whip: asst govt 1993-94, govt 1993-97. Select cttees incl: vice-chair Defence 1991-93, member Chairmen's Panel 2001-, chair Accommodation and Works 2001-. Chair all-party groups 2001-. Joint sec 1922 cttee 2001-02. Member Con party NEC 1971-81. Cllr Gateshead BC 1974-87, Tyne and Wear Metropolitan BC 1977-83: leader 1979-82. Advertising manager. Ed Newcastle upon Tyne Poly.

Sir Edward Heath was this area's MP from 1950 until he stood down to Tory MP Derek Conway in 2001. The constituency is affluent, residential and borders Kent. The owner-occupancy rate is among the highest in London and is eighth in the country and unemployment is low. 40 per cent of workers are either professional or managerial/technical; a further 22 per cent are skilled non-manual workers, ranking first in the country for this classification.

OLDHAM EAST AND SADDLEWORTH — Lab hold

		Electorate	Turnout	Change from	2001	Electorate	Turnout
		75,680	57.3%	2001		74,511	61%
Woolas P	**Lab**	**17,968**	**41.4%**	**2.8%**	**Lab**	**17,537**	**38.6%**
Dawson T	LD	14,378	33.2%	0.6%	LD	14,811	32.6%
Chapman K	C	7,901	18.2%	2.1%	C	7,304	16.1%
Treacy M	BNP	2,109	4.9%	-6.3%	BNP	5,091	11.2%
Nield V	UKIP	873	2%	0.5%	UKIP	677	1.5%
O'Grady P	Ind	138	0.3%				
LD to Lab swing	**1.1%**	**43,367**		**Lab maj 3,590**		**45,420**	**Lab maj 2,726**
				8.3%			6%

PHIL WOOLAS b 11 Dec 1959. MP 1997-. Minister of State ODPM 2005-, Dep Leader HoC 2003-05. PPS to Lord Macdonald of Tradeston 1999-2001. Whip: asst govt 2001-02, govt 2002-03. Chair Tribune newspaper 1997-2001. Dep leader leadership campaign team 1997-99. Pres NUS 1984-86. TV producer 1988-90 (RTS award for political coverage 1990). Head of communication GMB 1991-97. Ed Walton Lane High Sch; Nelson and Colne Coll; BA philosophy, Manchester Univ.

A Labour/Liberal Democrat marginal, Oldham East and Saddleworth, since its creation in 1983, has returned MPs from each major party. Despite its name, the seat contains little of the town of Oldham. Situated to the south of Rochdale and on the eastern edge of Greater Manchester, the overwhelming part of the seat's geographical area is in the Saddleworth region, the umbrella name for a group of commuter villages in the south Pennines including Diggle, Uppermill and Delph.

OLDHAM WEST AND ROYTON — Lab hold

		Electorate 70,496	Turnout 53.3%	Change from 2001	2001	Electorate 69,409	Turnout 57.6%
Meacher M	**Lab**	**18,452**	**49.1%**	**-2.1%**	**Lab**	**20,441**	**51.2%**
Moore S	C	7,998	21.3%	3.6%	C	7,076	17.7%
Bodsworth S	LD	7,519	20%	7.6%	BNP	6,552	16.4%
Corbett A	BNP	2,606	6.9%	-9.5%	LD	4,975	12.4%
Short D	UKIP	987	2.6%		Greens	918	2.3%
Lab to C swing	**2.9%**	**37,562**		**Lab maj 10,454** 27.8%		**39,962**	**Lab maj 13,365** 33.4%

MICHAEL MEACHER b 4 Nov 1939. MP for Oldham West 1970-97, for Oldham West and Royton 1997-. Minister of State: Dept for Environ, Food and Rural Affairs/Dept of Environment, Transport and Regions 1997-2003. Parly Under-Sec: Dept of Trade 1976-79, DHSS 1975-76, Dept of Industry 1974-75. Opposition spokes/Shadow Cabinet member 1983-97. Member Environmental Audit select cttee 1997-2003. Lab Party: dep leader candidate 1983, NEC member 1983-89. University lecturer/visiting professor. PC 1997. Ed BA Greats, New Coll, Oxford; Dip soc admin, LSE.

Oldham West and Royton is situated to the north and east of the Manchester city seats. It contains the majority of the old industrial town of Oldham and the smaller towns of Royton and Chadderton. Few cotton-spinning firms have survived but engineering, defence-related industries and food processing have all grown in their place. The Labour Party is firmly entrenched in this constituency and it would take something extraordinary for them to lose this seat.

ORKNEY AND SHETLAND — LD hold

		Electorate 33,048	Turnout 53.7%	Change from 2001	2001 (as Western Isles)		Turnout 52.4%
Carmichael A	**LD**	**9,138**	**51.5%**	**10.2%**	**LD**	**6,919**	**41.3%**
Meade R	Lab	2,511	14.2%	-6.4%	Lab	3,444	20.6%
Nairn F	C	2,357	13.3%	-5.4%	C	3,121	18.7%
Mowat J	SNP	1,833	10.3%	-4.5%	SNP	2,473	14.8%
Aberdein J	SSP	992	5.6%	1%	SSP	776	4.6%
Dyble S	UKIP	424	2.4%				
Cruickshank P	LCA	311	1.8%				
Nugent B	Free Scot	176	1%				
Lab to LD swing	**8.3%**	**17,742**		**LD maj 6,627** 37.4%		**16,733**	**LD maj 3,475** 20.1%

ALISTAIR CARMICHAEL b 15 July 1965. MP for Orkney and Shetland 2001-. Lib Dem dep spokes: Northern Ireland 2002-, Home Affairs 2004-. Scottish Lib Dem spokes energy review 2001-02. Member select cttees: Scottish Affairs 2001-, Internat Devt 2001-02. Vice-chair all-party telecommunications group 2004-. Member Lib Dem federal policy cttee 2004-. Solicitor 1996-2001. Hotel manager 1984-89; procurator fiscal depute Procurator Fiscal Service 1993-96. Ed Aberdeen Univ Scots law: LLB, Dip LP.

The Orkney and Shetland Islands are the UK's northernmost constituency. Orkney has two main towns, Kirkwall, the capital and administrative centre, and Stromness. Apart from the oil terminal at Flotta, the main industry is beef production. The main town of Lerwick is a centre for the oil industry in the Shetland Islands and further to the north is Sullom Voe oil terminal. There has been a return to traditional industries such as fishing and knitware. Other industries that continue to provide employment are tourism and the salmon farming industry.

ORPINGTON — C hold

		Electorate 78,276	Turnout 69.9%	Change from 2001	2001	Electorate 74,423	Turnout 68.4%
Horam J	**C**	**26,718**	**48.8%**	**4.9%**	**C**	**22,334**	**43.9%**
Maines C	LD	21,771	39.8%	-3.5%	LD	22,065	43.3%
Bird E	Lab	4,914	9%	-1.8%	Lab	5,517	10.8%
Greenhough J	UKIP	1,331	2.4%	0.4%	UKIP	996	2%
LD to C swing	**4.2%**	**54,734**		**C maj 4,947** 9%		**50,912**	**C maj 269** 0.5%

JOHN HORAM b 7 March 1939. MP for Gateshead West 1970-83 (Lab 1970-81, SDP 1981-83), for Orpington 1992- (Con). Parly Under-Sec Dept of Health 1995-97; Parly Sec Office of Public Service 1995; Parly Under-Sec Dept of Transport 1976-79. Lab spokes econ affairs 1979-81; SDP spokes 1981-83. Member select cttees: Public Accounts 1992-95, Liaison 1997-2003, Environmental Audit 1997- (chair 1997-2003). Member exec 1922 cttee 2004-. Journalist/market research officer/MD/dep chair. ED MA econ, St Catherine's Coll, Cambridge.

An affluent seat, over 80 per cent owner-occupied, with an almost all-white population, low unemployment and few manual workers, Orpington is the largest seat in the largest London stockbroker-belt borough of Bromley, both in acreage and electorate. The major landmark is Biggin Hill airfield, which played an important role in the Battle of Britain and now hosts an internationally recognised annual air show.

OXFORD EAST — Lab hold

		Electorate 72,234	Turnout 57.8%	Change from 2001	2001	Electorate 71,357	Turnout 55.8%
Smith A	**Lab**	**15,405**	**36.9%**	**-12.5%**	**Lab**	**19,681**	**49.4%**
Goddard S	LD	14,442	34.6%	11.2%	LD	9,337	23.4%
Morris V	C	6,992	16.7%	-2%	C	7,446	18.7%
Sanders J	Greens	1,813	4.3%	0.5%	Greens	1,501	3.8%
Blair H	Ind	1,485	3.6%	3.4%	SA	708	1.8%
Leen M	IWCA	892	2.1%		UKIP	570	1.4%
Gardner P	UKIP	715	1.7%	0.3%	SLP	274	0.7%
Mylvaganam P	Ind	46	0.1%		ProLife	254	0.6%
					Ind	77	0.2%
Lab to LD swing	**11.9%**	**41,790**		**Lab maj 963** 2.3%		**39,848**	**Lab maj 10,344** 26%

ANDREW SMITH b 1 Feb 1951. MP 1987-. Sec of State Work and Pensions 2002-04; Chief Sec to Treasury 1999-2002; Minister of State Dept for Education and Employment 1997-99. Shadow: Sec of State for Transport 1996-97, Chief Sec to Treasury 1994-96. Opposition spokes: Education 1988-92, Treasury and economic affairs 1992-96. Member Lab Party Parly Cttee 1999-2002. Cllr Oxford City 1976-87. Oxford/Swindon Co-op Soc relations officer 1979-87. PC 1997. Ed BA/BPhil econ/pol/sociology, St John's Coll, Oxford.

This is the industrial, marginal half of the city rather than the Oxford of dreaming spires. Cowley has a long history as a manufacturing centre, particularly of cars. The Rover factory has been the largest employer in the region by far. 26 per cent of accommodation is council-housing, and there is a far greater proportion of ethnic minorities than in the West half of the city. The seat is also home to a number of teaching hospitals.

OXFORD WEST AND ABINGDON — LD hold

		Electorate 80,195	Turnout 65.6%	Change from 2001	2001	Electorate 79,915	Turnout 64.5%
Harris E	**LD**	**24,336**	**46.3%**	**-1.5%**	**LD**	**24,670**	**47.8%**
McLean A	C	16,653	31.7%	1.7%	C	15,485	30%
Bance A	Lab	8,725	16.6%	-1.1%	Lab	9,114	17.7%
Lines T	Greens	2,091	4%	1.2%	Greens	1,423	2.8%
Watney M	UKIP	795	1.5%	0.6%	UKIP	451	0.9%
					Ind	332	0.6%
					EC	93	0.2%
LD to C swing	**1.6%**	**52,600**		**LD maj 7,683** 14.6%		**51,568**	**LD maj 9,185** 17.8%

EVAN HARRIS b 21 Oct 1965. MP 1997-. Spokes: NHS 1997-99, higher education, science and women's issues 1999-2001, health 2001-03. Member select cttees: Education and Employment 1999-2001, Science and Technology 2003-. Chair all-party kidney group 2000-. Hon. pres Lib Dems for gay and lesbian rights 2000. BMA nat council 1991-94. Junior doctors cttee exec 1995-97. Member: Medical Ethics cttee/Industry and Parliament Trust 2001. Doctor/registrar 1991-97. Ed BA physiology, Wadham Coll, Oxford; BM/BCh, Oxford Univ Medical Sch.

This liberally-inclined, Lib-Dem voting seat contains most of the historic walled city of Oxford, the bulk of the university, the main shopping centre and the well-known intellectual and professional residential areas of north Oxford. The rural areas on the outskirts of the city contain a high number of commuters both to Oxford itself and London.

PAISLEY AND RENFREWSHIRE NORTH — Lab hold

		Electorate 63,076	Turnout 64.8%		2001
Sheridan J	**Lab**	**18,697**	**45.7%**		No comparable results due to boundary changes
Wilson B	SNP	7,696	18.8%		
Hutton L	LD	7,464	18.3%		
Lardner P	C	5,566	13.6%		
McGregor A	SSP	646	1.6%		
McGavigan K	SLP	444	1.1%		
Pearson J	UKIP	372	0.9%		
Lab to SNP swing (notional)	**1.3%**	**40,885**		**Lab maj 11,001** 26.9%	

JIM SHERIDAN b 24 Nov 1952. MP for West Renfrewshire 2001-05, for Paisley and North Renfrewshire 2005-. Member select cttees: Information 2001-04, Broadcasting 2003-, Public Accounts 2003-. Chair all-party Scottish football group 2003-. Cllr Renfrewshire Council 1999-. TGWU 1984-: convener 1984-99, stand down official 1998-99. Print room asst, painter, M/C operator, material handler. Ed St Pius Sec Sch.

Most of Paisley North and a sizeable north-eastern chunk of West Renfrewshire combine in this Clydeside constituency, which includes Glasgow airport and a mixture of suburban and industrial conurbations. Labour was stronger in the old Paisley North constituency (centred on Renfrew, Paisley and Linwood) than it is in the eight wards which are obtained from West Renfrewshire, where the SNP has signiificant support, especially in Bridge of Weir, whilst the Conservatives do well in Bishopton.

PAISLEY AND RENFREWSHIRE SOUTH — Lab hold

		Electorate	Turnout		2001
		60,181	62.9%		
Alexander D	**Lab**	**19,904**	**52.6%**		No comparable results due to boundary changes
McCartin E	LD	6,672	17.6%		
Doig A	SNP	6,653	17.6%		
Begg T	C	3,188	8.4%		
Hogg I	SSP	789	2.1%		
Matthew G	Paisley	381	1%		
Rodgers R	Ind	166	0.4%		
Broadbent H	SLP	107	0.3%		
Lab to LD swing (notional)	**6.2%**	**37,860**		**Lab maj 13,232** 35%	

DOUGLAS ALEXANDER b 26 Oct 1967. MP for Paisley South Nov 1997 (by-election) -2005, for Paisley and South Renfrewshire 2005-. Minister of State: Europe, FCO 2005-, Trade, Investment and Foreign Affairs, FCO, DTI 2004-05. Minister: Cabinet Office, Chancellor Duchy of Lancaster 2003-04, of State 2002-03, Cabinet Office 2002-04, DTI 2001-02. Gen election campaign co-ordinator 1999-2001. Gordon Brown MP parly researcher 1990-91. Solicitor. PC 2005. Ed MA, LLB, Dip Legal Practice, Edinburgh Univ; Pennsylvania Univ, USA.

The combination of Paisley and west Renfrewshire gives an interesting demographic mix. The seat begins in the urban centre of southern Paisley, on the western rim of Greater Glasgow, taking in Paisley University and the hub of Paisley town centre. It spreads west to Elderslie then out to rural towns of Kilbarchan and Howwood and countryside around Kilbarchan and Lochwinnoch, forming part of Muirshiel Country Park.

PENDLE — Lab hold

		Electorate	Turnout	Change from	2001	Electorate	Turnout
		64,917	63.4%	2001		62,870	63.2%
Prentice G	**Lab**	**15,250**	**37.1%**	**-7.5%**	**Lab**	**17,729**	**44.6%**
Ellison J	C	13,070	31.8%	-2.1%	C	13,454	33.9%
Anwar S	LD	9,528	23.2%	9.4%	LD	5,479	13.8%
Boocock T	BNP	2,547	6.2%	1.2%	BNP	1,976	5%
Cannon G	UKIP	737	1.8%	-1%	UKIP	1,094	2.8%
Lab to C swing	**2.7%**	**41,132**		**Lab maj 2,180** 5.3%		**39,732**	**Lab maj 4,275** 10.8%

GORDON PRENTICE b 28 Jan 1951. MP 1992-. PPS to Gavin Strang 1997. Member select cttees: Deregulation 1995-97, Agriculture 1996-97, Modernisation of HoC 1999-2001, Public Admin 2001-. Member: Lab Party Nat Policy Forum 1999-2001, Parly Lab Party Parly Cttee 2001-03. Exec cttee member Inter-Parly Union British Group. Member British Delegation to Council of Europe/WEU 2001-. Cllr Hammersmith and Fulham 1982-90: leader 1984-88. Lab Party Policy Directorate 1982-92. Ed MA pol/econ, Glasgow Univ.

A mainly urban constituency, Pendle includes the towns of Nelson and Colne, and the small towns that appeared as a result of the Pennine textile industry of the nineteenth century. The seat is to the east of Burnley and goes up to the Yorkshire border. Areas of natural beauty abound, with the Yorkshire Dales to the North and the Forest of Bowland in the west. A slightly marginal Labour seat, this is a key Conservative/Labour battleground.

PENRITH AND THE BORDER — C hold

		Electorate	Turnout	Change from	2001	Electorate	Turnout
		70,922	66.1%	2001		68,605	64.5%
Maclean D	**C**	**24,046**	**51.3%**	**-3.6%**	**C**	**24,302**	**54.9%**
Walker G	LD	12,142	25.9%	4.1%	LD	9,625	21.8%
Boaden M	Lab	8,958	19.1%	0.6%	Lab	8,177	18.5%
Robinson W	UKIP	1,187	2.5%	0.4%	UKIP	938	2.1%
Gibson M	LCA	549	1.2%	-0.8%	LCA	870	2%
					Ind	337	0.8%
C to LD swing	**3.9%**	**46,882**		**C maj 11,904** 25.4%		**44,249**	**C maj 14,677** 33.2%

DAVID MacLEAN b 16 May 1953. MP July 1983- (by-election). Minister of State: Home Office 1993-97, Dept of Environment 1992-93. Parly Sec MAFF 1989-92. Whip: opposition chief 2001-03, 2003-, govt 1988-89, asst govt 1987-89. Highland Volunteers, TA. Securicor worker. PC 1995. Ed Fortrose Academy; law, Aberdeen Univ.

Penrith and the Border is the largest constituency in England and is surrounded by beautiful scenery. This massive northern Cumbrian constituency stretches from the Solway Firth to the Yorkshire Dales, from the Scottish border at Gretna Green to Helvellyn in the heart of the Lakes. The only towns of note are Penrith and Appleby, with its 'gypsy' horse fair. A rural seat, it has been solidly Conservative for more than half a century.

PERTH AND NORTH PERTHSHIRE — SNP hold

		Electorate	Turnout	2001
		70,895	64.8%	
Wishart P	**SNP**	**15,469**	**33.7%**	No comparable results due to boundary changes
Taylor D	C	13,948	30.4%	
Maughan D	Lab	8,601	18.7%	
Campbell G	LD	7,403	16.1%	
Stott P	SSP	509	1.1%	
SNP to C swing (notional)	**3.8%**	**45,930**	**SNP maj 1,521** 3.3%	

PETER WISHART b 9 March 1962. MP for North Tayside 2001-05, for Perth and North Perthshire 2005-. SNP chief whip 2001-. SNP spokes: transport, rural affairs, culture, media and sport 2001-05, for constitution, culture and sport and overseas aid 2005-. Member Catering select cttee 2004-. Vice-chair all-party Scottish football 2004-. Member: nat council 1997-, NEC 1999-. Exec vice-convener fundraising SNP 1999-2001. Member European standing cttee B 2005-. Musician (Big Country, Runrig), community worker. Scotland against drugs campaign ctee. Ed Dip CommEd, Moray House Coll of Education.

This vast seat ranges from the Tay just east of Dundee, through Perth and the Carse of Gowrie then inland across rich Strathmore farmland (including the snug hamlets of Coupar Angus and Blairgowrie) sprawling out to the Grampians in the north-west. The Labour party attracts some support in Perth, which is politically varied, while the SNP and the Tories do battle in the spectacular mountains glens and lochs of the north.

PETERBOROUGH — C gain

		Electorate	Turnout	Change from	2001	Electorate	Turnout
		67,499	61%	2001		64,874	61.4%
Jackson S	**C**	**17,364**	**42.1%**	**4.1%**	**Lab**	**17,975**	**45.1%**
Clark H	Lab	14,624	35.5%	-9.6%	C	15,121	38%
Sandford N	LD	6,876	16.7%	2.2%	LD	5,761	14.5%
Herdman M	UKIP	1,242	3%	0.6%	UKIP	955	2.4%
Blackham T	NF	931	2.3%				
Potter M	MNP	167	0.4%				
Lab to C swing	**6.9%**	**41,204**		**C maj 2,740** 6.6%		**39,812**	**Lab maj 2,854** 7.2%

STEWART JACKSON b 31 March 1965. MP 2005-. Contested Brent South 1997 and Peterborough 2001 general elections. Bank manager Lloyds TSB 1993-98; Business services manager Aztec training and enterprise council for SW London 1998-2000; Business adviser human resources Business Link for London 2000-. Ed London Nautical School; Chatham House Grammar School, Ramsgate; economics, Royal Holloway College; human resources management, Thames Valley University

Peterborough lies halfway between the East Anglian coast and the Midlands. The East Coast Mainline provides travel to London in 50 minutes and, as a result, Peterborough has started to develop into something of a commuter town. Peterborough is a new town based on the old cathedral city and as such has a small tourist industry. A large swing away from Labour was enough to allow the Conservatives to seize Peterborough back in 2005.

PLYMOUTH DEVONPORT — Lab hold

		Electorate	Turnout	Change from	2001	Electorate	Turnout
		72,848	57.7%	2001		73,666	56.6%
Seabeck A	**Lab**	**18,612**	**44.3%**	**-14%**	**Lab**	**24,322**	**58.3%**
Cuming R	C	10,509	25%	-2.1%	C	11,289	27.1%
Jolly J	LD	8,000	19%	8.2%	LD	4,513	10.8%
Wakeham B	UKIP	3,324	7.9%	5.6%	UKIP	958	2.3%
Greene K	Ind	747	1.8%		SA	334	0.8%
Hawkins R	SLP	445	1.1%	0.4%	SLP	303	0.7%
Staunton T	Respect	376	0.9%				
Lab to C swing	**6%**	**42,013**		**Lab maj 8,103** 19.3%		**41,719**	**Lab maj 13,033** 31.2%

ALISON SEABECK b 20 Feb 1954. MP 2005-. Member/official Amicus-MSF; Member Fawcett Society; Parliamentary adviser

Compromising the northern part of the western docklands area of the famous naval city, Plymouth Devonport is a largely urban working-class constituency with a stable population. It has a high proportion of council housing spread out on the hillsides, with spectacular views over the river Tamar. Despite a swing away from them in the recent election this remains a safe seat for Labour and its new MP.

PLYMOUTH SUTTON — Lab hold

		Electorate 67,202	Turnout 56.8%	Change from 2001	2001	Electorate 68,438	Turnout 57.1%
Gilroy L	**Lab/C**	**15,497**	**40.6%**	**-10.1%**	**Lab/C**	**19,827**	**50.7%**
Colvile O	C	11,388	29.8%	-1.7%	C	12,310	31.5%
Gillard K	LD	8,685	22.7%	8.4%	LD	5,605	14.3%
Cumming R	UKIP	2,392	6.3%	3.8%	UKIP	970	2.5%
Hawkins R	SLP	230	0.6%	-0.3%	SLP	361	0.9%
Lab/C to C swing	**4.2%**	**38,192**		**Lab/C maj 4,109** 10.8%		**39,073**	**Lab/C maj 7,517** 19.2%

LINDA GILROY b 19 July 1949. MP 1997-. PPS to Nick Raynsford 2001-. Member European Scrutiny select cttee 1998. Vice-chair all-party fireworks group 2002-. Member: Nat Policy Forum 2001-04. Dep dir Age Concern, Scotland 1972-79. Regional manager Gas Consumers Council 1979-96. Member: Health Policy Commission, Inst of Trading Standards Administration. Ed Stirling High Sch; MA hist, Edinburgh Univ; postgrad dip secretarial studies, Strathclyde Univ.

Taking in the centre and most of the outskirts of this Devon town, Plymouth Sutton has many of the problems of constituencies in much higher profile cities, but has had to fight hard to get the same level of funding to tackle key social issues. The boundaries were redrawn for the 1997 general election, changing the make-up of the electorate from a Tory-leaning one to solidly pro-New Labour.

PONTEFRACT AND CASTLEFORD — Lab hold

		Electorate 61,871	Turnout 53.2%	Change from 2001	2001	Electorate 63,181	Turnout 49.7%
Cooper Y	**Lab**	**20,973**	**63.7%**	**-6%**	**Lab**	**21,890**	**69.7%**
Jones S	C	5,727	17.4%	-0.2%	C	5,512	17.6%
Paxton W	LD	3,942	12%	4.6%	LD	2,315	7.4%
Cass S	BNP	1,835	5.6%		UKIP	739	2.4%
Hague B	Green S	470	1.4%		SLP	605	1.9%
					SA	330	1.1%
Lab to C swing	**2.9%**	**32,947**		**Lab maj 15,246** 46.3%		**31,391**	**Lab maj 16,378** 52.2%

YVETTE COOPER b 20 March 1969. MP 1997-. ODPM: Minister of State 2005-, Parly Under-Sec 2003-05; Parly Sec Lord Chancellor's Dept 2002-03; Parly Under-Sec for Public Health, Dept of Health 1999-2002. Member Education and Employment select cttee 1997-99. John Smith MP economic researcher 1990-92. Domestic policy specialist Bill Clinton presidential campaign 1992. Policy adviser to Lab Treasury teams 1992-94. Economist. Leader writer The Independent 1995-97. Ed BA PPE, Balliol Coll, Oxford; Kennedy Scholar, Harvard Univ; MSc econ, LSE.

This constituency in the far north west corner of West Yorkshire includes Knottingley as well as the eponymous towns. The seat is a Labour stronghold and has a strong coalmining history, but only one of its pits remains open. Despite the decline of coal the seat is still as industrial and working-class as they come.

PONTYPRIDD — Lab hold

		Electorate 65,074	Turnout 60.9%	Change from 2001	2001	Electorate 66,891	Turnout 57.3%
Howells K	**Lab**	**20,919**	**52.8%**	**-7.1%**	**Lab**	**22,963**	**59.9%**
Powell M	LD	7,728	19.5%	8.7%	PIC	5,279	13.8%
Edwards Q	C	5,321	13.4%	0.1%	C	5,096	13.3%
Richards J	PIC	4,420	11.2%	-2.6%	LD	4,152	10.8%
Bevan D	UKIP	1,013	2.6%	1%	UKIP	603	1.6%
Griffiths R	Comm	233	0.6%		ProLife	216	0.6%
Lab to LD swing	**7.9%**	**39,634**		**Lab maj 13,191** 33.3%		**38,309**	**Lab maj 17,684** 46.2%

KIM HOWELLS b 27 Nov 1946. MP Feb 1989- (by-election). Minister of State: FCO 2005-, Dept for Education and Skills 2004-05, Dept for Transport 2003-04. Parly Under-Sec: Dept for Culture, Media and Sport 2001-03, Dept of Trade and Industry 1998-2001, Dept for Education and Employment 1997-98. Opposition spokes 1993-97. Member select cttees 1989-90, 1993-94. Research officer/newspaper editor NUM 1982-89, univ research officer, radio/tv presenter and writer. Ed BA Eng/hist, Cambridge CAT; PhD UK coal industry, Warwick Univ.

Based around the market town of Pontypridd, the constituency includes former mining communities on the periphery of the valleys, as well as more affluent areas on the outskirts of Cardiff. It is scenic and contains pockets of prosperity and has been a safe Labour seat since the 1920s. It is unlikely that Plaid Cymru will ever be better positioned to challenge Dr Howells than they were at the time of his 1989 by-election success.

POOLE

C hold

		Electorate 64,178	Turnout 63.1%	Change from 2001	2001	Electorate 64,644	Turnout 60.7%
Syms R	**C**	**17,571**	**43.4%**	**-1.7%**	**C**	**17,710**	**45.1%**
Plummer M	LD	11,583	28.6%	3.1%	Lab	10,544	26.9%
Brown D	Lab	9,376	23.1%	-3.8%	LD	10,011	25.5%
Barnes J	UKIP	1,436	3.5%	1%	UKIP	968	2.5%
Pirnie P	BNP	547	1.4%				
C to LD swing	**2.4%**	**40,513**		**C maj 5,988** 14.8%		**39,233**	**C maj 7,166** 18.3%

ROBERT SYMS b 15 Aug 1956. MP 1997-. Shadow Minister: Local Govt Affairs and Communities 2005-, Local and Devolved Govt Affairs 2003-05. PPS to Michael Ancram 1999-2000. Opposition whip 2003. Opposition spokes 1999-2001. Member select cttees: Health 1997-2000, Procedure 1998-99, Transport 2002-03. Vice-chair Con Party 2001-03. Joint vice-chair Con Party Scotland/Wales constitutional affairs cttee 1997-99. Cllr: N Wilts DC 1983-87, Wilts CC 1985-87. Dir family building/plant hire/property group 1978-. Ed Colston's Sch, Bristol.

Set on the north bank of Poole harbour, Poole is an affluent and economically booming seat, from Sandbanks, which has some of the highest residential land value in Britain, to the town's many new industrial developments. Popular with the elderly and tourists alike, Poole's seaside resort ambience, and miles of sandy beaches makes it a popular location. A safe Conservative seat, it is likely to remain so for some time to come.

POPLAR AND CANNING TOWN

Lab hold

		Electorate 61,768	Turnout 63.2%	Change from 2001	2001	Electorate 84,593	Turnout 40.3%
Fitzpatrick J	**Lab**	**15,628**	**40.1%**	**-21.1%**	**Lab**	**20,866**	**61.2%**
Archer T	C	8,499	21.8%	2%	C	6,758	19.8%
Rahman O	Respect	6,573	16.8%		LD	3,795	11.1%
Ludlow J	LD	5,420	13.9%	2.8%	BNP	1,733	5.1%
McGrenera T	Greens	955	2.4%		SA	950	2.8%
Hoque A	Ind	815	2.1%				
Smith T	Veritas	650	1.7%				
Ademolake S	CPA	470	1.2%				
Lab to C swing	**11.6%**	**39,010**		**Lab maj 7,129** 18.3%		**34,102**	**Lab maj 14,108** 41.4%

JIM FITZPATRICK b 4 April 1952. MP 1997-. Parly Under-Sec ODPM 2005-. PPS to Alan Milburn 1999-2001. Whip: asst govt 2001-02, govt 2002-05. Member Selection select cttee 2003. Member London Lab Exec 1988-2000. Chair: Greater London Lab Party 1991-2000, Barking Constituency Lab Party 1989-90. Hon Treasurer London Lab MPs regional group 1999-2001. Member: Fire Brigades Union Nat Exec Council, GPMU parly group. Trainee/driver/firefighter 1970-97 (fire brigade long service and good conduct medal 1994). Ed Holyrood Senior Sec, Glasgow.

This is a recent, mixed staunch Labour seat in the Docklands area of London. High unemployment and over a quarter of the population partly skilled or unskilled contrast with around 1.5 million tourists annually, as well as offices for the London Underground, Mirror Group Newspapers, Telegraph Newspapers, and Credit Suisse. Britain's tallest building, Canary Wharf, lies in the constituency. London City Airport operates from within the constituency.

PORTSMOUTH NORTH

Lab hold

		Electorate 62,884	Turnout 60%	Change from 2001	2001	Electorate 64,256	Turnout 57.4%
McCarthy-Fry S	**Lab/C**	**15,412**	**40.9%**	**-9.8%**	**Lab**	**18,676**	**50.7%**
Mordaunt P	C	14,273	37.8%	1.1%	C	13,542	36.7%
Lawson G	LD	6,684	17.7%	7.4%	LD	3,795	10.3%
Smith M	UKIP	1,348	3.6%	2.1%	UKIP	559	1.5%
					Ind	294	0.8%
Lab/C to C swing	**5.5%**	**37,717**		**Lab/C maj 1,139** 3%		**36,866**	**Lab maj 5,134** 13.9%

SARAH McCARTHY-FRY b 4 Feb 1955. MP 2005-. Contested Wight and Hants South 1994 and South East England 1999 European Parliament elections. Cllr Portsmouth City Council 1994-2002; deputy leader 1995-2000. Financial accountant 1988-2000; financial analyst (Europe) 2000-03; financial controller 2002-05. Ed Portsmouth High School.

This largely working-class Hampshire seat takes in the outlying estates and suburbs on the mainland as well as the northern part of Portsea Island, with the ferry terminal. Portsmouth is densely populated, but people are generally more affluent here than in the southern half of the city. In some ways Portsmouth North is a conservative place, which tends to favour the incumbent, and with the departure of Syd Rapson the seat became marginal.

PORTSMOUTH SOUTH — LD hold

		Electorate	Turnout	Change from	2001	Electorate	Turnout
		70,969	56.9%	2001		77,095	50.9%
Hancock M	**LD**	**17,047**	**42.2%**	**-2.4%**	**LD**	**17,490**	**44.6%**
Dinenage C	C	13,685	33.9%	4.8%	C	11,397	29.1%
Button M	Lab	8,714	21.6%	-2.3%	Lab	9,361	23.9%
Pierson D	UKIP	928	2.3%	1.5%	SA	647	1.6%
					UKIP	321	0.8%
LD to C swing	**3.6%**	**40,374**		**LD maj 3,362**		**39,216**	**LD maj 6,093**
				8.3%			15.5%

MIKE HANCOCK b 9 April 1946. MP (SDP) for Portsmouth South 1984-87, for Portsmouth South (Lib Dem) 1997-. Spokes 1997-99, 2000-01. Member select cttees: Public Admin 1997-99, Defence 1999-, Chairmen's Panel 2000-. Vice-chair various all-party groups. Member: Lab Party 1968-81, Soc Dem Party 1981-87, Lib Dem Party 1987-, Council of Europe, Western European Union, NATO. Cllr Portsmouth CC 1971, Hants CC 1973-97 (leader 1993-97). Dir BBC Daytime. Mencap district officer 1989-97. Vice-chair Portsmouth Docks 1992-2002. CBE 1992.

This Hampshire constituency covers the densely populated area of central Portsmouth, the smart and gentrified area of Old Portsmouth with the historic dockyard and the resort of Southsea. The constituency has high numbers of students attending the university and other colleges of higher education. The voters show a certain volatility. For most of the second half of the twentieth century they returned Conservative MPs but on present evidence the Liberal Democrats appear fairly secure.

PRESELI PEMBROKESHIRE — C gain

		Electorate	Turnout	Change from	2001	Electorate	Turnout
		55,502	69.5%	2001		54,283	67.8%
Crabb S	**C**	**14,106**	**36.6%**	**3.3%**	**Lab**	**15,206**	**41.3%**
Hayman S	Lab	13,499	35%	-6.3%	C	12,260	33.3%
Smith D	LD	4,963	12.9%	2.3%	PlC	4,658	12.7%
Mathias M	PlC	4,752	12.3%	-0.4%	LD	3,882	10.6%
Carver J	UKIP	498	1.3%	0.4%	SLP	452	1.2%
Scott-Cato M	Greens	494	1.3%		UKIP	319	0.9%
Bowen T	SLP	275	0.7%	-0.5%			
Lab to C swing	**4.8%**	**38,587**		**C maj 607**		**36,777**	**Lab maj 2,946**
				1.6%			8%

STEPHEN CRABB b 20 January 1973. MP 2005-. Contested Preseli Pembrokeshire 2001 general election. Chair North Southwark and Bermondsey Conservative Association 1998-2000. Parliamentary affairs officer National Council for Voluntary Youth Services 1996-98; London Chamber of Commerce: campaigns executive 1998-2000, campaigns manager 2000-. Ed Tasker Milward VC School, Haverfordwest; politics, Bristol University.

A predominantly rural seat in south west Wales, comprising parts of English-speaking south Pembrokeshire, including much of the port town of Milford Haven, combined with the Welsh-speaking northern part of the county. Growth is hampered by the closure of the direct train line to London in 2003. The Tories' partial recovery in Wales in 2005 included the recapture of this seat from Labour who won the seat in 1997.

PRESTON — Lab hold

		Electorate	Turnout	Change from	2001	Electorate	Turnout
		63,351	53.8%	2001		72,650	49.6%
Hendrick M	**Lab/C**	**17,210**	**50.5%**	**-6.5%**	**Lab/C**	**20,540**	**57%**
Bryce F	C	7,803	22.9%	-0.1%	C	8,272	23%
Parkinson W	LD	5,701	16.7%	3.5%	LD	4,746	13.2%
Lavalette M	Respect	2,318	6.8%		Ind	1,241	3.4%
Boardman E	UKIP	1,049	3.1%		Greens	1,019	2.8%
					Ind	223	0.6%
Lab/C to C swing	**3.2%**	**34,081**		**Lab/C maj 9,407**		**36,041**	**Lab/C maj 12,268**
				27.6%			34%

MARK HENDRICK b 2 Nov 1958. MP Nov 2000- (by-election). PPS to Margaret Beckett 2003-. Member European Scrutiny select cttee 2001-04. Member Preston and District Co-operative Party 1994-. Chair Eccles constituency Lab Party 1990-94. Cllr Salford CC 1987-95. Hon vice-pres Central and W Lancs chamber of commerce/industry 1994-96, 2001-. Engineer/lecturer. MEP Lancs Central 1994-99. Ed Salford Grammar Sch; BSc electrical/electronic engineering, Liverpool Poly; MSc computer science/CertEd, Manchester Univ.

Preston, in the heart of Lancashire, is in the Ribble valley just to the east of the Fylde peninsula. An old industrial centre originally based on cotton, engineering and light industry has now replaced it. A Labour stronghold since its creation in 1983, Preston was the only English town to be conferred city status as part of the 2002 Golden Jubilee celebrations.

PUDSEY — Lab hold

		Electorate	Turnout	Change from	2001	Electorate	Turnout
		70,411	66%	2001		71,576	63.1%
Truswell P	**Lab**	**21,261**	**45.8%**	**-2.3%**	**Lab**	**21,717**	**48.1%**
Singleton P	C	15,391	33.1%	-2.5%	C	16,091	35.6%
Keeley J	LD	8,551	18.4%	4.2%	LD	6,423	14.2%
Daniel D	UKIP	1,241	2.7%	0.6%	UKIP	944	2.1%
C to Lab swing	**0.1%**	**46,444**		**Lab maj 5,870**		**45,175**	**Lab maj 5,626**
				12.6%			12.5%

PAUL TRUSWELL b 17 Nov 1955. MP 1997-. Member Environmental Audit select cttee 1997-99. Sec all-party mobile communications group 2001-. Cllr Leeds CC 1982-97. Member Leeds: Eastern Health Auth 1982-90, Community Health Council 1990-92, Family Health Services Auth 1992-96. Journalist Yorkshire Post Newspapers 1977-88. Local govt officer Wakefield MDC 1988-97. Ed Firth Park Comp Sch; BA hist, Leeds Univ.

Nestled between Leeds and Bradford, this safe Labour seat comprises the towns of Pudsey, Guiseley, Yeadon and the Leeds suburb of Horsforth. The constituency, one of Labour's biggest prizes in 1997 when they took it from the Conservatives, has an almost equal percentage of manual and non-manual workers, but an unusually low number of unskilled. Unemployment, too, is very low, and adds to the image of solid, stable white Yorkshireness.

PUTNEY — C gain

		Electorate	Turnout	Change from	2001	Electorate	Turnout
		61,498	59.5%	2001		60,643	56.5%
Greening J	**C**	**15,497**	**42.4%**	**4%**	**Lab**	**15,911**	**46.5%**
Colman T	Lab	13,731	37.5%	-9%	C	13,140	38.4%
Ambache J	LD	5,965	16.3%	2.7%	LD	4,671	13.6%
Magnum K	Greens	993	2.7%		UKIP	347	1%
Gahan A	UKIP	388	1.1%	0.1%	ProLife	185	0.5%
Lab to C swing	**6.5%**	**36,574**		**C maj 1,766**		**34,254**	**Lab maj 2,771**
				4.8%			8.1%

JUSTINE GREENING b 30 April 1969. MP 2005-. Contested Ealing, Acton and Shepherd's Bush 2001 general election. Auditor PriceWaterhouse 1991-96; Finance manager SmithKline Beecham 1996-2001; Business strategy manager GlaxoSmithKline 2001-02; Sales and marketing finance manager Centrica 2002-. Ed Oakwood Comprehensive, Rotherham; business economics and accounting, Southampton University; MBA, London Business School

This seat, which Labour took from the Conservatives in 1997, is in south-west London. Bordered by well-heeled Richmond Park to the west, Wimbledon to the south and Tooting to the east, Putney is on the cusp between inner and outer London. It has become increasingly affluent and middle class. It returned to the Tories in 2005.

RAYLEIGH — C hold

		Electorate	Turnout	Change from	2001	Electorate	Turnout
		71,996	64.2%	2001		70,653	60.5%
Francois M	**C**	**25,609**	**55.4%**	**5.3%**	**C**	**21,434**	**50.1%**
Ware-Lane J	Lab	10,883	23.6%	-7.1%	Lab	13,144	30.7%
Cumberland S	LD	7,406	16%	0.5%	LD	6,614	15.5%
Davies J	UKIP	2,295	5%	1.3%	UKIP	1,581	3.7%
Lab to C swing	**6.2%**	**46,193**		**C maj 14,726**		**42,773**	**C maj 8,290**
				31.9%			19.4%

MARK FRANCOIS b 14 Aug 1965. MP 2001-. Shadow Min: Treasury 2005-, Economic Affairs 2004-05. Opposition whip 2002-04. Member Environmental Audit select cttee 2001-. Cllr Basildon DC 1991-95. Member: European Standing Cttee A 2002-, Royal Utd Services Institute for Defence Studies 1991-, Internat Institute for Strategic Studies 1999-. TA 1983-89. Lloyds Bank management trainee 1987. Public affairs consultant 1988-95, 1996-2001. Ed Nicholas Comp Sch, Basildon; BA hist, Bristol Univ; MA war studies, King's Coll, London.

This safe Tory seat was mainly rural villages and picturesque countryside before the war, but has seen rapid population growth since then. Rayleigh is already a sizeable town and the new development of South Woodham Ferrers expands apace. Nearly all new housing developments have been private, explaining the highest proportion in England and Wales of owner-occupied accommodation here, at 90 per cent. The Rayleigh constituents are not particularly prosperous, and working-class voters are numerous.

READING EAST — C gain

		Electorate 72,806	Turnout 60.3%	Change from 2001	2001	Electorate 74,637	Turnout 58.4%
Wilson R	**C**	**15,557**	**35.4%**	**3.4%**	**Lab**	**19,538**	**44.8%**
Page T	Lab	15,082	34.4%	-10.4%	C	13,943	32%
Howson J	LD	10,619	24.2%	5.7%	LD	8,078	18.5%
White R	Greens	1,548	3.5%	1.1%	Greens	1,053	2.4%
Lamb D	UKIP	849	1.9%	0.7%	UKIP	525	1.2%
Lloyd J	Ind	135	0.3%		SA	394	0.9%
Hora R	Ind	122	0.3%	0.1%	Ind	94	0.2%
Lab to C swing	**6.9%**	**43,912**		**C maj 475** 1.1%		**43,625**	**Lab maj 5,595** 12.8%

ROBERT WILSON MP 2005-. Councillor Reading Borough Council 1992-96, 2004-. Conservative campaign manager 1992 general election campaign. Entrepreneur in health and communications; adviser to David Davis MP. Ed Reading University

Reading lies in the affluent Thames corridor and the M4. This division contains the town centre and the more commercial and business-orientated parts. It has expanded its light and service industries greatly in recent years. Most of the workforce are non-manual, with a high proportion of professionals and fairly low unemployment. Only 10 per cent of accommodation is council-rented. The surrounding area is mostly pleasant suburbia, housing commuters. It reverted to the Tories in 2005.

READING WEST — Lab hold

		Electorate 69,011	Turnout 61%	Change from 2001	2001	Electorate 71,089	Turnout 59.1%
Salter M	**Lab**	**18,940**	**45%**	**-8.1%**	**Lab**	**22,300**	**53.1%**
Cameron E	C	14,258	33.9%	1.9%	C	13,451	32%
Gaines D	LD	6,663	15.8%	3%	LD	5,387	12.8%
Williams P	UKIP	1,180	2.8%	0.8%	UKIP	848	2%
Windisch A	Greens	921	2.2%				
Boyle D	Veritas	141	0.3%				
Lab to C swing	**5%**	**42,103**		**Lab maj 4,682** 11.1%		**41,986**	**Lab maj 8,849** 21.1%

MARTIN SALTER b 19 April 1954. MP 1997-. Member select cttees: Northern Ireland Affairs 1997-99, Modernisation of HoC 2001-. Sec all-party Panjabis in Britain group 2001-. Parly shooting/fishing adviser to Richard Caborn 2002-. Member Co-operative Party. Chair SE regional Lab MPs group 1998-. Representative SE PLP campaign team 1999-. Cllr Reading BC 1984-96: dep leader 1987-96. Former TGWU/UCATT shop steward. Co-ordinator Reading Centre for Unemployed. Regional manager housing assocn 1987-96. Ed Sussex Univ.

Reading, the county town of Berkshire, forms a crossroads where the river Kennet joins the Thames. Good motorway links and the town's proximity to London have attracted national companies, particularly computer companies, to set up headquarters here. This commercial growth has added to the more traditional industries of beer, bulbs and biscuits. Low unemployment matches comparatively high owner occupation (72.9 per cent). Labour have successfully consolidated here, since winning the traditionally Tory seat in 1997.

REDCAR — Lab hold

		Electorate 66,947	Turnout 58%	Change from 2001	2001	Electorate 67,150	Turnout 56.9%
Baird V	**Lab**	**19,968**	**51.4%**	**-8.9%**	**Lab**	**23,026**	**60.3%**
Swales I	LD	7,852	20.2%	7.6%	C	9,583	25.1%
Lehrle J	C	6,954	17.9%	-7.2%	LD	4,817	12.6%
McGlade C	Ind	2,379	6.1%		SLP	772	2%
Harris A	BNP	985	2.5%				
Walker E	UKIP	564	1.4%				
Taylor J	SLP	159	0.4%	-1.6%			
Lab to LD swing	**8.3%**	**38,861**		**Lab maj 12,116** 31.2%		**38,198**	**Lab maj 13,443** 35.2%

VERA BAIRD b 13 Feb 1951. MP 2001-. PPS to Home Secretary 2005-. Member select cttees: Joint Cttee on Human Rights 2001-03, Work and Pensions 2003-. Chair all-party groups: Burma 2002-, sexual abuse 2003-, domestic violence 2004-, equalities 2004-. Vice-chair Soc of Lab Lawyers. Chair Lab Criminal Justice Forum. Barrister 1975-. QC (2000) North Eastern Circuit. Vice-Pres Assocn of Women Barristers. Ed LLB law, Newcastle Poly; BA lit/hist, Open Univ; MA mod hist, London Guildhall Univ.

A coastal constituency, Redcar includes the eponymously named seaside resort. It is sandwiched in between Middlesbrough to the south and Hartlepool and Stockton to the north. Most of the constituency is urban and heavily industrialised. ICI chemicals have a plant in Wilton, as does Corus, in Redcar. A safe seat, its voters will continue to vote for whoever wears the red rosette for the foreseeable future.

REDDITCH — Lab hold

		Electorate	Turnout	Change from	2001	Electorate	Turnout
		64,121	62.8%	2001		62,565	59.2%
Smith J	**Lab**	**18,012**	**44.7%**	**-0.9%**	**Lab**	**16,899**	**45.6%**
Lumley K	C	15,296	38%	-0.9%	C	14,415	38.9%
Hicks N	LD	5,602	13.9%	3.6%	LD	3,808	10.3%
Ison J	UKIP	1,381	3.4%		UKIP	1,259	3.4%
					Greens	651	1.8%
C to Lab swing	**0%**	**40,291**		**Lab maj 2,716**		**37,032**	**Lab maj 2,484**
				6.7%			6.7%

JACQUI SMITH b 3 Nov 1962. MP 1997-. Minister of State: Dept for Education and Skills 2005-, Industry and the Regions and Dep Minister Women and Equality, Dept of Trade and Industry 2003-05, Community, Dept of Health 2001-03. Parly Under-Sec Dept for Education and Employment 1999-2001. Member Treasury select cttee 1998-99. Cllr Redditch BC 1991-97. Member British East-West Centre. Economics teacher/teacher/head of economics/GNVQ co-ordinator 1986-97. PC 2003. Ed BA PPE, Hertford Coll, Oxford; PGCE, Worcester Coll of Higher Education.

Redditch was designated a new town in 1964, and was developed largely to cope with the overspill from the West Midlands conurbation. Nearly 30 per cent of homes in the seat remain council-rented, offering a solid foundation for Labour support, and there is a diverse mix of industry. In the south of the seat there are a couple of rural commuter villages. This Labour seat was classed vulnerable after a swing to the Conservatives in 2001 and remained so after the 2005 election.

REGENT'S PARK AND KENSINGTON NORTH — Lab hold

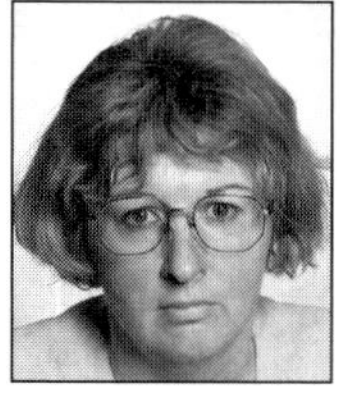

		Electorate	Turnout	Change from	2001	Electorate	Turnout
		55,824	72.9%	2001		75,886	48.8%
Buck K	**Lab**	**18,196**	**44.7%**	**-9.9%**	**Lab**	**20,247**	**54.6%**
Bradshaw J	C	12,065	29.7%	2.8%	C	9,981	26.9%
Martins R	LD	7,569	18.6%	6%	LD	4,669	12.6%
Miller P	Greens	1,985	4.9%	1.5%	Greens	1,268	3.4%
Perrin P	UKIP	456	1.1%	0.1%	SA	459	1.2%
Boufas R	CP	227	0.6%		UKIP	354	1%
Dharamsey A	Ind	182	0.4%	0.2%	Ind	74	0.2%
Lab to C swing	**6.4%**	**40,680**		**Lab maj 6,131**		**37,052**	**Lab maj 10,266**
				15.1%			27.7%

KAREN BUCK b 30 Aug 1958. MP 1997-. Parly Under-Sec Dept for Transport 2005-. Member select cttees: Soc Security 1997-2001, Selection 1999-2001, Work and Pensions 2001-. Chair all-party groups, London regional group of Lab MPs 1999-. Lab Party: policy directorate (health), campaign strategy co-ordinator. Cllr Westminster CC 1990-97. Disabled people services/employment charity worker/Borough of Hackney specialist officer. Public health officer. Ed BSc/MSc econ, MA soc policy/admin, LSE.

This safe Labour seat is a typically cosmopolitan London constituency. Mansion flats, bedsits and council estates mingle, offering accommodation to a similarly diverse range of ethnic groups, including the large black community in Notting Hill, home of the carnival. 29 per cent of homes are council-rented, and over 15 per cent are rented from housing associations – the second highest proportion in the country. Famous landmarks include Lords, home of cricket, the MCC, and Madame Tussaud's.

REIGATE — C hold

		Electorate	Turnout	Change from	2001	Electorate	Turnout
		65,719	64.8%	2001		65,023	60.7%
Blunt C	**C**	**20,884**	**49%**	**1.2%**	**C**	**18,875**	**47.8%**
Kulka J	LD	9,896	23.2%	2.1%	Lab	10,850	27.5%
Townend S	Lab	8,896	20.9%	-6.6%	LD	8,330	21.1%
Wraith J	UKIP	1,921	4.5%	1.8%	UKIP	1,062	2.7%
Green H	EDP	600	1.4%		RefUK	357	0.9%
Selby M	Ind	408	1%				
C to LD swing	**0.5%**	**42,605**		**C maj 10,988**		**39,474**	**C maj 8,025**
				25.8%			20.3%

CRISPIN BLUNT b 15 July 1960. MP 1997-. Shadow Minister Trade and Industry 2002-03. Opposition whip 2004-05. Opposition Northern Ireland spokes 2001-02. Member select cttees: Defence 1997-2000, 2003-04, Environment, Transport and Regional Affairs 2000-01. Vice-chair various all-party groups. Exec member 1922 cttee 2000-01. District agent Forum of Private Business. Political consultant. Special adviser to Malcolm Rifkind 1993-97. Ed Wellington Coll; RMA Sandhurst; BA pol, University Coll, Durham Univ; MBA Cranfield Inst of Tech.

This Surrey constituency runs from Banstead in the north to the village of Salfords in the south, with the main conurbation of Reigate and Redhill at its heart. Since the end of the Second World War, Reigate the town has grown significantly, and Reigate the constituency has an unbroken record of Conservative representation throughout the same period. Conservative majorities nowadays are not as generous as they used to be, but still generous enough.

EAST RENFREWSHIRE — Lab hold

		Electorate 65,714	Turnout 72.1%	Change from 2001	2001 (as Eastwood)		Turnout 70.8%
Murphy J	**Lab**	**20,815**	**43.9%**	**-3.7%**	**Lab**	**23,036**	**47.6%**
Cook R	C	14,158	29.9%	1.2%	C	13,895	28.7%
MacDonald G	LD	8,659	18.3%	5.4%	LD	6,239	12.9%
Bhutta O	SNP	3,245	6.8%	-1.8%	SNP	4,137	8.6%
Henderson I	SSP	528	1.1%	-0.6%	SSp	814	1.7%
Lab to C swing	**2.5%**	**47,405**		**Lab maj 6,657** 14%		**48,368**	**Lab maj 9,141** 18.9%

JIM MURPHY b 23 Aug 1967. MP for Eastwood 1997-2005, for East Renfrewshire 2005-. Parly Sec Cabinet Office 2005-, PPS to Helen Liddell 2001-02. Whip: asst govt 2002-03, govt 2003-05. Member Public Accounts select cttee 1999-2001. Sec all-party consumer affairs and trading standards group 2001-. Member Co-operative Party. Chair Lab Friends of Israel 2001-02. Scottish Lab Party project manager 1996-97. Pres NUS: Scotland 1992-94, 1994-96. Dir Endlseigh Insurance 1994-96. Ed Minerton High Sch, Cape Town; Strathclyde Univ.

Sharing its perimeter with the East Renfrewshire council, East Renfrewshire extends south and west from a cluster of prosperous commuter towns on the southern edge of Glasgow, taking in industrial Barrhead. The rest of the seat is rural: Eaglesham, the first conservation village in Scotland, is the only sizeable town in the south. This was once the safest Conservative seat in Scotland and the Labour majority, which peaked at 20 per cent in 2001, is rather anomalous.

RHONDDA — Lab hold

		Electorate 51,041	Turnout 61%	Change from 2001	2001	Electorate 56,091	Turnout 60.6%
Bryant C	**Lab**	**21,198**	**68.1%**	**-0.2%**	**Lab**	**23,230**	**68.3%**
Jones L	PlC	4,956	15.9%	-5.2%	PlC	7,183	21.1%
Roberts K	LD	3,264	10.5%	6%	C	1,557	4.6%
Stuart-Smith P	C	1,730	5.6%	1%	LD	1,525	4.5%
					Ind	507	1.5%
PlC to Lab swing	**2.5%**	**31,148**		**Lab maj 16,242** 52.1%		**34,002**	**Lab maj 16,047** 47.2%

CHRIS BRYANT b 11 Jan 1962. MP 2001-. Team PPS Dept Const Affairs 2005-. Member select cttees: Culture, Media and Sport 2001-, Joint Cttee on House of Lords Reform 2003-. Lab Party: agent 1991-93, local govt devt officer 1993-94. Chair: Lab Movement for Europe 2002-, Christian Socialist Movement 1993-98. Cllr Hackney 1993-98. Ordained priest (C of E) 1987. Freelance author. BBC European Affairs head 1998-2000. Ed BA Eng, MA, Mansfield Coll, Oxford; MA Cert Theol, Ripon Coll, Cuddesdon.

Situated in the South Wales valleys to the north west of Cardiff, Rhondda incorporates communities such as Tonypandy and Treorchy. This is one of the most famous place names in Wales. The name Rhondda conjures up an image of coalmining and village communities though the mines closed in the mid-1980s. Aside from in the 1999 National Assembly elections, the Rhondda has always been one of the very safest of all Labour seats.

RIBBLE VALLEY — C hold

		Electorate 75,692	Turnout 65.8%	Change from 2001	2001	Electorate 74,319	Turnout 66.2%
Evans N	**C**	**25,834**	**51.9%**	**0.4%**	**C**	**25,308**	**51.5%**
Young J	LD	11,663	23.4%	-5.2%	LD	14,070	28.6%
Davenport J	Lab	10,924	22%	2.1%	Lab	9,793	19.9%
Henry K	UKIP	1,345	2.7%				
LD to C swing	**2.8%**	**49,766**		**C maj 14,171** 28.5%		**49,171**	**C maj 11,238** 22.9%

NIGEL EVANS b 10 Nov 1957. MP 1992-. Shadow Sec of State Wales 2001-03. PPS to: William Hague 1996-97, Tony Baldry 1995-96, David Hunt 1993-95. Opposition spokes 1997-2001. Member select cttees: Welsh Affairs 2003-, Trade/Industry 2003-. Chair all-party Malaysia group 2004-. Vice-chair: Con Party 2004, Con Party (Conservatives Abroad) 2004-. Cllr W Glamorgan CC 1985-91. Management family retail newsagent/convenience store 1979-90. Worked on 3 US presidential elections in New York, Florida, California. Ed BA pol, Univ Coll of Wales.

This rock-solid Conservative seat is situated, as the name suggests, along the Ribble Valley in Lancashire. Tourism is a growing industry here with agriculture declining, as many farmers begin to diversify. Most of the constituency's population is concentrated near the River Ribble in small towns and villages. Although this mainly residential seat is centred on the town of Clitheroe, the largest urban community is Fulwood in the south-west of the seat at the Preston border.

SOUTH RIBBLE — Lab hold

		Electorate	Turnout	Change from	2001	Electorate	Turnout
		75,357	63%	2001		73,794	62.5%
Borrow D	**Lab**	**20,428**	**43%**	**-3.4%**	**Lab**	**21,386**	**46.4%**
Fullbrook L	C	18,244	38.4%	0.3%	C	17,584	38.1%
Alcock M	LD	7,634	16.1%	0.6%	LD	7,150	15.5%
Jones K	UKIP	1,205	2.5%				
Lab to C swing	**1.9%**	**47,511**		**Lab maj 2,184**		**46,120**	**Lab maj 3,802**
				4.6%			8.2%

DAVID BORROW b 2 Aug 1952. MP 1997-. PPS to Kim Howells 2003-. Member select cttees: Agriculture 1999-2001, Environment, Food and Rural Affairs 2001-03. Chair all-party aerospace group 1999-. Member: Co-operative Party, Lab campaign for electoral reform, European Standing Cttee C 1999-. Cllr Preston BC 1987-98: leader 1992-94, 1995-97. Merseyside Valuation Tribunal clerk 1983-97. Pres Soc of Clerks 1990-92, 1996-97. Ed Mirfield Grammar Sch; BA economics, Lanchester Poly.

The marginal Lancashire constituency of South Ribble can be divided into three distinct parts, town, suburb and country. The principal town is Leyland, an old manufacturing town, which has traditionally depended on the commercial vehicle industry. The southern suburbs of Preston, lying to the south of the river Ribble, and the small rural villages stretching between Preston and Southport form a commuter belt, but are in many respects agricultural, specialising in horticulture and market gardening.

RICHMOND PARK — LD hold

		Electorate	Turnout	Change from	2001	Electorate	Turnout
		70,555	72.8%	2001		72,251	68%
Kramer S	**LD**	**24,011**	**46.7%**	**-1%**	**LD**	**23,444**	**47.7%**
Forgione M	C	20,280	39.5%	1.9%	C	18,480	37.6%
Butler J	Lab	4,768	9.3%	-2%	Lab	5,541	11.3%
Page J	Greens	1,379	2.7%	0.2%	Greens	1,223	2.5%
Dul P	UKIP	458	0.9%	0.2%	UKIP	348	0.7%
Flower P	CPA	288	0.6%		Ind	115	0.2%
Harrison M	Ind	83	0.2%				
Weiss R	Vote Dream	63	0.1%				
Meacock R	Ind	44	0.1%				
LD to C swing	**1.5%**	**51,374**		**LD maj 3,731**		**49,151**	**LD maj 4,964**
				7.3%			10.1%

SUSAN KRAMER b 21 July 1950. MP 2005-. Chair Twickenham and Richmond Liberal Democrats 2001-02. Director, Infrastructure Capital Partners Ltd 1999-, Speciality Scanners Plc 2001-. Ed St Paul's Girls' School, Hammersmith; BA PPE St Hilda's College, Oxford; MBA Illinois University, USA

This solid Lib-Dem seat includes the towns of Richmond, Barnes and some of Kingston-upon-Thames as well as the Royal Botanic Gardens at Kew and Richmond Park. The constituency has one of the highest proportions of professional and managerial households in the country (over 66 per cent). The seat also has a relatively low number of children of school age, a relatively small percentage of people in part-time work and very few on government schemes.

RICHMOND (YORKSHIRE) — C hold

		Electorate	Turnout	Change from	2001	Electorate	Turnout
		69,521	65%	2001		65,360	67.4%
Hague W	**C**	**26,722**	**59.1%**	**0.2%**	**C**	**25,951**	**58.9%**
Foster N	Lab	8,915	19.7%	-2.2%	Lab	9,632	21.9%
Bell J	LD	7,982	17.7%	-0.2%	LD	7,890	17.9%
Rowe L	Greens	1,581	3.5%		Loony	561	1.3%
Lab to C swing	**1.2%**	**45,200**		**C maj 17,807**		**44,034**	**C maj 16,319**
				39.4%			37.1%

WILLIAM HAGUE b 26 March 1961. MP Feb 1989- (by-election). Leader Con Party/Opposition 1997-2001. Sec of State Wales 1995-97. DSS: Joint Parly Under-Sec 1993-94, Minister of State (Soc Security and Disabled People) 1994-95. PPS to Norman Lamont 1990-93. Member Joint select cttee on House of Lords Reform 2003-. Vice-pres British-American group 1997-2001. Political adviser to: Sir Geoffrey Howe, Leon Brittan. Shell UK/McKinsey and Co/JCB political and economic adviser. PC 1995. Ed PPE, Magdalen Coll, Oxford; INSEAD Business Sch, France.

William Hague, the former Leader of the Opposition, sits comfortably here having won a 1989 by-election. The two main towns are Northallerton (county town) and Richmond. The constituency is cut in half by the A1M and has a large army presence at Catterick Garrison near Richmond.

ROCHDALE LD gain

		Electorate 69,894	Turnout 58.4%	Change from 2001	2001	Electorate 69,506	Turnout 56.7%
Rowen P	**LD**	**16,787**	**41.1%**	**6.2%**	**Lab**	**19,406**	**49.2%**
Fitzsimons L	Lab	16,345	40%	-9.2%	LD	13,751	34.9%
Hussain K	C	4,270	10.5%	-2.9%	C	5,274	13.4%
Adams D	BNP	1,773	4.3%		Greens	728	1.8%
Whittaker J	UKIP	499	1.2%		None	253	0.6%
Chatterjee S	Greens	448	1.1%	-0.7%			
Salim M	IZB	361	0.9%				
Faulkner C	Veritas	353	0.9%				
Lab to LD swing	**7.7%**	**40,836**		**LD maj 442** 1.1%		**39,412**	**Lab maj 5,655** 14.3%

PAUL ROWEN b 11 May 1955. MP 2005-. Contested Rochdale 2001 general election. Leader, Rochdale Metropolitan Borough Council, 1992-96. Ed Bishop Henshaw RC Memorial High School, Rochdale; Nottingham University

The birthplace of the co-operative movement, Rochdale is a manufacturing centre where engineering and textiles are the most important industries. The greater Manchester constituency consists of the industrial town of Rochdale as well as the attractive, Pennine-hugging town of Littleborough and its environs. A former Liberal/Labour marginal, boundary changes in Labour's favour before the 1997 general election could not stop the Liberal Democrats retaking this safe seat in 2005 and re-establishing its marginal status.

ROCHFORD AND SOUTHEND EAST C hold

		Electorate 71,186	Turnout 55.4%	Change from 2001	2001	Electorate 70,328	Turnout 53.3%
Duddridge J	**C**	**17,874**	**45.3%**	**-8.3%**	**C**	**20,058**	**53.6%**
Grindrod F	Lab	12,380	31.4%	-3.4%	Lab	13,024	34.8%
Longley G	LD	5,967	15.1%	7.7%	LD	2,780	7.4%
Croft J	UKIP	1,913	4.8%		Greens	990	2.6%
Vaughan A	Greens	1,328	3.4%	0.8%	Lib	600	1.6%
C to Lab swing	**2.5%**	**39,462**		**C maj 5,494** 13.9%		**37,452**	**C maj 7,034** 18.8%

JAMES DUDDRIDGE b 26 August 1971. MP 2005-. Contested Rother Valley 2001 general election. Research assistant to Bernard Jenkin 1991-93; Campaign manager for Stephen Shakespeare 1997; Executive committee Conservative Way Forward 1998. Barclays Bank Head Office 1995-96; Barclays Bank of Swaziland 1995-96; Sales director Banque Belgolaise Ivory Coast 1997-98; National sales manager Barclays 1998. Ed Huddersfield New College; Wells Blue School; BA government, Essex University

This recent, safe Tory constituency combines part of the residential district of Rochford, with its many open spaces and waterways, with the eastern part of the popular Essex seaside resort of Southend-on-Sea, including areas such as Shoeburyness and Southchurch. There are excellent rail connections with London Liverpool Street and some 70 per cent of the homes are owner-occupied. The area now has many businesses and public offices providing employment in the town and adjacent communities.

ROMFORD C hold

		Electorate 58,571	Turnout 62.3%	Change from 2001	2001	Electorate 60,040	Turnout 59.5%
Rosindell A	**C**	**21,560**	**59.1%**	**6.1%**	**C**	**18,931**	**53%**
Mullane M	Lab	9,971	27.3%	-9%	Lab	12,954	36.3%
Seeff G	LD	3,066	8.4%	0.4%	LD	2,869	8%
McCaffrey J	BNP	1,088	3%	1.8%	UKIP	533	1.5%
Murray T	UKIP	797	2.2%	0.7%	BNP	414	1.2%
Lab to C swing	**7.6%**	**36,482**		**C maj 11,589** 31.8%		**35,701**	**C maj 5,977** 16.7%

ANDREW ROSINDELL b 17 March 1966. MP 2001-. Member select cttees: Regulatory Reform 2001-, Joint Cttee on Statutory Instruments 2002-03, Constitutional Affairs 2004-. Vice-chair Con Party 2004-. Member Nat Union Exec Cttee Con Party 1986-88, 1992-94. Chair: Con Friends of Gibraltar 2002-, Internat Young Democrat Union 1998-2002. Cllr Havering 1990-2002. Central Press Features, freelance journalist. Parly researcher Vivian Bendall MP. Dir/internat dir European Foundation 1997-2001. Ed Marshalls Park Comp Sch, Romford.

Romford has a 750 year old market. It is an important office and retail centre for north London and Essex and is home to the administrative headquarters of the London Borough of Havering. The seat largely comprises owner-occupied homes, middle-class, white collar workers, and skilled manual workers, amount to 30 per cent of the workforce. The tough-campaigning, Eurosceptic MP Andrew Rosindell resecured this seat for the Tories in 2001, after Romford had succumbed to Labour in 1997.

ROMSEY — LD hold

		Electorate 72,177	Turnout 69.7%	Change from 2001	2001	Electorate 72,574	Turnout 66.8%
Gidley S	**LD**	**22,465**	**44.6%**	**-2.4%**	**LD**	**22,756**	**47%**
Nokes C	C	22,340	44.4%	2.3%	C	20,386	42.1%
Stevens M	Lab	4,430	8.8%	0.6%	Lab	3,986	8.2%
Wigley M	UKIP	1,076	2.1%	0.6%	UKIP	730	1.5%
					LCA	601	1.2%
LD to C swing	**2.4%**	**50,311**		**LD maj 125** 0.2%		**48,459**	**LD maj 2,370** 4.9%

SANDRA GIDLEY b 26 March 1957. MP May 2000- (by-election). Shadow Minister Women 2003-. Lib Dem spokes: health and women's issues 2001-02, older people 2003-. Member Health select cttee 2001-03. Chair all-party groups: mental health 2001-, health 2003-, housing, care and support 2004-. Cllr Test Valley BC 1995-2003. Mayor Romsey Town 1997-98. Pharmacist. Ed BPharm, Bath Univ.

Romsey is a well-preserved medieval town, which attracts tourists to its abbey and the nearby country house of Broadlands. The landscape of the seat as a whole is typified by high quality agricultural land, olde world villages, and affluent Southampton suburbs. The needs of commuters are well-served by the M27. In the 2000 by-election the Conservatives suffered a massive shock, being swept away by the Liberal Democrats in this previously safe seat.

ROSS, SKYE AND LOCHABER — LD hold

		Electorate 50,507	Turnout 64.4%		2001
Kennedy C	**LD**	**19,100**	**58.7%**		No comparable results due to boundary changes
Conniff C	Lab	4,851	14.9%		
Hodgson J	C	3,275	10.1%		
Will M	SNP	3,119	9.6%		
Jardine D	Greens	1,097	3.4%		
Anderson P	UKIP	500	1.5%		
McLeod A	SSP	412	1.3%		
Grant M	Ind	184	0.6%		
Lab to LD swing (notional)	**11.3%**	**32,538**		**LD maj 14,249** 43.8%	

CHARLES KENNEDY b 25 Nov 1959. MP for Ross, Cromarty and Skye 1983-97, for Ross, Skye and Inverness West 1997-2005, for Ross, Skye and Lochaber 2005-. Alliance/SDP/Lib Dem spokes 1987-99. Member Standards and Privileges select cttee 1997-99. Vice-pres all-party British-American group 2000-. Lib Dem Party: leader 1999-, pres 1990-94. Member Lib Dem: federal exec cttee, policy cttee. Journalist, broadcaster. PC 1999. Ed Lochaber High Sch, Fort William; MA politics, philosophy, English, Glasgow Univ; Indiana Univ.

Geographically this is the biggest constituency in the UK. It sprawls across the lochs, glens and mountains of western and central portion of the Scottish highlands to Dingwall and the Black Isle in the north-east, Ullapool and the Isle of Skye in the north-west and Glencoe and Fort William in the south. It is largely the old Ross, Skye and Inverness seat, with Inverness swapped for Lochaber. The Liberal Democrats substantially outweigh Labour in Parliamentary elections.

ROSSENDALE AND DARWEN — Lab hold

		Electorate 72,207	Turnout 61.5%	Change from 2001	2001	Electorate 70,683	Turnout 58.9%
Anderson J	**Lab**	**19,073**	**42.9%**	**-5.8%**	**Lab**	**20,251**	**48.7%**
Adams N	C	15,397	34.6%	-2.1%	C	15,281	36.7%
Carr M	LD	6,670	15%	0.4%	LD	6,079	14.6%
Wentworth A	BNP	1,736	3.9%				
McIver G	Greens	821	1.8%				
Duthie D	UKIP	740	1.7%				
Lab to C swing	**1.9%**	**44,437**		**Lab maj 3,676** 8.3%		**41,611**	**Lab maj 4,970** 11.9%

JANET ANDERSON b 6 Dec 1949. MP 1992-. Parly Under-Sec Dept for Culture, Media and Sport 1998-2001. PPS to Margaret Beckett as Lab Party dep leader 1992-93. Whip: opposition 1995-96, govt 1997-98. Opposition spokes for women 1996-97. Member select cttees 1994-. Chair various all-party groups 2003-. Parly Lab Party: representative HoC Commission 1993-94. Vice-chair Lab campaign for electoral reform. PA to: Barbara Castle 1974-81, Jack Straw 1981-87. Secretary. Ed bi-lingual business studies dip, Central London Poly; Nantes Univ.

Situated to the north of Greater Manchester, the semi-safe Labour seat of Rossendale and Darwen includes the towns of Rawenstall, Whitworth, and Darwen. Traditional employment in the textiles industry and mining has now virtually disappeared, but there is still an industrial base with jobs provided in engineering and in the manufacture of paint, plastics and wallpaper. The pleasant Lancashire countryside outside the towns also attracts visitors who provide employment in tourism.

ROTHER VALLEY — Lab hold

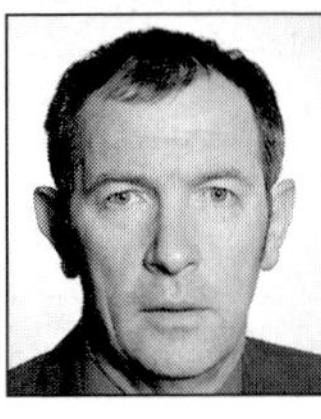

		Electorate 67,973	Turnout 58.1%	Change from 2001	2001	Electorate 69,174	Turnout 53.2%
Barron K	**Lab**	**21,871**	**55.4%**	**-6.7%**	**Lab**	**22,851**	**62.1%**
Phillips C	C	7,647	19.4%	-2.3%	C	7,969	21.7%
Bristow P	LD	6,272	15.9%	3.4%	LD	4,603	12.5%
Cass N	BNP	2,020	5.1%		UKIP	1,380	3.7%
Brown G	UKIP	1,685	4.3%	0.6%			
Lab to C swing	**2.2%**	**39,495**		**Lab maj 14,224** 36%		**36,803**	**Lab maj 14,882** 40.4%

KEVIN BARRON b 26 Oct 1946. MP 1983-. PPS to Neil Kinnock 1985-88. Opposition spokes: energy 1988-92, employment 1993-95, health 1995-97. Chair all-party groups: pharmaceutical industry 1997-, Bulgaria 1999-, connecting communities 2003-, infertility 2003-. Chair Yorkshire regional group of Lab MPs 1987-. National Coal Board 1962-83. PC 2001. Ed Maltby Hall Sec; dip Labour studies, Ruskin Coll, Oxford.

This is a working-class safe Labour seat with an industrial heritage based on coal. Unemployment is not a grave problem, however. More unusual is the high level (70 per cent) of owner-occupation and the corresponding dearth of council-rented homes. This, combined with large areas of open countryside would normally point to a Conservative threat. The lack of threat results from a working-class electorate that feels alienated by the pit closure programme.

ROTHERHAM — Lab hold

		Electorate 54,410	Turnout 55.1%	Change from 2001	2001	Electorate 57,931	Turnout 50.7%
MacShane D	**Lab**	**15,840**	**52.8%**	**-11.1%**	**Lab**	**18,759**	**63.9%**
Gordon T	LD	5,159	17.2%	6.6%	C	5,682	19.4%
Rotherham L	C	4,966	16.6%	-2.8%	LD	3,117	10.6%
Guest M	BNP	1,986	6.6%		UKIP	730	2.5%
Cutts D	UKIP	1,122	3.7%	1.2%	Greens	577	2%
Penycate D	Greens	905	3%	1%	SA	352	1.2%
					JLDP	137	0.5%
Lab to LD swing	**8.9%**	**29,978**		**Lab maj 10,681** 35.6%		**29,354**	**Lab maj 13,077** 44.5%

DENIS MacSHANE b 21 May 1948. MP May 1994- (by-election). FCO: Minister of State 2002-05, Parly Under-Sec 2001-02. Joint PPS to Ministers of State Foreign and Commonwealth Office 1999-2001. PPS to: Geoff Hoon 1999, Joyce Quin, Derek Fatchett, Tony Lloyd 1997-99. Member Deregulation select cttee 1996-97. Pres NUJ 1978-79. BBC producer 1969-77, Internat Metal Workers Federation policy dir, dir European Policy Institute 1992-94. Ed MA mod hist, Merton Coll, Oxford; PhD international economics, London Univ.

Rotherham's Labour-voting tradition is part of the South Yorkshire town's industrial working-class heritage. The local economy was built on coal, steel and heavy manufacturing industries, and with their decline has come a more fervent endorsement of Labour at elections. There was, though, a notable decline in that vote in 2005.

RUGBY AND KENILWORTH — C gain

		Electorate 83,303	Turnout 68.4%	Change from 2001	2001	Electorate 79,764	Turnout 67.4%
Wright J	**C**	**23,447**	**41.2%**	**1.5%**	**Lab**	**24,221**	**45%**
King A	Lab	21,891	38.4%	-6.6%	C	21,344	39.7%
Allanach R	LD	10,143	17.8%	4%	LD	7,444	13.8%
Thurley J	UKIP	911	1.6%	0.1%	UKIP	787	1.5%
Hadland B	Ind	299	0.5%				
Pallikaropoulos L	Ind	258	0.4%				
Lab to C swing	**4.1%**	**56,949**		**C maj 1,556** 2.7%		**53,796**	**Lab maj 2,877** 5.3%

JEREMY WRIGHT b 24 October 1972. MP 2005-. Chair, Warwick and Leamington Conservative Association 2002-03. Criminal law barrister 1996-; Ed Taunton School, Somerset; Trinity School, New York; law, Exeter University; Bar vocational course, Inns of Court School of Law.

Situated to the south east of the West Midlands conurbation, the two towns that give this Tory-Labour marginal seat its name are quite detached in geography and character. Industry in the seat is centred around Rugby, with its good motorway and rail links. GEC are big employers, as are Peugeot-Talbot whose main factory is in Ryton-on-Dunsmore. Dairy farming is widespread too. Kenilworth is most famous for its twelfth-century castle.

RUISLIP NORTHWOOD — C hold

		Electorate 60,774	Turnout 65.3%	Change from 2001	2001	Electorate 60,777	Turnout 61.1%
Hurd N	**C**	**18,939**	**47.7%**	**-1.1%**	**C**	**18,115**	**48.8%**
Cox M	LD	10,029	25.3%	6%	Lab	10,578	28.5%
Riley A	Lab	8,323	21%	-7.5%	LD	7,177	19.3%
Lee G	Greens	892	2.2%	0.3%	Greens	724	1.9%
Edward I	NF	841	2.1%		BNP	547	1.5%
Courtenay R	UKIP	646	1.6%				
C to LD swing	**3.6%**	**39,670**		**C maj 8,910** 22.5%		**37,141**	**C maj 7,537** 20.3%

NICK HURD b 1962. MP 2005-. Kensington and Chelsea borough champion for Steve Norris 2003. Member Vote No to the EU Constitution Campaign. Business consultant. Chief of staff to Tim Yeo MP. Ed Oxford University.

This safe Tory constituency is mainly suburban and semi-rural, bordering the Hertfordshire and Buckinghamshire countryside, but with such metropolitan affinities as tube lines. Housing is largely owner-occupied in the prosperous commuter suburbs. There is no major industry in the area, the biggest local employer outside the public sector is Express Dairies, with only 500 employees. The majority of constituents work in finance, commerce or retail in the West End or City.

RUNNYMEDE AND WEYBRIDGE — C hold

		Electorate 74,172	Turnout 58.7%	Change from 2001	2001	Electorate 75,569	Turnout 56.1%
Hammond P	**C**	**22,366**	**51.4%**	**2.7%**	**C**	**20,646**	**48.7%**
Greenwood P	Lab	10,017	23%	-6%	Lab	12,286	29%
Bolton H	LD	7,771	17.8%	1.5%	LD	6,924	16.3%
Micklethwait T	UKIP	1,719	4%	0.9%	UKIP	1,332	3.1%
Gilman C	Greens	1,180	2.7%	-0.2%	Greens	1,238	2.9%
Collett A	Loony	358	0.8%				
Osman K	UKC	113	0.3%				
Lab to C swing	**4.4%**	**43,524**		**C maj 12,349** 28.4%		**42,426**	**C maj 8,360** 19.7%

PHILIP HAMMOND b 4 Dec 1955. MP 1997-. Shadow Chief Sec to Treasury 2005-. Shadow Minister: Local/Devolved Govt Affairs 2003-05, ODPM 2002-03. Opposition spokes: health/soc services 1998-2001, trade and industry 2001-02. Member select cttees: Unopposed Bills (Panel) 1997-2004, Environment, Transport and Regional Affairs 1998, Trade/Industry 2002. Chair: all-party group, East Lewisham Con Assocn 1989-96. Member European standing cttee B 1997-98. Company director/Malawi govt consultant. Ed MA PPE, Univ Coll, Oxford.

The constituency of Runnymede and Weybridge, in the affluent commuter belt ringing London, is part suburban and part rural in character. The borough of Runnymede is named after the meadows where King John signed the Magna Carta in 1215. The meadows have changed little since then. The constituency includes towns such as Chertsey, Egham, Virginia Water and Weybridge, a major engineering centre until the 1960s. This is a safe Conservative seat.

RUSHCLIFFE — C hold

		Electorate 79,913	Turnout 70.5%	Change from 2001	2001	Electorate 81,847	Turnout 66.5%
Clarke K	**C**	**27,899**	**49.5%**	**2%**	**C**	**25,869**	**47.5%**
Gamble E	Lab	14,925	26.5%	-7.5%	Lab	18,512	34%
Khan K	LD	9,813	17.4%	3.8%	LD	7,385	13.6%
Anthony S	Greens	1,692	3%	0.7%	UKIP	1,434	2.6%
Faithfull M	UKIP	1,358	2.4%	-0.2%	Greens	1,236	2.3%
Moss D	Veritas	624	1.1%				
Lab to C swing	**4.8%**	**56,311**		**C maj 12,974** 23%		**54,436**	**C maj 7,357** 13.5%

KENNETH CLARKE b 2 July 1940. MP 1970-. Chancellor of Exchequer 1993-97; Home Sec 1992-93; Sec of State: Education/Science 1990-92, Health 1988-90; Chancellor Duchy of Lancaster, Minister of Trade & Industry 1987-88; Paymaster General, Employment Minister 1985-87; Minister Health 1982-85; Transport Parly Under-Sec/Parly Sec 1979-82; PPS 1971-72. Whip 1972-74. Opposition spokes 1974-79. Member HoL Reform select cttee 2003-. Contested Con Party leadership 1997, 2001. Barrister. PC 1984. Ed BA/LLB, Gonville and Caius Coll, Cambridge.

The main town is West Bridgford, a middle-class commuter suburb on the south-eastern edge of Nottingham. The rest of the seat is rural with prosperous small villages. Coal-mining, gypsum-mining and gravel pits are the main industries and the constituency has a C category prison at Watton. This is a safe Conservative seat.

RUTHERGLEN AND HAMILTON WEST — Lab hold

		Electorate	Turnout	2001
		73,998	58.5%	
McAvoy T	**Lab/C**	**24,054**	**55.6%**	No comparable results due to boundary changes
Robertson I	LD	7,942	18.4%	
Park M	SNP	6,023	13.9%	
Crerar P	C	3,621	8.4%	
Bonnar B	SSP	1,164	2.7%	
Murdoch J	UKIP	457	1.1%	
Lab/C to LD swing (notional)	**5.4%**	**43,261**	**Lab/C maj 16,112** 37.2%	

THOMAS McAVOY b 14 Dec 1943. MP for Glasgow Rutherglen 1987-2005, for Rutherglen and Hamilton West 2005-. Whip: opposition 1991-93, 1996-97, govt (pairing whip) 1997-. Member select cttees: Northern Ireland Affairs 1994-96, Finance and Services 1997-. Member Co-operative Party. Chair Rutherglen Community Council 1980-82, Strathclyde regional cllr Rutherglen and Toryglen 1982-87. Chair tenants assocns 1980-82: Fernhill, Rutherglen. Engineering storeman. AEU shop steward 1974-87. PC 2003. Ed secondary schools.

Spreading south-east from the margins of Glasgow, this seat was formed in 2005 when the dozen South Lanarkshire wards from Glasgow Rutherglen were combined with nine more from Hamilton South. It is densely urban in the north-west, centred on Rutherglen and Cambuslang. In the south, it extends along the west side of the M74, taking in Blantyre and west Hamilton. Still marked by heavy industry, this is natural Labour territory, and the party dominates the area.

RUTLAND AND MELTON — C hold

		Electorate	Turnout	Change from	2001	Electorate	Turnout
		75,823	65%	2001		73,264	64.2%
Duncan A	**C**	**25,237**	**51.2%**	**3.1%**	**C**	**22,621**	**48.1%**
Arnold L	Lab	12,307	25%	-4.8%	Lab	14,009	29.8%
Hudson G	LD	9,153	18.6%	0.8%	LD	8,386	17.8%
Baker P	UKIP	1,554	3.2%	0.6%	UKIP	1,223	2.6%
Shelley D	Veritas	696	1.4%		Greens	817	1.7%
Pender H	Ind	337	0.7%				
Lab to C swing	**4%**	**49,284**		**C maj 12,930** 26.2%		**47,056**	**C maj 8,612** 18.3%

ALAN DUNCAN b 31 March 1957. MP 1992-. Shadow Sec of State: Transport 2005-, Internat Devt 2003-05. Parly Political Sec to William Hague 1997-98; PPS to Dr Brian Mawhinney 1993-94. Opposition spokes: health 1998-99, trade/industry 1999-2001, foreign/Commonwealth affairs 2001-03. Member Soc Security select cttee 1992-95. Chair all-party Oman group 2000-. Vice-chair Con Party 1997-98. Shell trainee/oil trader. Govt/companies oil supply, shipping, refining adviser. Ed BA PPE, St John's Coll, Oxford; Kennedy Scholar, Harvard Univ.

Lying just south of Nottingham, Rutland and Melton is one of the most rural constituencies in the country. It is a typical rural Tory seat, with much agriculture industry (food processing and animal feed production), and no large centres of population. Most of the inhabitants are white and middle-class, and only 12 per cent of homes council-rented. The unemployment rate, at 1 per cent, is among the very lowest in the country.

RYEDALE — C hold

		Electorate	Turnout	Change from	2001	Electorate	Turnout
		67,770	65.1%	2001		66,849	65.7%
Greenway J	**C**	**21,251**	**48.2%**	**1%**	**C**	**20,711**	**47.2%**
Beever G	LD	10,782	24.4%	-11.7%	LD	15,836	36.1%
Blanchard P	Lab	9,148	20.7%	6%	Lab	6,470	14.7%
Feaster S	UKIP	1,522	3.4%	1.4%	UKIP	882	2%
Clarke J	Lib	1,417	3.2%				
LD to C swing	**6.4%**	**44,120**		**C maj 10,469** 23.7%		**43,899**	**C maj 4,875** 11.1%

JOHN GREENWAY b 15 Feb 1946. MP 1987-. PPS to Baroness Trumpington 1991-92. Opposition spokes: home affairs 1997-2000, culture, media and sport 2000-03. Member select cttees: Home Affairs 1987-97, Education and Skills 2005-. Chair all-party groups: insurance/financial services 1992-, opera 1994. Member: exec 1922 cttee 1997, 2004-, 92 group. Cllr N Yorks CC 1985-87. Police officer/insurance broker/financial consultant. Pres Inst of Insurance Brokers. Ed Sir John Dean's Grammar Sch, Northwich; Hendon Police Coll; London Coll of Law.

Ryedale, a Conservative stronghold, extends over a huge area, from the suburbs of north York to the coast at Filey, just below Scarborough, including a large part of the North York Moors National Park, and has few towns of any size. The unemployment rate is lower than the national average. There is thoroughbred racehorse training at Malton, and the stately home of Castle Howard.

SAFFRON WALDEN — C hold

		Electorate 77,600	Turnout 68.3%	Change from 2001	2001	Electorate 76,724	Turnout 65.2%
Haselhurst A	**C**	**27,263**	**51.4%**	**2.5%**	**C**	**24,485**	**48.9%**
Tealby-Watson E	LD	14,255	26.9%	2%	LD	12,481	24.9%
Nandanwa S	Lab	8,755	16.5%	-6.1%	Lab	11,305	22.6%
Brown R	Eng Dem	1,412	2.7%		UKIP	1,769	3.5%
Tyler R	UKIP	860	1.6%	-1.9%			
Hackett T	Veritas	475	0.9%				
LD to C swing	**0.3%**	**53,020**		**C maj 13,008** 24.5%		**50,040**	**C maj 12,004** 24%

SIR ALAN HASELHURST b 23 June 1937. MP for Middleton and Prestwich 1970-74, for Saffron Walden 1977-. PPS to Mark Carlisle 1979-81. Member Catering select cttee 1991-97. Chair Ways and Means/Dep Speaker 1997-. Hon sec all-party parly cricket group 1993-. Dep chair Con group for Europe 1982-85. Chair Commonwealth Youth Exchange Council 1978-81. Sec/treasurer/librarian Oxford Union Soc. Chemicals/plastics exec. Public affairs consultant. Kt 1995; PC 1999. Ed Cheltenham Coll; Oriel Coll, Oxford.

This safe Conservative constituency in Essex is mainly rural with agriculture and tourism forming important industries. There are some jobs in manufacturing and services based around the towns of Saffron Walden, Great Dunmow and Halstead. The biggest employer is Stansted Airport: 10,000 people work there. Unemployment is very low at 1.1 per cent.

ST ALBANS — C gain

		Electorate 64,595	Turnout 70.4%	Change from 2001	2001	Electorate 66,040	Turnout 66.3%
Main A	**C**	**16,953**	**37.3%**	**2.1%**	**Lab**	**19,889**	**45.4%**
Pollard K	Lab	15,592	34.3%	-11.1%	C	15,423	35.2%
Green M	LD	11,561	25.4%	7.5%	LD	7,847	17.9%
Evans R	UKIP	707	1.6%	0.2%	UKIP	602	1.4%
Girsman J	St Albans	430	1%				
Reynolds M	Ind	219	0.5%				
Lab to C swing	**6.6%**	**45,462**		**C maj 1,361** 3%		**43,761**	**Lab maj 4,466** 10.2%

ANNE MAIN b 17 May 1957. MP 2005-. Cllr: Beaconsfield Parish Council 1999-2002, South Buckinghamshire District Council 2001-; Teaching and family 1979-80; Home-maker 1980-90; Carer for terminally ill husband 1990-91; Single parent and supply teacher 1991-95; Ed Bishop of Llandaff Secondary School, Cardiff; BA English, Swansea University; PGCE Sheffield University

This Tory-Labour marginal seat in Hertfordshire contains the cathedral city of St Albans to the north and the towns of London Colney, Bricket Wood to the south and is home to many commuters into London. Three motorways dissect the constituency, the M25, M10 and M1. These communication links have facilitated diversification away from traditional businesses such as printing and musical instrument manufacture into electronics and service industries.

ST HELENS NORTH — Lab hold

		Electorate 69,834	Turnout 56.2%	Change from 2001	2001	Electorate 71,313	Turnout 52.7%
Watts D	**Lab**	**22,329**	**56.9%**	**-4.2%**	**Lab**	**22,977**	**61.1%**
Beirne J	LD	8,367	21.3%	3.7%	C	7,076	18.8%
Oakley P	C	7,410	18.9%	0.1%	LD	6,609	17.6%
Hall S	UKIP	1,165	3%		SLP	939	2.5%
Lab to LD swing	**4%**	**39,271**		**Lab maj 13,962** 35.6%		**37,601**	**Lab maj 15,901** 42.3%

DAVID WATTS b 26 Aug 1951. MP 1997-. PPS to: John Prescott as Dep PM 2003-05, John Spellar 1999-2002. Govt whip 2005-. Member Finance and Services select cttee 1997-2001. Membership sec all-party India group 2004-. Chair PLP north west regional group 2000-01. Lab Party organiser. Cllr St Helens MBC 1979-97: leader 1993-97. Vice-chair assocn of metropolitan authorities. UK pres Euro group of industrial regions 1989-93. MP research asst 1992-97. Shop steward Utd Biscuits AEU. Ed Seel Road Sec Mod Sch.

The slightly more affluent of the St Helens constituencies, St Helens North, like its neighbour, is a staunch Labour stronghold. Change does not come naturally to these Merseyside voters, and Labour candidates have been winning here for decades. A mainly industrial seat, glass manufacture is the predominant industry. There is also a history of coalmining here, further strengthening its bond with the Labour Party.

ST HELENS SOUTH — Lab hold

		Electorate 65,441	Turnout 54.2%	Change from 2001	2001	Electorate 65,741	Turnout 51.4%
Woodward S	**Lab**	**19,345**	**54.5%**	**4.8%**	**Lab**	**16,799**	**49.7%**
Spencer B	LD	10,036	28.3%	5.2%	LD	7,814	23.1%
Riley U	C	4,602	13%	-0.8%	C	4,675	13.8%
Nightingale M	UKIP	847	2.4%	1.4%	SA	2,325	6.9%
Perry M	SLP	643	1.8%	-2.6%	SLP	1,504	4.4%
					UKIP	336	1%
					Ind	271	0.8%
					Ind	80	0.2%
Lab to LD swing	**0.2%**	**35,473**		**Lab maj 9,309** 26.2%		**33,804**	**Lab maj 8,985** 26.6%

SHAUN WOODWARD b 26 Oct 1958. MP for Witney 1997-2001 (Con 1997-99, Lab 1999-2001), for St Helens South 2001-. Parly Under-Sec NI Office 2005-. Opposition environment, transport and regions spokes 1999. Member select cttees: Broadcasting 1997-99, 2000-01, European Scrutiny 1998-99, Foreign Affairs 1999, Joint Cttee on Human Rights 2001-. Dir Con Party communications 1991-92. BBC TV news/current affairs 1982-98. Dir English Nat Opera. Ed Bristol Grammar Sch; MA Eng lit, Jesus Coll, Cambridge.

St Helens is noted mainly for two things – glass manufacture and its rugby league team. The giant Pilkington glass factory is found in this seat which helps make St Helens the largest glass producing area in the country, although there are also a number of other manufacturing industries in the town. Although not as safe as its northern counterpart, Labour is firmly entrenched here.

ST IVES — LD hold

		Electorate 74,716	Turnout 67.5%	Change from 2001	2001	Electorate 74,256	Turnout 66.3%
George A	**LD**	**25,577**	**50.7%**	**-0.9%**	**LD**	**25,413**	**51.6%**
Mitchell C	C	13,968	27.7%	-3.5%	C	15,360	31.2%
Dooley M	Lab	6,583	13.1%	-0.2%	Lab	6,567	13.3%
Faulkner M	UKIP	2,551	5.1%	1.2%	UKIP	1,926	3.9%
Slack K	Greens	1,738	3.4%				
C to LD swing	**1.3%**	**50,417**		**LD maj 11,609** 23%		**49,266**	**LD maj 10,053** 20.4%

ANDREW GEORGE b 2 Dec 1958. MP 1997-. Lib Dem Shadow: Sec of State Internat Devt 2005-, Minister Food and Rural Affairs 2002-05. PPS to Charles Kennedy as Lib Dem Party Leader 2001-02. Lib Dem Shadow Minister: Disabilities 1999-2001, Fisheries 1997-99. Lib Dem spokes 1997-. Member Agriculture select cttee 1997-2000. Rural community devt charity worker. Dep dir Cornwall Rural Community Devt Council 1994-97. Ed BA cultural/community studies, Sussex Univ; MSc agricultural economics, Univ Coll, Oxford.

St Ives, Britain's most south westerly constituency, is a rural seat where agriculture, horticulture, tourism and fishing are the most important industries. The attractiveness of the constituency as a place to live is reflected in the high figure of retired residents and the number of second homes. A Conservative stronghold for over 60 years, it fell to the Liberal Democrats in 1997 and now looks even safer for them.

SALFORD — Lab hold

		Electorate 53,294	Turnout 42.4%	Change from 2001	2001	Electorate 54,152	Turnout 41.6%
Blears H	**Lab**	**13,007**	**57.6%**	**-7.5%**	**Lab**	**14,649**	**65.1%**
Owen N	LD	5,062	22.4%	6.2%	LD	3,637	16.2%
Cash L	C	3,440	15.2%	-0.1%	C	3,446	15.3%
Duffy L	UKIP	1,091	4.8%		SA	414	1.8%
					Ind	216	1%
					Ind	152	0.7%
Lab to LD swing	**6.9%**	**22,600**		**Lab maj 7,945** 35.2%		**22,514**	**Lab maj 11,012** 48.9%

HAZEL BLEARS b 14 May 1956. MP 1997-. Minister of State Home Office 2003-. Parly Under-Sec: Public Health 2002-03, Health 2001-02. PPS to Alan Milburn 1998-99. Member: Nat Policy Reform 1997-2001, leadership campaign team 1997-98, leader parly campaign team 2003. Chair NW regional group of Lab MPs 1998-99. Cllr Salford CC 1984-92. Solicitor. Branch sec UNISON 1981-85. Chair Salford Community Health Council 1993-97. PC 2005. Ed BA law, Trent Poly; Law Soc part II, Chester Coll of Law.

Although part of Greater Manchester, Salford, lying on the left bank of the river Irwell, is technically a city in its own right. The industrial image depicted in the paintings of L S Lowry has almost disappeared following the decline of the textiles and coal mining industries, and manufacturing companies such as Colgate Palmolive are now major employers. This has long been a safe Labour seat, having returned members continuously since 1945.

SALISBURY C hold

		Electorate	Turnout	Change from	2001	Electorate	Turnout
		80,385	67.6%	2001		80,527	65.3%
Key R	**C**	**25,961**	**47.8%**	**1.2%**	**C**	**24,527**	**46.6%**
Denton-White R	LD	14,819	27.3%	-2.8%	LD	15,824	30.1%
Moody C	Lab	9,457	17.4%	-0.1%	Lab	9,199	17.5%
Howard F	UKIP	2,290	4.2%	0.5%	UKIP	1,958	3.7%
Soutar H	Greens	1,555	2.9%	0.8%	Greens	1,095	2.1%
Holme J	Ind	240	0.4%				
LD to C swing	**2%**	**54,322**		**C maj 11,142**		**52,603**	**C maj 8,703**
				20.5%			16.5%

ROBERT KEY b 22 April 1945. MP 1983-. Shadow Min: Econ Affairs/Environ and Transport 2004-05, Internat Devt 2002-03. Parly Under-Sec Depts of: Transport 1993-94, Nat Heritage 1992-93, Environ 1990-92. PPS to: Christopher Patten 1987-90, Alick Buchanan-Smith 1985-87. Edward Heath Political Sec 1984-85. Opposition spokes 1997-2003. Member select cttees 1994- (chair Information 2004-). Member 1922 cttee exec 2003-04, UK UNESCO nat commission 1984-85. Assistant school master 1967-83. Ed BA econ/MA/CertEd, Clare Coll, Cambridge.

The two most famous aspects of this constituency are Stonehenge and Salisbury Cathedral. It was also the seat of the 18th-century Prime Minister, William Pitt the younger. Salisbury has strong military links, and large parts of the constituency are marked as danger areas on maps due to their use in military training exercises. After an increase in their majority in Election 2005 Salisbury is once again safe Conservative territory.

SCARBOROUGH AND WHITBY C gain

		Electorate	Turnout	Change from	2001	Electorate	Turnout
		73,806	63.6%	2001		75,213	63.2%
Goodwill R	**C**	**19,248**	**41%**	**1.4%**	**Lab**	**22,426**	**47.2%**
Quinn L	Lab	18,003	38.4%	-8.8%	C	18,841	39.6%
Exley-Moore T	LD	7,495	16%	7.6%	LD	3,977	8.4%
Dixon J	Greens	1,214	2.6%	0.4%	Greens	1,049	2.2%
Abbott P	UKIP	952	2%		UKIP	970	2%
					ProLife	260	0.5%
Lab to C swing	**5.1%**	**46,912**		**C maj 1,245**		**47,523**	**Lab maj 3,585**
				2.6%			7.5%

ROBERT GOODWILL b 31 Dec 1956. MP 2005-. Contested Redcar 1992 general election, Richmond and N Yorkshire 1994 European Parliament election, NW Leicestershire 1997 general election and Yorkshire (S) European Parliament election 1998. MEP for Yorkshire and the Humber 1999-2004: Conservative environment spokesperson 2001-04; Environment, Public Health and Consumer Policy Committee member 1999-2004. Farmer 1979-. Ed Bootham School, York; crop production, Newcastle University

This is a peaceful and ruggedly picturesque constituency, steeped in history. The seat has (in Scarborough) Yorkshire's premier resort, a busy port and a certain amount of light industry. Whitby is also an active port, with fishing being the main industry. Beyond, farming is the predominant occupation, while tourism also features, especially around the North York Moors National Park. A notable sight in the region is the Fylingdale Early Warning Station. The seat is a Tory-Labour marginal.

SCUNTHORPE Lab hold

		Electorate	Turnout	Change from	2001	Electorate	Turnout
		62,669	52.1%	2001		59,367	56.6%
Morley E	**Lab**	**17,355**	**53.1%**	**-6.7%**	**Lab**	**20,096**	**59.8%**
Sturdy J	C	8,392	25.7%	-3.2%	C	9,724	28.9%
Poole N	LD	5,556	17%	7.6%	LD	3,156	9.4%
Baxendale D	UKIP	1,361	4.2%		None	347	1%
					Ind	302	0.9%
Lab to C swing	**1.8%**	**32,664**		**Lab maj 8,963**		**33,625**	**Lab maj 10,372**
				27.4%			30.8%

ELLIOT MORLEY b 6 July 1952. MP for Glanford and Scunthorpe 1987-97, for Scunthorpe 1997-. Dept for Environment, Food and Rural Affairs: Minister of State 2003-, Parly Under-Sec 2001-03; Parly Sec MAFF 1997-2001. Opposition spokes 1989-97. Member select cttees: Agriculture 1987-89, Environmental Audit 2003-. Cllr Hull CC 1979-86. Vice-pres federation of economic devt authorities. Former pres Hull teachers assocn. Teacher. Ed BEd, Hull Coll of Education.

Scunthorpe in Lincolnshire, with its ironstone reserves, grew up as a steel town and that industry survives in a reduced form. In considerable industrial and commercial expansion in the late 1980s firms like Citizen, Hygena and McKeys Foods set up, along with companies similarly associated with food and electronics. Heavy industry in this safe Labour seat produces the largest proportion of skilled manual workers in the country (over 40 per cent of the workforce).

SEDGEFIELD — Lab hold

		Electorate	Turnout	Change from	2001	Electorate	Turnout
		66,666	62.2%	2001		64,925	62%
Blair T	**Lab**	**24,429**	**58.9%**	**-6%**	**Lab**	**26,110**	**64.9%**
Lockwood A	C	5,972	14.4%	-6.5%	C	8,397	20.9%
Browne R	LD	4,935	11.9%	2.9%	LD	3,624	9%
Keys R	Ind	4,252	10.2%		UKIP	974	2.4%
Brown W	UKIP	646	1.6%	-0.8%	SLP	518	1.3%
Farrell M	NF	253	0.6%		RNRL	375	0.9%
Luckhurst-Matthews F	Veritas	218	0.5%		Ind	260	0.6%
Abraham B	Ind	209	0.5%				
Maroney B	Loony	157	0.4%				
Cockburn J	BMG	103	0.2%				
Pattinson T	Senior	97	0.2%				
Gilham C	UKPP	82	0.2%				
John H	Ind	68	0.2%				
Barker J	Ind	45	0.1%				
Brennan J	Ind	17	0%				
C to Lab swing	**0.3%**	**41,483**		**Lab maj 18,457**		**40,258**	**Lab maj 17,713**
				44.5%			44%

TONY BLAIR b 6 May 1953. MP 1983-. PM 1997-. Leader: Opposition 1994-97, Lab Party 1994-. Shadow Home Sec 1992-94, Shadow Sec of State: Employment 1989-92, Energy 1988-89. Opposition spokes: Treasury/econ affairs 1984-87, trade/industry 1987-88. All-party groups: chair British-American, pres tennis club 2003-. Barrister (trade union/industrial law specialist) 1976-83. Spectator Parliamentarian of Year 2002. TGWU-sponsored to March 1996. PC 1994. Ed Durham Choristers Sch; Fettes Coll, Edinburgh; MA law, St John's Coll, Oxford.

The Prime Minister's safe constituency of Sedgefield almost completely surrounds Darlington on the southern edge of County Durham, and takes in a number of former colliery villages in the north east, including the new town of Newton Aycliffe and Sedgefield itself. Once heavily industrial, Sedgefield's economy is now recovering from the decline of traditional industries by diversifying into light engineering, distributive trades and the service sector. Tony Blair has represented Sedgefield since it was recreated in 1983.

SELBY — Lab hold

		Electorate	Turnout	Change from	2001	Electorate	Turnout
		78,111	67.3%	2001		77,391	65%
Grogan J	**Lab**	**22,623**	**43.1%**	**-2%**	**Lab**	**22,652**	**45.1%**
Menzies M	C	22,156	42.2%	1.4%	C	20,514	40.8%
Cuthbertson I	LD	7,770	14.8%	3.7%	LD	5,569	11.1%
					Greens	902	1.8%
					UKIP	635	1.3%
Lab to C swing	**1.7%**	**52,549**		**Lab maj 467**		**50,272**	**Lab maj 2,138**
				0.9%			4.3%

JOHN GROGAN b 24 Feb 1961. MP 1997-. Member Northern Ireland Affairs select cttee 1997-2001. Chair all-party groups: BBC 1999-, liquor licensing reform panel of parly beer 1998-, beer 2003-. Lab Party European Parliament press officer 1995. Member: Institute of public policy research, John Smith Institute. Commnications co-ordinator Leeds CC 1987-94. Self-employed conference organiser 1996-97. Ed St Michael's Coll, Leeds; BA mod hist/econ, St John's Coll, Oxford.

This vulnerable Labour seat is of mixed constitution. Situated on good quality agricultural land, it contained the coutry's largest worked coalfield until its closure in 2004. However, this field only dated back to 1982, so the seat has a limited mining tradition. Numerous other sites of interest in Selby include the town's 900 year-old abbey, the Drax power station, Samuel Smith's brewery at Tadcaster, the University of York at Heslington and the Archbishop of York's palace at Bishopthorpe.

SEVENOAKS — C hold

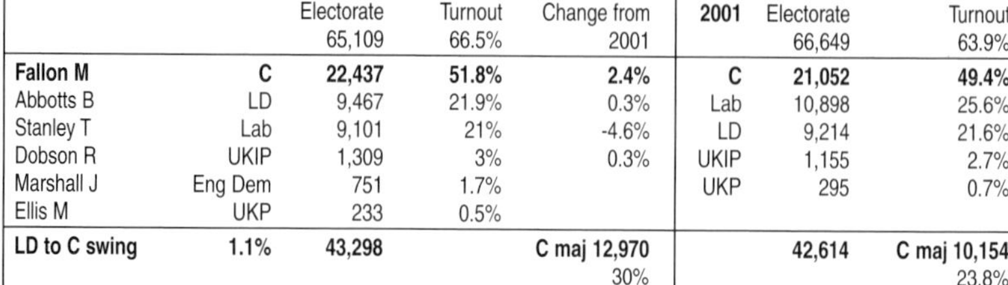

		Electorate	Turnout	Change from	2001	Electorate	Turnout
		65,109	66.5%	2001		66,649	63.9%
Fallon M	**C**	**22,437**	**51.8%**	**2.4%**	**C**	**21,052**	**49.4%**
Abbotts B	LD	9,467	21.9%	0.3%	Lab	10,898	25.6%
Stanley T	Lab	9,101	21%	-4.6%	LD	9,214	21.6%
Dobson R	UKIP	1,309	3%	0.3%	UKIP	1,155	2.7%
Marshall J	Eng Dem	751	1.7%		UKP	295	0.7%
Ellis M	UKP	233	0.5%				
LD to C swing	**1.1%**	**43,298**		**C maj 12,970**		**42,614**	**C maj 10,154**
				30%			23.8%

MICHAEL FALLON b 14 May 1952. MP for Darlington 1983-92, for Sevenoaks 1997-. Parly Under-Sec Dept of Education and Science 1990-92. PPS to Cecil Parkinson 1987-88. Whip: asst govt 1988-90, govt 1990. Opposition spokes: trade/industry 1997, Treasury 1997-98. Member Treasury select cttee 1999- (chair 2001-). Vice-chair all-party parliamentarians for global action group 2002-. Research 1974-79 (incl Con research dept). Cttee sec/MEP asst/company dir. Member deregulation task force 1994-97. Ed MA classics/ancient hist, St Andrews Univ.

Just to the south of London, Sevenoaks in Kent has fast become commuter country, although it can still lay claim to being the 'Garden of England'. The main centres of population are Sevenoaks itself, Swanley, Westerham and New Ash Green. The scenery is picturesque. Undulating and often wooded countryside is home to many country houses and small towns with great historical associations. As ever, this remains a very safe Conservative seat.

SHEFFIELD ATTERCLIFFE — Lab hold

		Electorate	Turnout	Change from	2001	Electorate	Turnout
		67,815	54.6%	2001		67,697	52.9%
Betts C	**Lab**	**22,250**	**60.1%**	**-7.7%**	**Lab**	**24,287**	**67.8%**
Moore K	LD	6,283	17%	2.8%	C	5,443	15.2%
Critchlow T	C	5,329	14.4%	-0.8%	LD	5,092	14.2%
Arnott J	UKIP	1,680	4.5%	1.7%	UKIP	1,002	2.8%
Jones B	BNP	1,477	4%				
Lab to LD swing	**5.3%**	**37,019**		**Lab maj 15,967**		**35,824**	**Lab maj 18,844**
				43.1%			52.6%

CLIVE BETTS b 13 Jan 1950. MP 1992-. Whip: opposition 1996-97, asst govt 1997-98, govt 1998-2001. Member select cttees: Treasury 1996-97, Selection 1997-2001, Transport, Local Govt and Regions 2001-02, ODPM 2002-. Chair all-party football club group 2004-. Member: Lab leader campaign team 1995-96, Lab housing group. Cllr Sheffield CC 1976-92: leader 1987-92. Economist: TUC, Derbyshire CC, S Yorks CC, Rotherham BC. Chair S Yorks Pensions Authority 1989-92. Ed King Edward VII Sch, Sheffield; BA PPE, Pembroke Coll, Oxford.

Attercliffe, a very safe Labour seat, is the area where most of Sheffield's steel was manufactured. Several of the steelworks have been closed for some time now and while steel and engineering are still important employers, other industries also offer a more diverse base for the local economy. That economy was boosted significantly with the building of the giant Meadowhall shopping complex. The seat is no longer an unemployment blackspot.

SHEFFIELD BRIGHTSIDE — Lab hold

		Electorate	Turnout	Change from	2001	Electorate	Turnout
		51,379	47.9%	2001		54,134	47.2%
Blunkett D	**Lab**	**16,876**	**68.5%**	**-8.4%**	**Lab**	**19,650**	**76.9%**
Harston J	LD	3,232	13.1%	4.3%	C	2,601	10.2%
Clark T	C	2,205	9%	-1.2%	LD	2,238	8.8%
Hartigan C	BNP	1,537	6.2%		SA	361	1.4%
Clark J	UKIP	779	3.2%	1.8%	SLP	354	1.4%
					UKIP	348	1.4%
Lab to LD swing	**6.4%**	**24,629**		**Lab maj 13,644**		**25,552**	**Lab maj 17,049**
				55.4%			66.7%

DAVID BLUNKETT b 6 June 1947. MP 1987-. Sec of State Work and Pensions 2005-. Home Sec 2001-04, Sec of State Education/Employment 1997-2001. Shadow Sec of State: Education/Employment 1995-97, Education 1994-95, Health 1992-94. Opposition spokes 1988-92. Lab Party: member NEC 1983-98, chair 1993-94. Cllr Sheffield CC 1970-88: leader 1980-87. Indust relats/politics tutor. Shop steward. PC 1997. Ed Shrewsbury Tech Coll; Sheffield Richmond Further Ed Coll; BA political theory/institutions, Sheffield Univ; PGCE, Huddersfield Coll of Ed.

This seat contains central and north-eastern Sheffield with a high percentage of council housing (over 53 per cent) including the Longley Estate. It is predominately urban residential with some industry on the eastern side of the constituency. The seat is mainly working-class with extensive inner city council estates and is traditionally a safe Labour seat. Sheffield Wednesday's famous Hillsborough stadium (the scene of the 1989 tragedy) is in this constituency.

SHEFFIELD CENTRAL — Lab hold

		Electorate 59,862	Turnout 50.1%	Change from 2001	2001	Electorate 60,765	Turnout 49.5%
Caborn R	**Lab**	**14,950**	**49.9%**	**-11.5%**	**Lab**	**18,477**	**61.4%**
Qadar A	LD	7,895	26.3%	6.6%	LD	5,933	19.7%
George S	C	3,094	10.3%	-0.6%	C	3,289	10.9%
Little B	Greens	1,808	6%	2.6%	Greens	1,008	3.4%
Bowler M	Respect	1,284	4.3%		SA	754	2.5%
Payne M	BNP	539	1.8%		SLP	289	1%
Arnott C	UKIP	415	1.4%	0.5%	UKIP	257	0.9%
					WRP	62	0.2%
Lab to LD swing	**9.1%**	**29,985**		**Lab maj 7,055** 23.5%		**30,069**	**Lab maj 12,544** 41.7%

RICHARD CABORN b 6 Oct 1943. MP 1983-. Minister of State: Dept for Culture, Media and Sport 2001-, Dept of Trade and Industry 1999-2001, Dept of Environ, Transport and Regions 1997-99. Opposition spokes: 1988-90, 1990-92, 1995-97. Select cttees: member Liaison 1992-95, chair Trade and Industry 1992-95. Chair Sheffield district Lab Party. Shop stewards convenor AEEU. Engineer. MEP Sheffield District 1979-84. Joint chair British Trade Internat Board 2000-01. Member BBC advisory council 1975-78. PC 1999. Ed engineering, Sheffield Poly.

Significant redevelopment in recent years has turned Sheffield Central into a major conference and retail centre, bringing about much-needed economic up-lift. Unemployment is still twice the national average with 42 per cent of homes council-rented. A significant 15 per cent of the population stem from non-white ethnic groups. Despite widespread apathy (only half the electorate bothered to vote in 2005) this seat's Labour credentials are deep-rooted.

SHEFFIELD HALLAM — LD hold

		Electorate 59,606	Turnout 67.8%	Change from 2001	2001	Electorate 58,982	Turnout 64.8%
Clegg N	**LD**	**20,710**	**51.2%**	**-4.2%**	**LD**	**21,203**	**55.4%**
Pitfield S	C	12,028	29.8%	-1.2%	C	11,856	31%
Hussain M	Lab	5,110	12.6%	0.2%	Lab	4,758	12.4%
Cole R	Greens	1,331	3.3%		UKIP	429	1.1%
Cordle S	CPA	441	1.1%				
James N	UKIP	438	1.1%				
Senior I	BNP	369	0.9%				
LD to C swing	**1.5%**	**40,427**		**LD maj 8,682** 21.5%		**38,246**	**LD maj 9,347** 24.4%

NICK CLEGG b 7 Jan 1967. MP 2005-. MEP for East Midlands 1999-2004: member Maghreb and Arab Maghreb Union Delegation 2002-04. European Commission official 1994-96. Ed MA social anthropology, Cambridge University

Over half the constituency falls in rural land. It was the only Conservative seat in South Yorkshire and in 1997 it fell to the Liberal Democrats. Hallam includes all the most affluent of Sheffield's suburbs and has the highest proportion of professional workers in England and Wales with an almost complete lack of manual workers. 78 per cent of homes are owner-occupied and unemployment is by far the lowest of the Sheffield seats.

SHEFFIELD HEELEY — Lab hold

		Electorate 59,748	Turnout 57.1%	Change from 2001	2001	Electorate 61,949	Turnout 55.1%
Munn M	**Lab/C**	**18,405**	**54%**	**-3%**	**Lab/C**	**19,452**	**57%**
Ross C	LD	7,035	20.6%	-2.1%	LD	7,748	22.7%
Crawshaw A	C	4,987	14.6%	0.4%	C	4,864	14.2%
Beatson J	BNP	1,314	3.8%		Greens	774	2.3%
Unwin R	Greens	1,312	3.8%	1.5%	SLP	667	2%
Suter M	UKIP	775	2.3%	0.4%	UKIP	634	1.9%
Dunnell M	SAP	265	0.8%				
Lab/C to LD swing	**0.5%**	**34,093**		**Lab/C maj 11,370** 33.4%		**34,139**	**Lab/C maj 11,704** 34.3%

MEG MUNN b 24 Aug 1959. MP 2001-. Parly Under-Sec Dept of Trade and Industry 2005-. PPS to Margaret Hodge 2004-05. Team PPS Dept for Education and Skills 2003-04. Member select cttees 2001-03. Chair all-party voice group 2004-. Member Co-operative Party 1975-. Chair: women's parly Lab Party, Co-op parly group 2005-. Cllr Nottingham CC 1987-91. NALGO shop steward 1982-84. Soc worker. Asst dir City of York Council 1999-2000. BA languages, York Univ; MA soc work, Nottingham Univ; Soc Work Qualification Cert; Management Studies Cert/Dip.

This secure Labour constituency lies immediately south of the city centre. Much of Heeley is made up of post-war council estates – 43 per cent of homes are council-rented, although there are also some owner-occupied Victorian terraces. The seat was as badly affected as any other by the decline of Sheffield's traditional steel industry, and unemployment today remains above average. Most residents are working-class, and there are few of the more well-paid non-manual workers.

SHEFFIELD HILLSBOROUGH — Lab hold

		Electorate 75,706	Turnout 60.6%	Change from 2001	2001	Electorate 74,180	Turnout 57.3%
Smith A	**Lab/C**	**23,477**	**51.2%**	**-5.6%**	**Lab**	**24,170**	**56.8%**
Commons J	LD	12,234	26.7%	4.1%	LD	9,601	22.6%
Doyle-Price J	C	6,890	15%	-3.3%	C	7,801	18.3%
Wright D	BNP	2,010	4.4%		UKIP	964	2.3%
Patterson M	UKIP	1,273	2.8%	0.5%			
Lab to LD swing	**4.9%**	**45,884**		**Lab maj 11,243** 24.5%		**42,536**	**Lab maj 14,569** 34.3%

ANGELA SMITH b 16 August 1961. MP 2005-. Sheffield City Council: Councillor, cabinet member for education, member regional education and skills commission, chair 14-19 board; Sheffield First for Learning and Work. Ed Nottingham University; Newnham College, Cambridge

This traditionally Labour-supporting seat is a large constituency containing part of the old city area on its north western side, some of the towns on the outskirts including Stocksbridge and a large rural area of farms and small villages which includes part of the Peak District. It is primarily a residential seat from which people commute into other parts of the city. The largest employer is the steel works at Stocksbridge.

SHERWOOD — Lab hold

		Electorate 75,913	Turnout 62.1%	Change from 2001	2001	Electorate 75,558	Turnout 60.7%
Tipping P	**Lab**	**22,824**	**48.4%**	**-5.8%**	**Lab**	**24,900**	**54.2%**
Laughton B	C	16,172	34.3%	0.5%	C	15,527	33.8%
Harris P	LD	6,384	13.6%	1.7%	LD	5,473	11.9%
Dawkins M	UKIP	1,737	3.7%				
Lab to C swing	**3.2%**	**47,117**		**Lab maj 6,652** 14.1%		**45,900**	**Lab maj 9,373** 20.4%

PADDY TIPPING b 24 Oct 1949. MP 1992-. Parly Sec Privy Council Office 1999-2001. PPS to Jack Straw 1997-99, 2005-. Member Environ, Food and Rural Affairs select cttee 2001-. Chair all-party groups: forestry 2002-, energy studies 2002-, wood panel industry 2005-. Member: Co-operative Party. Chair: central region of Lab MPs 1997-2001, E Mids group of Lab MPs to 1999. Cllr Notts CC 1981-93. Dir: Notts Co-operative Devt Agency 1983-93, Nottingham Devt Enterprise 1987-93. Soc worker/project leader 1972-83. Ed BA philosophy, Nottingham Univ.

Nottinghamshire's Sherwood became one of the more profitable and modern of British coalfields. Tory success here in the 1980s was due to lack of support among local miners for the nationwide strike, but when even their most reliable pits were earmarked for closure and the job losses came, so Labour reaped the benefit. Coal remains the prime industry in the region. Sherwood Forest remains a big tourist attraction in the seat.

SHIPLEY — C gain

		Electorate 69,575	Turnout 68.5%	Change from 2001	2001	Electorate 69,576	Turnout 66.1%
Davies P	**C**	**18,608**	**39%**	**-1.9%**	**Lab**	**20,243**	**44%**
Leslie C	Lab	18,186	38.2%	-5.8%	C	18,815	40.9%
Briggs J	LD	7,018	14.7%	3.8%	LD	4,996	10.9%
Linden T	BNP	2,000	4.2%		Greens	1,386	3%
Deakin Q	Greens	1,665	3.5%	0.5%	UKIP	580	1.3%
Crabtree D	Iraq	189	0.4%				
Lab to C swing	**2%**	**47,666**		**C maj 422** 0.9%		**46,020**	**Lab maj 1,428** 3.1%

PHILIP DAVIES b 5 Jan 1972. MP 2005-. Contested Colne Valley 2001 general election. Asda Stores 1995-: Management trainee 1995-97, Manager 1997-. Ed Old Swinford Hospital School, Stourbridge; historical and political studies, Huddersfield University

This vulnerable Tory seat in West Yorkshire is mainly residential but industries include textiles and light engineering with some agriculture. Owner-occupation levels are well above the national average at 78 per cent, as are the proportion of those in white collar occupational groups. The seat has become more middle class and residential as the woollen industry has declined.

SHREWSBURY AND ATCHAM — C gain

		Electorate 73,193	Turnout 68.7%	Change from 2001	2001	Electorate 74,964	Turnout 66.6%
Kawczynski D	**C**	**18,960**	**37.7%**	**0.3%**	**Lab**	**22,253**	**44.6%**
Ion M	Lab	17,152	34.1%	-10.5%	C	18,674	37.4%
Burt R	LD	11,487	22.8%	10.4%	LD	6,173	12.4%
Lewis P	UKIP	1,349	2.7%	-0.5%	UKIP	1,620	3.2%
Bullard E	Greens	1,138	2.3%	0.4%	Greens	931	1.9%
Gollins J	Ind	126	0.2%	-0.3%	Ind	258	0.5%
Harris N	Online	84	0.2%				
Lab to C swing	**5.4%**	**50,296**		**C maj 1,808** 3.6%		**49,909**	**Lab maj 3,579** 7.2%

DANIEL KAWCZYNSKI MP 2005-. Contested Ealing Southall 2001 general election. Chairman Stirling University Conservative Association 1991. Ed business studies with languages, Stirling University.

This Shropshire constituency is dominated by the market town of Shrewsbury, an important shopping and tourist attraction, with some of the finest medieval buildings in the country. Agriculture is important but the attractive countryside with its large houses and historical associations is supporting a growing tourist industry. This is a Conservative–Labour marginal.

NORTH SHROPSHIRE — C hold

		Electorate 73,477	Turnout 63.3%	Change from 2001	2001	Electorate 71,700	Turnout 64.9%
Paterson O	**C**	**23,061**	**49.6%**	**1%**	**C**	**22,631**	**48.6%**
Samuels S	Lab	12,041	25.9%	-9.3%	Lab	16,390	35.2%
Bourne S	LD	9,175	19.7%	6.9%	LD	5,945	12.8%
Smith I	UKIP	2,233	4.8%	2.3%	UKIP	1,165	2.5%
					Ind	389	0.8%
Lab to C swing	**5.2%**	**46,510**		**C maj 11,020** 23.7%		**46,520**	**C maj 6,241** 13.4%

OWEN PATERSON b 24 June 1956. MP 1997-. Shadow Minister: Environment, Food and Rural Affairs 2005-, Environ/Transport 2003-05. PPS: Iain Duncan Smith 2001-03. Opposition whip 2000-01. Member select cttees: Welsh Affairs 1997-2001, European Scrutiny 1999-2000, Agriculture 2000-01. Exec member 1922 cttee 2000. Member 92 and No Turning Back groups. Member Con: Friends of Israel, Way Forward, 2000. Member Commonwealth Parly Assocn 1997-. Tanner. British Leather Co Ltd 1985-99. Ed Radley Coll; MA hist, Corpus Christi Coll, Cambridge.

This is a large, rural, safe Tory constituency of small towns and villages stretching from the Welsh border to Market Drayton. Other small towns in the constituency include Wem, Whitchurch and Ellesmere. The main centre is the market town of Oswestry which has been part of Wales at different times in its long history. The main economic activities are agriculture and its associated industries, tourism and some light industry in the towns.

SITTINGBOURNE AND SHEPPEY — Lab hold

		Electorate 62,950	Turnout 64.8%	Change from 2001	2001	Electorate 65,824	Turnout 57.5%
Wyatt D	**Lab**	**17,051**	**41.8%**	**-4%**	**Lab**	**17,340**	**45.8%**
Henderson G	C	16,972	41.6%	5.1%	C	13,831	36.5%
Nelson J	LD	5,183	12.7%	-1.4%	LD	5,353	14.1%
Dean S	UKIP	926	2.3%	0.6%	RNRL	673	1.8%
Young M	Loony	479	1.2%	-0.6%	UKIP	661	1.7%
Cassidy D	Veritas	192	0.5%				
Lab to C swing	**4.6%**	**40,803**		**Lab maj 79** 0.2%		**37,858**	**Lab maj 3,509** 9.3%

DEREK WYATT b 4 Dec 1949. MP 1997-. Rugby union adviser to Richard Caborn 2002-. Member Culture, Media and Sport select cttee 1997-. Chair all-party groups incl: British Council 2001-, Zimbabwe 2003-, Olympics 2004-. Cllr Haringey 1994-96. Founder: Oxford Internet Inst 2000, women's sports foundation (UK) 1985. UN special commendation 1987. Publisher/head of Wire TV programmes/BSkyB dir. Ed CertEd, St Luke's Coll, Exeter; BA art/architecture, Open Univ; research, St Catherine's Coll, Oxford; management, Univ of California, Berkeley.

At the point on the north Kent coast where the Thames estuary meets the sea proper, this is one of the less well-known regions in that county. Sittingbourne is an expanding country town, while the bleak, marshy Isle Of Sheppey, including the port of Sheerness, is now linked to the mainland by a new £100 million bridge. It was one of the most remarkable New Labour success stories but is now extremely vulnerable to the Conservatives again.

SKIPTON AND RIPON — C hold

		Electorate	Turnout	Change from	2001	Electorate	Turnout
		76,485	66%	2001		74,326	66.1%
Curry D	**C**	**25,100**	**49.7%**	**-2.7%**	**C**	**25,736**	**52.4%**
English P	LD	13,480	26.7%	0.6%	LD	12,806	26.1%
Baptie P	Lab	9,393	18.6%	1.2%	Lab	8,543	17.4%
Bannister I	UKIP	2,274	4.5%	0.3%	UKIP	2,041	4.2%
Leakey R	Currency	274	0.5%				
C to LD swing	**1.7**	**50,521**		**C maj 11,620**		**49,126**	**C maj 12,930**
				23%			26.3%

DAVID CURRY b 13 June 1944. MP 1987-. Shadow: Sec of State Local and Devolved Govt Affairs 2003-04, Minister MAFF 1997. Minister of State Dept of Environ 1993-97. MAFF: Minister of State 1992-93, Parly Sec 1989-92. Spokes 1984-89. Member select cttees; select cttee chair: Agriculture 2000-01, Environ, Food and Rural Affairs 2001-03. Exec member 1922 cttee 2001-02. Chair Con group for Europe. Vice-pres Local Govt Assocn. MEP NE Essex 1979-89. Journalist. PC 1996. Ed BA mod hist, Corpus Christi Coll, Oxford; Kennedy Sch of Govt, Harvard Univ.

Typically for a North Yorkshire constituency, its economy is dependent largely on tourism and farming. It covers the southern portion of the Yorkshire Dales National Park. Income from tourism goes a long way to up-holding an economy that would otherwise be largely based on sheep farming. The inhabitants are middle-class owner occupiers, with only 10 per cent of accommodation council-rented and unemployment is low, giving rise to a solid foundation for Tory support.

SLEAFORD AND NORTH HYKEHAM — C hold

		Electorate	Turnout	Change from	2001	Electorate	Turnout
		79,612	67.1%	2001		75,033	64.9%
Hogg D	**C**	**26,855**	**50.3%**	**0.6%**	**C**	**24,190**	**49.7%**
Bull K	Lab	14,150	26.5%	-5.5%	Lab	15,568	32%
Harding-Price D	LD	9,710	18.2%	2%	LD	7,894	16.2%
Croft G	UKIP	2,682	5%	2.8%	UKIP	1,067	2.2%
Lab to C swing	**3.1%**	**53,397**		**C maj 12,705**		**48,719**	**C maj 8,622**
				23.8%			17.7%

DOUGLAS HOGG b 5 Feb 1945. MP for Grantham 1979-97, for Sleaford and North Hykeham 1997-. Minister MAFF 1995-97; Minister of State: FCO 1990-95, DTI 1989-90; Parly Under-Sec Home Office 1986-89; PPS to Leon Brittan 1982-83. Govt whip 1983-84. Member Home Affairs select cttee 1997-98. Barrister. QC 1990. PC 1992. Ed Eton Coll; MA hist, Christ Church, Oxford.

Much of the land on which this Lincolnshire seat lies was reclaimed from the Fenland marshes and consists of rich alluvial soil, making it ideal for arable farming. Cereal, root and market garden crops are all cultivated here, and agriculture is the region's main industry, although it is in decline. Some 76 per cent of householders are owner-occupiers and unemployment is well below the national average. This is a stereotypical Tory stronghold.

SLOUGH — Lab hold

		Electorate	Turnout	Change from	2001	Electorate	Turnout
		71,595	51.8%	2001		73,008	53.4%
Mactaggart F	**Lab**	**17,517**	**47.2%**	**-11.1%**	**Lab**	**22,718**	**58.3%**
Gunn S	C	9,666	26.1%	-0.1%	C	10,210	26.2%
McCann T	LD	5,739	15.5%	5%	LD	4,109	10.5%
Khan A	Respect	1,632	4.4%		Ind	859	2.2%
Howard G	UKIP	1,415	3.8%	1.9%	UKIP	738	1.9%
Wood D	Greens	759	2.1%		Ind	364	0.9%
Janik P	Ind	367	1%				
Lab to C swing	**5.5%**	**37,095**		**Lab maj 7,851**		**38,998**	**Lab maj 12,508**
				21.2%			32.1%

FIONA MACTAGGART b 12 Sept 1953. MP 1997-. Parly Under-Sec Home Office 2003-. PPS to Chris Smith 1997-2001. Member Public Administration select cttee 1997-98. Chair Parly Lab Party women's cttee 2001-. Cllr Wandsworth 1986-90. Vice-pres, national sec NUS 1978-81. Press/PR officer NCVO 1981. Gen sec joint council for immigrants welfare 1982-86. Teacher/PR officer/lecturer 1987-97. Chair Liberty 1994-96. Ed London Univ: BA Eng, King's Coll; Postgrad teaching cert, Goldsmith's Coll; MA, Inst of Education.

Slough in Berkshire has a vigorous and energetic business sector helped by its proximity to Heathrow, the M4 and M25. In part this sector is boosted by the highly entrepreneurial Asian community – nearly a quarter of the population are Asian in origin – the twelfth highest proportion in the country. Labour have managed to draw on a core of support here to turn the once marginal seat into safe Labour territory.

SOLIHULL — LD gain

		Electorate	Turnout	Change from	2001	Electorate	Turnout
		77,910	67.2%	2001		76,298	63.3%
Burt L	**LD**	**20,896**	**39.9%**	**13.9%**	**C**	**21,935**	**45.4%**
Taylor J	C	20,617	39.4%	-6%	LD	12,528	26%
Vaughan R	Lab	8,058	15.4%	-10.2%	Lab	12,373	25.6%
Carr D	BNP	1,752	3.4%		UKIP	1,061	2.2%
Moore A	UKIP	990	1.9%	-0.3%	ProLife	374	0.8%
C to LD swing	**10%**	**52,313**		**LD maj 279**		**48,271**	**C maj 9,407**
				0.5%			19.5%

LORELY BURT b 1957. Contested Dudley South 2001 general election. Personnel management; Prison Service; Director, Marketing consultancy company; Former founder, Licensed retail company. Ed economics; MBA

Although Land Rovers are built here this seat is overwhelmingly residential, white and middle-class – 51 per cent can be classed as professional or managerial/technical. It has one of the highest levels of owner-occupation (85 per cent) and only nearby Sutton Coldfield has a lower level of unskilled people in England and Wales. It borders Birmingham in the west and in the north near the International Airport.

SOMERTON AND FROME — LD hold

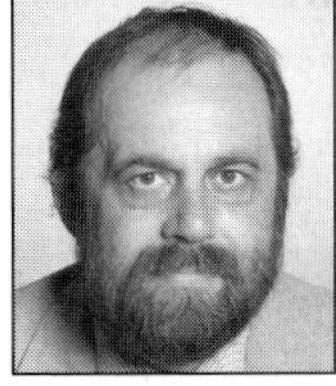

		Electorate	Turnout	Change from	2001	Electorate	Turnout
		77,806	69.5%	2001		75,815	69.5%
Heath D	**LD**	**23,759**	**44.1%**	**0.5%**	**LD**	**22,983**	**43.6%**
Allen C	C	22,947	42.6%	0.2%	C	22,315	42.4%
Pestell J	Lab	5,865	10.8%	-0.8%	Lab	6,113	11.6%
Lukins W	UKIP	1,047	1.9%	0.2%	UKIP	919	1.7%
Beaman C	Veritas	484	0.9%		Lib	354	0.7%
C to LD swing	**0.2%**	**54,102**		**LD maj 812**		**52,684**	**LD maj 668**
				1.5%			1.3%

DAVID HEATH b 16 March 1954. MP 1997-. Lib Dem spokes 1997-. Member select cttees: Foreign Affairs 1997-99, 1997-98, Standards and Privileges 2001-, Science and Technology 2001-03. Chair all-party eye health/visual impairment group 2002-. Member: Liberal Party Nat Exec 1988-89, Lib Dem Federal Exec 1990-92, 1993-95, Audit Commission 1995-97. Cllr Somerset CC 1985-97: leader 1985-89. Chair Avon/Somerset Police Authority 1993-96. Optician. CBE 1989. Ed MA physiological sciences, St John's Coll, Oxford; ophthalmic optics, City Univ.

Somerton and Frome is one of the largest rural constituencies in England, covering almost 900 square miles. The seat, which is predominantly based in agriculture, borders Bath to the north and Dorset to the south. The Tories controlled Somerton and Frome until 1997, when the Liberal Democrats won by a mere 130 votes. Despite strong Conservative challenges the Lib Dems have since managed to hang on the seat with slender majorities.

SOUTH HOLLAND AND THE DEEPINGS — C hold

		Electorate	Turnout	Change from	2001	Electorate	Turnout
		77,453	62.3%	2001		73,922	62.5%
Hayes J	**C**	**27,544**	**57.1%**	**1.7%**	**C**	**25,611**	**55.4%**
Woodings L	Lab	11,764	24.4%	-7%	Lab	14,512	31.4%
Jarvis S	LD	6,244	12.9%	2.6%	LD	4,761	10.3%
Corney J	UKIP	1,950	4%	1.1%	UKIP	1,318	2.9%
Poll P	Ind	747	1.6%				
Lab to C swing	**4.4%**	**48,249**		**C maj 15,780**		**46,202**	**C maj 11,099**
				32.7%			24%

JOHN HAYES b 23 June 1958. MP 1997-. Shadow Minister: Transport 2005-, Local and Devolved Govt 2003-05, Agriculture 2002-03. Opposition: whip 2001-02, spokes 2000-01. Member select cttees: Agriculture 1997-99, Education and Employment 1998-99, 1999-2000, Selection 2001-02, Admin 2001-02. Chair all-party groups: (joint chair) disability 2000-, housing, care and support 2004-. Vice-chair Con Party 1999-2000. Member 1992 group. Cllr Notts CC 1985-88. IT company director. Ed BA pol, PGCE history/Eng, Nottingham Univ.

Its hugely fertile alluvial soil makes this solid Tory seat in Lincolnshire a prime area for crop production. Dutch engineers and scientists played their part in reclamation schemes, lending it the name of their native country. Another similarity is the cultivation of tulips, particularly around Spalding, once an inland port, an old market town on the river Welland whose owner-occupying residents are typical of those living throughout the seat.

SOUTH SHIELDS — Lab hold

		Electorate	Turnout	Change from	2001	Electorate	Turnout
		59,403	50.8%	2001		61,112	49.8%
Miliband D	**Lab**	**18,269**	**60.5%**	**-2.7%**	**Lab**	**19,230**	**63.2%**
Psallidas S	LD	5,957	19.7%	2.9%	C	5,140	16.9%
Lewis R	C	5,207	17.2%	0.3%	LD	5,127	16.8%
Afshari-Naderi N	Ind	773	2.6%	1.7%	UKIP	689	2.3%
					SNH	262	0.9%
Lab to LD swing	**2.8%**	**30,206**		**Lab maj 12,312**		**30,448**	**Lab maj 14,090**
				40.8%			46.3%

DAVID MILIBAND b 15 July 1965. MP 2001-. Minister of State ODPM 2005-; Minister for Cabinet Office 2004-05; Minister of State for School Standards, Dept for Education and Skills 2002-04. Founder Centre for European Reform. Parly officer NCVO 1987-88. Research fellow Inst for Public Policy Research 1989-94. Sec Commission on Social Justice 1992-94. Head: Leader of Opposition policy office 1994-97, PM's policy unit 1997-2001. Ed BA PPE, Corpus Christi Coll, Oxford; MSc political science, Massachussets Inst of Technology.

The seaside town of South Shields, north of Jarrow, has many problems associated with the decline of traditional local industries, but the area remains solidly Labour. All the coal mines have closed, and ships are no longer built here, but the Tyne is still busy with ship repairs and offshore oil platforms. Light engineering and electronic companies have also replaced some of the heavy industry.

SOUTHAMPTON ITCHEN — Lab hold

		Electorate	Turnout	Change from	2001	Electorate	Turnout
		78,818	54.8%	2001		78,066	53%
Denham J	**Lab**	**20,871**	**48.3%**	**-6.2%**	**Lab**	**22,553**	**54.5%**
Drummond F	C	11,569	26.8%	-0.6%	C	11,330	27.4%
Goodall D	LD	9,162	21.2%	6.2%	LD	6,195	15%
Rose K	UKIP	1,623	3.8%	1.8%	UKIP	829	2%
					SA	241	0.6%
					SLP	225	0.5%
Lab to C swing	**2.8%**	**43,225**		**Lab maj 9,302**		**41,373**	**Lab maj 11,223**
				21.5%			27.1%

JOHN DENHAM b 15 July 1953. MP 1992-. Minister of State: Home Office 2001-03, Dept of Health 1999-2001, Dept of Social Security 1998-99. Parly Under-Sec Dept of Social Security 1997-98. Opposition social security spokesman 1995-97. Select cttees: member Liaison 2003-, chair Home Affairs 2003-. Cllr: Hants CC 1981-89, Southampton CC 1989-92. Advice worker, transport campaigner, head of youth affairs, consultant to voluntary organisations. War on Want campaigner 1984-88. PC 2000. Ed BSc chemistry, Southampton Univ.

The Southampton constituencies are named after the two rivers flowing through the city. Itchen is the city's eastern side. It contains the town centre, most of the docks, marina and inner-city council estates. Itchen was one of the narrowest Labour gains in 1992 and was then one of the party's few southern seats. Now it has plenty for company, including the neighbouring constituency of Southampton Test. Itchen should remain a Labour seat for some time.

SOUTHAMPTON TEST — Lab hold

		Electorate	Turnout	Change from	2001	Electorate	Turnout
		72,833	57.4%	2001		75,485	55.1%
Whitehead A	**Lab**	**17,845**	**42.7%**	**-9.8%**	**Lab**	**21,824**	**52.5%**
MacLoughlin S	C	10,827	25.9%	0.4%	C	10,617	25.5%
Sollitt S	LD	10,368	24.8%	6.7%	LD	7,522	18.1%
Spottiswoode J	Greens	1,482	3.6%		UKIP	792	1.9%
Day P	UKIP	1,261	3%	1.1%	SA	442	1.1%
					SLP	378	0.9%
Lab to C swing	**5.1%**	**41,783**		**Lab maj 7,018**		**41,575**	**Lab maj 11,207**
				16.8%			27%

ALAN WHITEHEAD b 15 Sept 1950. MP 1997-. Parly Under-Sec Dept of Transport 2001-02. PPS to: Baroness Blackstone 1999-2001, (joint) to David Blunkett 1999-2000. Member select cttees: Environment, Transport and Regional Affairs 1997-99, Constitutional Affairs 2003-. Chair all-party groups 2002-. Member Lab Party Nat Policy Forum 1999-2001. Cllr Southampton CC 1980-92: leader 1984-92. Prof of public policy. Dir: Outset/BIIT/Southampton Environment Centre. Ed BA politics/philosophy, PhD politics science, Southampton Univ.

Southampton's livelihood has largely come from its position as a thriving seaport, but this half of the city contains little of the dockyards. Instead Test harbours the more middle-class elements of Southampton in the leafy northern suburbs. However, there are also a number of council estates here. Unlike neighbouring Itchen, Test waited until 1997 to return to the Labour fold, but now appears to be equally safe for Labour.

SOUTHEND WEST — C hold

		Electorate 64,915	Turnout 61.4%	Change from 2001	2001	Electorate 64,328	Turnout 58.1%
Amess D	**C**	**18,408**	**46.2%**	**-0.1%**	**C**	**17,313**	**46.3%**
Wexham P	LD	9,449	23.7%	-1.2%	Lab	9,372	25.1%
Etienne J	Lab	9,072	22.8%	-2.3%	LD	9,319	24.9%
Sampson C	UKIP	1,349	3.4%	-0.3%	UKIP	1,371	3.7%
Velmurugan M	Ind	745	1.9%				
Moss J	England	701	1.8%				
Anslow D	Power	106	0.3%				
LD to C swing	**0.6%**	**39,830**		**C maj 8,959** 22.5%		**37,375**	**C maj 7,941** 21.2%

DAVID AMESS b 26 March 1952. MP for Basildon 1983-97, for Southend West 1997-. PPS to: Michael Portillo 1988-97, Lord Skelmersdale 1988, Edwina Currie 1987-88. Member select cttees: Broadcasting 1994-97, Health 1998-, Chairmen's Panel 2001-. Chair all-party groups incl solvent abuse 2001-, fire safety 2001-, health 2003-. Member exec 1922 cttee 2004-. Hon sec Con Friends of Israel. Cllr Redbridge Council 1982-86. Teacher, underwriter, consultant to agencies supplying accountants. Ed BSc econ, Bournemouth Coll of Tech.

In recent years this Essex constituency has grown into a major office and retailing centre and this plus the effect of London commuters is reflected in the high level of skilled non-manual groups in the constituency. Pensioners form about a quarter of the population. The level of owner occupation is high. The town centre and main offices fall outside the seat.

SOUTHPORT — LD hold

		Electorate 67,977	Turnout 60.6%	Change from 2001	2001	Electorate 70,259	Turnout 58.6%
Pugh J	**LD**	**19,093**	**46.3%**	**2.5%**	**LD**	**18,011**	**43.8%**
Bigley M	C	15,255	37%	0.5%	C	15,004	36.5%
Brant P	Lab	5,277	12.8%	-3.8%	Lab	6,816	16.6%
Durrance T	UKIP	749	1.8%	0.5%	Lib	767	1.9%
Givens B	YPB	589	1.4%		UKIP	555	1.3%
Forster H	Veritas	238	0.6%				
C to LD swing	**1%**	**41,201**		**LD maj 3,838** 9.3%		**41,153**	**LD maj 3,007** 7.3%

JOHN PUGH b 28 June 1948. MP 2001-. Lib Dem education spokes 2002-. Member select cttees: Transport, Local Govt and the Regions 2001-02, ODPM 2002-03. Vice-chair all-party Burma group 2002-. Former chair Southport Lib Dem assocn, Merseyside Police Authority. Member: North West Arts Board, Merseyside Partnership. Teacher/philosophy head Merchant Taylors Boys Sch, Crosby 1983-. Ed Prescott Grammar Sch; Maidstone Grammar Sch; BA phil, MA, MEd, MPhil, PhD logic, Durham Univ.

Situated on the north west coast of England, the seat of Southport is west of Manchester, and north of Liverpool. After boundary changes in the 1970s it moved into Merseyside from Lancashire, and has remained a marginal seat ever since; swinging from the Conservatives to the Liberal Democrats. Tourism is the main focus for this seaside town and it is an industry that generates millions of pounds and thousands of jobs.

NORTH SOUTHWARK AND BERMONDSEY — LD hold

		Electorate 77,084	Turnout 49.2%	Change from 2001	2001	Electorate 73,529	Turnout 50.1%
Hughes S	**LD**	**17,874**	**47.1%**	**-9.8%**	**LD**	**20,991**	**56.9%**
McNeill K	Lab	12,468	32.8%	2%	Lab	11,359	30.8%
Branch D	C	4,752	12.5%	4.9%	C	2,800	7.6%
Poorun S	Greens	1,137	3%	1%	Greens	752	2%
Robson L	UKIP	791	2.1%	1.4%	NF	612	1.7%
Winnett P	NF	704	1.8%	0.1%	UKIP	271	0.7%
Lawanson S	CPA	233	0.6%		Ind	77	0.2%
LD to Lab swing	**5.9%**	**37,959**		**LD maj 5,406** 14.2%		**36,862**	**LD maj 9,632** 26.1%

SIMON HUGHES b 17 May 1951. MP for Southwark and Bermondsey 1983-97, for North Southwark and Bermondsey 1997. Lib Dem Shadow ODPM 2005-. Lib Dem dep whip: 1988-99. Lib/Alliance/LD spokes 1983-. Member Accommodation and Works 1992-97 select cttee. Pres: LD Party 2004-, Nat Young Liberals League 1986-92. Member Liberal Lawyers Assocn. Barrister. Trainee EEC Brussels 1976. London mayoral candidate 2002/2004. Ed BA law/MA, Selwyn Coll, Cambridge; Inns of Court Sch of Law; Cert in Higher European Studies, Coll of Europe, Bruges.

This safe Lib-Dem seat has the smallest proportion of owner-occupied homes in England and Wales. Unemployment tends to run at about twice the national average. Development of previously derelict docklands, flats for example, is breathing new life into the region. As well as the Surrey and Rotherhithe docks the seat includes Southwark Cathedral, London Bridge station, Guy's Hospital, the Elephant and Castle shopping centre and the Labour Party's Walworth Road headquarters.

SPELTHORNE — C hold

		Electorate	Turnout	Change from	2001	Electorate	Turnout
		69,650	61.5%	2001		68,731	60.8%
Wilshire D	**C**	**21,620**	**50.5%**	**5.4%**	**C**	**18,851**	**45.1%**
Dibble K	Lab	11,684	27.3%	-10%	Lab	15,589	37.3%
James S	LD	7,318	17.1%	2.4%	LD	6,156	14.7%
Browne C	UKIP	1,968	4.6%	1.7%	UKIP	1,198	2.9%
Schwark C	UKC	239	0.6%				
Lab to C swing	**7.7%**	**42,829**		**C maj 9,936**		**41,794**	**C maj 3,262**
				23.2%			7.8%

DAVID WILSHIRE b 16 Sept 1943. MP 1987-. PPS to: Peter Lloyd 1992-94, Alan Clark 1991-92. Opposition whip 2001-05. Member select cttees: Northern Ireland Affairs 1994-97, Foreign Affairs 1997-2000. Chair all-party fairs/showgrounds group 2002-. Cllr: Wansdyke DC 1976-87 (leader 1981-87), Avon CC 1977-81. Member: British-Irish inter-parly body 1990-2001, exec ctee British-American parly group 2001-. Publisher, printer, MEPs' asst 1979-85, research services companies partner. Ed BA geog, Fitzwilliam Coll, Cambridge.

Although this constituency does have its plush commuter suburbs, it is not as sought-after as neighbouring Surrey seats. Just south of Heathrow airport and north of the Thames, Spelthorne is a very built-up area encompassing the Middlesex towns and villages of Staines, Ashford, Sunbury, Shepperton, Stanwell, Stanwell Moor and Laleham. The days of Conservative majorities in the tens of thousands appeared to have gone, but the current majority is again all but five figure.

STAFFORD — Lab hold

		Electorate	Turnout	Change from	2001	Electorate	Turnout
		70,359	64.8%	2001		67,934	65.3%
Kidney D	**Lab**	**19,889**	**43.7%**	**-4.3%**	**Lab**	**21,285**	**48%**
Chambers D	C	17,768	39%	2.4%	C	16,253	36.6%
Stamp B	LD	6,390	14%	4.5%	LD	4,205	9.5%
Goode F	UKIP	1,507	3.3%	-1.9%	UKIP	2,315	5.2%
					RNRL	308	0.7%
Lab to C swing	**3.4%**	**45,554**		**Lab maj 2,121**		**44,366**	**Lab maj 5,032**
				4.7%			11.3%

DAVID KIDNEY b 21 March 1955. MP 1997-. Team Parly Private Sec to Ministers of State 2002-03. Member select cttees: Treasury 1998-2001, Modernisation of HoC 2001-. All-party groups: chair conservation and wildlife 2002-, vice-chair Myodil 2002-. Co-chair parly transport safety advisory council. Member Society of Lab Lawyers. Cllr Stafford BC 1987-97. Solicitor. Ed Longton High Sch; sixth form coll, Stoke-on-Trent; LLB law, Bristol Univ.

Stafford has a long history of heavy engineering but in recent years has experienced a large growth in light industry and other commercial activities. This is based on the M6 motorway and the west coast main railway line and the town's proximity to the West Midlands conurbation. The number of both professionals and people between 40 and retirement age is comparatively high. Unemployment is low at 3 per cent. It is a vulnerable Labour seat.

STAFFORDSHIRE MOORLANDS — Lab hold

		Electorate	Turnout	Change from	2001	Electorate	Turnout
		69,136	64%	2001		66,760	63.9%
Atkins C	**Lab**	**18,126**	**41%**	**-8%**	**Lab**	**20,904**	**49%**
Hayes M	C	15,688	35.4%	0.1%	C	15,066	35.3%
Fisher J	LD	6,927	15.6%	1.7%	LD	5,928	13.9%
Povey S	UKIP	3,512	7.9%	6.1%	UKIP	760	1.8%
Lab to C swing	**4.1%**	**44,253**		**Lab maj 2,438**		**42,658**	**Lab maj 5,838**
				5.5%			13.7%

CHARLOTTE ATKINS b 24 Sept 1950. MP 1997-. Parly Under-Sec Dept for Transport 2004-05. PPS to Baroness Symons 2001-02. Asst govt whip 2002-04. Member select cttees: Education and Employment 1997-2001, Selection 1997-2000. Former member Nat Policy Forum. Vice-chair W Mids regional group of Lab MPs to 2002. Cllr Wandsworth 1982-86. Asst community relations officer Luton CRC 1974-76. Research/political officer UCATT/AUEW (TASS) 1976-84. Press/parly officer COHSE/UNISON 1984-97. Ed BSc econ, LSE; MA area studies, London Univ.

This Labour-Tory marginal seat is a mix of agricultural, urban and industrial land, and contains a fair part of the Peak District National Park. There are some small affluent towns that house commuters to Stoke-on-Trent, and the countryside attracts many tourists. Other than tourism and farming, local industry includes textiles, cement, pottery, copper and the quarrying of sand and gravel. Leek, home to the Britannia Building Society and Kerrygold spread factory, is the main centre of population.

STAFFORDSHIRE SOUTH — Lab hold

(By-election 23 June 2005)		Electorate 68,763	Turnout 37.3%	Change from 2001	2001	Electorate 69,959	Turnout 60.3%
Cormack P	**C**	**13,343**	**52.1%**	**1.6%**	**C**	**21,295**	**50.5%**
Kalinauckas P	Lab	4,496	17.5%	-16.7%	Lab	14,414	34.2%
Crotty J	LD	3,540	13.8%	2.2%	LD	4,891	11.6%
Hurst M	UKIP	2,675	10.4%	6.7%	UKIP	1,580	3.7%
Bushell G	Eng Dem	643	2.5%				
Spohrer K	Green	437	1.7%				
Davies A	FP	434	1.7%				
Braid Rev D	Clause 28	67	0.3%				
Lab to C swing	**9.1%**	**25,635**		**C maj 8,847** 34.5%		**42,180**	**C maj 6,881** 16.3%

SIR PATRICK CORMACK b 18 May 1939. MP for Cannock 1970-74, for SW Staffs 1974-83, for S Staffs 1983-. Deputy to Shadow HoC Leader 1997-2000. PPS to Joint Parly Secs DHSS 1970-73. Opposition spokes 1997-2000. Member select cttees. Chair all-party groups. Member: exec 1922 cttee 2002-, council for peace in the Balkans, Royal Historical Manuscripts Commission, gen C of E synod, HoC Commission. Dir Parly Broadcasting Unit. Schoolmaster/editor/lecturer/industrial consultant. Governor English Speaking Union 1999-. Kt 1995. BA Eng/hist, Hull Univ.

This prosperous, rural, natural Tory seat lies around the western and northern fringes of the West Midlands conurbation. Although there are no major towns, the seat is not wholly rural, containing as it does a string of commuter dormitory villages for places like Wolverhampton. Typically for a West Midlands constituency, manufacturing accounts for a higher percentage of work (20 per cent) than the national average. The death of the Lib Dem candidate during the 2005 general election campaign caused the poll to be deferred to a by-election in June.

STALYBRIDGE AND HYDE — Lab hold

		Electorate 66,013	Turnout 53.5%	Change from 2001	2001	Electorate 66,265	Turnout 48.4%
Purnell J	**Lab**	**17,535**	**49.6%**	**-5.9%**	**Lab**	**17,781**	**55.5%**
Boardman L	C	9,187	26%	-1.8%	C	8,922	27.8%
Bingham V	LD	5,532	15.7%	2.2%	LD	4,327	13.5%
Byrne N	BNP	1,399	4%		UKIP	1,016	3.2%
Smee M	Greens	1,088	3.1%				
Whittaker J	UKIP	573	1.6%	-1.6%			
Lab to C swing	**2.1%**	**35,314**		**Lab maj 8,348** 23.6%		**32,046**	**Lab maj 8,859** 27.6%

JAMES PURNELL b 2 March 1970. MP 2001-. Parly Under-Sec Dept for Culture, Media and Sport 2005-. PPS to Ruth Kelly 2003-04. Asst govt whip 2004-05. Member Work and Pensions select cttee 2001-03. Member Co-op Party. Chair Lab Friends of Israel 2002-. Cllr Islington. Tony Blair: researcher 1989-92, culture, media, sport, knowledge economy adviser 1997-2001. Strategy consultant, research fellow, BBC corporate planning head. Ed Lycee International, Coll Pierre et Marie Curie, France; BA PPE, Balliol Coll, Oxford.

The constituency of Stalybridge and Hyde lies right on the eastern outskirts of Manchester, at the foot of the Pennines and even includes some areas of barren moorland. Held safely by Labour since the Second World War, this mainly residential seat is made up of a number of towns and villages that nestle along the Pennine belt, as well as the old towns of Hyde, in the southern end of the seat, and Stalybridge.

STEVENAGE — Lab hold

		Electorate 66,889	Turnout 62.7%	Change from 2001	2001	Electorate 69,203	Turnout 61.3%
Follett B	**Lab**	**18,003**	**42.9%**	**-9%**	**Lab**	**22,025**	**51.9%**
Freeman G	C	14,864	35.4%	3.7%	C	13,459	31.7%
Davies J	LD	7,610	18.2%	4%	LD	6,027	14.2%
Peebles V	UKIP	1,305	3.1%		SA	449	1.1%
Losonczi A	Ind	152	0.4%	-0.4%	Ind	320	0.8%
					ProLife	173	0.4%
Lab to C swing	**6.4%**	**41,934**		**Lab maj 3,139** 7.5%		**42,453**	**Lab maj 8,566** 20.2%

BARBARA FOLLETT b 25 Dec 1942. MP 1997-. Member select cttees: International Development 1997-2001, Modernisation of HoC 2001-. Chair all-party retail industry group. Member: Lab electoral reform campaign, SERA. Chair eastern regional group of Lab MPs 1999-. Bank clerk, teacher, farm manager, S African Race Relats Inst regional sec, Kupugani regional manager/nat health education director, lecturer, research associate, dir EMILY's list UK. Ed fine art, Capetown Univ; govt, Open Univ; BSc econ hist, LSE.

Once the seat of Shirley Williams in her Labour days (she described it as 'a microcosm of the new Britain') the country's first post-Second World War, and now largely white-collar, new town has borne out her analysis by swinging with the party in power. True to form, it fell to New Labour and Barbara Follett in 1997 after 18 years in Conservative hands.

STIRLING — Lab hold

		Electorate 64,554	Turnout 67.7%		2001
McGuire A	**Lab**	**15,729**	**36%**		No comparable results due to boundary changes
Kerr S	C	10,962	25.1%		
Holdsworth K	LD	9,052	20.7%		
McGlinchey F	SNP	5,503	12.6%		
Illingworth D	Greens	1,302	3%		
Sheret R	SSP	458	1.1%		
McDonald J	Ind	261	0.6%		
Willis M	OCV	215	0.5%		
Desmond M	UKIP	209	0.5%		
Lab to C swing (notional)	**4.2%**	**43,691**		**Lab maj 4,767** 10.9%	

ANNE McGUIRE b 26 May 1949. MP for Stirling 1997-2005, for new Stirling 2005-. Parly Under-Sec: Dept for Work and Pensions 2005-, Scotland Office 2002-05. PPS to Donald Dewar 1997-98. Whip: asst govt 1998-2001, govt 2001-02. Member Lab Party Scottish exec 1984-97, chair Lab Party Scotland 1992-93. Cllr Strathclyde RC 1980-82. Teacher, voluntary sector devt worker/senior manager. Dep dir Scottish Council for Voluntary Organisations. GMB nat exec 1987-91. Ed MA politics with hist, Glasgow Univ; Dip Secondary Ed, Notre Dame Coll of Ed.

Labour and the Conservatives do battle for Stirling which is centred on the historic Scottish capital and includes Bannockburn and Stirling Bridge. The Conservatives have strong support in the rural north-west which stretches up to the Trossachs and Ben Lomond while Stirling, Bannockburn, and the old pit villages of the south-east largely vote Labour. Agriculture and tourism are important industries, though the chipboard factory at Cowie is a major employer.

STOCKPORT — Lab hold

		Electorate 65,593	Turnout 54.5%	Change from 2001	2001	Electorate 66,395	Turnout 53.3%
Coffey A	**Lab**	**18,069**	**50.5%**	**-8.1%**	**Lab**	**20,731**	**58.6%**
Berridge E	C	8,906	24.9%	-1%	C	9,162	25.9%
Floodgate L	LD	7,832	21.9%	6.4%	LD	5,490	15.5%
Simpson R	UKIP	964	2.7%				
Lab to C swing	**3.6%**	**35,771**		**Lab maj 9,163** 25.6%		**35,383**	**Lab maj 11,569** 32.7%

ANN COFFEY b 31 Aug 1946. MP 1992-. PPS to Alistair Darling 1998-. Joint PPS to Tony Blair as PM 1997-98. Opposition whip 1995-96. Opposition health spokes 1996-97. Member select cttees: Trade and Industry 1993-95, Modernisation of HoC 2000. Vice-chair all-party markets industry group 2002-. Cllr Stockport MBC 1984-92. Social worker, fostering team leader. Ed Bodmin and Bushey Grammar Schs; BSc sociology, South Bank Poly, London; Postgrad Education Cert, Walsall Coll of Education; MSc psychiatric social work, Manchester Univ.

Part of Greater Manchester, Stockport very much has its own identity, but since the 1980s local Stopfordians have remorselessly followed the regional swing to Labour in the north west, and is now regarded as a safe Labour seat. Stockport is a largely residential seat, though it has grown recently as the preferred site for many firms' regional offices. Traditional industries, like much of the region, have declined sharply, but some light engineering plants do remain.

STOCKTON NORTH — Lab hold

		Electorate 63,271	Turnout 57.6%	Change from 2001	2001	Electorate 64,629	Turnout 54.8%
Cook F	**Lab**	**20,012**	**54.9%**	**-8.5%**	**Lab**	**22,470**	**63.4%**
Baldwin H	C	7,575	20.8%	-1.3%	C	7,823	22.1%
Hughes N	LD	6,869	18.9%	7%	LD	4,208	11.9%
Parkin G	UKIP	986	2.7%				
Hughes K	BNP	986	2.7%				
Lab to C swing	**3.6%**	**36,428**		**Lab maj 12,437** 34.1%		**35,427**	**Lab maj 14,647** 41.3%

FRANK COOK b 3 Nov 1935. MP 1983-. Dep Speaker Westminster Hall 1999-2001, 2002-. Opposition whip 1987-92. Member select cttees: Procedure 1989-92, Defence 1992-97, Chairmen's Panel 1997-. Chair all-party groups: landmine eradication 2002-, Turkey 2002-. Vice-pres NATO parly assembly 1998-2000. Member organisation for security/co-operation in Europe parly body 1991-2001. MSF-sponsored. Career incl schoolmaster, postman, steel works transport manager, cost engineer, project manager. Ed Education Inst, Leeds.

This Teesside constituency has remained staunchly Labour since the town of Stockton was split into two seats in 1983. Heavily industrial, most prominantly featuring the giant ICI plant at Billingham, Stockton North is the more impoverished and working-class of the two Stockton seats, and unsurprisingly, it has been the more loyal of the two in its support of Labour.

STOCKTON SOUTH

Lab hold

		Electorate 71,286	Turnout 63%	Change from 2001	2001	Electorate 70,337	Turnout 62.9%
Taylor D	**Lab**	**21,480**	**47.8%**	**-5.2%**	**Lab**	**23,414**	**53%**
Gaddas J	C	15,341	34.2%	1.8%	C	14,328	32.4%
Barker M	LD	7,171	16%	2.4%	LD	6,012	13.6%
Allison S	UKIP	931	2.1%		SA	455	1%
Lab to C swing	**3.5%**	**44,923**		**Lab maj 6,139** 13.7%		**44,209**	**Lab maj 9,086** 20.6%

DARI TAYLOR b 13 Dec 1944. MP 1997-. PPS to: Hazel Blears 2003-, Lewis Moonie and Lord Bach 2001-03. Member Defence select cttee 1997-99. Chair all-party adoption group 2001-. Member leadership campaign team. Cllr Sunderland MC 1986-97. Lecturer 1970-81, 1986-87. GMB union: research support 1990, regional education officer northern region 1993-97. Regional/local NATFHE representative. Ed Ynyshir Girls' Sch; Burnley Municipal Coll; BA politics, Nottingham Univ; MA social policy, Durham Univ.

The congenial brother of the Stockton North seat contains the town centre, a focal point for shoppers from all over the region, and also houses many commuters to Middlesbrough. With lower unemployment and a workforce less centred upon manual labour, it is little surprise that Stockton South flirted with the Conservatives, albeit briefly and by narrow margins. However, it now appears to be a safe Labour seat.

STOKE-ON-TRENT CENTRAL

Lab hold

		Electorate 57,643	Turnout 48.4%	Change from 2001	2001	Electorate 59,750	Turnout 47.4%
Fisher M	**Lab**	**14,760**	**52.9%**	**-7.8%**	**Lab**	**17,170**	**60.7%**
Redfern J	LD	4,986	17.9%	3.2%	C	5,325	18.8%
Baroudy E	C	4,823	17.3%	-1.5%	LD	4,148	14.7%
Coleman M	BNP	2,178	7.8%		Ind	1,657	5.9%
Bonfiglio J	UKIP	914	3.3%				
Cessford J	SAP	246	0.9%				
Lab to LD swing	**5.5%**	**27,907**		**Lab maj 9,774** 35%		**28,300**	**Lab maj 11,845** 41.9%

MARK FISHER b 29 Oct 1944. MP 1983-. Parly Under-Sec: Dept for Culture, Media and Sport 1997-98, National Heritage 1997. Opposition whip 1985-86. Opposition spokes 1987-97. Chair all-party Tunisia group 2001-. Chair Parliament First 2001-. Cllr Staffs CC 1981-85. Member: BBC Gen Advisory Council 1987-97, Policy Studies Inst Council 1989-97, Museums/Galleries Commission 1998-2000. Academic, documentary film producer/scriptwriter. Ed Eton Coll; MA Eng lit, Trinity Coll, Cambridge.

Stoke-on-Trent, a city composed of several tight-knit towns forming the area known as The Potteries, has three constituencies, all perennially won by Labour. This Central seat, the retail centre for much of Staffordshire, contains the greatest proportion of council housing of the three seats. Most of the town's Asian population lives here. There is an extremely high proportion of skilled manual workers which make up 40 per cent of the economically active population.

STOKE-ON-TRENT NORTH

Lab hold

		Electorate 58,422	Turnout 52.6%	Change from 2001	2001	Electorate 57,998	Turnout 51.9%
Walley J	**Lab**	**16,191**	**52.6%**	**-5.4%**	**Lab**	**17,460**	**58%**
Browning B	C	6,155	20%	1.2%	C	5,676	18.8%
Jebb H	LD	4,561	14.8%	2.9%	LD	3,580	11.9%
Cartlidge S	BNP	2,132	6.9%		Ind	3,399	11.3%
Braithwaite E	UKIP	696	2.3%				
Taylor I	Veritas	689	2.2%				
Chesters H	Ind	336	1.1%	-10.2%			
Lab to C swing	**3.3%**	**30,760**		**Lab maj 10,036** 32.6%		**30,115**	**Lab maj 11,784** 39.1%

JOAN WALLEY b 23 Jan 1949. MP 1987-. Opposition spokes: environmental protection and devt 1988-90, transport 1990-95. Member select cttees: Trade and Industry 1995-97, 1997-98, Environmental Audit 1997-. Chair all-party groups: regeneration 2001-, lighting 2003-. Member SERA. Cllr Lambeth 1981-85. Alcoholics recovery project 1970-73. Local govt officer 1974-79. NACRO devt officer 1979-82. UNISON-sponsored. Vice-pres Inst Environmental Health Officers. Ed BA social admin, Hull Univ; community work devt dip, Univ Coll of Wales.

This seat is dominated by pottery and related industries and holds the highest proportion of skilled manual workers in England and Wales, at 46 per cent. This, and the corresponding lack of professional or managerial workers, gives Labour all the support it needs. Stoke North may have relatively low unemployment and a high level of owner-occupancy but the Tories know they will struggle to succeed in such a traditional, working-class, Labour stronghold.

STOKE-ON-TRENT SOUTH — Lab hold

		Electorate	Turnout	Change from	2001	Electorate	Turnout
		70,612	53.6%	2001		70,032	51.4%
Flello R	**Lab**	**17,727**	**46.9%**	**-6.9%**	**Lab**	**19,366**	**53.8%**
Deaville M	C	9,046	23.9%	-0.7%	C	8,877	24.6%
Martin A	LD	5,894	15.6%	2.5%	LD	4,724	13.1%
Leat M	BNP	3,305	8.7%	4.9%	Ind	1,703	4.7%
Benson N	UKIP	1,043	2.8%		BNP	1,358	3.8%
Allen G	Veritas	805	2.1%				
Lab to C swing	**3.1%**	**37,820**		**Lab maj 8,681**		**36,028**	**Lab maj 10,489**
				23%			29.1%

ROBERT FLELLO b 14 Jan 1966. MP 2005-. Birmingham City councillor 2002-04; Chair Birmingham Northfield CLP. Regional organiser Labour Party 2004-05; CEO Malachi Community Trust 2003-04. Ed King's Norton Boys' School; University of Wales, Bangor

For 26 years parliamentary home to Jack Ashley, Stoke South is one of the steadiest Labour seats in the country. Besides pottery, the seat also has a history of coal-mining and is still known for tyre-making. The area is undeniably working-class – it has the second highest proportion of skilled manual workers, after Stoke North, in England and Wales – yet it also has below average unemployment and a 70 per cent rate of owner-occupancy.

STONE — C hold

		Electorate	Turnout	Change from	2001	Electorate	Turnout
		70,359	66.8%	2001		68,847	66.3%
Cash W	**C**	**22,733**	**48.3%**	**-0.8%**	**C**	**22,395**	**49.1%**
Davis M	Lab	13,644	29%	-6.8%	Lab	16,359	35.8%
Stevens R	LD	9,111	19.4%	4.3%	LD	6,888	15.1%
Nattrass M	UKIP	1,548	3.3%				
Lab to C swing	**3%**	**47,036**		**C maj 9,089**		**45,642**	**C maj 6,036**
				19.3%			13.2%

WILLIAM CASH b 10 May 1940. MP for Stafford 1984-97, for Stone 1997-. Shadow Attorney General 2001-03. Member European Scrutiny 1998-. All-party groups: chair Uganda 1998, vice-chair: Tanzania 2001-, coalfields communities 2001-, solvent abuse 2001-, Kenya 2002-, Malaysia 2004-. Chair Friends of Bruges Group in HoC 1989-. Vice-pres Con Small Business Bureau. Founder/chair The European Foundation. Solicitor. Ed Stonyhurst Coll; MA, Lincoln Coll, Oxford.

Staffordshire's newest constituency, Stone was formed from three Tory seats. Named after the town of Stone, it covers a large and fairly rural area that stretches east to west across the county. Good road and rail links have helped the promotion of industry, especially around Stone, Cheadle and Eccleshall. The inhabitants are mainly white, many of the workers are in the management/technical social group, unemployment runs very low, and most homes are owner-occupied.

STOURBRIDGE — Lab hold

		Electorate	Turnout	Change from	2001	Electorate	Turnout
		64,479	64.7%	2001		64,610	61.8%
Waltho L	**Lab**	**17,089**	**41%**	**-6.1%**	**Lab**	**18,823**	**47.1%**
Coad D	C	16,682	40%	2.4%	C	15,011	37.6%
Bramall C	LD	6,850	16.4%	4.3%	LD	4,833	12.1%
Mau D	UKIP	1,087	2.6%	0.7%	UKIP	763	1.9%
					SLP	494	1.2%
Lab to C swing	**4.3%**	**41,708**		**Lab maj 407**		**39,924**	**Lab maj 3,812**
				1%			9.5%

LYNDA WALTHO b 19 May 1960. MP 2005-. Regional organiser West Midlands Labour Party. Principal adviser to Neena Gill MEP; Assistant to Sylvia Heal MP. Member GMB. Ed Keele University; PGCE University of Central England

Stourbridge marks the western extent of the West Midlands conurbation and the countryside of Worcestershire is tantalisingly close. Glass is the main industry in this constituency, with a large works at Amblecote, which is also home to much new private housing. There is a low proportion of council-rented accommodation and below average unemployment, suggesting reasons for earlier Tory election successes. A Labour-Tory marginal, Stourbridge is a barometer seat.

STRANGFORD — DUP hold

		Electorate	Turnout	Change from	2001	Electorate	Turnout
		69,040	53.6%	2001		72,192	59.9%
Robinson I	**DUP**	**20,921**	**56.5%**	**13.7%**	**DUP**	**18,532**	**42.8%**
McGimpsey G	UUP	7,872	21.3%	-19%	UUP	17,422	40.3%
McCarthy K	All	3,332	9%	2.3%	All	2,902	6.7%
Boyle J	SDLP	2,496	6.7%	0.6%	SDLP	2,646	6.1%
Dick T	C	1,462	4%		SF	930	2.2%
Kennedy D	SF	949	2.6%	0.4%	NIUP	822	1.9%
UUP to DUP swing	**16.4%**	**37,032**		**DUP maj 13,049**		**43,254**	**DUP maj 1,110**
				35.2%			2.6%

IRIS ROBINSON b 6 Sept 1949. MP 2001-. DUP spokes health, social services and public safety. New NI Assembly 1998-2002. Cllr Castlereagh BC 1989-: mayor Castlereagh 1992, 1995, 2000. Dir: Ballybeen Square Regeneration Board, Tullycarnet Community Enterprises Ltd. Ed Knockbreda Intermediate Sch; Castelreagh Tech Coll.

The constituency partly surrounds Strangford Lough (renowned for its superb oysters) and dominates the Ards Peninsula. It covers parts of Castlereagh, Ards and Down district councils and is acclaimed by the MP, Iris Robinson of the DUP, as 'God's own country'. While that may be arguable it is certainly DUP country and they look to have established a strong lead over the UUP in recent years.

STRATFORD-ON-AVON — C hold

		Electorate	Turnout	Change from	2001	Electorate	Turnout
		84,591	68.8%	2001		83,757	65.6%
Maples J	**C**	**28,652**	**49.2%**	**-1.1%**	**C**	**27,606**	**50.3%**
Juned S	LD	16,468	28.3%	-0.5%	LD	15,804	28.8%
Blackmore R	Lab/C	10,145	17.4%	0.7%	Lab	9,164	16.7%
Cottam H	UKIP	1,621	2.8%	0.6%	UKIP	1,184	2.2%
Davies M	Greens	1,354	2.3%	0.2%	Greens	1,156	2.1%
C to LD swing	**0.3%**	**58,240**		**C maj 12,184**		**54,914**	**C maj 11,802**
				20.9%			21.5%

JOHN MAPLES b 22 April 1943. MP for Lewisham West 1983-92, for Stratford-on-Avon 1997-. Shadow Sec of State: Foreign and Commonwealth Affairs 1999-2000, Defence 1998-99, Health 1997-98. Econ Sec Treasury 1990-92. PPS to Norman Lamont 1987-90. Member Foreign Affairs select cttee 2000-. Dep chair Con Party 1994-95. Joint vice-chair British-American Parly Internat Group 1999-2003. Council member Royal Internat Affairs Inst. Barrister, company director/chairman. Ed BA law, MA, Downing Coll, Cambridge; Harvard Business Sch.

This safest of Conservative seats fell briefly into Labour hands after sitting MP Alan Howarth crossed the floor in October 1995. Former Treasury minister John Maples won it back into favoured Tory hands in 2001. This is a rural constituency, Stratford-upon-Avon being the only big town in a seat that covers almost half of Warwickshire. Tourist centre, Stratford, markets its Shakespeare connections for all their considerable worth.

STREATHAM — Lab hold

		Electorate	Turnout	Change from	2001	Electorate	Turnout
		79,193	51.3%	2001		76,021	48.7%
Hill K	**Lab**	**18,950**	**46.7%**	**-10.2%**	**Lab**	**21,041**	**56.9%**
Sanders D	LD	11,484	28.3%	10%	LD	6,771	18.3%
Sproule J	C	7,238	17.8%	-0.1%	C	6,639	17.9%
Collins S	Greens	2,245	5.5%	1.1%	Greens	1,641	4.4%
Gittings T	UKIP	396	1%		SA	906	2.4%
Colvill W	World Rev	127	0.3%				
Stone P	Ind	100	0.2%				
West R	Ind	40	0.1%				
Acheng S	Ind	35	0.1%				
Lab to LD swing	**10.1%**	**40,615**		**Lab maj 7,466**		**36,998**	**Lab maj 14,270**
				18.4%			38.6%

KEITH HILL b 28 July 1943. MP 1992-. PPS to Tony Blair as PM 2005-. Minister of State Housing and Planning, ODPM 2003-05. PPS to Hilary Armstrong 1997-98, 1999-2001. Whip: asst govt 1998-99, deputy chief 2001-03. Member select cttees: Selection 2001-03, Accommodation and Works 2001-03, Finance and Services 2001-03. Chair Lab Movt for Europe 1997-98. Hon Sec London Lab MPs group 1997-98. Politics research asst/lecturer. Political liaison officer RMT union 1976-92. PC 2003. Ed MA PPE, Corpus Christi Coll, Oxford; DipEd, Univ Coll of Wales.

To the south of this mixed, but safe Labour south London seat are found the leafier, more select suburbs, while in the north and east are the more cramped, inner-city flats and bedsits of parts of Clapham and Brixton. Over one third of homes are council-rented. It has one of the highest proportions of 25-39 year olds in England and Wales (nearly a third of the population) and a correspondingly small number of middle-aged and pensioner voters.

STRETFORD AND URMSTON — Lab hold

		Electorate	Turnout	Change from	2001	Electorate	Turnout
		61,979	61.5%	2001		71,222	54.8%
Hughes B	**Lab**	**19,417**	**51%**	**-10.1%**	**Lab**	**23,836**	**61.1%**
Hinds D	C	11,566	30.4%	3.3%	C	10,565	27.1%
Bhatti F	LD	5,323	14%	4%	LD	3,891	10%
Krantz M	Respect	950	2.5%		Ind	713	1.8%
McManus M	UKIP	845	2.2%				
Lab to C swing	**6.7%**	**38,101**		**Lab maj 7,851**		**39,005**	**Lab maj 13,271**
				20.6%			34%

BEVERLEY HUGHES b 30 March 1950. MP 1997-. Minister of State Dept for Education and Skills 2005-, Home Office: Minister of State 2002-04, Parly Under-Sec 2001-02. Parly Under-Sec Dept of Environ, Transport and Regions 1999-2001. PPS to Hilary Armstrong 1998-99. Member Home Affairs select cttee 1997-98. Cllr Trafford MBC: leader 1995-97. Dir Manchester Airport plc 1995-97. Probation officer, research associate, lecturer. PC 2004. Ed Ellesmere Port Girls' Grammar Sch; BSc, MSc, Manchester Univ; applied social studies dip, Liverpool Univ.

A south-west suburb of Manchester, Stretford and Urmston is industrial as well as residential in character. The best known sites in the seat, however, are undoubtedly the Old Trafford cricket and football grounds. Although this seat was only created before the 1997 general election, it has become a safe Labour seat and is a prime example of how Labour has changed the electoral geography of the country.

STROUD — Lab hold

		Electorate	Turnout	Change from	2001	Electorate	Turnout
		79,748	71.3%	2001		78,818	70%
Drew D	**Lab/C**	**22,527**	**39.6%**	**-7%**	**Lab/C**	**25,685**	**46.6%**
Carmichael N	C	22,177	39%	1.6%	C	20,646	37.4%
Hirst P	LD	8,026	14.1%	3.2%	LD	6,036	10.9%
Whiteside M	Greens	3,056	5.4%	1.9%	Greens	1,913	3.5%
Noble E	UKIP	1,089	1.9%	0.3%	UKIP	895	1.6%
Lab/C to C swing	**4.3%**	**56,875**		**Lab/C maj 350**		**55,175**	**Lab/C maj 5,039**
				0.6%			9.1%

DAVID DREW b 13 April 1952. MP 1997-. Member select cttees: Procedure 1997-2001, Modernisation of HoC 1998-99, Agriculture 1999-2001, Environment, Food and Rural Affairs 2001-. Chair all-party group. Member: Co-operative Party, Christian Socialist Movt, Lab Electoral Reform Campaign. Cllr: Stevenage BC 1981-82, Stroud DC 1987-95, Stonehouse TC 1987-Glos CC 1993-97. NAS/UWT branch sec 1984-86. Teacher/lecturer. Ed BA econ, Nottingham Univ; PGCE, Birmingham Univ; MA historical studies, Bristol Poly; MEd, W of Eng Univ.

The town of Stroud and its adjacent urban areas dominate the constituency. Cloth mills used to provide employment but in recent times other light industry has grown in response to the easy access to Bristol, the West Country and Wales. After controlling Stroud for over 40 years the Tories were swept aside by the Labour landslide in 1997. What is more surprising is that they have since been able to hang on to this seat.

SUFFOLK COASTAL — C hold

		Electorate	Turnout	Change from	2001	Electorate	Turnout
		77,423	67.9%	2001		75,963	66.4%
Gummer J	**C**	**23,415**	**44.6%**	**1.3%**	**C**	**21,847**	**43.3%**
Rowe D	Lab	13,730	26.1%	-8.7%	Lab	17,521	34.8%
Young D	LD	11,637	22.1%	3.9%	LD	9,192	18.2%
Curtis R	UKIP	2,020	3.8%	0.1%	UKIP	1,847	3.7%
Whitlow P	Greens	1,755	3.3%				
Lab to C swing	**5%**	**52,557**		**C maj 9,685**		**50,407**	**C maj 4,326**
				18.4%			8.6%

JOHN GUMMER b 26 Nov 1939. MP for Lewisham West 1970-74, for Eye 1979-83, for Suffolk Coastal 1983-. Sec of State Environ 1993-97; Minister MAFF 1989-93; Minister Local Govt 1988-89; Minister of State MAFF 1985-88; Paymaster Gen 1984-85; Dept of Employment: Minister of State 1983-84, Parly Under-Sec 1983. PPS 1979-81, 1971-72. Whip: asst govt 1981, govt 1981-83. Vice-chair all-party groups 2002-. Con Party: chair 1983-85, vice-chair 1972-74. Cllr ILEA 1967-70. Company chairman/dir. PC 1985. BA hist, MA, Selwyn Coll, Cambridge.

Running along the Suffolk coast from Felixstowe, a container port and seaside resort in the south, to Southwold in the north, this fairly safe Tory seat includes the towns of Saxmundham and Woodbridge and borders Ipswich. The area's economy is spread between the poles of tourism and industry. The Sizewell A Magnox nuclear power station and the Sizewell B PWR reactor are in the constituency, as is Hollesley Bay Open Prison.

CENTRAL SUFFOLK AND NORTH IPSWICH — C hold

		Electorate 76,271	Turnout 66.7%	Change from 2001	2001	Electorate 74,200	Turnout 63.5%
Lord M	**C**	**22,333**	**43.9%**	**-0.5%**	**C**	**20,924**	**44.4%**
MacDonald N	Lab	14,477	28.5%	-8.6%	Lab	17,455	37.1%
Houseley A	LD	10,709	21.1%	5%	LD	7,593	16.1%
West J	UKIP	1,754	3.4%	1%	UKIP	1,132	2.4%
Wolfe M	Greens	1,593	3.1%				
Lab to C swing	**4.1%**	**50,866**		**C maj 7,856** 15.4%		**47,104**	**C maj 3,469** 7.4%

SIR MICHAEL LORD b 17 Oct 1938. MP for Central Suffolk 1983-97, for Central Suffolk and North Ipswich 1997-. PPS to John MacGregor 1984-87. Second deputy chair Ways and Means and deputy speaker 1997-. Chair all-party rugby union football club group 2003-. Parly delegate, Council of Europe and the Western European Union 1987-91. Cllr: North Beds Borough Council 1974-77, Beds County Council 1981-83. Arboricultural consultant. Ed MA agriculture, Christ's Coll, Cambridge.

The most rural of the Suffolk constituencies, with 70 per cent of the population living in villages and rural areas, Central Suffolk and North Ipswich is a largely prosperous region of golden cornfields, commuter homes and picturesque retirement residences. The economic pursuits are therefore mainly agricultural, and associated industries can be found in towns such as Framlingham and Wickham Market. The Tories have held this seat since 1951, and it remains solid Conservative territory.

SOUTH SUFFOLK — C hold

		Electorate 67,799	Turnout 71.8%	Change from 2001	2001	Electorate 68,456	Turnout 66.2%
Yeo T	**C**	**20,471**	**42%**	**0.6%**	**C**	**18,748**	**41.4%**
Pollard K	LD	13,865	28.5%	3.6%	Lab	13,667	30.2%
Craig K	Lab	11,917	24.5%	-5.7%	LD	11,296	24.9%
Carver J	UKIP	2,454	5%	1.5%	UKIP	1,582	3.5%
C to LD swing	**1.5%**	**48,707**		**C maj 6,606** 13.6%		**45,293**	**C maj 5,081** 11.2%

TIM YEO b 20 March 1945. MP 1983-. Shadow Sec of State: Environ and Transport 2004-05, Public Services, Health and Education 2003-04, Trade and Industry 2002-03, Culture, Media and Sport 2001-02. Shadow Minister MAFF 1998-2001. Joint Parly Under-Sec: Dept of Environ 1990-92, 1993-94, Dept of Health 1992-93. PPS to Douglas Hurd 1988-90. Opposition spokes 1997-98. Member Treasury select cttee 1996-97. Vice-chair Con Party 1998. Investment banker/company dir. Cambridge Univ Air Squadron. Ed MA hist, Emmanuel Coll, Cambridge.

This seat styles itself as 'Constable country', and was also the setting for some of Gainsborough's most famous paintings. The medieval wool towns of Lavenham, Long Melford and Nayland are tourist attractions. Sudbury, Gainsborough's birthplace, and Hadleigh are the largest towns, and both have modern industrial estates, although agriculture and tourism form the basis of the local economy. Unsurprisingly, this most English and rural of seats is solid Tory territory.

WEST SUFFOLK — C hold

		Electorate 72,856	Turnout 60.7%	Change from 2001	2001	Electorate 70,129	Turnout 60.5%
Spring R	**C**	**21,682**	**49.1%**	**1.5%**	**C**	**20,201**	**47.6%**
Jefferys M	Lab	12,773	28.9%	-8.6%	Lab	15,906	37.5%
Graves A	LD	7,573	17.1%	5.3%	LD	5,017	11.8%
Smith I	UKIP	2,177	4.9%	1.8%	UKIP	1,321	3.1%
Lab to C swing	**5.1%**	**44,205**		**C maj 8,909** 20.2%		**42,445**	**C maj 4,295** 10.1%

RICHARD SPRING b 24 Sept 1946. MP for Bury St Edmunds 1992-97, for W Suffolk 1997-. Shadow Minister: Transport 2005-, Economic Affairs 2004-05, Internat Affairs 2003-04. PPS to: Nicholas Soames, James Arbuthnot 1996-97, Tim Eggar 1995-96, Sir Patrick Mayhew 1994-95. Opposition spokes 1997-2003. Member select cttees: NI Affairs 1995-97, Health 1995-96, Deregulation 1997. Vice-chair Con Industrial Fund 1993-96. Dep chair small business bureau 1992-. Vice-pres Merrill Lynch Ltd 1976-86. Ed Cape Town Univ; Magdalene Coll, Cambridge.

Composed of prosperous provincial towns and rural communities, West Suffolk was created in 1995 from the former Bury St Edmunds seat and takes in areas that previously lay in South Suffolk. The region has been natural Conservative territory for over 50 years. Significant Labour gains in 1997 were reversed in 2001 and 2005 and seem unlikely to be repeated.

SUNDERLAND NORTH

Lab hold

		Electorate 58,146	Turnout 49.7%	Change from 2001	2001	Electorate 60,846	Turnout 49%
Etherington B	**Lab**	**15,719**	**54.4%**	**-8.3%**	**Lab**	**18,685**	**62.7%**
Daughton S	C	5,724	19.8%	1.9%	C	5,331	17.9%
Hollern J	LD	4,277	14.8%	2.7%	LD	3,599	12.1%
Herron N	Ind	2,057	7.1%	2%	Ind	1,518	5.1%
Hiles D	BNP	1,136	3.9%	1.6%	BNP	687	2.3%
Lab to C swing	**5.1%**	**28,913**		**Lab maj 9,995** 34.6%		**29,820**	**Lab maj 13,354** 44.8%

BILL ETHERINGTON b 17 July 1941. MP 1992-. Member select cttees: Catering 1995-97, Court of Referees 1997-2001. Vice-chair all-party groups: FRAME 2000-, coalfield communities 2001-. CLP exec cttee member 1981-87. Dep leader UK delegation to Council of Europe and Western European Union 2001. TUC: N regional representative 1985-92, NUM delegate 1990-91. Vice-pres NE area NUM 1988-92. Member RMT parly campaigning group 2002-04. Mechanical fitter. Ed Monkwearmouth Grammar Sch; Industrial Relations Studies Cert, Durham Univ.

This industrial base of the North East has maintained its strong support for the Labour party since abandoning its marginal days in the 1950s. Situated at the eastern coastal side of the Tyne and Wear conurbation, Sunderland North's loyalty to Labour is historically more consistent than that of its southerly neighbour; however, both are now safe Labour seats.

SUNDERLAND SOUTH

Lab hold

		Electorate 62,256	Turnout 49.3%	Change from 2001	2001	Electorate 64,577	Turnout 48.3%
Mullin C	**Lab**	**17,982**	**58.6%**	**-5.3%**	**Lab**	**19,921**	**63.9%**
Oliver R	C	6,923	22.5%	2.4%	C	6,254	20.1%
Kane G	LD	4,492	14.6%	2.8%	LD	3,675	11.8%
Guynan D	BNP	1,166	3.8%	2%	BNP	576	1.8%
Warner R	Loony	149	0.5%	-0.4%	UKIP	470	1.5%
					Loony	291	0.9%
Lab to C swing	**3.9%**	**30,712**		**Lab maj 11,059** 36%		**31,187**	**Lab maj 13,667** 43.8%

CHRIS MULLIN b 12 Dec 1947. MP 1987-. Parly Under-Sec: FCO 2003-05, Dept for International Development 2001, Dept of Environment, Transport and Regions 1999-2001. Chair Home Affairs select cttee 1997-99, 2001-03 (member 1992-97). Member Liaison select cttee 1997-99, 2001-03. Member parly Lab Party parly cttee 1997-99, 2001-. Author/journalist: BBC World Service 1974-78; editor Tribune 1982-84. Channel 4/House Questioner of the Year award 1999. Ed St Joseph's Coll, Ipswich; LLB, Hull Univ.

Sunderland South, unlike its northern counterpart, has not experienced an unbroken chain of post-war Labour representation. However, as it last yielded a non-Labour victory in 1960 it is safe to say that Sunderland South is now a safe Labour constituency. Once the world's largest shipbuilding town, with a thriving local coal industry, the decline of traditional industries has been alleviated to some extent by the arrival of Nissan in the neighbouring Houghton and Washington East seat.

SURREY HEATH

C hold

		Electorate 76,090	Turnout 62.9%	Change from 2001	2001	Electorate 75,858	Turnout 59.5%
Gove M	**C**	**24,642**	**51.5%**	**1.8%**	**C**	**22,401**	**49.7%**
Harper R	LD	13,797	28.8%	3.1%	LD	11,582	25.7%
Lowe C	Lab	7,989	16.7%	-4.7%	Lab	9,640	21.4%
Smith S	UKIP	1,430	3%	-0.3%	UKIP	1,479	3.3%
C to LD swing	**0.7%**	**47,858**		**C maj 10,845** 22.7%		**45,102**	**C maj 10,819** 24%

MICHAEL GOVE b 26 Aug 1967. MP 2005-. Reporter Aberdeen Press and Journal 1989; Researcher/reporter, Scottish Television 1990-91; reporter BBC News and Current Affairs 1991-96; writer and editor The Times 1996-2005; writer The Times 2005-. Ed Robert Gordon's College, Aberdeen; BA English, Oxford University.

This constituency, suburban in character despite the presence of the eponymous heath, is on the western edge of Surrey, bordering Hampshire and Berkshire. Created overwhelmingly from the old Surrey North West, but with additions from Woking and Guildford, the seat encompasses the communities of Camberley and Frimley and smaller towns such as Bagshot and Windlesham. Despite recent turmoil within the local party, Michael Gove has inherited a very safe Conservative seat.

EAST SURREY — C hold

		Electorate 73,948	Turnout 66.6%	Change from 2001	2001	Electorate 74,338	Turnout 63.3%
Ainsworth P	**C**	**27,659**	**56.2%**	**3.7%**	**C**	**24,706**	**52.5%**
Pursehouse J	LD	11,738	23.8%	-0.6%	LD	11,503	24.4%
Bridge J	Lab	7,288	14.8%	-4.3%	Lab	8,994	19.1%
Stone A	UKIP	2,158	4.4%	0.5%	UKIP	1,846	3.9%
Matthews W	LCA	410	0.8%				
LD to C swing	**2.2%**	**49,253**		**C maj 15,921** 32.3%		**47,049**	**C maj 13,203** 28.1%

PETER AINSWORTH b 16 Nov 1956. MP 1992-. Shadow Sec of State: Environm, Food and Rural Affairs 2001-02, Culture, Media and Sport 1998-2001. PPS to: Virginia Bottomley 1995-96, Jonathan Aitken 1994-95. Whip: asst govt 1996-97, opposition dep chief 1997-98. Member select cttees: Consolidation Bills Joint Cttee 1993-96, Selection 1997-98, Environmental Audit (chair) 2003-, Liaison 2003-. Cllr Wandsworth 1986-94. Research asst to MEP 1979-81. SG Warburg Securities 1985-92 (director 1990-92). Ed MA Eng lit and lang, Lincoln Coll, Oxford.

This constituency covers the eastern most section of Surrey, bordering Kent, and includes the small towns of Caterham, Horley and Warlingham. Essentially a London commuter seat, but with development limited to narrow valleys and established upland settlements by the North Downs, this is as safe for the Conservatives as they come, and not even the traumas of the last decade or so have dented an impressive Conservative majority.

SOUTH WEST SURREY — C hold

		Electorate 72,977	Turnout 71.8%	Change from 2001	2001	Electorate 70,570	Turnout 70.3%
Hunt J	**C**	**26,420**	**50.4%**	**5.1%**	**C**	**22,462**	**45.3%**
Cordon S	LD	20,709	39.5%	-4.1%	LD	21,601	43.6%
Sleigh T	Lab	4,150	7.9%	-0.8%	Lab	4,321	8.7%
Clark T	UKIP	958	1.8%	-0.6%	UKIP	1,208	2.4%
Platt G	Veritas	172	0.3%				
LD to C swing	**4.6%**	**52,409**		**C maj 5,711** 10.9%		**49,592**	**C maj 861** 1.7%

JEREMY HUNT b 1 November 1966. MP 2005-. Management consultant Outram Cullinan and Co 1988-89; English teacher Japan 1990-91; Founder/managing director Hot Courses Ltd 1991-. Ed Charterhouse, Surrey; MA PPE, Magdalen College, Oxford

Situated towards the Sussex and Hampshire borders, the South West Surrey seat combines countryside and residential areas. The main towns are Farnham, Godalming and Haslemere providing bases for mainly affluent London commuters, but it is predominantly wooded and rural. Local landmarks include the Devil's Punchbowl and Frensham Ponds. Formerly safe for the Conservatives, the seat became marginal in recent times, but the 2005 result suggests that the Liberal Democrat challenge may now have been repulsed.

MID SUSSEX — C hold

		Electorate 72,114	Turnout 68.6%	Change from 2001	2001	Electorate 70,623	Turnout 64.9%
Soames N	**C**	**23,765**	**48%**	**1.8%**	**C**	**21,150**	**46.2%**
Tierney S	LD	17,875	36.1%	5%	LD	14,252	31.1%
Fromant R	Lab	6,280	12.7%	-6.3%	Lab	8,693	19%
Piggott H	UKIP	1,574	3.2%	0.7%	UKIP	1,126	2.5%
					Loony	601	1.3%
C to LD swing	**1.6%**	**49,494**		**C maj 5,890** 11.9%		**45,822**	**C maj 6,898** 15.1%

NICHOLAS SOAMES b 12 Feb 1948. MP for Crawley 1983-97, for Mid Sussex 1997-. Shadow Sec of State Defence 2003-05. Min of State Armed Forces 1994-97, Joint Parly Sec MAFF 1992-94. PPS to: Nicholas Ridley 1987-89, John Gummer 1984-86. Member select cttees: Public Administration 1999, Joint Cttee on Consolidation of Bills Etc 2001-. Member 1922 cttee exec 2000-03. 11th Hussars 1967-72. Equerry to Prince of Wales 1970-72. Stockbroker 1972-74. PA 1974-78 (Sir James Goldsmith 1974-76). Asst dir Sedgewick Group 1979-81. Ed Eton Coll.

Mid Sussex is dominated by three towns: East Grinstead situated on the edge of Ashdown forest in the north, Haywards Heath in the centre and the fast growing Burgess Hill in the south. The seat also contains a few small villages set in some beautiful countryside, including the High Weald, and is, on balance, one of the most rural of the West Sussex districts. A loyal core vote keeps it safe for the Conservatives.

SUTTON AND CHEAM — LD hold

		Electorate 63,319	Turnout 66.2%	Change from 2001	2001	Electorate 63,648	Turnout 62.4%
Burstow P	**LD**	**19,768**	**47.1%**	**-1.7%**	**LD**	**19,382**	**48.8%**
Willis R	C	16,922	40.4%	2.4%	C	15,078	38%
Shukla A	Lab	4,954	11.8%	-1.4%	Lab	5,263	13.2%
Weiss R	Vote Dream	288	0.7%				
LD to C swing	**2.1%**	**41,932**		**LD maj 2,846**		**39,723**	**LD maj 4,304**
				6.8%			10.8%

PAUL BURSTOW b 13 May 1962. MP 1997-. Lib Dem Shadow Health Sec of State 2003-05. Lib Dem spokes: disabled people 1997-98, local govt 1997-99, older people 1999-2003. Member Health select cttee 2003-04. Chair all-party groups: back care 2002-, primary care and public health 2003-. Former member: SDP/Liberal Alliance, London regional Lib Dem exec, federal policy cttee. Political sec Lib Dem Cllrs Assocn 1996-97. Cllr Sutton 1986-: dep leader 1994-99. Organising sec, buyer. Ed Carshalton Further Ed Coll; BA business studies, South Bank Poly.

Cheam and the southern half of this Lib-Dem/Conservative marginal is the most affluent part of this seat, being near the borders of the South Downs yet within easy commuting distance of central London. Sutton and Cheam has one of the highest levels of owner occupation (82 per cent) and one of the lowest for council housing (6.9 per cent). Over two thirds of households are headed by white collar workers, mainly in managerial or technical jobs.

SUTTON COLDFIELD — C hold

		Electorate 72,995	Turnout 63.4%	Change from 2001	2001	Electorate 71,856	Turnout 60.5%
Mitchell A	**C**	**24,308**	**52.5%**	**2.1%**	**C**	**21,909**	**50.4%**
Pocock R	Lab	12,025	26%	-1.2%	Lab	11,805	27.2%
Drury C	LD	7,710	16.6%	-2.4%	LD	8,268	19%
Shorrock S	UKIP	2,275	4.9%	2.2%	UKIP	1,186	2.7%
					Ind	284	0.7%
Lab to C swing	**1.7%**	**46,318**		**C maj 12,283**		**43,452**	**C maj 10,104**
				26.5%			23.3%

ANDREW MITCHELL b 23 March 1956. MP for Gedling 1987-97, for Sutton Coldfield 2001-. Shadow Sec of State Internat Devt 2005-. Shadow Minister: Home Affairs 2004-05, Econ Affairs 2003-04. Parly Under-Sec DSS 1995-97. PPS to: John Wakeham 1990-92, William Waldegrave 1988-90. Whip: asst govt 1992-93, govt 1993-95. Member select cttees: Work and Pensions 2001-03, Modernisation of HoC 2002-04. Lazard Bros consultant/dir, strategy adviser, supervisory board member. UN Cyprus peacekeeping forces. Ed MA hist, Jesus Coll, Cambridge.

Sutton Coldfield has been held by the Conservatives since its creation in 1945. Owner occupiers form 84.3 per cent of all households – only nine constituencies have a higher proportion; unemployment is low and 80 per cent have access to at least one car. Sutton Coldfield is one of the most middle class areas in the Great Britain – 56 per cent can be classed professional, managerial or technical and only 1.4 per cent are unskilled – the lowest figure for any constituency in England and Wales.

SWANSEA EAST — Lab hold

		Electorate 58,813	Turnout 52.4%	Change from 2001	2001	Electorate 56,821	Turnout 52.9%
James S	**Lab**	**17,457**	**56.6%**	**-8.6%**	**Lab**	**19,612**	**65.2%**
Speht R	LD	6,208	20.1%	9.9%	PIC	3,464	11.5%
Bland E	C	3,103	10.1%		LD	3,064	10.2%
Couch C	PIC	2,129	6.9%	-4.6%	C	3,026	10.1%
Holloway K	BNP	770	2.5%		Greens	463	1.5%
Jenkins T	UKIP	674	2.2%	0.7%	UKIP	443	1.5%
Young T	Greens	493	1.6%	0.1%			
Lab to LD swing	**9.3%**	**30,834**		**Lab maj 11,249**		**30,072**	**Lab maj 16,148**
				36.5%			53.7%

SÎAN JAMES b 24 June 1959. MP 2005-. Nat Fed Young Farmers' Clubs 1990-91; Save the Children 1991-94; National Trust 1994-99; Lobbyist 1999-2003; Director Welsh Women's Aid 2003-. Ed Welsh, Univ of Wales, Swansea

Swansea East covers the old industrial east end of the city. A historically safe Labour seat in Wales' second city, this is an urban division that will never elect anybody but a Labour candidate. It has very strong roots and traditions in the party. The opposition parties all poll at similar low levels and regeneration projects including many new sports facilities being built here under Labour should maintain support.

SWANSEA WEST — Lab hold

		Electorate	Turnout	Change from	2001	Electorate	Turnout
		57,946	57.1%	2001		57,520	55.8%
Williams A	**Lab**	**13,833**	**41.8%**	**-6.9%**	**Lab**	**15,644**	**48.7%**
Kinzett R	LD	9,564	28.9%	12.3%	C	6,094	19%
Abdel-Haq M	C	5,285	16%	-3%	LD	5,313	16.6%
Roberts H	PIC	2,150	6.5%	-4.1%	PIC	3,404	10.6%
Shrewsbury M	Greens	738	2.2%	0.2%	UKIP	653	2%
Ford M	UKIP	609	1.8%	-0.2%	Greens	626	2%
Holley Y	Veritas	401	1.2%		SA	366	1.1%
Williams R	SAP	288	0.9%				
Pank S	LCA	218	0.7%				
Lab to LD swing	**9.6%**	**33,086**		**Lab maj 4,269**		**32,100**	**Lab maj 9,550**
				12.9%			29.8%

ALAN WILLIAMS b 14 Oct 1930. MP 1964-. Father of the House 2005-. Dep Shadow Leader of House/Campaigns Co-ordinator 1983-87. Shadow Sec of State Wales 1987-88. Minister of State 1974-79. Joint Parly Sec 1969-70, Parly Under-Sec 1967-69. PPS to Edward Short 1966-67. Opp spokes 1970-74, 1979-87. Select cttees member: Public Accounts, Parly Privilege 1997-2000, Standards and Privileges 1997-2003, chair Liaison. Economics lecturer. PC 1977. Ed BSc economics, Cardiff Coll of Tech; BA PPE, Univ Coll, Oxford.

This is the western division of Wales' second city. A study by Glasgow University rated Swansea as one of the best places to live in the UK, a judgment presumably endorsed by the Father of the House, its MP for 40 years. This is historically the affluent division of the city. It contains the university and the city centre. It also has prosperous suburbs out towards Mumbles. Despite this it is a solid Labour seat.

NORTH SWINDON — Lab hold

		Electorate	Turnout	Change from	2001	Electorate	Turnout
		73,636	61%	2001		70,471	60.1%
Wills M	**Lab**	**19,612**	**43.7%**	**-9.2%**	**Lab**	**22,371**	**52.9%**
Tomlinson J	C	17,041	38%	4.3%	C	14,266	33.7%
Evemy M	LD	6,831	15.2%	3.6%	LD	4,891	11.6%
Tingey R	UKIP	998	2.2%	0.3%	UKIP	800	1.9%
Newman A	Soc Unity	208	0.5%				
Reynolds E	Ind	195	0.4%				
Lab to C swing	**6.8%**	**44,885**		**Lab maj 2,571**		**42,328**	**Lab maj 8,105**
				5.7%			19.1%

MICHAEL WILLS b 20 May 1952. MP 1997-. Parly Under-Sec Home Office 2002-03: for Criminal Justice System IT 2002, IT in the Criminal Justice System 2003; Parly Sec Lord Chancellor's Dept 2001-02; Parly Under-Sec: Dept for Education and Employment 1999-2001, DTI (Min for Small Firms, Trade and Industry) 1999. Chair non-ministerial cross-party advisory group on preparation for EMU 1998-. HM Diplomatic Service 1976-80. TV researcher/producer/director. Ed Haberdashers Aske's, Elstree; BA hist, Clare Coll, Cambridge.

Swindon is situated in north Wiltshire between London and Bristol and linked to both by major motorway and rail routes. Its accessibility has turned it into a centre for business, shopping, and increasingly, tourism. Swindon North is still held by Labour, but, if the economy does falter in the next few years, their small majority will begin to look increasingly under threat from the Conservatives.

SOUTH SWINDON — Lab hold

		Electorate	Turnout	Change from	2001	Electorate	Turnout
		72,267	60.2%	2001		72,439	59.9%
Snelgrove A	**Lab**	**17,534**	**40.3%**	**-11%**	**Lab**	**22,260**	**51.3%**
Buckland R	C	16,181	37.2%	2.8%	C	14,919	34.4%
Stebbing S	LD	7,322	16.8%	4.9%	LD	5,165	11.9%
Hughes B	Greens	1,234	2.8%		UKIP	713	1.6%
Halden S	UKIP	955	2.2%	0.6%	RNRL	327	0.8%
Hayward A	Ind	193	0.4%				
Williams J	Ind	53	0.1%				
Lab to C swing	**6.9%**	**43,472**		**Lab maj 1,353**		**43,384**	**Lab maj 7,341**
				3.1%			16.9%

ANNE SNELGROVE b 7 Aug 1957. MP 2005-. Member, Amensty International, The Co-operative party. Ed Bracknell Ranelagh School; King Alfred's College, Winchester

While Swindon itself is an industrial town, the seat of Swindon South also includes a number of outlying rural areas. The railway and its associated industries were once the major employers in the town, but with their decline other industries, particularly hi-tech manufacturing, have taken their place. Despite a swing away from Labour in the election the Conservatives were still unable to take the seat from them.

TAMWORTH — Lab hold

		Electorate 71,675	Turnout 61%	Change from 2001	2001	Electorate 69,596	Turnout 57.8%
Jenkins B	**Lab**	**18,801**	**43%**	**-6%**	**Lab**	**19,722**	**49%**
Pincher C	C	16,232	37.1%	-0.5%	C	15,124	37.6%
Bennion P	LD	6,175	14.1%	2.4%	LD	4,721	11.7%
Eston P	Veritas	1,320	3%		UKIP	683	1.7%
Simpson T	UKIP	1,212	2.8%	1.1%			
Lab to C swing	**2.8%**	**43,740**		**Lab maj 2,569** 5.9%		**40,250**	**Lab maj 4,598** 11.4%

BRIAN JENKINS b 19 Sept 1942. MP for SE Staffs 1996-97, for Tamworth 1997-. PPS to: Joyce Quin 1999-2001, 1997-98, Joyce Quin, Geoff Hoon, Tony Lloyd 1999, Joyce Quin, Derek Fatchett, Tony Lloyd 1998-99. Member select cttees: Unopposed Bills (Panel) 1997-, Standing Orders 1998-, Public Accounts 2001-, Broadcasting 2001-03. Cllr Tamworth BC 1985-96: mayor 1993-94. Engineer/college lecturer 1961-96. Ed Kingsbury High Sch, Tamworth; Coventry Coll; Coleg Harlech; BSc econ, LSE; PGCE, Wolverhampton Poly.

Tamworth's population has trebled in 30 years largely as a result of Birmingham overspill developments. Private residential developments are still generating a slower growth. The old town centre is now dominated by tower blocks. There is some light industry on many new industrial estates. The skilled manual and partly skilled groups are over-represented, helping Labour's power here. Areas outside the town are rural and residential.

TATTON — C hold

		Electorate 64,140	Turnout 64.6%	Change from 2001	2001	Electorate 64,954	Turnout 63.5%
Osborne G	**C**	**21,447**	**51.8%**	**3.7%**	**C**	**19,860**	**48.1%**
Madders J	Lab	9,716	23.5%	-3.8%	Lab	11,249	27.3%
Arnold A	LD	9,016	21.8%	3.2%	LD	7,685	18.6%
Bowler D	UKIP	996	2.4%	0.5%	UKIP	769	1.9%
Gibson M	Ind	239	0.6%		Ind	734	1.8%
					Ind	505	1.2%
					Ind	322	0.8%
					Ind	154	0.4%
Lab to C swing	**3.8%**	**41,414**		**C maj 11,731** 28.3%		**41,278**	**C maj 8,611** 20.9%

GEORGE OSBORNE b 23 May 1971. MP 2001-. Shadow: Chancellor of Exchequer 2005-, Chief Sec of Treasury 2004-05, Minister for Economic Affairs 2003-04. Opposition whip 2003. Member select cttees: Public Accounts 2001-04, Transport 2002-03. Head of Con Research Dept political section 1994-95. Special adviser MAFF 1995-97. 10 Downing St political office 1997. Shadow Cabinet sec 1997-2001. William Hague political sec 1997-2001. Member Public Accounts Commission 2002-. Journalist. Ed BA mod hist, Magdalen Coll, Oxford.

In rural Cheshire, south west of Manchester, Tatton is one of the few constituencies to be named after a building, Tatton Park, which was formerly the ancestral home of the Lords Egerton, but is now the National Trust's most visited property. The prosperous commuter and market towns of Wilmslow, Knutsford and Alderley Edge are the principal centres of population in Tatton, and typical of nearly all other towns and villages in this safe Conservative seat.

TAUNTON — LD gain

		Electorate 85,466	Turnout 69.6%	Change from 2001	2001	Electorate 81,651	Turnout 67.6%
Browne J	**LD**	**25,764**	**43.3%**	**2%**	**C**	**23,033**	**41.7%**
Flook A	C	25,191	42.3%	0.6%	LD	22,798	41.3%
Govier A	Lab	7,132	12%	-2.9%	Lab	8,254	14.9%
Miles H	UKIP	1,441	2.4%	0.3%	UKIP	1,140	2.1%
C to LD swing	**0.7%**	**59,528**		**LD maj 573** 1%		**55,225**	**C maj 235** 0.4%

JEREMY BROWNE b 17 May 1970. MP 2005-. Contested Enfield Southgate 1997. Dewe Rogerson Ltd 1994-96; Lib Dem director of press and broadcasting 1997-2000; Edelman Worldwide 2000-02; ReputationInc 2003-04. Ed politics Nottingham University

Taunton, named after the county town of Somerset, is a traditional staging post for those travelling to the south west. Both the M5 and main-line rail services pass through the constituency. There is some light industry and The Vale of Taunton Deane is fertile and famous for its cider. Previously a Conservative stronghold, in recent years Taunton has become a highly marginal seat, with the Liberal Democrats claiming it in 2005.

TEIGNBRIDGE — LD hold

		Electorate	Turnout	Change from	2001	Electorate	Turnout
		88,674	68.7%	2001		85,533	69.3%
Younger-Ross R	**LD**	**27,808**	**45.7%**	**1.3%**	**LD**	**26,343**	**44.4%**
Johnson S	C	21,593	35.5%	-3.8%	C	23,332	39.3%
Sherwood C	Lab	6,931	11.4%	-1%	Lab	7,366	12.4%
Colman T	UKIP	3,881	6.4%	2.6%	UKIP	2,269	3.8%
Wills R	Lib	685	1.1%				
C to LD swing	**2.6%**	**60,898**		**LD maj 6,215**		**59,310**	**LD maj 3,011**
				10.2%			5.1%

RICHARD YOUNGER-ROSS b 29 Jan 1953. MP 2001-. Lib Dem whip 2002-03, 2004-. Lib Dem ODPM spokes 2004-. Parly researcher 1981. South West economics spokes 1994-97. Member: British Kurdish Friendship Society, Anti-Slavery International, Howard League for Penal Reform, European Standing Cttee C. Architectural asst 1970-90, design consultant 1990-2001. Ed Walton on Thames Sec Mod Sch; HNC building construction, Ewell Tech Coll.

Teignbridge consists of nearly 700 square miles of rolling Devon countryside from the granite tors on Dartmoor to the long stretches of sandy beach by the coastal towns of Dawlish and Teignmouth. Employment is mostly found in a declining agricultural sector and a growing tourism industry. This used to be a safe Tory seat, but is now held by the Liberal Democrats – although it may disappear entirely under new Boundary Commission proposals.

TELFORD — Lab hold

		Electorate	Turnout	Change from	2001	Electorate	Turnout
		59,277	57.7%	2001		59,431	52%
Wright D	**Lab**	**16,506**	**48.2%**	**-6.4%**	**Lab**	**16,854**	**54.6%**
Kyriazis S	C	11,100	32.4%	5%	C	8,471	27.4%
Jenkins I	LD	4,941	14.4%	1.5%	LD	3,983	12.9%
McCartney T	UKIP	1,659	4.8%	1.2%	UKIP	1,098	3.6%
					SA	469	1.5%
Lab to C swing	**5.7%**	**34,206**		**Lab maj 5,406**		**30,875**	**Lab maj 8,383**
				15.8%			27.2%

DAVID WRIGHT b 22 Dec 1966. MP 2001-. PPS to: Rosie Winterton 2004-05, David Miliband 2005-. Member select cttees: Administration 2001-02, Environmental Audit 2001-, Procedure 2001-. All-party groups: chair world heritage sites 2004-, vice-chair architecture and planning 2003-. Cllr: Wrekin DC 1989-97, Oakengates Town Council 1989-2000. Local govt officer. Housing strategy manager Sandwell MBC 1988-2001. Ed Wrockwardine Wood Comp Sch, Shropshire; New Coll, Telford, Shropshire; BA humanities, Wolverhampton Poly.

Telford in Shropshire is a New Town based on some of the oldest industrial communities in the country. Iron was smelted at Coalbrookdale in the early eighteenth century and Thomas Telford built the first iron bridge at Ironbridge. Today industry is mainly light, including plastics, textile and electronic companies while the service sector has grown. 53.4 per cent of Telford's youthful population are from either skilled or partly skilled manual groups, who tend to vote Labour.

TEWKESBURY — C hold

		Electorate	Turnout	Change from	2001	Electorate	Turnout
		72,145	63%	2001		70,465	64.1%
Robertson L	**C**	**22,339**	**49.2%**	**3.1%**	**C**	**20,830**	**46.1%**
Cameron A	LD	12,447	27.4%	1.2%	Lab	12,167	26.9%
Mannan C	Lab	9,179	20.2%	-6.7%	LD	11,863	26.2%
Rendell R	Greens	1,488	3.3%		None	335	0.7%
LD to C swing	**1%**	**45,453**		**C maj 9,892**		**45,195**	**C maj 8,663**
				21.8%			19.2%

LAURENCE ROBERTSON b 29 March 1958. MP 1997-. Shadow Minister: NI 2005-, Economic Affairs 2003-05, Trade and Industry 2003. Opposition whip 2001-03. Member select cttees: Environmental Audit 1997-99, Joint Cttee on Consolidation of Bills Etc 1997-2001, Soc Security 1999-2001, European Scrutiny 1999-2002, Education and Skills 2001. Former member: Con Way Forward, Con 2000 foundation. Consultant: industrial management, charity fundraising, PR, special events. Factory owner. Ed Management Service Dip, Bolton Higher Ed Inst.

This constituency takes its name from its major town, situated on the northern periphery of the seat. Lying at the north end of Gloucestershire, Tewkesbury contains a mix of suburban and rural areas. It is more middle class than average with high levels of owner-occupation, low unemployment, and nearly half the total population in the 40-plus age group. This is solid Conservative territory and the Tory MP's continued tenure here is assured.

NORTH THANET — C hold

		Electorate 72,734	Turnout 60.1%	Change from 2001	2001	Electorate 71,012	Turnout 59%
Gale R	**C**	**21,699**	**49.6%**	**-0.7%**	**C**	**21,050**	**50.3%**
Johnston I	Lab	14,065	32.2%	-2.2%	Lab	14,400	34.4%
Barnard M	LD	6,279	14.4%	3.4%	LD	4,603	11%
Stocks T	UKIP	1,689	3.9%	1.6%	UKIP	980	2.3%
					Ind	440	1.1%
					NF	395	0.9%
Lab to C swing	**0.8%**	**43,732**		**C maj 7,634** 17.5%		**41,868**	**C maj 6,650** 15.9%

ROGER GALE b 20 Aug 1943. MP 1983-. PPS to: Jeremy Hanley 1993-94, Archibald Hamilton 1992-93. Member select cttees: Home Affairs 1990-92, Broadcasting 1997-, Chairmen's Panel 1997-. Vice-chair Con Party 2001-03. Delegate: Council of Europe 1987-89, Western European Union 1987-89. International election observer. Radio/TV dir/producer/reporter/editor. Universal Films PA. Special constable (BTP) 2003. City of London Freeman. RSPCA animal welfare award. Ed Hardye's Sch, Dorchester; LGSM&D, Guildhall Sch of Music and Drama.

North Thanet consists of a 13-mile long coastal strip in northern Kent that contains the resorts of Birchington and Margate, along with Herne Bay. Tourism is therefore an important factor in the local economy, as is agriculture inland and a certain amount of light industry in the larger towns. This is a relatively safe Conservative seat.

SOUTH THANET — Lab hold

		Electorate 63,436	Turnout 65%	Change from 2001	2001	Electorate 61,680	Turnout 63.9%
Ladyman S	**Lab**	**16,660**	**40.4%**	**-5.3%**	**Lab**	**18,002**	**45.7%**
MacGregor M	C	15,996	38.8%	-2.3%	C	16,210	41.1%
Voizey G	LD	5,431	13.2%	3.8%	LD	3,706	9.4%
Farage N	UKIP	2,079	5%	3.7%	Ind	770	2%
Green H	Greens	888	2.2%		UKIP	502	1.3%
Kinsella M	Ind	188	0.5%	-1.5%	NF	242	0.6%
Lab to C swing	**1.5%**	**41,242**		**Lab maj 664** 1.6%		**39,432**	**Lab maj 1,792** 4.5%

STEPHEN LADYMAN b 6 Nov 1952. MP 1997-. Minister of State Dept for Transport 2005-, Parly Under-Sec Dept of Health 2003-05, PPS to Adam Ingram 2001-03. Member Environment, Transport and Regional Affairs select cttee 2000-01. Cllr Thanet DC 1995-99. Netherlands liaison MP. Member European standing cttee C 1999-2003. Computer manager Pfizer Central Research. Ed BSc applied biology, Liverpool Poly; PhD research into isotopic abundances in soil devt, Strathclyde Univ.

South Thanet lies on the north-east corner of Kent. It includes the coastal towns of Broadstairs and Ramsgate plus the former Cinque Port of Sandwich and a number of smaller towns and villages such as Minster, Ash and Wingham. Represented by Jonathan Aitken before the 1997 Labour landslide, this is now a volatile and marginal seat.

THURROCK — Lab hold

		Electorate 79,545	Turnout 54.9%	Change from 2001	2001	Electorate 76,180	Turnout 49%
Mackinlay A	**Lab**	**20,636**	**47.2%**	**-9.3%**	**Lab**	**21,121**	**56.5%**
Hague G	C	14,261	32.6%	2.8%	C	11,124	29.8%
Palmer E	LD	4,770	10.9%	0.6%	LD	3,846	10.3%
Geri N	BNP	2,526	5.8%		UKIP	1,271	3.4%
Jackson C	UKIP	1,499	3.4%				
Lab to C swing	**6.1%**	**43,692**		**Lab maj 6,375** 14.6%		**37,362**	**Lab maj 9,997** 26.8%

ANDREW MACKINLAY b 24 April 1949. MP 1992-. Opposition whip 1993-94. Member select cttees: Foreign Affairs 1997-, Unopposed Bills (Panel) 1997-2004. Chair all-party Belarus group 2004-. Member: parly Lab Party parly cttee 2001-, parly OSCE delegation. Cllr Kingston upon Thames 1971-78. Surrey CC local govt officer 1965-75; NALGO official 1975-92. Chartered sec. Ed Salesian Coll, Surrey; dip municipal administration.

Thurrock was Labour's only Essex seat until the 1997 election. Thurrock's focal points include Tilbury docks and the Lakeside Centre, one of Europe's largest indoor shopping malls. The centre, which attracts shoppers from Kent, East London and other parts of Essex, has brought a large number of jobs to Thurrock. A high proportion of constituents live in council houses although in recent years more private developments have been built.

TIVERTON AND HONITON — C hold

		Electorate	Turnout	Change from	2001	Electorate	Turnout
		83,375	69.8%	2001		79,880	69.8%
Browning A	**C**	**27,838**	**47.9%**	**0.8%**	**C**	**26,258**	**47.1%**
Nation D	LD	16,787	28.9%	-6.9%	LD	19,974	35.8%
Bentley F	Lab	7,944	13.7%	1.8%	Lab	6,647	11.9%
Edwards R	UKIP	2,499	4.3%	2%	UKIP	1,281	2.3%
Collins R	Lib	1,701	2.9%	1.8%	Greens	1,030	1.8%
Matthews C	Greens	1,399	2.4%	0.6%	Lib	594	1.1%
LD to C swing	**3.9%**	**58,168**		**C maj 11,051**		**55,784**	**C maj 6,284**
				19%			11.3%

ANGELA BROWNING b 4 Dec 1946. MP for Tiverton 1992-97, for Tiverton and Honiton 1997-. Shadow: Leader of House 2000-01, Sec of State Trade and Industry 1999-2000. Parly Sec MAFF 1994-97. PPS to Michael Forsyth 1993-94. Opposition spokes 1997-98. Member select cttees: Agriculture 1992-93, Modernisation of HoC 2000-01, Public Accounts 2004-, Standards and Privileges 2004-. Vice-chair Con Party 2001-. Teacher, nurse, manufacturing/management consultant, dir/chair. Alzheimer's Disease Soc nat vice-pres. Ed Bournemouth Tech Coll.

This Devon constituency is predominantly rural and its towns are small, the largest being Tiverton, which serves the local area as a shopping, industrial and distribution centre. There is a tradition of manufacturing here which was started by mill owners from northern England harnessing the water power of the river valleys. Tiverton and Honiton has been solidly Conservative since the Second World War, and is likely to remain so for some time to come.

TONBRIDGE AND MALLING — C hold

		Electorate	Turnout	Change from	2001	Electorate	Turnout
		68,444	67.3%	2001		65,979	64.3%
Stanley J	**C**	**24,357**	**52.9%**	**3.5%**	**C**	**20,956**	**49.4%**
Hayman V	Lab	11,005	23.9%	-6%	Lab	12,706	29.9%
Barstow J	LD	8,980	19.5%	1.6%	LD	7,605	17.9%
Waller D	UKIP	1,721	3.7%	0.9%	UKIP	1,169	2.8%
Lab to C swing	**4.8%**	**46,063**		**C maj 13,352**		**42,436**	**C maj 8,250**
				29%			19.4%

SIR JOHN STANLEY b 19 Jan 1942. MP 1974-. Minister: of State, NI Office 1987-88, Armed Forces 1983-87, Housing and Construction 1979-83. PPS to Margaret Thatcher 1976-79. Member Foreign Affairs select cttee 1992-97, 1997-. Chair all-party groups: Republic of Korea 1997-, Nepal 1997-. Con research dept 1967-68. Exec cttee member Commonwealth Parly Assocn UK branch 1999-. Strategic Studies Inst research associate 1968-69. Rio Tinto-Zinc Corp Ltd 1969-79. PC 1984. Kt 1988. Ed Repton Sch; Lincoln Coll, Oxford.

Within the boundaries of this constituency, which stretches across a wide expanse of west Kent, there are numerous towns and villages including Edenbridge, East and West Peckham, East and West Malling, as well as Tonbridge itself. It is a fairly diverse constituency, home to commuters and light industry, farmers and apple growers, castles and country houses. New Labour probably peaked here in 2001 and this remains a safe Tory seat.

TOOTING — Lab hold

		Electorate	Turnout	Change from	2001	Electorate	Turnout
		70,504	59%	2001		68,447	54.9%
Khan S	**Lab**	**17,914**	**43.1%**	**-11%**	**Lab**	**20,332**	**54.1%**
Bethell J	C	12,533	30.2%	3.8%	C	9,932	26.4%
Dearden S	LD	8,110	19.5%	4.6%	LD	5,583	14.9%
Vitelli S	Greens	1,695	4.1%	-0.5%	Greens	1,744	4.6%
Zaidi A	Respect	700	1.7%				
McDonald S	UKIP	424	1%				
Perkin I	Ind	192	0.5%				
Lab to C swing	**7.4%**	**41,568**		**Lab maj 5,381**		**37,591**	**Lab maj 10,400**
				13%			27.7%

SADIQ KHAN b 18 August 1970. MP 2005-. Cllr Wandsworth Borough Council 1994-: deputy leader Labour Group 1996-2001. Chair legal affairs committee, Muslim Council of Britain; vice-chair Legal Action Group 1999-2004. Ed Ernest Bevin School, London

Tooting, a relatively affluent seat in the heart of south London, was a marginal Labour seat for years, but in 1997 the party's vote rose to a 15,000 majority. Over a quarter of residents are non-white, and the large South Asian population are helping Tooting overtake Brick Lane's reputation as London's curry capital. 13 per cent of homes are council-rented and two-thirds of workers are in non-manual jobs.

TORBAY

LD hold

		Electorate	Turnout	Change from	2001	Electorate	Turnout
		76,474	61.9%	2001		76,072	62.5%
Sanders A	**LD**	**19,317**	**40.8%**	**-9.7%**	**LD**	**24,015**	**50.5%**
Wood M	C	17,288	36.6%	0.2%	C	17,307	36.4%
Pedrick-Friend D	Lab	6,972	14.7%	5.3%	Lab	4,484	9.4%
Booth G	UKIP	3,726	7.9%	4.7%	UKIP	1,512	3.2%
					Ind	251	0.5%
LD to C swing	**5%**	**47,303**		**LD maj 2,029**		**47,569**	**LD maj 6,708**
				4.3%			14.1%

ADRIAN SANDERS b 25 April 1959. MP 1997-. Lib Dem whip 1997-2001. Lib Dem spokes: housing 1997-2001, environ, transport, the regions and social justice 1999-2001, transport, local govt and regions 2001-02, tourism 2002-. Chair all-party diabetes group 1998-. Liberal Cllrs Assocn info officer 1986-89. Parly officer Lib Dem whips' office 1989-90. Paddy Ashdown asst 1992-93. Cllr Torbay BC 1984-86. NCVO policy officer 1992-93. Member: CPA, IPU, British American parly group. Grants adviser to charities. Ed Torquay Boys' Grammar Sch.

The three coastal towns which make up the Devon constituency of Torbay are known as the 'English Riviera', and tourism is certainly a major industry here. Also known as a pensioners' paradise, Torbay is trying hard to change its image to attract a new younger generation of residents. Previously a Tory stronghold, the Liberal Democrats snatched Torbay in 1997 with a wafer-thin majority of 12 votes and have since managed to hold off the Conservative challenge.

TORFAEN

Lab hold

		Electorate	Turnout	Change from	2001	Electorate	Turnout
		60,669	59.3%	2001		61,110	57.7%
Murphy P	**Lab**	**20,472**	**56.9%**	**-5.2%**	**Lab**	**21,883**	**62.1%**
Ramsey N	C	5,681	15.8%	-0.1%	C	5,603	15.9%
Watkins V	LD	5,678	15.8%	4.6%	LD	3,936	11.2%
Preece A	PIC	2,242	6.2%	-1.5%	PIC	2,720	7.7%
Rowlands D	UKIP	1,145	3.2%	1.3%	UKIP	657	1.9%
Turner-Thomas R	Ind	761	2.1%		SA	443	1.3%
Lab to C swing	**2.5%**	**35,979**		**Lab maj 14,791**		**35,242**	**Lab maj 16,280**
				41.1%			46.2%

PAUL MURPHY b 25 Nov 1948. MP 1987-. Sec of State: Northern Ireland 2002-05, Wales 1999-2002. Minister of State NI Office 1997-99. Opposition spokes 1988-97. Vice-chair all-party British-America group 2002-. Chair Welsh group of Lab MPs 1996-97. Cllr Torfaen BC 1973-87. Member Royal Inst of Internat Affairs 1997-. Management trainee CWS 1970-71, lecturer in govt 1971-87. Knight of St Gregory (papal award); PC 1999. Ed St Francis Sch, Abersychan; West Monmouth Sch, Pontypool; MA mod hist, Oriel Coll, Oxford.

This seat is situated in the Gwent Valleys and within its boundaries are the towns of Cwmbran and Pontypool and their surrounding communities. Formerly called Pontypool, the seat has coterminous boundaries with the Torfaen local authority area. Historically this is a very safe Labour seat. It has been continuously held by the Labour Party since long before the Second World War and this seems unlikely to change.

TOTNES

C hold

		Electorate	Turnout	Change from	2001	Electorate	Turnout
		74,744	67.7%	2001		72,548	67.9%
Steen A	**C**	**21,112**	**41.7%**	**-2.8%**	**C**	**21,914**	**44.5%**
Treleaven M	LD	19,165	37.9%	0.7%	LD	18,317	37.2%
Burns V	Lab	6,185	12.2%		Lab	6,005	12.2%
Knapman R	UKIP	3,914	7.7%	1.6%	UKIP	3,010	6.1%
Thompson M	Ind	199	0.4%				
C to LD swing	**1.8%**	**50,575**		**C maj 1,947**		**49,246**	**C maj 3,597**
				3.8%			7.3%

ANTHONY STEEN b 22 July 1939. MP for Liverpool Wavertree 1974-83, for South Hams 1983-97, for Totnes 1997-. PPS to Peter Brooke 1992-94. Member select cttees: Regulatory Reform 1997-, European Scrutiny 1998-, Joint Cttee on Consolidation of Bills Etc 2001-, Public Admin 2001-02. Joint sec 1922 cttee 2001-. Chair Minority Party Unit 1999-2000. Barrister, youth leader, soc/community worker, law lecturer, Canadian govt adviser. MoD Court Martials Defence Counsel. Nat charities founder. Ed Westminster Sch; Grays Inn; London Univ.

Totnes is now a marginal Tory seat on the south Devon coast, taking in Dartmouth on the coast and Dartmoor further inland. In many ways this is a typical Devon constituency, possessing an aging population with tourism making up the bulk of its income. Fishing has suffered in recent years but there are still fishing fleets based at Salcombe and Brixham, as well as a growing number of people who sail for pleasure.

TOTTENHAM — Lab hold

		Electorate 66,231	Turnout 47.8%	Change from 2001	2001	Electorate 65,568	Turnout 48.2%
Lammy D	**Lab**	**18,343**	**57.9%**	**-9.6%**	**Lab**	**21,317**	**67.5%**
Hoban W	LD	5,309	16.8%	7.3%	C	4,401	13.9%
MacDougall W	C	4,278	13.5%	-0.4%	LD	3,008	9.5%
Alder J	Respect	2,014	6.4%		Greens	1,443	4.6%
McAskie P	Greens	1,457	4.6%		SA	1,162	3.7%
Durrani J	SLP	263	0.8%		R2000	270	0.9%
Lab to LD swing	**8.5%**	**31,664**		**Lab maj 13,034** 41.2%		**31,601**	**Lab maj 16,916** 53.5%

DAVID LAMMY b 19 July 1972. MP June 2000- (by-election). Parly Under-Sec: Dept for Culture, Media and Sport 2005-, Dept for Constitutional Affairs 2003-05, Health 2002-03. PPS to Estelle Morris 2001-02. Member select cttees: Public Administration 2001, Procedure 2001. Member: Soc of Lab Lawyers, Christian Socialist Movement. Member: Greater London Assembly 2000, Archbishops' Council 1999-2002. Barrister. Ed The King's Sch, Peterborough; LLB, School of Oriental and African Studies, London Univ; LLM, Harvard Law Sch, USA.

This is one of the most deprived and safest Labour constituencies in the country, with a high number of income support claimants, a large ethnic minority populations, and high crime. Nearly a quarter of the population is of Afro-Caribbean descent, 150 languages are spoken and the constituency also houses large Turkish, Cypriot and Irish communities. Unusually for a London constituency Tottenham has a strong industrial nature, with engineering, clothing, confectionery, and hi-tech firms.

TRURO AND ST AUSTELL — LD hold

		Electorate 80,256	Turnout 64.2%	Change from 2001	2001	Electorate 79,219	Turnout 63.5%
Taylor M	**LD**	**24,089**	**46.7%**	**-1.6%**	**LD**	**24,296**	**48.3%**
Kemp F	C	16,686	32.4%	0.1%	C	16,231	32.3%
Mackenzie C	Lab	6,991	13.6%	-0.1%	Lab	6,889	13.7%
Noakes D	UKIP	2,736	5.3%	2%	UKIP	1,664	3.3%
Jenkin C	MebK	1,062	2.1%	-0.2%	MebK	1,137	2.3%
					Ind	78	0.2%
LD to C swing	**0.9%**	**51,564**		**LD maj 7,403** 14.4%		**50,295**	**LD maj 8,065** 16%

MATTHEW TAYLOR b 3 Jan 1963. MP for Truro 1987-97, for Truro and St Austell 1997-. Lib Dem spokes: economy 1999-2003, environment and transport 1997-99, environment 1994-97, Citizen's Charter 1992-94, education 1990-92, trade and industry 1989-90, England 1988-89. Liberal energy spokes 1987-88. Member Broadcasting select cttee 1992-94. Chair: Lib Dem parly party 2003-, Lib Dem campaigns and communications 1989-95. Parly Liberal Party economic policy researcher 1986-87. Ed Univ Coll Sch, London; BA PPE, Lady Margaret Hall, Oxford.

Truro is Cornwall's county town and acts as a retailing, business and administrative centre. But the main centre of population and industry is St Austell with its china clay mining. Tourism is concentrated around the northern and southern coasts, with agriculture not being as important as in other Cornish seats. Truro and St Austell is a strong Liberal Democrat seat, but it will disappear when the Boundary Commission's proposals are implemented.

TUNBRIDGE WELLS — C hold

		Electorate 64,630	Turnout 65.7%	Change from 2001	2001	Electorate 65,730	Turnout 61.2%
Clark G	**C**	**21,083**	**49.6%**	**0.7%**	**C**	**19,643**	**48.9%**
Murphy L	LD	11,095	26.1%	1.4%	LD	9,913	24.7%
Jedrzejewski J	Lab	8,736	20.6%	-2.6%	Lab	9,332	23.2%
Webb V	UKIP	1,568	3.7%	0.4%	UKIP	1,313	3.3%
C to LD swing	**0.4%**	**42,482**		**C maj 9,988** 23.5%		**40,201**	**C maj 9,730** 24.2%

GREG CLARK b 1967. MP 2005-. Director of policy Conservative Party 2001-; Special adviser Ian Lang MP 1996-97; Chief adviser, commercial policy BBC; Boston Consulting Group. Ed BA economics, Cambridge University, PhD London School of Economics.

The town of Tunbridge Wells was founded in 1606 with the discovery of the Chalybeate Spring, is still a functioning spa town and attracts tourists to its architecturally or historically important buildings. Apart from the outlying communities of Sherwood, Southborough and Pembury, all relatively favourable to Labour, the town is surrounded by a fairly large agricultural hinterland. Royal Tunbridge Wells is for some the epitome of Conservatism, and seems set to remain a Conservative stronghold.

TWICKENHAM — LD hold

		Electorate 72,015	Turnout 71.8%	Change from 2001	2001	Electorate 75,225	Turnout 66.4%
Cable V	**LD**	**26,696**	**51.6%**	**2.9%**	**LD**	**24,344**	**48.7%**
Maynard P	C	16,731	32.4%	-1%	C	16,689	33.4%
Whitington B	Lab	5,868	11.4%	-2.4%	Lab	6,903	13.8%
Gower H	Greens	1,445	2.8%		Greens	1,423	2.8%
Orchard D	UKIP	766	1.5%	0.3%	UKIP	579	1.2%
Gilbert B	Ind	117	0.2%				
Weiss R	Vote Dream	64	0.1%				
C to LD swing	**2%**	**51,687**		**LD maj 9,965** 19.3%		**49,938**	**LD maj 7,655** 15.3%

VINCENT CABLE b 9 May 1943. MP 1997-. Lib Dem Shadow Chancellor of Exchequer 2003-. Lib Dem spokes 1997-2003. Member Treasury select cttee 1998-99. Cllr (Lab) Glasgow CC 1971-74. Adviser: (special) John Smith 1979, (special) Commonwealth Gen Sec 1983-90, World Environ and Devt Commission 1985-87. Chief economist Shell Internat 1995-97. Finance officer, economics lecturer, Diplomatic Service. Dep dir Overseas Devt Inst. BA natural science/economics, Fitzwilliam Coll, Cambridge; PhD internat economics, Glasgow Univ.

This leafy, largely residential constituency in the affluent borough of Richmond-upon-Thames was one of the most remarkable examples of the Liberal Democrats' sensational takeover of much of south-west London in 1997. Previously strongly Conservative, it fell to the Lib Dems after a 20-year third-party advance in local government. In 2001 and 2005 Vincent Cable consolidated into a comfortable majority, turning Twickenham into what may now be regarded as a safe Lib Dem seat.

TYNE BRIDGE — Lab hold

		Electorate 53,565	Turnout 49.2%	Change from 2001	2001	Electorate 58,900	Turnout 44.2%
Clelland D	**Lab**	**16,151**	**61.2%**	**-9.3%**	**Lab**	**18,345**	**70.5%**
Boyle C	LD	5,751	21.8%	9.5%	C	3,456	13.3%
Fairhead T	C	2,962	11.2%	-2.1%	LD	3,213	12.3%
Scott K	BNP	1,072	4.1%		SLP	533	2%
Russell J	Respect	447	1.7%		SA	485	1.9%
Lab to LD swing	**9.4%**	**26,383**		**Lab maj 10,400** 39.4%		**26,032**	**Lab maj 14,889** 57.2%

DAVID CLELLAND b 27 June 1943. MP December 1985- (by-election). Adviser to Richard Caborn 2002-. Whip: opposition 1995-97, asst govt 1997-2001, govt 2001. Member ODPM select cttee 2002-. Chair all-party Turks and Caicos Islands group 2004. Chair northern regional Lab MPs group 2002-. Cllr Gateshead BC 1972-86: leader 1984-86. Vice-chair Gateshead Health Authority 1982-84. AEEU shop steward 1967-81. Electrical fitter 1964-81. Local govt assocn sec 1981-85. Ed City and Guilds, electrical technician courses, Charles Trevelyan Tech Coll.

This seat, which spans the Tyne, links the centre of Newcastle with the heart of Gateshead. It is a dense, small, inner-city seat, with a working-class population and relatively high unemployment. Tyne Bridge has delivered healthy majorities for Labour since the constituency's creation in 1983.

TYNEMOUTH — Lab hold

		Electorate 64,023	Turnout 66.9%	Change from 2001	2001	Electorate 65,184	Turnout 67.4%
Campbell A	**Lab**	**20,143**	**47%**	**-6.2%**	**Lab**	**23,364**	**53.2%**
McIntyre M	C	16,000	37.3%	3.8%	C	14,686	33.5%
Finlay C	LD	6,716	15.7%	4.1%	LD	5,108	11.6%
					UKIP	745	1.7%
Lab to C swing	**5%**	**42,859**		**Lab maj 4,143** 9.7%		**43,903**	**Lab maj 8,678** 19.8%

ALAN CAMPBELL b 8 July 1957. MP 1997-. PPS to: Adam Ingram 2003-05, Lord Macdonald of Tradeston 2001-03. Asst govt whip 2005-. Member Public Accounts select cttee 1997-2001. Hon sec/treasurer northern group of Lab MPs 1999-. Sec/campaign co-ordinator Tynemouth constituency Lab Party. School teacher. Ed Blackfyne Sec Sch, Consett; BA politics, Lancaster Univ; PGCE, Leeds Univ; MA hist, Newcastle Poly.

Tynemouth has a long coastline at the south eastern tip of the old Northumberland county. Held by Labour since 1997, it has lower majorities than many seats in the area. Before 1997 the Tories held the seat for 47 years, suggesting that if Labour's national fortunes ever faltered, so would their grip on Tynemouth. Like much of Tyneside, shipbuilding was the main industry, but now the service and public sector are the major employers.

NORTH TYNESIDE — Lab hold

		Electorate	Turnout	Change from	2001	Electorate	Turnout
		64,634	57.2%	2001		64,914	57.7%
Byers S	**Lab**	**22,882**	**62%**	**-7.5%**	**Lab**	**26,027**	**69.5%**
McLellan D	C	7,845	21.2%	6.6%	C	5,459	14.6%
Ferguson G	LD	6,212	16.8%	4.4%	LD	4,649	12.4%
					UKIP	770	2.1%
					SA	324	0.9%
					SLP	240	0.6%
Lab to C swing	**7.1%**	**36,939**		**Lab maj 15,037**		**37,469**	**Lab maj 20,568**
				40.7%			54.9%

STEPHEN BYERS b 13 April 1953. MP for Wallsend 1992-97, for N Tyneside 1997-. Sec of State: Transport, Local Govt and Regions 2001-02; Trade and Industry 1998-2001; Chief Sec Treasury 1998; Min of State Dept for Education and Employment 1997-98. Opposition whip 1994-95. Spokes education/employment 1995-97. Member Home Affairs select cttee 1993-94. Chair all-party council against anti-semitism group 2003-. Cllr N Tyneside Council 1980-92: dep leader 1985-92. Law lecturer. PC 1998. Ed Chester Further Education Coll; LLB, Liverpool Poly.

North Tyneside lies on the north bank of the river Tyne, east of Newcastle. A rock-solid Labour stronghold, this former mining community is mainly residential covering the town of Longbenton and the sprawling council estate of the Killingsworth Township. Officially it may be classed as rural, but much of the landscape is bleak and therefore agriculture plays a very small role in the local economy.

WEST TYRONE — SF hold

		Electorate	Turnout	Change from	2001	Electorate	Turnout
		60,286	72.1%	2001		60,739	79.9%
Doherty P	**SF**	**16,910**	**38.9%**	**-1.9%**	**SF**	**19,814**	**40.8%**
Deeny C	Ind	11,905	27.4%		UUP	14,774	30.4%
Buchanan T	DUP	7,742	17.8%		SDLP	13,942	28.7%
McMenamin E	SDLP	3,949	9.1%	-19.6%			
Hussey D	UUP	2,981	6.8%	-23.6%			
SF to Ind swing	**14.7%**	**43,487**		**SF maj 5,005**		**48,530**	**SF maj 5,040**
				11.5%			10.4%

PAT DOHERTY b 18 July 1945. MP 2001-. Sinn Fein spokes enterprise trade and investment 2000-. New NI Assembly 1998: member/chair Enterprise, Trade and Investment cttee 1999-. Sinn Féin: activist 1970-84, dir of elections 1984-85, nat organiser 1985-88, vice-pres 1988-. Leader delegation to Dublin Forum for Peace and Reconciliation 1994-96. Member Castle Building talks team 1997-98. Former member Local Credit Union 1992. Site engineer 1975.

This constituency, roughly mid-way between Belfast and Derry, is a mainly rural seat, with gently rolling hills, glens, forests, loughs and rivers. It covers two district councils centred around its two major towns, Strabane and Omagh. The constituency has one of the largest Catholic populations at 64 per cent.

MID ULSTER — SF hold

		Electorate	Turnout	Change from	2001	Electorate	Turnout
		62,666	72.5%	2001		61,390	81.3%
McGuinness M	**SF**	**21,641**	**47.6%**	**-3.5%**	**SF**	**25,502**	**51.1%**
McCrea I	DUP	10,665	23.5%	-7.6%	DUP	15,549	31.1%
McGlone P	SDLP	7,922	17.4%	0.6%	SDLP	8,376	16.8%
Armstrong B	UUP	4,853	10.7%		WP	509	1%
Donnelly F	WP	345	0.8%	-0.2%			
DUP to SF swing	**2.1%**	**45,426**		**SF maj 10,976**		**49,936**	**SF maj 9,953**
				24.2%			19.9%

MARTIN McGUINNESS b 23 May 1950. MP 1997-. Minister for Education, NI Assembly 1999-2003 (suspension). Member NI Assembly 1982, 1998-. Sinn Fein: chief negotiator mid-1980s, representative to Dublin Forum for Peace and Reconciliation 1994-95. Ed Christian Brothers' Technical Coll.

This largely rural and Catholic constituency in the west of Northern Ireland lies between the Sperrin Mountains in the west and Lough Neagh in the east. The border county has a high proportion of Irish speakers, just under one in five. It covers part of Dungannon and all of Cookstown and Magherafelt district councils. Its key towns are Cookstown, Magherafelt and Coalisland. It has become a solid Sinn Féin seat.

UPMINSTER — C hold

		Electorate 55,075	Turnout 63%	Change from 2001	2001	Electorate 56,932	Turnout 59.5%
Watkinson A	**C**	**16,820**	**48.5%**	**3%**	**C**	**15,410**	**45.5%**
Darvill K	Lab	10,778	31.1%	-10.8%	Lab	14,169	41.9%
Truesdale P	LD	3,128	9%	-0.4%	LD	3,183	9.4%
Ower R	RA	1,455	4.2%		UKIP	1,089	3.2%
Roberts C	BNP	1,174	3.4%				
Hindle A	UKIP	701	2%	-1.2%			
Collins M	Greens	543	1.6%				
Durant D	Third	78	0.2%				
Lab to C swing	**6.9%**	**34,677**		**C maj 6,042** 17.4%		**33,851**	**C maj 1,241** 3.7%

ANGELA WATKINSON b 18 Nov 1941. MP 2001-. Shadow Minister: Local Govt Affairs and Communities 2005-, Education 2004-05, Health and Education 2004. Opposition whip 2002-04. Member select cttees: Home Affairs 2001-02, European Scrutiny 2002-03. Member 1922 cttee 2001-. Vice-pres Billericay Con Assocn 1999-. Member Con: Cllrs Assocn, Way Forward group, Friends of Israel. European Foundation subscriber 1998-. Cllr: Havering 1994-98, Essex CC 1997-2001. Local govt officer. Cttee manager Basildon DC 1989-94. Ed HNC public admin, Anglia Univ.

Essex in essence, it is no surprise that Upminster lacks the cosmopolitan flair of seats closer to central London. The white population is higher than in any other London seat; countryside intermingles with commuter suburbs; and owner-occupied housing accounts for 73 per cent of the total. However, Harold Hill is a significant council-housing development. Most working residents are in non-manual jobs and unemployment is relatively low.

UPPER BANN — DUP gain

		Electorate 72,402	Turnout 61.4%	Change from 2001	2001	Electorate 72,574	Turnout 70.3%
Simpson D	**DUP**	**16,679**	**37.6%**	**8.1%**	**UUP**	**17,095**	**33.5%**
Trimble D	UUP	11,381	25.6%	-7.9%	DUP	15,037	29.5%
O'Dowd J	SF	9,305	21%	-0.1%	SF	10,771	21.1%
Kelly D	SDLP	5,747	12.9%	-2%	SLP	7,607	14.9%
Castle A	All	955	2.2%		WP	527	1%
French T	WP	355	0.8%	-0.2%			
UUP to DUP swing	**8%**	**44,422**		**DUP maj 5,298** 11.9%		**51,037**	**UUP maj 2,058** 4%

DAVID SIMPSON MP 2005-. MLA 2003-. Vice-president DUP; Vice-chair: DUP Victims Committee, DUP Council Association; Chair Upper Bann Constituency Association. Councillor Craigavon Borough Council 2001-. Ed Birches Primary School, Killicomaine High School, Portadown; College of Business Studies, Belfast

This largely rural seat, with pockets of industry, is situated in the middle of the province below Lough Neagh, the largest freshwater lake in the British Isles. It covers parts of Banbridge and all of Craigavon district councils and it includes the town of Lurgan. Until 2005 this was the constituency berth of UUP leader David Trimble. His defeat by the DUP highlighted the DUP advance at the expense of the UUP.

UXBRIDGE — C hold

		Electorate 57,878	Turnout 59.4%	Change from 2001	2001	Electorate 58,068	Turnout 57.5%
Randall J	**C**	**16,840**	**49%**	**1.9%**	**C**	**15,751**	**47.1%**
Dubrow-Marshall R	Lab	10,669	31%	-9.9%	Lab	13,653	40.9%
Mahmood T	LD	4,544	13.2%	2.9%	LD	3,426	10.3%
Le May C	BNP	763	2.2%		UKIP	588	1.8%
Young S	Greens	725	2.1%				
Kerby R	UKIP	553	1.6%	-0.2%			
Shaw P	NF	284	0.8%				
Lab to C swing	**5.9%**	**34,378**		**C maj 6,171** 18%		**33,418**	**C maj 2,098** 6.3%

JOHN RANDALL b 5 Aug 1955. MP July 1997- (by-election). Opposition whip 2000-03, 2003-. Member select cttees: Deregulation 1997-2001, Environment, Transport and Regional Affairs 1998-2000, Transport 2003-. Chair all-party kidney group 2001-. Chair Uxbridge Con Assocn 1994-97. Randall's of Uxbridge (dir 1980-, MD 1988-97). Chair: Uxbridge Retailers' Assocn to 1997, Uxbridge town centre steering cttee to1997. Tour leader 1986-97. Ornithologist. Ed BA Serbo-Croat, Slavonic and E European Studies Sch, London Univ.

Uxbridge in west London is a comfortable constituency with one of the country's highest levels of full-time employment. Nearly three-quarters of householders are owner-occupiers, with a trend for those in council houses to buy their properties. Strong Conservative support is hardly surprising with most of the population white and middle-class, and with few in manual work. The seat contains Brunel University, and the Battle of Britain was largely directed from an underground control centre at RAF Uxbridge.

VAUXHALL — Lab hold

		Electorate 79,637	Turnout 46.9%	Change from 2001	2001	Electorate 74,474	Turnout 44.8%
Hoey K	**Lab**	**19,744**	**52.9%**	**-6.2%**	**Lab**	**19,738**	**59.1%**
Anglin C	LD	9,767	26.2%	6.1%	LD	6,720	20.1%
Heckels E	C	5,405	14.5%	1.1%	C	4,489	13.4%
Summers T	Greens	1,705	4.6%	0.2%	Greens	1,485	4.4%
McWhirter R	UKIP	271	0.7%		SA	853	2.6%
Lambert D	Socialist	240	0.6%		Ind	107	0.3%
Polenceus J	Eng Dem	221	0.6%				
Lab to LD swing	**6.2%**	**37,353**		**Lab maj 9,977** 26.7%		**33,392**	**Lab maj 13,018** 39%

KATE HOEY b 21 June 1946. MP June 1989- (by-election). Parly Under-Sec: Dept for Culture, Media and Sport 1999-2001, Home Office 1998-99. PPS to Frank Field 1997-98. Member select cttees: Broadcasting 1991-97, Social Security 1994-97, Science and Technology 2004-. Member opposition Citizen's Charter and Women team 1992-93. Cllr: Hackney BC 1978-82, Southwark BC 1988-89. Senior lecturer. Educational adviser Arsenal FC 1985-89. Ed teaching dip, Ulster Coll of Physical Education; BSc economics, City of London Coll, London.

This diverse, solid Labour constituency faces the House of Commons from the south side of the Thames and includes the South Bank, Lambeth Palace, the Oval cricket ground, Kennington, Stockwell, Brixton and part of Clapham. It has large numbers of single-parent families (52.8 per cent) and unemployment is high. 50 per cent of all households rent from the council and 21 per cent of the largely young population are black.

WAKEFIELD — Lab hold

		Electorate 73,118	Turnout 59.3%	Change from 2001	2001	Electorate 75,750	Turnout 54.5%
Creagh M	**Lab**	**18,802**	**43.3%**	**-6.6%**	**Lab**	**20,592**	**49.9%**
Shelbrooke A	C	13,648	31.5%	0.9%	C	12,638	30.6%
Ridgway D	LD	7,063	16.3%	3.9%	LD	5,097	12.4%
Rowe G	BNP	1,328	3.1%		Greens	1,075	2.6%
Hardcastle D	Greens	1,297	3%	0.4%	UKIP	677	1.6%
Upex J	UKIP	467	1.1%	-0.5%	SLP	634	1.5%
McEnhill A	England	356	0.8%		SAP	541	1.3%
Griffiths M	SAP	319	0.7%				
Sheridan L	SLP	101	0.2%	-1.3%			
Lab to C swing	**3.8%**	**43,381**		**Lab maj 5,154** 11.9%		**41,254**	**Lab maj 7,954** 19.3%

MARY CREAGH b 2 Dec 1967. MP 2005-. London Borough of Islington: councillor 1998-2005, leader Labour group 2000-04. Lecturer in entrepreneurship Cranfield School of Management 1997-. Ed Bishop Ullathorne RC Comprehensive, Coventry; BA modern languages, Pembroke College, Oxford; MSC European studies, London School of Economics

This is a commercial and office centre in West Yorkshire, once heavily reliant on the coal industry but now attracting high technology firms. Unemployment is about average at 2.9 per cent and the workforce is now split between those in manual and non-manual jobs. Just under 30 per cent of housing in the seat is council-rented. Despite a large increase in Tory support in 2001 and a swing in their favour in 2005, this seat's Labour roots stand strong.

WALLASEY — Lab hold

		Electorate 63,764	Turnout 57.5%	Change from 2001	2001	Electorate 64,889	Turnout 57.6%
Eagle A	**Lab**	**20,085**	**54.8%**	**-6%**	**Lab**	**22,718**	**60.8%**
Fraser L	C	10,976	29.9%	1.9%	C	10,442	28%
Pemberton J	LD	4,770	13%	1.8%	LD	4,186	11.2%
Griffiths P	UKIP	840	2.3%				
Lab to C swing	**4%**	**36,671**		**Lab maj 9,109** 24.8%		**37,346**	**Lab maj 12,276** 32.9%

ANGELA EAGLE b 17 Feb 1961. MP 1992-. Parly Under-Sec: Home Office 2001-02, DSS 1998-2001, Dept of Environment, Transport and Regions 1997-98. Opposition whip 1996-97. Member select cttees: Public Accounts 1995-97, Public Accounts 2002-03, Treasury 2003-. Chair nat conference of Lab women 1991. COHSE 1984: researcher, nat press officer, parly liaison officer. Ed Formby High Sch; BA PPE, St John's Coll, Oxford.

The constituency of Wallasey is across the Mersey from Liverpool, on the northern tip of the Wirral peninsula. It encompasses residential areas, derelict docklands, council estates and the seaside resort of New Brighton. The contrasts have been illustrated by decades of Conservative representation suddenly terminating in Labour's strong grip on the seat after 1992.

WALSALL NORTH — Lab hold

		Electorate	Turnout	Change from	2001	Electorate	Turnout
		63,268	52.8%	2001		65,981	49%
Winnick D	**Lab**	**15,990**	**47.8%**	**-10.3%**	**Lab**	**18,779**	**58.1%**
Lucas I	C	9,350	28%	-1.1%	C	9,388	29.1%
Taylor D	LD	4,144	12.4%	3.4%	LD	2,923	9%
Locke W	BNP	1,992	6%		UKIP	812	2.5%
Lenton A	UKIP	1,182	3.5%	1%	SA	410	1.3%
Smith P	Dem Lab	770	2.3%				
Lab to C swing	**4.6%**	**33,428**		**Lab maj 6,640**		**32,312**	**Lab maj 9,391**
				19.9%			29.1%

DAVID WINNICK b 26 June 1933. MP for Croydon South 1966-70, for Walsall North 1979-. Member select cttees: Procedure 1989-97, Home Affairs 1997-. British co-chair British-Irish inter-parly body 1997-. Cllr: Willesden BC 1959-64, Brent BC 1964-66. Chair UK Immigrants advisory service 1984-90. Vice-president Association of Professional, Executive, Clerical and Computer Staff (APEX) 1983-88. Ed diploma social administration, LSE.

Walsall North is one of the two constituencies that make up the town on the north edge of the West Midlands conurbation, although some of the town's suburbs also fall in the more prosperous Aldridge Brownhills constituency. With some significant economic and social problems, the seat has been a very solid win for Labour apart from three years in the 1970s.

WALSALL SOUTH — Lab hold

		Electorate	Turnout	Change from	2001	Electorate	Turnout
		60,370	58.5%	2001		62,626	55.7%
George B	**Lab**	**17,633**	**49.9%**	**-9.1%**	**Lab**	**20,574**	**59%**
Sabar K	C	9,687	27.4%	-3.1%	C	10,643	30.5%
Asmal M	LD	3,240	9.2%	2.4%	LD	2,365	6.8%
Bennett D	UKIP	1,833	5.2%	2.4%	UKIP	974	2.8%
Smith K	BNP	1,776	5%		SA	343	1%
Fazal N	Respect	1,146	3.2%				
Lab to C swing	**3%**	**35,315**		**Lab maj 7,946**		**34,899**	**Lab maj 9,931**
				22.5%			28.5%

BRUCE GEORGE b 1 June 1942. MP 1974-. Member select cttees: Liaison 1997-, Defence 1997-. Chair all-party groups: skin 1997-, Azerbaijan 1997-. Chair political cttee N Atlantic assembly 1983-94. Parly organisation for security and co-operation in Europe 1992-: pres 2002. Member: Internat Strategic Studies Inst, American Soc for Industrial Security (UK). Joint founder HoC football club. Author, tutor, lecturer. PC 2001. Ed Mountain Ash Grammar Sch; BA political theory and govt, Univ of Wales; MA comparative politics, Warwick Univ.

The constituency contains the town centre and combines solid Labour-voting wards with more affluent Tory stalwarts in the south east. It is a very mixed seat with a large Asian population and includes both notable pockets of deprivation and a swathe of green belt between the town and outer Birmingham. Having managed to hold the seat throughout the danger years of the 1980s, Labour should be secure here in the future.

WALTHAMSTOW — Lab hold

		Electorate	Turnout	Change from	2001	Electorate	Turnout
		63,079	54.6%	2001		64,403	53.5%
Gerrard N	**Lab**	**17,323**	**50.3%**	**-11.9%**	**Lab**	**21,402**	**62.2%**
Ahmed F	LD	9,330	27.1%	12.5%	C	6,221	18.1%
Wright J	C	6,254	18.2%	0.1%	LD	5,024	14.6%
Brock R	UKIP	810	2.4%	1.5%	SAP	806	2.3%
Taaffe N	SAP	727	2.1%	-0.2%	BNP	389	1.1%
					UKIP	298	0.9%
					ProLife	289	0.8%
Lab to LD swing	**12.2%**	**34,444**		**Lab maj 7,993**		**34,429**	**Lab maj 15,181**
				23.2%			44.1%

NEIL GERRARD b 3 July 1942. MP 1992-. PPS to Dawn Primarolo 1997. Member select cttees: Deregulation 1995-97, Information 1997-, Environmental Audit 1999-2002. Chair all-party groups: refugees 1997-, AIDS 1997-. Sec PLP civil liberties group. Cllr Waltham Forest 1973-90: leader 1986-90. Schoolteacher, lecturer, 1965-92. Ed Manchester Grammar Sch; BA natural science, Wadham Coll, Oxford; MED, Chelsea Coll, London; DPSE, South Bank Poly, London.

This north-east London seat is traditional Labour territory, but not entirely immune from aberrant Tory victories. It is made up of eight wards from the borough of Waltham Forest. It lies between the extremely deprived Hackney North and Stoke Newington (to the south-west) and Chingford and Woodford Green (to the north-west), and is a mixture of urban grit and suburban greenery. It is likely to remain in Labour's grasp for some time to come.

WANSBECK

Lab hold

		Electorate 63,096	Turnout 58.3%	Change from 2001	2001	Electorate 63,149	Turnout 59.3%
Murphy D	**Lab**	**20,315**	**55.2%**	**-2.6%**	**Lab**	**21,617**	**57.8%**
Reed S	LD	9,734	26.4%	3.6%	LD	8,516	22.8%
Scrope G	C	5,515	15%	2.2%	C	4,774	12.8%
Best N	Greens	1,245	3.4%	0.9%	Ind	1,076	2.9%
					Greens	954	2.5%
					UKIP	482	1.3%
Lab to LD swing	**3.1%**	**36,809**		**Lab maj 10,581** 28.8%		**37,419**	**Lab maj 13,101** 35%

DENIS MURPHY b 2 Nov 1948. MP 1997-. Member Regulatory Reform select cttee 1998-. All-party groups: treasurer coalfield communities 2001- and energy studies 2001-, sec local govt cllrs 2001-. Cllr Wansbeck DC 1990-97. Electrician 1965-94. Gen sec Northumberland Colliery Mechanics Assocn 1989-97. Chair board of governors, Northumberland Aged Mineworkers Home Assocn. Ed St Cuthberts Grammar Sch, Newcastle upon Tyne; electrical engineering, Northumberland Coll.

Formerly known as Morpeth, this seat has been solidly Labour since 1945. The previous name derives from the middle-class market and commuting town, which makes up only a small percentage of the overall population. The seat was renamed Wansbeck, after the river which runs through it, in 1983. The new name more fittingly represents this industrial constituency, lying as it does in the heart of the former Northumberland coalfield.

WANSDYKE

Lab hold

		Electorate 70,359	Turnout 72.4%	Change from 2001	2001	Electorate 70,850	Turnout 69.9%
Norris D	**Lab**	**20,686**	**40.6%**	**-6.2%**	**Lab**	**23,206**	**46.8%**
Watt C	C	18,847	37%	1.5%	C	17,593	35.5%
Coleshill G	LD	10,050	19.7%	5.3%	LD	7,135	14.4%
Sandell P	UKIP	1,129	2.2%	0.9%	Greens	958	1.9%
Parkes G	Ind	221	0.4%		UKIP	655	1.3%
Lab to C swing	**3.9%**	**50,933**		**Lab maj 1,839** 3.6%		**49,547**	**Lab maj 5,613** 11.3%

DAN NORRIS b 28 Jan 1960. MP 1997-. Asst govt whip 2001-03. Member: Co-operative Party, Lab leader campaign team (health responsibility) 1998-99. Gen election campaign team with responsibility for campaigning against Lib Dems 1999-. Cllr: Bristol CC 1989-92, 1995-97, Avon CC 1994-96. Child protection officer, researcher, author. Ed MSW, Sussex Univ.

The population of Wansdyke, which borders both Bristol in the west and Bath in the east, is evenly split between rural and urban areas. Wansdyke is an ideal commuter area for both Bristol and Bath, and this gives it a residential and moderately affluent character. Since seizing the seat from the Conservatives in 1997 Labour have worked hard to consolidate their position in Wansdyke. However, they lost most of their majority in 2005.

WANTAGE

C hold

		Electorate 76,156	Turnout 68.2%	Change from 2001	2001	Electorate 76,129	Turnout 64.5%
Vaizey E	**C**	**22,354**	**43.1%**	**3.5%**	**C**	**19,475**	**39.6%**
Crawford A	LD	14,337	27.6%	-0.4%	Lab	13,875	28.2%
McDonald M	Lab	12,464	24%	-4.2%	LD	13,776	28%
Twine A	Greens	1,332	2.6%	0.4%	Greens	1,062	2.2%
Tolstoy-Miloslavsky N	UKIP	798	1.5%	-0.4%	UKIP	941	1.9%
Lambourne G	Eng Dem	646	1.2%				
LD to C swing	**2%**	**51,931**		**C maj 8,017** 15.4%		**49,129**	**C maj 5,600** 11.4%

ED VAIZEY b 1969. MP 2005-. Contested Bristol East 1997 general election. Speechwriter for Michael Howard as party leader; election aide to Iain Duncan Smith 2001 general election. Barrister specialising in family law and child care; director and partner Consolidated Communications; freelance journalist. Trustee the Trident Trust (work experience for children). Ed Merton College, Oxford

The constituency covers the south-western quarter of Oxfordshire, between Oxford and Swindon. The main towns are Didcot and Wallingford from the South Oxfordshire district and Faringdon and Wantage from the Vale of White Horse. It is historically a safe Tory seat, altough the Conservatives can no longer bank on a 50 per cent share of the vote.

WARLEY — Lab hold

		Electorate 56,171	Turnout 57.1%	Change from 2001	2001	Electorate 58,065	Turnout 54.1%
Spellar J	**Lab**	**17,462**	**54.4%**	**-6.1%**	**Lab**	**19,007**	**60.5%**
Bissell K	C	7,315	22.8%		C	7,157	22.8%
Ferguson T	LD	4,277	13.3%	2.7%	LD	3,315	10.6%
Smith S	BNP	1,761	5.5%		SLP	1,936	6.2%
Connigale M	SLP	637	2%	-4.2%			
Matthews D	UKIP	635	2%				
Lab to C swing	**3.1%**	**32,087**		**Lab maj 10,147** 31.6%		**31,415**	**Lab maj 11,850** 37.7%

JOHN SPELLAR b 5 Aug 1947. MP for Birmingham Northfield 1982-83, for Warley West 1992-97, for Warley 1997. Minister of State: NI Office 2003-05, Dept for Transport 2002-03, Dept of Transport, Local Govt and Regions 2001-02. MoD: Minister of State Armed Forces 1999-2001, Parly Under-Sec 1997-99. Opposition whip 1992-94. Opposition spokes: N Ireland 1994-95, defence, disarmament, arms control 1995-97. Nat officer Electrical, Telecommunication and Plumbing Union 1969-97. PC 2001. Ed BA PPE, St Edmund's Hall, Oxford.

Warley is an urban and strongly Labour seat on the western outskirts of Birmingham. Once a mainly white working-class area, the area now has a multi-racial population and a recent, small increase in middle-class residents.

WARRINGTON NORTH — Lab hold

		Electorate 73,352	Turnout 55.1%	Change from 2001	2001	Electorate 72,445	Turnout 53.7%
Jones H	**Lab**	**21,632**	**53.5%**	**-8.2%**	**Lab**	**24,026**	**61.7%**
Ferryman A	C	9,428	23.3%	0.5%	C	8,870	22.8%
Walker P	LD	7,699	19.1%	5.7%	LD	5,232	13.4%
Kirkham J	UKIP	1,086	2.7%	0.7%	UKIP	782	2%
Hughes M	CAP	573	1.4%				
Lab to C swing	**4.4%**	**40,418**		**Lab maj 12,204** 30.2%		**38,910**	**Lab maj 15,156** 39%

HELEN JONES b 24 Dec 1954. MP 1997-. Member select cttees: Catering 1997-98, Public Admin 1998-2000, Standing Orders 1999-2000, 2001-, Education and Employment 1999-2001, Unopposed Bills (Panel) 1999-, Education and Skills 2003-. Cllr Chester CC 1984-91. MSF Lab Party liaison officer NW coast region. Former member: Nat Women's Cttee, Nat Appeals Panel. Solicitor, Eng teacher, justice/peace officer, MIND devt officer. Ed BA, Univ Coll, London; Chester Coll; MEd, Liverpool Univ; Manchester Metropolitan Univ.

This North Cheshire constituency contains the inner-city core of the industrial town just north of the Mersey. While the southern seat in Warrington is an interesting marginal, Warrington North is not. The tradition of Labour representation here is over half a century old. Warrington North forms part of a belt of seats lying between Liverpool and Manchester which are solidly Labour.

WARRINGTON SOUTH — Lab hold

		Electorate 75,724	Turnout 61.8%	Change from 2001	2001	Electorate 74,283	Turnout 61.2%
Southworth H	**Lab**	**18,972**	**40.5%**	**-8.8%**	**Lab**	**22,419**	**49.3%**
Bruce F	C	15,457	33%		C	15,022	33%
Marks I	LD	11,111	23.7%	7.4%	LD	7,419	16.3%
Kelley G	UKIP	804	1.7%	0.3%	UKIP	637	1.4%
Kennedy P	Ind	453	1%				
Lab to C swing	**4.4%**	**46,797**		**Lab maj 3,515** 7.5%		**45,497**	**Lab maj 7,397** 16.3%

HELEN SOUTHWORTH b 13 Nov 1956. MP 1997-. PPS to Paul Boateng 2001-05. Member select cttees: Procedure 1997-99, Trade and Industry 1998-2001. Vice-chair all-party town centre management group 2001-. Cllr St Helens BC 1994-98. Non-exec member St Helens and Knowsley Health Authority. Governor Age Concern (former dir). Community health council representative. Ed Larkhill Convent Sch; BA, Lancaster Univ.

Won by a whisker in 1992 by Labour, this Cheshire constituency is the less safe of the two Warrington seats held by Labour and as such, is the more interesting. This used to be a solid Conservative seat and now it is a measure of how things have changed for the Conservative Party. There is some industry in the seat, mainly chemical and service industries, but it generally consists of quiet residential areas.

WARWICK AND LEAMINGTON — Lab hold

		Electorate 81,205	Turnout 67.5%	Change from 2001	2001	Electorate 81,515	Turnout 65.7%
Plaskitt J	**Lab**	**22,238**	**40.6%**	**-8.2%**	**Lab**	**26,108**	**48.8%**
White C	C	21,972	40.1%	2.5%	C	20,155	37.6%
Forbes L	LD	8,119	14.8%	3.7%	LD	5,964	11.1%
Davison I	Greens	1,534	2.8%		SA	664	1.2%
Warwick G	UKIP	921	1.7%	0.5%	UKIP	648	1.2%
Lab to C swing	**5.4%**	**54,784**		**Lab maj 266** 0.5%		**53,539**	**Lab maj 5,953** 11.1%

JAMES PLASKITT b 23 June 1954. MP 1997-. Parly Under-Sec Dept for Work and Pensions 2005-. Member select cttees: Joint Cttee on Consolidation of Bills Etc 1997-2001, Treasury 1999-. Chair all-party compassion in dying group 2002-. Cllr Oxfordshire CC 1985-97: leader 1990-96. Politics lecturer. Business analyst 1984-97. Non-exec dir De Brus Marketing Ltd. Ed Pilgrim Sch, Bedford; MA PPE, Univ Coll, Oxford.

The Warwick and Leamington constituency to the south east of Birmingham has existed since the 19th century, but it has contracted to become a more urban seat, dominated by the two towns that give it its name. The seat is a key target for the Conservatives. It represents the kind of economically independent, relatively prosperous, post-industrial community that they will need to win back in order to regain national power.

NORTH WARWICKSHIRE — Lab hold

		Electorate 75,435	Turnout 62.2%	Change from 2001	2001	Electorate 73,825	Turnout 60.2%
O'Brien M	**Lab**	**22,561**	**48.1%**	**-6%**	**Lab**	**24,023**	**54.1%**
Gibb I	C	15,008	32%	-0.4%	C	14,384	32.4%
Roodhouse J	LD	6,212	13.2%	1.8%	LD	5,052	11.4%
MacKenzie M	BNP	1,910	4.1%		UKIP	950	2.1%
Campbell I	UKIP	1,248	2.7%	0.6%			
Lab to C swing	**2.8%**	**46,939**		**Lab maj 7,553** 16.1%		**44,409**	**Lab maj 9,639** 21.7%

MIKE O'BRIEN b 19 June 1954. MP 1992-. Solicitor General 2005-. Minister of State DTI 2004-05; FCO: Minister of State Trade, Investment and Foreign Affairs (also DTI) 2003-04, Parly Under-Sec 2002-03; Parly Under-Sec Home Office 1997-2001. Shadow Treasury Economic Sec 1996-97. Opposition spokes Treasury/economic affairs 1995-96. Member Home Affairs select cttee 1992-93. Parly adviser to England and Wales Police Federation 1993-96. Branch sec NATFHE 1989-90. Solicitor/law lecturer. Ed BA hist and politics/PGCE, North Staffs Poly.

Bedworth is an industrial and manufacturing town with a long history of Labour support. The rest of the constituency covers a large part of the old North Warwickshire coalfield where the Labour voting tradition survives. More than half the households are headed by skilled or partly skilled workers, many working in the newer manufacturing, service and distribution industries, grown up as a result of the easy access to the M6, M41 and A5.

WATFORD — Lab hold

		Electorate 76,280	Turnout 64.8%	Change from 2001	2001	Electorate 75,872	Turnout 61.1%
Ward C	**Lab**	**16,575**	**33.6%**	**-11.7%**	**Lab**	**20,992**	**45.3%**
Brinton S	LD	15,427	31.2%	13.8%	C	15,437	33.3%
Miraj A	C	14,634	29.6%	-3.7%	LD	8,088	17.4%
Rackett S	Greens	1,466	3%	1.1%	Greens	900	1.9%
Wright K	UKIP	1,292	2.6%	1.4%	UKIP	535	1.2%
					SA	420	0.9%
Lab to LD swing	**12.8%**	**49,394**		**Lab maj 1,148** 2.3%		**46,372**	**Lab maj 5,555** 12%

CLAIRE WARD b 9 May 1972. MP 1997-. PPS to John Hutton 2001-05. Asst govt whip 2005-. Member Culture, Media and Sport select cttee 1997-2001. Chair all-party groups. Member: Co-operative Party, Lab Party nat policy commissions 1992-95. Lab Party NEC youth rep 1991-95. Cllr Elstree/Boreham Wood TC 1994-97: mayor 1996-97. TGWU: nat youth award 1990, delegate biennial delegate conference 1991. Solicitor. Howard Penal Reform League board member 2000-. Ed LLB, Herts Univ; MA Britain and European Union, Brunel Univ; Coll of Law, London.

Watford constituency lies about 25 miles north of London in the south-west corner of the county of Hertfordshire. It encompasses the town of Watford to the north and the communities of Abbots Langley, Leavesden, and Langleybury. In the south are the residential areas of Carpenders Park and Oxhey Hall. Previously a fairly safe Labour seat, it is now a three-way marginal.

WAVENEY — Lab hold

		Electorate 77,138	Turnout 64.4%	Change from 2001	2001	Electorate 76,585	Turnout 61.6%
Blizzard B	**Lab**	**22,505**	**45.3%**	**-5.4%**	**Lab**	**23,914**	**50.7%**
Aldous P	C	16,590	33.4%	0.8%	C	15,361	32.6%
Bromley N	LD	7,497	15.1%	3.7%	LD	5,370	11.4%
Aylett B	UKIP	1,861	3.8%	1.5%	UKIP	1,097	2.3%
Elliott G	Greens	1,200	2.4%	0.3%	Greens	983	2.1%
					SA	442	0.9%
Lab to C swing	**3.1%**	**49,653**		**Lab maj 5,915** 11.9%		**47,167**	**Lab maj 8,553** 18.1%

BOB BLIZZARD b 31 May 1950. MP 1997-. PPS to: Nick Brown 2001-03, Baroness Hayman 1999-2001. Member Environmental Audit select cttee 1997-2000. Chair all-party groups: Brazil 1997-, offshore oil and gas industry 1999-, Latin America 2004-. Cllr Waveney DC 1987-97: leader 1991-97. Teacher. Ed Culford Sch, Bury St Edmunds; BA, Birmingham Univ.

The most easterly seat in Britain, Waveney is situated in the north-eastern recess of Suffolk. The constituency contains the declining coastal town of Lowestoft and the market towns of Beccles and Bungay. It was taken by Labour in 1997 and shows no sign of reverting to its previous Tory allegiance.

WEALDEN — C hold

		Electorate 82,261	Turnout 67.6%	Change from 2001	2001	Electorate 83,940	Turnout 62.8%
Hendry C	**C**	**28,975**	**52.1%**	**2.3%**	**C**	**26,279**	**49.8%**
Wigley C	LD	13,054	23.5%	-0.2%	LD	12,507	23.7%
Rose D	Lab	9,360	16.8%	-3.5%	Lab	10,705	20.3%
Salmon J	Greens	2,150	3.9%	1.5%	UKIP	1,539	2.9%
Riddle K	UKIP	2,114	3.8%	0.9%	Greens	1,273	2.4%
					PCP	453	0.9%
LD to C swing	**1.3%**	**55,653**		**C maj 15,921** 28.6%		**52,756**	**C maj 13,772** 26.1%

CHARLES HENDRY b 6 May 1959. MP for High Peak 1992-97, for Wealden 2001-. Shadow Minister: Trade and Industry 2005, Higher Education 2005, Young People 2002-05. PPS to: Gillian Shepherd 1995, William Hague, Lord Mackay of Ardbrecknish 1994-95. Opposition whip 2001-02. Member select cttees: Procedure 1992-95, NI Affairs 1994-97, Culture, Media, Sport 2003-04. Dep chair Con Party 2003-. Adviser: Sec of State, Antony Newton. Senior public affairs cllr Burson-Marsteller. Pres British Youth Council. Ed BCom business studies, Edinburgh Univ.

There are no large towns in this traditional and rural constituency, (Crowborough and Hailsham are the largest) and countryside issues are predominant. The seat was named Wealden in 1983, and covers a large part of the Sussex High Weald, a patchwork of well-wooded ridges and valleys. It includes Ashdown Forest and many parts are designated as Areas of Outstanding Natural Beauty. Since 1945 the seat has been very safe for the Conservatives.

WEAVER VALE — Lab hold

		Electorate 69,072	Turnout 57.1%	Change from 2001	2001	Electorate 68,236	Turnout 57.6%
Hall M	**Lab**	**18,759**	**47.6%**	**-4.9%**	**Lab**	**20,611**	**52.5%**
Mackie J	C	11,904	30.2%	2.3%	C	10,974	27.9%
Griffiths N	LD	7,723	19.6%	5.2%	LD	5,643	14.4%
Swinscoe B	UKIP	1,034	2.6%	1.2%	Ind	1,484	3.8%
					UKIP	559	1.4%
Lab to C swing	**3.6%**	**39,420**		**Lab maj 6,855** 17.4%		**39,271**	**Lab maj 9,637** 24.5%

MIKE HALL b 20 Sept 1952. MP for Warrington South 1992-97, for Weaver Vale 1997-. PPS to John Reid 2003-05, Alan Milburn 2001-03, Ann Taylor 1997-98. Asst govt whip 1998-2001. Member select cttees: Public Accounts 1992-97, Modernisation of HoC 1997-98, Administration 1999-2001. Cllr Warrington BC 1979-93: leader 1985-92. Scientific asst. History/physical education/support teacher 1977-92. Ed Teacher's Cert, Padgate Higher Ed Coll; BEd, North Cheshire Coll; Dip Ed, Univ Coll of Wales, Bangor.

Held safely by Labour since its creation in 1997, the Cheshire constituency of Weaver Vale has an extremely varied landscape. Centred on industrial Northwich, the seat takes in rural Helsby, popular with hill-walkers and rock-climbers, and affluent commuter towns like Hartford. Salt mining is the key industry here, and the presence of salt led to the establishment of the huge ICI works at Winnington.

WELLINGBOROUGH — C gain

		Electorate	Turnout	Change from	2001	Electorate	Turnout
		79,679	66.5%	2001		77,323	66%
Bone P	**C**	**22,674**	**42.8%**	**0.6%**	**Lab**	**23,867**	**46.8%**
Stinchcombe P	Lab	21,987	41.5%	-5.3%	C	21,512	42.2%
Church R	LD	6,147	11.6%	2.3%	LD	4,763	9.3%
Wrench J	UKIP	1,214	2.3%	0.6%	UKIP	864	1.7%
Alex N	Veritas	749	1.4%				
Dickson A	SLP	234	0.4%				
Lab to C swing	**3%**	**53,005**		**C maj 687** 1.3%		**51,006**	**Lab maj 2,355** 4.6%

PETER BONE b 19 Oct 1952. MP 2005-. Contested Islwyn 1992 and Pudsey 1997 and Wellingborough 2001 general elections, Mid and West Wales 1994 European Parliament election. Cllr Southend-on-Sea BC 1977-86. Deputy chair Southend West Con Assn 1977-84; press sec Paul Channon MP 1982-84. Financial director Essex Electronics and Precision Engineering Group, 1977-83; chief exec High Tech Electronics Company, 1983-90; managing director international travel company. Ed Westcliff-on-Sea Grammar School, Essex.

The traditionally marginal town of Wellingborough lies to the east of Northampton and north of Bedford. Founded on ironworks and the leather industry, it has expanded into more diverse light and service industries. With good rail links to London, commuters settle here. Recent industrial development has included the creation and growth of the Park Farm estate, and the improvement of road links. Elsewhere, the seat is a mix of countryside and ironstone villages.

WELLS — C hold

		Electorate	Turnout	Change from	2001	Electorate	Turnout
		77,842	68%	2001		74,189	69.2%
Heathcoat-Amory D	**C**	**23,071**	**43.6%**	**-0.2%**	**C**	**22,462**	**43.8%**
Munt T	LD	20,031	37.8%	-0.5%	LD	19,666	38.3%
Whittle D	Lab	8,288	15.6%	0.2%	Lab	7,915	15.4%
Reed S	UKIP	1,575	3%	0.8%	UKIP	1,104	2.2%
					Wes R	167	0.3%
LD to C swing	**0.2%**	**52,965**		**C maj 3,040** 5.7%		**51,314**	**C maj 2,796** 5.4%

DAVID HEATHCOAT-AMORY b 21 March 1949. MP 1983. Shadow: Minister for Work and Pensions and Welfare Reform 2005-, Sec of State Trade and Industry 2000-01, Chief Sec Treasury 1997-2000. Paymaster Gen 1994-96, Minister of State FCO 1993-94. Parly Under-Sec: Dept of Energy 1990-92, Dept of Environ 1989-90. PPS to: Douglas Hurd 1987-88, Norman Lamont 1985-87. Whip: asst govt 1988-89, dep chief 1992-93. Member: select cttees 1992-93, 2003-, exec 1922 cttee 2001-. Chartered accountant. PC 1996. Ed MA PPE, Christ Church Coll, Oxford.

The Somerset city of Wells is England's smallest city, with a population of merely 10,000. The city has a magnificent Gothic cathedral but the constituency is perhaps more famous for containing the town of Glastonbury, home of the world renowned music festival. Despite being in Conservative hands since 1945 Wells has, at least recently, been far from a safe seat. It was therefore surprising the Liberal Democrats did not challenge more strongly in 2005.

WELWYN HATFIELD — C gain

		Electorate	Turnout	Change from	2001	Electorate	Turnout
		65,617	68.2%	2001		67,004	63.9%
Shapps G	**C**	**22,172**	**49.6%**	**9.2%**	**Lab**	**18,484**	**43.2%**
Johnson M	Lab	16,226	36.3%	-6.9%	C	17,288	40.4%
Bedford S	LD	6,318	14.1%		LD	6,021	14.1%
					UKIP	798	1.9%
					ProLife	230	0.5%
Lab to C swing	**8.1%**	**44,716**		**C maj 5,946** 13.3%		**42,821**	**Lab maj 1,196** 2.8%

GRANT SHAPPS b 14 Sept 1968. MP 2005-. Contested North Southwark and Bermondsey 1997 and Welwyn Hatfield 2001 general elections. Printhouse Corporation: director 1990-2000. Ed Watford Boys Grammar School; HND business and finance, Manchester Polytechnic

Created out of two towns, Welwyn and Hatfield, in 1974 this Hertfordshire constituency contains the New Town and Garden City as well as Brookmans Park. It is a volatile constituency which has changed parties four times since it was created.

WENTWORTH

Lab hold

		Electorate 63,561	Turnout 56%	Change from 2001	2001	Electorate 64,033	Turnout 52.8%
Healey J	**Lab**	**21,225**	**59.6%**	**-7.9%**	**Lab**	**22,798**	**67.5%**
Hughes M	C	6,169	17.3%	-1.5%	C	6,349	18.8%
Orrell K	LD	4,800	13.5%	2.7%	LD	3,652	10.8%
Pygott J	BNP	1,798	5.1%		UKIP	979	2.9%
Wilkinson J	UKIP	1,604	4.5%	1.6%			
Lab to C swing	**3.2%**	**35,596**		**Lab maj 15,056** 42.3%		**33,778**	**Lab maj 16,449** 48.7%

JOHN HEALEY b 13 Feb 1960. MP 1997-. Econ Secretary, Treasury 2002-. Parly Under-Sec Dept for Education and Skills 2001-02. PPS to Gordon Brown as Chancellor of Exchequer 1999-2001. Member Education and Employment select cttee 1997-99. Journalist/editor The House Magazine 1983-84. Disability charity campaigner 1984-90. Tutor, campaigns manager. MSF union communications head 1992-94. TUC campaigns/communications dir 1994-97. Ed Lady Lumley's Comp Sch, Pickering; St Peter's Sch, York; BA, Christ's Coll, Cambridge.

This former coalmining constituency in South Yorkshire is still a working-class seat with 60 per cent of breadwinners in manual occupations. The closure of Cortonwood colliery near Brampton was one of the elements that sparked the miners' strike in 1984-85, and served to fortify Labour's long-standing hold here. The urban settlements are small and separated by rural areas which broaden in the north west to enclose Wentworth House and Park.

WEST BROMWICH EAST

Lab hold

		Electorate 60,565	Turnout 58.6%	Change from 2001	2001	Electorate 61,180	Turnout 53.4%
Watson T	**Lab**	**19,741**	**55.6%**	**-0.3%**	**Lab**	**18,250**	**55.9%**
Bromwich R	C	8,089	22.8%	-3.2%	C	8,487	26%
Garrett I	LD	4,386	12.4%	-1.4%	LD	4,507	13.8%
Butler C	BNP	2,329	6.6%		UKIP	835	2.6%
Grey S	UKIP	607	1.7%	-0.9%	SLP	585	1.8%
Sambrook J	SLP	200	0.6%	-1.2%			
Macklin M	Ind	160	0.4%				
C to Lab swing	**1.5%**	**35,512**		**Lab maj 11,652** 32.8%		**32,664**	**Lab maj 9,763** 29.9%

TOM WATSON b 8 Jan 1967. MP 2001-. PPS to Dawn Primarolo 2003-04. Whip: asst govt 2004-05, govt 2005-. Member Home Affairs select cttee 2001-03. All-party groups: vice-treasurer music 2002-, treasurer e-democracy 2003-. Lab Party nat devt officer (youth) 1993-97. Nat co-ordinator Lab first past the post campaign 1997-. Dir: Tribune 2000-, Policy Network 2000-. AEEU nat political officer 1997-. Marketing officer Save the city of Wells 1987-88. Advertising account exec 1988-90. Ed King Charles I, Kidderminster.

West Bromwich is a populous residential area lying between Wednesbury and Handsworth in the Black Country, containing a long chain of villages and streets which form a widely spread town. It lies around three and a half miles from Birmingham and three miles east of Dudley and has been Labour since its creation in 1974.

WEST BROMWICH WEST

Lab hold

		Electorate 66,752	Turnout 52.3%	Change from 2001	2001	Electorate 66,765	Turnout 47.7%
Bailey A	**Lab/C**	**18,951**	**54.3%**	**-6.5%**	**Lab/C**	**19,352**	**60.8%**
Harker M	C	8,057	23.1%	-2%	C	7,997	25.1%
Smith M	LD	3,583	10.3%	3.5%	LD	2,168	6.8%
Lloyd J	BNP	3,456	9.9%	5.4%	BNP	1,428	4.5%
Walker K	UKIP	870	2.5%	0.9%	UKIP	499	1.6%
					SLP	396	1.2%
Lab/C to C swing	**2.3%**	**34,917**		**Lab/C maj 10,894** 31.2%		**31,840**	**Lab/C maj 11,355** 35.7%

ADRIAN BAILEY b 11 Dec 1945. MP Nov 2000- (by-election). PPS to John Hutton as Chancellor of Duchy of Lancaster 2005-. Member select cttees: NI Affairs 2001-, Unopposed Bills (Panel) 2001-. Chair all-party building societies and financial mutuals group 2003-. Chair parly group 2004. Co-operative Party political organiser 1982-2000. Cllr Sandwell BC 1991-: dep leader 1997-2000. Librarian Cheshire CC 1971-82. Ed Cheltenham Grammar Sch; BA economic history, Exeter Univ; postgrad librarianship dip, Loughborough Coll of Librarianship.

West Bromwich is typical of the industrial towns of the West Midlands with a manufacturing and engineering economic base and sturdy Labour tradition. It includes Tipton, Oldbury and Wednesbury as well as parts of the town of West Bromwich itself. It should be a reliable constituency for Labour for many years.

WEST HAM — Lab hold

		Electorate	Turnout	Change from	2001	Electorate	Turnout
		62,184	49.8%	2001		59,828	48.9%
Brown L	**Lab**	**15,840**	**51.2%**	**-18.7%**	**Lab**	**20,449**	**69.9%**
German L	Respect	6,039	19.5%		C	4,804	16.4%
Whitbread C	C	3,618	11.7%	-4.7%	LD	2,166	7.4%
Sugden A	LD	3,364	10.9%	3.5%	Greens	1,197	4.1%
Lithgow J	Greens	894	2.9%	-1.2%	UKIP	657	2.2%
Hammond S	CPA	437	1.4%				
Mayhew H	UKIP	409	1.3%	-0.9%			
Alcantara G	Veritas	365	1.2%				
Lab to Respect swing	**19.1%**	**30,966**		**Lab maj 9,801**		**29,273**	**Lab maj 15,645**
				31.6%			53.4%

LYN BROWN b 13 April 1960. MP 2005-. Founder London Library Development Board; Member London Region Sports Board, London Arts Board, Museums, Libraries and Archives Council, London

This impoverished east London seat includes the council wards of Stratford and New Town, Forest Gate North, Forest Gate South, Green Street West, Green Street East, West Ham, Plaistow North, Plaistow South and Boleyn. It is a multi-racial, multi-lingual area of staunch Labour support.

WESTBURY — C hold

		Electorate	Turnout	Change from	2001	Electorate	Turnout
		83,039	67%	2001		76,137	66.5%
Murrison A	**C**	**24,749**	**44.5%**	**2.4%**	**C**	**21,299**	**42.1%**
Hames D	LD	19,400	34.9%	3.3%	LD	16,005	31.6%
Gibby P	Lab	9,640	17.3%	-4.1%	Lab	10,847	21.4%
Williams L	UKIP	1,815	3.3%	0.8%	UKIP	1,261	2.5%
					Greens	1,216	2.4%
C to LD swing	**0.5%**	**55,604**		**C maj 5,349**		**50,628**	**C maj 5,294**
				9.6%			10.5%

ANDREW MURRISON b 24 April 1961. MP 2001-. Shadow Minister Health 2004-, Public Services, Health and Education 2003-04. Member Science and Technology select cttee 2001-. Research asst Lord Freeman 2000-. Parly Office of Science and Technology 2002-. Member PH7 magazine editorial advisory board. Surgeon Commander Royal Navy 1981-2000. Locum consultant occupational physician Gloucester Royal Hospital and GP 2000-01. Gilbert Blane Medal 1994. Ed medicine: MB CHB, MD, Bristol Univ; DPH, Cambridge Univ.

The Westbury seat consists of four towns on the Wiltshire plains. Spread across the constituency is the military town of Warminster, Bradford-on-Avon, the county town of Trowbridge and Westbury itself. Westbury, a market town on the western edge of Salisbury Plain, is famed for its White Horse carved into the chalk. The Conservatives have held the Westbury area continually since the 1920s and will probably do so for the foreseeable future.

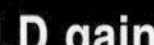

WESTMORLAND AND LONSDALE — LD gain

		Electorate	Turnout	Change from	2001	Electorate	Turnout
		69,363	71.6%	2001		70,637	67.2%
Farron T	**LD**	**22,569**	**45.5%**	**5.1%**	**C**	**22,486**	**46.9%**
Collins T	C	22,302	44.9%	-2%	LD	19,339	40.4%
Reardon J	Lab	3,796	7.6%	-3.3%	Lab	5,234	10.9%
Gibson R	UKIP	660	1.3%	0.1%	UKIP	552	1.2%
Kemp A	Ind	309	0.6%		Ind	292	0.6%
C to LD swing	**3.6%**	**49,636**		**LD maj 267**		**47,903**	**C maj 3,147**
				0.5%			6.6%

TIM FARRON b 27 May 1970. MP 2005-. Contested Westmorland and Lonsdale 2001 general election. South Lakeland District Councillor 2004-; Group deputy leader Lancashire County Council 1993-2000; Head of faculty administration, St Martin's College 2002-. Ed Lostock Hall High School, Preston, Lancashire; Newcastle University

Situated in the heart of the Lake District, Westmorland and Lonsdale contains some of the most beautiful countryside found anywhere within the United Kingdom. Unsurprisingly, tourism is the main industry here. Centred around the towns of Kendal and Windermere, the seat also includes parts of both the Lake District national park and the Yorkshire Dales national park. Considered safe Conservative territory since the 1940s, it is now marginal after a narrow win for the Liberal Democrats.

WESTON-SUPER-MARE — C gain

		Electorate	Turnout	Change from	2001	Electorate	Turnout
		74,900	65.6%	2001		74,322	62.8%
Penrose J	**C**	**19,804**	**40.3%**	**1.6%**	**LD**	**18,424**	**39.5%**
Cotter B	LD	17,725	36.1%	-3.4%	C	18,086	38.7%
Egan D	Lab	9,169	18.7%	-1.1%	Lab	9,235	19.8%
Spencer P	UKIP	1,207	2.5%	1.1%	UKIP	650	1.4%
Courtney C	BNP	778	1.6%		Ind	206	0.4%
Human W	Ind	225	0.5%		Ind	79	0.2%
Hemingway-Arnold P	Honesty	187	0.4%				
LD to C swing	**2.5%**	**49,095**		**C maj 2,079**		**46,680**	**LD maj 338**
				4.2%			0.7%

JOHN PENROSE b 22 June 1964. MP 2005-. Contested Ealing Southall 1997 and Weston-Super-Mare 2001 general elections. Publishing and general management: managing director schools publishing Europe Pearson plc 1996-2000, chair Logotron Ltd 2001-. Ed Ipswich School, Suffolk; BA law, Downing College, Cambridge; MBA, Columbia University, USA

This Somerset constituency stretches from the banks of the Severn Estuary in the north to the Mendip hills in the south. Although predominantly rural the constituency also has a light engineering base and the seaside town of Weston-Super-Mare is a famous tourist attraction. After decades of Conservative dominance Weston-Super-Mare fell to the Liberal Democrats in 1997. However, after a hard fought campaign, the Tories snatched it back in 2005.

WIGAN — Lab hold

		Electorate	Turnout	Change from	2001	Electorate	Turnout
		64,267	53.3%	2001		64,040	52.5%
Turner N	**Lab**	**18,901**	**55.1%**	**-6.6%**	**Lab**	**20,739**	**61.7%**
Coombes J	C	7,134	20.8%		C	6,996	20.8%
Capstick D	LD	6,051	17.6%	2.8%	LD	4,970	14.8%
Whittaker J	UKIP	1,166	3.4%		SA	886	2.6%
Williams K	CAP	1,026	3%				
Lab to C swing	**3.3%**	**34,278**		**Lab maj 11,767**		**33,591**	**Lab maj 13,743**
				34.3%			40.9%

NEIL TURNER b 16 Sept 1945. MP Sept 1999- (by-election). PPS to Ian McCartney 2001-. Member Public Administration 2000-01. Chair all-party local environmental quality 2004-. Cllr: Wigan County BC 1972-74, Wigan Metropolitan BC 1975-2000. Chair: Metropolitan Authorities Assocn 1995-97, Local Govt Assocn Quality Panel 1998-99. Quantity surveyor. Operations manager N Shropshire DC 1995-97. Ed Carlisle Grammar Sch.

It might easily be assumed that Wigan is very urban, but the constituency does not just include the town itself: on the constituency's northern edge, former pit villages such as Crooke, Standish and Haigh are surrounded by wonderful countryside. This is about as far as it is possible to get away from the chattering classes of metropolitan Labour, but the Labour Party has a secure hold here that is unlikely to be broken.

NORTH WILTSHIRE — C hold

		Electorate	Turnout	Change from	2001	Electorate	Turnout
		80,896	69.3%	2001		78,625	67.3%
Gray J	**C**	**26,282**	**46.9%**	**1.4%**	**C**	**24,090**	**45.5%**
Fox P	LD	20,979	37.4%	-0.8%	LD	20,212	38.2%
Nash D	Lab	6,794	12.1%	-2.2%	Lab	7,556	14.3%
Dowdney N	UKIP	1,428	2.6%	0.5%	UKIP	1,090	2.1%
Allnatt P	Ind	578	1%				
LD to C swing	**1.1%**	**56,061**		**C maj 5,303**		**52,948**	**C maj 3,878**
				9.5%			7.3%

JAMES GRAY b 7 Nov 1954. MP 1997-. Shadow Sec of State for Scotland May 2005; Shadow Min: Environment/ Transport 2003-05, Environment, Food, Rural Affairs 2001-03. Opposition: whip 2000-01, spokes: defence 2001-02, environment, food, rural affairs 2002-05. Member select cttees: Environment, Transport and Regional Affairs 1997-2001, Broadcasting 2001-03. Chair all-party groups 2003-. Special adviser to John Gummer, Michael Howard 1991-95. Management trainee/broker/MD/dir. Dir Baltic Futures Exchange 1989-91. Ed MA hist, Glasgow Univ; hist thesis, Christ Church, Oxford.

North Wiltshire is situated on the edge of the Cotswolds and is bisected by the M4. The major towns are Chippenham, Wootton Bassett, Corsham and Malmesbury. In the rural areas the closure of military bases and the decline of agriculture is being replaced by the growth of tourism. This constituency has been in Conservative hands continuously since 1945, and after the recent election it appears this situation will remain unchanged for the foreseeable future.

WIMBLEDON — C gain

		Electorate 63,714	Turnout 68.1%	Change from 2001	2001	Electorate 63,930	Turnout 64.3%
Hammond S	**C**	**17,886**	**41.2%**	**4.6%**	**Lab**	**18,806**	**45.7%**
Casale R	Lab	15,585	35.9%	-9.8%	C	15,062	36.6%
Gee S	LD	7,868	18.1%	5.1%	LD	5,341	13%
Barrow G	Greens	1,374	3.2%	0.8%	Greens	1,007	2.4%
Mills A	UKIP	408	0.9%	-0.1%	CPA	479	1.2%
Coverdale C	Ind	211	0.5%		UKIP	414	1%
Wilson A	TEPK	50	0.1%				
Weiss R	Vote Dream	22	0.1%				
Lab to C swing	**7.2%**	**43,404**		**C maj 2,301** 5.3%		**41,109**	**Lab maj 3,744** 9.1%

STEPHEN HAMMOND b 4 February 1962. MP 2005-. Contested North Warwickshire 1997 and Wimbledon 2001 general elections. Councillor, Merton Borough Council, 2002-: Environment spokesman 2002-04, Deputy group leader 2004-. Stockbroker UBS Philips and Drew 1988-91; Director UK equities Dresdner Kleinwort Benson Securities 1991-98; Director Pan European research Commerzbank Securities 1998. Ed King Edward VI School, Southampton; Richard Hale School, Hertford; Queen Mary College, London University

Wimbledon in south-west London is best known for its world-famous tennis courts, home to the annual tennis championships. From the predominantly Conservative village which skirts the Common in the north, the wards become more marginal as the constituency moves down Wimbledon Hill, with the strongest Labour support to be found in the south east on the border with Mitcham and Morden. Once safe Conservative territory, the constituency reverted to the Tories in 2005.

WINCHESTER — LD hold

		Electorate 85,810	Turnout 71.8%	Change from 2001	2001	Electorate 83,532	Turnout 70.8%
Oaten M	**LD**	**31,225**	**50.6%**	**-4%**	**LD**	**32,282**	**54.6%**
Hollingbery G	C	23,749	38.5%	0.2%	C	22,648	38.3%
Davies P	Lab	4,782	7.8%	1.9%	Lab	3,498	5.9%
Abbott D	UKIP	1,321	2.1%	1%	UKIP	664	1.1%
Pendragon A	Ind	581	0.9%		Wes R	66	0.1%
LD to C swing	**2.1%**	**61,658**		**LD maj 7,476** 12.1%		**59,158**	**LD maj 9,634** 16.3%

MARK OATEN b 8 March 1964. MP 1997- (declared invalid but confirmed Nov 1997 by-election). Lib Dem Shadow Home Sec 2003-. PPS to Charles Kennedy as Lib Dem Party leader 1999-2001. Lib Dem spokes: soc security, welfare 1997-99, foreign affairs, defence 1999-2001, Cabinet Office 2001-03. Member Public Admin select cttee 1999-2001. Chair: all-party civil contingency/preparedness group, Parly Party, Lib Dem Peel group. Cllr Watford BC 1986-94. Oasis Radio dir, public affairs consultant, MD. Ed BA hist, internat PR dip, Hatfield Poly.

On the edge of the South Downs, Winchester is England's ancient capital and the former seat of King Alfred. The constituency also encompasses the market towns of Twyford, New Alresford, Bishop's Waltham and Denmead. It is one of the wealthiest constituencies in the country and, although once a Conservative stronghold, has become a safe Liberal Democrat seat following Mark Oaten's narrow victory in one of the most dramatic twists of the 1997 general election.

WINDSOR — C hold

		Electorate 68,290	Turnout 64%	Change from 2001	2001	Electorate 73,854	Turnout 57%
Afriyie A	**C**	**21,646**	**49.5%**	**2.2%**	**C**	**19,900**	**47.3%**
Wood A	LD	11,354	26%	-0.1%	LD	11,011	26.1%
Muller M	Lab	8,339	19.1%	-5%	Lab	10,137	24.1%
Black D	UKIP	1,098	2.5%		UKIP	1,062	2.5%
Wall D	Greens	1,074	2.5%				
Hooper P	Ind	182	0.4%				
LD to C swing	**1.2%**	**43,693**		**C maj 10,292** 23.6%		**42,110**	**C maj 8,889** 21.1%

ADAM AFRIYIE b 4 Aug 1965. MP 2005-. Constituency branch chair 1999-2004; Chair (London region) 'No' to the Euro campaign 2001-04; Governor Museum of London; Non-exec chair: Connect Support Services, DeHavilland Information Services; Board member Policy Exchange 2003-. Ed Addey and Stanhope School, New Cross; agricultural economics, Imperial College, London

Home to Windsor Castle, Eton College and exclusive suburbs around Windsor, Sunningdale and Ascot, Windsor is one of the most wealthy and privileged constituencies in the country. Formerly Windsor and Maidenhead, the constituency was redrawn in the 1995 Boundary Commission review, and there was never much doubt that the new seat would be anything other than a very safe Tory seat.

WIRRAL SOUTH — Lab hold

		Electorate	Turnout	Change from	2001	Electorate	Turnout
		58,834	67.5%	2001		60,653	65.6%
Chapman B	**Lab**	**16,892**	**42.5%**	**-4.9%**	**Lab**	**18,890**	**47.4%**
Cross C	C	13,168	33.2%	-1.6%	C	13,841	34.8%
Holbrook S	LD	8,568	21.6%	3.8%	LD	7,087	17.8%
Scott D	UKIP	616	1.6%				
Jones L	Ind	460	1.2%				
Lab to C swing	**1.7%**	**39,704**		**Lab maj 3,724**		**39,818**	**Lab maj 5,049**
				9.4%			12.7%

BEN CHAPMAN b 8 July 1940. MP Feb 1997- (by-election). PPS to Richard Caborn 1997-. Chair all-party groups: cleaning and hygiene industry 2001-, China 2001-, Vietnam 2004-. Vice-chair all-party Cuba group 2003-. Dir Wirral Chamber of Commerce 1995-96. Hon ambassador for: Cumbria 1995-, Merseyside 1997-. Hon vice-pres Wirral Investment Network 1997-. Exec cttee UK-China forum 1999-. Civil servant. Pilot officer RAFVR 1959-61. Commercial counsellor, company director, partner, consultant. Ed Appleby Grammar Sch, Westmorland.

The Wirral has long been home to the more affluent sections of Merseyside society, containing the more comfortable suburbs of Liverpool and Birkenhead. Wirral South also contains is a fair sized element of the peninsula's petrochemical industry.

WIRRAL WEST — Lab hold

		Electorate	Turnout	Change from	2001	Electorate	Turnout
		61,050	67.5%	2001		62,294	65%
Hesford S	**Lab**	**17,543**	**42.6%**	**-4.6%**	**Lab**	**19,105**	**47.2%**
McVey E	C	16,446	39.9%	2.7%	C	15,070	37.2%
Clarke J	LD	6,652	16.1%	0.5%	LD	6,300	15.6%
Moore J	UKIP	429	1%				
Taylor R	AP	163	0.4%				
Lab to C swing	**3.7%**	**41,233**		**Lab maj 1,097**		**40,475**	**Lab maj 4,035**
				2.7%			10%

STEPHEN HESFORD b 27 May 1957. MP 1997-. Member select cttees: Deregulation 1997-98, Northern Ireland Affairs 1998-99, Health 1999-2001. Vice-chair all-party autism group 2001-. Member: NEC Socialist Health Assocn, European standing cttee C 1999-. Vice-chair North Manchester community health council. Barrister 1981-97. Asst to Joan Lestor MP 1992-93. GMB branch equal opps officer. Ed Urmston Grammar Sch; BSc social science, Bradford Univ; LLM, Central London Poly.

On the far side of the peninsula, Wirral West is the wealthier and most rural of the four constituencies, and therefore popular with commuters. Despite its name, this is in fact situated on the north-western corner of the peninsula facing the Irish Sea and the banks of the River Dee. A seat Labour did not expect to win in 1997 and yet have held on to, it is vulnerable to a Conservative comeback.

WITNEY — C hold

		Electorate	Turnout	Change from	2001	Electorate	Turnout
		78,053	69%	2001		74,612	65.9%
Cameron D	**C**	**26,571**	**49.3%**	**4.3%**	**C**	**22,153**	**45%**
Leffman L	LD	12,415	23.1%	2.8%	Lab	14,180	28.8%
Gray T	Lab	11,845	22%	-6.8%	LD	10,000	20.3%
Dossett-Davies R	Greens	1,682	3.1%	0.9%	Greens	1,100	2.2%
Wesson P	UKIP	1,356	2.5%	0.9%	Ind	1,003	2%
					UKIP	767	1.6%
LD to C swing	**0.8%**	**53,869**		**C maj 14,156**		**49,203**	**C maj 7,973**
				26.3%			16.2%

DAVID CAMERON b 9 Oct 1966. MP 2001-. Shadow Sec of State Ed and Skills 2005-. Member Shadow Cabinet 2004-. Shadow Minister: Local and Devolved Govt Affairs 2004, Privy Council Office 2003. Member select cttees 2001-04. Con Party: dep chair 2003, head policy co-ordination 2004-. Head political section Con research dept 1988-92, member John Major PM's Question Time briefing team. Special adviser to: Norman Lamont, Michael Howard. Carlton Communications plc corporate affairs dir. Ed Eton Coll; BA PPE, Brasenose Coll, Oxford.

The constituency covers the town of Witney itself, Eynsham, Chipping Norton, RAF Brize Norton, Carterton (which is the second largest town after Witney), Charlbury and Woodstock. A growing industrial and residential town 20 miles outside Oxford, Witney's population grew by 30 per cent in the 1980s, and the local economy is booming. Witney is a safe Tory seat.

WOKING

C hold

		Electorate 72,676	Turnout 63.4%	Change from 2001	2001	Electorate 71,254	Turnout 60.2%
Malins H	**C**	**21,838**	**47.4%**	**1.4%**	**C**	**19,747**	**46%**
Lee A	LD	15,226	33.1%	2.8%	LD	12,988	30.3%
Blagbrough E	Lab	7,507	16.3%	-4%	Lab	8,714	20.3%
Davies M	UKIP	1,324	2.9%	-0.5%	UKIP	1,461	3.4%
Osman M	UKC	150	0.3%				
C to LD swing	**0.7%**	**46,045**		**C maj 6,612** 14.4%		**42,910**	**C maj 6,759** 15.8%

HUMFREY MALINS b 31 July 1945. MP for Croydon North West 1983-92, for Woking 1997-. Shadow Minister: Home Affairs 2003, 2004-, Home, Constitutional and Legal Affairs 2003-04. PPS to: Virginia Bottomley 1989-92, Tim Renton 1987-89. Opposition home affairs 2001-03. Member select cttees: Home Affairs 1997-2002, Chairmen's Panel 1998-2001. Capt all-party golf group. Cllr Mole Valley DC 1973-82. Solicitor. Dep Metropolitan Stipendiary Magistrate 1992-97, Crown Court Recorder 1996-. CBE 1997. Ed MA jurisprudence, Brasenose Coll, Oxford.

Woking, the largest town in Surrey, has become the retail and service centre for the stockbroker belt. In addition to Woking itself, the constituency contains numerous villages, together with the Guildford borough wards of Normandy and Pirbright. Always staunchly Conservative, in 1997 the Conservative vote fell dramatically, partly due to the presence of an Independent Tory candidate, and the Liberal Democrats have been inching forward but remain some distance away.

WOKINGHAM

C hold

		Electorate 68,614	Turnout 67.2%	Change from 2001	2001	Electorate 68,430	Turnout 64.1%
Redwood J	**C**	**22,174**	**48.1%**	**2%**	**C**	**20,216**	**46.1%**
Bray P	LD	14,934	32.4%		LD	14,222	32.4%
Black D	Lab	6,991	15.2%	-2.2%	Lab	7,633	17.4%
Carstairs F	UKIP	994	2.2%	0.2%	UKIP	897	2%
Owen T	Loony	569	1.2%	-0.8%	Loony	880	2%
Colborne R	BNP	376	0.8%				
Hall M	telepath	34	0.1%				
LD to C swing	**1%**	**46,072**		**C maj 7,240** 15.7%		**43,848**	**C maj 5,994** 13.7%

JOHN REDWOOD b 15 June 1951. MP 1987-. Shadow Sec of State: Deregulation 2004-, Environ, Transport and Regions 1999-2000, Trade and Industry 1997-99. Sec of State Wales 1993-95. Minister of State: Dept of Environ 1992-93; 1990-92. Parly Under-Sec Dept of Trade and Industry 1989-90. Contested Con Party leadership 1995, 1997. Chair No Turning Back group. Cllr Oxon CC 1973-77. Tutor, lecturer, investment analyst, NM Rothschild dir. Chair Concentric plc 2003-. PC 1993. Ed Oxford: MA mod hist, Magdalen Coll, DPhil mod hist, St Antony's Coll.

Wokingham is a sprawling constituency south of the Thames in Berkshire, containing the historic market town of Wokingham and a wide area to the south-east of Reading, characterised by acres of mixed woodlands. It has traditionally been a safe Tory home counties seat, which houses an ever growing number of affluent commuters.

WOLVERHAMPTON NORTH EAST

Lab hold

		Electorate 60,595	Turnout 54.4%	Change from 2001	2001	Electorate 59,616	Turnout 52.8%
Purchase K	**Lab/C**	**17,948**	**54.5%**	**-5.8%**	**Lab/C**	**18,984**	**60.3%**
Robson A	C	9,792	29.7%	1.1%	C	9,019	28.6%
Jack D	LD	3,845	11.7%	3.8%	LD	2,494	7.9%
Simpson L	UKIP	1,371	4.2%	1%	UKIP	997	3.2%
Lab/C to C swing	**3.5%**	**32,956**		**Lab/C maj 8,156** 24.8%		**31,494**	**Lab/C maj 9,965** 31.6%

KEN PURCHASE b 8 Jan 1939. MP 1992-. PPS to Robin Cook as Leader of HoC 2001-03, as Foreign Sec 1997-2001. Member Trade and Industry select cttee 1993-97. Chair all-party export group 1993-. Cllr: Wolverhampton County BC 1970-74, Wolverhampton Metropolitan BC 1973-90. Member Wolverhampton community health council 1990-92. Apprentice toolmaker, component devt, toolroom machinist, Walsall metropolitan BC housing dept, business devt adviser. Ed BA social science, Wolverhampton Poly.

Wolverhampton North East is at the northern end of the industrial conurbation of the West Midlands. Although it borders the south Staffordshire countryside, industry still dominates Wolverhampton's urban landscape and the city is one of the great manufacturing centres in the West Midlands and a traditional Labour stronghold.

WOLVERHAMPTON SOUTH EAST — Lab hold

		Electorate	Turnout	Change from	2001	Electorate	Turnout
		54,047	52.3%	2001		53,243	51.3%
McFadden P	**Lab**	**16,790**	**59.4%**	**-8%**	**Lab/C**	**18,409**	**67.4%**
Fairbairn J	C	6,295	22.3%	0.5%	C	5,945	21.8%
Murray D	LD	3,682	13%	4.2%	LD	2,389	8.8%
Simmons K	UKIP	1,484	5.2%		NF	554	2%
Lab to C swing	**4.3%**	**28,251**		**Lab maj 10,495**		**27,297**	**Lab/C maj 12,464**
				37.2%			45.7%

PAT McFADDEN b 26 March 1965. MP 2005-. Political secretary, Prime Minister's Office 2002-05. Ed Holyrood Secondary School; Glasgow University

Situated north of Dudley, Wolverhampton South East is the closest of the city's three seats to the urban core of the West Midlands, going beyond the city boundaries to include parts of Dudley borough. It is heavily industrialised, with manufacturing industries to the fore, and a long-standing Labour seat.

WOLVERHAMPTON SOUTH WEST — Lab hold

		Electorate	Turnout	Change from	2001	Electorate	Turnout
		67,096	62.1%	2001		65,909	62.1%
Marris R	**Lab**	**18,489**	**44.4%**	**-3.9%**	**Lab**	**19,735**	**48.3%**
Verma S	C	15,610	37.4%	-2.3%	C	16,248	39.7%
Ross C	LD	5,568	13.4%	5%	LD	3,425	8.4%
Hope D	UKIP	1,029	2.5%	0.8%	Greens	805	2%
Mullins E	BNP	983	2.4%		UKIP	684	1.7%
Lab to C swing	**0.8%**	**41,679**		**Lab maj 2,879**		**40,897**	**Lab maj 3,487**
				6.9%			8.5%

ROB MARRIS b 8 April 1955. MP 2001-. Member Work and Pensions select cttee 2001-. Treasurer all-party Punjabis in Britain group 2001-. Member: New Democratic Party Canada 1980-82, European standing cttees A and B 2003-. Firefighter, labourer, trucker, bus driver, solicitor. Member Birmingham TUC club. Ed St Edwards Sch, Oxford; BA sociology/hist, MA hist, British Columbia Univ; law: Common Professional Examination, Law Society Finals, Birmingham Poly.

This seat is the most prosperous of the three Wolverhampton seats stretching out from the city centre into the residential, predominantly middle-class south west of the city. Suburban support helped the Conservatives hold the constituency from 1950 until 1997 when Labour took the seat.

WOODSPRING — C hold

		Electorate	Turnout	Change from	2001	Electorate	Turnout
		71,662	72%	2001		71,018	68.7%
Fox L	**C**	**21,587**	**41.8%**	**-1.9%**	**C**	**21,297**	**43.7%**
Bell M	LD	15,571	30.2%	6%	Lab	12,499	25.6%
Stevens C	Lab	11,249	21.8%	-3.8%	LD	11,816	24.2%
Lewis R	Greens	1,309	2.5%	-0.1%	Ind	1,412	2.9%
Butcher A	UKIP	1,269	2.5%	1.6%	Greens	1,282	2.6%
Howson M	BNP	633	1.2%		UKIP	452	0.9%
C to LD swing	**4%**	**51,618**		**C maj 6,016**		**48,758**	**C maj 8,798**
				11.6%			18%

LIAM FOX b 22 Sept 1961. MP 1992-. Shadow: Foreign Sec 2005-, Sec of State Health 1999-2003, Cabinet Member 1998-. Parly Under-Sec FCO 1996-97. PPS to Michael Howard 1993-94. Whip: asst govt 1994-95, govt 1995-96. Opposition spokes 1997-99. Member Scottish Affairs select cttee 1992-93. Co-chair Con Party 2003-. Member Families for Defence central cttee 1987-89. Guest of US state dept 1985. GP, divisional surgeon St John's Ambulance. Ed St Bride's Sch, East Kilbride; MB, ChB, MROGP, Glasgow Univ.

Woodspring is a tranquil and affluent constituency. The main towns of Clevedon and Portishead serve as resorts on the Bristol Channel coast and have large proportions of retired residents. The other main centres of population such as Nailsea and the Gordano Valley are communities based largely on farming. The Lib Dems will continue to challenge in Woodspring but the Tories should remain relatively safe.

WORCESTER — Lab hold

		Electorate 72,384	Turnout 64.1%	Change from 2001	2001	Electorate 71,255	Turnout 62%
Foster M	**Lab**	**19,421**	**41.9%**	**-6.7%**	**Lab**	**21,478**	**48.6%**
Harper M	C	16,277	35.1%	-0.4%	C	15,712	35.5%
Dhonau M	LD	7,557	16.3%	3.7%	LD	5,578	12.6%
Chamings R	UKIP	1,113	2.4%	-0.9%	UKIP	1,442	3.3%
Roberts M	BNP	980	2.1%				
Lennard C	Greens	921	2%				
Dowson P	Ind	119	0.3%				
Lab to C swing	**3.2%**	**46,388**		**Lab maj 3,144** 6.8%		**44,210**	**Lab maj 5,766** 13%

MICHAEL FOSTER b 14 March 1963. MP 1997-. PPS to Peter Hain 2005-; Team PPS Dept for Education and Skills 2004-05. PPS to Margaret Hodge 2001-04. Member Education and Employment select cttee 1999-2001. Chair all-party flood prevention group 2002-. Sec Worcester constituency Lab Party 1992-95. Agent Mid Worcester 1992. Financial planning/control dept Jaguar Cars Ltd, financial analyst, manager, accountancy lecturer. TGWU shop steward 1986-88. Ed BA economics, Wolverhampton Poly; PGCE, Wolverhampton Univ.

The constituency is very similar to the national average in its class composition, proportion of ethnic minority voters, average age and housing tenure. Unemployment, however, is below avarege. Employment in the service sector such as administration, hotels, distribution and shops takes up about 80 per cent of the total. Manufacturing employs around 14 per cent and includes companies such as Metal Box and Yamasaki (computerised machine tools). Both tourism and shopping are areas of economic growth.

MID WORCESTERSHIRE — C hold

		Electorate 71,546	Turnout 67.3%	Change from 2001	2001	Electorate 72,055	Turnout 62.3%
Luff P	**C**	**24,783**	**51.5%**	**0.4%**	**C**	**22,937**	**51.1%**
Gregson M	Lab	11,456	23.8%	-3.6%	Lab	12,310	27.4%
Rowley M	LD	9,796	20.4%	1.6%	LD	8,420	18.8%
Eaves A	UKIP	2,092	4.4%	1.7%	UKIP	1,230	2.7%
Lab to C swing	**2%**	**48,127**		**C maj 13,327** 27.7%		**44,897**	**C maj 10,627** 23.7%

PETER LUFF b 18 Feb 1955. MP for Worcester 1992-97, for Mid Worcs 1997-. PPS to: Ann Widdecombe 1996-97, Lord Mackay of Clashfern 1996-97, Tim Eggar 1993-96. Opposition whip 2000-05. Member various select cttees incl chair Agriculture 1997-2000. Chair all-party middle way group 1999-. Chair Con parly friends of India 2001-. Member exec cttee Commonwealth parly assocn. MP research asst/head of Edward Heath priv office/company sec/PR consultant/spec adviser Trade and Industry Sec of State. Ed BA econ, Corpus Christi Coll, Cambridge.

Apart from the towns of Droitwich and Evesham this is attractive, rural, loyal Tory territory with an important fruit growing and market gardening industry around Evesham. There is also some commuting from here to the West Midlands conurbation via the M5 which passes through the constituency. The motorway has also attracted some light industry. Car ownership is high (81 per cent) as are the numbers in managerial or technical occupations.

WEST WORCESTERSHIRE — C hold

		Electorate 66,999	Turnout 70.3%	Change from 2001	2001	Electorate 66,769	Turnout 67.1%
Spicer M	**C**	**20,959**	**45.4%**	**-0.6%**	**C**	**20,597**	**46%**
Wells T	LD	18,484	40%	6%	LD	15,223	34%
Bhatti Q	Lab	4,945	10.7%	-3.3%	Lab	6,275	14%
Bovey C	UKIP	1,590	3.4%	-0.1%	UKIP	1,574	3.5%
Victory M	Greens	1,099	2.3%	-0.2%	Greens	1,138	2.5%
C to LD swing	**3.3%**	**47,077**		**C maj 2,475** 5.3%		**44,807**	**C maj 5,374** 12%

SIR MICHAEL SPICER b 22 Jan 1943. MP for South Worcs 1974-97, for West Worcs 1997-. Minister of State Dept of Environ 1990. Parly Under-Sec Dept of Energy 1987-90. Aviation Minister 1985-87. Parly Under-Sec Transport 1984-87. PPS to Sally Oppenheim 1979-81. Member Treasury select cttee 1997-2001. Chair 1922 cttee 2001-. Chair/capt all-party Lords and Commons tennis club group 1997-. Con Party: vice-chair 1981-83, dep chair 1983-84, board member 2001-. Journalist, economic consultant, novelist. Kt 1996. Ed MA econ, Emmanuel Coll, Cambridge.

The historical home of Edward Elgar, West Worcestershire is a rural constituency that is truly part of England's green and pleasant land on the edge of the Cotswolds. The town of Great Malvern is the major settlement, known for its spring water which is exported across the world. The River Severn meanders through the constituency, overlooked by the Malvern hills, where the Conservatives hold sway at present.

WORKINGTON — Lab hold

		Electorate	Turnout	Change from	2001	Electorate	Turnout
		61,441	64.7%	2001		65,965	63.4%
Cunningham T	**Lab**	**19,554**	**49.2%**	**-6.3%**	**Lab**	**23,209**	**55.5%**
Pattinson J	C	12,659	31.9%	2.3%	C	12,359	29.6%
Clarkson K	LD	5,815	14.6%	2.1%	LD	5,214	12.5%
Richardson M	UKIP	1,328	3.3%		LCA	1,040	2.5%
Peacock J	LCA	381	1%	-1.5%			
Lab to C swing	**4.3%**	**39,737**		**Lab maj 6,895**		**41,822**	**Lab maj 10,850**
				17.4%			25.9%

TONY CUNNINGHAM b 16 Sept 1952. MP 2001-. PPS to Elliot Morley 2003-05. Asst govt whip 2005-. Member select cttees: Catering 2001-, European Scrutiny 2001-04. All-party groups: chair Afghanistan 2001-, press officer/sec rugby league 2004-. MEP Cumbria and North Lancashire 1994-99. Member European standing cttee C. Cllr Allerdale BC: leader 1992-94. NUT local sec 1985-94. Teacher, chief exec Human Rights NGO 1999-2000. Patron: Mines Advisory Group, VSO. Ed Workington Grammar Sch; Ba hist/politics, Liverpool Univ; PGCE, Didsbury Coll.

Much of this seat is made up of the Lake District's National Park and the glorious countryside stretching from the buzzing tourist town of Keswick on Derwentwater to Cockermouth. The rest of the seat is composed of bleak old coalmining villages such as Workington itself. Yet, however physically diverse the landscape may be, the constituency has remained solidly united behind Labour.

WORSLEY — Lab hold

		Electorate	Turnout	Change from	2001	Electorate	Turnout
		69,534	53.1%	2001		69,300	51%
Keeley B	**Lab**	**18,859**	**51%**	**-6.1%**	**Lab**	**20,193**	**57.1%**
Evans G	C	9,491	25.7%	1.9%	C	8,406	23.8%
Clayton R	LD	6,902	18.7%	1.2%	LD	6,188	17.5%
Gill B	UKIP	1,694	4.6%		SLP	576	1.6%
Lab to C swing	**4%**	**36,946**		**Lab maj 9,368**		**35,363**	**Lab maj 11,787**
				25.4%			33.3%

BARBARA KEELEY b 26 March 1952. MP 2005-. Trafford Borough councillor 1995-2004. Voluntary sector consultant. Ed Mount St Mary's RC College, Leeds; Politics and contemporary history, Salford University

The seat includes some of the most sought-after residential areas in Greater Manchester and half of its landscape is rural in character. Worsley town is renowned for its 'pastoral beauty', and its canal is lined with timbered buildings from the 19th century, including the Court House and Worsley Old Hall. Worsley is one of the many safe Labour seats in Greater Manchester that the Party has held for decades.

WORTHING WEST — C hold

		Electorate	Turnout	Change from	2001	Electorate	Turnout
		71,780	62.6%	2001		72,419	59.7%
Bottomley P	**C**	**21,383**	**47.6%**	**0.1%**	**C**	**20,508**	**47.5%**
Potter C	LD	12,004	26.7%	0.2%	LD	11,471	26.5%
Bignell A	Lab	8,630	19.2%	-2.3%	Lab	9,270	21.5%
Cross T	UKIP	2,374	5.3%	0.8%	UKIP	1,960	4.5%
Baldwin C	LCA	550	1.2%				
C to LD swing	**0.2%**	**44,941**		**C maj 9,379**		**43,209**	**C maj 9,037**
				20.9%			20.9%

PETER BOTTOMLEY b 20 July 1944. MP for Greenwich, Woolwich West 1975-83, for Eltham 1983-97, for Worthing West 1997-. PPS to Peter Brooke 1990. Parly Under-Sec: NI Office 1989-90, Dept of Transport 1986-89, Dept Employment 1984-86. PPS to Norman Fowler 1983-84, Cranley Onslow 1982-83. Member select cttees: Standards/Privileges 1997-2002, Unopposed Bills (Panel) 1997-, Constitutional Affairs 2003-. Chair numerous all-party groups. Industrial sales/relations/economics. Ed BA econ, Trinity Coll, Cambridge.

Worthing is a seaside resort with many elderly residents. Tourism is the main industry, but it is also a bustling modern commercial centre. The town, the largest in West Sussex, is bounded to the north by the South Downs and to the south by the English Channel. Worthing West contains most of the town of Worthing, including Goring-by-Sea, and some coastal villages. A Tory stronghold since 1945, it shows no signs of changing allegiance.

EAST WORTHING AND SHOREHAM — C hold

		Electorate 72,302	Turnout 61.6%	Change from 2001	2001	Electorate 71,890	Turnout 59.9%
Loughton T	**C**	**19,548**	**43.9%**	**0.7%**	**C**	**18,608**	**43.2%**
Yates D	Lab	11,365	25.5%	-3.5%	Lab	12,469	29%
Doyle J	LD	10,844	24.4%	1.5%	LD	9,876	22.9%
Jelf R	UKIP	2,109	4.7%	1.9%	UKIP	1,195	2.8%
Baldwin C	LCA	677	1.5%	-0.6%	LCA	920	2.1%
Lab to C swing	**2.1%**	**44,543**		**C maj 8,183** 18.4%		**43,068**	**C maj 6,139** 14.3%

TIM LOUGHTON b 30 May 1962. MP 1997-. Shadow Min: Children 2004-, Children and the Family 2003-04, Health and Education 2003. Opposition spokes: environment, transport and the regions 2000-01, health 2001-03. Member Environmental Audit select cttee 1997-2001. Chair all-party hockey team group 2004-. 1994-2004. Chair Con Disability group 1998-. Gen election PA to Tim Eggar 1987. Member Royal Inst of Internat Affairs. Fund manager. Ed BA classical civilisation, Warwick Univ; research Mesopotamian archaeology, Clare Coll, Cambridge.

East Worthing and Shoreham is a fairly recent seat in West Sussex, created in the 1995 boundary review. The constituency is an eclectic mix, containing four wards from the east of Worthing, Shoreham by Sea, and the smaller communities of Sompting, Lancing, Southwick and Fishergate. With a mix of seaside, pensioners, comfortable residential areas and inland farming, this constituency is typical of many Tory-held south coast resort seats.

THE WREKIN — C gain

		Electorate 67,291	Turnout 67%	Change from 2001	2001	Electorate 65,781	Turnout 63.1%
Pritchard M	**C**	**18,899**	**42%**	**3.6%**	**Lab**	**19,532**	**47.1%**
Bradley P	Lab	17,957	39.9%	-7.2%	C	15,945	38.4%
Tomlinson B	LD	6,608	14.7%	3.3%	LD	4,738	11.4%
Lawson B	UKIP	1,590	3.5%	0.4%	UKIP	1,275	3.1%
Lab to C swing	**5.4%**	**45,054**		**C maj 942** 2.1%		**41,490**	**Lab maj 3,587** 8.6%

MARK PRITCHARD MP 2005-. Contested Warley 2001 general election. Councillor: Harrow Council, Woking Borough Council. Ed Afan Comprehensive Shool, Cymmer; Aylestone School, Hereford; London Guildhall University

The Wrekin consists of a horseshoe shaped portion of mid-Shropshire that curves around the new town of Telford. The seat includes some of the northern areas of Telford, the market towns of Wellington and Newport, the old mining towns of Hadley and Donnington, and Shifnal and Albrighton in the south east. A Conservative-type territory in many ways it eventually fell to the Tories in 2005 after being held by Labour since its creation in 1997.

WREXHAM — Lab hold

		Electorate 48,016	Turnout 63.3%	Change from 2001	2001	Electorate 50,465	Turnout 59.5%
Lucas I	**Lab**	**13,993**	**46.1%**	**-6.9%**	**Lab**	**15,934**	**53%**
Rippeth T	LD	7,174	23.6%	6.5%	C	6,746	22.5%
Coffey T	C	6,079	20%	-2.5%	LD	5,153	17.1%
Owen S	PIC	1,744	5.7%	-0.2%	PIC	1,783	5.9%
Walker J	BNP	919	3%		UKIP	432	1.4%
Williams J	Forward Wales	476	1.6%				
Lab to LD swing	**6.7%**	**30,385**		**Lab maj 6,819** 22.4%		**30,048**	**Lab maj 9,188** 30.6%

IAN LUCAS b 18 Sept 1960. MP 2001-. Member select cttees: Environmental Audit 2001-03, Procedure 2001-02, Transport 2003-. Sec all-party packaging manufacturing industry group 2004-. Lab Party: chair Wrexham 1992-93, vice-chair N Shropshire 1993-2000. Soc of Lab lawyers 1996-. Member Gresford Community Council, Wrexham 1987-91. Solicitor. Ed Greenwell Comp Sch, Gateshead; Royal Grammar Sch, Newcastle upon Tyne; BA jurisprudence, New Coll, Oxford; Solicitor's Final Exam, Coll of Law, Christleton law.

Wrexham is the largest town in North Wales, situated close to the English border. It is an important regional centre for North Wales and was formerly reliant on its major mining industry, but its economy has diversified considerably in recent years. Labour has long dominated politics in this constituency and they will hope to regain the Assembly seat in 2007 that they lost to their former MP John Marek.

WYCOMBE — C hold

		Electorate 71,464	Turnout 62.2%	Change from 2001	2001	Electorate 74,297	Turnout 60.5%
Goodman P	**C**	**20,331**	**45.8%**	**3.4%**	**C**	**19,064**	**42.4%**
Wassell J	Lab	13,280	29.9%	-5.4%	Lab	15,896	35.3%
Oates J	LD	8,780	19.8%	2.8%	LD	7,658	17%
Davis R	UKIP	1,735	3.9%	1.5%	UKIP	1,059	2.4%
Fitton D	Ind	301	0.7%	0.2%	Greens	1,057	2.4%
					Ind	240	0.5%
Lab to C swing	**4.4%**	**44,427**		**C maj 7,051** 15.9%		**44,974**	**C maj 3,168** 7%

PAUL GOODMAN b 17 Nov 1959. MP 2001-. Shadow Minister: Economic Affairs 2004-, Disabled People 2003-04, Work and Pensions 2003. PPS to David Davis as chair Con Party 2001-02. Member select cttees: Work and Pensions 2001-, Regulatory Reform 2001-03. Vice-chair European secure vehicle alliance group 2002-. Chair Federation of Con students 1983-84. NUS exec cttee member 1981-83. Public affairs exec, researcher Tom King MP, journalist. Ed Cranleigh Sch, Surrey; BA Eng lit, York Univ.

This Buckinghamshire constituency is a combination of urban and rural. Around half of the seat is constituted by the town of High Wycombe, the rest consists of the small affluent villages around Marlow and the Chiltern Hills. Traditionally a very safe Tory seat, Wycombe remains under Conservative control, and Labour's chance here appears to have passed.

WYRE FOREST — Ind KHHC hold

		Electorate 73,192	Turnout 64.2%	Change from 2001	2001	Electorate 72,152	Turnout 68%
Taylor R	**IndK**	**18,739**	**39.9%**	**-18.2%**	**IndK**	**28,487**	**58.1%**
Garnier M	C	13,489	28.7%	9.6%	Lab	10,857	22.1%
Bayliss M	Lab	10,716	22.8%	0.7%	C	9,350	19.1%
Oborski F	Lib	2,666	5.7%		UKIP	368	0.8%
Lee R	UKIP	1,074	2.3%	1.5%			
Priest B	Loony	303	0.6%				
Ind KHHC to C swing	**13.9%**	**46,987**		**Ind KHHC maj 5,250** 11.2%		**49,062**	**Ind KHHC maj 17,630** 35.9%

RICHARD TAYLOR b 7 July 1934. MP 2001-. Member Health select cttee 2001-. All-party groups: chair health 2003-, vice-chair local hospitals 2002-, cancer 2002-, flood prevention 2002-. Chair: Save Kidderminster Hospital Campaign 1997-2000, Health Concern 2000-01. Medical career incl RAF medical officer 1961-64, gen medicine consultant with special rheumatology interest Kidderminster gen hospital/Droitwich rheumatic diseases centre 1972-95. Ed BA natural sciences, Clare Coll, Cambridge; BChir, MB, Westminster Medical Sch.

Wyre Forest is a mix of urban and rural areas in Worcestershire. It comprises the three towns of Kidderminster, Stourport and Bewdley and takes its name from the historic Forest of Wyre at the western side of the constituency. It fell to Labour in 1997 after nearly 50 Tory years, but in 2001 was taken by the only independent of that Parliament, Richard Taylor, standing on the local issue of hospital closure, with a huge majority.

WYTHENSHAWE AND SALE EAST — Lab hold

		Electorate 71,766	Turnout 50.4%	Change from 2001	2001	Electorate 72,127	Turnout 48.6%
Goggins P	**Lab**	**18,878**	**52.2%**	**-7.8%**	**Lab**	**21,032**	**60%**
Meehan J	C	8,051	22.2%	-1.8%	C	8,424	24%
Firth A	LD	7,766	21.5%	9.2%	LD	4,320	12.3%
Ford W	UKIP	1,120	3.1%		Greens	869	2.5%
Worthington L	SAP	369	1%		SLP	410	1.2%
Lab to C swing	**3%**	**36,184**		**Lab maj 10,827** 29.9%		**35,055**	**Lab maj 12,608** 36%

PAUL GOGGINS b 16 June 1953. MP 1997-. Parly Under-Sec Home Office 2003-. PPS to: David Blunkett 2000-03, John Denham 1998-2000. Member Social Security select cttee 1997-98. Cllr Salford CC 1990-98. Child worker, national charity director. Member CAFOD board. Ed St Bede's, Manchester; Ushaw Coll, Durham; Residential Care of Children and Young People Cert, Birmingham Poly; Social Work Cert of Qualification, Manchester Poly.

Wythenshawe and Sale East is a constituency whose two parts are quite different from one another. Wythenshawe, an overspill estate from the City of Manchester, is Labour Party territory. The eastern section of the seat includes Sale, a comfortable middle class part of Cheshire from which many commute into Manchester. Boundary changes have weakened Labour's control on balance, but this is still very much a constituency inclined to vote Labour.

YEOVIL — LD hold

		Electorate 77,668	Turnout 64.3%	Change from 2001	2001	Electorate 75,977	Turnout 63.4%
Laws D	**LD**	**25,658**	**51.4%**	**7.2%**	**LD**	**21,266**	**44.2%**
Jenkins I	C	17,096	34.2%	-1.8%	C	17,338	36%
Rolfe C	Lab	5,256	10.5%	-4.2%	Lab	7,077	14.7%
Livings G	UKIP	1,903	3.8%	1.5%	UKIP	1,131	2.3%
					Greens	786	1.6%
					Lib	534	1.1%
C to LD swing	**4.5%**	**49,913**		**LD maj 8,562** 17.2%		**48,132**	**LD maj 3,928** 8.2%

DAVID LAWS b 30 Nov 1965. MP 2001-. Lib Dem Shadow: Sec of State Work and Pensions 2005-, Chief Sec to Treasury 2002-05. Lib Dem defence spokes 2001-02. Member Treasury select cttee 2001-03. Lib Dem parly party: economics 1994-97, policy and research dir 1997-99. Investment banker: vice-pres JP Morgan and Co 1987-92, MD Barclays de Zoete Wedd Ltd 1992-94. Ed St George's Coll, Surrey; BA economics, King's Coll, Cambridge.

The Somerset constituency of Yeovil covers much more territory than merely the town after which it is named. Apart from Yeovil, it takes in Chard, Crewkerne and Ilminster, as well as many picturesque villages. It is home to Westland Helicopters and, until 2001, was represented by the then Liberal Democrat leader Paddy Ashdown. It will need a strong Conservative revival to seriously threaten the Lib Dems in Yeovil.

YNYS MÔN — Lab hold

		Electorate 52,512	Turnout 67.5%	Change from 2001	2001	Electorate 53,398	Turnout 63.7%
Owen A	**Lab**	**12,278**	**34.6%**	**-0.4%**	**Lab**	**11,906**	**35%**
Wyn E	PIC	11,036	31.1%	-1.5%	PIC	11,106	32.6%
Rogers P	Ind	5,216	14.7%	14%	C	7,653	22.5%
Roach J	C	3,915	11%	-11.5%	LD	2,772	8.1%
Green S	LD	2,418	6.8%	-1.3%	UKIP	359	1.1%
Gill E	UKIP	367	1%	-0.1%	Ind	222	0.7%
Evans T	LCA	232	0.6%				
PIC to Lab swing	**0.6%**	**35,462**		**Lab maj 1,242** 3.5%		**34,018**	**Lab maj 800** 2.4%

ALBERT OWEN b 10 Aug 1959. MP 2001-. Member select cttees: Welsh Affairs 2001-, Accommodation and Works 2001-. Constituency Lab Party: vice-chair 1992-96, press officer 1996-2000. Cllr 1997-99. RMT/NUS official 1976-97. Merchant seafarer, welfare rights and employment adviser, Isle of Anglesey CC centre manager. Member: WEA N Wales management cttee 1999-2001, Welsh Affairs Inst. Chair Anglesey regeneration partnership 2000-01. Ed Holyhead County Comp, Anglesey; dip industrial relations, Coleg Harlech; BA politics, York Univ.

Ynys Môn (Isle of Anglesey) is the largest island off the coast of England and Wales. The main town is Holyhead, which is a major port for transport across the Irish Sea. The Westminster seat is currently controlled by Labour, but it has had a mixed political past and is strongly challenged by Plaid Cymru, who hold the seat in the National Assembly for Wales. It seems likely to remain a key Labour–Plaid Cymru marginal.

CITY OF YORK — Lab hold

		Electorate 75,555	Turnout 61.7%	Change from 2001	2001	Electorate 80,431	Turnout 59.7%
Bayley H	**Lab**	**21,836**	**46.9%**	**-5.4%**	**Lab**	**25,072**	**52.3%**
Booth C	C	11,364	24.4%	0.9%	C	11,293	23.5%
Waller A	LD	10,166	21.8%	4%	LD	8,519	17.8%
D'Agorne A	Greens	2,113	4.5%	1.4%	Greens	1,465	3.1%
Jackson R	UKIP	832	1.8%	0.6%	SA	674	1.4%
Curran K	Ind	121	0.3%		UKIP	576	1.2%
Fleck D	DDTP	93	0.2%		Loony	381	0.8%
Hinkles A	Ind	72	0.2%				
Lab to C swing	**3.2%**	**46,597**		**Lab maj 10,472** 22.5%		**47,980**	**Lab maj 13,779** 28.7%

HUGH BAYLEY b 9 Jan 1952. MP for York 1992-97, for City of York 1997-. Soc Security Dept Parly Under-Sec 1999-2001. PPS to Frank Dobson 1997-99. Member select cttees: Health 1992-97, Internat Devt 2001-. Chair all-party Africa group 2003-. Member Inter-Parly Union exec cttee UK branch 1997-99, 2001. Cllr Camden Borough Council 1980-86; York Health Auth 1988-90. NALGO district/national officer 1975-82. General sec Internat Broadcasting Trust 1982-86. Research/lecturerYork Univ 1986-92. Ed BSc pol, Bristol Univ; BPhil York Univ.

The City of York has been attracting tourists for centuries, but there are also manufacturing companies based here, including the confectionery companies Nestlé-Rowntree, Terry's of York and Cadbury. York is a major centre for bioscience (Smith and Nephew, Nestlé, MAFF and others employ more than 1,500 research scientists). York University has established itself as one of the top-ranked universities for research and teaching. This seat was traditionally marginal although it has become more safe for Labour in recent years.

VALE OF YORK — C hold

		Electorate 76,000	Turnout 66.3%	Change from 2001	2001	Electorate 73,335	Turnout 66.1%
McIntosh A	**C**	**26,025**	**51.7%**	**0.1%**	**C**	**25,033**	**51.6%**
Scott D	Lab	12,313	24.4%	-1.4%	Lab	12,516	25.8%
Wilcock J	LD	12,040	23.9%	3.7%	LD	9,799	20.2%
					UKIP	1,142	2.4%
Lab to C swing	**0.8%**	**50,378**		**C maj 13,712** 27.2%		**48,490**	**C maj 12,517** 25.8%

ANNE McINTOSH b 20 Sept 1954. MP 1997-. Shadow Minister: Foreign Affairs 2005-, Environment and Transport 2003-05, Transport 2002-03. Opposition spokes 2001-02. Member select cttees incl: European Scrutiny 2000-03, Transport, Local Govt, Regions 2001-02, Transport 2003-. Exec member 1922 cttee 2000-01. MEP 1989-99. Con transport/tourism spokes 1992-99. Co-chair European transport safety council. Pres Anglia Enterprise in Europe 1989-99. Advocate/adviser. Ed LLB, Edinburgh Univ; European law, Rhus Univ, Denmark.

The mix of affluent market towns, farmland, scenic countryside and stately homes in this part of North Yorkshire is certainly conducive to Tory success. The unemployment rate is among the lowest in England and Wales, and council housing accounts for less than 10 per cent of the total.

YORKSHIRE EAST — C hold

		Electorate 76,648	Turnout 61.2%	Change from 2001	2001	Electorate 72,052	Turnout 60.1%
Knight G	**C**	**21,215**	**45.2%**	**-0.7%**	**C**	**19,861**	**45.9%**
Hoddinott E	Lab	14,932	31.8%	-3.2%	Lab	15,179	35%
Wastling J	LD	9,075	19.3%	4.8%	LD	6,300	14.5%
Tressider C	UKIP	1,703	3.6%	-0.2%	UKIP	1,661	3.8%
					Ind	313	0.7%
Lab to C swing	**1.3%**	**46,925**		**C maj 6,283** 13.4%		**43,314**	**C maj 4,682** 10.8%

GREG KNIGHT b 4 April 1949. MP for Derby North 1983-97, for Yorkshire East 2001-. Shadow Minister: Transport 2005-, Environ and Transport 2003-05, Culture, Media and Sport 2003; Dep Shadow Leader of House 2002-03; Minister of State: Dept of Trade and Industry 1996-97; David Mellor PPS 1987-89. Govt whip 1989-96. Select cttees: member, chair ODPM 1993-2002. Chair all-party groups. Vice-chair Con parly candidates assocn 1997-2001. Cllr: Leicester CC 1976-79, Leics CC 1977-83. Solicitor. PC 1995. Ed London and Guildford Law Colleges.

This safe Conservative seat comprises a large agricultural area touching the boundaries of York's unitary authority. There are a high number of owner-occupiers and private renters among the ageing population. Bridlington is a fishing port, seaside resort and shopping centre. To the north are the cliffs of Flamborough Head, a notable tourist attraction. Inland is the rolling countryside of the Wolds with numerous villages and the small towns of Driffield, Market Weighton and Pocklington.

NOT MANY CONTESTS BUT SOME MIGHTY RESULTS ALL THE SAME

by **Tim Hames**
Assistant Editor, The Times

The distinguishing features of by-elections during Tony Blair's first term of office were that they were relatively infrequent, mostly somewhat unspectacular in their outcomes and the turnout was often dire. A relatively modest number of 17 were held and in 1998 there were none at all, the first time that a year had passed without such a poll since the Great Reform Act of 1832. Labour held all the nine seats they were obliged to defend and in only two Scottish seats (Hamilton South and Falkirk West) did their majority fall below four figures. The Conservatives endured a spectacular defeat to the Liberal Democrats in Romsey. The level of voter participation plunged with the Leeds Central by-election witnessing a turnout of a meagre 19.6 per cent – the lowest ever figure for a peacetime by-election.

The 2001-05 Parliament was different. The number of contests held actually slumped further. A mere six were held in total. This is easily the lowest tally recorded for a four-year Parliament. Whether this reflects the fact that MPs are now healthier or younger or (improbably) working less hard is unclear, but it was still a striking pattern. Furthermore, two of the six by-elections which did occur were triggered by resignation and not the death of the sitting member. Had not Terry Davis and Peter Mandelson sought positions with the Council of Europe and the European Commission respectively then by-elections would have averaged one a year during this period. Not much for political enthusiasts to sink their teeth into.

Secondly, while these by-elections were few in number at least some of them were extremely interesting. Labour lost two seats (Brent East and Leicester South) and came very close to being defeated in Birmingham Hodge Hill as well. In each instance, nonetheless, the Liberal Democrats and not the Conservatives proved to be the principal challenger to the Government, pushing the Tories back into third place in every example. In Hartlepool, the hapless Conservative contender was forced into a humiliating fourth place by the candidate from the anti-EU UK Independence Party. Iain Duncan Smith and then Michael Howard must have been relieved that the Tories did not have to defend a single by-election in this Parliament. Had one occurred in any place where the Liberal Democrats were remotely credible then a damaging defeat could easily have occurred.

The most positive development, though, was that the collapse in turnout was partially reversed. Although participation rates ranging from 35.3 per cent (in the very solid Welsh Labour seat of Ogmore) to 46 per cent (in Hartlepool) can hardly be described as a triumph for democracy, these numbers were all better than six of the by-elections between 1997 and 2001.

The narrative of the by-elections of this Parliament runs as follows. The first was held within six months of the general election. Jamie Cann, the sitting Labour MP for **Ipswich**, had been ill for some time. His death might, in different political circumstances, have triggered a serious political battle between the two major parties. It did not. Chris Mole, an effective politician, held the seat for Mr Blair comfortably. The Liberal Democrats did not expend that much effort in the seat but were not very far from pushing the Tories into third place.

Less than three months later – in February 2002 – another campaign occurred in **Ogmore**. The death of the veteran Labour MP, Sir Raymond Powell, opened up a plum constituency. Although Plaid Cymru might have hoped to make a fist of it, Labour won by a street, the Welsh Nationalists were second, the Liberal Democrats came third and the Tories just held off the Socialist Labour contender to secure fourth place. Huw Irranca-Davies thus became the local MP and acquired employment for life.

A very long period then passed – 19 months in fact – before the next by-election. This was also a period in which Iraq dominated British politics with, first, the highly controversial build-up to war, then the conflict itself followed by the unexpectedly awkward aftermath and the failure to find actual weapons of mass destruction. Alas, one MP, Paul Daisley, could do little to influence proceedings. Having replaced Ken Livingstone as Labour MP for the safe seat of **Brent East** in June 2001 he almost immediately fell victim to a debilitating and evidently incurable disease. He finally succumbed to it in June 2003, a sad loss to his family and the Labour Party.

At this point Labour strategists made a major miscalculation. They had the option of calling a snap by-election in July but decided not to do so for fear of an embarrassingly feeble turnout. By delaying into the late summer, paradoxically, they enabled the Liberal Democrats to build up a local organisation and to acquire momentum. Charles Kennedy took the quite brave decision to make several early high-profile visits to the constituency. He found a young local candidate, Sarah Teather, with a popular touch and she in turn was helped by her leader's vocal opposition to the Iraq intervention. A phenomenal swing allowed Ms Teather to seize the seat – becoming the youngest member of the House of Commons as she did – and for the Liberal Democrats to seize a famous victory. The distinctly uninspiring Conservative showing put in train a series of events which would lead to Iain Duncan Smith's departure as the Tory leader.

Labour was now in legitimate fear of the 'yellow peril' in by-elections. Mr Kennedy's crew seemed well placed to run them close in almost any constituency. In the spring of 2004 Terry Davis, MP for **Birmingham Hodge Hill**, made it plain that he would stand down and the death of James Marshall in **Leicester South** forced Mr Blair's hand. This time it was decided that Labour had better hold the by-elections as quickly as possible and on the same date (15 July) in an attempt to stretch limited Liberal Democrat resources. The Labour team in Birmingham decided to run a no-holds-barred onslaught on the Liberal Democrats, while in Leicester South, a seat with a large anti-war Asian minority, it quickly became plain that the contest would be a referendum on the Government's decision to back George W. Bush in Iraq. Very large swings occurred in each seat but in Hodge Hill Labour started with a robust enough majority to survive by 460 votes. Liam Byrne was duly elected. In Leicester, by contrast, the Liberal Democrats stormed home by a rather comfortable 1,654 votes. Parmjit Singh Gill became the MP. The Tories finished a somewhat poor third in each constituency.

The final battle of the Parliament took place in **Hartlepool**. The resignation of Peter Mandelson left Labour with a dilemma. The party appealed to the deeply-held Labour sentiments of the seat, hoped that the character of the constituency (essentially white working-class) would limit the impact of the anti-war factor and roughed up the Liberal Democrat champion, Jody Dunn, with scant mercy. As a result, Iain Wright, a sturdy local Labour man, managed to succeed Mr Mandelson as the Member of Parliament. He claimed this to be a famous victory. In the context of the three previous campaigns alone then it was. By any other standard it brought to an end an extremely uncomfortable period at the by-election polls for the Prime Minister and the Labour Party

2001

22 November: IPSWICH

Caused by the death of Labour MP Jamie Cann

Chris Mole (Lab)	**11,881**
Paul West (C)	7,794
Tessa Munt (LD)	6,146
Dave Cooper (Christian People's Alliance)	581
Jonathan Wright (UKIP)	276
Tony Slade (Green Party)	255
John Ramirez (Legalise Cannabis Alliance)	236
Peter Leech (Socialist Alliance)	152
Nicholas Winskill (English Independence Party)	84

Lab majority 4,087 – Lab hold
Electorate 68,244 – Total vote 27,477
Turnout 40.1%

2002

14 February: OGMORE

Caused by the death of Labour MP Sir Raymond Powell

Huw Irranca-Davies (Lab)	**9,548**
Bleddyn Hancock (PlC)	3,827
Veronica Watkins (LD)	1,608
Guto Bebb (C)	1,377
Chris Herriot (Socialist Labour)	1,152
Jonathan Spink (Green)	250
Jeff Hurford (Socialist Alliance)	205
Leslie Edwards (Official Monster Raving Loony Party)	187
New Millennium Bean Party	122
David Braid (Ind)	100

Lab majority 5,721 – Lab hold
Electorate 52,209 – Total vote 18,410
Turnout 35.3%

2003

18 September: BRENT EAST

Caused by the death of Labour MP Paul Daisley

Sarah Teather (LD)	**8,158**
Robert Evans (Lab)	7,040
Uma Fernandes (C)	3,368
Noel Lynch (Green)	638
Brian Butterworth (Socialist Alliance)	361
Khidori Fawzi Ibrahim (Public Services Not War)	219
Winston McKenzie (Ind)	197
Kelly McBride (Ind)	189
Harold Immanuel (Ind Lab)	188
Brian Hall (UKIP)	140
Iris Cremer (Socialist Labour Party)	111
Alan Howling Lord Hope (Monster Raving Loony Party)	59
Aaron Barschack	37
Jiten Bardwaj	35
George Weiss (www.xat.org Rainbow)	11

LD majority 1,118 – LD gain from Lab
Turnout 36.4%

2004

15 July: BIRMINGHAM HODGE HILL

Caused by Labour MP Terry Davis standing down

Liam Byrne (Lab)	**7,451**
Nicola Davies (LD)	6,991
Stephen Eyre (C)	3,543
John Rees (Respect)	1,282
James Starkey (National Front)	805
Mark Wheatley (English Democrats)	277
James Hargreaves (Operation Christian Vote)	90

Lab majority 460 – Lab hold
Turnout 37.9%

15 July: LEICESTER SOUTH

Caused by the death of Labour MP James Marshall

Parmjit Singh Gill (LD)	**10,274**
Peter Soulsby (Lab)	8,620
Christopher Heaton-Harris (C)	5,796
Yvonne Ridley (Respect)	3,724
David Roberts (Socialist Labour)	263
RU Seerius (Official Monster Raving Loony Party)	225
Patrick Kennedy (Ind)	204
Paul Lord (Ind)	186
Mark Benson (Ind)	55
Jiten Bardwaj (Ind)	36
Alan Barratt (Ind)	25

LD majority 1,654 – LD gain from Lab
Turnout 41.6%

30 September: HARTLEPOOL

Caused by the resignation of Labour MP Peter Mandelson

Iain Wright (Lab)	**12,752**
Jody Dunn (LD)	10,719
Stephen Allison UKIP)	3,193
Jeremy Middleton (C)	3,044
John Bloom (Respect)	572
Iris Ryder (Green)	255
James Starkey (National Front)	246
Paul Watson (Fathers4Justice)	139
Christopher Herriot (Socialist Labour)	95
Richard Rodgers (Common Good)	91
Philip Berriman (Ind)	90
Alan Hope (Official Monster Raving Loony Party)	80
Ronnie Carroll (Ind)	45
Edward Abrams (English Democrats)	41

Lab majority 2,033 – Lab hold
Turnout 46%

STATISTICS

HOW THE NATION VOTED

MAY 2005			Lab	C	LD	Nat	Other	Total
UNITED KINGDOM								
Electorate	44,261,545	Votes	9,547,944*	8,772,473	5,981,874	587,105	2,234,256†	27,123,652
Lab to C swing %	3.1	% of vote/Turnout	35.2	32.3	22.1	2.2	8.2	61.3
		MPs	355	197	62	9	22	645
		Candidates	626	629	625	99	1,567	3,546
ENGLAND								
Electorate	36,963,191	Votes	8,045,874	8,102,537	5,197,549	0	1,333,484	22,679,444
Lab to C swing %	3.2	% of vote/Turnout	35.5	35.7	22.9	0	5.9	61.2
		MPs	286	193	47	0	2	528
		Candidates	528	528	527	0	1,226	2,809
SCOTLAND								
Electorate	3,851,290	Votes	907,249*	369,388	528,076	412,267	116,907†	2,333,887
Lab to LD swing %	5.6	% of vote/Turnout	38.9	15.8	22.6	17.7	5	60.6
		MPs	41	1	11	6	1	59
		Candidates	58	58	58	59	149	382
WALES								
Electorate	2,231,880	Votes	594,821	297,830	256,249	174,838	68,981	1,392,719
Lab to Con swing %	3.2	% of vote/Turnout	42.7	21.4	18.4	12.6	5.0	62.4
		MPs	29	3	4	3	1	40
		Candidates	40	40	40	40	90	250
NORTHERN IRELAND								
Electorate	1,148,003	Votes	0	2,718	0	0	714,884	717,602
SF to DUP swing %	6.9	% of vote/Turnout	0	0.4	0	0	99.6	62.5
		MPs	0	0	0	0	18	18
		Candidates	0	3	0	0	102	105

JUNE 2001			Lab	C	LD	Nat	Other	Total
UNITED KINGDOM								
Electorate	44,377,752	Votes	10,740,648*	8,357,292	4,816,137	660,207	1,794,246†	26,368,530
Lab to C swing %	1.8	% of vote/Turnout	40.7	31.7	18.3	2.5	6.8	59.4
		MPs	412	166	52	9	20	659
		Candidates	640	643	639	112	1,211	3,133
ENGLAND								
Electorate	36,976,985	Votes	9,056,466	7,705,589	4,246,849	0	861,225	21,870,129
Lab to C swing %	1.8	% of vote/Turnout	41.4	35.2	19.4	0	4.0	59.1
		MPs	323	165	40	0	1	529
		Candidates	529	529	528	0	1,002	2,588
SCOTLAND								
Electorate	3,980,974	Votes	1,017,226*	360,658	380,034	464,314	93,471†	2,315,703
C to Lab swing %	0.1	% of vote/Turnout	43.9	15.6	16.4	20.1	4.0	58.2
		MPs	55	1	10	5	1	72
		Candidates	71	71	71	72	48	333
WALES								
Electorate	2,228,723	Votes	666,956	288,623	189,254	195,893	31,598	1,372,324
Lab to C swing %	3.75	% of vote/Turnout	48.6	21	13.8	14.3	2.3	61.6
		MPs	34	0	2	4	0	40
		Candidates	40	40	40	40	64	224
NORTHERN IRELAND								
Electorate	1,191,070	Votes	0	2,422	0	0	807,952	810,374
		% of vote/Turnout	0.0	0.2	0.0	0.0	99.8	68.0
		MPs	0	0	0	0	18	18
		Candidates	0	3	0	0	97	100

*Excludes Speaker †Includes Speaker

METROPOLITAN AND COUNTY VOTING

by Tim Hames

Elections in Britain have become very complicated geographical affairs. The battle of 2005 proved no different, indeed it reinforced the trend. The performance of the three main parties varied considerably across the country. This was true for both metropolitan areas and the counties.

As far as metropolitan England is concerned, this was a tale of two elections. The pattern in the capital city was distinct from that of every other urban area. In London the Labour vote fell more sharply than anywhere else and the Conservative Party managed a modest but not an insignificant recovery. This was particularly true in the more affluent outer London area.

For the rest of metropolitan England, by contrast, the story was of a fall in the Labour vote, although not on the scale recorded in London, but also of a decline in backing for the Conservative Party as well and an increase for the Liberal Democrats in all of Greater Manchester, Merseyside, Tyne and Wear, the West Midlands, South Yorkshire and West Yorkshire. The various 'others' also pushed up their proportion of the vote in every area bar Merseyside. These are results about which Conservative strategists, in particular, should be concerned.

The results for the counties inevitably varied considerably but a few broad patterns emerge as well. The Tories did best in the places where they were very strong before the 1997 meltdown - with a clear improvement in their position all around the Home Counties. They were far less impressive in the west of England (with the exception of Cornwall), East Anglia, the East and West Midlands (with a counterexample in Warwickshire) and in the north of England as well.

If Michael Howard had been as popular (and Tony Blair as unpopular) north of Milton Keynes as he was south of that settlement, then a hung parliament would have been a very serious possibility. If the south had followed the north, on the other hand, Labour might had a majority of 120 seats. It is unlikely that the Conservatives will secure a majority in the House of Commons at the next election if they do not deal with the regional weaknesses which have been highlighted by this one.

INNER LONDON				Lab	C	LD	Other	Total
2005	**Electorate**	**1,658,296**	Votes	388,169	229,863	199,891	89,989	907,912
	Turnout %	**54.7**	Votes %	42.8	25.3	22	9.9	100
	Swing %	**5.5**	Seats	19	4	1	1	25
	Lab to C		Candidates	25	25	25	90	165
2001	**Electorate**	**1,681,441**	Votes	439,614	201,223	144,512	51,418	836,767
	Turnout %	**49.8**	Votes %	52.5	24	17.3	6.1	100
			Seats	22	2	1	0	25
			Candidates	25	25	25	70	145
			% Change 2001-05	-9.7	1.3	4.7	3.8	

Battersea, Bethnal Green and Bow, Camberwell and Peckham, Cities of London and Westminster, Dulwich and West Norwood, Eltham, Greenwich and Woolwich, Hackney North and Stoke Newington, Hackney South and Shoreditch, Hammersmith and Fulham, Hampstead and Highgate, Holborn and St Pancras, Islington North, Islington South and Finsbury, Kensington and Chelsea, Lewisham Deptford, Lewisham East, Lewisham West, North Southwark and Bermondsey, Poplar and Canning Town, Putney, Regent's Park and Kensington North, Streatham, Tooting, Vauxhall

OUTER LONDON				Lab	C	LD	Other	Total
2005	Electorate	3,351,992	Votes	748,418	702,103	438,442	122,217	2,011,180
	Turnout %	60	Votes %	37.2	34.9	21.8	6.1	100
	Swing %	4.8	Seats	25	17	7	0	49
	Lab to C		Candidates	49	49	49	145	292
2001	Electorate	3,334,339	Votes	867,211	640,528	338,376	77,447	1,923,562
	Turnout %	57.7	Votes %	45.1	33.3	17.6	4	100
			Seats	33	11	5	0	49
			Candidates	49	49	49	110	257
			% Change 2001-05	-7.9	1.6	4.2	2.1	

Barking, Beckenham, Bexleyheath and Crayford, Brent East, Brent North, Brent South, Brentford and Isleworth, Bromley and Chislehurst, Carshalton and Wallington, Chingford and Woodford Green, Chipping Barnet, Croydon Central, Croydon North, Croydon South, Dagenham, Ealing North, Ealing Southall, Ealing, Acton and Shepherd's Bush, East Ham, Edmonton, Enfield North, Enfield Southgate, Erith and Thamesmead, Feltham and Heston, Finchley and Golders Green, Harrow East, Harrow West, Hayes and Harlington, Hendon, Hornchurch, Hornsey and Wood Green, Ilford North, Ilford South, Kingston and Surbiton, Leyton and Wanstead, Mitcham and Morden, Old Bexley and Sidcup, Orpington, Richmond Park, Romford, Ruislip Northwood, Sutton and Cheam, Tottenham, Twickenham, Upminster, Uxbridge, Walthamstow, West Ham, Wimbledon

GREATER MANCHESTER				Lab	C	LD	Other	Total
2005	Electorate	1,887,012	Votes	484,104	243,162	239,389	59,663	1,026,318
	Turnout %	54.4	Votes %	47.2	23.7	23.3	5.8	100
	Swing %	3.0	Seats	23	1	4	0	28
	Lab to C		Candidates	28	28	28	68	152
2001	Electorate	1,904,994	Votes	540,982	245,361	184,334	37,573	1,008,250
	Turnout %	52.9	Votes %	53.7	24.3	18.3	3.7	100
			Seats	25	1	2	0	28
			Candidates	28	28	28	40	124
			% Change 2001-05	-6.5	-0.6	5	2.1	

Altrincham and Sale West, Ashton under Lyne, Bolton North East, Bolton South East, Bolton West, Bury North, Bury South, Cheadle - by election pending, Denton and Reddish, Eccles, Hazel Grove, Heywood and Middleton, Leigh, Makerfield, Manchester Blackley, Manchester Central, Manchester Gorton, Manchester Withington, Oldham East and Saddleworth, Oldham West and Royton, Rochdale, Salford, Stalybridge and Hyde, Stockport, Stretford and Urmston, Wigan, Worsley, Wythenshawe and Sale East

MERSEYSIDE				Lab	C	LD	Other	Total
2005	Electorate	1,027,745	Votes	299,373	108,038	127,213	21,758	556,382
	Turnout %	54.1	Votes %	53.8	19.4	22.9	3.9	100
	Swing %	5.0	Seats	15	0	1	0	16
	Lab to LD		Candidates	16	16	16	31	79
2001	Electorate	1,056,371	Votes	321,552	109,965	97,247	18,624	547,388
	Turnout %	51.8	Votes %	58.7	20.1	17.8	3.4	100
			Seats	15	0	1	0	16
			Candidates	16	16	16	22	70
			% Change 2001-05	-4.9	-0.7	5.1	0.5	

Birkenhead, Bootle, Crosby, Knowsley North and Sefton East, Knowsley South, Liverpool Garston, Liverpool Riverside, Liverpool Walton, Liverpool Wavertree, Liverpool West Derby, Southport, St Helens North, St Helens South, Wallasey, Wirral South, Wirral West

TYNE AND WEAR				Lab	C	LD	Other	Total
2005	Electorate	798,997	Votes	248,024	77,484	103,002	15,937	444,447
	Turnout %	55.6	Votes %	55.8	17.4	23.2	3.6	100
	Swing %	6.9	Seats	13	0	0	0	13
	Lab to LD		Candidates	13	13	13	17	56
2001	Electorate	827,233	Votes	277,905	78,088	73,339	12,280	441,612
	Turnout %	53.4	Votes %	62.9	17.7	16.6	2.8	100
			Seats	13	0	0	0	13
			Candidates	13	13	13	22	61
			% Change 2001-05	-7.1	-0.3	6.6	0.8	

Blaydon, Gateshead East and Washington West, Houghton and Washington East, Jarrow, Newcastle upon Tyne Central, Newcastle upon Tyne East and Wallsend, Newcastle upon Tyne North, North Tyneside, South Shields, Sunderland North, Sunderland South, Tyne Bridge, Tynemouth

WEST MIDLANDS				Lab	C	LD	Other	Total
2005	Electorate	1,887,180	Votes	483,278	320,802	196,894	87,804	1,088,778
	Turnout %	57.7	Votes %	44.4	29.5	18.1	8.1	100
	Swing %	2.9	Seats	24	3	2	0	29
	Lab to C		Candidates	29	29	29	66	153
2001	Electorate	1,908,113	Votes	535,187	319,267	136,493	53,085	1,044,032
	Turnout %	54.7	Votes %	51.3	30.6	13.1	5.1	100
			Seats	25	4	0	0	29
			Candidates	29	29	29	68	155
			% Change 2001-05	-6.9	-1.1	5	3	

Aldridge-Brownhills, Birmingham Edgbaston, Birmingham Erdington, Birmingham Hall Green, Birmingham Hodge Hill, Birmingham Ladywood, Birmingham Northfield, Birmingham Perry Barr, Birmingham Selly Oak, Birmingham Sparkbrook and Small Heath, Birmingham Yardley, Coventry North East, Coventry North West, Coventry South, Dudley North, Dudley South, Halesowen and Rowley Regis, Meriden, Solihull, Stourbridge, Sutton Coldfield, Walsall North, Walsall South, Warley, West Bromwich East, West Bromwich West, Wolverhampton North East, Wolverhampton South East, Wolverhampton South West

SOUTH YORKSHIRE				Lab	C	LD	Other	Total
2005	Electorate	949,043	Votes	273,199	93,223	110,683	41,287	518,392
	Turnout %	54.6	Votes %	52.7	18	21.4	8	100
	Swing %	4.8	Seats	13	0	1	0	14
	Lab to LD		Candidates	15	15	15	34	79
2001	Electorate	954,478	Votes	296,403	94,503	90,624	21,282	502,812
	Turnout %	52.7	Votes %	58.9	18.8	18	4.2	100
			Seats	14	0	1	0	15
			Candidates	15	15	15	30	75
			% Change 2001-05	-6.2	-0.8	3.4	3.8	

Barnsley Central, Barnsley East and Mexborough, Barnsley West and Penistone, Don Valley, Doncaster Central, Doncaster North, Rother Valley, Rotherham, Sheffield Attercliffe, Sheffield Brightside, Sheffield Central, Sheffield Hallam, Sheffield Heeley, Sheffield Hillsborough, Wentworth

WEST YORKSHIRE				Lab	C	LD	Other	Total
2005	Electorate	1,528,562	Votes	420,768	254,749	170,096	70,616	916,229
	Turnout %	59.9	Votes %	45.9	27.8	18.6	7.7	100
	Swing %	3.9	Seats	21	1	1	0	23
	Lab to C		Candidates	23	23	23	57	126
2005	Electorate	1,558,879	Votes	456,341	265,615	123,533	40,026	885,515
	Turnout %	56.8	Votes %	51.5	30	14	4.5	100
			Seats	23	0	0	0	23
			Candidates	23	23	23	52	121
			% Change 2001-05	-5.6	2.2	4.6	3.2	

Batley and Spen, Bradford North, Bradford South, Bradford West, Calder Valley, Colne Valley, Dewsbury, Elmet, Halifax, Hemsworth, Huddersfield, Keighley, Leeds Central, Leeds East, Leeds North East, Leeds North West, Leeds West, Morley and Rothwell, Normanton, Pontefract and Castleford, Pudsey, Shipley, Wakefield

NON-METROPOLITAN TABLES

As noted earlier, the Home Counties were more receptive to the Conservative message (and more hostile to Labour) than counties elsewhere. This difference was reflected in the results of the county council elections which, for the third time running, were held on the same day as the general election.

Constituencies in England do not necessarily fall within a single county, as they did before local government re-organisation in the late 1990s. County names for English seats are as they applied when current constituencies boundaries were established before the 1997 general election. Thus, for instance, 'Avon', 'Cleveland' and 'Humberside' appear, although they have since been abolished. The Isle of Wight is still one seat; its detailed analysis is in the election results.

AVON				Lab	C	LD	Other	Total
2005	Electorate	747,961	Votes	159,626	160,070	155,107	26,982	501,785
	Turnout %	67.1	Votes %	31.8	31.9	30.9	5.4	100
	Swing %	2.7	Seats	5	2	3	0	10
	Lab to C		Candidates	10	10	10	30	60
2001	Electorate	751,426	Votes	177,782	152,030	134,170	19,185	483,167
	Turnout %	64.3	Votes %	36.8	31.5	27.8	4	100
			Seats	6	1	3	0	10
			Candidates	10	10	10	25	55
			% Change 2001-05	-5	0.4	3.1	1.4	

Bath, Bristol East, Bristol North West, Bristol South, Bristol West, Kingswood, Northavon, Wansdyke, Weston-Super-Mare, Woodspring

BEDFORDSHIRE				Lab	C	LD	Other	Total
2005	Electorate	431,374	Votes	90,891	107,893	53,955	13,112	265,851
	Turnout %	61.6	Votes %	34.2	40.6	20.3	4.9	100
	Swing %	4.9	Seats	3	3	0	0	6
	Lab to C		Candidates	6	6	6	15	33
2001	Electorate	415,446	Votes	109,113	100,265	37,599	7,817	254,794
	Turnout %	61.3	Votes %	42.8	39.4	14.8	3.1	100
			Seats	3	3	0	0	6
			Candidates	6	6	6	10	28
			% Change 2001-05	-8.6	1.2	5.5	1.8	

Bedford, Luton North, Luton South, Mid Bedfordshire, North East Bedfordshire, South West Bedfordshire

BERKSHIRE				Lab	C	LD	Other	Total
2005	Electorate	570,854	Votes	87,628	158,796	99,829	18,286	364,539
	Turnout %	63.9	Votes %	24	43.6	27.4	5	100
	Swing %	1.0	Seats	2	6	0	0	8
	LD to C		Candidates	8	8	8	25	49
2001	Electorate	587,463	Votes	108,675	142,280	91,960	11,002	353,917
	Turnout %	60.2	Votes %	30.7	40.2	26	3.1	100
			Seats	3	4	1	0	8
			Candidates	8	8	8	16	40
			% Change 2001-05	-6.7	3.4	1.4	1.9	

Bracknell, Maidenhead, Newbury, Reading East, Reading West, Slough, Windsor, Wokingham

BUCKINGHAMSHIRE				Lab	C	LD	Other	Total
2005	Electorate	522,443	Votes	86,342	159,603	70,867	16,814	333,626
	Turnout %	63.9	Votes %	25.9	47.8	21.2	5	100
	Swing %	3.6	Seats	1	6	0	0	7
	Lab to C		Candidates	7	7	7	12	33
2001	Electorate	504,216	Votes	98,165	145,128	63,221	12,724	319,238
	Turnout %	63.3	Votes %	30.7	45.5	19.8	4	100
			Seats	2	5	0	0	7
			Candidates	7	7	7	14	35
			% Change 2001-05	-4.8	2.3	1.4	1	

Aylesbury, Beaconsfield, Buckingham, Chesham and Amersham, Milton Keynes North East, Milton Keynes South West, Wycombe

CAMBRIDGESHIRE				Lab	C	LD	Other	Total
2005	Electorate	549,192	Votes	89,334	147,938	93,177	15,419	345,868
	Turnout %	63	Votes %	25.8	42.8	26.9	4.5	100
	Swing %	2.9	Seats	0	6	1	0	7
	C to LD		Candidates	7	7	7	13	34
2001	Electorate	520,769	Votes	104,506	138,798	68,824	11,843	323,971
	Turnout %	62.2	Votes %	32.3	42.8	21.2	3.7	100
			Seats	2	5	0	0	7
			Candidates	7	7	7	15	36
			% Change 2001-05	-6.5	0	5.7	0.8	

Cambridge, Huntingdon, North East Cambridgeshire, North West Cambridgeshire, Peterborough, South Cambridgeshire, South East Cambridgeshire

CHESHIRE				Lab	C	LD	Other	Total
2005	Electorate	774,459	Votes	190,764	174,678	95,576	9,648	470,666
	Turnout %	60.8	Votes %	40.5	37.1	20.3	2	100
	Swing %	3.7	Seats	7	4	0	0	11
	Lab to C		Candidates	11	11	11	12	45
2001	Electorate	765,508	Votes	214,236	164,470	72,118	11,609	462,433
	Turnout %	60.4	Votes %	46.3	35.6	15.6	2.5	100
			Seats	7	4	0	0	11
			Candidates	11	11	11	16	49
			% Change 2001-05	-5.8	1.5	4.7	-0.5	

City of Chester, Congleton, Crewe and Nantwich, Eddisbury, Ellesmere Port and Neston, Halton, Macclesfield, Tatton, Warrington North, Warrington South, Weaver Vale

CLEVELAND				Lab	C	LD	Other	Total
2005	Electorate	408,087	Votes	120,218	53,136	44,709	13,421	231,484
	Turnout %	56.7	Votes %	51.9	23	19.3	5.8	100
	Swing %	2.1	Seats	6	0	0	0	6
	Lab to C		Candidates	6	6	6	18	36
2001	Electorate	408,974	Votes	138,520	61,092	28,966	5,015	233,593
	Turnout %	57.1	Votes %	59.3	26.2	12.4	2.1	100
			Seats	6	0	0	0	6
			Candidates	6	6	6	8	26
			% Change 2001-05	-7.4	-3.2	6.9	3.7	

Hartlepool, Middlesbrough, Middlesbrough South and East Cleveland, Redcar, Stockton North, Stockton South

CORNWALL				Lab	C	LD	Other	Total
2005	Electorate	394,026	Votes	41,140	82,543	115,241	20,509	259,433
	Turnout %	65.8	Votes %	15.9	31.8	44.4	7.9	100
	Swing %	0.2	Seats	0	0	5	0	5
	C to LD		Candidates	5	5	5	16	31
2001	Electorate	389,488	Votes	43,674	82,227	113,000	13,216	252,117
	Turnout %	64.7	Votes %	17.3	32.6	44.8	5.2	100
			Seats	1	0	4	0	5
			Candidates	5	5	5	10	25
			% Change 2001-05	-1.4	-0.8	-0.4	2.7	

Falmouth and Camborne, North Cornwall, South East Cornwall, St Ives, Truro and St Austell

CUMBRIA				Lab	C	LD	Other	Total
2005	Electorate	377,323	Votes	83,720	92,367	56,452	9,360	241,899
	Turnout %	64.1	Votes %	34.6	38.2	23.3	3.9	100
	Swing %	1.4	Seats	4	1	1	0	6
	Lab to C		Candidates	6	6	6	15	33
2001	Electorate	382,290	Votes	94,191	96,163	46,736	5,563	242,653
	Turnout %	63.5	Votes %	38.8	39.6	19.3	2.3	100
			Seats	4	2	0	0	6
			Candidates	6	6	6	9	27
			% Change 2001-05	-4.2	-1.4	4	1.6	

Barrow and Furness, Carlisle, Copeland, Penrith and The Border, Westmorland and Lonsdale, Workington

DERBYSHIRE				Lab	C	LD	Other	Total
2005	Electorate	739,067	Votes	205,740	140,870	100,008	21,723	468,341
	Turnout %	63.4	Votes %	43.9	30.1	21.4	4.6	100
	Swing %	2.6	Seats	8	1	1	0	10
	Lab to C		Candidates	10	10	10	21	51
2001	Electorate	746,633	Votes	227,768	141,717	79,845	6,392	455,722
	Turnout %	61	Votes %	50	31.1	17.5	1.4	100
			Seats	8	1	1	0	10
			Candidates	10	10	10	13	43
			% Change 2001-05	-6.1	-1	3.9	3.2	

Amber Valley, Bolsover, Chesterfield, Derby North, Derby South, Erewash, High Peak, North East Derbyshire, South Derbyshire, West Derbyshire

DEVON				Lab	C	LD	Other	Total
2005	Electorate	850,280	Votes	114,560	213,544	183,623	49,136	560,863
	Turnout %	66	Votes %	20.4	38.1	32.7	8.8	100
	Swing %	0.9	Seats	3	5	3	0	11
	C to LD		Candidates	11	11	11	25	58
2001	Electorate	829,623	Votes	128,599	212,576	173,639	30,182	544,996
	Turnout %	65.7	Votes %	23.6	39	31.9	5.5	100
			Seats	3	4	4	0	11
			Candidates	11	11	11	22	55
			% Change 2001-05	-3.2	-0.9	0.8	3.3	

East Devon, Exeter, North Devon, Plymouth Devonport, Plymouth Sutton, South West Devon, Teignbridge, Tiverton and Honiton, Torbay, Torridge and West Devon, Totnes

DORSET				Lab	C	LD	Other	Total
2005	Electorate	546,013	Votes	66,614	160,175	119,358	17,237	363,384
	Turnout %	66.6	Votes %	18.3	44.1	32.8	4.7	100
	Swing %	1.3	Seats	1	6	1	0	8
	C to LD		Candidates	8	8	8	16	40
2001	Electorate	538,076	Votes	72,715	156,222	108,426	7,339	344,702
	Turnout %	64.1	Votes %	21.1	45.3	31.5	2.1	100
			Seats	1	6	1	0	8
			Candidates	8	8	8	9	33
			% Change 2001-05	-2.8	-1.2	1.3	2.6	

Bournemouth East, Bournemouth West, Christchurch, Mid Dorset and Poole North, North Dorset, Poole, South Dorset, West Dorset

DURHAM				Lab	C	LD	Other	Total
2005	Electorate	467,642	Votes	153,042	45,247	57,993	15,786	272,068
	Turnout %	58.2	Votes %	56.3	16.6	21.3	5.8	100
	Swing %	6.9	Seats	7	0	0	0	7
	Lab to LD		Candidates	7	7	7	19	40
2001	Electorate	462,838	Votes	170,329	55,254	38,533	6,890	271,006
	Turnout %	58.6	Votes %	62.9	20.4	14.2	2.5	100
			Seats	7	0	0	0	7
			Candidates	7	7	7	11	32
			% Change 2001-05	-6.6	-3.8	7.1	3.3	

Bishop Auckland, City of Durham, Darlington, Durham North, Easington, North West Durham, Sedgefield

ESSEX				Lab	C	LD	Other	Total
2005	Electorate	1,253,913	Votes	226,309	359,535	149,310	47,046	782,200
	Turnout %	62.4	Votes %	28.9	46	19.1	6	100
	Swing %	4.5	Seats	3	13	1	0	17
	Lab to C		Candidates	17	17	17	37	88
2001	Electorate	1,236,293	Votes	255,526	315,589	122,663	42,887	736,665
	Turnout %	59.6	Votes %	34.7	42.8	16.7	5.8	100
			Seats	5	11	1	0	17
			Candidates	17	17	17	33	84
			% Change 2001-05	-5.8	3.2	2.4	0.2	

Basildon, Billericay, Braintree, Brentwood and Ongar, Castle Point, Chelmsford West, Colchester, Epping Forest, Harlow, Harwich, Maldon and Chelmsford East, North Essex, Rayleigh, Rochford and Southend East, Saffron Walden, Southend West, Thurrock

GLOUCESTERSHIRE				Lab	C	LD	Other	Total
2005	Electorate	444,198	Votes	85,714	122,002	68,243	16,784	292,743
	Turnout %	65.9	Votes %	29.3	41.7	23.3	5.7	100
	Swing %	2.6	Seats	2	3	1	0	6
	Lab to C		Candidates	6	6	6	15	33
2001	Electorate	432,432	Votes	94,693	114,812	61,656	9,855	281,016
	Turnout %	65	Votes %	33.7	40.9	21.9	3.5	100
			Seats	3	2	1	0	6
			Candidates	6	6	6	14	32
			% Change 2001-05	-4.4	0.8	1.4	2.2	

Cheltenham, Cotswold, Forest of Dean, Gloucester, Stroud, Tewkesbury

HAMPSHIRE				Lab	C	LD	Other	Total
2005	Electorate	1,257,923	Votes	185,136	341,071	235,917	34,933	797,057
	Turnout %	63.4	Votes %	23.2	42.8	29.6	4.4	100
	Swing %	0.3	Seats	3	10	4	0	17
	C to LD		Candidates	17	17	17	29	80
2001	Electorate	1,255,100	Votes	210,610	316,520	211,595	23,583	762,308
	Turnout %	60.7	Votes %	27.6	41.5	27.8	3.1	100
			Seats	3	10	4	0	17
			Candidates	17	17	17	32	83
			% Change 2001-05	-4.4	1.3	1.8	1.3	

Aldershot, Basingstoke, East Hampshire, Eastleigh, Fareham, Gosport, Havant, New Forest East, New Forest West, North East Hampshire, North West Hampshire, Portsmouth North, Portsmouth South, Romsey, Southampton Itchen, Southampton Test, Winchester

HEREFORD AND WORCESTER				Lab	C	LD	Other	Total
2005	Electorate	553,938	Votes	91,081	159,921	81,141	40,224	372,367
	Turnout %	67.2	Votes %	24.5	42.9	21.8	10.8	100
	Swing %	2.4	Seats	2	4	1	1	8
	Lab to C		Candidates	8	8	7	18	41
2001	Electorate	551,877	Votes	97,932	146,806	69,215	43,092	357,045
	Turnout %	64.7	Votes %	27.4	41.1	19.4	12.1	100
			Seats	2	4	1	1	8
			Candidates	8	8	7	14	37
			% Change 2001-05	-2.9	1.8	2.4	-1.3	

Bromsgrove, Hereford, Leominster, Mid Worcestershire, Redditch, West Worcestershire, Worcester, Wyre Forest

HERTFORDSHIRE				Lab	C	LD	Other	Total
2005	Electorate	768,115	Votes	153,044	226,763	108,326	18,222	506,355
	Turnout %	65.9	Votes %	30.2	44.8	21.4	3.6	100
	Swing %	5.9	Seats	2	9	0	0	11
	Lab to C		Candidates	11	11	11	18	51
2001	Electorate	771,858	Votes	188,308	202,569	81,899	11,878	484,654
	Turnout %	62.8	Votes %	38.9	41.8	16.9	2.5	100
			Seats	5	6	0	0	11
			Candidates	11	11	11	19	52
			% Change 2001-05	-8.7	3	4.5	1.1	

Broxbourne, Hemel Hempstead, Hertford and Stortford, Hertsmere, Hitchin and Harpenden, North East Hertfordshire, South West Hertfordshire, St Albans, Stevenage, Watford, Welwyn Hatfield

HUMBERSIDE				Lab	C	LD	Other	Total
2005	Electorate	676,560	Votes	158,181	126,930	80,098	20,166	385,375
	Turnout %	57	Votes %	41	32.9	20.8	5.2	100
	Swing %	2.9	Seats	7	3	0	0	10
	Lab to C		Candidates	10	10	10	22	52
2001	Electorate	661,507	Votes	173,958	122,005	63,664	12,528	372,155
	Turnout %	56.3	Votes %	46.7	32.8	17.1	3.4	100
			Seats	7	3	0	0	10
			Candidates	10	10	10	18	48
			% Change 2001-05	-5.7	0.1	3.7	1.8	

Beverley and Holderness, Brigg and Goole, Cleethorpes, Great Grimsby, Haltemprice and Howden, Hull East, Hull North, Hull West and Hessle, Scunthorpe, Yorkshire East

KENT				Lab	C	LD	Other	Total
2005	Electorate	1,183,827	Votes	248,465	351,052	132,419	34,022	765,958
	Turnout %	64.7	Votes %	32.4	45.8	17.3	4.4	100
	Swing %	3.9	Seats	7	10	0	0	17
	Lab to C		Candidates	17	17	17	37	88
2001	Electorate	1,177,155	Votes	272,877	314,496	112,024	24,460	723,857
	Turnout %	61.5	Votes %	37.7	43.4	15.5	3.4	100
			Seats	8	9	0	0	17
			Candidates	17	17	17	30	81
			% Change 2001-05	-5.3	2.4	1.8	1	

Ashford, Canterbury, Chatham and Aylesford, Dartford, Dover, Faversham and Mid Kent, Folkestone and Hythe, Gillingham, Gravesham, Maidstone and The Weald, Medway, North Thanet, Sevenoaks, Sittingbourne and Sheppey, South Thanet, Tonbridge and Malling, Tunbridge Wells

LANCASHIRE				Lab	C	LD	Other	Total
2005	Electorate	1,084,309	Votes	269,708	227,951	110,620	42,447	650,726
	Turnout %	60	Votes %	41.4	35	17	6.5	100
	Swing %	2.0	Seats	12	3	0	0	15
	Lab to C		Candidates	15	15	15	28	73
2001	Electorate	1,079,162	Votes	298,739	232,940	84,827	22,618	639,124
	Turnout %	59.2	Votes %	46.7	36.4	13.3	3.5	100
			Seats	13	2	0	0	15
			Candidates	15	15	15	22	67
			% Change 2001-05	-5.3	-1.4	3.7	3	

Blackburn, Blackpool North and Fleetwood, Blackpool South, Burnley, Chorley, Fylde, Hyndburn, Lancaster and Wyre, Morecambe and Lunesdale, Pendle, Preston, Ribble Valley, Rossendale and Darwen, South Ribble, West Lancashire

LEICESTERSHIRE				Lab	C	LD	Other	Total
2005	Electorate	717,672	Votes	164,232	169,919	94,530	26,249	454,930
	Turnout %	63.4	Votes %	36.1	37.4	20.8	5.8	100
	Swing %	2.4	Seats	5	5	0	0	10
	Lab to C		Candidates	10	10	10	22	52
2001	Electorate	707,320	Votes	182,290	167,748	74,964	14,779	439,781
	Turnout %	62.2	Votes %	41.5	38.1	17	3.4	100
			Seats	5	5	0	0	10
			Candidates	10	10	10	17	47
			% Change 2001-05	-5.4	-0.7	3.8	2.4	

Blaby, Bosworth, Charnwood, Harborough, Leicester East, Leicester South, Leicester West, Loughborough, North West Leicestershire, Rutland and Melton

LINCOLNSHIRE				Lab	C	LD	Other	Total
2005	Electorate	513,600	Votes	94,316	149,731	55,673	20,163	319,883
	Turnout %	62.3	Votes %	29.5	46.8	17.4	6.3	100
	Swing %	3.4	Seats	1	6	0	0	7
	Lab to C		Candidates	7	7	7	12	33
2001	Electorate	497,190	Votes	109,150	141,109	49,225	5,943	305,427
	Turnout %	61.4	Votes %	35.7	46.2	16.1	1.9	100
			Seats	1	6	0	0	7
			Candidates	7	7	7	6	27
			% Change 2001-05	-6.2	0.6	1.3	4.4	

Boston and Skegness, Gainsborough, Grantham and Stamford, Lincoln, Louth and Horncastle, Sleaford and North Hykeham, South Holland and The Deepings

NORFOLK				Lab	C	LD	Other	Total
2005	Electorate	635,137	Votes	122,650	163,224	103,805	19,371	409,050
	Turnout %	64.4	Votes %	30	39.9	25.4	4.7	100
	Swing %	1.9	Seats	3	4	1	0	8
	Lab to C		Candidates	8	8	8	17	41
2001	Electorate	615,188	Votes	141,129	165,174	78,050	13,068	397,421
	Turnout %	64.6	Votes %	35.5	41.6	19.6	3.3	100
			Seats	3	4	1	0	8
			Candidates	8	8	8	16	40
			% Change 2001-05	-5.5	-1.7	5.8	1.4	

Great Yarmouth, Mid Norfolk, North Norfolk, North West Norfolk, Norwich North, Norwich South, South Norfolk, South West Norfolk

NORTHAMPTONSHIRE				Lab	C	LD	Other	Total
2005	Electorate	486,972	Votes	117,824	135,440	47,821	13,061	314,146
	Turnout %	64.5	Votes %	37.5	43.1	15.2	4.2	100
	Swing %	4.1	Seats	2	4	0	0	6
	Lab to C		Candidates	6	6	6	18	36
2001	Electorate	473,057	Votes	131,835	123,986	37,831	7,535	301,187
	Turnout %	63.7	Votes %	43.8	41.2	12.6	2.5	100
			Seats	5	1	0	0	6
			Candidates	6	6	6	10	28
			% Change 2001-05	-6.3	1.9	2.6	1.7	

Corby, Daventry, Kettering, Northampton North, Northampton South, Wellingborough

NORTHUMBERLAND				Lab	C	LD	Other	Total
2005	Electorate	244,054	Votes	59,177	38,522	50,591	1,895	150,185
	Turnout %	61.5	Votes %	39.4	25.6	33.7	1.3	100
	Swing %	4.8	Seats	2	1	1	0	4
	Lab to LD		Candidates	4	4	4	3	15
2001	Electorate	242,515	Votes	65,067	39,368	41,986	4,269	150,690
	Turnout %	62.1	Votes %	43.2	26.1	27.9	2.8	100
			Seats	2	1	1	0	4
			Candidates	4	4	4	5	17
			% Change 2001-05	-3.8	-0.5	5.8	-1.5	

Berwick-upon-Tweed, Blyth Valley, Hexham, Wansbeck

NOTTINGHAMSHIRE				Lab	C	LD	Other	Total
2005	Electorate	771,485	Votes	203,832	151,478	74,009	28,663	457,982
	Turnout %	59.4	Votes %	44.5	33.1	16.2	6.3	100
	Swing %	5.5	Seats	9	2	0	0	11
	Lab to C		Candidates	11	11	11	22	55
2001	Electorate	781,234	Votes	228,843	152,826	58,956	9,153	449,778
	Turnout %	57.6	Votes %	50.9	34	13.1	2	100
			Seats	9	2	0	0	11
			Candidates	11	11	11	11	44
			% Change 2001-05	-6.4	-0.9	3.1	4.3	

Ashfield, Bassetlaw, Broxtowe, Gedling, Mansfield, Newark, Nottingham East, Nottingham North, Nottingham South, Rushcliffe, Sherwood

OXFORDSHIRE				Lab	C	LD	Other	Total
2005	Electorate	462,344	Votes	70,886	123,846	87,707	20,497	302,936
	Turnout %	65.5	Votes %	23.4	40.9	29	6.8	100
	Swing %	0.7	Seats	1	4	1	0	6
	LD to C		Candidates	6	6	6	18	36
2001	Electorate	455,468	Votes	84,269	108,296	78,007	15,092	285,664
	Turnout %	62.7	Votes %	29.5	37.9	27.3	5.3	100
			Seats	1	4	1	0	6
			Candidates	6	6	6	19	37
			% Change 2001-05	-6.1	3	1.7	1.5	

Banbury, Henley, Oxford East, Oxford West and Abingdon, Wantage, Witney

SHROPSHIRE				Lab	C	LD	Other	Total
2005	Electorate	337,810	Votes	68,630	92,999	51,163	9,814	222,606
	Turnout %	65.9	Votes %	30.8	41.8	23	4.4	100
	Swing %	5.1	Seats	1	4	0	0	5
	Lab to C		Candidates	5	5	5	9	24
2001	Electorate	335,390	Votes	80,814	82,711	39,459	8,934	211,918
	Turnout %	63.2	Votes %	38.1	39	18.6	4.2	100
			Seats	3	1	1	0	5
			Candidates	5	5	5	10	25
			% Change 2001-05	-7.3	2.8	4.4	0.2	

Ludlow, North Shropshire, Shrewsbury and Atcham, Telford, The Wrekin

SOMERSET				Lab	C	LD	Other	Total
2005	Electorate	394,572	Votes	39,312	109,545	106,152	9,608	264,617
	Turnout %	67.1	Votes %	14.9	41.4	40.1	3.6	100
	No swing		Seats	0	2	3	0	5
			Candidates	5	5	5	7	22
2001	Electorate	381,711	Votes	42,162	104,502	101,080	7,458	255,202
	Turnout %	66.9	Votes %	16.5	40.9	39.6	2.9	100
			Seats	0	3	2	0	5
			Candidates	5	5	5	9	24
			% Change 2001-05	-1.6	0.5	0.5	0.7	

Bridgwater, Somerton and Frome, Taunton, Wells, Yeovil

STAFFORDSHIRE				Lab	C	LD	Other	Total
2005	Electorate	755,935	Votes	193,225	154,856	70,546	33,012	451,639
	Turnout %	59.7	Votes %	42.8	34.3	15.6	7.3	100
	Swing %	1.8	Seats	9	2	0	0	11
	Lab to C		Candidates	11	11	11	24	57
2001	Electorate	809,070	Votes	229,216	171,434	59,678	17,086	477,414
	Turnout %	59	Votes %	48	35.9	12.5	3.6	100
			Seats	9	3	0	0	12
			Candidates	12	12	12	14	50
			% Change 2001-05	-5.2	-1.6	3.1	3.7	

Burton, Cannock Chase, Lichfield, Newcastle-under-Lyme, South Staffordshire, Stafford, Staffordshire Moorlands, Stoke-on-Trent Central, Stoke-on-Trent North, Stoke-on-Trent South, Stone, Tamworth

SUFFOLK				Lab	C	LD	Other	Total
2005	Electorate	519,970	Votes	108,140	141,827	70,168	20,350	340,485
	Turnout %	65.5	Votes %	31.8	41.7	20.6	6	100
	Swing %	4.5	Seats	2	5	0	0	7
	Lab to C		Candidates	7	7	7	13	34
2001	Electorate	509,677	Votes	127,762	130,802	51,370	11,612	321,546
	Turnout %	63.1	Votes %	39.7	40.7	16	3.6	100
			Seats	2	5	0	0	7
			Candidates	7	7	7	13	34
			% Change 2001-05	-7.9	1	4.6	2.4	

Bury St Edmunds, Central Suffolk and North Ipswich, Ipswich, South Suffolk, Suffolk Coastal, Waveney, West Suffolk

SURREY				Lab	C	LD	Other	Total
2005	Electorate	801,420	Votes	87,469	264,112	148,620	23,125	523,326
	Turnout %	65.3	Votes %	16.7	50.5	28.4	4.4	100
	Swing %	0.8	Seats	0	11	0	0	11
	LD to C		Candidates	11	11	11	26	59
2001	Electorate	793,762	Votes	107,897	236,024	133,636	17,878	495,435
	Turnout %	62.4	Votes %	21.8	47.6	27	3.6	100
			Seats	0	10	1	0	11
			Candidates	11	11	11	15	48
			% Change 2001-05	-5.1	2.9	1.4	0.8	

East Surrey, Epsom and Ewell, Esher and Walton, Guildford, Mole Valley, Reigate, Runnymede and Weybridge, South West Surrey, Spelthorne, Surrey Heath, Woking

EAST SUSSEX				Lab	C	LD	Other	Total
2005	Electorate	561,086	Votes	93,432	146,504	96,731	31,822	368,489
	Turnout %	65.7	Votes %	25.4	39.8	26.3	8.6	100
	Swing %	1.0	Seats	4	3	1	0	8
	C to LD		Candidates	8	8	8	29	53
2001	Electorate	571,482	Votes	105,937	138,652	84,232	22,053	350,874
	Turnout %	61.4	Votes %	30.2	39.5	24	6.3	100
			Seats	4	3	1	0	8
			Candidates	8	8	8	28	52
			% Change 2001-05	-4.8	0.3	2.3	2.3	

Bexhill and Battle, Brighton Kemptown, Brighton Pavilion, Eastbourne, Hastings and Rye, Hove, Lewes, Wealden

WEST SUSSEX				Lab	C	LD	Other	Total
2005	Electorate	585,852	Votes	80,481	176,547	98,651	22,605	378,284
	Turnout %	64.6	Votes %	21.3	46.7	26.1	6	100
	Swing %	1.2	Seats	1	7	0	0	8
	C to LD		Candidates	8	8	8	16	40
2001	Electorate	581,724	Votes	92,261	164,009	82,152	18,405	356,827
	Turnout %	61.3	Votes %	25.9	46	23	5.2	100
			Seats	1	7	0	0	8
			Candidates	8	8	8	17	41
			% Change 2001-05	-4.6	0.7	3.1	0.8	

Arundel and South Downs, Bognor Regis and Littlehampton, Chichester, Crawley, East Worthing and Shoreham, Horsham, Mid Sussex, Worthing West

WARWICKSHIRE				Lab	C	LD	Other	Total
2005	Electorate	397,974	Votes	96,780	106,744	46,826	11,842	262,192
	Turnout %	65.9	Votes %	36.9	40.7	17.9	4.5	100
	Swing %	3.4	Seats	3	2	0	0	5
	Lab to C		Candidates	5	5	5	10	25
2001	Electorate	390,962	Votes	106,093	98,531	39,084	6,262	249,970
	Turnout %	63.9	Votes %	42.4	39.4	15.6	2.5	100
			Seats	4	1	0	0	5
			Candidates	5	5	5	7	22
			% Change 2001-05	-5.5	1.3	2.3	2	

North Warwickshire, Nuneaton, Rugby and Kenilworth, Stratford-on-Avon, Warwick and Leamington

WILTSHIRE				Lab	C	LD	Other	Total
2005	Electorate	476,391	Votes	75,556	137,467	83,410	14,057	310,490
	Turnout %	65.2	Votes %	24.3	44.3	26.9	4.5	100
	Swing %	0.2	Seats	2	4	0	0	6
	LD to C		Candidates	6	6	6	14	32
2001	Electorate	461,124	Votes	85,496	124,260	73,853	11,531	295,140
	Turnout %	64	Votes %	29	42.1	25	3.9	100
			Seats	2	4	0	0	6
			Candidates	6	6	6	11	29
			% Change 2001-05	-4.7	2.2	1.9	0.6	

Devizes, North Swindon, North Wiltshire, Salisbury, South Swindon, Westbury

NORTH YORKSHIRE				Lab	C	LD	Other	Total
2005	Electorate	582,870	Votes	105,858	165,550	93,828	13,899	379,135
	Turnout %	65	Votes %	27.9	43.7	24.7	3.7	100
	Swing %	0.9	Seats	2	5	1	0	8
	Lab to C		Candidates	8	8	8	15	39
2005	Electorate	578,064	Votes	110,412	162,679	87,841	12,571	373,503
	Turnout %	64.6	Votes %	29.6	43.6	23.5	3.4	100
			Seats	3	4	1	0	8
			Candidates	8	8	8	15	39
			% Change 2001-05	-1.7	0.1	1.2	0.3	

City of York, Harrogate and Knaresborough, Richmond (Yorkshire), Ryedale, Scarborough and Whitby, Selby, Skipton and Ripon, Vale of York

SCOTLAND

The massive changes to the constituency boundaries in Scotland make direct comparisons between 2005 and 2001 a very risky enterprise and for this reason that is not attempted in these tables. A few observations can, nonetheless, be made. This was not an impressive performance by Labour. Indeed, in its traditional bastions of the central belt of Scotland it is plainly not performing as well as it did at times during the 1980s. The same also appears to be true, however, for the Scottish Nationalist Party. Although it matched Alex Salmond's modest prediction of seats won, he must have been disappointed with the lack of momentum in terms of votes cast. With the Conservative Party still unpopular north of the border, it appears to be the Liberal Democrats and the others who have exploited the comparative unpopularity of Labour.

Constituencies in Scotland are allocated to regions used by the Scottish Parliament. Asterisked constituencies fall substantially within the region indicated but not entirely.

CENTRAL SCOTLAND				Lab	C	LD	Nat	Other	Total
2005	Electorate	559,840	Votes	177,429	30,165	46,790	62,110	12,332	328,826
	Turnout %	58.7	Votes %	53.95	9.173	14.22	18.88	3.750	100
			Seats	8	0	0	0	0	8
			Candidates	8	8	8	8	16	48

Airdrie and Shotts; Coatbridge, Chryston and Bellshill; Cumbernauld, Kilsyth and Kirkintilloch East; *East Kilbride, Strathaven and Lesmahagow; Falkirk; Kilmarnock and Loudoun; Motherwell and Wishaw; *Rutherglen and Hamilton West

GLASGOW				Lab	C	LD	Nat	Other	Total
2005	Electorate	438,366	Votes	96,848	16,217	33,884	32,342	39,493	218,784
	Turnout %	49.9	Votes %	44.26	7.412	15.48	14.78	18.05	100
			Seats	6	0	0	0	1	7
			Candidates	6	6	6	7	24	49

Glasgow Central; Glasgow East; Glasgow North; Glasgow North East; Glasgow North West; Glasgow South; Glasgow South West

HIGHLANDS AND ISLANDS				Lab	C	LD	Nat	Other	Total
2005	Electorate	355,392	Votes	49,220	32,326	84,367	41,755	10,388	218,056
	Turnout %	61.3	Votes %	22.57	14.82	38.69	19.14	4.763	100
			Seats	0	0	5	2	0	7
			Candidates	7	7	7	7	17	45

*Argyll and Bute; Caithness, Sutherland and Easter Ross; Inverness, Nairn, Badenoch and Strathspey; *Moray; Na h-Eileanan An Iar; Orkney and Shetland; Ross, Skye and Lochaber

LOTHIANS				Lab	C	LD	Nat	Other	Total
2005	Electorate	540,469	Votes	132,524	54,926	91,413	49,396	14,409	342,668
	Turnout %	63.4	Votes %	38.67	16.02	26.67	14.41	4.204	100
			Seats	7	0	1	0	0	8
			Candidates	8	8	8	8	16	48

Edinburgh East; Edinburgh North and Leith; Edinburgh South; Edinburgh South West; Edinburgh West; *Linlithgow and East Falkirk; Livingston; *Midlothian

MID SCOTLAND AND FIFE				Lab	C	LD	Nat	Other	Total
2005	Electorate	477,181	Votes	107,679	53,783	61,488	61,759	11,721	296,430
	Turnout %	62.1	Votes %	36.32	18.14	20.74	20.83	3.954	100
			Seats	5	0	1	1	0	7
			Candidates	7	7	7	7	23	51

Dunfermline and West Fife; Glenrothes; Kirkcaldy and Cowdenbeath; North East Fife; Ochil and South Perthshire; *Perth and North Perthshire; Stirling

NORTH EAST SCOTLAND				Lab	C	LD	Nat	Other	Total
2005	Electorate	528,054	Votes	87,400	56,815	83,412	81,767	6,784	316,178
	Turnout %	59.8	Votes %	27.64	17.96	26.38	25.86	2.145	100
			Seats	3	0	2	3	0	8
			Candidates	8	8	8	8	13	45

Aberdeen North; Aberdeen South; *Angus; Banff and Buchan; Dundee East; Dundee West; Gordon; West Aberdeenshire and Kincardine

SOUTH SCOTLAND				Lab	C	LD	Nat	Other	Total
2005	Electorate	498,836	Votes	121,926	80,044	65,008	38,784	12,417	318,179
	Turnout %	63.7	Votes %	38.31	25.15	20.43	12.18	3.902	100
			Seats	5	1	1	0	0	7
			Candidates	7	7	7	7	23	51

Ayr, Carrick and Cumnock; Berwickshire, Roxburgh and Selkirk; Central Ayrshire; Dumfries and Galloway; Dumfriesshire, Clydesdale and Tweeddale; *East Lothian; *Lanark and Hamilton East

WEST OF SCOTLAND				Lab	C	LD	Nat	Other	Total
2005	Electorate	454,567	Votes	134,223	45,112	61,714	44,354	9,363	294,766
	Turnout %	64.8	Votes %	45.53	15.30	20.93	15.04	3.176	100
			Seats	6	0	1	0	0	7
			Candidates	7	7	7	7	17	45

*East Dunbartonshire; East Renfrewshire; Inverclyde; *North Ayrshire and Arran; Paisley and Renfrewshire North; Paisley and Renfrewshire South; West Dunbartonshire

WALES

The results of the general election in Wales can be divided into five principal regions. Between them they provide for an interesting picture. While the swing between the Labour Party and the Conservatives in the principality was not dissimilar to that of the nation as a whole, the trend in Wales was closer to that of Scotland than its much larger neighbour. The Labour vote fell back, but to assert that it slumped in the manner that it really did in parts of London would be an exaggeration. After holding no Welsh seats since their 1997 collapse, the Conservative Party managed to win three seats – one of them by a very narrow margin – but to claim that this constitutes a genuine recovery would be extremely optimistic at this stage. Plaid Cymru, which performed extremely well in the Welsh Assembly election of 1999, has not been able to record anything like as impressive a result since. It is thus the Liberal Democrats who have emerged as the main beneficiaries from the discontent that exists towards the Labour Party nationally.

MID AND WEST WALES				Lab	C	LD	Nat	Other	Total
2005	Electorate	409,782	Votes	72,416	65,608	66,554	64,243	6,289	275,110
	Turnout %	67.1	Votes %	26.3	23.8	24.2	23.4	2.3	100
	Swing %	4.7	Seats	2	1	3	2	0	8
	Lab to LD		Candidates	8	8	8	8	13	45
2001	Electorate	409,568	Votes	83,261	63,275	52,322	65,834	5,425	270,117
	Turnout %	66	Votes %	30.8	23.4	19.4	24.4	2	100
			Seats	3	0	2	3	0	8
			Candidates	8	8	8	8	13	45
			% Change 2001-05	-4.5	0.4	4.8	-1	0.3	

Brecon and Radnorshire, Carmarthen East and Dinefwr, Carmarthen West and South Pembrokeshire, Ceredigion, Llanelli, Meirionnydd Nant Conwy, Montgomeryshire, Preseli Pembrokeshire

NORTH WALES				Lab	C	LD	Nat	Other	Total
2005	Electorate	472,590	Votes	121,618	72,299	45,734	42,395	15,815	297,861
	Turnout %	63	Votes %	40.8	24.3	15.4	14.2	5.3	100
	Swing %	1.5	Seats	7	1	0	1	0	9
	Lab to C		Candidates	9	9	9	9	24	60
2001	Electorate	478,968	Votes	134,761	76,520	35,880	45,627	5,196	297,984
	Turnout %	62.2	Votes %	45.2	25.7	12	15.3	1.7	100
			Seats	8	0	0	1	0	9
			Candidates	9	9	9	9	12	48
			% Change 2001-05	-4.4	-1.4	3.4	-1.1	3.6	

Alyn and Deeside, Caernarfon, Clwyd South, Clwyd West, Conwy, Delyn, Vale of Clwyd, Wrexham, Ynys Môn

SOUTH WALES CENTRAL				Lab	C	LD	Nat	Other	Total
2005	Electorate	481,040	Votes	141,953	62,458	60,186	25,160	7,961	297,718
	Turnout %	61.9	Votes %	47.7	21	20.2	8.5	2.7	100
	Swing %	3.4	Seats	7	0	1	0	0	8
	Lab to C		Candidates	8	8	8	8	21	53
2001	Electorate	482,779	Votes	156,386	58,819	42,192	29,446	5,526	292,369
	Turnout %	60.6	Votes %	53.5	20.1	14.4	10.1	1.9	100
			Seats	8	0	0	0	0	8
			Candidates	8	8	8	8	13	45
			% Change 2001-05	-5.8	0.9	5.8	-1.6	0.8	

Cardiff Central, Cardiff North, Cardiff South and Penarth, Cardiff West, Cynon Valley, Pontypridd, Rhondda, Vale of Glamorgan

SOUTH WALES EAST				Lab	C	LD	Nat	Other	Total
2005	Electorate	464,419	Votes	139,141	57,664	38,919	20,327	28,459	284,510
	Turnout %	61.3	Votes %	48.9	20.3	13.7	7.1	10	100
	Swing %	5.1	Seats	6	1	0	0	1	8
	Lab to C		Candidates	8	8	8	8	14	46
2001	Electorate	466,683	Votes	161,044	52,282	30,680	27,949	8,025	279,980
	Turnout %	60	Votes %	57.5	18.7	11	10	2.9	100
			Seats	8	0	0	0	0	8
			Candidates	8	8	8	8	13	45
			% Change 2001-05	-8.6	1.6	2.7	-2.9	7.1	

Blaenau Gwent, Caerphilly, Islwyn, Merthyr Tydfil and Rhymney, Monmouth, Newport East, Newport West, Torfaen

SOUTH WALES WEST				Lab	C	LD	Nat	Other	Total
2005	Electorate	402,656	Votes	119,693	39,801	44,856	22,713	10,457	237,520
	Turnout %	59	Votes %	50.4	16.8	18.9	9.6	4.4	100
	Swing %	6.5	Seats	7	0	0	0	0	7
	Lab to LD		Candidates	7	7	7	7	18	46
2001	Electorate	392,483	Votes	131,504	37,767	28,360	27,037	7,426	232,094
	Turnout %	59.1	Votes %	56.7	16.3	12.2	11.6	3.2	100
			Seats	7	0	0	0	0	7
			Candidates	7	7	7	7	13	41
			% Change 2001-05	-6.3	0.5	6.7	2.0	1.2	

Aberavon, Bridgend, Gower, Neath, Ogmore, Swansea East, Swansea West

NORTHERN IRELAND

As has long been the trend, the mainland political parties made no effort to speak of in Northern Ireland. Three souls stood on behalf of the Conservative Party and secured a handful of votes for their troubles.

This was, nonetheless, a momentous election. The movement in votes between the Democratic Unionist Party and the Ulster Unionist Party between 2001 and 2005 was staggering. In crude terms it amounted to a swing within this section of the community of slightly more than 10 per cent. It is hardly surprising that the party led by David Trimble, traditionally the dominant force in Unionist politics, was all but wiped out.

The movement on the nationalist side of the divide was stark but not as sweeping. It amounted to a 2.5 per cent swing to the advantage of Sinn Féin and to the cost of the moderate nationalist SDLP. The 'others' in Northern Ireland were marginalised by this process. Ulster is thus left with the prospect of an emerging two-party dominant system with the DUP and Sinn Féin establishing clear command in their respective electorates. It is this context that any new attempt at power-sharing will have to be framed.

N IRELAND				DUP	UUP	SDLP	SF	Other	Total
2005	Electorate	1,148,486	Votes	241,856	127,414	125,626	174,530	48,176	717,602
	Turnout %	62.5	Votes %	33.7	17.8	17.5	24.3	6.7	100
	Swing %	6.9	Seats	9	1	3	5	0	18
	SF to DUP		Candidates	18	18	18	18	33	105
2001	Electorate	1,191,009	Votes	181,999	216,839	162,258	175,933	73,345	810,374
	Turnout %	68	Votes %	22.5	26.8	20	21.7	9.1	100
			Seats	5	6	3	4	0	18
			Candidates	14	17	17	18	34	100
			% Change 2001-05	11.2	-0.9	-2.5	2.6	2.4	

Belfast East, Belfast North, Belfast South, Belfast West, East Antrim, East Londonderry, Fermanagh and South Tyrone, Foyle, Lagan Valley, Mid Ulster, Newry and Armagh, North Antrim, North Down, South Antrim, South Down, Strangford, Upper Bann, West Tyrone

MANIFESTOS

LABOUR MANIFESTO

ECONOMY

Labour's economic record is unprecedented – the highest employment ever, longest period of uninterrupted growth in modern history, lowest sustained interest and inflation rates for a generation.Our economic policies will build on the platform of stability and growth in three ways:entrenching a low-debt/high-employment economy which generates investment in public services; supporting enterprise and wealth creation by making Britain the best place to do business; and helping every part of Britain and every person in Britain to contribute to and gain from the strength of our economy. And as we work globally to tackle climate change we recognise the challenge and the opportunity of achieving sustainable development at home.

The new Labour case

Our economic record has finally laid to rest the view that Labour could not be trusted with the economy. We are winning the argument that economic dynamism and social justice must go hand in hand. In the future the countries that do best will be those with a shared purpose about the long-term changes and investments they need to make – and have the determination to equip their people for that future. So, we approach new challenges with a progressive strategy for growth. In our third term we will build new ladders of social mobility and advancement on the firm foundations of stability, investment and growth.

Low debt and high employment

In the last eight years we have pioneered a British way to economic stability. Our economy has grown in every quarter with this Government. Interest rates have averaged 5.3 per cent since 1997, saving mortgage payers on average nearly £4,000 per year compared to the Tory years.

Only with Labour, which constructed this framework, will this continue. We will maintain our inflation target at two per cent. We will continue to meet our fiscal rules: over the economic cycle, we will borrow only to invest, and keep net debt at a stable and prudent level.

Public spending and taxation

The longest period of uninterrupted economic growth in modern times has enabled the Government to deliver the longest period of sustained investment in public services for a generation. Social security bills for unemployment have been halved since 1997, saving £5 billion a year, and we are also saving £4 billion a year on debt interest payments. Over the ten-year period 1997-98 to 2007-08, real-terms investment per year in education will have risen by 4.8 per cent and in health by 6.5 per cent.

Every pound we invest goes further because of our drive for efficiency and reform. Labour will complete the implementation of Sir Peter Gershon's recommendations to improve public-service efficiency and root out waste, liberating over £21 billion for investment in front-line services.

Labour believes tax policy should continue to be governed by the health of the public finances, the requirement for public investment and the needs of families, business and the environment.

We will not raise the basic or top rates of income tax in the next Parliament. We renew our pledge not to extend VAT to food,children's clothes,books, newspapers and public transport fares. We will continue to make targeted tax cuts for families and to support work. As a result of personal tax and benefit measures introduced since 1997, by October 2005 families with children will be on average £1,400 a year better off in real terms. Living standards in Britain have been rising, on average, by 2.5 per cent per year since 1997 – a total increase of nearly 20 per cent.

We want a tax regime that supports British business. That is why we have cut corporation tax to its lowest ever level, introduced the best regime of capital gains tax in any industrialised country, and introduced a new Research and Development tax credit.

Full employment

Our goal is employment opportunity for all – the modern definition of full employment. Britain has more people in work than ever before, with the highest employment rate in the G7. Our long-term aim is to raise the employment rate to 80 per cent. And, as we move more people from welfare to work, the savings on unemployment benefits will go towards investing more in education.

We will make work pay. With Labour's tax credits a family with two children pays no net tax until their earnings reach £21,000.

We will implement the recommendations of the Low Pay Commission to raise the minimum wage to £5.05 from October 2005 and £5.35 from October 2006.

The New Deals and the creation of JobCentre Plus have made a major contribution to cutting unemployment. The active welfare state created since 1997 is working.

The Tories trebled the number on incapacity benefits. We will help people who can work into rehabilitation and eventually into employment, recognising the practical assistance to disabled people of the Access to Work scheme. We will build on the successful Pathways to Work programme and reform Incapacity Benefit, with the main elements of the new benefit regime in place from 2008. The majority of claimants with more manageable conditions will be required to engage in both work-focused interviews and in activity to help them prepare for a return to work. Those with the most severe conditions will also be encouraged to engage in activity and should receive more money than now. We will continue to welcome new independent and voluntary sector partners to provide job-seeking services.

Supporting enterprise

Government does not create wealth but it must support the wealth creators. That is why our priorities are the national infrastructure of skills, science, regulation and planning, and transport. The economy of the future will be based on knowledge, innovation and creativity. That applies both to manufacturing and services.

In a fast changing global economy, government cannot postpone or prevent change. The modern role for government – the case for a modern employment and skills policy – is to equip people to succeed, to be on their side, helping them become more skilled, adaptable and flexible for the job ahead rather than the old Tory way of walking away leaving people unaided to face change.

Successful manufacturing industries are vital to our future prosperity. The Labour Government backs manufacturing: from launch investment for Airbus A380 Super Jumbo to the successful Manufacturing Advisory Service helping 13,000 of our smaller manufacturing businesses in its first year. In a third term we will continue to do so.

Public procurement is a big opportunity for business in Britain and the source of many jobs. We will promote a public procurement strategy that safeguards UK jobs and skills, under EU rules, to ensure that British industry can compete fairly with the rest of Europe.

Britain has some of the strongest capital markets in the world. We are determined they – and our financial services industry – should prosper. We will ensure that companies have the right framework of corporate governance and relationships with the institutions that invest our pension funds and savings in them.

Skills at work

Our reforms to 14-19 education will raise the quality and quantity of apprenticeships and vocational education. We are now putting in place a comprehensive and ambitious strategy to help everyone get on at work:

- All adults to get free access to basic skills in literacy, language and numeracy.
- A new national programme, working with employers, to ensure that employees who did not reach GCSE standard (level 2) at school will get time off for free training up to level 2.
- A new partnership between government and employers to fund workplace training at level 3 (technician level)
- A genuinely employer-driven training system – in every sector there will be a Sector Skills Council determining the training strategy and a leading edge Skills Academy.
- A nationwide system of advice – bringing together support on skills, jobs and careers – helping people to get on at work.
- A strong partnership with trade unions to boost workplace training including a new TUC Academy and continued support for Union Learning Reps.

Supporting science

The alliance of scientific research and business creativity is key to our continued prosperity.

Looking ahead, we are committed to a ten-year strategy on science and innovation that will continue to invest in our science and industrial base at least in line with trend GDP. Our ambition now is to raise the UK's total private and public sector investment in research and development, as a proportion of national income, from its current 1.9 per cent to 2.5 per cent by 2014.

Our pharmaceutical and biotechnology industries are world leaders. We have created one of the world's best environments for stem-cell research. We have now passed legislation to protect our researchers from the activities of animal rights extremists.

Across a range of environmental issues – from soil erosion to the depletion of marine resources, from water scarcity to air pollution – it is clear now not just that economic activity is their cause but that these problems in themselves threaten future economic activity and growth. We will continue to work with the environmental goods and services sector – which is already worth £25 billion to the economy to promote new green technologies and industries in the UK and internationally, and use the purchasing power of government to support environmental improvement.

Competition, planning and regulation

Competition is a driving force for innovation. Our competition regime has been toughened with independent competition bodies and stronger penalties.

To the benefit of business and household consumers we are liberalising the postal services market, while protecting the universal service at a uniform tariff.

As we said in our policy document Britain is Working, we have given the Royal Mail greater commercial freedom and have no plans to privatise it. Our ambition is to see a publicly owned Royal Mail fully restored to good health, providing customers with an excellent service and its employees with rewarding employment. We will review the impact on the Royal Mail of market liberalisation, which is being progressively introduced under the Postal Services Act 2000 and which allows alternative carriers to the Royal Mail to offer postal services.

We have reformed our energy markets to make them open and competitive. And we are a leading force in the campaign to make Europe's energy markets the same. Our wider energy policy has created a framework that places the challenge of climate change – as well as the need to achieve security of supply – at the heart of our energy policy. We have a major programme to promote renewable energy, as part of a strategy of having a mix of energy sources from nuclear power stations to clean coal to micro-generators.

We will only regulate where necessary and will set exacting targets for reducing the costs of administering regulations. We will rationalise business inspections. The merger of the Inland Revenue and Customs and Excise will cut the administrative costs of tax compliance for small businesses.

We will take further action in Europe to ensure that EU regulations are proportionate and better designed. We strongly support the creation of an EU single market in services to match the single market in goods – and want an effective directive to provide real benefits to consumers and new opportunities to British business. We will protect our employment standards. In developing the directive we will want to avoid any undermining of our regulatory framework.

We will continue to work to protect the rights of consumers, bringing forward proposals to strengthen and streamline consumer advocacy. We look forward to action from the banking industry to remove delays in processing cheques and other payments and, if necessary, will legislate to ensure this early in the next Parliament.

There are many bank accounts that are lying dormant and unclaimed, often because people have forgotten about them or because the owner has died. We will work with the financial services industry to establish a common definition and a comprehensive record of unclaimed assets. We will then expect banks, over the course of the Parliament, to either reunite those assets with their owners or to channel them back into the community.

An effective planning regime protects the environment while promoting economic growth – and does so quickly and responsively. In the next term, we will ensure that our planning system continues to protect the sustainability of local and regional environments – and we will continue to develop a regime which is simpler, faster and more responsive to local and business needs including the need to create jobs and regenerate our cities.

Fostering entrepreneurship

There are 300,000 more businesses now than in 1997. We are tackling barriers to financing for small and growing businesses – especially enterprises in deprived areas. Through Business Links we will offer start-ups, social enterprises and small businesses access to tailored intensive support and coaching. To foster the entrepreneurs of tomorrow, by 2006 every school in the country will offer enterprise education, and every college and university should be twinned with a business champion.

Modern transport infrastructure

An efficient transport system is vital to the country's future, to our economy and to our quality of life. We welcome the freedom that additional travel provides and support the continuing development of a competitive and efficient freight sector. Investment, better management of road and rail, and planning ahead are vital to deal with the pressures on the system in a way that respects our environmental objectives.

We have doubled transport spending since 1997 and will increase it year on year – committing over £180 billion in public money between now and 2015 as well as private investment. The Eddington Review will work with the Government to advise on how this investment should be targeted – in particular, where transport is vital to underpin economic growth.

We are now taking charge of setting the strategy for rail to further raise the standard of service and reliability. We will examine options for increasing capacity, including a new generation of high-speed trains on intercity routes and a new life for rural branch lines as community railways. We are committed to continuing to work to develop a funding and finance solution for the Crossrail project; and will look at the feasibility and affordability of a new North-South high-speed link.

We will support light-rail improvements where they represent value for money and are part of the best integrated transport solution. To that end, we are working with cities across the country and have committed £520 million to Manchester for Metrolink. We will support the continuing upgrade of the London Underground and the extension of the East London line.

Major investment is planned to expand capacity on the M1, M6 and M25. We must also manage road space better. We are examining the potential benefits of a parallel Expressway on the M6 corridor. We will introduce car-pool lanes for cars with more than one passenger on suitable roads and explore other ways to lock in the benefit of new capacity. We will complete the introduction of Traffic Management Officers to keep traffic flowing. Because of the long-term nature of transport planning, we will seek political consensus in tackling congestion, including examining the potential of moving away from the current system of motoring taxation towards a national system of road-pricing.

We will give all over-60s, and disabled people, free off-peak local bus travel and give local authorities the freedom to provide more generous schemes. We will continue to support growth in bus provision including innovation in school transport, with greater opportunity for local authorities to control their bus networks where they are demonstrating value for money and taking strong measures to tackle congestion. To facilitate improved public transport provision, we will explore giving Passenger Transport Executives greater powers over local transport.

We will continue funding local authorities and voluntary groups to make cycling and walking more attractive. We are committed to reducing child deaths and serious injuries on the road by 50 per cent,and we will continue to work to reduce dangerous driving, especially drink driving and uninsured driving. We will work with industry to make travel on public transport safer and more secure.

Government will continue to support technological innovation to reduce carbon emissions such as the hydrogen fuel-cell buses in London. We will explore the scope for further use of economic instruments as well as other measures to promote lower vehicle emissions.

We will continue to support air travel by implementing the balanced policies set out in our aviation white paper. We are committed to using the UK's 2005 presidency of the European Union to promote the inclusion of aviation in the EU's emissions trading scheme.

For shipping, our introduction of the tonnage tax has led to a trebling in size of the fleet since 1997. We want more ships to fly the British flag, to boost jobs and training, and to increase shipping and port capacity.

Opportunity for all

We are determined to spread the benefits of enterprise to every community in the country.Every regional economy has different strengths, and Regional Development Agencies now play an essential role in regional economic development.

We have given local authorities a direct incentive to promote local business creation, allowing them to keep up to £1 billion over three years of increased rate revenues to spend on their own priorities. The Local Enterprise Growth Initiative will work through local authorities to remove barriers to enterprise in the most deprived areas of England.

In 1997, many parts of our towns and cities were suffering from deeply entrenched and multiple disadvantage. To tackle this we established a ten-year programme, the New Deal for Communities, empowering local communities – and this is already delivering improvements in education outcomes and crime reduction.

No area in our country should be excluded from the opportunity to get ahead, to benefit from improving public services, and to be secure and safe. We will maintain our commitment to tackling issues of worklessness, low skills, crime, poor environment and health in our poorest neighbourhoods.

Fairness at work

Since 1997, the Labour Government has introduced new rights for people at work and new opportunities for trade unions to represent their members. We see modern, growing trade unions as an important part of our society and economy. They provide protection and advice for employees, and we welcome the positive role they have played in developing a modern model of social partnership with business representatives. The Labour Party has agreed a set of policies for the work-place (the Warwick Agreement) and we will deliver them in full. They will be good for employees and for the economy.

We have introduced, for the first time, an entitlement for every employee to four weeks' paid holiday, and we propose to extend this by making it additional to bank holiday entitlement.

Promoting equality at work

A strong economy draws on the talents of all. We have extended legislation to protect people from discrimination at work to cover not only gender, disability, race and ethnicity but also religion and sexual orientation and – from 2006 – age. Labour has transformed legal rights for disabled people. We will empower disabled people further by joining up services and expanding personalised budgets.

We will take further action to narrow the pay and promotion gap between men and women. The Women and Work Commission will report to the Prime Minister later this year.

We will implement the National Employment Panel's report on measures to promote employment and small business growth for ethnic and faith minorities. We will take forward the Strategy for Race Equality to ensure that we combat discrimination on the grounds of race and ethnicity across a range of services. The Equalities Review reporting to the Prime Minister in 2006 will make practical recommendations on the priorities for tackling disadvantage and promoting equality of opportunity for all groups.

Thriving rural areas

Since 1997, Labour has made it more difficult to close rural schools, put in £750 million to support rural post offices and introduced a 50 per cent rate relief on village shops. Through our £51 million Rural Bus Subsidy Grant we have delivered over 2,200 new bus services in rural areas this year.

We set targets for the creation of affordable homes in rural areas,which we have now exceeded. We will explore how to ensure a proportion of all new housing development is made available and affordable to local residents and their families.

Because of our success in achieving extensive reforms in the Common Agricultural Policy (CAP), 2005 will be the first year for decades when farmers will be free to produce for the market and not simply for subsidy. We will continue to push for further reform of the CAP in the next Parliament, starting with the sugar regime.

We will continue to promote the competitiveness of the whole food sector, and assure the safety and quality of its products. We will introduce an explicit policy for schools, hospitals and government offices to consider local sourcing of fresh produce. We will continue to improve the environmental performance of agriculture, rewarding every farmer in England for environmental protection and enhancement work through our new Stewardship schemes. We will also promote biomass, biofuels and non-food crops. We will work to tackle diffuse water pollution through addressing impacts across water catchments without the costs falling on water customers.

Under difficult circumstances, Labour is working with the fishing industry to create a sustainable long-term future for the fishing communities of the United Kingdom. We have reformed the Common Fisheries Policy and will continue to protect the marine environment and ensure fish stocks and their exploitation are set at sustainable levels.

We will introduce the Animal Welfare Bill as soon as possible in the new Parliament.

The choice for 2010

The Conservatives are the party of high interest rates, high inflation, mass unemployment and house repossessions. Their tax-and-spend promises do not add up; and they would cut £35 billion from public investment. With new Labour, Britain can seize the opportunities of globalisation, creating jobs and prosperity for people up and down the country. We can only do so if we build a clear sense of shared national economic purpose, not just around economic stability but also investment in infrastructure, skills, science and enterprise. The choice is to go forward to economic stability, rising prosperity and wider opportunities with new Labour. Or go back to the bad old days of Tory cuts, insecurity and instability.

EDUCATION

Education is still our number one priority. In our first term, we transformed recruitment, training and methods of teaching, with record results in primary schools. In our second term we have driven fundamental reform in secondary provision – more teachers and support staff, more money, specialist schools and the Academies programmes. Our plan now is to tailor our education system to individual pupil needs, with parents supporting teachers and support staff in further raising standards. That means music, art, sport and languages as well as English and maths in primary school; a good secondary school for every child, with modern buildings and excellent specialist teaching; catch-up support for all children who need it; the guarantee of a sixth-form place, apprenticeship or further education at 16; sufficient quality and quantity in higher education. At each stage we send a clear message – every child has a right to a good education, but no child has the right to disrupt the education of other children.

The new Labour case

For generations our country has been held back by an education system that excelled for the privileged few but let down the majority. Every child can and should be able to fulfil their potential. We will achieve this by uniting our commitment to equal opportunities for all children with a reform programme which gives every child and young person, from pre-school to sixth-form or apprenticeship and beyond, the personalised package of learning and support they need. In a third term, we will entrench high expectations for every child, ensure the flexibility of provision to meet all needs and make parents true partners as we aim for the highest ever school standards.

Every pupil with better teaching

There is no greater responsibility than teaching the next generation. Head teachers, teachers and support staff deserve support and respect. There are now over 28,000 more teachers and 105,000 more support staff than in 1997; graduate teacher applications are up 70 per cent; average salaries are up by more than 30 per cent. The remodelling of the school workforce is benefiting staff and helping to tailor provision to pupil need. We will now go further – to intensify in-service training for teachers, to widen further routes into teaching, to help more teachers and pupils get the benefit of the range of support staff now working in schools, from learning mentors to music and arts specialists. The goal is clear: every pupil with extra support in their weakest subjects and extra opportunities in their strongest.

We want to see every pupil mastering the basics. If they are not mastered by 11, there will be extra time in the secondary curriculum to get them right: schools will be judged on how pupils do in English and maths at the ages of 11, 14 and 16.

We want every pupil to be stretched, including the brightest, so we will develop extended projects at A-level, harder A-level questions to challenge the most able, and give universities the individual module marks – as well as overall grades – of A-level students.

Every school with more money and effective leadership

Since 1997, school funding has risen by £1,000 per pupil. Education spending that was 4.7 per cent of national income in 1997 will rise to 5.5 per cent this year. We will continue to raise the share of national income devoted to education. And we will continue to recognise the additional needs of disadvantaged pupils. We will also ensure fundamental reform in the way the money is spent. Funding will be allocated on a multi-year timescale. There will be a dedicated national schools budget set by central government, with a guaranteed per pupil increase for every school. Heads and governors will be in control. Successful schools and colleges will have the independence to take decisions about how to deploy resources and develop their provision. Schools will work together to raise standards. New provision will be created where standards are too low or innovation is needed. Local authorities have a vital role in championing the parent interest and providing support services.

A strong, effective governing body is essential to the success of every school and governors must be given support to help them play this role. We will allow more flexibility in the structure of governing bodies, including the ability to have smaller governing bodies, of ten members or less, to streamline management while strengthening the position of parents.

Parents as partners

Our aim for the education system is to nurture the unique talents of every child. But children and schools do best with real and effective parental engagement. Parents should have the information and support they need to encourage their children, from the first reading book to the key choices they make at 14 and 16. And parents should be central to the process of assessing school performance and driving improvement, as well as their vital role in promoting good behaviour and raising the quality of school meals.

All schools should have good home-school links, building on the new school and pupil profiles. Some schools are using ICT to make contact between parents and schools easier and better for both sides. We will encourage all schools to follow suit.

Ofsted now actively seeks the views of parents when undertaking inspections. Ofsted will be given new powers to respond to parental complaints and where necessary to close failing schools or replace failing management.

Enriching primary schools

International studies show that our ten-year-olds are the third highest achievers in literacy in the world and the fastest improving in maths. Three-quarters of 11-year-olds now reach high standards in reading, writing and maths. We will intensify our literacy and numeracy programme to help an extra 50,000 pupils achieve high standards at age 11, reaching our targets of 85 per cent of pupils succeeding at the basics.

All primary school children will have access to high-quality tuition in the arts, music, sport and foreign languages. We have set aside funds for this purpose, working with head teachers to develop support programmes and modernise the school workforce.

We have abolished infant class sizes of more than 30, and almost all primary schools have gained improved facilities since 1997. We will now upgrade primary schools nationwide in a 15-year Building Schools for the Future programme, including under-fives and childcare facilities where needed. Primary schools will become the base for a massive expansion of out-of-school provision.

Foundation schools operate within the local family of state schools, and are funded in the same way as others, but manage their own assets and employ their staff directly. We will allow successful primary schools, like secondary schools, to become foundation schools by a simple vote of their governing body following consultation with their parents.

Every secondary school an independent specialist school

We want all secondary schools to be independent specialist schools with a strong ethos, high-quality leadership,good discipline (including school uniforms), setting by ability and high-quality facilities as the norm.

The way to achieve this is not a return to the 11-plus or a free-for-all on admissions policies. It is to ensure that independent specialist schools tailor education to the needs, interests and aptitudes of each pupil within a fair admissions system.

There are over 2,000 specialist schools – schools which teach the entire national curriculum and also have a centre of excellence. Their results are improving faster than those of non-specialist schools. We want every secondary school to become a specialist school and existing specialist schools will be able to take on a second specialism. Over time all specialist schools will become extended schools, with full programmes of after-school activities.

Every part of the country will benefit, over fifteen years, from the Building Schools for the Future programme. This is a once in a generation programme to equip the whole country with modern secondary education facilities, open five days a week, ten hours a day.

Good schools will be able to expand their size and also their influence – by taking over less successful schools. We will develop a system to create rights for successful schools to establish sixth-form provision where there is pupil and parent demand, extending quality and choice for local students.

Britain has a positive tradition of independent providers within the state system, including church and other faith schools. Where new educational providers can help boost standards and opportunities in a locality we will welcome them into the state system, subject to parental demand, fair funding and fair admissions.

We strongly support the new Academies movement. Seventeen of these independent non-selective schools are now open within the state system; their results are improving sharply, and 50 more are in the pipeline. Within the existing allocation of resources our aim is that at least 200 Academies will be established by 2010 in communities where low aspirations and low performance are entrenched.

We will encourage more small schools and boarding schools as ways of helping the most disadvantaged children. We will make sure schools in deprived areas receive the resources they need. To enable all young people to enjoy the opportunities previously enjoyed by the few,we are developing a nationwide week-long summer residential programme for school students. We support partnership between the state and private sectors to bridge the unhealthy historic divide between the two.

Good discipline

Every pupil has the right to learn without disruption; no teacher should be subject to abuse or disrespect. We have given head teachers the powers needed to maintain discipline and the highest standards of conduct. Violent behaviour,including the use of knives will not be tolerated. We are also working with schools and teacher organisations to implement a zero tolerance approach to lower-level disruption. The number of places in out-of-school units has almost doubled, and the quality of provision has been enhanced. We will give head teachers within each locality direct control of the budgets for out-of-school provision, so they can expand and improve it as needed. We will encourage more dedicated provision for disruptive and excluded pupils, including by charities and voluntary groups with expertise in this area, and no school will become a dumping ground for such pupils.

Parents have a duty to get their children to attend school. We have introduced parenting orders and fines and will continue to advocate truancy sweeps.

Special educational needs

Children with special educational needs require appropriate resources and support from trained staff. For some this will be in mainstream schools; for others, it will be in special schools. Parents should have access to the special education appropriate for their child. It is the role of local authorities to make decisions on the shape of local provision, in consultation with local parents.

No more dropping out at 16

The historic problems of our education system at 14-plus have been an academic track that has been too narrow and a vocational offer too weak.

We are determined to raise the status and quality of vocational education. Beyond the age of 14, GCSEs and A-levels will be the foundation of the system in which high-quality vocational programmes will be available to every pupil. Designed in collaboration with employers, specialised diplomas will be established in key areas of the economy, leading to apprenticeships, to further and higher education and to jobs with training. We will review progress on the development of the 14-19 curriculum in 2008.

We will not let economic disadvantage stand in the way of young people staying in education beyond the age of 16. We have rolled out Educational Maintenance Allowances, providing lower income students with a £30-a-week staying-on allowance. We believe that everyone up to the age of 19 should be learning, so we will expand sixth-form, college and apprenticeship places, and ensure that all 16-to 19-year-olds in employment get access to training.

We believe that every 16- to 19-year-old should have dedicated supervision and support, including in the further education sector. We will support sixth-form colleges and expect FE colleges to have dedicated centres for 16- to 19-year-olds.

Further education is vital to vocational lifelong learning. Achieving a transformation of FE colleges requires both our increased investment and serious reform. Every FE college will develop a centre for vocational excellence, and we will establish new skills academies led by leading entrepreneurs and employers from the relevant skill sectors. Sir Andrew Foster's review will help shape the reform process.

Children's Trusts

Ofsted reports show that local government is continuing to improve the vital services on which schools and families rely. Education and social services should collaborate to help youngsters, especially the most vulnerable, achieve their potential. Local government should be the champion of parents and high-quality provision, including special needs education, school transport, and other support services. We are reforming local education authorities to form Children's Trusts to provide seamless support to children and families and work in partnership with the private and voluntary sectors.

World-class higher education, open to all

Universities are critical to Britain's future prosperity. We need a bigger, better higher education system. We are investing £1 billion more in the science base, and increasing public spending on higher education by 34 per cent in real terms. But graduates and employers must also play their part. Our funding reforms will generate £1 billion of extra funds by 2010; the abolition of up-front fees and the creation of grants will help poorer students. A quarter of the income from the new student finance system will go to bursaries for students from poorer families. The maximum annual fee paid by students will not rise above £3,000 (uprated annually for inflation) during the next Parliament.

As school standards rise we maintain our aim for 50 per cent of young people to go on to higher education by 2010. Two-year foundation degrees in vocational disciplines have a key part to play.

PhD students are vital to universities and the nation's research base.

The number of PhD students in the UK has risen by nearly 10,000 since 1997, and we are carrying through a 30 per cent increase in average PhD stipends to make doctoral research still more attractive to high-flyers.

We will incentivise all universities to raise more charitable and private funding for student bursaries and endowments.

The choice for 2010

Under their last government the Conservatives spent more on unemployment and debt interest than on education. Their priority now is to take at least £1 billion from state schools to subsidise private education for the privileged few. In addition they would allow a free-for-all in school admissions – including an extension of selection – for five- and 11-year-olds, cap the number of pupils who can succeed at GCSE and A-level, and reduce places in higher education. The choice for 2010 is forward with new Labour: pupils with quality and opportunity through the system from three to 18; parents with the confidence that where there is no improvement there will be intervention; teachers knowing that quality will be supported and rewarded; and employers with a system that gets the basics right and provides the skills that industry needs. Or back with the Tories to an education system designed to look after the few but fail the many.

CRIME AND SECURITY

Today, there is less chance of being a victim of crime than for more than 20 years. But our security is threatened by major organised crime; volume crimes such as burglary and car theft, often linked to drug abuse; fear of violent crime; and anti-social behaviour. Each needs a very different approach. We are giving the police and local councils the power to tackle anti-social behaviour; we will develop neighbourhood policing for every community and crack down on drug dealing and hard drug use to reduce volume crime; we are modernising our asylum and immigration system; and we will take the necessary measures to protect our country from international terrorism.

The new Labour case

The modern world offers freedoms and opportunities unheralded a generation ago. But with new freedoms come new fears and threats to our security. Our progressive case is that to counter these threats we need strong communities built on mutual respect and the rule of law. We prize the liberty of the individual; but that means protecting the law-abiding majority from the minority who abuse the system. We believe in being tough on crime and its causes so we will expand drugs testing and treatment, and tackle the conditions – from lack of youth provision to irresponsible drinking – that foster crime and anti-social behaviour. In a third term we will make the contract of rights and responsibilities an enduring foundation of community life.

A neighbourhood policing team for every community

Overall crime as measured by the authoritative British Crime Survey is down 30 per cent – the equivalent of almost five million fewer crimes a year. Record numbers of police – almost 13,000 more than in 1997 – working with 4,600 new Community Support Officers (CSOs), local councils, and the Crown Prosecution Service deserve the credit. But local people want a more visible police presence and a role in setting local police priorities. So our pledge is a neighbourhood policing team for every community. We will carry on funding the police service to enable it to continue to employ historically high numbers of police officers.

Hard-working police officers should be supported by professional and trained support staff. So a new £340 million a year fund will take CSO numbers up to 24,000 – to work alongside the equivalent of an additional 12,000 police officers freed up for frontline duties. And we will work with representatives of police officers and other police staff to develop a modern career framework for the whole police team.

Not all problems need a 999 response, so a single phone number staffed by police, local councils and other local services will be available across the country to deal with anti-social behaviour and other non-emergency problems.

Empowering communities against anti-social behaviour

People want communities where the decent law-abiding majority are in charge. The experience of almost 4,000 Anti-Social Behaviour Orders, nearly 66,000 Penalty Notices for Disorder, and the closure of over 150 crack houses shows that communities can fight back against crime. We are ready to go further.

Parish Council wardens, like those working for local authorities, will be given the power to issue Penalty Notices for Disorder for noise, graffiti and throwing fireworks. Victims of anti-social behaviour will be able to give evidence anonymously. Local people will be able to take on 'neighbours from hell' by triggering action by councils and the police.

We have reformed housing and planning legislation to ensure that councils plan for the needs of genuine Gypsies and travellers. But with rights must go responsibilities so we have provided tough new powers for councils and the police to tackle the problem of unauthorised sites.

Excessive alcohol consumption fuels anti-social behaviour and violence. The new Licensing Act will make it easier for the police and councils to deal with pubs and clubs that cause problems. Local councils and police will be able to designate Alcohol Disorder Zones to help pay for extra policing around city centre pubs and clubs, with new powers to immediately shut down premises selling alcohol to under-age drinkers, and bans from town and city centres for persistent offenders. Police will be able to exclude yobs from town centres for 24 hours when they issue a Penalty Notice for Disorder.

We will continue to overhaul our youth justice system and improve Young Offender Institutions. We will make more use of intensive community programmes, including electronic tagging and tracking to deal with the most persistent young offenders, and will increase the number of parents of young offenders getting help with their children's behaviour. We will increase, by at least a half, programmes targeted at young people most at risk of offending and will expand drug treatment services for young people.

Cutting crime through cutting drug dependency

Communities know that crime reduction depends on drug reduction. There are now 54 per cent more drug users in treatment and new powers for the police to close crack houses and get drug dealers off our streets. We will introduce compulsory drug testing at arrest for all property and drugs offenders, beginning in high-crime areas, with compulsory treatment assessment for those who test positive. Offenders under probation supervision will be randomly drug tested to mirror what already happens to offenders in custody.

From 2006, the Serious Organised Crime Agency will bring together over 4,000 specialist staff to tackle terrorism, drug dealers, people traffickers and other national and international organized criminals. And in consultation with local police authorities and chief constables we will restructure police resources in order to develop strong leadership, streamline all police support services, and focus upon national and regional organised crime.

Reducing the use of guns and knives

Dangerous weapons fuel violence. We have banned all handguns, introduced five-year minimum sentences for those caught with an unlawful firearm and raised the age limit for owning an air gun. Now we will go further. We will introduce a Violent Crime Reduction Bill to restrict the sale of replica guns, raise the age limit for buying knives to 18 and tighten the law on air guns. Head teachers will have legal rights to search pupils for knives or guns. At-risk pubs and clubs will be required to search for them and we will introduce tougher sentences for carrying replica guns, for those involved in serious knife crimes and for those convicted of assaulting workers serving the public.

Punishing criminals, reducing offending

As court sentences have got tougher, we have built over 16,000 more prison places than there were in 1997. The most high-risk violent offenders will now be detained in custody indefinitely and our 2003 Criminal Justice Act confirmed that life sentences must mean life for the most heinous murders. Where significant new evidence comes to light we have abolished the 'double jeopardy' rule so that serious criminals who have been unjustly acquitted can be tried again. And we will introduce much tougher penalties for those who cause death by careless driving or who kill while driving without a licence or while disqualified.

We will tackle reoffending. By 2007 every offender will be supervised after release; we will increase the use of electronic tagging; and we will test the use of compulsory lie detector tests to monitor convicted sex offenders. Our new National Offender Management Service will ensure that every offender is individually case-managed from beginning to end of their sentence, both in and out of custody – with increased effort targeted on drugs treatment, education and basic skills training to reduce reoffending. Voluntary organisations and the private sector will be offered greater opportunities to deliver offender services and we will give local people a greater say in shaping community punishment.

Making sure crime does not pay

Those who commit crimes should not profit from them. Already we have introduced laws that enable the courts to confiscate the assets and property of drug dealers and other major criminals. We will enable the police and prosecuting authorities to keep at least half of all the criminal assets they seize to fund local crime-fighting priorities. And we will develop new proposals to ensure that criminals are not able to profit from publishing books about their crimes. In addition we will support magistrates effectively in fighting crime and improve the enforcement of court decisions – including the payment of fines.

Where a defendant fails to turn up for court without good excuse, the presumption should be that the trial and sentencing should go ahead anyway.

We will overhaul laws on fraud and the way that fraud trials are conducted to update them for the 21st century and make them quicker and more effective.

Backing the victim

The legal system must dispense justice to the victim as well as the accused. We have invested to create a modern, self-confident prosecution service. With new powers and new technology to bring more offenders to justice more speedily and effectively. We will improve the way the courts work for victims, witnesses and jurors by:

- Building a nationwide network of witness and victim support units that provide practical help.
- Expanding specialist courts to deal with domestic violence and specialist advocates to support the victims of such crime and of other serious crimes like murder and rape.

We will extend the use of restorative justice schemes and Community Justice Centres to address the needs of victims, resolve disputes and help offenders to make recompense to victims for their crimes.

Legal aid will be reformed to better help the vulnerable. We will ensure independent regulation of the legal profession, and greater competition in the legal services market to ensure people get value for money. We will tackle the compensation culture – resisting invalid claims, but upholding people's rights.

Following consultation on the draft Bill we have published, we will legislate for a new offence of corporate manslaughter.

Migration: The facts

Over seven million people entered the UK from outside the EU in 2003: of whom 180,000 came here to work and over 300,000 to study, with the rest coming here as business visitors and tourists. People from overseas spent almost £12 billion in the UK, and overseas students alone are worth £5 billion a year to our economy. At a time when we have over 600,000 vacancies in the UK job market, skilled migrants are contributing 10-15 per cent of our economy's overall growth.

Since 1997, the time taken to process an initial asylum application has been reduced from 20 months to two months in over 80 per cent of cases. The number of asylum applications has been cut by two-thirds since 2002. The backlog of claims has been cut from over 50,000 at the end of 1996 to just over 10,000. There are 550 UK Immigration Officers posted in France and Belgium to check passports of people boarding boats and trains, and Airline Liaison Officers and overseas entry clearance staff are helping to stop 1,000 people a day improperly entering the UK.

Building a strong and diverse country

For centuries Britain has been a home for people from the rest of Europe and further afield. Immigration has been good for Britain. We want to keep it that way.

Our philosophy is simple: if you are ready to work hard and there is work for you to do, then you are welcome here. We need controls that work and a crackdown on abuse to ensure that we have a robust and fair immigration system fit for the 21st century that is in the interests of Britain.

A points system for immigration

We need skilled workers. So we will establish a points system for those seeking to migrate here. More skills mean more points and more chance of being allowed to come here.

We will ensure that only skilled workers are allowed to settle long-term in the UK, with English language tests for everyone who wants to stay permanently and an end to chain migration.

Where there has been evidence of abuse from particular countries, the immigration service will be able to ask for financial bonds to guarantee that migrants return home. We will continue to improve the quality and speed of immigration and asylum decisions. Appeal rights for non-family immigration cases will be removed and we will introduce civil penalties on employers of up to £2,000 for each illegal immigrant they employ.

Strong and secure borders

While the Tories would halve investment in our immigration services, we would invest in the latest technology to keep our borders strong and secure.

By 2008, those needing a visa to enter the UK will be fingerprinted. We will issue ID cards to all visitors planning to stay for more than three months. Over the next five years we will implement a new electronic borders system that will track visitors entering or leaving the UK.

Across the world there is a drive to increase the security of identity documents and we cannot be left behind. From next year we are introducing biometric 'ePassports'. It makes sense to provide citizens with an equally secure identity card to protect them at home from identity theft and clamp down on illegal working and fraudulent use of public services. We will introduce ID cards, including biometric data like fingerprints, backed up by a national register and rolling out initially on a voluntary basis as people renew their passports.

Fair rules

We can and should honour our obligations to victims of persecution without allowing abuse of the asylum system. We will:

- Fast-track all unfounded asylum seekers with electronic tagging where necessary and more use of detention as we expand the number of detention places available.
- Remove more failed applicants. We have more than doubled the number of failed asylum seekers we remove from the UK compared to 1996. By fingerprinting every visa applicant and prosecuting those who deliberately destroy their documents we will speed up the time taken to redocument and remove people and will take action against those countries that refuse to co-operate. By the end of 2005, our aim is for removals of failed asylum seekers to exceed new unfounded claims.

Tough action to combat international terrorism

We know that there are people already in the country and who seek to enter the United Kingdom who want to attack our way of life. Our liberties are prized but so is our security.

Police and other law enforcement agencies now have the powers they need to ban terrorist organisations, to clampdown on their fundraising and to hold suspects for extended questioning while charges are brought. Over 700 arrests have been made since 2001. Wherever possible, suspects should be prosecuted through the courts in the normal way. So we will introduce new laws to help catch and convict those involved in helping to plan terrorist activity or who glorify or condone acts of terror. But we also need to disrupt and prevent terrorist activity. New control orders will enable police and security agencies to keep track on those they suspect of planning terrorist outrages including bans on who they can contact or meet, electronic tagging and curfew orders, and for those who present the highest risk, a requirement to stay permanently at home.

We will continue to improve coordination between enforcement agencies and co-operation with other countries so that every effort is made to defeat the terrorists.

The choice for 2010

Labour's goals for 2010 are clear. Overall crime down, the number of offenders brought to justice up, with a neighbourhood policing team in every community to crack down on crime and disorder and a modern criminal justice system fit for the 21st century. And to reduce threats from overseas: secure borders backed up by ID cards and a crackdown on abuse of our immigration system. The Conservative threat is equally clear. Savage cuts to our border controls, 'fantasy island' asylum policies and a return to the days of broken promises on police numbers and crime investment.

THE NHS

The NHS is being restored to good health: more doctors, more nurses, better facilities. Waiting times are coming down and the survival rates for the biggest killers are improving. The revolution in quantity of care must be matched by a revolution in quality of care. With equal access for all and no charges for operations. That means new types of health provision, more say for patients in how, where and when they are treated, and tackling ill-health at source.

The new Labour case

Healthcare is too precious to be left to chance, too central to life chances to be left to your wealth. Access to treatment should be based on your clinical need not on your ability to pay. This means defeating those who would dismantle the NHS. But it also means fundamentally reforming the NHS to meet new challenges – a more demanding citizenry with higher expectations, major advances in science and medical technology, changes in the composition and needs of the population.

So our aim is an NHS free to all of us and personal to each of us. We will deliver through high national standards backed by sustained investment, by using new providers where they add capacity or promote innovation, and most importantly by giving more power to patients over their own treatment and over their own health.

We promised to revive the NHS; we have. In our third term we will make the NHS safe for a generation.

New investment

NHS spending has doubled since 1997, and will triple by 2008; already we have an extra 27,000 doctors in post or in training and 79,000 extra nurses; over 100 new hospital building projects under way; 500,000 more operations a year. We are proud of the dedication and commitment of NHS staff. We have widened the responsibilities of nurses and pharmacists, paramedics and porters, creating health services more convenient for patients.

Together with our organisational reforms, the investment is paying off. The maximum time that people waited for operations in 1997 was well over 18 months. Now virtually no one waits longer than nine months, and this year it will fall further to six months. For a heart operation or for cataract removal no one is waiting longer than three months; 97 per cent of people wait less than four hours in Accident and Emergency before treatment, admission or discharge.And speedier treatment saves lives. Death rates from heart disease are down by 27 per cent since 1996; from cancer by 12 per cent.

We will do even better. For too long waiting times have only counted the time after diagnosis. We will be the first Government to include all waiting times in this calculation, including waiting for outpatient appointments and for test results. There will be no hidden waits. So:

- By the end of 2008, no NHS patient will have to wait longer than a maximum of 18 weeks from the time they are referred for a hospital operation by their GP until the time they have that operation. This would mean an average wait of nine to ten weeks.
- We will commit to faster test results for cervical smears.
- We will go further in improving cancer waiting times.

All this with equal access for all, free at the point of need with no charges for hospital operations.

We have tightened the rules on NHS operations so that 'health tourists' now have to pay for treatment.

We will deal with the challenge of MRSA. Infections acquired in hospital are not new. The time to destroy MRSA was in the early 1990s – when only five per cent of the bacteria were resistant to antibiotics. At that time the Tory government did not even keep records about the incidence of MRSA and were forcing hospitals to contract out cleaning services. We were the first government to publish statistics on the problem. Now, thanks to the tough measures we have already taken, including the end to a two-tier workforce for contracted-out cleaning services, MRSA rates are on their way down. But there is still some way to go. We all want clean hospitals, free of infection. We have already reintroduced hospital matrons and given them unprecedented powers to deal with cleanliness and infections in their wards; we shall reinforce this by consulting on new laws to enforce higher hygiene standards.

And by strengthening accountability and cutting bureaucracy, we shall ensure that the new investment is not squandered. We are decreasing the numbers of staff in the Department of Health by a third, and are halving the numbers of quangos – freeing up £500 million for front-line staff. Given the pace of change within medical services we will ensure that it is possible for the NHS to change the way in which it organises its services as quickly as possible.Further streamlining measures will allow us to release an additional £250 million a year for front-line services by 2007.

In the light of the findings of the Shipman Inquiry, we will strengthen clinical governance in the NHS to ensure that professional activity is fully accountable to patients, their families and the wider public. Following the recommendation of the Health Select Committee, we will require registration of all clinical trials and publication of their findings for all trials of medicinal products with a marketing authorisation in the UK.

Innovation and reform

To achieve our goals we need to expand and develop different types of provision. We will put more money into the frontline, develop practice-based commissioning, and so ensure that family doctors have more power over their budgets. We will create more services in primary care. We will build on our family doctor service with more GPs delivering more advanced services more locally; new walk-in centres for commuters; specialised diagnostic and testing services; comprehensive out-of-hours services; high-street drop-in centres for chiropody, physiotherapy and check-ups. And we will continue to expand the role of nurses. These changes will result in more quality, convenience and care.

Expansion in NHS capacity will come both from within the National Health Service – where we will develop the NHS Foundation Trust model and the new freedom for GPs to expand provision – as well as from the independent and voluntary sector, where specialist services are available at NHS standards to meet NHS need.

To help create an even greater range of provision and further improve convenience, we will over the next five years develop a new generation of modern NHS community hospitals. These state-of-the-art centres will provide diagnostics, day surgery and outpatients facilities closer to where people live and work.

We shall continue to encourage innovation and reform through the use of the independent sector to add capacity to, and drive contestability within, the NHS. We have already commissioned 460,000 operations from the independent sector, which will all be delivered free – with equal access for all based on need, not the ability to pay.

Whenever NHS patients need new capacity for their healthcare, we will ensure that it is provided from whatever source.

Empowering patients: choosing not waiting

One principle underpins our reforms – putting patients centre stage. And extending patient power and choice is crucial to achieving this. We shall be embedding both throughout the NHS. So:

- By the end of 2008, patients whose GPs refer them for an operation will be able to choose from any hospital that can provide that operation to NHS medical and financial standards. There will be the choice of a convenient time and place for a non-urgent operation for example a location close to relatives.
- We will expand capacity and choice in primary care too. Where GPs' lists are full we will expand provision by encouraging entrepreneurial GPs and other providers to expand into that location.
- By 2009 all women will have choice over where and how they have their baby and what pain relief to use. We want every woman to be supported by the same midwife throughout her pregnancy. Support will be linked closely to other services that will be provided in Children's Centres.
- In order to increase choices for patients with cancer we will double the investment going into palliative care services, giving more people the choice to be treated at home.

By October 2005 we will have recruited more than 1,000 new NHS dentists and will have increased the number of dental school places by 25 per cent. We will undertake a fundamental review of the scope and resourcing of NHS dentistry.

We will provide more information and advice. Through NHS Direct, Health Direct,interactive TV, print media and the internet we will give more convenient access to much better information about health and health services, including the performance of doctors and hospitals.

Empowering patients: long-term conditions and social care

We will promote the integration of health and social care at local level, so that older people and those with long-term conditions can retain their independence. We will continue to provide healthcare free in long-term care establishments, and provide the right framework for schemes such as equity release which make staying at home an attractive option. We will develop our policy of community matrons for those with severe conditions, helping to keep people out of hospital by providing better care at home.

- We will develop personalised budgets in social care where people can decide for themselves what they need and how it should be provided.
- We shall extend case-management for the 18 million people with long-term conditions. We will treble the investment in the Expert Patients Programme, and help many more patients take control of their own care plans.
- Almost a third of people attending GP surgeries have mental health problems and mental health occupies approximately one third of a GP's time. So we will continue to invest in and improve our services for people with mental health problems at primary and secondary levels, including behavioural as well as drug therapies.
- We shall provide safeguards for the few people with long-term mental health problems who need compulsory treatment coupled with appropriate protection for the public. We shall also strengthen the system for protecting the public from offenders who have served their sentence but may still pose a threat because they have a serious psychopathic disorder.

Living healthier lives

People want to take responsibility for their own health outside the NHS as well as within it. They have the right to expect help from government. The killer diseases of the heart and the many forms of cancer are often the product of poor diet, lack of exercise and above all smoking. By 2010 we aim to reduce deaths from coronary heart disease and strokes by 40 per cent from 1997. And we want death rates from cancer to be cut by 20 per cent.

Healthy choices for children

We will start the drive for better health early – at school. We have already extended the provision of free fruit to all 4- to 6-year-olds at school. We will invest more in renovating and building new kitchens as well as investing an extra £210 million in school meals, guaranteeing that at least 50p per meal is spent on ingredients in primary schools, and at least 60p in secondary schools. We are introducing an independent School Food Trust, better training for dinner ladies and Ofsted inspection of healthy eating. We will legislate for tougher standards of nutrition for school meals and will encourage schools to teach more about healthy eating. We will ban certain products that are high in fat/salt content from school meals and ensure that fresh fruit and vegetables are part of every school meal. We will encourage secondary schools to keep pupils on the premises to ensure that they have a healthy meal. We will ensure that all school children have access to a school nurse.

Healthy choices for all

We will put in place a simple system of labelling to make it easier for busy shoppers to see at a glance how individual foods contribute to a healthy balanced diet. We will help parents by restricting further the advertising and promotion to children of those foods and drinks that are high in fat, salt and sugar.

We recognise that many people want smoke-free environments and need regulation to help them get this. We therefore intend to shift the balance significantly in their favour. We will legislate to ensure that all enclosed public places and workplaces other than licensed premises will be smoke-free. The legislation will ensure that all restaurants will be smoke-free; all pubs and bars preparing and serving food will be smoke-free; and other pubs and bars will be free to choose whether to allow smoking or to be smoke-free. In membership clubs the members will be free to choose whether to allow smoking or to be smoke-free. However, whatever the general status, to protect employees, smoking in the bar area will be prohibited everywhere.

These restrictions will be accompanied by an expansion of NHS smoking cessation services to encourage and support smokers to improve their own health by giving up smoking.

Starting with the poorest areas of the country we will introduce health trainers to help people maintain their healthy choices. By 2010, through this activity we plan to reduce the health inequalities that exist between rich and poor.

All this will be free at the point of need.

The choice for 2010

Today's Conservatives want to do what not even Margaret Thatcher would countenance – introducing charges for hospital operations so that those who can afford to pay thousands of pounds can push ahead of those who cannot. As well as ending the founding principle of the health service, this would take more than £1 billion out of the system to subsidise those who can afford to pay. For the rest of us, the Tories would abandon waiting list targets and allow a return to the 18-month waits that were their NHS legacy. The choice is forward with new Labour to a health system with patients in the driving seat, free to all and personal to each of us. Or back with the Tories to longer waits, and to a health system where treatment depends not on your condition but on your bank balance.

OLDER PEOPLE

Our priority since 1997 has been to tackle pensioner poverty. Nearly two million pensioners have been lifted out of absolute poverty as a result of Labour's measures, which are now getting on average an extra £2,000 a year to the poorest third. Our priorities now are to build a national consensus for tomorrow's pensioners, combining public and private pension schemes to build security in retirement, and to extend the quality of life of older people.

The new Labour case

By 2020 there will be more people over the age of 80 than under the age of five. For a progressive government there can be no compromise of our duty to today's pensioners. But while we fulfil that duty we must also see old age as a time of independence and opportunity. On pensions, our aim is a system that provides security and decency for all, which encourages and rewards saving, and is financially sustainable. And because, more than anything, people need certainty to plan for the future we will seek a national consensus – cross-party, cross-generation – for long-term reform.

Tackling pensioner poverty

In 1997, 2.8 million pensioners were living in poverty – with the poorest expected to live on just £69 per week. Labour's Pension Credit now means that no pensioner need live on less than £109 per week. It rewards saving and helps over three million pensioners, with women in particular benefiting. We will increase Pension Credit in line with earnings up to and including 2007-08.

All pensioners have benefited from improved universal benefits like the state pension,the Winter Fuel Payment (now worth £300 per year for the over-80s), help with council tax and free TV licences for the over-75s. This year, all households expected to pay council tax that include anyone over 65 will receive £200 towards the cost of council tax,and the following year there will be free,off-peak local bus travel in England for the over-60s.

Millions of pensioners have benefited from our fuel poverty programme. Our goal is to eliminate fuel poverty for vulnerable groups by 2010, and for all by 2015.

Pensions for the generation of tomorrow

The generation retiring in the future will be different in many ways from its predecessors. Their jobs will have been different; the expectations of women will be transformed;their retirements will be longer and healthier. We have begun to lay the foundations for the pensions system of tomorrow, for example, by: introducing the State Second Pension to ensure carers, low earners and disabled people have a chance to build up a decent pension for the first time; encouraging automatic enrolment into company pension schemes; creating the Pension Protection Fund; enabling pensioners for the first time to work part time and draw down their occupational pension; as well as offering an increased state pension or lump sum for those deferring their pension. We will work to increase the proportion of pension fund trustees nominated by scheme members, along with access to proper training. We will keep this issue under review, with consultation in the expectation of further progress to 50 per cent member-nominated trustees.

We need to forge a national consensus about how we move from a pension system designed for today's pension problems to one that is right for tomorrow's. We appointed the Pensions Commission to look into the future of pensions and its second report is due in autumn 2005. We are clear about the goals of a reformed system. It must tackle poverty,provide everyone with the opportunity to build an adequate retirement income, and be affordable, fair and simple to understand. In particular it must address the disadvantages faced by women.

New rights, new choices

Many older people want to carry on working in their 50s and 60s. The welfare state should be there to help them. Older people with their skills and experience are potentially an enormous resource. That is why we set up the New Deal for the Over-50s,with over 150,000 older people helped back to work.

We also need to put the force of the law on the side of older people who wish to continue working. Companies will no longer be able to force people to retire before the age of 65 except where specifically justified. All employees over the age of 65 will have the right to request of their employer that they be allowed to carry on working. After five years we will review whether there should be any fixed retirement ages.

We will give older people greater choice over their care. For every older person receiving care or other support, we want to offer transparent, individual budgets which bring funding for a range of services, including social care, care homes, and housing support such as adaptations, maintenance and cleaners together in one place. We will pilot individual budgets for older people by the end of this year.

We will make the most of the opportunities of an older population by creating a new programme for older people to be mentors and coaches to gifted and talented young people. We will also work with voluntary organisations to help expand grandparent and toddler groups across the country.

Support across the generations

The challenge of balancing work and family applies to parents but also to people looking after an elderly or sick relative – now one in five adults. Since the introduction of the right to request from their employer flexible working arrangements, a million parents have changed their working hours. We are consulting on a similar right for carers of elderly or sick relatives.

The choice for 2010

The Tories are the party of pensioner poverty. When they left office in 1997, one in four pensioners was living in poverty and the poorest pensioners were expected to get by on just £69 a week. They would phase out the Pension Credit and abolish the State Second Pension, hurting most those most in need. When the one thing we all need is certainty, the Tories have admitted they have absolutely no plans for how to fund their pensions policy beyond four years. The choice is whether we go forward with new Labour with today's pensioners provided for and poverty falling, a national consensus on fair and sustainable long-term reform and the policies to give older people enhanced rights and choices. Or back with the Tories to rising levels of pensioner poverty and unending insecurity for tomorrow's pensioners.

FAMILIES

It is impossible to fulfil the potential of our country – never mind promoting social mobility and equality of life chances – unless every child gets the best possible start in life. Government does not bring up children, but it must support parents in their key role. We will help parents balance work and family, expand paid leave, deliver the biggest ever expansion in childcare and end child poverty in a generation.

The new Labour case

Strong families are the bedrock of a strong society. Children cannot be the forgotten constituency of politics; parents put their children first and they deserve support from government.Yet fear of seeming to 'nanny' has in the past meant British law and culture have not supported parents and children. Government cannot shirk its responsibilities. Our starting point is that for children to come first parents need to be given choices: a tax and benefit system to raise family incomes and tackle child poverty; legal changes to promote a healthy balance between work and family; and services built around the needs of children. Our third-term commitment – not a nanny state but a family-friendly government.

Tackling child poverty

We will end child poverty, starting by halving it – both in terms of relative low-income and in terms of material deprivation – by 2010-11.

Work is the best anti-poverty strategy. Tailored help, especially for lone parents, is key but we are also committed to making work pay – with a guaranteed income of at least £258 per week for those with children and in full-time work.

The benefits system needs to support all children, and those in greatest need the most. That is the rationale for universal child benefit and targeted tax credits, and why we have committed to increasing the Child Tax Credit at least in line with earnings up to and including 2007-08. By October 2005, families with children will be on average £1,400 per year better off, and those in the poorest fifth of the population on average £3,200 a year better off compared to 1997. Labour's Child Trust Fund creates a nest egg for newborns that they can access at age 18. It is the world's first example of a government ensuring that all children grow up with a financial stake. We are determined to see it grow and are consulting on making payments at age seven and at secondary school age, in addition to those made at birth.

We are supporting local authorities in the radical reform of children's services, above all to ensure there is one professional with lead responsibility for each vulnerable child. We will also ensure that services are designed to meet the additional needs of disabled children and their families.

Universal childcare

Since 1997, the Government has funded an additional 520,000 sustainable childcare places and now every family with a three- or four-year-old child has access to a free nursery place. By 2010, we will create 3,500 Sure Start Children's Centres for children under five years – five in every constituency – a universal local service that brings together childcare and services for families. By 2010, all parents of three- and four-year-olds will have increased rights to flexible, free, part-time nursery provision for 15 hours a week over the whole school year. Over the longer term we will increase free provision to 20 hours.

For older children up to the age of 14 extended schools, working in partnership with the private and voluntary sectors, will offer affordable out-of-school childcare from 8am to 6pm throughout the year, with a range of arts, music, sport and study support.

We will help families with incomes of up to £59,000 a year with their childcare costs through more generous Working Tax Credit, including help for those using a nanny or au pair. Parents using childcare sup-ported by their employer will be able to get a tax break worth up to £50 a week each. We are working with the GLA and the Mayor to bring down the cost of childcare in London.

Creating time

Over 350,000 mothers and 80,000 fathers each year are using new rights to paid maternity and paternity leave. Parents consistently say their top priority is more choice of whether to stay at home with their baby in the first year of its life. We will therefore increase paid maternity leave to nine months from 2007 – worth an extra £1,400 – with the goal of achieving a year's paid leave by the end of the Parliament while simplifying the system for employers. We want to give fathers more opportunities to spend time with their children, and are consulting on how best to do this including the option of sharing paid leave. We have already introduced the right to request flexible working to parents of children under six and nearly a million parents have benefited. We need to balance the needs of parents and carers, with those of employers, especially small businesses. We are consulting on extending the right to request flexible working to carers of sick and disabled adults as a priority, and also on whether we should extend the right to parents of older children.

Supporting family life

Common sense, as well as research, says that children need to be able to depend on the love and support of both parents. The financial support we are giving families, along with new rights to flexible working and access to childcare, are all designed to support family life. Government can and should support those public and voluntary agencies that support families and parents. We are examining the development of a new information service – Parents Direct – to provide advice on all aspects of children's services and parental entitlements.

For those parents who do separate or divorce, both have a responsibility for a meaningful relationship with their children where that is safe. We are introducing reforms to minimise conflict and encourage conciliation by greater and early use of mediation. We stand by the principle that absent parents should make a fair contribution to the cost of the upkeep of their children, and we are committed to tackling the backlog of Child Support Agency claims as efficiently and fairly as possible. We also need to ensure court orders on access are enforced according to the best interests of the child, which ideally gives both parents an important role.

Increasing home ownership

A decent home is crucial to family well-being. Home ownership has increased by over one million with Labour and by the end of our third term we aim for it to have risen by another million to two million. Rising house prices in many areas of the country have made it difficult for people on lower incomes to get a foot on the housing ladder. So we have raised the stamp duty threshold from £60,000 to £120,000 for residential properties, exempting an extra 300,000 homebuyers from stamp duty every year.

We will continue to respond to the challenges of local housing markets across the UK. In the South we will invest in extra housing in London and the wider South East, with particular emphasis on the Thames Gateway and other growth areas. In the Midlands and North we will tackle the problems of low demand and abandonment that threaten communities.

We want to widen the opportunity to own or part own, especially for more young people and those tenants who rent in the private or public sector. Our comprehensive plan includes:

- A new Homebuy scheme offering up to 300,000 council and housing association tenants the opportunity to buy part of their home, increasing their equity over time if they wish.
- A First Time Buyers Initiative to help over 15,000 first-time buyers who could not own or part-own a home without extra help. We will use surplus public land for new homes, enabling the buyer to take out a mortgage for only the building.
- Strengthening existing home ownership schemes, such as the Key Worker Living scheme and Shared Ownership.

Social housing

The increased supply and quality of social housing is central to Labour's belief in mixed, sustainable communities.

Since 1997, we have cut the number of substandard social-rented homes by one million; installing 300,000 new kitchens, 220,000 new bathrooms and 720,000 new boilers and central heating systems into council homes. By 2010 we will ensure that all social tenants benefit from a decent, warm home with modern facilities.

For too long, tenants have had little say over where they live. In a third term, Labour will offer greater flexibility and choice for those who rent. We will increase the annual supply of new social homes by 50 per cent by 2008, an extra 10,000 homes a year, and give local authorities the ability to start building homes again and bring empty homes back into use. And we will end the 'take it or leave it' approach to social renting by expanding choice-based lettings nationwide.

The choice for 2010

The Tories are all talk and no action on family policy. They opposed our increases in maternity and paternity pay and the introduction of flexible working rights. Even the measures they have proposed wouldn't come in until 2009, by which time the Tories are committed to making deep cuts in spending. The choice is forward with new Labour to a universal, affordable, good-quality childcare, a million more homeowners, more choice for all parents and an end to child poverty. Or back to the risky economic policies of a Tory government that would let families sink or swim whatever the pressures they face.

INTERNATIONAL POLICY

Globalisation means that events elsewhere have a direct impact at home. So we will pursue British interests by working with our allies to make the world a safer, fairer place. This means reforming Europe. It means fighting terrorism and stopping the spread of weapons of mass destruction. It means modernising our armed forces. And it means using our leading role in the G8, EU, the Commonwealth and UN to promote global action on climate change and poverty.

The new Labour case

Domestic interests and international action are entwined more than ever before. Action on drugs, terrorism, people trafficking, AIDS, climate change, poverty, migration and trade all require us to work with other countries and through international organisations. The best defence of our security at home is the spread of liberty and justice overseas. In a third term we will secure Britain's place in the EU and at the heart of international decision-making. We will always uphold the rule of international law.

Making Europe work better for Britain

We are proud of Britain's EU membership and of the strong position Britain has achieved within Europe. British membership of the EU brings jobs, trade and prosperity; it boosts environmental standards, social protection and international clout. Since 1997 we have gone from marginal players, often ignored, to leaders in the European Union. Working hard with Labour MEPs, we are determined to remain leaders. Outside the EU, or on its margins, we would unquestionably be weaker and more vulnerable.

The EU now has 25 members and will continue to expand. The new Constitutional Treaty ensures the new Europe can work effectively, and that Britain keeps control of key national interests like foreign policy, taxation, social security and defence. The Treaty sets out what the EU can do and what it cannot. It strengthens the voice of national parliaments and governments in EU affairs. It is a good treaty for Britain and for the new Europe. We will put it to the British people in a referendum and campaign whole-heartedly for a 'Yes' vote to keep Britain a leading nation in Europe.

We will also work to reform Europe. During Britain's EU presidency this year, we will work to promote economic reform, bear down on regulation; make progress in the Doha development trade round; bring closer EU membership for Turkey, the Balkans and Eastern Europe; and improve the focus and quality of EU aid so it better helps the poorest countries.

We will continue to lead European defence co-operation. We will build stronger EU defence capabilities, in harmony with NATO – the cornerstone of our defence policy – without compromising our national ability to act independently. We will ensure the new EU battle groups are equipped and organised to act quickly to save lives in humanitarian crises.

On the euro, we maintain our common sense policy. The determining factor underpinning any government decision is the national economic interest and whether the case for joining is clear and unambiguous. The five economic tests must be met before any decision to join can be made. If the Government were to recommend joining, it would be put to a vote in Parliament and a referendum of the British people.

Protecting British interests and British citizens abroad

We will continue to provide effective support to British businesses and trade unions abroad, and we will continue to improve our ability to respond quickly to international crises and disasters which affect our citizens. The Foreign Office already provides a wide range of services for British people in difficulty overseas, and we will consult widely before drawing up a comprehensive statement spelling out the rights and responsibilities of British travellers abroad. This will include the help that people can expect from their government in times of need.

Helping make you more secure

We have worked closely with the US and other nations to combat the threat of terrorism in Afghanistan and in Iraq. The threat of the proliferation of chemical, biological and nuclear weapons – and their use by rogue states or terrorist groups – is a pressing issue for the world today. We have worked with the US to ensure that Libya has given up its WMD, and we will continue with France and Germany to ensure that Iran does not develop nuclear weapons. In North Korea we will support the multilateral approach of the Six Parties talks. We will continue to strongly support the peace process between India and Pakistan, and back moves to resolve the long-running dispute over Kashmir. And we will work to put an end to the international network of trade in weapons of mass destruction. Labour has already introduced a strict regime to control the export of conventional weapons, and we led moves for EU-wide measures. We will work actively to secure an international treaty on the arms trade.

Promoting human rights, peace and democracy

We need to be tough on terrorism and its causes. The threat of terrorism and the danger to British citizens is proven, not just by September 11th but by repeated attacks in Europe and around the world. So we cannot sit back and hope that we will be unaffected. It is right that we do everything in our power to disrupt terrorist networks, and to challenge the conditions that help terrorism to breed.

The UN Charter proclaims the universal principles of human rights and democracy. In an uncertain world they are not only right in principle, they are important guarantees of our national security and prosperity too.

There have been major strides forward in recent years: in Indonesia, Afghanistan and many parts of Africa and Latin America, democracy is being extended.

We mourn the loss of life of innocent civilians and coalition forces in the war in Iraq and the subsequent terrorism. But the butchery of Saddam is over and across Iraq, eight million people risked their lives to vote earlier this year. Many people disagreed with the action we took in Iraq. We respect and understand their views. But we should all now unite to support the fledgling democracy in Iraq. British troops should remain in Iraq under a United Nations mandate as long as the democratically elected government there wants them. They will continue to train Iraqi security forces to take responsibility for their own future.

We welcome the wider process of democratic reform across the Middle East, and we will work with our allies to encourage and promote economic and political change.

We strongly support the peace process between Israel and Palestine. Resolution of the conflict is crucial to peace in the region and the wider world. The conference held in London in March 2005 has started the process of helping a democratic government in Palestine build security and prosperity. We will work tirelessly to bring about a peace settlement in which a viable and independent state of Palestine lives alongside a safe and secure Israel.

Supporting our armed forces

Britain's armed forces are among the best in the world. They are able to play a key role in advancing our interests and values. We want to keep it that way.

We are immensely proud of the bravery, skill and dedication our armed forces have demonstrated in Afghanistan, Iraq, Sierra Leone, the Balkans and elsewhere across the world. They are a force for good. We will never commit forces to battle unless it is essential; but when they are committed they will have the investment, strategy, training and preparation they need. That is one reason we have given the armed forces the biggest sustained increase in funding since the end of the Cold War. But we also know that modern demands on our armed forces are changing. That is why reform and modernisation are essential. A reduction in the number of infantry battalions, made possible because of the improved security situation in Northern Ireland, has allowed extra resources for the vital support services such as signals, engineers, intelligence and logistics units – the parts of the army most under pressure. This is essential to allow our infantry soldiers to be fully supported when they go into action on our behalf. We will continue with the investment and reform that make our fighting forces the most flexible and effective in the world.

We are also committed to retaining the independent nuclear deterrent and we will continue to work, both bilaterally and through the UN, to urge states not yet party to non-proliferation treaties, notably the Nuclear Non-Proliferation Treaty, to join.

Veterans

Labour has always recognised the sacrifice and bravery of our servicemen and women. That is why we were the first government to appoint a Minister for Veterans Affairs. This has enabled us to put veterans' affairs at the heart of decision-making at the Ministry of Defence. Labour has also put more money than ever before into veterans' issues, including £27 million of Lottery funding over the last two years. We will continue to give priority to veterans' affairs as we mark 60 years since the end of the Second World War.

Reforming the United Nations

The UN is crucial to our efforts to build a more secure and more prosperous world. We support the reform of the Security Council so it becomes more representative and has a stronger focus on conflict prevention. We support the recommendation of the Secretary-General's High-level Panel for a Peace-building Commission to assist countries emerging from conflict and to develop mechanisms to enhance conflict prevention. We will press for more radical reform of the UN humanitarian system, so it is better equipped to saves lives. We will also press for reform of the World Bank and IMF to improve transparency, give more say to developing countries and, with the EU better focus their efforts on the poorest countries, particularly in Africa.

Climate change and Africa

Britain has the chair of the G8 this year. We will use the summit for two particular purposes.

First, climate change is the one of the most pressing challenges that the world faces. We will continue to lead internationally on climate change, and to strive for wider acceptance of the science and the steps needed to combat the problem. We will look beyond Kyoto and promote an international dialogue to reach agreement on the long-term goals and action needed to stabilise the level of greenhouse gases in the atmosphere. We will also work for effective international action to adapt to the impacts of climate change.

The UK has already met its obligations under the Kyoto Protocol. We remain committed to achieving a 20 per cent reduction in carbon dioxide emissions on 1990 levels by 2010, and our review of progress this summer will show us how to get back on track. A 60 per cent reduction by 2050 remains necessary and achievable.

We will continue to promote and develop renewable energy sources, to seek high standards of energy efficiency in the public and private sectors, and to support emissions trading in Europe and beyond.

Secondly we will focus on Africa and the global fight against poverty.

We have more than doubled aid since 1997. We have cancelled the debts of the poorest countries and are now pushing others to follow our lead and offer 100 per cent debt relief for the poorest. We are proud to have established a Department for International Development, with a clear mission to reduce poverty. Now, for the first time ever the UK has a clear timetable – 2013 – for achieving the UN target of 0.7 per cent of national income devoted to development. Globally we are pressing for a doubling of aid backed by getting international agreement to an International Finance Facility as supported by the Commission for Africa.

But aid will not be successful without conflict prevention, good governance and zero tolerance of corruption. We will work for faster repatriation of stolen assets from UK financial institutions, ratification of the UN Convention on corruption, and more open and accountable reporting of revenues from oil and mining – that so often fuel local conflicts. Our commitment is to the people of the developing world; our contract is with their governments for reform. But if poor countries are committed to good governance and poverty reduction we then believe they should be in control of their own policies. We will end the practice of making aid conditional on sensitive economic policy choices, such as trade liberalisation and privatisation.

With this leadership and extra money, we can now work to ensure all children go to school, and millions of people in Asia and Africa suffering from AIDS, tuberculosis and malaria have access to treatment. In particular, we will press for an international agreement on universal access to AIDS treatment by 2010 and for all people in poor countries to have access to free basic healthcare and education.

Our long-term aim is to help lift a billion people out of poverty.

Fair trade

We also know that without fairer trade rules and private investment, poor countries will not generate the growth needed to lift themselves out of poverty. We will press for the conclusion of an ambitious trade deal that will completely open markets to exports from poorer countries; for further reform of rich countries' agricultural subsidies, including the EU's Common Agricultural Policy and a 2010 timetable to end agricultural export subsidies. We do not believe poor countries should be forced to liberalise. We will allow them to sequence their trade reforms, so they can build their capacity to compete globally.

The choice for 2010

In 1997 the Tories had left Britain isolated in Europe, overseas aid had declined and we lacked any coherent vision of our place in the world. With Labour, a strong Britain will force international terrorism into retreat and help spread democracy and freedom around the world. We will be leaders in a reformed Europe, and, with others, make significant progress towards raising a billion people out of extreme poverty. We will fight for a new global agreement on climate change, an arms trade treaty, and a trade deal that makes trade work for the many, not just the few. Our armed forces will continue to be the best in the world. The alternative is to go back to the Tories with their record of cuts in aid and defence and their policies of tearing up the Social Chapter, and marginalising Britain in Europe and the world.

QUALITY OF LIFE

Arts, culture and sport are thriving around Britain – enriching individual lives and transforming communities, towns and cities. They are important in their own right – as nourishment for our imagination or a source of plain enjoyment and our local environment should be a source of pride. We will work to improve the quality of life of every community in Britain.

The new Labour case

We believe in the inherent value of arts, culture and sport. Our towns and cities are being energised by sports and culture and as they are regenerated the quality of life for all is transformed. As we build on this change, our progressive challenge is to broaden participation as widely as possible, making the links between sport and health, and culture and well-being. We must combine the broadest base of participation with the ability for the most talented to progress to the very top. Our third term will embed the expectation that every child and every adult have the maximum chance to develop their creative or sporting talents.

Creative cities

Art and culture are valuable for their own sake; they are also crucial to our national prosperity. Britain's cultural industries now make up over eight per cent of our national income; and from computer games to the fine arts, British talent is gaining global recognition and generating real wealth. This is one of the fastest growing and fastest changing areas of the economy. And the transformation of our great cities is, in great part, a story of culture-led regeneration. We are proud of the record of Labour-led councils in leading this transformation, from Gateshead to Greenwich.

To help young talent get the right start we will work to establish Creative Apprenticeships. Through the National Endowment for Science, Technology and the Arts (NESTA) we are funding the Creative Pioneer Academy which will develop the entrepreneurial skills of recent graduates with outstanding talents and original business ideas – and for some there will be the offer of up to £35,000 to start their own business.

From 2006 we will provide £12 million over two years to the Arts Council England to promote leadership and management in the cultural sector. We want to invest in high-flyers developing commercial and business skills, encourage the talents of leading ethnic minority figures and improve the links between arts and business.

Arts, culture and museums

Since 1997 we have increased funding for the arts by 73 per cent in real terms. We will continue to support our finest artists and institutions to achieve worldclass standards.

Thanks to our policy of free admissions the number of people visiting formerly charging national museums and galleries has risen by 75 per cent over three years. Many are first-time visitors, with the biggest increases among children.

Victorian City leaders left us a legacy of great local and regional museums, and through our investment programme 'Renaissance in the Regions', we are recreating them as centres of excellence. By 2008 we will have invested £147 million in partnerships across the country, modernising museum collections,broadening access to new audiences and providing a comprehensive service to schools. We will explore further ways to encourage philanthropy to boost the quality of our public art collections.

We will legislate, as soon as time allows, to implement the findings of the Heritage Protection Review, which allows the public a greater say in listing decisions.

Creative Sparks

Our aim is that everyone should have the opportunity to participate in cultural life, and we want that involvement to start as early as possible. Creative Partnerships, our programme of support for art in schools in our most disadvantaged areas, has already reached over 150,000 children. We will build on this approach by rolling out our new programme Creative Sparks to guarantee that all children and young people will be given the chance to experience the very best of culture every year.

Sport for all

Our aim is to increase participation in sport year on year. Central to this is having modern, high-quality facilities close to where people live. £1.5 billion is being invested in sports facilities in every community. By 2008 our aim is that almost everyone will be within 20 minutes of a good multi-sport facility.

Grassroots clubs are the lifeblood of sports in Britain, and week in, week out,they are sustained by an army of volunteers. Reform of Sport England will continue, to reduce overheads and ensure that more money reaches the grassroots. We have put sports clubs at the forefront of our investment plans with the £100 million Community Club Development Scheme and mandatory rate relief at 80 per cent for registered Community Amateur Sports Clubs already worth about £5 million. As we review the operation of the new licensing regime we will ensure that there is not an unfair burden on local community groups, including sports clubs.

Investment in school sports will ensure that by 2010 all children will receive two hours high-quality PE or sport per week. Building on that, we pledge that by 2010 every child who wants it will have access to a further two to three hours sport per week.

Every child should have the chance to compete at school. We have clamped down on the sale of playing fields: 96 per cent of schools in School Sport Partnerships now hold at least one sports day or sports festival each year. All secondary schools will be expected to field teams in regular competitive fixtures. We will also establish individual and team rankings in all the main sports, with clear and transparent success criteria.

Sport in the community

To make it easier to get access to sports in your local area we will establish Sport Direct – a single point of access for sports in the UK. One website and one phone number will help you find out what's going on in your area. Together with £155 million from the Big Lottery Fund, the Government will ensure that children who have had little access to play facilities and those with a disability have much better access to safe, modern playgrounds.

Building on the lessons of the Football Foundation, we will develop a National Sports Foundation to bring resources from the private and voluntary sectors together with public money to invest in grassroots sporting facilities. We will work with the Premier League and the FA to find innovative ways of assisting community sport, including Supporters Direct. Having passed the necessary legislation, we remain committed to completing the sale of the Tote to a Racing Trust.

The Olympics

Britain's medal hauls at the Sydney Olympics in 2000 and in Athens in 2004 were the best for over 80 years, and we maintained our position as one of the leading nations in the Paralympics. Now we are supporting the bid to bring the Olympics to London in 2012.Our plans would bring regeneration to the East End of London and will leave lasting sporting, economic and cultural legacies. As we approach the Olympics we will continue to invest in elite athletes through the Talented Athlete Scholarship Scheme for young athletes. In addition we have launched 2012 Scholarships worth around £10,000 a year each for our most talented 12- to 18-year-olds.

Libraries in the information age

Where they offer new services like childcare, after-school education for pupils, and IT learning our libraries are successful. We will develop a strategy for the modernisation of our libraries which builds on the best, strengthens library leadership, sharpens customer focus and harnesses local popular support. We will encourage further co-operation in back-office functions and identify the best ways to improve our library infrastructure.

Public service broadcasting and the BBC

We support a strong, independent and world-class BBC with clearly defined public purposes at the heart of a healthy public broadcasting system. We will replace the BBC Governors with a BBC Trust to ensure that the BBC's governance and regulation is accountable to the licence-fee payers to whom it belongs. The licence fee will be guaranteed for the whole of the ten-year Royal Charter that will take effect on 1January 2007. Channel 4 will continue to be a publicly owned broadcaster providing distinctive competition to the BBC. ITV and Five will also be retained in our public service broadcasting system.

Digital switchover

The success of satelite and cable television in driving take-up of digital shows how changes in technology bring real benefits – in terms of greater choice, and increasingly, in access to services. Our aim is to make those benefits available to all. We will achieve digital switchover between 2008 and 2012 ensuring universal access to high-quality, free-to-view and subscription digital TV. This will happen region by region, and we will make sure that the interests of elderly people and other vulnerable groups are protected.

Digital challenge

We will deliver our cross-government strategy for closing the digital divide and using ICT to further transform public services:

- By 2006 every school supported to offer all pupils access to computers at home.
- A Digital Challenge for a local authority to be a national and international pathfinder in universal digital service provision.
- A new National Internet Safety Unit to make Britain the safest place in the world to access the internet.

Copyright in a digital age

We will modernise copyright and other forms of protection of intellectual property rights so that they are appropriate for the digital age. We will use our presidency of the EU to look at how to ensure content creators can protect their innovations in a digital age. Piracy is a growing threat and we will work with industry to protect against it.

Film

The strength of Britain's film industry is a source of pride, and employment. We will continue to make the UK the right place to invest in film production. We will legislate to provide new tax reliefs that will ensure support is delivered directly and efficiently to those who produce films.

We will work with the UK Film Council to achieve a higher priority for funding film festivals around the country, in particular for the Edinburgh Film Festival, the oldest in Britain.

The Lottery

Every single part of British life has been touched by the £15 billion generated for good causes by the Lottery. Labour has made the Lottery more inclusive and more in tune with people's priorities. We have created the Big Lottery Fund and given it an explicit mandate to involve people not just in setting strategy but also in awarding grants. Our Lottery Bill will give a duty and a power to every Lottery distributor to involve the public more radically in decision-making at every level.

By the end of 2005 we will put in place a new, national consultation on the way that the National Lottery good causes proceeds are spent after the new Lottery Licence is awarded in 2009.

The local environment

The quality of our local environment is vital to our well-being and our natural environment is a key part of our national heritage.

The environment starts at the front door, and we have made action to improve the cleanliness of public spaces and communities a priority. The 2005 Clean Neighbourhoods and Environment Act will give local authorities and regulators the powers they have asked for to tackle litter, graffiti, abandoned cars, fly-tipping, noise pollution and other environmental concerns. We will further crack down on environmental crime, minimising litter, cleaning up graffiti and tackling fly-tipping. We will extend kerbside collection of at least two types of recyclable materials to all households in England by 2010. Polluters will have the opportunity to invest in environmental remediation or new local environmental projects rather than just pay fines. Rather than 'polluter pays' this new system would mean the 'polluter improves'.

Britain's beaches, rivers and drinking water are now of the highest ever quality. We have added 30,000 hectares to the green belt while exceeding our target of building 60 per cent of new houses on brownfield sites. We have established the first National Park in England since the 1950s. To enhance our children's understanding of the environment we will give every school student the opportunity to experience out-of-classroom learning in the natural environment.

All newly developed communities – such as the Thames Gateway Development – will be built to high environmental standards on issues such as energy efficiency and water use, and we will develop a clear plan to minimise the impact of new communities on the environment. From April 2006, all new homes receiving government funding will meet the new Code for Sustainable Buildings and we will encourage local authorities to apply similar standards to private homes.

Through a Marine Act, we will introduce a new framework for the seas, based on marine spatial planning, that balances conservation, energy and resource needs. To obtain best value from different uses of our valuable marine resources, we must maintain and protect the ecosystems on which they depend.

The choice for 2010

The Tories have always neglected the arts, seeing them as an easy target for cuts. They do not understand the role that culture can play in the lives of individuals, in the futures of our towns and cities, and in the prosperity of our country. The choice is forward with new Labour to more sport in schools, arts for all children and young people,and continued investment in culture.Or back to the Tories and cuts of £207 million across culture, arts and sport.

DEMOCRACY

In our first two terms we enshrined a new constitutional settlement between the nations of the United Kingdom. In our next term we will complete the reform of the House of Lords so that it is a modern and effective revising Chamber. And we will devolve more power to local authorities and local communities, giving people real power over the issues that matter most to them.

The new Labour case

Widening access to power is as important as widening access to wealth and opportunity. National standards are important to ensure fairness. But the best way to tackle exclusion is to give choice and power to those left behind. Our political institutions – including our own party – must engage a population overloaded with information, diverse in its values and lifestyles, and sceptical of power. However, people are passionate about politics – when they see it affects them. So our challenge is to bridge the chasm between government and governed. Our third term will build upon our unprecedented programme of constitutional reform embedding a culture of devolved government at the centre and self-government in our communities.

Building from the neighbourhood up

People want a sense of control over their own neighbourhood. Not a new tier of neighbourhood government, but new powers over the problems that confront them when they step outside their front door – issues like litter, graffiti and anti-social behaviour. That is why we will offer neighbourhoods a range of powers from which they can choose, including:

- New powers for parish councils to deal with anti-social behaviour.
- Powers for local people to trigger action in response to persistent local problems.
- Community funds for local neighbourhoods to spend on local priorities.
- New opportunities for communities to assume greater responsibility or even ownership of community assets like village halls, community centres, libraries or recreational facilities.

Good parish councils engage communities and make a real difference, so we will extend the right to establish parish councils to communities in London.

A vibrant civil society

We believe that enterprises in the mutual and co-operative sector have an important role to play in the provision of local services, from health to education, from leisure to care for the vulnerable. As democratic, not-for-profit organisations, they can help to involve local people in shaping the services they want, unleash creativity and innovation, create jobs and provide new services – especially in neighbourhoods where traditional services have failed local people in the past.

We have introduced a new legal form – the Community Interest Company (CIC) – and want to support new enterprises. As a major stimulus to this sector, central government and local authorities will work with these 'social enterprises' wherever possible. Where services can be provided by mutuals, co-operatives or CICs to the required standards of quality and value for money, they should be positively encouraged to develop and be included in procurement policies. We will discuss with local authorities the best way to achieve this.

In a range of services the voluntary and community sector has shown itself to be innovative, efficient and effective. Its potential for service delivery should be considered on equal terms. We will continue to improve the context in which the gifting of time and resources to the voluntary sector takes place. We will reintroduce the widely supported reforms in the Charities Bill.

We understand that often the spark for local innovation and change comes from one or two dedicated, visionary individuals. These people, sometimes dubbed 'social entrepreneurs', deserve our full support. We will develop a framework of incentives and rewards, to recognise the special people in every community whose voluntary efforts transform the lives of others.

A better alternative for young people

We know that parents and young people think that there should be more things to do and places to go for teenagers. We will publish plans to reform provision in order to ensure that all young people have access to a wider set of activities after the school day such as sport and the arts. We are determined that better provision will be allied to a stronger voice for the young themselves in designing and managing local provision. We will establish the first ever national framework for youth volunteering, action and engagement – a modern national youth community service, led by young people themselves – with an investment over the next three years of up to £100 million with matched funding from business, the voluntary sector and the Lottery.

Councils: more freedom, less bureaucracy

Strong communities ultimately require strong local government. We will give councils further freedoms to deliver better local services, subject to minimum national standards, with even greater freedoms for top-performing councils. We will reduce unnecessary bureaucracy by cutting both the cost of inspection and the total number of inspectorates, and we will dramatically simplify the many funding streams available to local areas through new Local Area Agreements. We will also give councils greater stability by providing three-year funding. We will continue to deliver efficiency savings and improvements to local services through joint procurement, shared services, streamlining administrative structures while promoting decision-making at the level that will make a difference. We will continue to strengthen the community leadership role of local authorities working in partnership with public, voluntary and private bodies.

Stronger leadership

Strong local government requires strong leadership. We will ensure that councils are organised in the most effective way to lead and support local partnerships and deliver high-quality services. We will explore giving people a more direct opportunity to express a view about whether they would like to have a directly elected mayor. We will also consult with city councils on the powers needed for a new generation of city mayors. And we will examine the case for simplifying the current local government election cycle by moving towards 'whole council' elections every four years.

Council tax under control

Labour recognises the concerns that have been raised about the level of council tax. This year we have delivered the lowest council tax increase in over a decade through a combination of extra investment and tough action to cap excessive increases.

We will continue to invest in local services with year-on-year increases in grants to local councils, and will not hesitate to use our capping powers to protect council taxpayers from excessive rises in council tax.

We remain concerned that many council taxpayers are not claiming reductions in their council tax bills to which they are already entitled. We will therefore introduce measures to make it easier for pensioners and people on low incomes to claim Council Tax Benefit.

In the longer term, we are committed to reforming council tax and will consider carefully the conclusions of the Lyons Review into local government finance.

The nations and regions of the UK

In our first term, we devolved power to Scotland and Wales and restored city-wide government to London. Britain is stronger as a result. In the next Parliament, we will decentralise power further. In Wales we will develop democratic devolution by creating a stronger Assembly with enhanced legislative powers and a reformed structure and electoral system to make the exercise of Assembly responsibilities clearer and more accountable to the public. We will also review the powers of the London Mayor and the Greater London Authority. And we will devolve further responsibility to existing regional bodies in relation to planning, housing, economic development and transport.

Northern Ireland

The Belfast Agreement on Good Friday 1998, was a remarkable achievement. Life in Northern Ireland is immeasurably better as a result. A huge programme of reform in policing, justice and rights, together with the lowest ever unemployment has helped address the inequalities of the past and has created a new confidence.

It is unacceptable that seven years after the agreement there are still paramilitary groups involved in criminality and punishment attacks. This has to end. The period of transition is over. Unionist politicians have made it clear that they are prepared to share power with nationalists and republicans if violence is ended once and for all. It is time for all groups in Northern Ireland to make it clear they will only use democratic and peaceful means to advance their aims.

We will work tirelessly with the parties in Northern Ireland and with the Irish government to re-establish the devolved institutions. But this can only happen on an inclusive basis if the IRA ends paramilitarism and criminality for good and decommissions its weapons. Bringing this about so that normal politics can take over in the Province will be our principal aim.

Loyalist paramilitary violence and criminality is equally intolerable. We will ensure that it is dealt with severely while providing the assistance necessary to Loyalist communities to ensure that prosperity is spread throughout Northern Ireland.

Parliamentary reform

Labour has already taken steps to make the House of Commons more representative, through all-women shortlists. Labour will also continue to support reforms that improve parliamentary accountability and scrutiny led by the successful Modernisation Committee.

In our first term, we ended the absurdity of a House of Lords dominated by hereditary peers. Labour believes that a reformed Upper Chamber must be effective, legitimate and more representative without challenging the primacy of the House of Commons.

Following a review conducted by a committee of both Houses, we will seek agreement on codifying the key conventions of the Lords, and developing alternative forms of scrutiny that complement rather than replicate those of the Commons; the review should also explore how the upper chamber might offer a better route for public engagement in scrutiny and policy-making. We will legislate to place reasonable limits on the time bills spend in the second chamber – no longer than 60 sitting days for most bills.

As part of the process of modernisation, we will remove the remaining hereditary peers and allow a free vote on the composition of the House.

Labour remains committed to reviewing the experience of the new electoral systems – introduced for the devolved administrations, the European Parliament and the London Assembly. A referendum remains the right way to agree any change for Westminster.

Having been the first government to take action to clean up the funding of political parties, we will continue to work with the independent Electoral Commission to explore how best to support the vital democratic role of political parties while recognising that campaigning activity must always be funded by parties from their own resources.

Since 1997 there has been a flowering of innovative forms of public engagement, for example, the Citizens Council used by the National Institute for Clinical Excellence to advise on ethical dilemmas. With the growing importance of new public policy issues and dilemmas – particularly those arising from scientific advances – we will continue to explore new and innovative forms of public engagement raising their profile and status in policy-making.

A voice for all

A fully democratic society depends on giving everyone a voice and stake. Only Labour governments have ever introduced race relations legislation, and laws passed in 2000 are ensuring that all public bodies promote diversity and tackle discrimination against black and Asian Britons. We will continue to promote civil rights for disabled people, ensuring full implementation of the new positive duty on the public sector to promote equality of opportunity for disabled people. We will also introduce a similar duty to promote equality of opportunity between women and men, and will further extend protection against discrimination on the grounds of religion and belief. We are committed to improving the rights and opportunities of gays and lesbians, that's why we brought in legislation on civil partnerships, reducing the age of consent, repealed Section 28 and reformed the sexual offences legislation so that it was no longer discriminatory.

It remains our firm and clear intention to give people of all faiths the same protection against incitement to hatred on the basis of their religion. We will legislate to outlaw it and will continue the dialogue we have started with faith groups from all backgrounds about how best to balance protection, tolerance and free speech.

We are proud to have brought in the Human Rights Act, enabling British citizens to take action in British courts rather than having to wait years to seek redress in Strasbourg. But rights must be balanced by responsibilities. So we will continue to bear down on abusive or frivolous claims.

In the next Parliament we will establish a Commission on Equality and Human Rights to promote equality for all and, tackle discrimination, and introduce a Single Equality Act to modernise and simplify equality legislation.

The choice for 2010

The Tories have only one policy on democratic reform – opportunism. Arch centralisers when in office, they now claim to be localists. Having refused for decades to accept any reform of the archaic House of Lords, some of them now claim to support a fully elected House. The choice is forward with new Labour to modern institutions and more power than ever devolved to communities and successful local authorities. Or back with the Tories to a government indifferent to the health of our democracy and negligent of our institutions.

CONSERVATIVE MANIFESTO

ECONOMY: VALUE FOR MONEY AND LOWER TAXES

A strong economy is the foundation for everything we do. It provides higher living standards so that people can look to the future with optimism. It creates the jobs we all depend on – enabling families to build their financial independence. It should guarantee our pensions in old age. It provides a safety net for the least fortunate. It is essential in tackling poverty, including child poverty. It pays for our public services – our children's education and our parents' healthcare. And it allows us to invest in our nation's security – defence, the police and border controls.

Our economic success over generations has been built on the hard work, enterprise and creativity of the British people.

Today, government is spending too much, wasting too much and taxing too much. Britain cannot continue indefinitely to spend more than she is earning without higher taxes or higher interest rates – either of which will harm our economic prospects. If we are to secure our future prosperity, government must once again start to live within its means.

The consequences of Labour's profligacy are now plain to see. Last year, average living standards fell for the first time in over a decade – and the poorest 10 per cent of Britons became poorer.

We need to change direction.

The way in which a government allocates taxpayers' money demonstrates its values. By going to war on waste and ending ineffective public spending programmes, we will achieve three simple aims.

First, we will give taxpayers value for money. We will spend the same as Labour would on the NHS, schools, transport and international development, and more than Labour on police, defence and pensions. But we will save £12 billion a year by 2007-8 by cutting back other expenditure. We will freeze civil service recruitment, remove 235,000 bureaucratic posts, and cut or abolish 168 public bodies.

Over the period to 2011-12, we will increase government spending by 4 per cent a year, compared to Labour's plans (on current trends) to increase spending by 5 per cent a year.

Second, we will avoid further Labour stealth taxes by reducing government borrowing. Of our £12 billion savings, we will use £8 billion to reduce Labour's excessive borrowing, so that we can avoid the tax rises that would otherwise be needed.

Third, we will lower taxes. We believe that people should choose how their money is spent. They should be rewarded for their hard work and be given peace of mind in old age. We will use the remaining £4 billion of our £12 billion savings to cut taxes in our first Budget.

Lower taxes promote enterprise and growth. But they also promote the right values. Hard-working families have suffered from Labour's tax raids on mortgages and marriage, pensions and petrol, buying a home and having a job.

We will change direction. Whereas Labour want to make people more dependent on the State, we believe that lower taxes help families build their financial independence and security. For those on low incomes we will retain the minimum wage, together with proposed increases.

After a lifetime of paying taxes, we believe people deserve dignity in retirement. Rising council tax bills, which are up by 76 per cent since Labour came to power, have hit pensioners particularly hard. That is why our tax plans include halving council tax bills for millions of pensioners. Our new, permanent discount, reducing council tax bills by up to £500 for households where all residents are over 65 will be fully funded by central government.

A Conservative Government will increase the basic state pension in line with earnings rather than prices, reversing the spread of means-testing. Over four years, this will increase the value of the pension by around £7 a week for single pensioners and £11 a week for couples – on top of increases in line with inflation. We will also keep all the other benefits that pensioners currently receive, including the Winter Fuel Payment, free television licences for the over-75s, and this year's one-off £200 council tax payment.

The financial security of pensioners tomorrow will be vastly improved by encouraging more saving today. To get more people into the saving habit, we will create a new Lifetime Savings Account in which government contributions top up the money that people save themselves. And we will take a series of steps to strengthen company pensions. We will abolish the rules that stop firms promoting pension schemes to their staff, encouraging employers to make pension schemes 'opt-out' rather than 'opt-in'. We will also use the unclaimed assets of banks and other financial institutions to replenish the pension funds of people who lose out when a scheme fails.

The best guarantee of future prosperity is a dynamic economy. The growth of China, India and other Asian economies poses a direct challenge to our future competitiveness. New technology and the speed of global capital flows punish the inflexible and the sluggish. We need to reward risk-taking and innovation so that Britain becomes the best place in the world to start and grow a business.

As well as keeping taxes low, we must reduce the burdens on business through deregulation.

A Conservative Government will negotiate to restore our opt-out from the European Social Chapter and liberate small businesses from job-destroying employment legislation.

We will set regulatory budgets for each department, capping and then cutting the cost of the regulations that they can introduce in any one year. All new regulation will have to have benefits exceeding costs, and regulations will be given 'Sunset Reviews' to check that this remains the case. A Conservative Government will end the elaboration or 'gold-plating' of EU directives.

A Conservative Government will lock in economic stability. We will maintain the independence of the Bank of England in setting interest rates. We will not join the Euro. By keeping the pound as our currency, control of our interest rates will continue to be set to meet the needs of the British economy. As the other major parties are committed to joining the euro, only the Conservatives can make this pledge.

FLEXIBLE CHILDCARE AND SCHOOL DISCIPLINE

It's not easy bringing up a family in modern Britain. Parents who work hard to give their children the best start in life need a government that is on their side. That means access to flexible childcare and schools with good discipline and high standards.

Juggling work and family life can be a struggle. Under Labour, Britain has the most expensive childcare in Europe, and many working families receive no help.

Conservatives trust families to make the right decisions about childcare. We will reform the system to increase choice, flexibility and support for working families.

We will provide more flexible maternity pay – giving mothers a choice of whether to receive it over nine months, or a higher amount paid over six months.

During the next Parliament, we will ensure that all working families who qualify for the working tax credit will receive up to £50 a week for each child under the age of five, irrespective of the type of childcare they choose. We will end Labour's insistence on endless form-filling and enable families to choose between formal and informal childcare.

We will also give extra support for workplace nurseries and provide a new network of clubs for older children.

Education enriches lives and provides us all, whatever our background, with the tools to achieve our ambitions.

Providing good education costs money – and our plans provide for an extra £15 billion a year for schools by 2009-10. Even more important than extra money, we must get the fundamentals right.

Classrooms need to be disciplined environments where children can learn. Teachers must be free to follow their vocation and inspire young minds. Standards must be maintained so that pupils, colleges and employers have examinations they can trust. Our education system should encourage excellence and ambition.

Today, these basics have been completely neglected. Over one million children play truant each year. Head teachers have been denied the final say on expulsions, and good schools will be further punished by being forced to admit a quota of disruptive pupils.

Last year a third of children left primary school unable to write properly and more than 40,000 teenagers left school without a single GCSE. Examinations have been devalued so that it is possible to secure a 'C' Grade at GCSE maths with just 16 per cent.

A Conservative Government will put the right values at the heart of our education system. We will ensure proper discipline in schools by giving heads and governors full control over admissions and expulsions. We will not allow a minority to ruin the education of the majority. Instead of disrupting the education of others, difficult pupils will be given the chance to get their lives back on track in special Turnaround Schools.

The respect due to teachers will be enhanced by protecting them against malicious allegations of abuse and, most importantly, reducing the massive burden of paperwork.

Schools will be liberated to set their own priorities and budgets. The current proliferation of funding streams will be replaced by a simple system, with funds allocated on the basis of pupil numbers. Money will follow the pupil. Head teachers will then have the freedom to spend money in accordance with their school's own needs, without interference from Whitehall.

The examination system will be made more transparent and accountable. The targets which encourage examiners to award higher and higher grades for the same level of performance will be scrapped. Marks will be published alongside grades. And schools will be free to offer internationally-recognised qualifications alongside GCSEs and A-Level. We will slim down and improve the National Curriculum, root out political correctness, restore rigour and give teachers the scope once again to be creative and imaginative.

Many children leave school at 16 because they are bored and because vocational education does not have the status that it deserves. We will end the snobbery that has damaged vocational education. New grants will be made available to help pupils who wish to combine GCSEs with vocational study at a wide range of colleges, businesses and other enterprises. We will introduce 300,000 vocational grants of £1,000 each for 14-16 year olds.

Education should be about more than academic learning. Under Labour, sport has been squeezed out of the curriculum and child obesity has risen alarmingly.

Our schools should be places where children also learn other skills for life, such as healthy living, being part of a team and respecting others. We will give every child the right to two hours of after-school sport with our Club2School programme, at no cost to parents. We support improvements to school dinners, and will go further by banning junk food in schools.

Children need to be taught how to deal with risks in life. We will encourage learning outside the classroom and provide protection for teachers worried about school trips.

Parents know their children best and are increasingly frustrated at not being able to exercise more choice and control over their children's education. We will give parents the right to choose the school best suited to their child's needs, and our school expansion fund will provide an additional 600,000 places in our first term. This will ensure that in our first five years 100,000 more parents get their first choice of school.

Schools will have responsibility for admissions, good schools will be allowed to grow and support will be given to new schools set up to respond to parental demand. Parents will also be able to send their children free of charge to any independent school that offers a place at no more than the cost of a state-funded school.

We will pay particular attention to children with special needs. Under Labour, the dogmatic pursuit of inclusion has led to the closure of special schools and children have suffered as a result. A Conservative Government will introduce a moratorium on the closure of special schools and give parents proper information and choice so they can secure the best opportunities for their children.

Labour have ignored the further education sector. We will simplify funding, replace the bureaucratic Learning and Skills Councils, ensure that money follows the student and allow colleges to apply for 'Super college' status with greater freedom to manage budgets, specialise and innovate.

We will restore real choice in higher education by scrapping fees and abolishing Labour's admissions regulator. University funding will depend on attracting new students and so excellence will be encouraged. We will also help universities move towards greater financial independence by building up their individual endowments.

BETTER HEALTHCARE AND CLEANER HOSPITALS

We believe that everyone has the right to high quality healthcare, free at the point of use, delivered when and where they need it.

Record amounts of taxpayers' money have been spent on the NHS. Yet over a million people are still waiting for treatment, and average waiting times have gone up. More people die each year from infections they pick up in hospitals than on Britain's roads.

Taxpayers have not received value for money because the NHS has not been reformed. It is too impersonal, too inflexible, too centralised and too bureaucratic to respond to the needs of patients.

Staff in the health service – from doctors and nurses to porters and cleaners – work hard to deliver world class healthcare. But the system lets them down.

We have a clear plan of action to cut waiting times and clean up hospitals. We will increase funding, reduce bureaucracy, empower local professionals to operate local services and give greater choice to patients.

We will increase the NHS budget by £34 billion a year during our first Parliament – at least as much as Labour – from £1,450 per head to £2,000 per head. And we will ensure that the money reaches the front line.

We will radically reduce the number of Primary Care Trusts, abolish the Strategic Health Authorities and cut the number of quangos, inspectorates and commissions.

Centrally set targets on hospitals will be abolished. Patients will be treated according to clinical needs, not government targets.

We will give power and responsibility to local professionals. All hospitals will have the freedom to hire staff, specialise and borrow to invest. In response to local demand, hospitals will have the flexibility to increase the number of individual rooms and invest in infection control teams. We will bring back matron, who will have the power to close wards for cleaning.

We will give patients and local GPs the right to choose the hospital or care provider that is right for them.

Funding will follow the patient and go directly to front-line care. Hospitals will be paid according to the treatments they deliver, rather than by Whitehall budgets. Small community hospitals which have the support of local patients and GPs will not be closed by bureaucrats.

Each year around 220,000 people without health insurance pay for important operations. We believe that providing a contribution based on the cost of half the NHS operation when people make these choices both recognises the tax they have paid towards the NHS and will help further reduce waiting lists.

Choice gives people power, a sense of purpose and control. It makes those who offer a service accountable to those who use it. It will give patients the clean hospitals and the shorter waiting times they want. Our policies will give everyone the kind of choice in healthcare that today only money can buy.

We believe that increased choice, combined with extra resources and freedom for local professionals, will end waiting lists as we know them during the life of the next Parliament.

As we live longer and expect more treatment and care to be available at home and in the community, social services will inevitably face greater demands. We will give people more control over their social care and introduce a partnership scheme so that no one is compelled to sell their home to pay for long-term care.

Carers who look after elderly or disabled relatives, including those suffering from long-term conditions, deserve more support. We will boost respite for carers and give them more choice and information about the support available.

We will ensure greater access to NHS dentistry by changing the way in which dentists are paid and offering patients a low monthly payment system to cover against large and unplanned bills.

We will introduce health checks for immigrants in order to curb the spread of diseases such as TB and to protect access to our NHS. It is, after all, a national health service not a world health service. People coming to Britain for over 12 months from outside the EU will be required to undergo a full medical test. And anyone settling permanently here from outside the EU will have to demonstrate that they have an acceptable standard of health and that they are unlikely to impose significant costs or demands on Britain's health system.

Public health is important – it affects every family in our country. That is why a Conservative Government will take action to tackle sexually transmitted infections (STIs). In Britain today we face an STI epidemic. Today's sexually transmitted infections are tomorrow's NHS bills. It's time for a clear, bold and very public health TV campaign – young people need to know the risks involved and the precautions they can take.

SAFER COMMUNITIES AND MORE POLICE

Ensuring order is the first priority of government. Crime blights lives and ruins communities: it should not be excused, but condemned and punished. That means drawing a clear distinction between right and wrong, and restoring respect, discipline and decent values.

Crime today is out of control. There is a gun crime every hour. A million violent crimes are committed each year. Fewer than one in four crimes are now cleared up.

Criminals have a better chance of getting away with breaking the law today than at any time in the last 25 years.

Anti-social behaviour – vandalism, graffiti, binge-drinking, threatening behaviour – is a growing concern in all our communities.

Too many of Mr Blair's responses have been gimmicks, some of which, like marching yobs to cash machines, were never even introduced.

It doesn't have to be that way. Crime can be cut. Anti-social behaviour can be confronted. Communities can and should be made safe for the law-abiding. It requires active community policing and a relentless focus on catching, convicting and punishing criminals.

Labour's centralised control of the police has sapped officers' morale, increased bureaucracy and undermined public confidence.

It is time to change direction. We will recruit 5,000 new police officers each year, radically cut paperwork and introduce genuine local accountability, through elected police commissioners.

Giving local people a say over police priorities will lead to genuine neighbourhood policing with officers based in the locality clearly focused on zero tolerance.

When criminals are caught they should be punished properly. If appropriate they should be sent to prison, and in any event encouraged to reform their ways. None of these things happens properly today.

So, we will end Labour's early release from prison scheme and provide 20,000 extra prison places.

We will introduce honesty in sentencing so that criminals serve the full sentence handed down by the court. They will be told, in open court, the minimum time that they will serve behind bars.

There is much that can be done to improve the justice system – the police, courts and the prison and probation services. But they only pick up the pieces of problems whose roots often lie elsewhere.

Our goal is to reverse the drift towards communities that are blighted by crime, where people live in fear. We will deliver safer neighbourhoods where the streets belong to the law-abiding.

We will start at school by ensuring proper discipline.

We will break the link between drugs and crime by massively expanding treatment programmes, including 25,000 residential rehab places (compared with fewer than 2,500 places today), and by giving all young users of hard drugs a straight choice – effective treatment or appearing in court. We will stop sending mixed messages on drugs by reversing Labour's reclassification of cannabis as a less serious drug, changing it from class 'C' back to class 'B'.

We will support the social institutions – families, schools, voluntary bodies and youth clubs – that can prevent crime and drug dependency before it starts.

A Conservative Government will place the highest possible priority on combating the threat from terrorism. This requires a co-ordinated response right across government, including funding for the intelligence services, training for the emergency services, robust anti-terror laws, controlled immigration and rigorous arrangements for the extradition and deportation of terrorist suspects. That's why we will appoint a Homeland Security Minister to co-ordinate our national response.

SECURE BORDERS AND CONTROLLED IMMIGRATION

Britain has benefited from immigration. We all gain from the social diversity, economic vibrancy and cultural richness that immigration brings.

But if those benefits are to continue to flow we need to ensure that immigration is effectively managed, in the interests of all Britons, old and new.

This Government has lost effective control of our borders. More than 150,000 people (net) come to Britain every year, a population the size of Peterborough. Labour see 'no obvious upper limit to legal immigration'.

Our asylum system is in chaos. Instead of offering a safe haven to those most in need, the current system encourages illegality. Desperate individuals are forced into the hands of people smugglers and when they reach Britain they are open to continuing exploitation in the underground economy. Only two out of every ten asylum seekers are found to have a genuine claim.

Britain has reached a turning-point. That is why a Conservative Government will bring immigration back under control. We have set out a series of practical and considered steps to restore control and fairness to our immigration system.

First of all we will take proper control of our borders. We will ensure 24-hour surveillance at our ports, and restore full embarkation controls. Border security is currently divided between seven different bodies reporting to three different cabinet ministers. We believe that the time has now come to establish a British Border Control Police, whose sole job will be to secure Britain's borders.

We will introduce a points-based system for work permits similar to the one used in Australia. This will give priority to people with the skills Britain needs.

On asylum, a Conservative Government will not allow outdated and inflexible rules to prevent us shaping a system which is more humane, more likely to improve community relations and better managed. So we will take back powers from Brussels to ensure national control of asylum policy, withdraw from the 1951 Geneva Convention, and work for modernised international agreements on migration.

Our objective is a system where we take a fixed number of refugees from the UNHCR rather than simply accepting those who are smuggled to our shores. Asylum seekers' applications will be processed outside Britain.

We will set an overall annual limit on the numbers coming to Britain, including a fixed quota for the number of asylum seekers we accept. Parliament will set, and review, that number every year.

We are committed to making a continued success of Britain's diversity. There should be popular consent for further demographic change. And the best way to secure continuing support for future migration is by showing that government has control of our borders. Refusing to set a limit on new migrants is irresponsible politics. Only the Conservatives take this issue seriously enough to insist on a limit, and will introduce the policies necessary to police it.

ACCOUNTABILITY

In the real world, if you say you're going to do something, you do it. And if you fail, you can lose your job. That is accountability. Accountability is at the heart of good government and a healthy democracy. We all know that when people think they can get away with it, they won't do things as well as they should.

That's why we've published a Timetable for Action that sets out clearly what we will do, and when we will do it. And Michael Howard has made clear that ministers who fail to deliver will lose their jobs.

Under Mr Blair, the way we are governed has become less accountable, more complex and, ultimately, less democratic. Ministers don't take responsibility for their failures. Unprecedented powers have been given to new, unelected and remote bodies, including regional assemblies for which there is no popular support. The House of Commons has been steadily undermined, and proper reform of the House of Lords has been repeatedly promised but never delivered.

Conservatives understand that people identify with their town, city or county, not with arbitrary 'regions'. We will abolish Labour's regional assemblies. Powers currently exercised at a regional level covering planning, housing, transport and the fire service will all be returned to local authorities.

The House of Commons needs to be made more capable of standing up to the executive. We will strengthen select committees and make time for proper scrutiny of all legislation. As part of our drive for efficiency across Whitehall and Westminster, we will cut the number of MPs by 20 per cent. We will seek cross-party consensus for a substantially elected House of Lords.

Conservatives believe that the Union of England, Scotland, Wales and Northern Ireland brings benefits to all parts of our United Kingdom.

We remain strongly committed to making a success of devolution in Scotland, so that it delivers for the Scottish people. In Wales we will work with the Assembly and give the Welsh people a referendum on whether to keep the Assembly in its current form, increase its powers or abolish it.

But devolution has brought problems of accountability at Westminster.

Now that exclusively Scottish matters are decided by the Scottish Parliament in Edinburgh, exclusively English matters should be decided in Westminster without the votes of MPs sitting for Scottish constituencies who are not accountable to English voters. We will act to ensure that English laws are decided by English votes.

We are committed to supporting Northern Ireland's position within the United Kingdom in accordance with the consent principle. We will continue to work for a comprehensive political settlement, based on the principles of the Belfast Agreement. We will not accept any party into the government of Northern Ireland linked to a paramilitary organisation that holds on to illegal weapons and is engaged in any criminal activity. In the absence of devolved government, we will make direct rule more accountable.

Communities, Transport and the Environment

Britain draws great strength from its diversity. We are a country of vibrant urban centres, historic towns and an evolving countryside. It is both inefficient and insensitive to local communities to impose uniform control from Whitehall.

We believe in devolving power down to the lowest level so that local people are given greater control over their own lives.

Local councils should be accountable to voters. But under Labour, people's priorities have taken second place to centrally imposed targets and Whitehall inspection regimes. The cost to local taxpayers has increased rapidly, with council tax levels up 76 per cent since 1997. It has been a vicious circle – less representation and more taxation.

The Conservatives will liberate local government.

Local communities will have a greater say over planning decisions. We will also give new powers to help local councils to deal with those incidents, such as illegal traveller encampments, which breach planning laws. Together with clear guidance for police and our review of the Human Rights Act, this will ensure fairness for all, rather than special rules for different groups.

With greater power for local people will come less interference from central government. We will radically cut the burdens on local councils.

A Conservative Government will support creativity and excellence in the arts. Instead of Labour's centralised bureaucracy and political interference, including in the National Lottery, we will devolve funding and decision-making while ensuring that the lottery supports the arts, heritage, sport and charities.

The most powerful form of devolution is to individuals and families. The Right to Buy for council tenants extended home ownership, transformed many of Britain's housing estates and expanded our property-owning democracy.

A Conservative Government will extend this right to tenants of housing associations. Our plans to boost shared ownership schemes, and give social housing tenants the right to own a share of their home, will also benefit first-time buyers.

Empowering individuals also means giving them the opportunity to get around Britain more quickly and safely. A modern economy depends on it.

A Conservative Government will end Labour's war on the motorist. We will modernise Britain's road network and review all speed cameras to ensure they are there to save lives, not make money.

We will bring stability to the rail network, avoiding further costly and inefficient re-organisation. Successful train operating companies will have their franchises extended to allow companies to invest in improved stations, car parks, facilities and rolling stock.

A commitment to safeguarding our environment lies deep in Conservative thinking. We instinctively understand the importance of conservation, natural beauty and our duty of stewardship of the earth.

A Conservative Government will call a halt to Labour's plans to concrete over our green fields. We will promote development on brownfield sites and establish more Green Belts with tighter development rules.

To ensure Britain plays its part in combating climate change, we will phase out the use of harmful HFCs and deliver greater incentives to make homes more energy-efficient. Through cuts in Vehicle Excise Duty and increased grants, we will significantly reduce the cost of cars with low carbon emissions. We believe that households and businesses should recycle an increasing amount of their waste.

A Conservative Government will guarantee the security and sustainability of Britain's energy supplies. We will do this by supporting the development of a broad range of renewable energy sources. We also recognise that energy efficiency must play an increasingly important role in our energy policy.

Conservatives understand the pressures on the livelihoods of those who work in rural areas.

We value the diverse nature of our nation and believe in defending traditional liberties. A Conservative Government will therefore introduce a Bill, and offer Parliament a free vote, to overturn the Government's ban on hunting with dogs.

Britain's farmers operate to some of the highest animal welfare standards in the world and help to preserve the countryside for all of us to enjoy. We will introduce a Bill to ensure honest labelling of food and stem the flow of expensive new regulation. We will support initiatives, such as farmers' markets and local food projects, that enable British customers to support Britain's farmers. The Little Red Tractor mark denotes high British animal welfare and production standards. We will insist that all publicly procured food carries this mark.

We will press for further reform of the Common Agricultural Policy, to make it less burdensome for farmers and taxpayers alike. And we will promote legislation to strengthen and update animal welfare.

DEFENDING OUR FREEDOMS

Britain plays a unique role in the world. We are the only nation that is one of the five permanent members of the United Nations Security Council, a net contributor to the European Union, a member of the G8, at the centre of the Commonwealth family of nations and a leading member of NATO. We are a global trading nation with interests in every continent. As the world's fourth largest economy, we have the potential to be a powerful force for good.

These durable strengths allow Britain to defend our interests and promote our values across the globe.

As a country, we have been in the vanguard of freedom's advance, a friend to the growth of democracy, an advocate of the rule of law, a defender of the oppressed and a robust protector of our people's security.

But, under this Government, Britain's ability to defend its interests and secure valuable freedoms has been undermined. Our Armed Forces, the vital muscle which allows us to punch above our weight, have been allowed to weaken. And our relations with the European Union have been mismanaged in a way which threatens not just British interests, but the capacity of the continent to adapt flexibly to the future.

A Conservative Government will strengthen our Armed Forces within NATO by spending £2.7 billion more than Labour on the front line by 2007-08.

Those serving in our Armed Forces are vitally important to us, so we must take care of the people most important to them. A Conservative Government will support service families. They deserve decent homes, good schools for their children, and the chance to spend as much time as possible with their families.

We will make the Army stronger. A Conservative Government will preserve the regiments Labour would abolish and improve the supply and procurement of weaponry.

We will save warships Mr Blair would scrap. A Conservative Government will support European co-operation on defence but we strongly believe that such co-operation should take place within the framework of NATO.

If a Conservative Government ever has to take the country to war, we will tell the British people why. Mr Blair misrepresented intelligence to make the case for war in Iraq, and failed to plan for the aftermath of Saddam Hussein's downfall. It is nevertheless the case that a democratic Iraq would be a powerful beacon of hope in a troubled part of the world. So we believe that Britain must remain committed to rebuilding Iraq and allowing democracy to take hold. And a Conservative Government will work to achieve peace in the Middle East based on the principle of Israel secure within its borders and a viable Palestinian state.

Conservatives support the cause of reform in Europe and we will co-operate with all those who wish to see the EU evolve in a more flexible, liberal and decentralised direction. We oppose the EU Constitution and would give the British people the chance to reject its provisions in a referendum within six months of the General Election. We also oppose giving up the valuable freedom which control of our own currency gives us. We will not join the Euro.

In a reformed Europe, the restrictive employment laws of the Social Chapter will have to give way to more flexible working. We will ensure that Britain once again leads the fight for a deregulated Europe by negotiating the restoration of our opt-out from the Social Chapter.

The common policies on agriculture and fisheries are unsustainable, damaging to free trade and conservation, and waste huge sums of money. The CAP needs further and deeper reform. And, because fisheries would be better administered at the national level, we will negotiate to restore national and local control over British fishing grounds. We are determined to ensure national control in this area.

We will also build on the success of enlargement, making Europe more diverse by working to bring in more nations, including Turkey.

We value Britain's membership of the European Union, but our horizons extend much further. A key element of British foreign policy under a Conservative Government will be fighting world poverty. We will support further action on debt relief and will work to meet the UN target of spending 0.7 per cent of national income on overseas aid by 2013. We believe that British aid programmes are among the best in the world, so we will negotiate to increase British national control over our international aid spending.

Above all, we recognise that there is a vital thread that links open markets, free trade, property rights, the rule of law, democracy, economic development and social progress. We will use our global influence to champion these principles in the interests of the developing world.

LIBERAL DEMOCRAT MANIFESTO

GREEN ACTION

The environment features on every page of this manifesto – a strong green thread running through everything we do and promise.

HEALTH

Free personal care

Those towards the end of their lives deserve the best possible care. Liberal Democrats will provide free personal care for elderly people and people with disabilities, for as long as they need it, funded out of our new 50 per cent rate on that part of people's incomes over £100,000. In short, we will implement the recommendations of the independent Royal Commission on Long-Term Care. Liberal Democrats in government in Scotland have already achieved this for elderly people.

Quicker diagnosis for serious conditions - so your NHS treatment is not delayed

Your chances of surviving life-threatening and debilitating illnesses improve the swifter the diagnosis. When a GP considers you may have a serious illness we will make sure you are offered diagnosis by the quickest practical route, public or private, so that the NHS can treat you more quickly. More tests and scans will be available in places like GPs'surgeries and community pharmacies. We will tackle the scandal of expensive scanners being under-used by investing in training, recruitment and retention of the key staff needed to operate them. We will provide more scans at weekends and in the evenings. We will publish waiting times for tests and scans – figures which the Labour Government has refused to make public.

Cut unfair charges - free eye and dental checks, fewer prescription charges

To reduce the risk of illness going undetected we will end the charges for eye and dental check-ups which deter people from coming forward for testing. It is also unfair that some people living with long-term conditions pay no prescription charges, while people with other, equally serious, conditions (such as cystic fibrosis and multiple sclerosis) have to pay. We will extend the range of long-term conditions which qualify for exemption from prescription charges, based on an independent review.

Put patients first - more doctors and nurses, free from Whitehall meddling

We will complete NHS plans to recruit at least an extra 8,000 more doctors, 12,000 more nurses and 18,000 more therapists and scientists by 2008. That will cut waiting times and improve the quality of care. Doctors, nurses and therapists are highly trained and dedicated health professionals, while ministers and civil servants are not. Liberal Democrats will hack away the red tape and abolish the absurd targets set by government, and free frustrated health professionals from demoralising government meddling. Clinical decisions should be taken by health professionals and local investment will be determined by locally elected and accountable people who can be removed by local people if they get it wrong. Scrapping unnecessary centralised targets will mean that your local hospital will have the time and flexibility to put patients first, providing personalised care and cleaner hospitals and treating the sickest the quickest.

High-quality dental care

Many people can't find an NHS dentist to take them on. We will reform NHS dental contracts so that more dentists are encouraged to do more NHS work. This will rebuild the relationship between the dental profession and government which has been badly damaged under Conservatives and Labour. Personal Dental Plans will set out how frequently people should have a check-up, how better to look after their teeth and, for those with serious dental problems, their future course of treatment.

Give people more control over their healthcare

We will encourage regular health 'MoTs' tailored to individual patients'needs, with wider access to screening and blood pressure and cholesterol tests. Tens of thousands of patients die in the NHS every year without access to specialised care and pain management. We will prioritise extending choice and access to these services, including more support for hospices. People with long-term conditions should be entitled to an agreed Personal Care Plan, setting out their course of treatment, where and when they will be treated, and what other help, such as social care, they will receive. We will introduce new legislation to safeguard the rights and welfare of people with mental health problems, allowing them to exercise more control over their treatment. We will end inappropriate age discrimination within the NHS; for example, many older women are not currently invited for the routine breast cancer screening which could save their lives.

Prevention is as important as cure

We will concentrate on helping people stay healthy, as well as caring for them when they fall ill. According to the NHS report, Securing our Future Health, the Government's failure to tackle the unnecessary causes of ill-health will cost the NHS an extra £30 billion a year by 2022. If the causes of ill-health aren't tackled, the NHS of the future won't be able to cope – so we will give people the information and opportunities to make healthy choices, for example through clearer food and alcohol labelling. To improve children's health, on top of plans to increase funding for school meals, we will introduce minimum nutrition standards for school meals, as we already have in Scotland; we will restrict advertising of unhealthy food during children's television programmes; and we will require food and drink sold in vending machines on school premises to meet minimum health and nutrition standards. Because second-hand smoke kills, we will ban smoking in all enclosed public places. Our policies as a whole will help tackle other causes of ill-health, such as poverty, pollution and poor housing.

GREEN ACTION

Clean air and water

Pollution in the air, in water and in the food chain causes or aggravates many illnesses as well as destroying the environment. We support the adoption of the EU Registration, Evaluation and Authorisation of Chemicals (REACH) Directive. This will mean that information becomes available to the public on the consequences of exposure to all chemicals in daily use and that those of high concern are replaced by safer alternatives.

Promote walking and cycling

Fewer school-run car journeys means less pollution, less congestion and fewer road deaths. Children walking or cycling to school also get fitter – but the journey must be safe. Liberal Democrats will encourage and promote nationally what many Liberal Democrat councils already do locally, such as 'Safe Routes to School'with calmed traffic, safe pavements, good lighting and adults on hand to conduct 'walking buses'. We will also provide more cycle routes and reform planning rules to make sure that key services are more easily accessible by foot or bicycle. This will benefit adults as well as children.

EDUCATION AND SKILLS

No tuition fees, no top-up fees, fair grants – university affordable for every student

Labour broke their promise on tuition fees. The result: tens of thousands of able students are saddled with mortgage-sized debts or deterred altogether from going to university. Funded from part of our new 50 per cent rate on incomes over £100,000, Liberal Democrats will abolish all tuition fees and make grants available to help poorer students with maintenance costs. That will build on the achievements of Liberal Democrats in government in Scotland. No one will be denied the opportunity of a university education because of the fear of debt, while universities will receive the increased funds they need.

Cut class sizes – using the £1.5 billion Child Trust Fund

Expert opinion confirms what common sense tells us: children well taught and well-cared-for in their early years have a better opportunity to lead successful and rewarding lives. The Government has the wrong priorities, handing out a one-off cash windfall to 18 year-olds at taxpayers'expense through the Child Trust Fund. Liberal Democrats will use this money better by recruiting 21,000 more teachers to cut infant class sizes from the present maximum of 30 to an average of 20, and junior class sizes to an average of 25. We will extend before and after school provision from 8 a.m. to 6 p.m. for all children and complete 3500 Children's Centres by 2010. Building on our Maternity Income Guarantee, which will raise maternity pay for the first six months to £170 a week instead of £102.80 at present, these policies will give every child the best possible start.

Every child taught English, Maths, Science, Modern Languages, plus Information and Communication Technology, by suitably qualified teachers

The teacher recruitment crisis means that thousands of children are being taught key subjects by staff who are not trained specialists in that subject. Liberal Democrats will guarantee that all children will be taught the core subjects of English, Maths, Science, Modern Languages and ICT by suitably qualified teachers through funding secondary schools to provide the necessary high-quality teacher-training courses in these subjects.

School discipline

Children need to learn in a safe and orderly environment, where high standards of behaviour are upheld, where bullying is challenged effectively and where teachers are able to teach without disruption. Our smaller class sizes will help reduce discipline problems. To deal with more persistent disruption schools will agree externally-monitored 'positive behaviour plans'with parents and pupils. If necessary, local education authorities' Behavioural Support Units will tackle exceptional problems in particular schools. When all else fails we will guarantee that head teachers will have local education authority support for 'managed transfer' to other schools or special units for pupils whose behaviour remains unacceptable.

Time to teach

Children in England are now the most tested in Europe, yet there is little evidence that the Government's obsession with testing and targets has improved standards. Liberal Democrats believe that teachers should be given more time to teach and that testing should have a clear purpose: to improve learning for individual children. We will reduce the level of external testing, replacing compulsory tests at seven and eleven with a system of sampling against national standards. Teachers will regularly assess pupils'performance, using the results to inform teaching and give parents accurate information on their child's progress.

Special educational needs

Children with special educational needs should be schooled in an environment appropriate to their needs – usually in local schools with appropriate support, or in specialist schools for those who need them. Parents'wishes must be considered when making decisions about type of schooling. A designated teacher in each school will have responsibility to identify and plan for children with special needs, and act as a contact point for parents and other teachers. We will make sure that all teachers and teaching assistants working with children with special educational needs are appropriately trained. Special schools will act as resource centres to support local schools with their specialist provision. In turn special schools will be linked to research departments in universities so that they can benefit directly from, and be involved with, the latest research in special education.

Skills for work

School-leavers should be equipped with the skills they need to succeed in the workplace. We will combine GCSE, A-level and vocational programmes of study within a new diploma system, stretching the most gifted and engaging those previously turned off by schooling. We will give all students over the age of 14 the opportunity to combine vocational and academic learning, as Liberal Democrats in government in Scotland are already doing.

World-class skills for a world-class economy

We are committed to closing the funding gap between schools and colleges, starting by providing equal funding for equivalent courses, wherever they are taught. To deliver world-class skills, world-class facilities are needed. We will implement plans to invest in the modern, high-quality college facilities needed to deliver high-quality skills training.

School transport

We will maintain the right of children to free school transport when they live more than two miles from their designated primary school and three miles from their secondary school – a right which is being taken away by the Labour Government. For those who live nearer school, there still need to be safe alternatives to the car; we will promote 'Safe Routes to School', with calmed traffic, safe pavements, good lighting and adults on hand to conduct 'walking buses'.

GREEN ACTION

Green every school, college and university

All plans for new educational buildings must be good for the environment as well as good for education, for example by minimising the need for heating and using sustainable building materials. By putting the two together, children and students can learn about caring for the environment by seeing green projects in real action in their own school or college. We also believe that out-of-classroom learning is a key part of a good education, and will include the quality of out-of-classroom education in the criteria on which schools are inspected.

JUSTICE AND CRIME

10,000 more police on the streets - cut crime and the fear of crime

By getting rid of Labour's expensive, illiberal and ineffective ID card scheme, we will pay for 10,000 police on top of Labour's plans. We will also complete existing plans for an extra 20,000 community support officers to back them up. The average police officer today spends more time in the police station than they do on the streets. We will give the police the technology they need, and simplify the bureaucracy they face, to allow them to spend more time on patrol and less time tied to the desk. We will concentrate more police efforts on tackling drug traffickers and those drug users who resort to crime to feed their habits, rather than criminalising people possessing cannabis only for their own personal use.

Make offenders pay back to victims and their communities

Liberal Democrats will make more non-violent criminals, such as fine defaulters, shoplifters and petty vandals, do tough community work as an alternative to jail. Experience shows that this reduces re-offending, gives them skills for legitimate work, and means that they pay back to the community. Through Community Justice Panels, local people will have more say in the punishment offenders carry out in the community – for example, by making them clean off graffiti or repair damage to victims'property.

Get tough on anti-social behaviour

Many towns and cities are becoming no-go areas at the weekend. We will tackle excessive drinking by cracking down on licensees who serve people when clearly drunk or under-age. We will make big late-night venues contribute to the cost of extra late-night policing. Unacceptable noise and offensive behaviour will be tackled through Acceptable Behaviour Contracts agreed between the individual, their family, the police and the local authority. Where individuals do not co-operate we will use Anti-Social Behaviour Orders, plus appropriate measures to tackle underlying causes.

Give prisoners skills for work, not crime

With four out of five prisoners functionally illiterate, and over half of prisoners re-offending, it's time to make prison work. Prisoners will be subject to a tough working day, with increased resources for education and training a top priority so that they learn the skills to acquire a legitimate job. The effort a prisoner puts into their education and work-related skills will be one of the factors used when considering their release date, as part of our emphasis on tackling the causes of crime.

Quality investigations, safe convictions, fighting crime and terror

We will increase police resources to improve the detection and investigation of crime. We will create a co-ordinated UK Border Force to strengthen the country's borders against terrorism, people-trafficking and drug smuggling. We oppose moves to reduce or remove rights to jury trial, and the routine use of hearsay evidence or revelation of previous convictions. We opposed Labour's plans to allow the Home Secretary to order house arrest and other restrictions on personal liberty. A British citizen's liberty must only be removed through a fair judicial process, not on the command of politicians. Liberal Democrats achieved substantial amendment of the Prevention of Terrorism Act, but it still has serious flaws, and we will repeal it. Effective action against terrorism is vital, and our priority will be to extend the criminal law to enable terrorist suspects to be prosecuted in the mainstream courts. We will admit evidence from communications interception. If control orders are still required they must be granted by a judge, be time-limited and be subject to a high standard of proof.

Firm but fair on asylum

For centuries Britain has had a proud record of granting safe refuge to those fleeing persecution. In turn, refugees have enriched the UK's culture and wealth immeasurably. The Home Office has a record of delays and bad decisions on asylum, so we will transfer responsibility for assessing asylum claims to a dedicated agency to sort out the mess, ensuring that those who need help get it, whilst those who don't can't abuse the system. We will work within the EU to develop common standards so that all EU countries take their fair share of refugees. We will also end asylum-seekers'dependence on benefits, allowing them to work so they can pay their own way and use their skills to benefit everyone.

Strengthen the fight against discrimination

We will introduce a Single Equality Act to outlaw all unfair discrimination, (including on the grounds of race, gender, religion or belief, sexual orientation, disability, age or gender identity), thus giving equal protection for all. We will establish hate-crimes investigation units in each police force to co-ordinate information and action against racism, homophobia and other hate crimes. Liberal Democrats led the call for an amendment to the laws on incitement to racial hatred, to criminalise those who use religious words as a pretext for race hate. Our Equality Act will stop same-sex couples in civil partnerships being treated unfairly compared with married couples in pension arrangements.

GREEN ACTION

Tougher action to enforce high environmental standards

The courts have struggled to enforce the rules in environmental cases that are often highly technical and specialised. We will improve the enforcement of pollution controls through a specialist Environmental Tribunal to deal with enforcing environmental rules. We will also make sure that the level of penalties that polluters have to pay are appropriate to the offence – at present they are often trivial compared to the profits from environmental crime.

THE ECONOMY

All our policies are costed and affordable

Unlike the other parties, we have consistently set out costings for our manifesto pledges, explaining how much money they will need and how they will all be paid for. So this manifesto includes a specific section outlining our main costings. Our package of tough choices on spending, and fairer taxes, means that most people will be better off. There is only one proposed net tax rise (to 50 per cent on the proportion of incomes over £100,000 a year, affecting just one per cent of taxpayers) which will pay for the abolition of student tuition fees, free personal care for the elderly, and lower local taxes. Most people's tax will be cut by replacing Council Tax with a system based on ability to pay, saving the typical household around £450 per year.

Tough choices in public spending

Liberal Democrats have different spending priorities from Labour. We believe that in order to concentrate resources on currently under-funded areas such as pensions, policing and early years education, funding should be switched from lower priority areas. That means reducing unnecessary subsidies to industry, and cutting wasteful new initiatives like the ID card and the Child Trust Fund handouts for future 18 year-olds. This will allow us to spend more on the things that really matter, like better pensions, more police and smaller class sizes.

A stable, well-managed economy

We welcome the greater economic stability that has been established since interest rates were set independently by the Bank of England (which the Liberal Democrats were the first party to advocate). Now, there needs to be more independent scrutiny and discipline in fiscal policy. We will give the National Audit Office the power to scrutinise the budget figures, including public borrowing, so that no Chancellor can fiddle the figures. We will make sure that the Office for National Statistics is independent and accountable to parliament, not subservient to ministers. We will tackle irresponsible credit expansion in mortgages and personal loans by curbing misleading advertising and anti-competitive practices by promoters of insurance for mortgages and loans, and of credit cards. We oppose the increasing complexity of business taxes and we will consult with business on a simpler and fairer system, giving priority to helping small businesses.

Fairer taxes

Under Labour, ordinary hard-working families pay more as a share of their incomes in tax than the very rich. Under Labour, the elderly have to sell their homes to pay for their care, while rising Council Tax and university top-up fees are making the system even more unfair. Taking all taxes together, the poorest 20 per cent of the population pay 38 per cent of their income in tax, compared to just 35 per cent for the richest 20 per cent. That's not what people expected from a Labour Government. Liberal Democrats will make the tax system fairer and simpler. As a first step towards reducing tax paid by low earners, we will axe the unfair Council Tax and replace it with a Local Income Tax based on people's ability to pay. This will cut the typical household's tax bill by over £450. To pay for our policies of abolishing student top-up and tuition fees, ending elderly and disabled people needing to pay for their care, and cutting Council Tax, the richest one per cent of the population will pay 50 per cent tax (up from 41 per cent) on that part of their income over £100,000 per year.

Cut stamp duty

People are increasingly struggling to afford their first home. We will raise the starting point for stamp duty from £120,000 to £150,000. This step will take 150,000 mainly first-time buyers out of paying stamp duty altogether, and cuts the cost of home ownership.

An outward-looking economy

Liberal Democrats support a liberal economic approach to trade, investment and migration in the national interest. We want Britain to be at the centre of a liberalised, reformed European Union. Liberal Democrats believe that Britain should work to create the right economic conditions to join the euro (subject to a referendum) in order to safeguard investment in the UK and reduce the cost and risk of trade with the rest of Europe. We will work to break down the trade barriers that prevent the poorest countries in the world selling their goods to the richer countries on fair terms.

Economic migration

Economic migrants have helped make Britain one of the richest countries in the world, both economically and culturally. There remains a positive economic benefit from managed immigration to fill the demand for skills and labour that are in short supply. We will consult with business and the public services to agree numbers of work permits for economic migration to make sure that Britain continues to prosper.

BUSINESS

Cut the red tape that stops businesses from growing. Liberal Democrats will slash the red tape, bureaucracy and over-regulation that are holding British businesses – especially small businesses – back. We will start with these three measures:

- No new regulation will be passed until a full assessment of its costs and necessity is published.
- New regulations affecting business will automatically be scrapped unless Parliament specifically approves their renewal after a period specified in a 'sunset clause'.
- Endless visits by all sorts of inspectors will be replaced in most cases by one all-purpose inspection.

Introduce small-business rate relief

Many small businesses pay a disproportionate amount in rates – as much as 35 per cent of their profits. We will help small businesses by reforming the business rates system to allow firms with a rateable value of less than £25,000 to claim a business rate allowance of up to £1,500. This would represent a saving of over £600 a year for the majority of small businesses. We will also reform the valuation system to base rates on site values, rather than rental value, which penalises businesses that invest in improving their premises.

Scrap the Department of Trade and Industry

There is no need for a big department that interferes in the economy and subsidises failing companies at taxpayers'expense. The DTI is irrelevant to most enterprises, so in abolishing it Liberal Democrats will cut away its bureaucratic and wasteful functions. We will transfer its useful roles to more appropriate departments, such as support for scientific research to our Department for Education, Skills and Science. The Chief Secretary to the Treasury will take on the role of advocate for business at the Cabinet table. Overall, this will save £8 billion of taxpayers'money over the life of a parliament. We will invest this saving in our priorities, including improving education and training – which are of far more real benefit to business.

Protect consumers from rip-offs

We will introduce a new legal duty on businesses to trade fairly, while cutting back unnecessary red tape and bureaucracy. Enforced by the courts, this will require less form-filling than Labour's complex rules, yet provide more effective protection for consumers, and promote free competition.

Boost tourism

We will promote domestic tourism opportunities, starting by creating an English Tourism Board to match those in Scotland, Wales and Northern Ireland, with increased resources for marketing England. These measures will help reduce the 'tourism deficit'– the difference between the amount spent by overseas visitors in the UK and the amount spent by UK tourists abroad – which has quadrupled under Labour and now stands at £17 billion.

GREEN ACTION

Using economic instruments to benefit the environment

Green tax reforms and traded permits should be used to encourage people to act in a more environmentally responsible way. We will change the Climate Change Levy into a Carbon Tax, making it more effective at discouraging the use of the polluting fuels and energy sources that harm the environment. We will also strengthen tax incentives to use smaller and less polluting vehicles and create more energy-efficient homes. We will launch a Treasury-led Environmental Incentive Programme, examining tax reforms that will reduce pollution and protect the environment, on the clear principle of taxing differently, not taxing more.

Promote clean energy

Liberal Democrats will make sure that at least 20 per cent of the UK's electricity comes from a full range of renewable sources by the year 2020, by increasing and reforming the obligation on energy suppliers to use renewable energy. Liberal Democrats will not replace existing nuclear power stations as they come to the end of their safe and economic operating lives – instead we will use renewables and conserve energy. We will encourage the use of alternatives, such as hydrogen fuels, as technology develops.

PENSIONS AND BENEFITS

Over £100 more on the pension every month at 75 – a million pensioners off means-testing

Millions of elderly people are failing to receive the pensions they've earned – and deserve and need – because of demeaning and unworkable means tests. Liberal Democrats will simplify the system, immediately guaranteeing a basic pension at 75 of at least £109.45 per week, with future increases linked to earnings. That's over £100 a month more at 75 for every single pensioner. Every pensioner couple over 75 will receive at least £167.05 per week state pension – over £140 a month more than at present. This will abolish the need for means tests altogether for a million people.

Citizen's Pension

Many women who gave up work to bring up their children receive as little as a penny a week because they haven't paid enough national insurance. From the age of 75 we will give pensioners our increased 'Citizen's Pension' as of right, making sure that 2.8 million women pensioners have security and dignity in retirement.

Help pensioners by axing the Council Tax

Too often, pensioners are forced to pay huge Council Tax bills despite being on low incomes, and many will be faced with further massive increases due to revaluation. Replacing Council Tax with Local Income Tax means eight out of ten pensioners will be better off and six million poorer pensioners will pay no local tax at all. Unlike the other parties' proposals, no one will be denied help simply because of their age or who they live with – everyone will only pay what they can afford.

Help working parents spend more time with their children

Becoming a parent for the first time is a daunting and expensive task. Giving new working parents more support has benefits for them, their babies, their employers and the economy. Liberal Democrats will give working families having their first child increased maternity pay for the first six months at the rate of the minimum wage – that's £170 a week instead of £102.80 at present, a lot more just when parents really need it.

Reform the New Deal to get more people into work

The present New Deal leaves too many people on unnecessary or ineffective schemes rather than getting them into real jobs. Liberal Democrats will instead tailor the assistance so that jobseekers receive the package of support they need to get proper, permanent work. We will also scrap benefit sanctions which leave genuine claimants unable to feed and house themselves.

Scrap the Child Support Agency

The CSA is failing. Some parents are required to pay an unrealistic amount for maintenance, whilst other payments are never enforced. We would scrap the CSA and hand over its initial assessment and enforcement functions to the Inland Revenue so that payment is enforced fairly and effectively. Special circumstances would be addressed by appeal to a specialist tribunal able to take account of individual circumstances, instead of the present unfair rigid formula.

Provide more support for people with disabilities

Many severely disabled people feel the cold intensely and cannot afford to heat their homes adequately, despite the fact that the cold will often make their conditions worse. We will help severely disabled people of working age with their fuel bills by giving them the same £200 a year Winter Fuel Payment that pensioners receive. We will also implement the recommendations of the Royal Commission on Long-Term Care to guarantee free personal care for people with disabilities who need it.

Private and public sector pensions

More than 60,000 workers worked for companies that have gone out of business leaving insufficient money in their pension funds. We will bolster the government's compensation scheme to make sure that these workers are compensated at the same level available under the new Pension Protection Fund. Unlike Labour, we will give proper time for consultation before making changes to existing public sector pension schemes, and we will honour the entitlements already built up.

Beating fraud and error

Each year, around £3 billion is lost to the taxpayer due to fraud and error in the social security system – £100 for every taxpayer every year. The new tax credits could add a further £1.6 billion to that loss. We will reverse the spread of mass means-testing, simplify the benefits and tax credit system, and extend fraud prevention and detection activities to all benefits, reducing both fraud and error.

GREEN ACTION

Save energy and cut fuel bills

Thousands of people – mostly pensioners – die each year from preventable cold-related illnesses. On average, around fifty people die unnecessarily in each constituency every year. Poor home insulation and poor-quality housing lead to cold homes and high fuel bills, the main causes of this 'fuel poverty', while the average pensioner household spends £500 a year on energy. We will help pensioners and severely disabled people cut this bill by allowing them to take a year's Winter Fuel Payment as a voucher redeemable against insulation and energy saving materials. These would be made available at about half price through a partnership with fuel suppliers. A pensioner could save more than £100 from their energy bill every year by investing just one year's Winter Fuel Payment, and help the environment as well. In this way we will invest in cutting energy use and at the same time help pensioners and severely disabled people stay warm and save money.

LOCAL COMMUNITIES

Axe the unfair Council Tax – Local Income Tax is fair and affordable

On top of the Chancellor's plans to increase Council Tax yet again, Council Tax revaluation in England in 2007 threatens one in three households with huge and arbitrary rises, as is already happening in Wales. The Council Tax penalises pensioners and people on low incomes, who pay a far higher proportion of their income in Council Tax than the very rich. A Local Income Tax is based very simply on the ability to pay. It would be run through the existing Inland Revenue Income Tax mechanism, so saving hundreds of millions of pounds by abolishing Council Tax administration. The typical household will save around £450 per year, and eight out of ten pensioners will have lower bills.

Affordable homes

We will help tackle the affordable housing crisis by making available public sector land currently owned by the Ministry of Defence, the Department of Health and English Partnerships, sufficient to build 100,000 more homes both for rent and for affordable purchase through shared ownership schemes for local people. We will reform VAT to encourage developers to repair and reuse empty buildings and brownfield land, rather than building on greenfields and eroding the countryside. We will take 150,000 homebuyers a year out of paying stamp duty altogether, by raising the threshold to £150,000. In areas where second homes are overwhelming the local housing market, we will require people to get planning permission before turning another full-time home into a holiday home.

Art, heritage and sport

Liberal Democrats have a proud tradition of championing the arts, culture and heritage, which successive governments have undervalued. This Government's move towards greater state interference in the arts has threatened to stifle artistic freedom. We will restore the National Lottery funds' independence, requiring the Department for Culture, Media and Sport to separate clearly government spending from independently determined Lottery spending in its annual reports. We will end Labour's freeze in the core Arts Council budget, guaranteeing that growth in core arts funding at least matches inflation. We will help protect the built environment by reducing VAT on historic building repairs. We will increase grassroots sports funding, and support the UK's 2012 Olympic and Paralympic bid.

Set communities free from Whitehall

We will free local councils from many of the stifling controls of central government so that they can innovate and deliver services that meet local people's real needs. Councils will become genuinely accountable to their local communities rather than being agents of Whitehall. To cut bureaucracy and increase effectiveness we would go much further than Labour or the Tories to cut the burden of inspections, merging eight government inspectorates into one, a streamlined and independent Audit Commission.

Protect the post office network and universal mail delivery

Over 3,500 post offices have closed under Labour, and hundreds more are due to be axed. Thousands also closed under the Conservatives. Our priority is to secure a viable future for the post office network, by developing a business plan based on providing a combination of commercial services, benefits transactions and government information. This will help keep more post offices open. We will maintain the obligation on Royal Mail to provide universal same-price delivery of letters throughout the UK.

GREEN ACTION

Tackle waste

Liberal Democrats will set a long-term goal of zero municipal waste, through waste minimisation, reuse and recycling. As a first step, we will make sure that within seven years 60 per cent of all household waste is recycled and we will aim to offer every household regular kerbside recycling. Manufacturers will be held responsible for disposing of their products and materials that are difficult to reuse or recycle. We will not allow new incinerators for municipal waste unless they can be shown to be the best environmental option after considering all alternatives, including new technologies where waste reduction and reuse are not possible.

Planning for sustainability

We will reform the planning system to make sure that local authority development plans are sustainable. That means incorporating targets for CO_2 emission reductions to encourage the development of renewable energy facilities, and accounting for the climate change consequences of policies, including transport. We will also use building regulations to improve the environmental quality of new buildings.

INTERNATIONAL AFFAIRS

We should not have gone to war in Iraq

There were no weapons of mass destruction, there was no serious and current threat, and inspectors were denied the time they needed to finish their job. Thousands of soldiers and civilians have been killed and it has cost the UK over £3.5 billion. Britain must never again support an illegal military intervention. But by invading Iraq the Government has imposed on us a moral obligation to work towards a stable, secure and free Iraq. We welcome the recent elections. We will seek to strengthen and enlarge Iraqi security forces so that they can assume greater responsibility, include Sunni leaders in the political process, and ensure adequate provision of food, water, sanitation and health care for all the Iraqi people. We will support the transition to a fully democratic and legitimate government, aiming to withdraw British troops by the expiry of the UN mandate at the end of the year; the open-ended presence of coalition forces is destabilising and fuels the insurgency.

Build security at home and abroad

The best way to achieve security and to tackle the threat from terrorism is through international action. Britain must work through the United Nations, as a committed member of the EU, and with the US to promote international law, democracy and respect for human rights. We will work to reform the UN and the EU to make them more responsive to international challenges.

EUROPE

Make Europe more effective and democratic

Membership of the EU has been hugely important for British jobs, environmental protection, equality rights, and Britain's place in the world. But with enlargement to twenty-five member states, the EU needs reform to become more efficient and more accountable. The new constitution helps to achieve this by improving EU coherence, strengthening the powers of the elected European Parliament compared to the Council of Ministers, allowing proper oversight of the unelected Commission, and enhancing the role of national parliaments. It also more clearly defines and limits the powers of the EU, reflecting diversity and preventing over-centralisation. We are therefore clear in our support for the constitution, which we believe is in Britain's interest – but ratification must be subject to a referendum of the British people.

DEFENCE

Our troops protect the nation – we must protect them

Britain's armed forces protect the country and are a force for good in the world. But with increasing overseas commitments, they are overstretched. The Government should not be cutting the size of the armed forces while at the same time asking them to take on ever more difficult tasks. New equipment continues to arrive late and over-budget, so we will make military procurement more open and competitive. By switching funding from unnecessary programmes, for example by cutting the third tranche of the Eurofighter programme, we will be able to invest more in protecting the welfare of the armed forces, ensuring that they are well-trained and well-equipped. We will seek new ways of sharing the military burden, by working with allies through NATO and the EU. Liberal Democrats will be realistic about what Britain can, and should, take on, and British forces must always be able to deal with emergencies at home, such as terrorism or natural disasters.

Work for the elimination of nuclear weapons and tackle the arms trade

We will press for a new round of multilateral arms reduction talks, retaining the UK's current minimum nuclear deterrent for the foreseeable future, until sufficient progress has been made towards the global elimination of such weapons. Arms sales contribute to conflict, so we will establish a cross-party Parliamentary Arms Export Committee to monitor arms exports and scrutinise individual licence applications. We will require arms brokers to register under a code of conduct and revoke the licences of those who break the code. We will support the establishment of an International Arms Trade Treaty.

INTERNATIONAL DEVELOPMENT

Meet Britain's promise on aid

Liberal Democrats are committed to realising a world free from poverty. In order to achieve the UN Millennium Development Goals by 2015 (which include tackling extreme poverty and hunger, providing universal primary education, and combating HIV/AIDS) the UK needs to provide more effective international assistance. Liberal Democrats will increase British aid spending from 0.35 per cent of Gross National Income today to at least 0.5 per cent by 2007/08, and set out detailed plans for it to reach 0.7 per cent by 2011 at the latest.

Fair and sustainable trade and investment

Working through the EU and the World Trade Organisation, we will seek to remove the subsidies and tariff barriers that prevent the poorest countries in the world selling their goods on fair terms. We will work to end the dumping of subsidised agricultural exports by developed economies which is wrecking farming in Africa and other parts of the world. We will work to make sure that agreements to liberalise new sectors proceed on a genuinely voluntary basis, without undue pressure on developing countries. We will require companies benefiting from open markets to behave responsibly, and we will promote a new international agreement to encourage investment, particularly in the poorest countries.

GREEN ACTION

Promote environmentally sustainable development

We will make sure that development assistance, whether delivered from the UK, EU, or multilateral institutions, not only meets the needs of the poor, but does so in ways that contribute to environmental sustainability. This means, in particular, targeting aid on renewable energy, clean water and sustainable agriculture, and increasing market access for green products from the developing world. We will devote resources to protecting biodiversity in developing countries, where many species of rare plants and wildlife are seriously endangered.

Take effective action to protect the global environment

We will work through the EU to promote effective and enforceable international agreements to protect the global environment, such as the Cartagena Protocol (on GM products). We will support international agreements and activities designed to stop international environmental crime, such as illegal logging or illegal trade in endangered wildlife, and improve customs training to tackle these illegal activities more effectively. We will argue for reforms of the World Trade Organisation, World Bank and International Monetary Fund to make sure that trade and development policies support rather than hinder environmental sustainability.

Put Britain at the forefront of climate change negotiations

Catastrophic climate change is the major environmental threat to the planet. Urgent action is needed. Liberal Democrat plans will make sure that Britain achieves its targets from the Kyoto Protocol (the international agreement on the pollution that causes climate change) well before the deadline. Britain and the EU must take the lead on negotiations for the next set of targets for greenhouse gas emissions. It is vital that we include the US and Australia but we also need to work with developing countries. Our long-term goal is 'contraction and convergence' – which means agreeing for every country a sustainable population-related allowance for emissions.

RURAL AFFAIRS

Fair prices for food

Of every pound consumers spend on food in supermarkets just eight pence goes to the farmer. Liberal Democrats will introduce a legal duty to trade fairly, supported by a Food Trade Inspector within the Office of Fair Trading. This will protect farmers and consumers from unfair practices by supermarkets and processing companies.

Speed up reform of the Common Agricultural Policy

The CAP fails to protect the interests of rural communities, family farms and the environment. We will press within the EU to speed up reform so that the public funding available is used to provide public benefits. These should include improved access and environmental protection, support for traditional farming and organic systems and new opportunities for agricultural products and local markets. We will use the UK's CAP flexibility to support family farms and aid new entrants more effectively.

Save the UK's fish and marine environment

We will seek early further reform of the Common Fisheries Policy to give local fishermen and other stakeholders a real say in the management of their own regional waters. We will introduce a Marine Act to create a marine planning system to resolve problems of conflicting uses of the sea and sea bed. This would establish conservation zones for highly sensitive areas and strengthen protection of commercial fish stocks, dolphins, porpoises and other endangered marine wildlife.

Improve animal welfare

Liberal Democrats will establish an Animal Protection Commission, bringing all animal welfare matters under the responsibility of a dedicated, expert body, with the duty to make sure that animal protection laws are properly enforced and kept up to date. We will introduce a new Animal Welfare Act to guarantee high standards of animal welfare across the board for farm livestock, working animals and domestic pets, and will close the loophole in existing legislation which allows people who have been banned from keeping animals still to own them if someone else has 'custody'.

GREEN ACTION

No commercial GM crops unless we know they're safe for the environment

We support the right of communities to create GM-free zones. We will insist on rigorous schemes of labelling and traceability in food to guarantee consumer choice. At the same time we will introduce measures to promote organic farming.

TRANSPORT

Make the railways work again

Conservative privatisation left the railways in a mess, but Labour hasn't solved the problems. Whilst delays have doubled, bureaucracy has increased fivefold, while services are being cut. Liberal Democrats will streamline the system, with fewer, larger franchises, given longer contracts in return for more investment and better services. We will use savings from the roads budget to prioritise safety at stations, and to restore the key rail upgrades postponed or cancelled under Labour.

Reward owners of less polluting cars with lower taxes

For many people, particularly in rural areas, cars are a necessity and cannot be replaced by public transport. But they can be far less damaging to the environment when they use less fuel or alternative fuels. We will start by reforming the Vehicle Excise Duty system ('road tax') to cut tax altogether on cars that pollute least, funded by increasing it on those that pollute more. Congestion charging in London (first proposed by the Liberal Democrats) has cut pollution, cut traffic jams and paid for new investment in buses. We will encourage more cities and towns where traffic congestion is a problem to extend congestion charging, linked to up-front investment in better public transport to give millions real alternatives to the car and to reduce the need to drive. In the longer term, as technology allows, we will scrap petrol duties and VED altogether, replacing the revenue with a national road user charging system based on location, congestion and pollution (including the level of pollution of the particular vehicle). As a result, pollution and congestion will be better targeted, with no need for the present system of heavy taxes on every journey.

Free off-peak local bus travel for all pensioners and disabled people

Liberal Democrats were the first to make the case for giving all pensioners and disabled people free off-peak local bus travel, and have already done so in Scotland and Wales. We will implement this policy, and we will in addition provide all pensioners, disabled people, families and young people with their rail discount cards free.

Cut lorry traffic, reduce pollution, and make towns and villages safer

In office, Labour has now increased road building, while the Conservatives' plans would concrete over an area half the size of London with new roads. Both their approaches mean more traffic and pollution, not less. We will not proceed with major new road-building schemes unless the benefits are clear, including environmental and safety factors and a full assessment of alternative public transport schemes. Resources switched from the roads programme will be used to increase investment in public transport, and we will promote safer cycle and pedestrian routes throughout towns and cities. In addition, we will encourage the development of freight interchanges to facilitate growth in rail freight, and we will develop a shipping, ports and waterways strategy.

Reform aviation taxes

To encourage more fuel-efficient aircraft and discourage half-empty planes we will press for international agreement on extending emissions trading to aviation, while at the same time implementing per-aircraft rather than per-passenger charges. We will oppose the construction of international airports on new sites, and also the expansion of airports in the South East. We will end the regulation on busy national airports which results in retail rents subsidising landing charges and encouraging congestion and pollution. We will protect essential 'lifeline' routes to remote UK communities.

GREEN ACTION

Green transport policies

All our transport policies are designed to encourage more environmental transport options, including cutting the cost of using more environmentally friendly vehicles, boosting public transport, discouraging heavily polluting vehicles and reforming aviation policies to cut emissions.

BETTER GOVERNMENT

Curb the power of the Prime Minister

In recent decades Prime Ministers have exercised a growing domination over the political system, insufficiently accountable to Parliament or the people. We will curb this excessive concentration of power. We will cut back the powers of patronage, in particular through our plans for a predominantly elected second chamber. We will make the Royal Prerogative powers which the Prime Minister exercises – such as decisions over war and peace – subject to parliamentary accountability, including bringing in a War Powers Act to require parliament's authority before a government takes Britain to war. A Civil Service Act will introduce a barrier to politicisation of the civil service. We will also strengthen the powers of parliament to scrutinise the actions of the government, enhancing the Select Committee system.

Cut back central government

We will cut the excessive number of government departments and reduce the number of government ministers by over a third. We will also move government bureaucracy out of London, saving money on office rents and spreading wealth and jobs more equally through the UK. The savings will be ploughed back into better public services.

More power for local communities

Our priority is to make local services, like health and education, work better for people. That means that local communities need to have more influence and say over the major issues affecting them. So we will strengthen local democracy, taking power down from Whitehall and reducing central interference and the burden of inspection. The powers of many unelected regional and national quangos and administrators will be given to local cities and counties, including returning to County Councils their strategic planning role. The healthcare planning role of Primary Care Trusts will be given to elected local social services authorities. We will streamline remaining regional functions into a single agency, increasing accountability to the local community through an executive comprising councillors elected from the cities and counties, rather than appointed by the Secretary of State. Underpinning these reforms will be a new system for dividing up government funding fairly within the UK, so that the system is fair for the nations and regions according to their real needs.

A more democratic Britain

Liberal Democrats will improve and strengthen the UK's democratic systems. Liberal Democrats in government in Scotland are already bringing in the single transferable vote (STV) system for local elections, so that local councillors will genuinely represent their community. We will extend this fair voting system to all local elections in Britain, and to the House of Commons, Scottish Parliament and National Assembly for Wales. At the age people can marry, leave school and start work, they will have the right to vote. We will review the European electoral system so people can choose their MEPs personally, rather than just vote by party list as at present. Reform of the House of Lords has been botched by Labour, leaving it unelected and even more in the patronage of the Prime Minister. We will replace it with a predominantly elected second chamber.

Better government in the nations of the UK

Liberal Democrats have led the way in arguing for devolution to Scotland, Wales and Northern Ireland. We believe that people in those parts of the UK, rather than the government in London, should take the decisions on issues that affect them directly. We will therefore strengthen the powers of the Northern Ireland Assembly and extend primary legislative powers to the National Assembly for Wales. In consultation with the Scottish Parliament, we will consider how to extend its role.

Make the BBC more independent from government

The BBC has, over the last eighty years, made a major contribution to Britain's democracy, culture and standing in the world. The Liberal Democrats will make sure it remains the world's leading public service broadcaster – strong, independent, and securely funded. But the regulation of the BBC has been insufficiently independent of its own management, and of the government. Labour's proposals fail to address this. Liberal Democrats will scrap the current government-appointed Board of Governors, and introduce a new, independent external regulator appointed by parliament, to make sure that all public service broadcasters live up to their obligations to the public.

GREEN ACTION

Make government take the environment seriously

It is vital that government and business are made to take their environmental obligations seriously. We will strengthen reporting obligations for government and business as part of an Environmental Responsibility Act, holding government as well as business to account. We will use the purchasing power of government to boost the market for green products and services. We will unite those areas of government with the biggest impact on the environment in a single Environment, Transport and Energy department.

GREEN ACTION

Concern for the environment has always been a core Liberal Democrat value. Our policies are focused on three main areas:

Tackle climate change

Catastrophic climate change is the major environmental threat to the planet. Urgent action is needed. Liberal Democrat plans will make sure that Britain achieves its targets from the Kyoto Protocol (the international agreement on the pollution that causes climate change) well before the deadline. Britain and the EU must take the lead on negotiations for the next set of targets for greenhouse gas emissions. It is vital that we include the US and Australia but we also need to work with developing countries. Our long-term goal is 'contraction and convergence' – which means agreeing for every country a sustainable population-related allowance for emissions.

Cleaner transport and environment

Pollution and congestion have a major impact on people's health and quality of life, as well as on climate change. Many of the solutions to these problems involve transport and this document includes plans to promote public transport, especially the railways. However, pollution can also be cut by reducing domestic waste and promoting recycling. Pioneering Liberal Democrat controlled local authorities are leading the way in cutting unnecessary waste and we will expand these practices nationally.

Cleaner power

Energy use is the main source of greenhouse gas emissions and hazardous waste. We will introduce measures to reduce energy use overall – for example through better home insulation which will also tackle the 'fuel poverty' faced in particular by pensioners. We will make sure that at least 20 per cent of the UK's electricity derives from a range of renewable sources by the year 2020. Finally, given their long-term problems of cost, pollution and safety, we will not replace existing nuclear power stations as they reach the end of their safe and economic operating lives. We will use renewables and save energy instead.

OTHER MANIFESTOS

Summarised by Gabriel Rozenberg

DEMOCRATIC UNIONIST PARTY

After topping the poll in Assembly elections in 2003, the Democratic Unionist Party entered the Westminster election claiming its agenda now dominates the political process in Northern Ireland. The party would only accept Sinn Féin in a future Northern Ireland Executive after the complete, visible, verifiable decommissioning of the IRA's arms, a total end to all paramilitary and criminal activity, and after the Ulster community is convinced that the IRA has been stood down. It is vital that unionism has strong negotiators acting on its behalf, the DUP says, claiming that the UUP allowed republican parties to extract concessions. It calls on voters to rally behind the DUP to prevent Sinn Féin becoming Northern Ireland's largest party in Westminster.

Believing that Sinn Féin has proven itself incapable of ending its association with terror and criminality, the DUP wants a voluntary coalition that excludes the party to proceed with devolution.

On law and order, it opposes devolution of power without unionists's agreement. It opposes reductions in police numbers and supports rural police stations. It calls for zero tolerance initiatives, tougher sentences for attacks on the elderly and burglaries and greater resources to tackle drugs. The party calls for security forces to retain their emergency powers until the terrorist threat is eradicated. The DUP values a zero tolerance approach to racism.

The party wants to replace the Parades Commission and provide greater funding for Ulster-Scots culture.

The DUP wants to streamline bureaucracy in the health service and increase spending by 20 per cent, to achieve the same standards as in Great Britain. It would introduce a ban on smoking in public places.

The party supports grammar schools but says tests should be made less stressful for children. It is against water charges. Its agricultural policies include changes to the implementation of the Nitrates Directive and a sheep identification system.

The DUP maintains its opposition to the Euro, the European Constitution and unnecessary constitutional change, and repeats its support for the war on terrorism.

ULSTER UNIONIST PARTY

The manifestos of all of Northern Ireland's political parties are overshadowed by the failure of negotiations to bring about a return to devolution in 2004. In the absence of an Assembly, the Ulster Unionist Party proposes a policy programme to be carried out in Westminster. The UUP says it does not intend to re-enter an Executive with Sinn Féin, because it has concluded that the republicans are unwilling to give up their private army. Instead, it suggests repealing the formula that automatically gives parties ministerial appointments in the Assembly; the UUP would then form a coalition with the SDLP.

But the bulk of its manifesto is concerned with Ulster's economy, public services and law and order. A theme is the reduction of bureaucracy, to create flexibility in the public sector, cut waste, and encourage business. So the UUP advocates replacing Northern Ireland's five education boards with one authority, merging its four health boards into a single body, and amalgamating all of Northern Ireland's regulatory bodies. Primary care groups would allow GPs, not administrators, to make key decisions, it believes. In primary schools it would prioritise literacy and numeracy. It plans an increase in midwifery training, more flexibility in parental leave, and improved child protection legislation. The UUP proposes reform of employers' liability to reduce the insurance burden on business. Similarly in agriculture, the party wishes to see a reduction in red tape.

A scheme to levy charges on water is roundly criticised as an unfair tax on home ownership; the Ulster Unionists believe local taxes should be made more fair. They also propose a flat rate pension of £110 per week.

The party calls for more police officers on the streets and the introduction of a UK-wide ID card scheme.

The UUP is committed to abolishing the Parades Commission, which it sees as infringing the right to peaceful assembly. Ulster Unionists support strong and decisive action against regimes which support terrorism.

ALLIANCE PARTY OF NORTHERN IRELAND

Alliance, the anti-sectarian party in Northern Ireland, seeks to build a united community by opposing all forms of paramilitary and criminal activity. It plans to reform power-sharing government by allowing a weighted majority of parties in Northern Ireland to join a voluntary coalition; the rule which gives parties automatic rights to sit in the Executive should end. It wants tax-varying powers for the Assembly. The party believes that £1 billion a year is wasted dealing with the costs of managing a divided society. It wishes to see that money used for quality public services and to promote unity.

SOCIAL DEMOCRATIC AND LABOUR PARTY

The Social Democratic and Labour Party claim to be the only party in Northern Ireland to stand totally and positively by both the standards of inclusive democracy and lawful society set out in the Good Friday Agreement. But they reject the 'Comprehensive Agreement' negotiated by the DUP and Sinn Féin, which they say is a flawed renegotiation of the earlier settlement. The SDLP demands the full implementation of the Good Friday Agreement, including the Joint Declaration's commitments on human rights, equality, demilitarisation, community relations and the Irish language.

Their goal is a United Ireland, secured by a referendum, which it hopes can be won when the Agreement's institutions are operating stably and it is clear that its protections for unionists will remain.

Their hallmark of the SDLP agenda is the building of all-Ireland institutions of government. For the economy, an all-Ireland marketing co-operation and investment strategy is recommended, coupled with the removal of all cross-border trading agreements. An all-Ireland Law Commission, all-Ireland police training, and an all-Ireland register of sex offenders will strengthen policing and justice. Energy should be run in an all-Ireland market under a single planning framework. Island-wide public safety and food marketing bodies will be set up.

The SDLP will work to agree an all-Ireland charter of rights, as well as north-south co-operation to tackle racism. It supports an all-Ireland victim-centred mechanism for truth and remembrance. In cultural policy, the party supports all-Ireland coverage of RTE television and TG4, and calls to increase all-Ireland funding for Irish-medium television. The SDLP wants to cut bureaucracy and spend more on front-line services. It opposes water privatisation and charging. The party calls for greater investment in education, a preventative agenda in the health services, a detailed anti-poverty strategy, and speedy demilitarisation from the North.

SINN FÉIN

Sinn Féin calls for political independence for the Six Counties, and Irish unity. Its manifesto focuses attention on Gerry Adams's speech in April 2005 in which the Sinn Féin president appealed to the IRA to commit itself to purely political and democratic methods. IRA acceptance would revive the peace process, Sinn Féin believes; the party likewise calls on unionists to reject 'sectarianism' and says the British government must accept its responsibilities on equal rights and demilitarisation. That includes a ban on the use of plastic bullets, the repeal of legislation Sinn Féin sees as repressive, and new policing arrangements controlled by the devolved Assembly.

Equality plays a pivotal role in Sinn Féin's campaign. It claims nationalists are more likely to suffer from poverty, unemployment and multiple deprivation, and demands an all-Ireland anti-poverty strategy and compliance by employers with affirmative action measures. The party wants to see taxes reformed in favour of the low paid, with a 50 per cent tax band for incomes in excess of £100,000.

An island-wide approach is demanded for a range of measures. The 18 Westminster MPs should be accorded automatic membership of the Dáil, with voters in the Six Counties also having the vote in the Republic's Seanad and Presidential elections, the party says. Sinn Féin calls on the Irish Taoiseach to commission a Green Paper on Irish unity, in an attempt to provide practical steps towards a united Ireland. An all-Ireland economy with one tax regime and one currency should be developed.

Other Sinn Féin plans include additional funding for small rural primary schools and an end to academic selection. The party would ban smoking in the workplace and reject incineration as a means of disposing of waste. It calls for Irish speakers' rights to be strengthened with an Irish Language Bill.

In a heartening display of unity, Sinn Féin joins with the SDLP, Alliance, the UUP and the DUP in opposing proposals to introduce water charges.

SCOTTISH NATIONAL PARTY

The theme of the Scottish National Party's manifesto is that with independence from the UK, Scotland can compete and flourish. It proposes a Scottish Oil Fund, to invest a share of North Sea revenues for Scotland's future, modelled along the lines of a similar fund in Norway. The SNP commits itself to business rates below English levels, a lowering of corporation tax to 20 per cent, and a welcoming immigration policy as a way of improving growth and competitiveness. A pension of at least £110 for single retirees is proposed, rising in line with earnings, with residency in Scotland the sole qualification.

On health, the SNP plans to train 100 extra doctors every year and keep vital services local. It want to encourage doctors from abroad to study in Scotland and work in the Scottish NHS.

It plans to freeze council tax this year and replace it with a progressive local income tax as soon as possible. The SNP opposes ID cards and will invest instead in more community police officers.

Internationally, a SNP-led Scotland would oppose wars waged without international legal authority, but would 'join the world community where necessary to preserve peace and security'. The SNP wants to preserve Scotland's historic regiments and airforce bases; it would also set up a centre to promote peaceful alternatives to conflict. It supports reform for international trade organisations to level the playing field between rich and poor nations.

PLAID CYMRU – THE PARTY OF WALES

The Welsh separatist party sets out a manifesto for what it sees as a fairer tax system, a fair funding deal for Wales, better use of environmental technology, a campaign for a 'real Parliament' and an ethical foreign policy.

Like its Scottish counterpart, Plaid Cymru is committed to a local income tax replacing the council tax. Additionally, it calls for a 50 per cent income tax on incomes above £50,000 a year. A citizen's pension of £106 for a single pensioner, a review of the allocation of regional spending and compensation for former slate quarrymen suffering from respiratory diseases are proposed.

Noting a 'crisis in the countryside', the party wants to keep Less Favoured Area status for Wales to maintain eligibility for support for farmers. A planning framework which respects the environment and the need for development for agricultural diversification is also called for.

The party plans a full Parliament for Wales with primary law-making powers and a changed voting system. Its ambition for Wales is independence in Europe, backed by a referendum, which would involve full national status for Wales within the United Nations and the European Union.

Plaid Cymru, which is campaigning to impeach the Prime Minister for what it sees as his twisting of the truth to justify the war in Iraq, pledges never to support a war without approval from the UN. It plans to establish a Ministry for Peace to tackle the causes of war. It opposes Britain's nuclear weapons and supports a much fairer system of international trade.

Other policies include public ownership of the railways, an end to university tuition fees, free long-term care for the elderly, congestion charging in urban centres, stricter controls on town centre binge drinking, enhanced rights for the Welsh language, and a ban on the advertising of unhealthy food and drink on children's' television.

UNITED KINGDOM INDEPENDENCE PARTY

Flush from coming third in elections to the European Parliament in 2004, the UK Independence Party sets out a complete programme of policies with withdrawal from the European Union at their heart. It plans to repeal the 1972 European Communities Act immediately and stop paying into the EU budget. Bilateral trade and co-operation agreements will be agreed with the remaining EU states and farming and fishing policies will be replaced over a two-year period.

The UKIP will use the £12 billion saved from leaving the EU to raise state pensions by £25 a week. It will raise government borrowing to provide £30 billion a year for tax cuts and focused spending. Council tax will be halved, the starting rate of income tax scrapped and other taxes simplified.

The UKIP calls for government to be removed from day to day management of NHS facilities. It wants state schools to have more autonomy, with decisions over excluding unruly pupils left to headteachers. It plans to cancel university top-up fees but withdraw funding from courses which are of 'insufficient standard'.

On immigration, the UKIP pledges a points system to evaluate work permits, embarkation controls, quotas and 'Britishness' tests.

The party would keep Britain in NATO. It supports guaranteed minimum prices for British farmers, who it says should be protected from big business. The UKIP also plans an immediate end to the erection of wind turbines.

GREEN PARTY

Ambitiously, the Greens promise 'a political programme for at least the next hundred years' – set out in a manifesto which, to save natural resources, is only available on the internet. Economics and climate change are its central concerns.

Economic inequality, overuse of the world's resources and 'short term' wealth creation are contributing to poor health and declining self-sufficiency, the Greens believe. They propose wealth redistribution via a 60 per cent tax on earnings over £100,000 and a land value tax to undermine unequal land ownership. They call for eco-taxes to limit pollution and waste, and moot local currencies, along with other trade policies promoting economic localisation. The Greens want to extend workers' rights and reduce their working hours. To combat climate change, they want Britain to lead Europe in carbon emissions trading, while reducing its demand for energy and investing in renewable fuel. By 2030 they hope fossil fuel emissions will be reduced to 15 per cent of their 1990 levels.

The Greens advocate a national basic income as a universal right, an increase in the basic state pension, and measures to tackle housing shortages. They seek to return a service ethos to public services. Charges should be phased out from the NHS. Money raised from substantial cuts in military spending – such as the scrapping of nuclear weapons – will go towards the health service. The Greens would aim to cut care use by restoring the railways to public ownership, extend congestion charging and research more sustainable forms of transport. Finally, there is support for an internationalist and 'truly ethical' foreign policy.

RESPECT – THE UNITY COALITION

In the words of its manifesto, Respect 'sprang directly from the great anti-war movement that brought millions onto the streets.' A coalition formed by the former Labour MP George Galloway in 2004, its full name – Respect Equality Socialism Peace Environment Community Trade Unionism – gives some idea of its chief concerns. Defining itself against what it sees as a rightward march in British politics, Respect's organising priority at this election is to end the occupation of Iraq, a country it claims is in ruins as a result of an illegal war.

The group believes that public services should be publicly owned and democratically controlled by those who use them. It rejects what it sees as attacks on civil liberties and the demonisation of Muslim communities.

VERITAS

Veritas is the party set up by Robert Kilroy-Silk, the MEP and former talk show host, after he defected from the UKIP shortly after his election in 2004. In the introduction to its manifesto, Mr Kilroy-Silk pledges: 'We will, believe me, change the face of British politics forever.' Veritas calls for 'straight-talking', withdrawal from the European Union and fearless support for the British way of life. Policies include heavy control of immigration, tough sentencing, an end to the 'nonsense' of multiculturalism, a voucher scheme for schools and a flat income tax.

COMMUNIST PARTY OF BRITAIN

The Communist Party continues to view the world through the prism of its guiding ideology, Marxist-Leninism. It claims that 'imperialist powers' like the USA, Britain and France have promoted globalisation in order to further the interests of their own transnational corporations, a process which will inevitably lead to war as resources are progressively plundered. In that context, it sees the USA as the world's greatest threat to peace, accusing it of pursuing a strategy of worldwide military domination, and claims that the British government has talked up a 'Big Lie' – an imminent threat from terrorists – to divert attention from the corporations and banks which hold the levers of power. In response, it proposes socialist revolution led by a united working class.

The Communists call for a strategy to defend Britain's manufacturing, including public ownership of essential industries and the outlawing of mass redundancies from profitable firms. It advocates leaving the European Union, which it sees as a vehicle for imperialism and oppression. All privatisation in public services must end, the party says, and the state pension should be increased to £114 a week. The Communist Party wants to strengthen anti-discrimination laws. Policies such as greater investment in renewable energy and a higher minimum wage will be paid for with tax rises on banks, oil companies and the rich.

SCOTTISH SOCIALIST PARTY

The Scottish Socialist Party stands for a fully independent, socialist republic of Scotland and stands against the war on terror and the war in Iraq. It claims that 'to make poverty history, we will need to make capitalism history'.
It wants an £8 minimum wage as part of a programme for shifting wealth and power from the wealthy to the poor. Its goal is a four-day, 32 hour working week with five weeks minimum annual leave and an extra five public holidays for every worker.

All private medical facilities and resources would be incorporated into an expanded NHS under SSP rule, and it would put an end to PFI and all private contractors in hospitals. Fossil fuels and nuclear power would be phased out to protect the environment. The SSP would decriminalise all drug use, but run a propaganda war on Scotland's binge drinking culture.

LIBERAL PARTY

The offspring of the old Liberal Party continues some philosophical tenets of its parent. It believes in liberty of the individual, protection of the planet and free trade, although it stresses that the latter must not be used as a device by which developing economies are suppressed. Greenhouse gases must be drastically reduced to counter climate change, the party believes. It opposes the European Union and the euro. Health care should be locally controlled and animal welfare improved. The basic pension should be increased to £120 for a single person, the party says. It would promote 'fair market access' and a tax system which redistributes wealth as well as income. Counter-terrorism legislation should be repealed, the party thinks. Internationally, it stresses the importance of non-military security, rejecting nuclear weapons and the right of any nation to unilateral military action. Instead the UN General Assembly should be strengthened as a step towards the creation of legitimate global government.

BRITISH NATIONAL PARTY

The British National Party believes in the right of the indigenous peoples of the British Isles to self-determination. In its 25,000-word manifesto it sets out plans to restore power to national parliaments from Europe, lobbyists and corporate giants.

Leaving the EU is key, particularly given its plans to expand into Turkey, which the party claims would mark the beginning of the end of secular democratic government in the West.

The BNP would call an immediate halt to immigration, which it calls 'a crisis without parallel' that threatens Britain's existence. Immigrants and their descendants who are legally in the country would be given generous financial incentives to leave. The party says it will 'seek to emphasise the importance of the prior status of the aboriginal people' in areas such as housing and school places lists.

The BNP opposes globalisation, saying that the government's duty is to proactively run the economy for the benefit of the nation. While the party believes that 'creeping Islamification' presents a danger to Britain, it opposes attempts by the US and the 'Zionist lobby' to drag Britain to war in the Middle East.

NATIONAL FRONT

The National Front, which is what remains after the split in 1980 eventually led to the formation of the British National Party, claims that mainstream political parties have reduced Britain to bankruptcy and impotence, and advocates the repatriation of all non-white people living in Britain.

ENGLISH DEMOCRATS PARTY

The English Democrats Party, whose best-known candidate is Garry Bushell, the former TV editor of The Sun, was created to campaign for an English Parliament. The party advocates traditional English civil liberties, recognition of traditional counties, economic independence and promotion of the English way of life, such as making St George's Day a Bank Holiday.

MEBYON KERNOW – THE PARTY FOR CORNWALL

Mebyon Kernow describes itself as Cornish, green, left-of-centre and decentralist. Its chief priority is the creation of a Cornish Assembly and a Cornish Development Agency. It calls for sustainable policies for Cornwall to protect the global environment, and a tolerant and inclusive society for one and all.

THE CO-OPERATIVE PARTY

This party, which promotes and supports co-operatives and all forms of mutual organisations that empower employees and citizens, is closely allied to the Labour Party and supports that party in its aims.

CHRISTIAN PEOPLES ALLIANCE

This party, fighting its first general election campaign, seeks to use Christian principles to renew society and 'heal its relationships'. It believes that stable marriages are the bedrock of society and proposes financial incentives to encourage marriage. The CPA, which models itself on continental Christian Democratic parties, strongly opposes abortion and supports moral values in schools.

LEGALISE CANNABIS ALLIANCE

This single-issue party calls for cannabis to be removed from the Misuse of Drugs Act. Possession, cultivation and use of the drug would be free from prosecution, which, the group believes, would increase social well being, spirit, health and happiness. Hemp could also be used as a cheap fuel, while a levy on sales of the weed could go towards lowering council tax.

VOTE FOR YOURSELF RAINBOW DREAM TICKET

This 'mystically directed' grouping, led by Rainbow George, advocates government by 'preferendum', which promises to make party politics redundant. Voters in constituencies where the VFYRDT is standing can govern themselves by ticking off on a checklist any policies they like the look of. The party also calls for money to be replaced with an electronic currency called the Wonder.

OFFICIAL MONSTER RAVING LOONY PARTY

Income tax is to be replaced by people lending the government a bob or two at the end of the week, as soon as the Official Monster Raving Loony Party takes office. Its invisible platform (designed so that people cannot see the floors in its policies) includes a 99p coin to save on change, pram lanes for shopping centres, and the abolition of the number 13, due to its longstanding unpopularity.

The party's proposals for schools are broadly egalitarian. Bright pupils will be provided with dimmer switches to prevent them distracting the rest of the class, and all children will automatically receive full marks in their exams, in the interests of fairness. The party plans to reduce class sizes by making pupils sit closer to each other.

Home affairs policies follow the party's belief that anyone caught breaking the law must be made to mend it. Any kerbs that are caught crawling will be arrested. The country's borders will be open to anybody, as long as they are over 85 and accompanied by both parents.

Showing a commitment to the environment, the party promises that all foxes will be issued with sheep's clothing. All houses built on flood plains will have foundations made of sponge, in order to soak up surplus water.

The House of Lords will be replaced with a House of Cards, to make it easier for the government to deal with. An inquiry is promised to find out why there is a polar bear on Fox's Glacier Mints. The party also plans to strengthen Britain's defences with a pledge that the white cliffs of Dover will be painted blue, for camouflage.

INDEX TO CANDIDATES

INDEX TO CANDIDATES

Names in bold are of winners

H

I

J

N

T

Y

Z

RECORD OF BY-ELECTIONS IN THE PARLIAMENT OF 2005–